Seventh Edition

Global Edition

MACROECONOMICS

Olivier Blanchard

Boston   Columbus   Indianapolis   New York   San Francisco   Amsterdam
Cape Town   Dubai   London   Madrid   Milan   Munich   Paris   Montréal   Toronto   Delhi
Mexico City   São Paulo   Sydney   Hong Kong   Seoul   Singapore   Taipei   Tokyo

Vice President, Business Publishing: Donna Battista

Editor-in-Chief: Adrienne D'Ambrosio

Senior Acquisitions Editor: Christina Masturzo

Editorial Assistant: Diana Tetterton

Associate Acquisitions Editor, Global Edition: Ananya Srivastava

Associate Project Editor, Global Edition: Paromita Banerjee

Vice President, Product Marketing: Maggie Moylan

Director of Marketing, Digital Services and Products: Jeanette Koskinas

Field Marketing Manager: Ramona Elmer

Product Marketing Assistant: Jessica Quazza

Team Lead, Program Management: Ashley Santora

Program Manager: Nancy Freihofer

Team Lead, Project Management: Jeff Holcomb

Project Manager: Heather Pagano

Project Manager, Global Edition: Sudipto Roy

Senior Manufacturing Controller, Global Edition: Trudy Kimber

Operations Specialist: Carol Melville

Creative Director: Blair Brown

Art Director: Jonathan Boylan

Vice President, Director of Digital Strategy and Assessment: Paul Gentile

Manager of Learning Applications: Paul DeLuca

Digital Editor: Denise Clinton

Director, Digital Studio: Sacha Laustsen

Digital Studio Manager: Diane Lombardo

Digital Studio Project Managers: Melissa Honig, Alana Coles, Robin Lazrus

Digital Content Team Lead: Noel Lotz

Digital Content Project Lead: Courtney Kamauf

Media Production Manager, Global Edition: Vikram Kumar

Assistant Media Producer, Global Edition: Pallavi Pandit

Full-Service Project Management and Composition: Integra Software Services

Cover Designer: Lumina Datamatics

Cover image: gst/Shutterstock

Acknowledgments of third-party content appear on the appropriate page within the text.

Pearson Education Limited
KAO Two
KAO Park
Harlow
Essex CM 17 9NA
England

and Associated Companies throughout the world

Visit us on the World Wide Web at: www.pearsonglobaleditions.com

ISBN 10: 1-292-16050-0
ISBN 13: 978-1-292-16050-4

British Library Cataloguing-in-Publication Data
A catalogue record for this book is available from the British Library

10 9 8 7
20 19

Typeset in Photina MT Pro by Integra Software Services, Inc.
Printed and bound by Vivar in Malaysia (CTP-VVP)

To Noelle

About the Authors

A citizen of France, **Olivier Blanchard** has spent most of his professional life in Cambridge, U.S.A. After obtaining his Ph.D. in economics at the Massachusetts Institute of Technology in 1977, he taught at Harvard University, returning to MIT in 1982. He was chair of the economics department from 1998 to 2003. In 2008, he took a leave of absence to be the Economic Counsellor and Director of the Research Department of the International Monetary Fund. Since October 2015, he is the Fred Bergsten Senior Fellow at the Peterson Institute for International Economics, in Washington. He also remains Robert M. Solow Professor of Economics emeritus at MIT.

He has worked on a wide set of macroeconomic issues, from the role of monetary policy, to the nature of speculative bubbles, to the nature of the labor market and the determinants of unemployment, to transition in former communist countries, and to forces behind the recent global crisis. In the process, he has worked with numerous countries and international organizations. He is the author of many books and articles, including a graduate level textbook with Stanley Fischer.

He is a past editor of the Quarterly Journal of Economics, of the NBER Macroeconomics Annual, and founding editor of the AEJ Macroeconomics. He is a fellow and past council member of the Econometric Society, a past vice president of the American Economic Association, and a member of the American Academy of Sciences.

Brief Contents

THE CORE

Introduction 21
Chapter 1   A Tour of the World 23
Chapter 2   A Tour of the Book 41

The Short Run 65
Chapter 3   The Goods Market 67
Chapter 4   Financial Markets I 87
Chapter 5   Goods and Financial Markets; The *IS-LM* Model 109
Chapter 6   Financial Markets II: The Extended *IS-LM* Model 131

The Medium Run 155
Chapter 7   The Labor Market 157
Chapter 8   The Phillips Curve, the Natural Rate of Unemployment, and Inflation 177
Chapter 9   From the Short to the Medium Run: The *IS-LM-PC* Model 197

The Long Run 217
Chapter 10   The Facts of Growth 219
Chapter 11   Saving, Capital Accumulation, and Output 237
Chapter 12   Technological Progress and Growth 261
Chapter 13   Technological Progress: The Short, the Medium, and the Long Run 283

EXTENSIONS

Expectations 303
Chapter 14   Financial Markets and Expectations 305
Chapter 15   Expectations, Consumption, and Investment 331
Chapter 16   Expectations, Output, and Policy 351

The Open Economy 367
Chapter 17   Openness in Goods and Financial Markets 369
Chapter 18   The Goods Market in an Open Economy 389
Chapter 19   Output, the Interest Rate, and the Exchange Rate 411
Chapter 20   Exchange Rate Regimes 431

Back to Policy 453
Chapter 21   Should Policy Makers Be Restrained? 455
Chapter 22   Fiscal Policy: A Summing Up 473
Chapter 23   Monetary Policy: A Summing Up 497
Chapter 24   Epilogue: The Story of Macroeconomics 517

Contents

Preface   13

THE CORE

Introduction 21

Chapter 1   **A Tour of the World 23**

1-1   The Crisis 24

1-2   The United States 26

Low Interest Rates and the Zero Lower Bound 27 • How Worrisome Is Low Productivity Growth? 28

1-3   The Euro Area 29

Can European Unemployment Be Reduced? 31 • What Has the Euro Done for Its Members? 32

1-4   China 33

1-5   Looking Ahead 35

Appendix: Where to Find the Numbers 38

Chapter 2   **A Tour of the Book 41**

2-1   Aggregate Output 42

GDP: Production and Income 42 • Nominal and Real GDP 44 • GDP: Level versus Growth Rate 46

2-2   The Unemployment Rate 47

Why Do Economists Care about Unemployment? 49

2-3   The Inflation Rate 51

The GDP Deflator 51 • The Consumer Price Index 51 • Why Do Economists Care about Inflation? 53

2-4   Output, Unemployment, and the Inflation Rate: Okun's Law and the Phillips Curve 53

Okun's Law 54 • The Phillips Curve 54

2-5   The Short Run, the Medium Run, and the Long Run 55

2-6   A Tour of the Book 56

The Core 56 • Extensions 57 • Back to Policy 58 • Epilogue 58

Appendix: The Construction of Real GDP and Chain-Type Indexes 62

The Short Run 65

Chapter 3   **The Goods Market 67**

3-1   The Composition of GDP 68

3-2   The Demand for Goods 70

Consumption (C) 70 • Investment (I) 72 • Government Spending (G) 72

3-3   The Determination of Equilibrium Output 73

Using Algebra 74 • Using a Graph 75 • Using Words 77 • How Long Does It Take for Output to Adjust? 78

3-4   Investment Equals Saving: An Alternative Way of Thinking about Goods-Market Equilibrium 80

3-5   Is the Government Omnipotent? A Warning 82

Chapter 4   **Financial Markets I 87**

4-1   The Demand for Money 88

Deriving the Demand for Money 89

4-2   Determining the Interest Rate: I 91

Money Demand, Money Supply, and the Equilibrium Interest Rate 91 • Monetary Policy and Open Market Operations 94 • Choosing Money or Choosing the Interest Rate? 96

4-3   Determining the Interest Rate: II 96

What Banks Do 96 • The Demand and Supply for Central Bank Money 98 • The Federal Funds Market and the Federal Funds Rate 99

4-4   The Liquidity Trap 100

Appendix: The Determination of the Interest Rate When People Hold Both Currency and Checkable Deposits 105

Chapter 5   **Goods and Financial Markets; The *IS-LM* Model 109**

5-1   The Goods Market and the *IS* Relation 110

Investment, Sales, and the Interest Rate 110 • Determining Output 111 • Deriving the *IS* Curve 113 • Shifts of the *IS* Curve 113

5-2 Financial Markets and the *LM* Relation 114

Real Money, Real Income, and the Interest Rate 114 • Deriving the *LM* Curve 115

5-3 Putting the *IS* and the *LM* Relations Together 116

Fiscal Policy 116 • Monetary Policy 118

5-4 Using a Policy Mix 119

5-5 How Does the *IS-LM* Model Fit the Facts? 124

Chapter 6 Financial Markets II: The Extended *IS-LM* Model 131

6-1 Nominal versus Real Interest Rates 132

Nominal and Real Interest Rates in the United States since 1978 134 • Nominal and Real Interest Rates: The Zero Lower Bound and Deflation 135

6-2 Risk and Risk Premia 136

6-3 The Role of Financial Intermediaries 137

The Choice of Leverage 138 • Leverage and Lending 139

6-4 Extending the IS-LM 141

Financial Shocks and Policies 142

6-5 From a Housing Problem to a Financial Crisis 143

Housing Prices and Subprime Mortgages 143 • The Role of Financial Intermediaries 145 • Macroeconomic Implications 147 • Policy Responses 147

The Medium Run 155

Chapter 7 The Labor Market 157

7-1 A Tour of the Labor Market 158

The Large Flows of Workers 158

7-2 Movements in Unemployment 161

7-3 Wage Determination 163

Bargaining 164 • Efficiency Wages 164 • Wages, Prices, and Unemployment 166 • The Expected Price Level 166 • The Unemployment Rate 166 • The Other Factors 167

7-4 Price Determination 167

7-5 The Natural Rate of Unemployment 168

The Wage-Setting Relation 168 • The Price-Setting Relation 169 • Equilibrium Real Wages and Unemployment 170

7-6 Where We Go from Here 171

Appendix: Wage- and Price-Setting Relations versus Labor Supply and Labor Demand 175

Chapter 8 The Phillips Curve, the Natural Rate of Unemployment, and Inflation 177

8-1 Inflation, Expected Inflation, and Unemployment 178

8-2 The Phillips Curve and Its Mutations 180

The Early Incarnation 180 • The Apparent Trade-Off and Its Disappearance 180

8-3 The Phillips Curve and the Natural Rate of Unemployment 183

8-4 A Summary and Many Warnings 185

Variations in the Natural Rate across Countries 186 • Variations in the Natural Rate over Time 186 • High Inflation and the Phillips Curve Relation 188 • Deflation and the Phillips Curve Relation 190

Appendix: Derivation of the Relation to a Relation between Inflation, Expected Inflation, and Unemployment 195

Chapter 9 From the Short to the Medium Run: The *IS-LM-PC* Model 197

9-1 The IS-LM-PC model 178

9-2 Dynamics and the Medium Run Equilibrium 201

The Role of Expectations Revisited 203 • The Zero Lower Bound and Debt Spirals 203

9-3 Fiscal Consolidation Revisited 206

9-4 The Effects of an Increase in the Price of Oil 207

Effects on the Natural Rate of Unemployment 209

9-5 Conclusions 212

The Short Run versus the Medium Run 212 • Shocks and Propagation Mechanisms 212

The Long Run 217

Chapter 10   The Facts of Growth 219

10-1 Measuring the Standard of Living 220

10-2 Growth in Rich Countries since 1950 223

The Large Increase in the Standard of Living since 1950 225 • The Convergence of Output per Person 226

10-3 A Broader Look across Time and Space 227

Looking across Two Millennia 227 • Looking across Countries 227

10-4 Thinking about Growth: A Primer 229

The Aggregate Production Function 229 • Returns to Scale and Returns to Factors 230 • Output per Worker and Capital per Worker 231 • The Sources of Growth 231

Chapter 11   Saving, Capital Accumulation, and Output 237

11-1 Interactions between Output and Capital 238

The Effects of Capital on Output 238 • The Effects of Output on Capital Accumulation 239 • Output and Investment 239 • Investment and Capital Accumulation 240

11-2 The Implications of Alternative Saving Rates 241

Dynamics of Capital and Output 241 • The Saving Rate and Output 243 • The Saving Rate and Consumption 247

11-3 Getting a Sense of Magnitudes 248

The Effects of the Saving Rate on Steady-State Output 250 • The Dynamic Effects of an Increase in the Saving Rate 251 • The U.S. Saving Rate and the Golden Rule 253

11-4 Physical versus Human Capital 254

Extending the Production Function 254 • Human Capital, Physical Capital, and Output 255 • Endogenous Growth 256

Appendix: The Cobb-Douglas Production Function and the Steady State 259

Chapter 12   Technological Progress and Growth 261

12-1 Technological Progress and the Rate of Growth 262

Technological Progress and the Production Function 262

Interactions between Output and Capital 264 • Dynamics of Capital and Output 266 • The Effects of the Saving Rate 267

12-2 The Determinants of Technological Progress 268

The Fertility of the Research Process 269 • The Appropriability of Research Results 270 • Management, Innovation, and Imitation 272

12-3 Institutions, Technological Progress, and Growth 273

12-4 The Facts of Growth Revisited 276

Capital Accumulation versus Technological Progress in Rich Countries since 1985 276 • Capital Accumulation versus Technological Progress in China 277

Appendix: Constructing a Measure of Technological Progress 281

Chapter 13   Technological Progress: The Short, the Medium, and the Long Run 283

13-1 Productivity, Output, and Unemployment in the Short Run 284

The Empirical Evidence 286

13-2 Productivity and the Natural Rate of Unemployment 287

Price Setting and Wage Setting Revisited 287 • The Natural Rate of Unemployment 288 • The Empirical Evidence 289

13-3 Technological Progress, Churning, and Inequality 291

The Increase in Wage Inequality 292 • The Causes of Increased Wage Inequality 294 • Inequality and the Top 1% 297

EXTENSIONS

Expectations 303

Chapter 14   Financial Markets and Expectations 305

14-1 Expected Present Discounted Values 306

Computing Expected Present Discounted Values 306 • A General Formula 307

- Using Present Values: Examples 308
- Constant Interest Rates 308 •
Constant Interest Rates and
Payments 308 • Constant Interest
Rates and Payments Forever 309
- Zero Interest Rates 309 • Nominal
versus Real Interest Rates and Present
Values 309

14-2 Bond Prices and Bond Yields 310

Bond Prices as Present Values 312
- Arbitrage and Bond Prices 313
- From Bond Prices to Bond Yields 314
- Reintroducing Risk 315
- Interpreting the Yield Curve 316

14-3 The Stock Market and Movements in
Stock Prices 318

Stock Prices as Present Values 318
- The Stock Market and Economic
Activity 321 • A Monetary Expansion
and the Stock Market 321 • An
Increase in Consumer Spending and
the Stock Market 322

14-4 Risk, Bubbles, Fads, and Asset
Prices 324

Stock Prices and Risk 324 • Asset
Prices, Fundamentals, and
Bubbles 324

Appendix: Deriving the Expected Present
Discounted Value Using Real or Nominal
Interest Rates 330

Chapter 15   **Expectations, Consumption,
and Investment 331**

15-1 Consumption 332

The Very Foresighted Consumer 332
- An Example 333 • Toward
a More Realistic Description 334
- Putting Things Together: Current
Income, Expectations, and
Consumption 337

15-2 Investment 338

Investment and Expectations of
Profit 338 • Depreciation 339
- The Present Value of Expected
Profits 339 • The Investment
Decision 340 • A Convenient
Special Case 340 • Current versus
Expected Profit 342 • Profit and
Sales 344

15-3 The Volatility of Consumption and
Investment 346

Appendix: Derivation of the Expected
Present Value of Profits under Static
Expectations 350

Chapter 16   **Expectations, Output,
and Policy 351**

16-1 Expectations and Decisions: Taking
Stock 352

Expectations, Consumption, and
Investment Decisions 352
- Expectations and the *IS*
Relation 352

16-2 Monetary Policy, Expectations, and
Output 355

Monetary Policy Revisited 355

16-3 Deficit Reduction, Expectations, and
Output 358

The Role of Expectations about the
Future 359 • Back to the Current
Period 359

The Open Economy 367

Chapter 17   **Openness in Goods and Financial
Markets 369**

17-1 Openness in Goods Markets 370

Exports and Imports 370 • The Choice
between Domestic Goods and Foreign
Goods 372 • Nominal Exchange
Rates 372 • From Nominal to Real
Exchange Rates 374 • From Bilateral to
Multilateral Exchange Rates 377

17-2 Openness in Financial Markets 378

The Balance of Payments 379 • The
Choice between Domestic and Foreign
Assets 381 • Interest Rates and
Exchange Rates 383

17-3 Conclusions and a Look Ahead 385

Chapter 18   **The Goods Market in an Open
Economy 389**

18-1 The *IS* Relation in the Open
Economy 390

The Demand for Domestic Goods 390
- The Determinants of *C*, *I*, and *G* 390
- The Determinants of Imports 391
- The Determinants of Exports 391
- Putting the Components
Together 391

18-2 Equilibrium Output and the Trade
Balance 393

18-3 Increases in Demand—Domestic or
Foreign 394

Increases in Domestic Demand 394
- Increases in Foreign Demand 396
- Fiscal Policy Revisited 397

18-4 Depreciation, the Trade Balance, and Output 399

Depreciation and the Trade Balance: The Marshall-Lerner Condition 400 • The Effects of a Real Depreciation 400 • Combining Exchange Rate and Fiscal Policies 401

18-5 Looking at Dynamics: The J-Curve 404

18-6 Saving, Investment, and the Current Account Balance 406

Appendix: Derivation of the Marshall-Lerner Condition 410

Chapter 19 Output, the Interest Rate, and the Exchange Rate 411

19-1 Equilibrium in the Goods Market 412

19-2 Equilibrium in Financial Markets 413

Domestic Bonds versus Foreign Bonds 413

19-3 Putting Goods and Financial Markets Together 417

19-4 The Effects of Policy in an Open Economy 419

The Effects of Monetary Policy in an Open Economy 419 • The Effects of Fiscal Policy in an Open Economy 419

19-5 Fixed Exchange Rates 423

Pegs, Crawling Pegs, Bands, the EMS, and the Euro 423 • Monetary Policy when the Exchange Rate Is Fixed 424 • Fiscal Policy when the Exchange Rate Is Fixed 424

Appendix: Fixed Exchange Rates, Interest Rates, and Capital Mobility 429

Chapter 20 Exchange Rate Regimes 431

20-1 The Medium Run 432

The IS Relation under Fixed Exchange Rates 433 • Equilibrium in the Short and the Medium Run 433 • The Case for and against a Devaluation 434

20-2 Exchange Rate Crises under Fixed Exchange Rates 436

20-3 Exchange Rate Movements under Flexible Exchange Rates 439

Exchange Rates and the Current Account 440 • Exchange Rates and Current and Future Interest Rates 441 • Exchange Rate Volatility 441

20-4 Choosing between Exchange Rate Regimes 442

Common Currency Areas 443 • Hard Pegs, Currency Boards, and Dollarization 445

Appendix 1: Deriving the IS Relation under Fixed Exchange Rates 451

Appendix 2: The Real Exchange Rate and Domestic and Foreign Real Interest Rates 451

Back to Policy 453

Chapter 21 Should Policy Makers Be Restrained? 455

21-1 Uncertainty and Policy 456

How Much Do Macroeconomists Actually Know? 456 • Should Uncertainty Lead Policy Makers to Do Less? 458 • Uncertainty and Restraints on Policy Makers 458

21-2 Expectations and Policy 459

Hostage Takings and Negotiations 460 • Inflation and Unemployment Revisited 460 • Establishing Credibility 461 • Time Consistency and Restraints on Policy Makers 463

21-3 Politics and Policy 463

Games between Policy Makers and Voters 463 • Games between Policy Makers 465 • Politics and Fiscal Restraints 468

Chapter 22 Fiscal Policy: A Summing Up 473

22-1 What We Have Learned 474

22-2 The Government Budget Constraint: Deficits, Debt, Spending, and Taxes 475

The Arithmetic of Deficits and Debt 475 • Current versus Future Taxes 477 • The Evolution of the Debt-to-GDP Ratio 479

22-3 Ricardian Equivalence, Cyclical Adjusted Deficits, and War Finance 482

Ricardian Equivalence 482 • Deficits, Output Stabilization, and the Cyclically Adjusted Deficit 483 • Wars and Deficits 484

22-4 The Dangers of High Debt 486

High Debt, Default Risk, and Vicious Cycles 486 • Debt Default 488 • Money Finance 488

Contents

Chapter 23 Monetary Policy: A Summing Up 497

23-1   What We Have Learned 498

23-2   From Money Targeting to Inflation Targeting 499

Money Targeting 499 • Inflation Targeting 501 • The Interest Rate Rule 502

23-3   The Optimal Inflation Rate 503

The Costs of Inflation 503 • The Benefits of Inflation 506 • The Optimal Inflation Rate: The State of the Debate 507

23-4   Unconventional Monetary Policy 508

23-5   Monetary Policy and Financial Stability 510

Liquidity Provision and Lender of Last Resort 510 • Macroprudential Tools 510

Chapter 24 Epilogue: The Story of Macroeconomics 517

24-1   Keynes and the Great Depression 518

24-2   The Neoclassical Synthesis 518

Progress on All Fronts 519 • Keynesians versus Monetarists 520

24-3   The Rational Expectations Critique 521

The Three Implications of Rational Expectations 522 • The Integration of Rational Expectations 523

24-4   Developments in Macroeconomics up to the 2009 Crisis 524

New Classical Economics and Real Business Cycle Theory 525 • New Keynesian Economics 525 • New Growth Theory 526 • Toward an Integration 527

24-5   First Lessons for Macroeconomics after the Crisis 528

Appendix 1 An Introduction to National Income and Product Accounts A-1

Appendix 2 A Math Refresher A-7

Appendix 3 An Introduction to Econometrics A-12

Glossary   G-1

Index   I-1

Credits   C-1

Focus Boxes

Real GDP, Technological Progress, and the Price of
   Computers   47

Unemployment and Happiness   50

The Lehman Bankruptcy, Fears of Another Great Depression,
   and Shifts in the Consumption Function   79

The Paradox of Saving   83

Semantic Traps: Money, Income, and Wealth   89

Who Holds U.S. Currency?   91

The Liquidity Trap in the United Kingdom   101

The German and French Recessions of 2001–02   120

Deficit Reduction: Good or Bad for Investment?   123

Bank Runs   140

The Australian Monthly Population Survey   160

Henry Ford and Efficiency Wages   165

Theory ahead of Facts: Milton Friedman
   and Edmund Phelps   184

What Explains European Unemployment?   187

Why is the Natural Rate of Unemployment in Japan so
   Low?   189

Okun's Law across Time and Countries   200

Deflation in the Great Depression   205

Plummeting Oil Price and Consumer Price Expectations   211

The Construction of PPP Numbers   222

Does Money Lead to Happiness?   224

Capital Accumulation and Growth in France
   in the Aftermath of World War II   244

Ageing, Contractual Mandatory Retirement, and Slow Growth in
   Japan   249

Foreign Direct Investment, Technological Change,
   and Economic Growth   270

Management Practices: Another Dimension
   of Technological Progress   272

The Importance of Institutions: North Korea
   and South Korea   274

What Is behind Chinese Growth?   275

Job Destruction, Churning, and Earnings Losses   293

The Role of Technology in the Decrease in Income Inequality
   in Latin America in the 2000s   295

The Vocabulary of Bond Markets   312

The Yield Curves for AAA-rated Central Government Bonds   317

Making (Some) Sense of (Apparent) Nonsense: Why the
   Stock Market Moved Yesterday and Other Stories   323

Famous Bubbles: From Tulipmania in 17th-Century Holland to
   Russia in 1994   325

The Increase in U.S. Housing Prices: Fundamentals
   or Bubble?   326

Understanding Aggregate Consumption Patterns:
   The Eurosystem Household Finance and Consumption
   Survey   333

How Much Do Expectations Matter in Estonia?   336

Investment and the Stock Market   341

Profitability versus Cash Flow   344

Rational Expectations   357

Can a Budget Deficit Reduction Lead to an Output Expansion?
   Ireland in the 1980s   361

Can Exports Exceed GDP?   372

GDP versus GNP: The Example of Kuwait   382

Buying Brazilian Bonds   384

Fiscal Stimulus and Structural Reforms amid Negative Interest
   Rates   398

The Disappearance of Current Account Deficits in Euro
   Periphery Countries: Good News or Bad News?   402

Does the Interest Rate Parity Condition Always Hold
   for Transitional Economies?   414

Fiscal and Monetary Policies Coordination in France
   (2008–2015)   422

German Reunification, Interest Rates, and the EMS   425

The Return of Britain to the Gold Standard:
   Keynes versus Churchill   435

The 1992 EMS Crisis   438

The Euro: A Short History   445

Lessons from Argentina's Currency Board   446

Was Alan Blinder Wrong in Speaking the Truth?   463

Euro Area Fiscal Rules: A Short History   466

Inflation Accounting and the Measurement of Deficits   476

How Countries Decreased Their Debt Ratios after
   World War II   481

Irresistible Growth of Public Spending Worldwide   485

Rules versus Discretion: New Absolute Budgetary
   Rules in the EU   490

How Japan Could Stand Such a Huge Debt?   491

Money Illusion   505

LTV Ratios and Housing Price Increases from 2000 to 2007   512

Preface

I had two main goals in writing this book:

- To make close contact with current macroeconomic events. What makes macroeconomics exciting is the light it sheds on what is happening around the world, from the major economic crisis which has engulfed the world since 2008, to monetary policy in the United States, to the problems of the Euro area, to growth in China. These events—and many more—are described in the book, not in footnotes, but in the text or in detailed boxes. Each box shows how you can use what you have learned to get an understanding of these events. My belief is that these boxes not only convey the "life" of macroeconomics, but also reinforce the lessons from the models, making them more concrete and easier to grasp.

- To provide an integrated view of macroeconomics. The book is built on one underlying model, a model that draws the implications of equilibrium conditions in three sets of markets: the goods market, the financial markets, and the labor market. Depending on the issue at hand, the parts of the model relevant to the issue are developed in more detail while the other parts are simplified or lurk in the background. But the underlying model is always the same. This way, you will see macroeconomics as a coherent whole, not a collection of models. And you will be able to make sense not only of past macroeconomic events, but also of those that unfold in the future.

New to this Edition

The crisis that started in 2008, and is still lingering, forced macroeconomists to rethink much of macroeconomics. They clearly had understated the role of the financial system. They also had too optimistic a view of how the economy returned to equilibrium. Eight years later, I believe the main lessons have been absorbed, and this edition reflects the deep rethinking that has taken place. Nearly all chapters have been rewritten, and the main changes are as follows:

- A modified Chapter 5, and a modified presentation of the IS-LM. The traditional treatment of monetary policy assumed that the central bank chose the money supply and then let the interest rate adjust. In fact, modern central banks choose the interest rate and then let the money supply adjust. In terms of the IS-LM model used to describe the short run, the LM curve, instead of being upward sloping, should be treated as flat. This makes for a more realistic and a simpler model.

- A new Chapter 6. The chapter focuses on the role of the financial system in the economy. It extends the IS-LM model to allow for two interest rates, the interest rate set by monetary policy and the cost of borrowing for people or firms, with the state of the financial system determining the relation between the two.

- A new Chapter 9. The traditional aggregate supply-aggregate demand model was cumbersome and gave too optimistic a view of the return of output to potential. The model has been replaced by an IS-LM-PC model (where PC stands for Phillips curve), which gives a simpler and more accurate description of the role of monetary policy, and of output and inflation dynamics.

- The constraints on monetary policy, coming from the zero lower bound, and the constraints on fiscal policy, coming from the high levels of public debt, are recurring themes throughout the book.

- Many Focus boxes are new or extended. Among them: "Unemployment and Happiness" in Chapter 2; "The Liquidity Trap in the United Kingdom" in Chapter 4; Bank Runs in Chapter 6; "Why is the Natural Rate of Unemployment in Japan so Low?" in Chapter 8; "Okun's Law" and "Deflation in the Great Depression" in Chapter 9; "The Construction of PPP Numbers" in Chapter 10; "The Role of Technology in the Decrease in Income Inequality in Latin America in the 2000s" in Chapter 13; "The Yield Curves for AAA-rated Central Government Bonds" in Chapter 14; "The Disappearance of Current Account Deficits in Euro Periphery Countries: Good News or Bad News?" in Chapter 18; "Euro Area Fiscal Rules: A Short History" in Chapter 21; and "Rules versus Discretion: New Absolute Budgetary Rules in the EU" and "How Japan Could Stand Such a Huge Debt?" in Chapter 22.

- Figures and tables have been updated using the latest data available.

In short, I see this edition as the first true post-crisis macroeconomics textbook. I hope it gives a clear guide not only to what has happened, and also to what may happen in the future.

Organization

The book is organized around two central parts: A core, and a set of two major extensions. An introduction precedes the core. The two extensions are followed by a review of the role of policy. The book ends with an epilogue. A flowchart on the front endpaper makes it easy to see how the chapters are organized, and fit within the book's overall structure.

■ Chapters 1 and 2 introduce the basic facts and issues of macroeconomics. Chapter 1 focuses first on the crisis, and then takes a tour of the world, from the United States, to Europe, to China. Some instructors will prefer to cover Chapter 1 later, perhaps after Chapter 2, which introduces basic concepts, articulates the notions of short run, medium run, and long run, and gives the reader a quick tour of the book.

While Chapter 2 gives the basics of national income accounting, I have put a detailed treatment of national income accounts to Appendix 1 at the end of the book. This decreases the burden on the beginning reader, and allows for a more thorough treatment in the appendix.

■ Chapters 3 through 13 constitute the **core**.

Chapters 3 through 6 focus on the **short run**. These four chapters characterize equilibrium in the goods market and in the financial markets, and they derive the basic model used to study short–run movements in output, the *IS–LM* model. Chapter 6 is new, and extends the basic *IS-LM* model to take into account the role of the financial system. It then uses it to describe what happened during the initial phase of the crisis.

Chapters 7 through 9 focus on the **medium run**. Chapter 7 focuses on equilibrium in the labor market and introduces the notion of the natural rate of unemployment. Chapter 8 derives and discusses the relation between unemployment and inflation, known as the Phillips curve. Chapter 9 develops the IS-LM-PC (PC for Phillips curve) model which takes into account equilibrium in the goods market, in the financial markets, and in the labor market. It shows how this model can be used to understand movements in activity and movements in inflation, both in the short and in the medium run.

Chapters 10 through 13 focus on the long run. Chapter 10 describes the facts, showing the evolution of output across countries and over long periods of time. Chapters 11

and 12 develop a model of growth and describe how capital accumulation and technological progress determine growth. Chapter 13 focuses on the effects of technological progress on unemployment and on inequality, not only in the long run, but also in the short run and in the medium run.

■ Chapters 14 through 20 cover the two major **extensions**.

Chapters 14 through 16 focus on the role of **expectations** in the short run and in the medium run. Expectations play a major role in most economic decisions, and, by implication, play a major role in the determination of output.

Chapters 17 through 20 focus on the implications of **openness** of modern economies. Chapter 20 focuses on the implications of different exchange rate regimes, from flexible exchange rates, to fixed exchange rates, currency boards, and dollarization.

■ Chapters 21 through 23 return to **macroeconomic** policy. Although most of the first 20 chapters constantly discuss macroeconomic policy in one form or another, the purpose of Chapters 21 through 23 is to tie the threads together. Chapter 21 looks at the role and the limits of macroeconomic policy in general. Chapters 22 and 23 review fiscal and monetary policy. Some instructors may want to use parts of these chapters earlier. For example, it is easy to move forward the discussion of the government budget constraint in Chapter 22 or the discussion of inflation targeting in Chapter 23.

■ Chapter 24 serves as an **epilogue**; it puts macroeconomics in historical perspective by showing the evolution of macroeconomics in the last 70 years, discussing current directions of research, and the lessons of the crisis for macroeconomics.

Alternative Course Outlines

Within the book's broad organization, there is plenty of opportunity for alternative course organizations. I have made the chapters shorter than is standard in textbooks, and, in my experience, most chapters can be covered in an hour and a half. A few (Chapters 5 and 9 for example) might require two lectures to sink in.

■ Short courses. (15 lectures or less)

A short course can be organized around the two introductory chapters and the core (Chapter 13 can be excluded at no cost in continuity). Informal presentations of one or two of the extensions, based, for example, on Chapter 16 for expectations (which can be taught as a stand alone), and on Chapter 17 for the open economy, can then follow, for a total of 14 lectures.

A short course might leave out the study of growth (the long run). In this case, the course can be organized around the introductory chapters and Chapters 3 through 9 in the core; this gives a total of 9 lectures, leaving enough time to cover, for example, Chapter 16 on expectations, Chapters 17 through 19 on the open economy, for a total of 13 lectures.

■ Longer courses (20 to 25 lectures)

A full semester course gives more than enough time to cover the core, plus one or both of the two extensions, and the review of policy.

The extensions assume knowledge of the core, but are otherwise mostly self-contained. Given the choice, the order in which they are best taught is probably the order in which they are presented in the book. Having studied the role of expectations first helps students to understand the interest parity condition, and the nature of exchange rate crises.

Features

I have made sure never to present a theoretical result without relating it to the real world. In addition to discussions of facts in the text itself, I have written a large number of Focus boxes, which discuss particular macroeconomic events or facts, from the United States or from around the world.

I have tried to re-create some of the student–teacher interactions that take place in the classroom by the use of margin notes, which run parallel to the text. The margin notes create a dialogue with the reader and, in so doing, smooth the more difficult passages and give a deeper understanding of the concepts and the results derived along the way.

For students who want to explore macroeconomics further, I have introduced the following two features:

■ Short appendixes to some chapters, which expand on points made within the chapter.
■ A Further Readings section at the end of most chapters, indicating where to find more information, including a number of key Internet addresses.

Each chapter ends with three ways of making sure that the material in the chapter has been digested:

■ A summary of the chapter's main points.
■ A list of key terms.
■ A series of end-of-chapter exercises. "Quick Check" exercises are easy. "Dig Deeper" exercises are a bit harder, and "Explore Further" typically require either access to the Internet or the use of a spreadsheet -program.
■ A list of symbols on the back endpapers makes it easy to recall the meaning of the symbols used in the text.

MyEconLab

MyEconLab is a powerful assessment and tutorial system that works hand-in-hand with Macroeconomics. It includes comprehensive homework, quiz, test, and tutorial options, allowing students to test their knowledge and instructors to manage all assessment needs in one program. Students and instructors can register, create, and access all of their MyLab courses, regardless of discipline, from one convenient online location: http://www.pearsonmylab.com.

Key innovations in the MyEconLab course for Macroeconomics, seventh edition, include the following resources for students and instructors:

■ **MyEconLab** Animation—The key figures in the seventh edition have been converted to digital figure animations where the figures from the textbook are presented in step-by-step animations with audio explanations of the action. The goal of this digital resource is to help students understand shifts in curves, movements along curves, and changes in equilibrium values. Having animated versions of a graph helps students who have difficulty interpreting the static version found in the printed text.

■ **MyEconLab** Video—There are approximately 100 videos featured in the new enhanced eText for the seventh edition. They provide real world explanations of key concepts with videos from the International Monetary Fund's "World Economic Outlook" press conferences and interviews with author Olivier Blanchard. The videos include in depth market analysis and are accompanied by graded practice exercises to ensure mastery. These new videos are embedded in the eText and are accessible through MyEconLab

■ **Pearson eText**—The Pearson eText gives students access to their textbook anytime, anywhere. In addition to notetaking, highlighting, and bookmarking, the Pearson eText offers interactive and sharing features. Students actively read and learn, through embedded and auto-graded practice, real-time data-graphs, animations, author videos, and more. Instructors can share comments or highlights, and students can add their own, for a tight community of learners in any class.

■ **NEW: Math Review Exercises in MyEconLab.** MyEconLab now offers a rich array of assignable and auto-graded exercises covering fundamental math concepts geared for macroeconomics students. Aimed at increasing student confidence and success, the new math skills review in Chapter R is accessible from the assignment manager and contains over 150 graphing, algebra, and calculus exercises for homework, quiz, and test use.

- **Practice.** Algorithmically generated homework and study plan exercises with instant feedback ensure varied and productive practice that helps students improve their understanding and prepare for quizzes and tests. Exercises that require drawing figures encourage students to practice the language of economics.

- **Learning Resources.** Personalized learning aids such as Help Me Solve This Problem walkthroughs, Teach Me explanations of the underlying concept, and figure animations provide on-demand help when students need it most.

- **Study Plan.** Customized study plans show students which sections to study next, give easy access to practice problems, and provide an automatically generated quiz to prove mastery of the course material.

- **Current News Exercises.** These exercises provide a turnkey approach to assign gradable news-based exercises in MyEconLab. Every week, Pearson scours the news, finds a current article appropriate for a macroeconomics course, creates an exercise based on this news article, and then automatically adds it to MyEconLab.

- **MyEconLab** Real-time data—Real-time data figures **FRED** and exercises allow students and instructors to use the very latest data from the Federal Reserve Bank of St. Louis's FRED site. These figures and exercises communicate directly with the FRED® site and update as new data are available.

- **Digital Interactives.** Focused on a single core topic and organized in progressive levels, each interactive immerses students in an assignable and auto-graded activity. Digital Interactives are lecture tools for traditional, online, and hybrid courses, many incorporating real-time data, data displays, and analysis tools for rich classroom discussions.

- **Experiments in MyEconLab.** Flexible, easy to assign, auto-graded, and available in Single and Multiplayer versions, the Experiments in MyEconLab make learning fun and engaging.

- **Learning Catalytics.** Learning Catalytics™ is a "bring your own device" student engagement, assessment, and classroom intelligence system that lets learners use their smartphone, tablet, or laptop to participate in and stay engaged in lecture. It allows instructors to generate classroom discussion, guides lectures, and promotes peer-to-peer learning with real-time analytics. Now students can use any device to interact in the classroom, engage with content and even draw and share graphs.

Instructors can divide classes into pairs or groups based on learners' response patterns, and learners with greater proficiency help motivate other learners while allowing instructors time to provide individualized and focused attention to learners who will benefit from it.

- **Reporting Dashboard.** Faculty can view, analyze, and report learning outcomes clearly and easily using the Reporting Dashboard. It is available via the Gradebook and fully mobile-ready. The Reporting Dashboard presents student performance data at the class, section, and program levels in an accessible, visual manner.

- **LMS Integration.** Faculty can link from any LMS platform to access assignments, rosters, and resources, and synchronize MyLab grades with your LMS gradebook. For students, a new direct, single sign-on provides easier access to all the personalized learning MyLab resources.

- **Mobile Ready.** Students and instructors can access multimedia resources and complete assessments from any mobile device.

For more information, visit http://www.myeconlab.com.

Supplements

The book comes with a number of supplements that support teaching and learning.

- **Instructor's Manual.** The Online Instructor's Manual, prepared by LaTanya Brown-Robertson, discusses pedagogical choices, alternative ways of presenting the material, and ways of reinforcing students' understanding. Chapters in the manual include six main sections: objectives, in the form of a motivating question; why the answer matters; key tools, concepts, and assumptions; summary; and pedagogy. Many chapters also include sections focusing on extensions and observations. The Instructor's Manual also includes the answers to all end-of-chapter questions and exercises. The Instructor's Manual is available for download as Word files or as PDFs from the Instructor Resource Center at www.pearsonglobaleditions.com/Blanchard.

- **Test Bank.** The online test bank, updated by Liping Zheng is completely revised with additional new multiple–choice questions for each chapter. The Test Item File can be downloaded from the Instructor Resource Center at www.pearsonglobaleditions.com/Blanchard.

- **Computerized Test Bank**—The Computerized Test Item File is designed for use with the computerized Test-Gen package, which allows instructors to customize, save, and generate classroom tests. The test program permits instructors to edit, add, or delete questions from the test bank; edit existing graphics and create new graphics; analyze test results; and organize a database of tests and student results. This software allows for extensive flexibility and ease of use. It provides many options for organizing and displaying tests, along with search and sort features. The software and the Test Item File can be downloaded from the Instructor's Resource Center at www.pearsonglobaleditions.com/Blanchard, and all questions can be assigned via MyEconLab.

- **PowerPoint Lecture Slides**—These electronic slides, prepared by Jim Lee provide section lecture notes including tables, equations, and graphs for each chapter and can be downloaded from the Instructor's Resource Center at www.pearsonglobaleditions.com/Blanchard.

Acknowledgments and Thanks

This book owes much to many. I thank Adam Ashcraft, Peter Berger, Peter Benczur, Efe Cakarel, Francesco Furno, Harry Gakidis, Ava Hong, David Hwang, Kevin Nazemi, David Reichsfeld, Jianlong Tan, Stacy Tevlin, Gaurav Tewari, Corissa Thompson, John Simon, and Jeromin Zettelmeyer for their research assistance over the years. I thank the generations of students in 14.02 at MIT who have freely shared their reactions to the book over the years.

I have benefited from comments from many colleagues and friends. Among them are John Abell, Daron Acemoglu, Tobias Adrian, Chuangxin An, Roland Benabou, Samuel Bentolila, and Juan Jimeno (who have adapted the book for a Spanish edition); Francois Blanchard, Roger Brinner, Ricardo Caballero, Wendy Carlin, Martina Copelman, Henry Chappell, Ludwig Chincarini, and Daniel Cohen (who has adapted the book for a French edition); Larry Christiano, Bud Collier, Andres Conesa, Peter Diamond, Martin Eichenbaum, Gary Fethke, David Findlay, Francesco Giavazzi, and Alessia Amighini (who adapted the book first for an Italian edition, and then for a European edition); Andrew Healy, Steinar Holden, and Gerhard Illing (who has adapted the book for a German edition); Yannis Ioannides, Angelo Melino (who has adapted the book for a Canadian edition); P. N. Junankar, Sam Keeley, Bernd Kuemmel, Paul Krugman, Antoine Magnier, Peter Montiel, Bill Nordhaus, Tom Michl, Dick Oppermann, Athanasios Orphanides, and Daniel Pirez Enri (who has adapted the book for a Latin American edition); Michael Plouffe, Zoran Popovic, Jim Poterba, and Jeff Sheen (who has adapted the book for an Australasian edition); Ronald Schettkat, and Watanabe Shinichi (who has adapted the book for a Japanese edition); Francesco Sisci, Brian Simboli, Changyong Rhee, Julio Rotemberg, Robert Solow, Andre Watteyne (who kindly agreed to be the first reader of this edition), and Michael Woodford. Particular thanks go to David Johnson, who coauthored the sixth edition while I was the chief economist at the IMF and did not have enough time to do it alone, and wrote the end of chapter exercises for this edition, and to Francesco Giavazzi, with whom I worked closely in preparing this edition.

I have benefited from comments from many readers, reviewers, and class testers. Among them:

- John Abell, Randolph, Macon Woman's College
- Carol Adams, Cabrillo College
- Gilad Aharonovitz, School of Economic Sciences
- Terence Alexander, Iowa State University
- Roger Aliaga-Diaz, Drexel University
- Robert Archibald, College of William & Mary
- John Baffoe-Bonnie, La Salle University
- Fatolla Bagheri, University of North Dakota
- Stephen Baker, Capital University
- Erol Balkan, Hamilton College
- Jennifer Ball, Washburn University
- Richard Ballman, Augustana College
- King Banaian, St. Cloud State University
- Charles Bean, London School of Economics and Political Science
- Scott Benson, Idaho State University
- Gerald Bialka, University of North Florida
- Robert Blecker, American University
- Scott Bloom, North Dakota State University
- Pim Borren, University of Canterbury, New Zealand
- LaTanya Brown-Robertson, Bowie State University
- James Butkiewicz, University of Delaware
- Colleen Callahan, American University
- Bruce Carpenter, Mansfield University
- Kyongwook Choi, Ohio University College
- Michael Cook, William Jewell College
- Nicole Crain, Lafayette College
- Rosemary Cunningham, Agnes Scott College
- Evren Damar, Pacific Lutheran University
- Dale DeBoer, University of Colorado at Colorado Springs

- Adrian de Leon-Arias, Universidad de Guadalajara
- Brad DeLong, UC Berkeley
- Firat Demir, University of Oklahoma
- Wouter Denhaan, UC San Diego
- John Dodge, King College
- F. Trenery Dolbear, Brandeis University
- Patrick Dolenc, Keene State College
- Brian Donhauser, University of Washington
- Michael Donihue, Colby College
- Vincent Dropsy, California State University
- Justin Dubas, St. Norbert College
- Amitava Dutt, University of Notre Dame
- John Edgren, Eastern Michigan University
- Eric Elder, Northwestern College
- Sharon J. Erenburg, Eastern Michigan University
- Antonina Espiritu, Hawaii Pacific University
- J. Peter Federer, Clark University
- Rendigs Fels, Vanderbilt University
- John Flanders, Central Methodist University
- Marc Fox, Brooklyn College
- Yee-Tien (Ted) Fu, Stanford University
- Yee-Tien Fu, National Cheng-Chi University, Taiwan
- Scott Fullwiler, Wartburg College
- Julie Gallaway, University of Missouri–Rolla
- Bodhi Ganguli, Rutgers, The State University of NJ
- Fabio Ghironi, Boston College
- Alberto Gomez-Rivas, University of Houston–Downtown
- Fidel Gonzalez, Sam Houston State University
- Harvey Gram, Queen College, City University of New York
- Randy Grant, Linfield College
- Alan Gummerson, Florida International University
- Reza Hamzaee, Missouri Western State College
- Michael Hannan, Edinboro University
- Kenneth Harrison, Richard Stockton College
- Mark Hayford, Loyola University
- Thomas Havrilesky, Duke University
- George Heitmann, Muhlenberg College
- Ana Maria Herrera, Michigan State University
- Peter Hess, Davidson College
- Eric Hilt, Wellesley College
- John Holland, Monmouth College
- Mark Hopkins, Gettysburg College
- Takeo Hoshi, University of California, San Diego
- Ralph Husby, University of Illinois, Urbana–Champaign
- Yannis Ioannides, Tufts University
- Aaron Jackson, Bentley College
- Bonnie Johnson, California Lutheran University
- Louis Johnston, College of St. Benedict
- Barry Jones, SUNY Binghamton
- Fred Joutz, George Washington University
- Cem Karayalcin, Florida International University
- Okan Kavuncu, University of California
- Miles Kimball, University of Michigan
- Paul King, Denison University
- Michael Klein, Tufts University
- Mark Klinedinst, University of Southern Mississippi
- Shawn Knabb, Western Washington University
- Todd Knoop, Cornell College
- Paul Koch, Olivet Nazarene University
- Ng Beoy Kui, Nanyang Technical University, Singapore
- Leonard Lardaro, University of Rhode Island
- James Leady, University of Notre Dame
- Charles Leathers, University of Alabama
- Hsien-Feng Lee, National Taiwan University
- Jim Lee, Texas A&M University–Corpus Christi
- John Levendis, Loyola University New Orleans
- Frank Lichtenberg, Columbia University
- Mark Lieberman, Princeton University
- Shu Lin, Florida Atlantic University
- Maria Luengo-Prado, Northeastern University

- Mathias Lutz, University of Sussex
- Bernard Malamud, University of Nevada, Las Vegas
- Ken McCormick, University of Northern Iowa
- William McLean, Oklahoma State University
- B. Starr McMullen, Oregon State University
- Mikhail Melnik, Niagara University
- O. Mikhail, University of Central Florida
- Fabio Milani, University of California, Irvine
- Rose Milbourne, University of New South Wales
- Roger Morefield, University of Saint Thomas
- Shahriar Mostashari, Campbell University
- Eshragh Motahar, Union College
- Nick Noble, Miami University
- Ilan Noy, University of Hawaii
- John Olson, College of St. Benedict
- Brian O'Roark, Robert Morris University
- Jack Osman, San Francisco State University
- Emiliano Pagnotta, Northwestern University
- Biru Paksha Paul, SUNY Cortland
- Andrew Parkes, Mesa State College
- Allen Parkman, University of Mexico
- Jim Peach, New Mexico State University
- Gavin Peebles, National University of Singapore
- Michael Quinn, Bentley College
- Charles Revier, Colorado State University
- Jack Richards, Portland State University
- Raymond Ring, University of South Dakota
- Monica Robayo, University of North Florida
- Malcolm Robinson, Thomas Moore College
- Brian Rosario, University of California, Davis
- Kehar Sangha, Old Dominion University
- Ahmad Saranjam, Bridgewater State College
- Carol Scotese, Virginia Commonwealth University
- John Seater, North Carolina State University
- Peter Sephton, University of New Brunswick
- Ruth Shen, San Francisco State University
- Kwanho Shin, University of Kansas
- Tara Sinclair, The George Washington University
- Aaron Smallwood, University of Texas, Arlington
- David Sollars, Auburn University
- Liliana Stern, Auburn University
- Edward Stuart, Northeastern Illinois University
- Abdulhanid Sukaar, Cameron University
- Peter Summers, Texas Tech University
- Mark Thomas, University of Maryland Baltimore County
- Brian Trinque, The University of Texas at Austin
- Marie Truesdell, Marian College
- David Tufte, Southern Utah University
- Abdul Turay, Radford University
- Frederick Tyler, Fordham University
- Pinar Uysal, Boston College
- Evert Van Der Heide, Calvin College
- Kristin Van Gaasbeck, California State University, Sacramento
- Lee Van Scyoc, University of Wisconsin, Oshkosh
- Paul Wachtel, New York University Stern Business School
- Susheng Wang, Hong Kong University
- Donald Westerfield, Webster University
- Christopher Westley, Jacksonville State University
- David Wharton, Washington College
- Jonathan Willner, Oklahoma City University
- Mark Wohar, University of Nebraska, Omaha
- Steven Wood, University of California, Berkeley
- Michael Woodford, Princeton University
- Ip Wing Yu, University of Hong Kong
- Chi-Wa Yuen, Hong Kong University of Science and Technology
- Christian Zimmermann, University of Connecticut
- Liping Zheng, Drake University

They have helped us beyond the call of duty, and each has made a difference to the book.

I have many people to thank at Pearson Christina Masturzo, senior acquisitions editor; Nancy Freihofer, program manager; Diana Tetterton, editorial assistant; Heather Pagano, project manager; and Maggie Moylan, VP, product marketing.

Finally, I want to single out Steve Rigolosi, the editor for the first edition; Michael Elia, the editor to the second and third editions. Steve forced me to clarify. Michael forced me to simplify. Together, they have made all the difference to the process and to the book. I thank them deeply. I thank John Arditi for his absolute reliability and his help, from the first edition to this one. I have also benefited from often-stimulating suggestions from my daughters, Serena, Giulia, and Marie: I did not, however, follow all of them. At home, I continue to thank Noelle for preserving my sanity.

Olivier Blanchard
Washington,
December 2015

Global Edition Acknowledgments

Pearson would like to thank the following people for their contributions and reviews for this Global Edition

Contributors

- Monal Abdelbaki, Durban University of Technology
- Olivier Butzbach, The Second University of Naples
- Patrick Terroir, Institut D'études Politiques de Paris

Reviewers

- Natalie Chen, University of Warwick
- Eliane Haykal, University of Balamand
- Glenn Otto, UNSW Business School

Introduction

The first two chapters of this book introduce you to the issues and the approach of macroeconomics.

Chapter 1

Chapter 1 takes you on a macroeconomic tour of the world. It starts with a look at the economic crisis that has shaped the world economy since the late 2000s. The tour then stops at each of the world's major economic powers: the United States, the Euro area, and China.

Chapter 2

Chapter 2 takes you on a tour of the book. It defines the three central variables of macroeconomics: output, unemployment, and inflation. It then introduces the three time periods around which the book is organized: the short run, the medium run, and the long run.

A Tour of the World

hat is macroeconomics? The best way to answer is not to give you a formal definition, but rather to take you on an economic tour of the world, to describe both the main economic evolutions and the issues that keep macroeconomists and macroeconomic policy makers awake at night.

At the time of this writing (the fall of 2015), policy makers are sleeping better than they did just a few years ago. In 2008, the world economy entered a major macroeconomic crisis, the deepest since the Great Depression. World output growth, which typically runs at 4 to 5% a year, was actually negative in 2009. Since then, growth has turned positive, and the world economy is slowly recovering. But the crisis has left a number of scars, and some worries remain.

My goal in this chapter is to give you a sense of these events and of some of the macroeconomic issues confronting different countries today. I shall start with an overview of the crisis, and then focus on the three main economic powers of the world: the United States, the Euro area, and China.

Section 1-1 looks at the crisis.

Section 1-2 looks at the United States.

Section 1-3 looks at the Euro area.

Section 1-4 looks at China.

Section 1-5 concludes and looks ahead.

Read this chapter as you would read an article in a newspaper. Do not worry about the exact meaning of the words or about understanding the arguments in detail: The words will be defined, and the arguments will be developed in later chapters. Think of this chapter as background, intended to introduce you to the issues of macroeconomics. If you enjoy reading this chapter, you will probably enjoy reading this book. Indeed, once you have read it, come back to this chapter; see where you stand on the issues, and judge how much progress you have made in your study of macroeconomics.

MyEconLab Video

◄ If you do not, please accept my apologies…

1-1 The Crisis

Figure 1-1 shows output growth rates for the world economy, for advanced economies, and for other economies, separately, since 2000. As you can see, from 2000 to 2007 the world economy had a sustained expansion. Annual average world output growth was 4.5%, with advanced economies (the group of 30 or so richest countries in the world) growing at 2.7% per year, and other economies (the other 150 or so countries in the world) growing at an even faster 6.6% per year.

In 2007 however, signs that the expansion might be coming to an end started to appear. U.S. housing prices, which had doubled since 2000, started declining. Economists started to worry. Optimists believed that, although lower housing prices might lead to lower housing construction and to lower spending by consumers, the Fed (the short name for the U.S. central bank, formally known as the *Federal Reserve Board*) could lower interest rates to stimulate demand and avoid a recession. Pessimists believed that the decrease in interest rates might not be enough to sustain demand and that the United States may go through a short recession.

Even the pessimists turned out not to be pessimistic enough. As housing prices continued to decline, it became clear that the problems were deeper. Many of the mortgages that had been given out during the previous expansion were of poor quality. Many of the borrowers had taken too large a loan and were increasingly unable to make the monthly payments on their mortgages. And, with declining housing prices, the value of their mortgage often exceeded the price of the house, giving them an incentive to default. This was not the worst of it: The banks that had issued the mortgages had often bundled and packaged them together into new securities and then sold these securities to other banks and investors. These securities had often been repackaged into yet new securities, and so on. The result is that many banks, instead of holding the mortgages themselves, held these securities, which were so complex that their value was nearly impossible to assess.

This complexity and opaqueness turned a housing price decline into a major financial crisis, a development that few economists had anticipated. Not knowing the quality of the assets that other banks had on their balance sheets, banks became reluctant to lend to each other for fear that the bank to which they lent might not be able to repay.

"Banks" here actually means "banks and other financial institutions." But this is too long to write and I do not want ▶ to go into these complications in Chapter 1.

Figure 1-1

Output Growth Rates for the World Economy, for Advanced Economies, and for Emerging and Developing Economies, 2000–2014

Source: World Economic Outlook Database, July 2015. NGDP_RPCH.A.

MyEconLab Real-time data

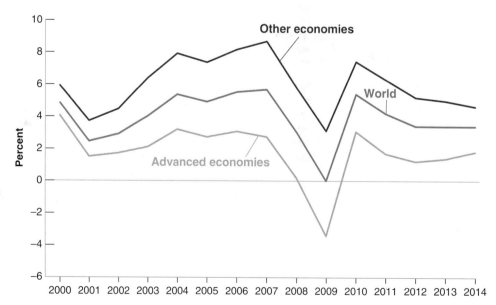

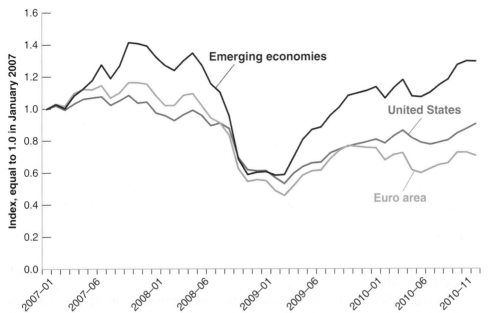

Figure 1-2

Stock Prices in the United States, the Euro Area, and Emerging Economies, 2007–2010

Source: Haver Analytics USA (S111ACD), Eurogroup (S023ACD), all emerging markets (S200ACD), all monthly averages.

Unable to borrow, and with assets of uncertain value, many banks found themselves in trouble. On September 15, 2008, a major bank, Lehman Brothers, went bankrupt. The effects were dramatic. Because the links between Lehman and other banks were so opaque, many other banks appeared at risk of going bankrupt as well. For a few weeks, it looked as if the whole financial system might collapse.

◀ I started my job as chief economist at the International Monetary Fund two weeks before the Lehman bankruptcy. I faced a steep learning curve.

This financial crisis quickly turned into a major economic crisis. Stock prices collapsed. Figure 1-2 plots the evolution of three stock price indexes, for the United States, for the Euro area, and for emerging economies, from the beginning of 2007 to the end of 2010. The indexes are set equal to 1 in January 2007. Note how, by the end of 2008, stock prices had lost half or more of their value from their previous peak. Note also that, despite the fact that the crisis originated in the United States, European and emerging market stock prices decreased by as much as their U.S. counterparts; I shall return to this later.

Hit by the decrease in housing prices and the collapse in stock prices, and worried that this might be the beginning of another Great Depression, people sharply cut their consumption. Worried about sales and uncertain about the future, firms sharply cut back their investment. With housing prices dropping and many vacant homes on the market, very few new homes were built. Despite strong actions by the Fed, which cut interest rates all the way down to zero, and by the U.S. government, which cut taxes and increased spending, demand decreased, and so did output. In the third quarter of 2008, U.S. output growth turned negative and remained so in 2009.

One might have hoped that the crisis would remain largely contained in the United States. As Figures 1-1 and 1-2 both show, this was not the case. The U.S. crisis quickly became a world crisis. Other countries were affected through two channels. The first channel was trade. As U.S. consumers and firms cut spending, part of the decrease fell on imports of foreign goods. Looking at it from the viewpoint of countries exporting to the United States, their exports went down, and so, in turn, did their output. The second channel was financial. U.S. banks, badly needing funds in the United States, repatriated funds from other countries, creating problems for banks in those countries as well. As those banks got in trouble, lending came to a halt, leading to a decrease in spending and in output. Also, in a number of European countries, governments had accumulated high levels of debt and were now running large deficits. Investors began to worry about whether debt could be repaid and asked for much higher interest rates. Confronted with those high interest rates, governments drastically reduced their deficits, through a combination of lower spending and higher taxes. This led in turn to a further decrease in demand, and in output. In Europe, the decline in output was so bad that this particular aspect of the crisis acquired its own name, the *Euro Crisis*. In short, the U.S. recession turned into a world recession. By 2009, average growth in advanced economies was −3.4%, by far the lowest annual growth rate since the Great Depression. Growth in emerging and developing economies remained positive but was 3.5 percentage points lower than the 2000–2007 average.

MyEconLab Video

Since then, thanks to strong monetary and fiscal policies and to the slow repair of the financial system, most economies have turned around. As you can see from Figure 1-1, growth in advanced countries turned positive in 2010 and has remained positive since. The recovery is however both unimpressive and uneven. In some advanced countries, most notably the United States, unemployment has nearly returned to its pre-crisis level. The Euro area however is still struggling. Growth is positive, but it is low, and unemployment remains high. Growth in emerging and developing economies has also recovered, but, as you can see from Figure 1-1, it is lower than it was before the crisis and has steadily declined since 2010.

Having set the stage, let me now take you on a tour of the three main economic powers in the world, the United States, the Euro area, and China.

1-2 The United States

When economists look at a country, the first two questions they ask are: How big is the country from an economic point of view? And what is its standard of living? To answer the first, they look at output—the level of production of the country as a whole. To answer the second, they look at output per person. The answers, for the United States, are given in Figure 1-3: The United States is big, with an output of $17.4 trillion in 2014,

Figure 1-3

The United States, 2014

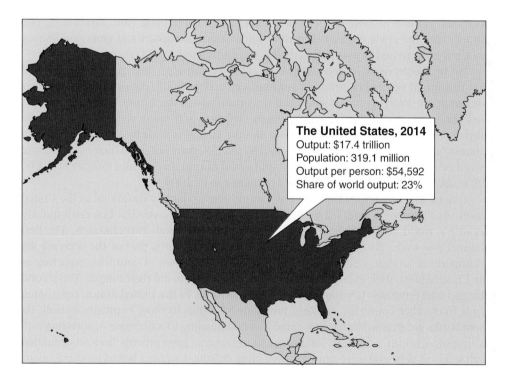

The United States, 2014
Output: $17.4 trillion
Population: 319.1 million
Output per person: $54,592
Share of world output: 23%

accounting for 23% of world output. This makes it the largest country in the world in economic terms. And the standard of living in the United States is high: Output per person is $54,600. It is not the country with the highest output per person in the world, but it is close to the top.

When economists want to dig deeper and look at the state of health of the country, they look at three basic variables:

■ *Output growth*—the rate of change of output
■ The *unemployment rate*—the proportion of workers in the economy who are not employed and are looking for a job
■ The *inflation rate*—the rate at which the average price of goods in the economy is increasing over time

Numbers for these three variables for the U.S. economy are given in Table 1-1. To put current numbers in perspective, the first column gives the average value of each of the three variables for the period 1990 up to 2007, the year before the crisis. The second column shows numbers for the acute part of the crisis, the years 2008 and 2009. The third column shows the numbers from 2010 to 2014, and the last column gives the numbers for 2015 (or more accurately, the forecasts for 2015 as of the fall of 2015).

By looking at the numbers for 2015, you can see why economists are reasonably optimistic about the U.S. economy at this point. Growth in 2015 is forecast to be above 2.5%, just a bit below the 1990–2007 average. Unemployment, which increased during the crisis and its aftermath (it reached 10% during 2010), is decreasing and, at 5.4%, is now back to its 1990–2007 average. Inflation is low, substantially lower than the 1990–2007 average. In short, the U.S. economy seems to be in decent shape, having largely left the effects of the crisis behind.

Not everything is fine however. To make sure demand was strong enough to sustain growth, the Fed has had to maintain interest rates very low, indeed, too low for comfort. And productivity growth appears to have slowed, implying mediocre growth in the future. Let's look at both issues in turn.

> Can you guess some of the countries with a higher standard of living than the United States? *Hint*: Think of oil producers and financial centers. For answers, look for "Gross Domestic Product per capita, in current prices" at http://www.imf.org/external/pubs/ft/weo/2015/01/weodata/weoselgr.aspx

Low Interest Rates and the Zero Lower Bound

When the crisis started, the Fed tried to limit the decrease in spending by decreasing the interest rate it controls, the so-called *federal funds rate*. As you can see from Figure 1-4, on page 28 the federal funds rate went from 5.2% in July 2007 to nearly 0% (0.16% to be precise) in December 2008.

Why did the Fed stop at zero? Because the interest rate cannot be negative. If it were, then nobody would hold bonds, everybody would want to hold cash instead—because cash pays a zero interest rate. This constraint is known in macroeconomics as the *zero lower bound*, and this is the bound the Fed ran into in December 2008.

> Because keeping cash in large sums is inconvenient and dangerous, people might be willing to hold some bonds even if those pay a small negative interest rate. But there is a clear limit to how negative the interest rate can go before people find ways to switch to cash.

MyEconLab Real-time data

| Table 1-1 | Growth, Unemployment, and Inflation in the United States, 1990–2015 |

Percent	1990–2007 (average)	2008–2009 (average)	2010–2014 (average)	2015
Output growth rate	3.0	–1.5	2.2	2.5
Unemployment rate	5.4	7.5	8.0	5.4
Inflation rate	2.3	1.4	1.6	0.7

Output growth rate: annual rate of growth of output (GDP). Unemployment rate: average over the year. Inflation rate: annual rate of change of the price level (GDP deflator).

Source: IMF, *World Economic Outlook*, July 2015.

Figure 1-4

The U.S. Federal Funds Rate since 2000

Source: Haver Analytics.

MyEconLab Real-time data

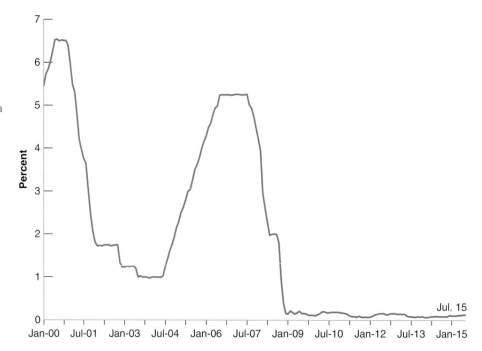

As you will see later in the book, central banks like the Fed can use a few other tools to increase demand. These tools ▶ are known as "unconventional monetary policy." But they do not work as well as the interest rate.

This sharp decrease in the interest rate, which made it cheaper for consumers to borrow, and for firms to invest, surely limited the fall in demand and the fall in output. But, as we saw earlier and you can see from Table 1-1, this was not enough to avoid a deep recession: U.S. growth was negative in both 2008 and 2009. To help the economy recover, the Fed then kept the interest rate close to zero, where it has remained until now (the fall of 2015). The Fed's plan is to start increasing the interest rate soon, so when you read this book, it is likely that the rate will have increased, but it will still be very low by historical standards.

Why are low interest rates a potential issue? For two reasons: The first is that low interest rates limit the ability of the Fed to respond to further negative shocks. If the interest rate is at or close to zero, and demand further decreases, there is little the Fed can do to increase demand. The second is that low interest rates appear to lead to excessive risk taking by investors. Because the return from holding bonds is so low, investors are tempted to take too much risk to increase their returns. And too much risk taking can in turn give rise to financial crises of the type we just experienced. Surely, we do not want to experience another crisis like the one we just went through.

How Worrisome Is Low Productivity Growth?

Although the Fed has to worry about maintaining enough demand to achieve growth in the short run, over longer periods of time, growth is determined by other factors, the main one being productivity growth: Without productivity growth, there just cannot be a sustained increase in income per person. And, here, the news is worrisome. Table 1-2 shows average U.S. productivity growth by decade since 1990 for the private sector as a whole and for the manufacturing sector. As you can see, productivity growth in the 2010s has so far been about half as high as it was in the 1990s.

How worrisome is this? Productivity growth varies a lot from year to year, and some economists believe that it may just be a few bad years and not much to worry about. Others believe that measurement issues make it difficult to measure output and that productivity growth may be underestimated. For example, how do you measure

Table 1-2 Labor Productivity Growth, by Decade

Percent change; year on year (average)	1990s	2000s	2010–2014
Nonfarm Business Sector	2.0	2.6	1.2
Business Sector	2.1	2.6	1.2
Manufacturing	4.0	3.1	2.4

Source: Haver Analytics.

the real value of a new smartphone relative to an older model? Its price may be higher, but it probably does many things that the older model could not do. Yet others believe that the United States has truly entered a period of lower productivity growth, that the major gains from the current IT innovations may already have been obtained, and that progress is likely to be less rapid, at least for some time.

IT stands for information technology.

One particular reason to worry is that this slowdown in productivity growth is happening in the context of growing inequality. When productivity growth is high, most everybody is likely to benefit, even if inequality increases. The poor may benefit less than the rich, but they still see their standard of living increase. This is not the case today in the United States. Since 2000, the real earnings of workers with a high school education or less have actually decreased. If policy makers want to invert this trend, they need either to raise productivity growth or limit the rise of inequality, or both. These are two major challenges facing U.S. policy makers today.

1-3 The Euro Area

In 1957, six European countries decided to form a common European market—an economic zone where people and goods could move freely. Since then, 22 more countries have joined, bringing the total to 28. This group is now known as the **European Union**, or EU for short.

Until a few years ago, the official name was the European Community, or EC. You may still encounter that name.

In 1999, the EU decided to go a step further and started the process of replacing national currencies with one common currency, called the *euro*. Only 11 countries participated at the start; since then, 8 more have joined. Some countries, in particular, the United Kingdom, have decided not to join, at least for the time being. The official name for the group of member countries is the **Euro area**. The transition took place in steps. On January 1, 1999, each of the 11 countries fixed the value of its currency to the euro. For example, 1 euro was set equal to 6.56 French francs, to 166 Spanish pesetas, and so on. From 1999 to 2002, prices were quoted both in national currency units and in euros, but the euro was not yet used as currency. This happened in 2002, when euro notes and coins replaced national currencies. Nineteen countries now belong to this *common currency area*.

The area also goes by the names of "Euro zone" or "Euroland." The first sounds too technocratic, and the second reminds one of Disneyland. I shall avoid them.

MyEconLab Real-time data

Table 1-3 Growth, Unemployment, and Inflation in the Euro Area, 1990–2015

Percent	1990–2007 (average)	2008–2009 (average)	2010–2014 (average)	2015
Output growth rate	2.1	−2.0	0.7	1.5
Unemployment rate	9.4	8.6	11.1	11.1
Inflation rate	2.1	1.5	1.0	1.1

Output growth rate: annual rate of growth of output (GDP). Unemployment rate: average over the year.
Inflation rate: annual rate of change of the price level (GDP deflator).

Source: IMF, *World Economic Outlook*, July 2015.

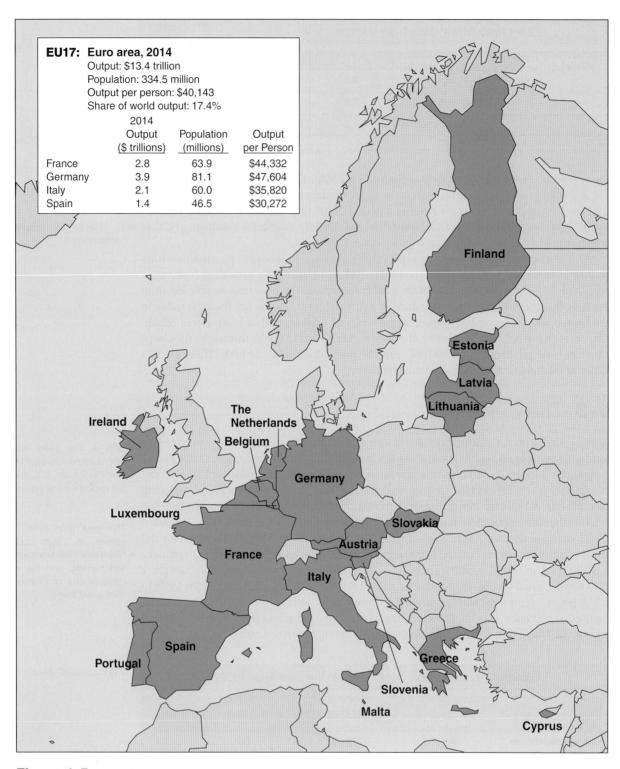

EU17: Euro area, 2014
Output: $13.4 trillion
Population: 334.5 million
Output per person: $40,143
Share of world output: 17.4%

	2014 Output ($ trillions)	Population (millions)	Output per Person
France	2.8	63.9	$44,332
Germany	3.9	81.1	$47,604
Italy	2.1	60.0	$35,820
Spain	1.4	46.5	$30,272

Figure 1-5

The Euro Area, 2014

As you can see from Figure 1-5, the Euro area is also a strong economic power. Its output is nearly equal to that of the United States, and its standard of living is not far behind. (The EU as a whole has an output that exceeds that of the United States.) As the numbers in Table 1-3 show, however, it is not doing very well.

MyEconLab Video

Just as in the United States, the acute phase of the crisis, 2008 and 2009, was characterized by negative growth. Whereas the United States recovered, growth in the Euro area remained anemic, close to zero over 2010 to 2014 (indeed two of these years again saw negative growth). Even in 2015, growth is forecast to be only 1.5%, less than in the United States, and less than the pre-crisis average. Unemployment, which increased from 2007 on, stands at a high 11.1%, nearly twice that of the United States. Inflation is low, below the target of the European Central Bank, the ECB.

The Euro area faces two main issues today. The first is how to reduce unemployment. Second is whether and how it can function efficiently as a **common currency area**. We consider these two issues in turn.

Can European Unemployment Be Reduced?

The high average unemployment rate for the Euro area, 11.1% in 2015, hides a lot of variations across Euro countries. At one end, Greece and Spain have unemployment rates of 25% and 23%, respectively. At the other, Germany's unemployment rate is less than 5%. In the middle are countries like France and Italy, with unemployment rates of 10% and 12%, respectively. Thus, it is clear that how to reduce unemployment must be tailored to the specifics of each country.

To show the complexity of the issues, it is useful to look at a particular country with high unemployment. Figure 1-6 shows the striking evolution of the Spanish unemployment rate since 1990. After a long boom starting in the mid 1990s, the unemployment rate had decreased from a high of nearly 25% in 1994 to 9% by 2007. But, with the crisis, unemployment exploded again, exceeding 25% in 2013. Only now, is it starting to decline, but it is still high. The graph suggests two conclusions:

■ Much of the high unemployment rate today is a result of the crisis, and to the sudden collapse in demand we discussed in the first section. A housing boom turned to

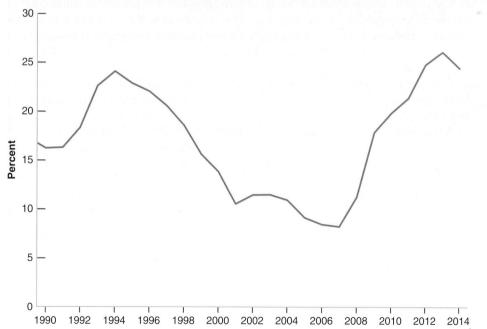

Figure 1-6

Unemployment in Spain since 1990

(*Source:* International Monetary Fund, *World Economic Outlook*, July 2015).

MyEconLab Real-time data

housing bust, plus a sudden increase in interest rates, triggered the increase in unemployment from 2008 on. One can hope that, eventually, demand will pick up, and unemployment will decrease.

■ How low can it get? Even at the peak of the boom however, the unemployment rate in Spain was around 9%, nearly twice the unemployment rate in the United States today. This suggests that more is at work than the crisis and the fall in demand. The fact that, for most of the last 20 years, unemployment has exceeded 10% points to problems in the labor market. The challenge is then to identify exactly what these problems are, in Spain, and in other European countries.

Some economists believe the main problem is that European states protect workers too much. To prevent workers from losing their jobs, they make it expensive for firms to lay off workers. One of the unintended results of this policy is to deter firms from hiring workers in the first place, and thus increasing unemployment. Also, to protect workers who become unemployed, European governments provide generous unemployment insurance. But, by doing so, they decrease the incentives for the unemployed to take jobs rapidly; this also increases unemployment. The solution, these economists argue, is to be less protective, to eliminate these *labor market rigidities*, and to adopt U.S.-style labor-market institutions. This is what the United Kingdom has largely done, and its unemployment rate is low.

Others are more skeptical. They point to the fact that unemployment is not high everywhere in Europe. Yet most countries provide protection and generous social insurance to workers. This suggests that the problem may lay not so much with the degree of protection but with the way it is implemented. The challenge, those economists argue, is to understand what the low unemployment countries are doing right, and whether what they do right can be exported to other European countries. Resolving these questions is one of the major tasks facing European macroeconomists and policy makers today.

What Has the Euro Done for Its Members?

Supporters of the euro point to its enormous symbolic importance. In light of the many past wars among European countries, what better proof of the permanent end to conflict than the adoption of a common currency? They also point to the economic advantages of having a common currency: no more changes in exchange rates for European firms to worry about; no more need to change currencies when crossing borders. Together with the removal of other obstacles to trade among European countries, the euro contributes, they argue, to the creation of a large economic power in the world. There is little question that the move to the euro was indeed one of the main economic events of the start of the twenty-first century.

Others worry, however, that the symbolism of the euro has come with substantial economic costs. Even before the crisis, they pointed out that a common currency means a common monetary policy, which means the same interest rate across the euro countries. What if, they argued, one country plunges into recession while another is in the middle of an economic boom? The first country needs lower interest rates to increase spending and output; the second country needs higher interest rates to slow down its economy. If interest rates have to be the same in both countries, what will happen? Isn't there the risk that one country will remain in recession for a long time or that the other will not be able to slow down its booming economy? And a common currency also means the loss of the exchange rate as an instrument of adjustment within the Euro area. What if, they argued, a country has a large trade deficit and needs to become more competitive? If it cannot adjust its exchange rate, it must adjust by decreasing prices relative to its competitors. This is likely to be a painful and long process.

Until the Euro crisis, the debate had remained somewhat abstract. It no longer is. As a result of the crisis, a number of Euro members, from Ireland and Portugal, to Greece, have gone through deep recessions. If they had their own currency, they could have depreciated their currency vis-à-vis other Euro members to increase the demand for their exports. Because they shared a currency with their neighbors, this was not possible. Thus, some economists conclude, some countries should drop out of the euro and recover control of their monetary policy and of their exchange rate. Others argue that such an exit would be both unwise because it would give up on the other advantages of being in the euro and be extremely disruptive, leading to even deeper problems for the country that exited. This issue is likely to remain a hot one for some time to come.

1-4 China

China is in the news every day. It is increasingly seen as one of the major economic powers in the world. Is the attention justified? A first look at the numbers in Figure 1-7 on page 34 suggests it may not be. True, the population of China is enormous, more than four times that of the United States. But its output, expressed in dollars by multiplying the number in yuans (the Chinese currency) by the dollar–yuan exchange rate, is still only 10.4 trillion dollars, about 60% of the United States. Output per person is about $7,600, only roughly 15% of output per person in the United States.

So why is so much attention paid to China? There are two main reasons: To understand the first, we need to go back to the number for output per person. When comparing output per person in a rich country like the United States and a relatively poor country like China, one must be careful. The reason is that many goods are cheaper in poor countries. For example, the price of an average restaurant meal in New York City is about 20 dollars; the price of an average restaurant meal in Beijing is about 25 yuans, or, at the current exchange rate, about 4 dollars. Put another way, the same income (expressed in dollars) buys you much more in Beijing than in New York City. If we want to compare standards of living, we have to correct for these differences; measures which do so are called PPP (for *purchasing power parity*) measures. Using such a measure, output per person in China is estimated to be about $12,100, roughly one-fourth of the output per person in the United States. This gives a more accurate picture of the standard of living in China. It is obviously still much lower than that of the United States or other rich countries. But it is higher than suggested by the numbers in Figure 1-7.

The issue is less important when comparing two rich countries. Thus, this was not a major issue when comparing standards of living in the United States and the Euro area previously.

Second, and more importantly, China has been growing very rapidly for more than three decades. This is shown in Table 1-4, which, like the previous tables for the United States and the Euro area, gives output growth, unemployment, and inflation for the periods 1990–2007, 2008–2009, 2010–2014, and the forecast for 2015.

The first line of the table tells the basic story. Since 1990 (indeed, since 1980, if we were to extend the table back by another 10 years), China has grown at close to 10% a year. This represents a doubling of output every 7 years. Compare this number to the numbers for the United States and for Europe we saw previously, and you understand why the weight of the emerging economies in the world economy, China being the main one, is increasing so rapidly.

There are two other interesting aspects to Table 1-4. The first is how difficult it is to see the effects of the crisis in the data. Growth barely decreased during 2008 and 2009, and unemployment barely increased. The reason is not that China is closed to the rest of the world. Chinese exports slowed during the crisis. But the adverse effect on demand was nearly fully offset by a major fiscal expansion by the Chinese government, with, in particular, a major increase in public investment. The result was sustained growth of demand and, in turn, of output.

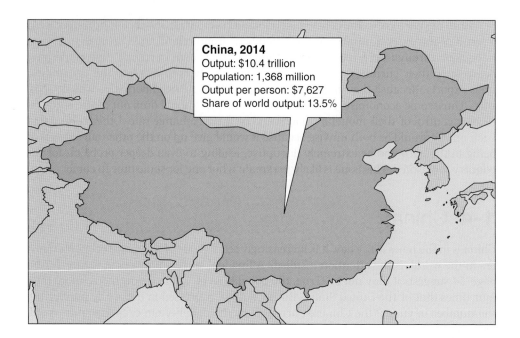

Figure 1-7

China, 2014

Source: World Economic Outlook, IMF.

The second is the decline in growth rates from 10% before the crisis to less than 9% after the crisis, and to the forecast 6.8% for 2015. This raises questions both about how China maintained such a high growth rate for so long, and whether it is now entering a period of lower growth.

A preliminary question is whether the numbers are for real. Could it be that Chinese growth was and is still overstated? After all, China is still officially a communist country, and government officials may have incentives to overstate the economic performance of their sector or their province. Economists who have looked at this carefully conclude that this is probably not the case. The statistics are not as reliable as they are in richer countries, but there is no major bias. Output growth is indeed very high in China. So where has growth come from? It has come from two sources: The first was high accumulation of capital. The investment rate (the ratio of investment to output) in China is 48%, a very high number. For comparison, the investment rate in the United States is only 19%. More capital means higher productivity and higher output. The second is rapid technological progress. One of the strategies followed by the Chinese government has been to encourage foreign firms to relocate and produce in China. As foreign firms are typically much more productive than Chinese firms,

MyEconLab Real-time data

Table 1-4 Growth, Unemployment, and Inflation in China, 1990–2015

Percent	1990–2007 (average)	2008–2009 (average)	2010–2014 (average)	2015
Output growth rate	10.2	9.4	8.6	6.8
Unemployment rate	3.3	4.3	4.1	4.1
Inflation rate	5.9	3.7	4.2	1.2

Output growth rate: annual rate of growth of output (GDP). Unemployment rate: average over the year.
Inflation rate: annual rate of change of the price level (GDP deflator).

Source: IMF, *World Economic Outlook*, July 2015.

this has increased productivity and output. Another aspect of the strategy has been to encourage joint ventures between foreign and Chinese firms. By making Chinese firms work with and learn from foreign firms, the productivity of the Chinese firms has increased dramatically.

When described in this way, achieving high productivity and high output growth appears easy and a recipe that every poor country could and should follow. In fact, things are less obvious. China is one of a number of countries that made the transition from central planning to a market economy. Most of the other countries, from Central Europe to Russia and the other former Soviet republics, experienced a large decrease in output at the time of transition. Most still have growth rates far below that of China. In many countries, widespread corruption and poor property rights make firms unwilling to invest. So why has China fared so much better? Some economists believe that this is the result of a slower transition: The first Chinese reforms took place in agriculture as early as 1980, and even today, many firms remain owned by the state. Others argue that the fact that the communist party has remained in control has actually helped the economic transition; tight political control has allowed for a better protection of property rights, at least for new firms, giving them incentives to invest. Getting the an- ◀ swers to these questions, and thus learning what other poor countries can take from the Chinese experience, can clearly make a huge difference, not only for China but for the rest of the world.

Tight political control has also allowed for corruption to develop, and corruption can also threaten investment. China is now in the midst of a strong anti-corruption campaign.

At the same time, the recent growth slowdown raises a new set of questions: Where does the slowdown come from? Should the Chinese government try to maintain high growth or accept the lower growth rate? Most economists and, indeed, the Chinese authorities themselves, believe that lower growth is now desirable, that the Chinese people will be better served if the investment rate decreases, allowing more of output to go to consumption. Achieving the transition from investment to consumption is the major challenge facing the Chinese authorities today.

1-5 Looking Ahead

This concludes our whirlwind world tour. There are many other regions of the world and many other macroeconomic issues we could have looked at:

- India, another poor and large country, with a population of 1,270 million people, which, like China, is now growing very fast and becoming a world economic power.
- Japan, whose growth performance for the 40 years following World War II was so impressive that it was referred to as an economic miracle, but it has done very poorly in the last two decades. Since a stock market crash in the early 1990s, Japan has been in a prolonged slump, with average output growth under 1% per year.
- Latin America, which went from high inflation to low inflation in the 1990s, and then sustained strong growth. Recently however, its growth has slowed, as a result, in part, of a decline in the price of commodities.
- Central and Eastern Europe, which shifted from central planning to a market system in the early 1990s. In most countries, the shift was characterized by a sharp decline in output at the start of transition. Some countries, such as Poland, now have high growth rates; others, such as Bulgaria, are still struggling.
- Africa, which has suffered decades of economic stagnation, but where, contrary to common perceptions, growth has been high since 2000, averaging 5.5% per year and reflecting growth in most of the countries of the continent.

MyEconLab Video

There is a limit to how much you can absorb in this first chapter. Think about the issues to which you have been exposed:

- The big issues triggered by the crisis: What caused the crisis? Why did it transmit so fast from the United States to the rest of the world? In retrospect, what could and should have been done to prevent it? Were the monetary and fiscal responses appropriate? Why is the recovery so slow in Europe? How was China able to maintain high growth during the crisis?
- Can monetary and fiscal policies be used to avoid recessions? How much of an issue is the zero lower bound on interest rates? What are the pros and cons of joining a common currency area such as the Euro area? What measures could be taken in Europe to reduce persistently high unemployment?
- Why do growth rates differ so much across countries, even over long periods of time? Can other countries emulate China and grow at the same rate? Should China slow down?

The purpose of this book is to give you a way of thinking about these questions. As we develop the tools you need, I shall show you how to use them by returning to these questions and showing you the answers the tools suggest.

Key Terms

European Union (EU), 29
Euro area, 29

common currency area, 31

Questions and Problems MyEconLab Real-time data exercises are marked .

QUICK CHECK

MyEconLab Visit www.myeconlab.com to complete similar Quick Check problems and get instant feedback.

1. *Using the information in this chapter, label each of the following statements true, false, or uncertain. Explain briefly.*

a. Output growth was negative in both advanced as well as emerging and developing countries in 2009.

b. World output growth recovered to its prerecession level after 2009.

c. Stock prices around the world fell between 2007 and 2010 and then recovered to their prerecession level.

d. The rate of unemployment in the United Kingdom is much lower than in much of the rest of Europe.

e. China's seemingly high growth rate is a myth; it is a product solely of misleading official statistics.

f. The high rate of unemployment in Europe started when a group of major European countries adopted a common currency.

g. The Federal Reserve lowers interest rates when it wants to avoid recession and raises interest rates when it wants to slow the rate of growth in the economy.

h. Output per person is different in the Euro area, the United States, and China.

i. Interest rates in the United States were at or near zero from 2009 to 2015.

2. *Macroeconomic policy in Europe*

   Beware of simplistic answers to complicated macroeconomic questions. Consider each of the following statements and comment on whether there is another side to the story.

a. There is a simple solution to the problem of high European unemployment: Reduce labor market rigidities.

b. What can be wrong about joining forces and adopting a common currency? Adoption of the euro is obviously good for Europe.

DIG DEEPER

MyEconLab Visit www.myeconlab.com to complete all Dig Deeper problems and get instant feedback.

3. *Chinese economic growth is the outstanding feature of the world economic scene over the past two decades.*

a. In 2014, U.S. output was $17.4 trillion, and Chinese output was $10.4 trillion. Suppose that from now on, the output of

China grows at an annual rate of 6.5% per year, whereas the output of the United States grows at an annual rate of 2.2% per year. These are the values in each country for the period 2010–2014 as stated in the text. Using these assumptions and a spreadsheet, calculate and plot U.S. and Chinese output from 2014 over the next 100 years. How many years will it take for China to have a total level of output equal to that of the United States?

b. When China catches up with the United States in total output, will residents of China have the same standard of living as U.S. residents? Explain.

c. Another term for *standard of living* is *output per person*. How has China raised its output per person in the last two decades? Are these methods applicable to the United States?

d. Do you think China's experience in raising its standard of living (output per person) provides a model for developing countries to follow?

4. *The rate of growth of output per person was identified as a major issue facing the United States as of the writing of this chapter. Go to the 2015 Economic Report of the President and find a table titled "Productivity and Related Data" (Table B-16). You can download this table as an Excel file.*

a. Find the column with numbers that describe the level of output per hour worked of all persons in the nonfarm business sector. This value is presented as an index number equal to 100 in 2009. Calculate the percentage increase in output per hour worked from 2009 to 2010. What does that value mean?

b. Now use the spreadsheet to calculate the average percent increase in output per hour worked for the decades 1970–1979, 1980–1989, 1990–1999, 2000–2009, and 2010–2014. How does productivity growth in the last decade compare to the other decades?

c. You may be able to find a more recent Economic Report of the President. If so, update your estimate of the average growth rate of output per hour worked to include years past 2014. Is there any evidence of an increase in productivity growth?

EXPLORE FURTHER

5. *U.S. postwar recessions*

This question looks at the recessions over the past 40 years. To work this problem, first obtain quarterly data on U.S. output growth for the period 1960 to the most recent date from the Web site www.bea.gov. Table 1.1.1 presents the percent change in real gross domestic product (GDP). This data can be downloaded to a spreadsheet. Plot the quarterly GDP growth rates from 1960:1 to the latest observations. Which, if any, quarters have negative growth? Using the definition of a recession as two or more consecutive quarters of negative growth, answer the following questions.

a. How many recessions has the U.S. economy undergone since 1960, quarter 2?

b. How many quarters has each recession lasted?

c. In terms of length and magnitude, which two recessions have been the most severe?

6. From Problem 5, write down the quarters in which the six traditional recessions started. Find the monthly series in the Federal Reserve Bank of St. Louis (FRED) database for the seasonally adjusted unemployment rate. Retrieve the monthly data series on the unemployment rate for the period 1969 to the end of the data. Make sure all data series are seasonally adjusted.

a. Look at each recession since 1969. What was the unemployment rate in the first month of the first quarter of negative growth? What was the unemployment rate in the last month of the last quarter of negative growth? By how much did the unemployment rate increase?

b. Which recession had the largest increase in the rate of unemployment? Begin with the month before the quarter in which output first falls and measure to the highest level of the unemployment rate before the next recession.

Further Reading

∙∙∙

■ The best way to follow current economic events and issues is to read *The Economist*, a weekly magazine published in England.

The articles in *The Economist* are well informed, well written, witty, and opinionated. Make sure to read it regularly.

APPENDIX: Where to Find the Numbers

Suppose you want to find the numbers for inflation in Germany over the past five years. Fifty years ago, the answer would have been to learn German, find a library with German publications, find the page where inflation numbers were given, write them down, and plot them by hand on a clean sheet of paper. Today, improvements in the collection of data, the development of computers and electronic databases, and access to the Internet make the task much easier. This appendix will help you find the numbers you are looking for, be it inflation in Malaysia last year, or consumption in the United States in 1959, or unemployment in Ireland in the 1980s. In most cases, the data can be downloaded to spreadsheets for further treatment.

For a Quick Look at Current Numbers

- The best source for the most recent numbers on output, unemployment, inflation, exchange rates, interest rates, and stock prices for a large number of countries is the last four pages of *The Economist*, published each week (www.economist.com). The Web site, like many of the Web sites listed throughout the text, contains both information available free to anyone and information available only to subscribers.

- A good source for recent numbers about the U.S. economy is *National Economic Trends*, published monthly by the Federal Reserve Bank of Saint Louis. (https://research.stlouisfed.org/datatrends/net/)

For More Detail about the U.S. Economy

- A convenient database, with numbers often going back to the 1960s, for both the United States and other countries, is the *Federal Reserve Economic Database* (called *FRED*), maintained by the Federal Reserve Bank of Saint Louis. Access is free, and much of the U.S. data used in this book comes from that database. (www.research.stlouisfed.org/fred2/)

- Once a year, the *Economic Report of the President*, written by the Council of Economic Advisers and published by the U.S. Government Printing Office in Washington, D.C., gives a description of current evolutions, as well as numbers for most major macroeconomic variables, often going back to the 1950s. (It contains two parts, a report on the economy, and a set of statistical tables. Both can be found at www.gpo.gov/erp/)

- A detailed presentation of the most recent numbers for national income accounts is given in the *Survey of Current Business*, published monthly by the U.S. Department of Commerce, Bureau of Economic Analysis (www.bea.gov). A user's guide to the statistics published by the Bureau of Economic Analysis is given in the *Survey of Current Business*, April 1996.

- The standard reference for national income accounts is the *National Income and Product Accounts of the United States*.

Volume 1, 1929–1958, and Volume 2, 1959–1994, are published by the U.S. Department of Commerce, Bureau of Economic Analysis (www.bea.gov).

- For data on just about everything, including economic data, a precious source is the *Statistical Abstract of the United States*, published annually by the U.S. Department of Commerce, Bureau of the Census (http://www.census.gov/library/publications/2011/compendia/statab/131ed.html).

Numbers for Other Countries

The **Organization for Economic Cooperation and Development**, OECD for short, located in Paris, France (www.oecd.org), is an organization that includes most of the rich countries in the world (Australia, Austria, Belgium, Canada, Chile, the Czech Republic, Denmark, Estonia, Finland, France, Germany, Greece, Hungary, Iceland, Israel, Italy, Japan, Korea, Luxembourg, Mexico, the Netherlands, New Zealand, Norway, Poland, Portugal, the Slovak Republic, Slovenia, Spain, Sweden, Switzerland, Turkey, the United Kingdom, and the United States). Together, these countries account for about 70% of the world's output. One strength of the OECD data is that, for many variables, the OECD tries to make the variables comparable across member countries (or tells you when they are not comparable). The OECD issues three useful publications, all available on the OECD site.

- The first is the *OECD Economic Outlook*, published twice a year. In addition to describing current macroeconomic issues and evolutions, it includes a data appendix, with data for many macroeconomic variables. The data typically go back to the 1980s and are reported consistently, both across time and across countries.

- The second is the *OECD Employment Outlook*, published annually. It focuses more specifically on labor-market issues and numbers.

- Occasionally, the OECD puts together current and past data, and publishes a set of OECD Historical Statistics in which various years are grouped together.

The main strength of the publications of the **International Monetary Fund** (IMF for short, located in Washington, D.C.) is that they cover nearly all of the countries of the world. The IMF has 187 member countries and provides data on each of them (www.imf.org).

- A particularly useful IMF publication is the *World Economic Outlook* (WEO for short), which is published twice a year and which describes major economic events in the world and in specific member countries. Selected series associated with the Outlook are available in the WEO database, available on the IMF site (www.imf.org/external/data.htm). Most of the data shown in this chapter come from this database.

■ Two other useful publications are the *Global Financial Stability Report* (GFSR for short), which focuses on financial developments, and the *Fiscal Monitor*, which focuses on fiscal developments. All three publications are available on the IMF Web site (www.imf.org/external/index.htm).

The World Bank also maintains a large data base (data.worldbank.org/), with a wide set of indicators, from climate change to social protection.

Historical Statistics

■ For long-term historical statistics for the United States, the basic reference is *Historical Statistics of the United States, Colonial Times to 1970*, Parts 1 and 2, published by the U.S. Department of Commerce, Bureau of the Census (www.census.gov/prod/www/statistical_abstract.html).

■ For long-term historical statistics for several countries, a precious data source is Angus Maddison's *Monitoring the World Economy, 1820–1992*, Development Centre Studies, OECD, Paris, 1995. This study gives data going back to 1820 for 56 countries. Two even longer and broader sources are *The World Economy: A Millenial Perspective*, Development Studies, OECD, 2001, and *The World Economy: Historical Statistics*, Development Studies, OECD 2004, both also by Angus Maddison.

Current Macroeconomic Issues

A number of Web sites offer information and commentaries about the macroeconomic issues of the day. In addition to *The Economist* Web site, the site maintained by Nouriel Roubini (www.rgemonitor.com) offers an extensive set of links to articles and discussions on macroeconomic issues (by subscription). Another interesting site is vox.eu (www.voxeu.org), in which economists post blogs on current issues and events.

If you still have not found what you were looking for, a site maintained by Bill Goffe at the State University of New York (SUNY) (www.rfe.org), lists not only many more data sources, but also sources for economic information in general, from working papers, to data, to jokes, to jobs in economics, and to blogs.

And, finally, the site called Gapminder (http://www.gapminder.org/) has a number of visually striking animated graphs, many of them on issues related to macroeconomics.

Key Terms

Organization for Economic Cooperation and Development (OECD), 38
International Monetary Fund (IMF), 38

A Tour of the Book

The words *output, unemployment*, and *inflation* appear daily in newspapers and on the evening news. So when I used these words in Chapter 1, you knew roughly what we were talking about. It is now time to define these words more precisely, and this is what we do in the first three sections of this chapter.

Section 2-1 looks at output.

Section 2-2 looks at the unemployment rate.

Section 2-3 looks at the inflation rate.

Section 2-4 introduces two important relations between these three variables: Okun's law and the Phillips curve.

Section 2-5 then introduces the three central concepts around which the book is organized:

- The *short run*: What happens to the economy from year to year

- The *medium run*: What happens to the economy over a decade or so

- The *long run*: What happens to the economy over a half century or longer

Building on these three concepts, Section 2-6 gives you a road map to the rest of the book.

2-1 Aggregate Output

Two economists, Simon Kuznets, from Harvard University, and Richard Stone, from Cambridge University, received the Nobel Prize for their contributions to the development of the national income and product accounts—a gigantic intellectual and empirical achievement.

Economists studying economic activity in the nineteenth century or during the Great Depression had no measure of aggregate activity (*aggregate* is the word macroeconomists use for *total*) on which to rely. They had to put together bits and pieces of information, such as the shipments of iron ore, or sales at some department stores, to try to infer what was happening to the economy as a whole.

It was not until the end of World War II that **national income and product accounts** (or national income accounts, for short) were put together. Measures of aggregate output have been published on a regular basis in the United States since October 1947. (You will find measures of aggregate output for earlier times, but these have been constructed retrospectively.)

Like any accounting system, the national income accounts first define concepts and then construct measures corresponding to these concepts. You need only to look at statistics from countries that have not yet developed such accounts to realize that precision and consistency in such accounts are crucial. Without precision and consistency, numbers that should add up do not; trying to understand what is going on feels like trying to balance someone else's checkbook. I shall not burden you with the details of national income accounting here. But because you will occasionally need to know the definition of a variable and how variables relate to each other, Appendix 1 at the end of the book gives you the basic accounting framework used in the United States (and, with minor variations, in most other countries) today. You will find it useful whenever you want to look at economic data on your own.

GDP: Production and Income

You may come across another term, **gross national product**, or **GNP**. There is a subtle difference between "domestic" and "national," and thus between GDP and GNP. We examine the distinction in Chapter 18 and in Appendix 1 at the end of the book. For now, ignore it.

The measure of **aggregate output** in the national income accounts is called the **gross domestic product**, or **GDP**, for short. To understand how GDP is constructed, it is best to work with a simple example. Consider an economy composed of just two firms:

In reality, not only workers and machines are required for steel production, but so are iron ore, electricity, and so on. I ignore these to keep the example simple.

- Firm 1 produces steel, employing workers and using machines to produce the steel. It sells the steel for $100 to Firm 2, which produces cars. Firm 1 pays its workers $80, leaving $20 in profit to the firm.
- Firm 2 buys the steel and uses it, together with workers and machines, to produce cars. Revenues from car sales are $200. Of the $200, $100 goes to pay for steel and $70 goes to workers in the firm, leaving $30 in profit to the firm.

We can summarize this information in a table:

Steel Company (Firm 1)		Car Company (Firm 2)		
Revenues from sales	$100	Revenues from sales		$200
Expenses	$80	Expenses		$170
Wages	$80	Wages	$70	
		Steel purchases	$100	
Profit	$20	Profit		$30

An intermediate good is a good used in the production of another good. Some goods can be both final goods and intermediate goods. Potatoes sold directly to consumers are final goods. Potatoes used to produce potato chips are intermediate goods. Can you think of other examples?

How would you define aggregate output in this economy? As the sum of the values of all goods produced in the economy—the sum of $100 from the production of steel and $200 from the production of cars, so $300? Or as just the value of cars, which is equal to $200?

Some thought suggests that the right answer must be $200. Why? Because steel is an **intermediate good**: It is used in the production of cars. Once we count the production of cars, we do not want to count the production of the goods that went into the production of these cars.

This motivates the first definition of GDP:

1. GDP Is the Value of the Final Goods and Services Produced in the Economy during a Given Period.

The important word here is *final*. We want to count only the production of **final goods**, not intermediate goods. Using our example, we can make this point in another way. Suppose the two firms merged, so that the sale of steel took place inside the new firm and was no longer recorded. The accounts of the new firm would be given by the following table:

Steel and Car Company	
Revenues from sales	$200
Expenses (wages)	$150
Profit	$50

All we would see would be one firm selling cars for $200, paying workers $80 + $70 = $150, and making $20 + $30 = $50 in profits. The $200 measure would remain unchanged—as it should. We do not want our measure of aggregate output to depend on whether firms decide to merge or not.

MyEconLab Video

This first definition gives us one way to construct GDP: by recording and adding up the production of all final goods—and this is indeed roughly the way actual GDP numbers are put together. But it also suggests a second way of thinking about and constructing GDP.

2. GDP Is the Sum of Value Added in the Economy during a Given Period.

The term **value added** means exactly what it suggests. The value added by a firm is defined as the value of its production minus the value of the intermediate goods used in production.

In our two-firms example, the steel company does not use intermediate goods. Its value added is simply equal to the value of the steel it produces, $100. The car company, however, uses steel as an intermediate good. Thus, the value added by the car company is equal to the value of the cars it produces minus the value of the steel it uses in production, $200 − $100 = $100. Total value added in the economy, or GDP, equals $100 + $100 = $200. (Note that aggregate value added would remain the same if the steel and car firms merged and became a single firm. In this case, we would not observe intermediate goods at all—because steel would be produced and then used to produce cars within the single firm—and the value added in the single firm would simply be equal to the value of cars, $200.)

This definition gives us a second way of thinking about GDP. Put together, the two definitions imply that the value of final goods and services—the first definition of GDP—can also be thought of as the sum of the value added by all the firms in the economy—the second definition of GDP.

So far, we have looked at GDP from the *production side*. The other way of looking at GDP is from the *income side*. Go back to our example and think about the revenues left to a firm after it has paid for its intermediate goods: Some of the revenues go to pay workers—this component is called *labor income*. The rest goes to the firm—that component is called *capital income* or *profit income* (the reason it is called capital income is that you can think of it as remuneration for the owners of the capital used in production).

Of the $100 of value added by the steel manufacturer, $80 goes to workers (labor income) and the remaining $20 goes to the firm (capital income). Of the $100 of value added by the car manufacturer, $70 goes to labor income and $30 to capital income. For the economy as a whole, labor income is equal to $150 ($80 + $70), capital income is equal to $50 ($20 + $30). Value added is equal to the sum of labor income and capital income is equal to $200 ($150 + $50).

The labor share in the example is thus 75%. In advanced countries, the share of labor is indeed typically between 60 ◀ and 75%.

This motivates the third definition of GDP.

3. GDP Is the Sum of Incomes in the Economy during a Given Period.

Two lessons to remember:

i. GDP is the measure of aggregate output, which we can look at from the production side (aggregate production), or the income side (aggregate income); and

ii. Aggregate production and aggregate income are always equal.

To summarize: You can think about aggregate output— *GDP*—in three different but equivalent ways.

- From the *production side*: GDP equals the value of the final goods and services produced in the economy during a given period.
- Also from the *production side*: GDP is the sum of value added in the economy during a given period.
- From the *income side*: GDP is the sum of incomes in the economy during a given period.

Nominal and Real GDP

U.S. GDP was $17,400 billion in 2014, compared to $543 billion in 1960. Was U.S. output really 32 times higher in 2014 than in 1960? Obviously not: Much of the increase reflected an increase in prices rather than an increase in quantities produced. This leads to the distinction between nominal GDP and real GDP.

Warning! People often use *nominal* to denote small amounts. Economists use *nominal* for variables expressed in current prices. And they surely do not refer to small amounts: The numbers typically run in the billions or trillions of dollars.

Nominal GDP is the sum of the quantities of final goods produced times their current price. This definition makes clear that nominal GDP increases over time for two reasons:

- First, the production of most goods increases over time.
- Second, the price of most goods also increases over time.

If our goal is to measure production and its change over time, we need to eliminate the effect of increasing prices on our measure of GDP. That's why **real GDP** is constructed as the sum of the quantities of final goods times *constant* (rather than *current*) prices.

If the economy produced only one final good, say, a particular car model, constructing real GDP would be easy: We would use the price of the car in a given year and then use it to multiply the quantity of cars produced in each year. An example will help here. Consider an economy that only produces cars—and to avoid issues we shall tackle later, assume the same model is produced every year. Suppose the number and the price of cars in three successive years are given by:

You may wonder why I chose these three particular years. Explanation given when I look at the actual numbers for the United States.

Nominal GDP, which is equal to the quantity of cars times their price, goes up from $200,000 in 2008 to $288,000 in 2009—a 44% increase—and from $288,000 in 2009 to $338,000 in 2010—a 16% increase.

Year	Quantity of Cars	Price of Cars	Nominal GDP	Real GDP (in 2009 dollars)
2008	10	$20,000	$200,000	$240,000
2009	12	$24,000	$288,000	$288,000
2010	13	$26,000	$338,000	$312,000

- To construct real GDP, we need to multiply the number of cars in each year by a *common* price. Suppose we use the price of a car in 2009 as the common price. This approach gives us in effect *real GDP in 2009 dollars*.
- Using this approach, real GDP in 2008 (in 2009 dollars) equals 10 cars × $24,000 per car = $240,000. Real GDP in 2009 (in 2009 dollars) equals 12 cars × $24,000 per car = $288,000, the same as nominal GDP in 2008. Real GDP in 2010 (in 2009 dollars) is equal to 13 × $24,000 = $312,000.

So real GDP goes up from \$240,000 in 2008 to \$288,000 in 2009—a 20% increase—and from \$288,000 in 2009 to \$312,000 in 2010—an 8% increase.

◼ How different would our results have been if we had decided to construct real GDP using the price of a car in, say, 2010 rather than 2009? Obviously, the level of real GDP in each year would be different (because the prices are not the same in 2010 as in 2009); but its rate of change from year to year would be the same as shown.

◀ To be sure, compute real GDP in 2010 dollars, and compute the rate of growth from 2008 to 2009, and from 2009 to 2010.

The problem when constructing real GDP in practice is that there is obviously more than one final good. Real GDP must be defined as a weighted average of the output of all final goods, and this brings us to what the weights should be.

The *relative prices* of the goods would appear to be the natural weights. If one good costs twice as much per unit as another, then that good should count for twice as much as the other in the construction of real output. But this raises the question: What if, as is typically the case, relative prices change over time? Should we choose the relative prices of a particular year as weights, or should we change the weights over time? More discussion of these issues, and of the way real GDP is constructed in the United States, is left to the appendix to this chapter. Here, what you should know is that the measure of real GDP in the U.S. national income accounts uses weights that reflect relative prices and which change over time. The measure is called **real GDP in chained (2009) dollars**. We use 2009 because, as in our example, at this point in time 2009 is the year when, by construction, real GDP is equal to nominal GDP. It is our best measure of the output of the U.S. economy, and its evolution shows how U.S. output has increased over time.

◀ The year used to construct prices, at this point the year 2009, is called the *base year*. The base year is changed from time to time, and by the time you read this book, it may have changed again.

Figure 2-1 plots the evolution of both nominal GDP and real GDP since 1960. By construction, the two are equal in 2009. The figure shows that real GDP in 2014 was about 5.1 times its level of 1960—a considerable increase, but clearly much less than the 32-fold increase in nominal GDP over the same period. The difference between the two results comes from the increase in prices over the period.

◀ Suppose real GDP was measured in 2000 dollars rather than 2009 dollars. Where would the nominal GDP and real GDP lines on the graph intersect?

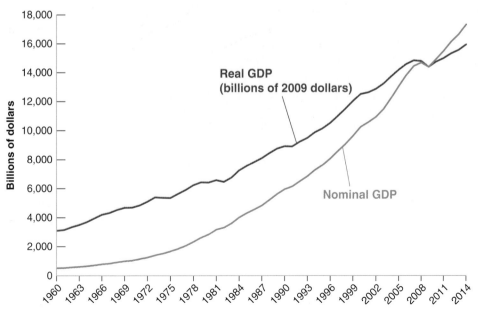

Figure 2-1

Nominal and Real U.S. GDP, 1960–2014

From 1960 to 2014, nominal GDP increased by a factor of 32. Real GDP increased by a factor of about 5.

Source: Series GDPCA, GDPA: Federal Reserve Economic Data (FRED) http://research.stlouisfed.org/fred2/.

MyEconLab Animation

MyEconLab Real-time data

The terms *nominal GDP* and *real GDP* each have many synonyms, and you are likely to encounter them in your readings:

■ Nominal GDP is also called **dollar GDP** or **GDP in current dollars**.
■ Real GDP is also called: **GDP in terms of goods**, **GDP in constant dollars**, **GDP adjusted for inflation**, or **GDP in chained (2009) dollars** or **GDP in 2009 dollars** —if the year in which real GDP is set equal to nominal GDP is 2009, as is the case in the United States at this time.

In the chapters that follow, unless I indicate otherwise,

■ GDP will refer to *real GDP* and Y_t will denote *real GDP in year t*.
■ Nominal GDP, and variables measured in current dollars, will be denoted by a dollar sign in front of them—for example, $\$Y_t$ for nominal GDP in year t.

GDP: Level versus Growth Rate

We have focused so far on the *level* of real GDP. This is an important number that gives the economic size of a country. A country with twice the GDP of another country is economically twice as big as the other country. Equally important is the level of **real GDP per person**, the ratio of real GDP to the population of the country. It gives us the average standard of living of the country.

Warning: One must be careful about how one does the comparison: Recall the discussion in Chapter 1 about the standard of living in China. This is discussed further in Chapter 10.

In assessing the performance of the economy from year to year, economists focus, however, on the rate of growth of real GDP, often called just **GDP growth**. Periods of positive GDP growth are called **expansions**. Periods of negative GDP growth are called **recessions**.

The evolution of GDP growth in the United States since 1960 is given in Figure 2-2. GDP growth in year t is constructed as $(Y_t - Y_{t-1})/Y_{t-1}$ and expressed as a percentage. The figure shows how the U.S. economy has gone through a series of expansions, interrupted by short recessions. Again, you can see the effects of the recent crisis: zero growth in 2008, and a large negative growth rate in 2009.

Figure 2-2

Growth Rate of U.S. GDP, 1960–2014

Since 1960, the U.S. economy has gone through a series of expansions, interrupted by short recessions. The 2008–2009 recession was the most severe recession in the period from 1960 to 2014.

Source: Calculated using series GDPCA in Figure 2-1.

MyEconLab Real-time data

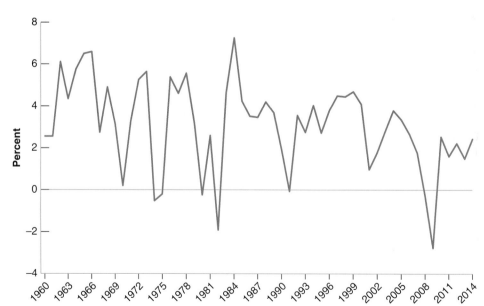

Real GDP, Technological Progress, and the Price of Computers

A tough problem in computing real GDP is how to deal with changes in quality of existing goods. One of the most difficult cases is computers. It would clearly be absurd to assume that a personal computer in 2015 is the same good as a personal computer produced, say 20 years ago: The 2015 version can clearly do much more than the 1995 version. But how much more? How do we measure it? How do we take into account the improvements in internal speed, the size of the random access memory (RAM) or of the hard disk, faster access to the Internet, and so on?

The approach used by economists to adjust for these improvements is to look at the market for computers and how it values computers with different characteristics in a given year. Example: Suppose the evidence from prices of different models on the market shows that people are willing to pay 10% more for a computer with a speed of 4 GHz (4,000 megahertz) rather than 3 GHz. The first edition of this book, published in 1996, compared two computers, with speeds of 50 and 16 megahertz, respectively. This change is a good indication of technological progress. (A further indication of the complexity of technological progress is that, for the past few years, progress has not been made not so much by increasing the speed of processors, but rather by using multicore processors. We shall leave this aspect aside here, but people in charge of national income accounts cannot; they have to take this change into account as well.) Suppose new computers this year have a speed of 4 GHz compared to a speed of 3 GHz for new computers last year. And suppose the dollar price of new computers this year is the same as the dollar price of new computers last year. Then economists in charge of computing the adjusted price of computers will conclude that new computers are in fact 10% cheaper than last year.

This approach, which treats goods as providing a collection of characteristics—for computers, speed, memory, and so on—each with an implicit price, is called **hedonic pricing** ("hedone" means "pleasure" in Greek). It is used by the Department of Commerce—which constructs real GDP—to estimate changes in the price of complex and fast changing goods, such as automobiles and computers. Using this approach, the Department of Commerce estimates for example, that, for a given price, the quality of new laptops has increased on average by 18% a year since 1995. Put another way, a typical laptop in 2015 delivers $1.18^{21} = 32$ times the computing services a typical laptop delivered in 1995. (Interestingly, in light of the discussion of slowing U.S. productivity growth in Chapter 1, the rate of improvement of quality has decreased substantially in the recent past, down closer to 10%.)

Not only do laptops deliver more services, they have become cheaper as well: Their dollar price has declined by about 7% a year since 1995. Putting this together with the information in the previous paragraph, this implies that their quality–adjusted price has fallen at an average rate of **18% + 7% = 25%** per year. Put another way, a dollar spent on a laptop today buys $1.25^{21} = 108$ times more computing services than a dollar spent on a laptop in 1995.

2-2 The Unemployment Rate

Because it is a measure of aggregate activity, GDP is obviously the most important macroeconomic variable. But two other variables, unemployment and inflation, tell us about other important aspects of how an economy is performing. This section focuses on the unemployment rate.

We start with two definitions: **Employment** is the number of people who have a job. **Unemployment** is the number of people who do not have a job but are looking for one. The **labor force** is the sum of employment and unemployment:

$$L \quad = \quad N \quad + \quad U$$

labor force = employment + unemployment

The **unemployment rate** is the ratio of the number of people who are unemployed to the number of people in the labor force:

$$u = \frac{U}{L}$$

unemployment rate = unemployment / labor force

Constructing the unemployment rate is less obvious than you might have thought. The cartoon notwithstanding, determining whether somebody is employed is relatively straightforward. Determining whether somebody is unemployed is more difficult. Recall from the definition that, to be classified as unemployed, a person must meet two conditions: that he or she does not have a job, and he or she is looking for one; this second condition is harder to assess.

Until the 1940s in the United States, and until more recently in most other countries, the only available source of data on unemployment was the number of people registered at unemployment offices, and so only those workers who were registered in unemployment offices were counted as unemployed. This system led to a poor measure of unemployment. How many of those looking for jobs actually registered at the unemployment office varied both across countries and across time. Those who had no incentive to register—for example, those who had exhausted their unemployment benefits—were unlikely to take the time to come to the unemployment office, so they were not counted. Countries with less generous benefit systems were likely to have fewer unemployed registering, and therefore smaller measured unemployment rates.

Today, most rich countries rely on large surveys of households to compute the unemployment rate. In the United States, this survey is called the **Current Population Survey (CPS)**. It relies on interviews of 60,000 households every month. The survey classifies a person as employed if he or she has a job at the time of the interview; it classifies a person as unemployed if he or she does not have a job *and has been looking for a job in the last four weeks.* Most other countries use a similar definition of unemployment. In the United States, estimates based on the CPS show that, in July 2015, an average of 148.9 million people were employed, and 8.3 million people were unemployed, so the unemployment rate was $8.3/(148.9 + 8.3) = 5.3\%$.

> The 60,000 households are chosen as a representative sample of the whole U.S. population. Thus, the sample provides good estimates of what is happening for the population as a whole.

Note that only those *looking for a job* are counted as unemployed; those who do not have a job and are not looking for one are counted as **not in the labor force**. When unemployment is high, some of the unemployed give up looking for a job and therefore are no longer counted as unemployed. These people are known as **discouraged workers**. Take an extreme example: If all workers without a job gave up looking for one, the unemployment rate would go to zero. This would make the unemployment rate a poor indicator of what is actually happening in the labor market. This example is too extreme; in practice, when the economy slows down, we typically observe both an increase in unemployment and an increase in the number of people who drop out of

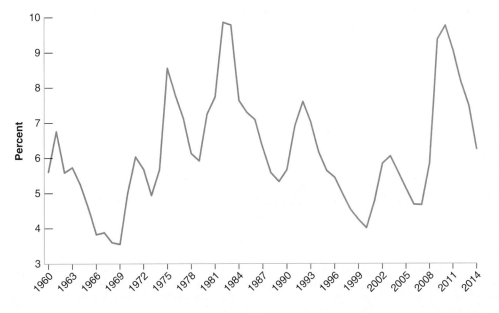

Figure 2-3

U.S. Unemployment Rate, 1960–2014

Since 1960, the U.S. unemployment rate has fluctuated between 3 and 10%, going down during expansions and going up during recessions. The effect of the recent crisis is highly visible, with the unemployment rate reaching close to 10% in 2010, the highest such rate since the early 1980s.

Source: Organization for Economic Co-operation and Development, Unemployment Rate: Aged 15-64: All Persons for the United States© [LRUN64TTUSA156N], retrieved from FRED, Federal Reserve Bank of St. Louis https://research.stlouisfed.org/fred2/series/LRUN64TTUSA156N/, January 13, 2016.

MyEconLab Real-time data

the labor force. Equivalently, a higher unemployment rate is typically associated with a lower **participation rate**, defined as the ratio of the labor force to the total population of working age.

During the crisis, as the U.S. unemployment rate increased, the participation rate decreased from 66% to 63%. But, surprisingly, as unemployment has decreased, the participation rate has not recovered. Why this is so is not fully understood. One hypothesis is the recession was so deep that some workers, who lost their job, have permanently given up on trying to become employed.

Figure 2-3 shows the evolution of unemployment in the United States since 1960. Since 1960, the U.S. unemployment rate has fluctuated between 3 and 10%, going up during recessions and down during expansions. Again, you can see the effect of the recent crisis, with the unemployment rate reaching a peak at nearly 10% in 2010, the highest such rate since the 1980s.

Why Do Economists Care about Unemployment?

Economists care about unemployment for two reasons. First, they care about unemployment because of its direct effect on the welfare of the unemployed. Although unemployment benefits are more generous today than they were during the Great Depression, unemployment is still often associated with financial and psychological suffering. How much suffering depends on the nature of unemployment. One image of unemployment is that of a stagnant pool, of people remaining unemployed for long periods of time. In normal times, in the United States, this image is not right: Every month, many people become unemployed, and many of the unemployed find jobs. When unemployment is high, however, as it was during the crisis, another image becomes more relevant. Not only are more people unemployed, but also many of them are unemployed for a long time. For example, the mean duration of unemployment, which was 16 weeks on average during 2000–2007, increased to 40 weeks in 2011; it has decreased since, but at the time of writing, remains at a relatively high 30 weeks. In short, when the unemployment increases, not only does unemployment become both more widespread, but it also becomes more painful for those who are unemployed.

Second, economists also care about the unemployment rate because it provides a signal that the economy may not be using some of its resources. When unemployment is high, many workers who want to work do not find jobs; the economy is clearly not using

Unemployment and Happiness

How painful is unemployment? To answer the question, one needs information about particular individuals, and how their happiness varies as they become unemployed. This information is available from the German Socio-Economic Panel survey. The survey has followed about 11,000 households each year since 1984, asking each member of the household a number of questions about their employment status, their income, and their happiness. The specific question in the survey about happiness is the following: "How satisfied are you at present with your life as a whole?", with the answer rated from 0 ("completely dissatisfied") to 10 ("completely satisfied").

The effect of unemployment on happiness defined in this way is shown in Figure 1. The figure plots the average life satisfaction for those individuals who were unemployed during one year, and employed in the four years before and in the four years after. Year 0 is the year of unemployment. Years -1 to -4 are the years before unemployment, years 1 to 4 the years after.

The figure suggests three conclusions. The first and main one is indeed that becoming unemployed leads to a large decrease in happiness. To give you a sense of scale, other studies suggest that this decrease in happiness is close to the decrease triggered by a divorce or a separation. The second

is that happiness declines before the actual unemployment spell. This suggests that either workers know they are more likely to become unemployed, or that they like their job less and less. The third is that happiness does not fully recover even four years after the unemployment spell. This suggests that unemployment may do some permanent damage, either because of the experience of unemployment itself, or because the new job is not as satisfying as the old one.

In thinking about how to deal with unemployment, it is essential to understand the channels through which unemployment decreases happiness. One important finding in this respect is that the decrease in happiness does not depend very much on the generosity of unemployment benefits. In other words, unemployment affects happiness not so much through financial channels than through psychological channels. To cite George Akerlof, a Nobel Prize winner, "A person without a job loses not just his income but often the sense that he is fulfilling the duties expected of him as a human being."

◄ The material in this box, and in particular the figure, comes in part from "Unemployment and happiness," by Rainer Winkelmann, *IZA world of labor*, 2014: 94, pp 1–9.

Figure 1

Effects of Unemployment on Happiness

Source: Winkelmann 2014.

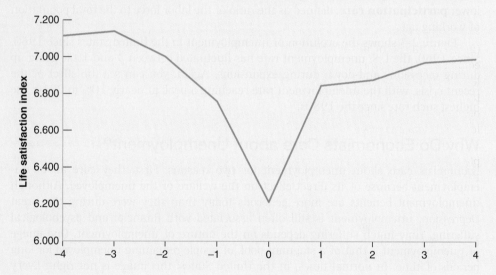

It is probably because of statements like this that ► economics is known as the "dismal science."

its human resources efficiently. What about when unemployment is low? Can very low unemployment also be a problem? The answer is yes. Like an engine running at too high a speed, an economy in which unemployment is very low may be overusing its resources and run into labor shortages. How low is "too low"? This is a difficult question, a question we will take up at more length later in the book. The question came up in 2000 in the United States. At the end of 2000, some economists worried that the unemployment rate, 4% at the time, was indeed too low. So, although they did not advocate triggering a recession, they favored lower (but positive) output growth for some time, so as to allow the unemployment rate to increase to a somewhat higher level. It turned out that they got more than they had asked for: a recession rather than a slowdown.

2-3 The Inflation Rate

Inflation is a sustained rise in the general level of prices—the **price level**. The **inflation rate** is the rate at which the price level increases. (Symmetrically, **deflation** is a sustained decline in the price level. It corresponds to a negative inflation rate.)

The practical issue is how to define the price level so the inflation rate can be measured. Macroeconomists typically look at two measures of the price level, at two *price indexes*: the GDP deflator and the Consumer Price Index.

Deflation is rare, but it happens. The United States experienced sustained deflation in the 1930s during the Great Depression (see the Focus box in Chapter 9). Japan has had deflation, off and on, since the late 1990s. More recently, the Euro area has had short spells of deflation.

The GDP Deflator

We saw how increases in nominal GDP can come either from an increase in real GDP, or from an increase in prices. Put another way, if we see nominal GDP increase faster than real GDP, the difference must come from an increase in prices.

This remark motivates the definition of the GDP deflator. The **GDP deflator** in year t, P_t, is defined as the ratio of nominal GDP to real GDP in year t:

$$P_t = \frac{\text{Nominal GDP}_t}{\text{Real GDP}_t} = \frac{\$Y_t}{Y_t}$$

Note that, in the year in which, by construction, real GDP is equal to nominal GDP (2009 at this point in the United States), this definition implies that the price level is equal to 1. This is worth emphasizing: The GDP deflator is called an **index number**. Its level is chosen arbitrarily—here it is equal to 1 in 2009—and has no economic interpretation. But its rate of change, $(P_t - P_{t-1})/P_{t-1}$ (which we shall denote by π_t in the rest of the book), has a clear economic interpretation: It gives the rate at which the general level of prices increases over time—the rate of inflation.

Index numbers are often set equal to 100 (in the base year) rather than to 1. If you look at the Economic Report of the President (see Chapter 1) you will see that the GDP deflator, reported in Table B3 is equal to 100 for 2009 (the base year), 102.5 in 2010, and so on.

One advantage to defining the price level as the GDP deflator is that it implies a simple relation between *nominal GDP*, *real GDP*, and the *GDP deflator*. To see this, reorganize the previous equation to get:

$$\$Y_t = P_t Y_t$$

Compute the GDP deflator and the associated rate of inflation from 2008 to 2009 and from 2009 to 2010 in our car example in Section 2-1, when real GDP is constructed using the 2009 price of cars as the common price.

Nominal GDP is equal to the GDP deflator times real GDP. Or, putting it in terms of rates of change: The rate of growth of nominal GDP is equal to the rate of inflation plus the rate of growth of real GDP.

For a refresher for going from levels to rates of change, see Appendix 2, Proposition 7.

The Consumer Price Index

The GDP deflator gives the average price of output—the final goods *produced* in the economy. But consumers care about the average price of consumption—the goods they *consume*. The two prices need not be the same: The set of goods produced in the economy is not the same as the set of goods purchased by consumers, for two reasons:

- Some of the goods in GDP are sold not to consumers but to firms (machine tools, for example), to the government, or to foreigners.
- Some of the goods bought by consumers are not produced domestically but are imported from abroad.

To measure the average price of consumption, or, equivalently, the **cost of living**, macroeconomists look at another index, the **Consumer Price Index**, **or CPI**. The CPI has been in existence in the United States since 1917 and is published monthly (in contrast, numbers for GDP and the GDP deflator are only constructed and published quarterly).

The CPI gives the cost in dollars of a specific list of goods and services over time. The list, which is based on a detailed study of consumer spending, attempts to represent the consumption basket of a typical urban consumer and is updated every two years.

Each month, Bureau of Labor Statistics (BLS) employees visit stores to find out what has happened to the price of the goods on the list; prices are collected for 211 items in 38 cities. These prices are then used to construct the CPI.

Like the GDP deflator (the price level associated with aggregate output, GDP), the CPI is an index. It is set equal to 100 in the period chosen as the base period and so its level has no particular significance. The current base period is 1982 to 1984, so the average for the period 1982 to 1984 is equal to 100. In 2014, the CPI was 236.7; thus, it cost more than twice as much in dollars to purchase the same consumption basket than in 1982–1984.

You may wonder how the rate of inflation differs depending on whether the GDP deflator or the CPI is used to measure it. The answer is given in Figure 2-4, which plots the two inflation rates since 1960 for the United States. The figure yields two conclusions:

■ The CPI and the GDP deflator move together most of the time. In most years, the two inflation rates differ by less than 1%.

■ But there are clear exceptions. In 1979 and 1980, the increase in the CPI was significantly larger than the increase in the GDP deflator. The reason is not hard to find. Recall that the GDP deflator is the price of goods *produced* in the United States, whereas the CPI is the price of goods *consumed* in the United States. That means when the price of imported goods increases relative to the price of goods produced in the United States, the CPI increases faster than the GDP deflator. This is precisely what happened in 1979 and 1980. The price of oil doubled. And although the United States is a producer of oil, it produces less than it consumes: It was and still is an oil importer. The result was a large increase in the CPI compared to the GDP deflator.

Figure 2-4

Inflation Rate, Using the CPI and the GDP Deflator, 1960–2014

The inflation rates, computed using either the CPI or the GDP deflator, are largely similar.

Source: Calculated using series USAGDPDEFAISMEI, CPALTT01USA659N Federal Reserve Economic Data (FRED) http://research.stlouisfed.org/fred2/.

MyEconLab Real-time data

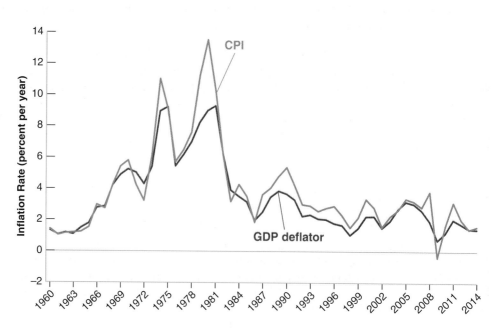

In what follows, we shall typically assume that the two indexes move together so we do not need to distinguish between them. We shall simply talk about *the price level* and denote it by P_t, without indicating whether we have the CPI or the GDP deflator in mind.

Why Do Economists Care about Inflation?

If a higher inflation rate meant just a faster but proportional increase in all prices and wages—a case called *pure inflation*—inflation would be only a minor inconvenience because relative prices would be unaffected.

Take, for example, the workers' *real wage*—the wage measured in terms of goods rather than in dollars. In an economy with 10% inflation, prices would, by definition, increase by 10% a year. But wages in dollars would also increase by 10% a year, so real wages would be unaffected by inflation. Inflation would not be entirely irrelevant; people would have to keep track of the increase in prices and wages when making decisions. But this would be a small burden, hardly justifying making control of the inflation rate one of the major goals of macroeconomic policy.

So why do economists care about inflation? Precisely because there is no such thing as pure inflation:

- During periods of inflation, not all prices and wages rise proportionately. Because they don't, inflation affects income distribution. For example, retirees in some countries receive payments that do not keep up with the price level, so they lose in relation to other groups when inflation is high. This is not the case in the United States, where Social Security benefits automatically rise with the CPI, protecting retirees from inflation. But during the very high inflation that took place in Russia in the 1990s, retirement pensions did not keep up with inflation, and many retirees were pushed to near starvation.

- Inflation leads to other distortions. Variations in relative prices also lead to more uncertainty, making it harder for firms to make decisions about the future, such as investment decisions. Some prices, which are fixed by law or by regulation, lag behind the others, leading to changes in relative prices. Taxation interacts with inflation to create more distortions. If tax brackets are not adjusted for inflation, for example, people move into higher and higher tax brackets as their nominal income increases, even if their real income remains the same.

This is known as bracket creep. In the United States, the tax brackets are adjusted automatically for inflation: If inflation is 5%, all tax brackets also go up by 5%—in other words, there is no bracket creep. By contrast, in Italy, where inflation averaged 17% a year in the second half of the 1970s, bracket creep led to a rise of almost 9 percentage points in the rate of income taxation. ◀

If inflation is so bad, does this imply that deflation (negative inflation) is good? ◀

The answer is no. First, high deflation (a large negative rate of inflation) would create many of the same problems as high inflation, from distortions to increased uncertainty. Second, as we shall see later in the book, even a low rate of deflation limits the ability of monetary policy to affect output. So what is the "best" rate of inflation? Most macroeconomists believe that the best rate of inflation is a low and stable rate of inflation, somewhere between 1 and 4%.

Newspapers sometimes confuse deflation and recession. They may happen together but they are not the same. Deflation is a decrease in the price level. A recession is a decrease in real output.

◀ *We shall look at the pros and cons of different rates of inflation in Chapter 23.*

2-4 Output, Unemployment, and the Inflation Rate: Okun's Law and the Phillips Curve

We have looked separately at the three main dimensions of aggregate economic activity: output growth, the unemployment rate, and the inflation rate. Clearly they are not independent, and much of this book will be spent looking at the relations among them in detail. But it is useful to have a first look now.

Figure 2-5

Changes in the Unemployment Rate versus Growth in the United States, 1960–2014

Output growth that is higher than usual is associated with a reduction in the unemployment rate; output growth that is lower than usual is associated with an increase in the unemployment rate.

Source: Series GDPCA,GDPA: Federal Reserve Economic Data (FRED) http://research.stlouisfed.org/fred2/.

MyEconLab Animation

MyEconLab Real-time data

Arthur Okun was an adviser to President John F. Kennedy in the 1960s. Okun's law is, ▶ of course, not a law, but an empirical regularity.

Such a graph, plotting one variable against another, is called a *scatterplot*. The line ▶ is called a *regression line*. For more on regressions, see Appendix 3.

MyEconLab Video

In recent years, the growth rate at which the unemployment rate remains constant has been lower, around 2.5%. This ▶ reflects again the decrease in productivity growth (the rate of growth of output per worker), discussed in Chapter 1.

It should probably be known as the Phillips relation, but it is too late to change that. ▶

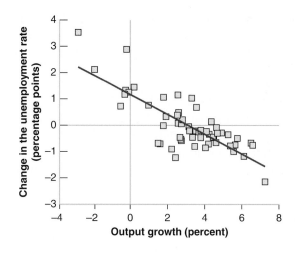

Okun's Law

Intuition suggests that if output growth is high, unemployment will decrease, and this is indeed true. This relation was first examined by U.S. economist Arthur Okun and for this reason has become known as **Okun's law**. Figure 2-5 plots the change in the unemployment rate on the vertical axis against the rate of growth of output on the horizontal axis for the United States since 1960. It also draws the line that best fits the cloud of points in the figure. Looking at the figure and the line suggests two conclusions:

■ The line is downward sloping and fits the cloud of points quite well. Put in economic terms: There is a tight relation between the two variables: Higher output growth leads to a decrease in unemployment. The slope of the line is −0.4. This implies that, on average, an increase in the growth rate of 1% decreases the unemployment rate by roughly −0.4%. This is why unemployment goes up in recessions and down in expansions. This relation has a simple but important implication: The key to decreasing unemployment is a high enough rate of growth.

■ This line crosses the horizontal axis at the point where output growth is roughly equal to 3%. In economic terms: It takes a growth rate of about 3% to keep unemployment constant. This is for two reasons. The first is that population, and thus the labor force, increases over time, so employment must grow over time just to keep the unemployment rate constant. The second is that output per worker is also increasing with time, which implies that output growth is higher than employment growth. Suppose, for example, that the labor force grows at 1% and that output per worker grows at 2%. Then output growth must be equal to 3%(1% + 2%) just to keep the unemployment rate constant.

The Phillips Curve

Okun's law implies that, with strong enough growth, one can decrease the unemployment rate to very low levels. But intuition suggests that, when unemployment becomes very low, the economy is likely to overheat, and that this will lead to upward pressure on inflation. And, to a large extent, this is true. This relation was first explored in 1958 by a ▶ New Zealand economist, A. W. Phillips, and has become known as the **Phillips curve**. Phillips plotted the rate of inflation against the unemployment rate. Since then, the Phillips curve has been redefined as a relation between the *change in the rate of inflation* and the unemployment rate. Figure 2-6 plots the change in the inflation rate (measured

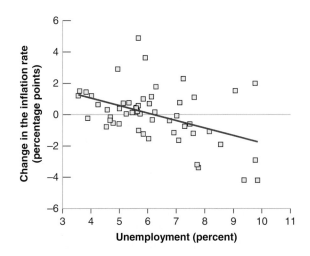

Figure 2-6

Changes in the Inflation Rate versus the Unemployment Rate in the United States, 1960–2014

A low unemployment rate leads to an increase in the inflation rate, a high unemployment rate to a decrease in the inflation rate.

Source: Series GDPCA,GDPA: Federal Reserve Economic Data (FRED) http://research.stlouisfed.org/fred2/.

MyEconLab Animation

MyEconLab Real-time data

using the CPI) on the vertical axis against the unemployment rate on the horizontal axis, together with the line that fits the cloud of points best, for the United States since 1960. Looking at the figure again suggests two conclusions:

■ The line is downward sloping, although the fit is not as good as it was for Okun's law: Higher unemployment leads, on average, to a decrease in inflation; lower unemployment leads to an increase in inflation. But this is only true on average. Sometimes, high unemployment is associated with an increase in inflation.

◀ As we shall see later in Chapter 8, the Phillips curve relation has evolved over time, in ways which cannot be captured in Figure 2-6. This explains why the fit is not as good as, say, for Okun's law.

■ The line crosses the horizontal axis at the point where the unemployment rate is roughly equal to 6%. When unemployment has been below 6%, inflation has typically increased, suggesting that the economy was overheating, operating above its potential. When unemployment has been above 6%, inflation has typically decreased, suggesting that the economy was operating below potential. But, again here, the relation is not tight enough that the unemployment rate at which the economy overheats can be pinned down precisely. This explains why some economists believe that we should try to maintain a lower unemployment rate, say 4 or 5%, and others believe that it may be dangerous, leading to overheating and increasing inflation.

Clearly, a successful economy is an economy that combines high output growth, low unemployment, and low inflation. Can all these objectives be achieved simultaneously? Is low unemployment compatible with low and stable inflation? Do policy makers have the tools to sustain growth, to achieve low unemployment while maintaining low inflation? These are the questions we shall take up as we go through the book. The next two sections give you the road map.

2-5 The Short Run, the Medium Run, and the Long Run

What determines the level of aggregate output in an economy? Consider three answers:

■ Reading newspapers suggests a first answer: Movements in output come from movements in the demand for goods. You probably have read news stories that begin like this: "Production and sales of automobiles were higher last month due to a surge in consumer confidence, which drove consumers to showrooms in record numbers." Stories like these highlight the role demand plays in determining aggregate output;

they point to factors that affect demand, ranging from consumer confidence to government spending to interest rates.

■ But, surely, no amount of Indian consumers rushing to Indian showrooms can increase India's output to the level of output in the United States. This suggests a second answer: What matters when it comes to aggregate output is the supply side—how much the economy can produce. How much can be produced depends on how advanced the technology of the country is, how much capital it is using, and the size and the skills of its labor force. These factors—not consumer confidence—are the fundamental determinants of a country's level of output.

■ The previous argument can be taken one step further: Neither technology, nor capital, nor skills are given. The technological sophistication of a country depends on its ability to innovate and introduce new technologies. The size of its capital stock depends on how much people have saved. The skills of workers depend on the quality of the country's education system. Other factors are also important: If firms are to operate efficiently, for example, they need a clear system of laws under which to operate and an honest government to enforce those laws. This suggests a third answer: The true determinants of output are factors like a country's education system, its saving rate, and the quality of its government. If we want to understand what determines the level of output, we must look at these factors.

MyEconLab Video

You might be wondering at this point, which of the three answers is right? The fact is that all three are right. But each applies over a different time frame:

■ In the **short run**, say, a few years, the first answer is the right one. Year-to-year movements in output are primarily driven by movements in demand. Changes in demand, perhaps as a result of changes in consumer confidence or other factors, can lead to a decrease in output (a recession) or an increase in output (an expansion).

■ In the **medium run**, say, a decade, the second answer is the right one. Over the medium run, the economy tends to return to the level of output determined by supply factors: the capital stock, the level of technology, and the size of the labor force. And, over a decade or so, these factors move sufficiently slowly that we can take them as given.

■ In the **long run**, say, a few decades or more, the third answer is the right one. To understand why China has been able to achieve such a high growth rate since 1980, we must understand why both the capital stock and the level of technology in China are increasing so fast. To do so, we must look at factors like the education system, the saving rate, and the role of the government.

This way of thinking about the determinants of output underlies macroeconomics, and it underlies the organization of this book.

2-6 A Tour of the Book

The book is organized in three parts: A core; two extensions; and, finally, a comprehensive look at the role of macroeconomic policy. This organization is shown in Figure 2-7. We now describe it in more detail.

The Core

The core is composed of three parts—the short run, the medium run, and the long run.

■ Chapters 3 to 6 look at how output is determined in the short run. To focus on the role of demand, we assume that firms are willing to supply any quantity at a given price. In other words, we ignore supply constraints. Chapter 3 shows

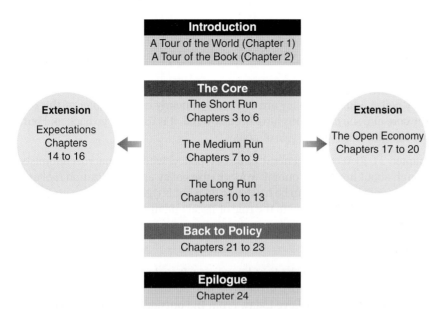

Figure 2-7

The Organization of the Book

how the demand for goods determines output. Chapter 4 shows how monetary policy determines the interest rate. Chapter 5 puts the two together, by allowing demand to depend on the interest rate, and then showing the role of monetary and fiscal policy in determining output. Chapter 6 extends the model by introducing a richer financial system, and using it to explain what happened during the recent crisis.

■ Chapters 7 to 9 develop the supply side and look at how output is determined in the medium run. Chapter 7 introduces the labor market. Chapter 8 builds on it to derive the relation between inflation and unemployment. Chapter 9 puts all the parts together, and shows the determination of output, unemployment, and inflation both in the short and the medium run.

■ Chapters 10 to 13 focus on the long run. Chapter 10 introduces the relevant facts by looking at the growth of output both across countries and over long periods of time. Chapters 11 and 12 discuss how both capital accumulation and technological progress determine growth. Chapter 13 looks at the interaction among technological progress, wages, unemployment, and inequality.

Extensions

The core chapters give you a way of thinking about how output (and unemployment, and inflation) is determined over the short, medium, and long run. However, they leave out several elements, which are explored in two extensions:

■ Expectations play an essential role in macroeconomics. Nearly all the economic decisions people and firms make depend on their expectations about future income, future profits, future interest rates, and so on. Fiscal and monetary policies affect economic activity not only through their direct effects, but also through their effects on people's and firms' expectations. Although we touch on these issues in the core, Chapters 14 to 16 offer a more detailed treatment and draw the implications for fiscal and monetary policy.

■ The core chapters treat the economy as *closed*, ignoring its interactions with the rest of the world. But the fact is, economies are increasingly *open*, trading goods and services and financial assets with one another. As a result, countries are becoming more and more interdependent. The nature of this interdependence and the implications for fiscal and monetary policy are the topics of Chapters 17 to 20.

Back to Policy

Monetary policy and fiscal policy are discussed in nearly every chapter of this book. But once the core and the extensions have been covered, it is useful to go back and put things together in order to assess the role of policy.

■ Chapter 21 focuses on general issues of policy, whether macroeconomists know enough about how the economy works to use policy as a stabilization tool at all, and whether policy makers can be trusted to do what is right.
■ Chapters 22 and 23 return to the role of fiscal and monetary policies.

Epilogue

Macroeconomics is not a fixed body of knowledge. It evolves over time. The final chapter, Chapter 24, looks at the history of macroeconomics and how macroeconomists have come to believe what they believe today. From the outside, macroeconomics sometimes looks like a field divided among schools—"Keynesians," "monetarists," "new classicals," "supply-siders," and so on—hurling arguments at each other. The actual process of research is more orderly and more productive than this image suggests. We identify what we see as the main differences among macroeconomists, the set of propositions that define the core of macroeconomics today, and the challenges posed to macroeconomists by the crisis.

Summary

■ We can think of GDP, the measure of aggregate output, in three equivalent ways: (1) GDP is the value of the final goods and services produced in the economy during a given period; (2) GDP is the sum of value added in the economy during a given period; and (3) GDP is the sum of incomes in the economy during a given period.
■ Nominal GDP is the sum of the quantities of final goods produced times their current prices. This implies that changes in nominal GDP reflect both changes in quantities and changes in prices. Real GDP is a measure of output. Changes in real GDP reflect changes in quantities only.
■ A person is classified as unemployed if he or she does not have a job and is looking for one. The unemployment rate is the ratio of the number of people unemployed to the number of people in the labor force. The labor force is the sum of those employed and those unemployed.
■ Economists care about unemployment because of the human cost it represents. They also look at unemployment because it sends a signal about how efficiently the economy is using its resources. High unemployment indicates that the country is not using its resources efficiently.
■ Inflation is a rise in the general level of prices—the price level. The inflation rate is the rate at which the price level

increases. Macroeconomists look at two measures of the price level. The first is the GDP deflator, which is the average price of the goods produced in the economy. The second is the Consumer Price Index (CPI), which is the average price of goods consumed in the economy.
■ Inflation leads to changes in income distribution, to distortions, and to increased uncertainty.
■ There are two important relations among output, unemployment, and inflation. The first, called Okun's law, is a relation between output growth and the change in unemployment: High output growth typically leads to a decrease in the unemployment rate. The second, called the Phillips curve, is a relation between unemployment and inflation: A low unemployment rate typically leads to an increase in the inflation rate.
■ Macroeconomists distinguish between the short run (a few years), the medium run (a decade), and the long run (a few decades or more). They think of output as being determined by demand in the short run. They think of output as being determined by the level of technology, the capital stock, and the labor force in the medium run. Finally, they think of output as being determined by factors like education, research, saving, and the quality of government in the long run.

Key Terms

national income and product accounts, 42
aggregate output, 42
gross domestic product (GDP), 42
gross national product (GNP), 42
intermediate good, 42
final good, 43
value added, 43
nominal GDP, 44
real GDP, 44
real GDP in chained (2009) dollars, 45
dollar GDP, GDP in current dollars, 46
GDP in terms of goods, GDP in constant dollars, GDP adjusted for inflation, GDP in chained (2009) dollars, GDP in 2009 dollars, 46
real GDP per person, 46
GDP growth, 46
expansions, 46
recessions, 46
hedonic pricing, 47
employment, 47

unemployment, 47
labor force, 47
unemployment rate, 47
Current Population Survey (CPS), 48
not in the labor force, 48
discouraged workers, 48
participation rate, 49
inflation, 51
price level, 51
inflation rate, 51
deflation, 51
GDP deflator, 51
index number, 51
cost of living, 52
Consumer Price Index (CPI), 52
Okun's law, 54
Phillips curve, 54
short run, 56
medium run, 56
long run, 56

Questions and Problems

QUICK CHECK

1. *Using the information in this chapter, label each of the following statements true, false, or uncertain. Explain briefly.*

   a. U.S. GDP was 32 times higher in 2014 than it was in 1960.

   b. When the unemployment rate is high, the participation rate is also likely to be high.

   c. The rate of unemployment tends to fall during expansions and rise during recessions.

   d. If the Japanese CPI is currently at 108 and the U.S. CPI is at 104, then the Japanese rate of inflation is higher than the U.S. rate of inflation.

   e. The rate of inflation computed using the CPI is a better index of inflation than the rate of inflation computed using the GDP deflator.

   f. Okun's law shows that when output growth is lower than normal, the unemployment rate tends to rise.

   g. Periods of negative GDP growth are called recessions.

   h. When the economy is functioning normally, the unemployment rate is zero.

   i. The Phillips curve is a relation between the level of prices and the level of unemployment.

2. *Suppose you are measuring annual U.S. GDP by adding up the final value of all goods and services produced in the economy. Determine the effect on GDP of each of the following transactions.*

   a. A seafood restaurant buys $100 worth of fish from a fisherman.

   b. A family spends $100 on a fish dinner at a seafood restaurant.

   c. Delta Air Lines buys a new jet from Boeing for $200 million.

   d. The Greek national airline buys a new jet from Boeing for $200 million.

   e. Delta Air Lines sells one of its jets to Jennifer Lawrence for $100 million.

3. *Suppose that an economy shows only the following activities in a specific year:*

   i. It costs an automobile manufacturing company €10 million to assemble 5,000 cars. The cars are then sold to stores for €12 million.

   ii. The stores pay their workers an annual wage of €1 million and then sell the cars directly to the consumers for €15 million. Please find other instances like this and correct them.

   a. Calculate the GDP in this economy using the production-of-final-goods approach.

   b. Calculate the GDP using the value-added approach. Show the value added at each stage of production.

   c. Calculate the GDP using the income approach. Show the costs incurred and profits earned.

4. *An economy produces three goods: cars, computers, and oranges. Quantities and prices per unit for years 2009 and 2010 are as follows:*

	2009		2010	
	Quantity	Price	Quantity	Price
Cars	10	$2,000	12	$3,000
Computers	4	$1,000	6	$500
Oranges	1,000	$1	1,000	$1

a. What is nominal GDP in 2009 and in 2010? By what percentage does nominal GDP change from 2009 to 2010?

b. Using the prices for 2009 as the set of common prices, what is real GDP in 2009 and in 2009? By what percentage does real GDP change from 2009 to 2010?

c. Using the prices for 2010 as the set of common prices, what is real GDP in 2009 and in 2010? By what percentage does real GDP change from 2009 to 2010?

d. Why are the two output growth rates constructed in (b) and (c) different? Which one is correct? Explain your answer.

5. Consider the economy described in Problem 4.

a. Use the prices for 2009 as the set of common prices to compute real GDP in 2009 and in 2010. Compute the GDP deflator for 2009 and for 2010, and compute the rate of inflation from 2009 to 2010.

b. Use the prices for 2010 as the set of common prices to compute real GDP in 2009 and in 2010. Compute the GDP deflator for 2009 and for 2010 and compute the rate of inflation from 2009 to 2010.

c. Why are the two rates of inflation different? Which one is correct? Explain your answer.

6. Consider the economy described in Problem 4.

a. Construct real GDP for years 2009 and 2010 by using the average price of each good over the two years.

b. By what percentage does real GDP change from 2009 to 2010?

c. What is the GDP deflator in 2009 and 2010? Using the GDP deflator, what is the rate of inflation from 2009 to 2010?

d. Is this an attractive solution to the problems pointed out in Problems 4 and 5 (i.e., two different growth rates and two different inflation rates, depending on which set of prices is used)? (The answer is yes and is the basis for the construction of chained-type deflators. See the appendix to this chapter for more discussion.)

7. The Consumer Price Index

The Consumer Price Index (CPI) is a measure of the average price of goods that a typical household consumes. To calculate the CPI, a basket of 700 goods and services that reflects the U.K. society's buying habits is used to construct the index. Assume that U.K. consumers buy only meat and movie tickets as their basket of goods and services. Below is a representation of the kind of data that the Office for National Statistics collects to construct the consumer price index. In the base year, 2010, both the prices and quantities of goods and services purchased are collected. In subsequent years, price changes are calculated for the same set of goods and services. The Office uses the Inflation Calculator to measure by how the cost of goods and services has changed over time. The Inflation Calculator can calculate the future cost of goods and services based on price changes from a date in the past. Alternatively, it can calculate the past cost of goods and services based on price changes from a date in the future.

The data: In an average week in 2010, the Office for National Statistics surveys thousands of households and determines that the average consumer purchases two pounds of meat and one ticket in a month. In subsequent years, the price per pound of meat and per movie ticket are found below:

Year	Price of Meat	Price of Movie Ticket
2010	£2	£5
2011	£1.9	£4.8
2012	£2	£4.9
2013	£2	£5
2014	£2	£5.2
2015	£2.1	£5.3

a. What is the cost of the consumer price basket in 2010?

b. What is the cost of the consumer price basket in 2011 and in subsequent years?

c. Represent the cost of the consumer price basket as an index number in the year 2008 to 2013. Set the value of the index number equal to 100 in 2008.

d. Calculate the annual rate of inflation using the percent change in the value of the index number between each year from 2010 through 2015.
You would find it helpful to fill in the table below

Year	Consumer Price Index 2010 = 100	Inflation Rate
2010		
2011		
2012		
2013		
2014		
2015		

e. Is there a year where inflation is negative? What does deflation imply?

f. The international price of oil has declined since 2014. What do you expect the response of consumers would be to such a decline in oil prices?

g. How many baskets of goods and services can £100 buy a household in 2010 and in 2014? What has happened to the purchasing power of money during this period? How can households ensure that their purchasing power does not decline?

h. Bank of England sets the target for the annual inflation rate of the Consumer Prices Index at 2%. Why would the Bank set such an inflation target?

i. Prices of oil and agricultural products decreased during the period 2010–2015. The Office for National Statistics calculates core inflation, which excludes energy and food prices. Complete the table below to calculate core inflation for the same period. How does core inflation compare to the CPI?

Year	Core Inflation Price Index 2013 = 100	Core Inflation Rate
2010	100	
2011	98.8	
2012	98.9	
2013	100.04	
2014	101.6	
2015	102.1	

8. Using macroeconomic relations:
   a. Okun's law stated that when output growth is higher than usual, the unemployment rate tends to fall. Explain why usual output growth is positive.
   b. In which year, a year where output growth is 2% or a year where output growth is −2%, will the unemployment rate rise more?
   c. The Phillips curve is a relation between the change in the inflation rate and the level of the unemployment rate. Using the Phillips curve, is the unemployment rate zero when the rate of inflation is neither rising nor falling?
   d. The Phillips curve is often portrayed as a line with a negative slope. In the text, the slope is about −0.5. In your opinion, is this a "better" economy if the line has a large slope, say −0.8, or a smaller slope, say −0.2?

DIG DEEPER

MyEconLab Visit www.myeconlab.com to complete all Dig Deeper problems and get instant feedback.

9. Hedonic pricing

   As the first Focus box in this chapter explains, it is difficult to measure the true increase in prices of goods whose characteristics change over time. For such goods, part of any price increase can be attributed to an increase in quality. Hedonic pricing offers a method to compute the quality-adjusted increase in prices.
   a. Consider the case of a routine medical check-up. Name some reasons you might want to use hedonic pricing to measure the change in the price of this service.

Now consider the case of a medical check-up for a pregnant woman. Suppose that a new ultrasound method is introduced. In the first year that this method is available, half of doctors offer the new method, and half offer the old method. A check-up using the new method costs 10% more than a check-up using the old method.
   b. In percentage terms, how much of a quality increase does the new method represent over the old method? (Hint: Consider the fact that some women choose to see a doctor offering the new method when they could have chosen to see a doctor offering the old method.)

Now, in addition, suppose that in the first year the new ultrasound method is available, the price of check-ups using the new method is 15% higher than the price of check-ups in the previous year (when everyone used the old method).
   c. How much of the higher price for check-ups using the new method (as compared to check-ups in the previous year) reflects a true price increase of check-ups and how much represents a quality increase? In other words, how much higher is the quality-adjusted price of check-ups using the new method as compared to the price of check-ups in the previous year?

In many cases, the kind of information we used in parts (b) and (c) is not available. For example, suppose that in the year the new ultrasound method is introduced, all doctors adopt the new method, so the old method is no longer used. In addition, continue to assume that the price of check-ups in the year the new method is introduced is 15% higher than the price of check-ups in the previous year (when everyone used the old method). Thus, we observe a 15% price increase in check-ups, but we realize that the quality of check-ups has increased.
   d. Under these assumptions, what information required to compute the quality-adjusted price increase of check-ups is lacking? Even without this information, can we say anything about the quality-adjusted price increase of check-ups? Is it more than 15%? less than 15%? Explain.

10. Measured and true GDP
Suppose that instead of cooking dinner for an hour, you decide to work an extra hour, earning an additional $12. You then purchase some (takeout) Chinese food, which costs you $10.
   a. By how much does measured GDP increase?
   b. Do you think the increase in measured GDP accurately reflects the effect on output of your decision to work? Explain.

EXPLORE FURTHER

11. Comparing the 2008 global financial crisis and the European Sovereign debt crisis.
EUROSTAT is the statistical agency of the European Commission that provides data to the institutions of the 28 nations (note, the number of nations may be affected by Brexit results) of the European Union (EU-28) and harmonizes statistical methods across member states. GDP at market prices and the GDP deflator can be downloaded from the database under the prefix: National accounts indicator ESA10.
   a. Look at the data on both the GDP deflator and GDP at market prices during the global financial crisis from 2007 till 2009 and then during the European Sovereign Debt Crisis from 2010 till 2015. Which of the two crises had a larger recessionary impact?
   b. According to the EUROSTAT's labor force survey, which of the two crises marked a higher level unemployment level?
   c. EUROSTAT presents statistical data on business demography in the nations of the EU-28, measuring the total number of active enterprises in the business economy, their birth rates, death rates, and the survival rates. While the enterprise birth rate is seen as an indicator of job creation and GDP growth, enterprise death rate is an indicator of a recession. The two recessions showed that the enterprise death rate was slightly higher than the birth rate. How does this relate to your answers in parts (a) and (b)?

For more on the impact of recessions on business activities and economic growth as well as the methodology of business demography, visit www.ec.europa.eu.

Further Readings

- If you want to learn more about the definition and the construction of the many economic indicators that are regularly reported on the news—from the help-wanted index to the retail sales index—two easy-to-read references are:
  The *Guide to Economic Indicators*, by Norman Frumkin, 3rd edition, M.E. Sharpe, 4th edition, New York, 2005.
  The Economist Guide to Economic Indicators, by the staff of *The Economist*, 6th edition, Bloomberg, New York, 2007.

- In 1995, the U.S. Senate set up a commission to study the construction of the CPI and make recommendations about potential changes. The commission concluded that the rate of inflation computed using the CPI was on average about 1% too high. If this conclusion is correct, this implies in particular that real wages (nominal wages divided by the CPI) have grown 1% more per year than is currently being reported. For more on the conclusions of the commission and some of the exchanges that followed, read *Consumer Prices, the Consumer Price Index, and the Cost of Living*, by Michael Boskin et al., *Journal of Economic Perspectives*, 1998, 12(1): pp. 3–26.

- For a short history of the construction of the National Income Accounts, read *GDP: One of the Great Inventions of the 20th Century*, Survey of Current Business, January 2000, 1–9. (http://www.bea.gov/scb/pdf/BEAWIDE/2000/0100od.pdf).

- For a discussion of some of the problems involved in measuring activity, read Katherine Abraham, "What We Don't Know Could Hurt Us; Some Reflections on the Measurement of Economic Activity," *Journal of Economic Perspectives*, 2005, 19(3): pp. 3–18.

- To see why it is hard to measure the price level and output correctly, read "Viagra and the Wealth of Nations" by Paul Krugman, 1998 (www.pkarchive.org/theory/viagra.html). (Paul Krugman is a Nobel Prize winner, and a columnist at the *New York Times*. His columns are opinionated, insightful, and fun to read.)

APPENDIX: The Construction of Real GDP and Chain-Type Indexes

The example we used in the chapter had only one final good—cars—so constructing real GDP was easy. But how do we construct real GDP when there is more than one final good? This appendix gives the answer.

To understand how real GDP in an economy with many final goods is constructed, all you need to do is look at an economy where there are just two final goods. What works for two goods works just as well for millions of goods.

Suppose that an economy produces two final goods, say wine and potatoes:

- In year 0, it produces 10 pounds of potatoes at a price of $1 a pound, and 5 bottles of wine at a price of $2 a bottle.
- In year 1, it produces 15 pounds of potatoes at a price of $1 a pound, and 5 bottles of wine at a price of $3 a bottle.
- Nominal GDP in year 0 is therefore equal to $20. Nominal GDP in year 1 is equal to $30.

This information is summarized in the following table.

Nominal GDP in Year 0 and in Year 1.

	Year 0		
	Quantity	$ Price	$ Value
Potatoes (pounds)	10	1	10
Wine (bottles),	5	2	10
Nominal GDP			20
	Year 1		
	Quantity	$ Price	$ Value
Potatoes (pounds)	15	1	15
Wine (bottles),	5	3	15
Nominal GDP			30

The rate of growth of nominal GDP from year 0 to year 1 is equal to $(\$30 - \$20)/(\$20) = 50\%$. But what is the rate of growth of real GDP?

Answering this question requires constructing real GDP for each of the two years. The basic idea behind constructing real GDP is to evaluate the quantities in each year using the *same set of prices*.

Suppose we choose, for example, the prices in year 0. Year 0 is then called the **base year**. In this case, the computation is as follows:

- Real GDP in year 0 is the sum of the quantity in year 0 times the price in year 0 for both goods: $(10 \times \$1) + (5 \times \$2) = \$20$.
- Real GDP in year 1 is the sum of the quantity in year 1 times the price in year 0 for both goods: $(15 \times \$1) + (5 \times \$2) = \$25$.
- The rate of growth of real GDP from year 0 to year 1 is then $(\$25 - \$20)/(\$20)$, or 25%.

This answer raises however an obvious issue: Instead of using year 0 as the base year, we could have used year 1, or any other year. If, for example, we had used year 1 as the base year, then:

- Real GDP in year 0 would be equal to $(10 \times \$1 + 5 \times \$3) = \$25$.
- Real GDP in year 1 would be equal to $(15 \times \$1 + 5 \times \$3) = \$30$.
- The rate of growth of real GDP from year 0 to year 1 would be equal to $\$5/\$25$, or 20%.

The answer using year 1 as the base year would therefore be different from the answer using year 0 as the base year. So if the choice of the base year affects the constructed percentage rate of change in output, which base year should one choose?

Until the mid-1990s in the United States—and still in most countries today—the practice was to choose a base year and change it infrequently, say, every five years or so. For example, in the United States, 1987 was the base year used from December 1991 to December 1995. That is, measures of real GDP published, for example, in 1994 for both 1994 and for all earlier years were constructed using 1987 prices. In December 1995, national income accounts shifted to 1992 as a base year; measures of real GDP for all earlier years were recalculated using 1992 prices.

This practice was logically unappealing. Every time the base year was changed and a new set of prices was used, all past real GDP numbers—and all past real GDP growth rates—were recomputed: Economic history was, in effect, rewritten every five years! Starting in December 1995, the U.S. Bureau of Economic Analysis (BEA)—the government office that produces the GDP numbers—shifted to a new method that does not suffer from this problem.

The method requires four steps:

- Constructing the rate of change of real GDP from year t to year $t + 1$ in two different ways. First using the prices from year t as the set of common prices; second, using the prices from year $t + 1$ as the set of common prices. For example, the rate of change of GDP from 2006 to 2007 is computed by:
  - (1) Constructing real GDP for 2006 and real GDP for 2007 using 2006 prices as the set of common prices, and computing a first measure of the rate of growth of GDP from 2006 to 2007.
  - (2) Constructing real GDP for 2006 and real GDP for 2007 using 2007 prices as the set of common prices, and computing a second measure of the rate of growth of GDP from 2006 to 2007.
- Constructing the rate of change of real GDP as the average of these two rates of change.
- Constructing an index for the level of real GDP by *linking*—or *chaining*—the constructed rates of change for each year. The index is set equal to 1 in some arbitrary year. At the time this

book is written, the arbitrary year is 2009. Given that the constructed rate of change from 2009 to 2010 by the BEA is 2.5%, the index for 2010 equals $(1 + 2.5\%) = 1.025$. The index for 2010 is then obtained by multiplying the index for 2009 by the rate of change from 2009 to 2010, and so on. (You will find the value of this index—multiplied by 100—in the second column of Table B3 in the Economic Report of the President. Check that it is 100 in 2009 and 102.6 in 2010, and so on.)

- Multiplying this index by nominal GDP in 2009 to derive *real GDP in chained (2009) dollars.* As the index is 1 in 2009, this implies that real GDP in 2009 equals nominal GDP in 2009.

Chained refers to the chaining of rates of change described previously. *(2009)* refers to the year where, by construction, real GDP is equal to nominal GDP. (You will find the value of real GDP in chained (2009) dollars in the first column of Table B2 of the Economic Report of the President.)

This index is more complicated to construct than the indexes used before 1995. (To make sure you understand the steps, construct real GDP in chained (year 0) dollars for year 1 in our example.) But it is clearly better conceptually: The prices used to evaluate real GDP in two adjacent years are the right prices, namely the average prices for those two years. And, because the rate of change from one year to the next is constructed using the prices in those two years rather than the set of prices in an arbitrary base year, history will not be rewritten every five years—as it used to be when, under the previous method for constructing real GDP, the base year was changed every five years.

(For more details, go to http://www.bea.gov/scb/pdf/national/nipa/1995/0795od.pdf.)

Key Term

base year, 62

The Short Run

In the short run, demand determines output. Many factors affect demand, from consumer confidence to the state of the financial system, to fiscal and monetary policy.

Chapter 3

Chapter 3 looks at equilibrium in the goods market and the determination of output. It focuses on the interaction among demand, production, and income. It shows how fiscal policy affects output.

Chapter 4

Chapter 4 looks at equilibrium in financial markets and the determination of the interest rate. It shows how monetary policy affects the interest rate.

Chapter 5

Chapter 5 looks at the goods market and financial markets together. It shows what determines output and the interest rate in the short run. It looks at the role of fiscal and monetary policy.

Chapter 6

Chapter 6 extends the model by introducing a richer financial system and uses it to explain what happened during the recent crisis.

The Goods Market

When economists think about year-to-year movements in economic activity, they focus on the interactions among *production, income, and demand*:

- **Changes in the demand for goods lead to changes in production.**

- **Changes in production lead to changes in income.**

- **Changes in income lead to changes in the demand for goods.**

Nothing makes the point better than this cartoon:

This chapter looks at these interactions and their implications.

Section 3-1 looks at the composition of GDP and the different sources of the demand for goods.

Section 3-2 looks at the determinants of the demand for goods.

Section 3-3 shows how equilibrium output is determined by the condition that the production of goods must be equal to the demand for goods.

Section 3-4 gives an alternative way of thinking about the equilibrium, based on the equality of investment and saving.

Section 3-5 takes a first pass at the effects of fiscal policy on equilibrium output.

3-1 The Composition of GDP

The terms *output* and *production* are synonymous. There is no rule for using one or the other. Use the one that sounds better.

The purchase of a machine by a firm, the decision to go to a restaurant by a consumer, and the purchase of combat airplanes by the federal government are clearly different decisions and depend on different factors. So, if we want to understand what determines the demand for goods, it makes sense to decompose aggregate output (GDP) from the point of view of the different goods being produced, and from the point of view of the different buyers for these goods.

The decomposition of GDP typically used by macroeconomists is shown in Table 3-1 (a more detailed version, with precise definitions, appears in Appendix 1 at the end of the book).

Warning! To most people, the term *investment* refers to the purchase of assets like gold or shares of General Motors. Economists use *investment* to refer to the purchase of *new capital goods*, such as (new) machines, (new) buildings, or (new) houses. When economists refer to the purchase of gold, or shares of General Motors, or other financial assets, they use the term *financial investment*.

■ First comes **consumption** (which we will denote by the letter C when we use algebra throughout this book). These are the goods and services purchased by consumers, ranging from food to airline tickets, to new cars, and so on. Consumption is by far the largest component of GDP. In 2014, it accounted for 68% of GDP.

■ Second comes **investment** (I), sometimes called **fixed investment** to distinguish it from inventory investment (which we will discuss later). Investment is the sum of **nonresidential investment**, the purchase by firms of new plants or new machines (from turbines to computers), and **residential investment**, the purchase by people of new houses or apartments.

MyEconLab Real-time data

Table 3-1 The Composition of U.S. GDP, 2014		Billions of Dollars	Percent of GDP
	GDP (Y)	17,348	100.0
1	Consumption (C)	11,865	68.3
2	Investment (I)	2,782	16.0
	Nonresidential	2,233	12.9
	Residential	549	3.1
3	Government spending (G)	3,152	18.1
4	Net exports	−530	−3.1
	Exports (X)	2,341	13.5
	Imports (IM)	−2,871	−16.6
5	Inventory investment	77	0.4

Source: Survey of Current Business, July 2015, Table 1-1-5.

Nonresidential investment and residential investment, and the decisions behind them, have more in common than might first appear. Firms buy machines or plants to produce output in the future. People buy houses or apartments to get *housing services* in the future. In both cases, the decision to buy depends on the services these goods will yield in the future, so it makes sense to treat them together. Together, nonresidential and residential investment accounted for 16% of GDP in 2014.

■ Third comes **government spending** (G). This represents the purchases of goods and services by the federal, state, and local governments. The goods range from airplanes to office equipment. The services include services provided by government employees: In effect, the national income accounts treat the government as buying the services provided by government employees—and then providing these services to the public, free of charge.

Note that G does not include **government transfers**, like Medicare or Social Security payments, nor interest payments on the government debt. Although these are clearly government expenditures, they are not purchases of goods and services. That is why the number for government spending on goods and services in Table 3-1, 18.1% of GDP, is smaller than the number for total government spending including transfers and interest payments. That number, in 2014, was approximately 33% of GDP when transfers and interest payments of federal, state, and local governments are combined.

■ The sum of lines 1, 2, and 3 gives the *purchases of goods and services by U.S. consumers, U.S. firms, and the U.S. government.* To determine the *purchases of U.S. goods and services*, two more steps are needed:

First, we must add **exports** (X), the purchases of U.S. goods and services by foreigners.

Second, we must subtract **imports** (IM) the purchases of foreign goods and services by U.S. consumers, U.S. firms, and the U.S. government.

The difference between exports and imports is called **net exports** ($X - IM$), or the **trade balance**. If exports exceed imports, the country is said to run a **trade surplus**. If exports are less than imports, the country is said to run a **trade deficit**. In 2014, U.S. exports accounted for 13.5% of GDP. U.S. imports were equal to 16.6% of GDP, so the United States was running a trade deficit equal to 3.1% of GDP.

■ So far we have looked at various sources of purchases (sales) of U.S. goods and services in 2014. To determine U.S. production in 2014, we need to take one last step:

In any given year, production and sales need not be equal. Some of the goods produced in a given year are not sold in that year but in later years. And some of the goods sold in a given year may have been produced in a previous year. The difference between goods produced and goods sold in a given year—the difference between production and sales, in other words—is called **inventory investment**.

If production exceeds sales and firms accumulate inventories as a result, then inventory investment is said to be positive. If production is less than sales and firms' inventories fall, then inventory investment is said to be negative. Inventory investment is typically small—positive in some years and negative in others. In 2014, inventory investment was positive, equal to just $77 billion. Put another way, production was higher than sales by an amount equal to $77 billion.

We now have what we need to develop our first model of output determination.

Exports > imports
⟺ trade surplus
Imports > exports
⟺ trade deficit

Although it is called 'inventory investment', the word *investment* is slightly misleading. In contrast to fixed investment, which represents decisions by firms, inventory investment is partly involuntary, reflecting the fact that firms did not anticipate sales accurately in making production plans.

Make sure you understand each of these three equivalent ways of stating the relations among production, sales, and inventory investment:

Inventory investment =
  production − sales
Production   =
  sales + inventory investment
Sales   =
  Production − inventory investment

3-2 The Demand for Goods

Denote the total demand for goods by Z. Using the decomposition of GDP we saw in Section 3-1, we can write Z as

$$Z \equiv C + I + G + X - IM$$

Recall that inventory investment is not part of demand. ▶

This equation is an **identity** (which is why it is written using the symbol "$\equiv$" rather than an equals sign). It *defines* Z as the sum of consumption, plus investment, plus government spending, plus exports, minus imports.

We now need to think about the determinants of Z. To make the task easier, let's first make a number of simplifications:

A model nearly always starts with "Assume" (or "Suppose"). This is an indication that reality is about to be simplified to focus on the issue at hand. ▶

■ Assume that all firms produce the same good, which can then be used by consumers for consumption, by firms for investment, or by the government. With this (big) simplification, we need to look at only one market—the market for "the" good—and think about what determines supply and demand in that market.

■ Assume that firms are willing to supply any amount of the good at a given price level P. This assumption allows us to focus on the role demand plays in the determination of output. As we shall see, this assumption is valid only in the short run. When we move to the study of the medium run (starting in Chapter 7), we shall abandon it. But for the moment, it will simplify our discussion.

■ Assume that the economy is *closed*—that it does not trade with the rest of the world: Both exports and imports are zero. This assumption clearly goes against the facts: Modern economies trade with the rest of the world. Later on (starting in Chapter 17), we will abandon this assumption as well and look at what happens when the economy is open. But, for the moment, this assumption will also simplify our discussion because we won't have to think about what determines exports and imports.

Under the assumption that the economy is closed, $X = IM = 0$, so the demand for goods Z is simply the sum of consumption, investment, and government spending:

$$Z \equiv C + I + G$$

Let's discuss each of these three components in turn.

Consumption (C)

Consumption decisions depend on many factors. But the main one is surely income, or, more precisely, **disposable income** (Y_D), the income that remains once consumers have received transfers from the government and paid their taxes. When their disposable income goes up, people buy more goods; when it goes down, they buy fewer goods.

We can then write:

$$C = C(Y_D) \tag{3.1}$$
$$(+)$$

This is a formal way of stating that consumption C is a function of disposable income Y_D. The function $C(Y_D)$ is called the **consumption function**. The positive sign below Y_D reflects the fact that when disposable income increases, so does consumption. Economists call such an equation a **behavioral equation** to indicate that the equation captures some aspect of behavior—in this case, the behavior of consumers.

We will use functions in this book as a way of representing relations between variables. What you need to know about functions—which is very little—is described in Appendix 2 at the end of the book. This appendix develops the mathematics you need to go through this book. Not to worry: We shall always describe a function in words when we introduce it for the first time.

It is often useful to be more specific about the form of the function. Here is such a case. It is reasonable to assume that the relation between consumption and disposable income is given by the simpler relation:

$$C = c_0 + c_1 Y_D \qquad (3.2)$$

In other words, it is reasonable to assume that the function is a **linear relation**. The relation between consumption and disposable income is then characterized by two **parameters**, c_0 and c_1:

◀ Think about your own consumption behavior. What are your values of c_0 and c_1?

■ The parameter c_1 is called the **propensity to consume**. (It is also called the *marginal propensity to consume*. I will drop the word *marginal* for simplicity.) It gives the effect an additional dollar of disposable income has on consumption. If c_1 is equal to 0.6, then an additional dollar of disposable income increases consumption by $\$1 \times 0.6 = 60$ cents.

A natural restriction on c_1 is that it be positive: An increase in disposable income is likely to lead to an increase in consumption. Another natural restriction is that c_1 be less than 1: People are likely to consume only part of any increase in disposable income and save the rest.

■ The parameter c_0 has a literal interpretation. It is what people would consume if their disposable income in the current year were equal to zero: If Y_D equals zero in equation (3.2), $C = c_0$. If we use this interpretation, a natural restriction is that, if current income were equal to zero, consumption would still be positive: With or without income, people still need to eat! This implies that c_0 is positive. How can people have positive consumption if their income is equal to zero? Answer: They dissave. They consume either by selling some of their assets or by borrowing.

■ The parameter c_0 has a less literal and more frequently used interpretation. Changes in c_0 reflect changes in consumption for a given level of disposable income. Increases in c_0 reflect an increase in consumption given income, decreases in c_0 a decrease. There are many reasons why people may decide to consume more or less, given their disposable income. They may, for example, find it easier or more difficult to borrow, or may become more or less optimistic about the future. An example of a decrease in c_0 is given in the Focus box, "The Lehman Bankruptcy, Fears of Another Great Depression, and Shifts in the Consumption Function."

The relation between consumption and disposable income shown in equation (3.2) is drawn in Figure 3-1. Because it is a linear relation, it is represented by a straight line.

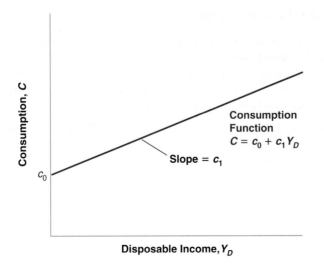

Disposable Income, Y_D

Figure 3-1

Consumption and Disposable Income

Consumption increases with disposable income but less than one for one. A lower value of c_0 will shift the entire line down.

MyEconLab Animation

Its intercept with the vertical axis is c_0; its slope is c_1. Because c_1 is less than 1, the slope of the line is less than 1: Equivalently, the line is flatter than a 45-degree line. If the value of c_0 increases, then the line shifts up by the same amount. (A refresher on graphs, slopes, and intercepts is given in Appendix 2.)

Next we need to define disposable income Y_D. Disposable income is given by

$$Y_D \equiv Y - T$$

where Y is income and T is taxes paid minus government transfers received by consumers. For short, we will refer to T simply as taxes—but remember that it is equal to taxes minus transfers. Note that the equation is an identity, indicated by "$\equiv$".

Replacing Y_D in equation (3.2) gives

$$C = c_0 + c_1(Y - T) \tag{3.3}$$

Equation (3.3) tells us that consumption C is a function of income Y and taxes T. Higher income increases consumption, but less than one for one. Higher taxes decrease consumption, also less than one for one.

Investment (*I*)

Models have two types of variables. Some variables depend on other variables in the model and are therefore explained within the model. Variables like these are called **endogenous variables**. This was the case for consumption given previously. Other variables are not explained within the model but are instead taken as given. Variables like these are called **exogenous variables**. This is how we will treat investment here. We will take investment as given and write:

$$I = \bar{I} \tag{3.4}$$

Putting a bar on investment is a simple typographical way to remind us that we take investment as given.

We take investment as given to keep our model simple. But the assumption is not innocuous. It implies that, when we later look at the effects of changes in production, we will assume that investment does not respond to changes in production. It is not hard to see that this implication may be a bad description of reality: Firms that experience an increase in production might well decide they need more machines and increase their investment as a result. For now, though, we will leave this mechanism out of the model. In Chapter 5 we will introduce a more realistic treatment of investment.

Government Spending (*G*)

The third component of demand in our model is government spending, G. Together with taxes T, G describes **fiscal policy**—the choice of taxes and spending by the government.

Just as we just did for investment, we will take G and T as exogenous. But the reason why we assume G and T are exogenous is different from the reason we assumed investment is exogenous. It is based on two distinct arguments:

- First, governments do not behave with the same regularity as consumers or firms, so there is no reliable rule we could write for G or T corresponding to the rule we wrote, for example, for consumption. (This argument is not airtight, though. Even if governments do not follow simple behavioral rules as consumers do, a good part of their behavior is predictable. We will look at these issues later, in particular in Chapters 22 and 23. Until then, I shall set them aside.)

- Second, and more importantly, one of the tasks of macroeconomists is to think about the implications of alternative spending and tax decisions. We want to be able to say, "If the government was to choose these values for G and T, this is what would happen." The approach in this book will typically treat G and T as variables chosen by the government and will not try to explain them within the model.

Because we will (nearly always) take G and T as exogenous, I won't use a bar to denote their values. This will keep the notation lighter.

3-3 The Determination of Equilibrium Output

Let's put together the pieces we have introduced so far.

Assuming that exports and imports are both zero, the demand for goods is the sum of consumption, investment, and government spending:

$$Z \equiv C + I + G$$

Replacing C and I from equations (3.3) and (3.4), we get

$$Z = c_0 + c_1(Y - T) + \bar{I} + G \tag{3.5}$$

The demand for goods Z depends on income Y, taxes T, investment $\bar{I}$ and government spending G.

MyEconLab Video

Let's now turn to **equilibrium** in the goods market, and the relation between production and demand. If firms hold inventories, then production need not be equal to demand: For example, firms can satisfy an increase in demand by drawing upon their inventories—by having negative inventory investment. They can respond to a decrease in demand by continuing to produce and accumulating inventories—by having positive inventory investment. Let's first ignore this complication, though, and begin by assuming that firms do not hold inventories. In this case, inventory investment is always equal to zero, and **equilibrium in the goods market** requires that production Y be equal to the demand for goods Z:

$$Y = Z \tag{3.6}$$

Think of an economy that produces only haircuts. There cannot be inventories of haircuts—haircuts produced but not sold?—so production must always be equal to demand.

This equation is called an **equilibrium condition**. Models include three types of equations: identities, behavioral equations, and equilibrium conditions. You now have seen examples of each: The equation defining disposable income is an identity, the consumption function is a behavioral equation, and the condition that production equals demand is an equilibrium condition.

There are three types of equations:

Identities
Behavioral equations
Equilibrium conditions

Replacing demand Z in (3.6) by its expression from equation (3.5) gives

$$Y = c_0 + c_1(Y - T) + \bar{I} + G \tag{3.7}$$

Equation (3.7) represents algebraically what we stated informally at the beginning of this chapter:

In equilibrium, production, Y (the left side of the equation), is equal to demand (the right side). Demand in turn depends on income, Y, which is itself equal to production.

Can you relate this statement to the cartoon at the start of the chapter?

Note that we are using the same symbol Y for production and income. This is no accident! As you saw in Chapter 2, we can look at GDP either from the production side or from the income side. Production and income are identically equal.

Having constructed a model, we can solve it to look at what determines the level of output—how output changes in response to, say, a change in government spending. Solving a model means not only solving it algebraically but also understanding why the results are what they are. In this book, solving a model will also mean characterizing the results using graphs—sometimes skipping the algebra altogether—and describing the results and the mechanisms in words. Macroeconomists always use these three tools:

1. Algebra to make sure that the logic is correct,
2. Graphs to build the intuition, and
3. Words to explain the results.

Make it a habit to do the same.

Using Algebra

Rewrite the equilibrium equation (3.7):

$$Y = c_0 + c_1 Y - c_1 T + \bar{I} + G$$

Move $c_1 Y$ to the left side and reorganize the right side:

$$(1 - c_1)Y = c_0 + \bar{I} + G - c_1 T$$

Divide both sides by $(1 - c_1)$:

$$Y = \frac{1}{1 - c_1}[c_0 + \bar{I} + G - c_1 T] \qquad (3.8)$$

Equation (3.8) characterizes equilibrium output, the level of output such that production equals demand. Let's look at both terms on the right, beginning with the term in brackets.

> Autonomous means independent—in this case, independent of output.

▶

- The term $[c_0 + \bar{I} + G - c_1 T]$ is that part of the demand for goods that does not depend on output. For this reason, it is called **autonomous spending**.

  Can we be sure that autonomous spending is positive? We cannot, but it is very likely to be. The first two terms in brackets, c_0 and $\bar{I}$, are positive. What about the last two, $G - c_1 T$? Suppose the government is running a **balanced budget**—taxes equal government spending. If $T = G$, and the propensity to consume (c_1) is less than 1 (as we have assumed), then $(G - c_1 T)$ is positive and so is autonomous spending. Only if the government were running a very large budget surplus—if taxes were much larger than government spending—could autonomous spending be negative. We can safely ignore that case here.

- Turn to the first term, $1/(1 - c_1)$. Because the propensity to consume (c_1) is between zero and 1, $1/(1 - c_1)$ is a number greater than one. For this reason, this number, which *multiplies* autonomous spending, is called the **multiplier**. The closer c_1 is to 1, the larger the multiplier.

  If $T = G$, then

$$(G - c_1 T) = (T - c_1 T) = (1 - c_1)T > 0$$

What does the multiplier imply? Suppose that, for a given level of income, consumers decide to consume more. More precisely, assume that c_0 in equation (3.3) increases by \$1 billion. Equation (3.8) tells us that output will increase by more than \$1 billion. For example, if c_1 equals 0.6, the multiplier equals $1/(1 - 0.6) = 1/0.4 = 2.5$. so that output increases by $2.5 \times$ \$1 billion = \$2.5 billion.

We have looked at an increase in consumption, but equation (3.8) makes it clear that any change in autonomous spending—from a change in investment, to a change in government spending, to a change in taxes—will have the same qualitative effect: It will change output by more than its direct effect on autonomous spending.

Where does the multiplier effect come from? Looking back at equation (3.7) gives us the clue: An increase in c_0 increases demand. The increase in demand then leads to an increase in production. The increase in production leads to an equivalent increase in income (remember the two are identically equal). The increase in income further increases consumption, which further increases demand, and so on. The best way to describe this mechanism is to represent the equilibrium using a graph. Let's do that.

Using a Graph

Let's characterize the equilibrium graphically.

- First, plot production as a function of income.

  In Figure 3-2, measure production on the vertical axis. Measure income on the horizontal axis. Plotting production as a function of income is straightforward: Recall that production and income are identically equal. Thus, the relation between them is the 45-degree line, the line with a slope equal to 1.

- Second, plot demand as a function of income.

  The relation between demand and income is given by equation (3.5). Let's rewrite it here for convenience, regrouping the terms for autonomous spending together in the term in parentheses:

$$Z = (c_0 + \bar{I} + G - c_1 T) + c_1 Y \qquad (3.9)$$

  Demand depends on autonomous spending and on income—via its effect on consumption. The relation between demand and income is drawn as ZZ in the graph. The intercept with the vertical axis—the value of demand when income is equal to zero—equals autonomous spending. The slope of the line is the propensity to consume, c_1: When income increases by 1, demand increases by c_1. Under the restriction that c_1 is positive but less than 1, the line is upward sloping but has a slope of less than 1.

- In equilibrium, production equals demand.

  Equilibrium output, Y, therefore occurs at the intersection of the 45-degree line and the demand function. This is at point A. To the left of A, demand exceeds production; to the right of A, production exceeds demand. Only at A are demand and production equal.

  Suppose that the economy is at the initial equilibrium, represented by point A in the graph, with production equal to Y.

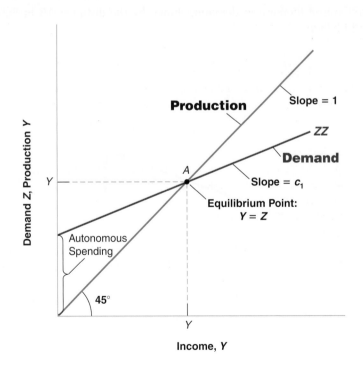

Figure 3-2

Equilibrium in the Goods Market

Equilibrium output is determined by the condition that production is equal to demand.

MyEconLab Animation

Now suppose c_0 increases by $1 billion. At the initial level of income (the level of disposable income associated with point A since T is unchanged in this example), consumers increase their consumption by $1 billion. This makes use of the second interpretation of the value of c_0. What happens is shown in Figure 3-3, which builds on Figure 3-2.

Equation (3.9) tells us that, for any value of income, if c_0 is higher by $1 billion, demand is higher by $1 billion. Before the increase in c_0, the relation between demand and income was given by the line ZZ. After the increase in c_0 by $1 billion, the relation between demand and income is given by the line ZZ', which is parallel to ZZ but higher by $1 billion. In other words, the demand curve shifts up by $1 billion. The new equilibrium is at the intersection of the 45-degree line and the new demand relation, at point A'.

Look at the vertical axis. The distance between Y and Y' on the vertical axis is larger than ▶ the distance between A and B—which is equal to $1 billion.

Equilibrium output increases from Y to Y'. The increase in output, $(Y' - Y)$, which we can measure either on the horizontal or the vertical axis, is larger than the initial increase in consumption of $1 billion. This is the multiplier effect.

With the help of the graph, it becomes easier to tell how and why the economy moves from A to A'. The initial increase in consumption leads to an increase in demand of $1 billion. At the initial level of income, Y, the level of demand is shown by point B: Demand is $1 billion higher. To satisfy this higher level of demand, firms increase production by $1 billion. This increase in production of $1 billion implies that income increases by $1 billion (recall: income = production), so the economy moves to point C. (In other words, both production and income are higher by $1 billion.) But this is not the end of the story. The increase in income leads to a further increase in demand. Demand is now shown by point D. Point D leads to a higher level of production, and so on, until the economy is at A', where production and demand are again equal. This is therefore the new equilibrium.

We can pursue this line of explanation a bit more, which will give us another way to think about the multiplier.

■ The first–round increase in demand, shown by the distance AB in Figure 3-3— equals $1 billion.

Figure 3-3

The Effects of an Increase in Autonomous Spending on Output

An increase in autonomous spending has a more than one-for-one effect on equilibrium output.

MyEconLab Animation

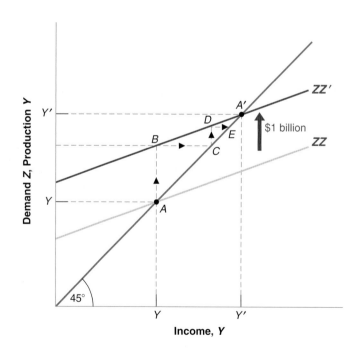

The Short Run   **The Core**

- This first-round increase in demand leads to an equal increase in production, or $1 billion, which is also shown by the distance AB.
- This first-round increase in production leads to an equal increase in income, shown by the distance BC, also equal to $1 billion.
- The second-round increase in demand, shown by the distance CD, equals $1 billion (the increase in income in the first round) times the propensity to consume, c_1—hence, $\$c_1$ billion.
- This second-round increase in demand leads to an equal increase in production, also shown by the distance CD, and thus an equal increase in income, shown by the distance DE.
- The third-round increase in demand equals $\$c_1$ billion (the increase in income in the second round), times c_1, the marginal propensity to consume; it is equal to $\$c_1 \times c_1 = \$c_1^2$ billion, and so on.

Following this logic, the total increase in production after, say, $n + 1$ rounds equals $1 billion times the sum:

$$1 + c_1 + c_1^2 + \cdots + c_1^n$$

Such a sum is called a **geometric series**. Geometric series will frequently appear in this book. A refresher is given in Appendix 2 at the end of the book. One property of geometric series is that, when c_1 is less than one (as it is here) and as n gets larger and larger, the sum keeps increasing but approaches a limit. That limit is $1/(1 - c_1)$, making the eventual increase in output $\$1/(1 - c_1)$ billion.

The expression $1/(1 - c_1)$ should be familiar: It is the multiplier, derived another way. This gives us an equivalent, but more intuitive way of thinking about the multiplier. We can think of the original increase in demand as triggering successive increases in production, with each increase in production leading to an increase in income, which leads to an increase in demand, which leads to a further increase in production, which leads … and so on. The multiplier is the sum of all these successive increases in production.

Trick question: Think about the multiplier as the result ◀ of these successive rounds. What would happen in each successive round if c_1, the propensity to consume, was larger than one?

Using Words

How can we summarize our findings in words?

Production depends on demand, which depends on income, which is itself equal to production. An increase in demand, such as an increase in government spending, leads to an increase in production and a corresponding increase in income. This increase in income leads to a further increase in demand, which leads to a further increase in production, and so on. The end result is an increase in output that is larger than the initial shift in demand, by a factor equal to the multiplier.

The size of the multiplier is directly related to the value of the propensity to consume: The higher the propensity to consume, the higher the multiplier. What is the value of the propensity to consume in the United States today? To answer this question, and more generally to estimate behavioral equations and their parameters, economists use **econometrics**, the set of statistical methods used in economics. To give you a sense of what econometrics is and how it is used, read Appendix 3 at the end of this book. This appendix gives you a quick introduction, along with an application estimating the propensity to consume. A reasonable estimate of the propensity to consume in the United States today is around 0.6 (the regressions in Appendix 3 yield two estimates, 0.5 and 0.8). In other words, an additional dollar of disposable income leads on average to an increase in consumption of 60 cents. This implies that the multiplier is equal to $1/(1 - c_1) = 1/(1 - 0.6) = 2.5$.

MyEconLab Video
The empirical evidence suggests that multipliers are typically smaller than that. This is because the simple model developed in this chapter leaves out a number of important mechanisms, for example, the reaction of monetary policy to changes in spending, or the fact that some of the demand falls on foreign goods. We shall come back to the issue as we ◀ go through the book.

How Long Does It Take for Output to Adjust?

Let's return to our example one last time. Suppose that c_0 increases by $1 billion. We know that output will increase by an amount equal to the multiplier $1/(1 - c_1)$ times $1 billion. But how long will it take for output to reach this higher value?

Under the assumptions we have made so far, the answer is: Right away! In writing the equilibrium condition (3.6), I have assumed that production is always equal to demand. In other words, I have assumed that production responds to demand instantaneously. In writing the consumption function (3.2) as I did, I have assumed that consumption responds to changes in disposable income instantaneously. Under these two assumptions, the economy goes instantaneously from point A to point A' in Figure 3-3: The increase in demand leads to an immediate increase in production, the increase in income associated with the increase in production leads to an immediate increase in demand, and so on. There is nothing wrong in thinking about the adjustment in terms of successive rounds as we did previously, even though the equations indicate that all these rounds happen at once.

This instantaneous adjustment isn't really plausible: A firm that faces an increase in demand might well decide to wait before adjusting its production, meanwhile drawing down its inventories to satisfy demand. A worker who gets a pay raise might not adjust her consumption right away. These delays imply that the adjustment of output will take time.

Formally describing this adjustment of output over time—that is, writing the equations for what economists call the **dynamics** of adjustment, and solving this more complicated model—would be too hard to do here. But it is easy to do it informally in words:

■ Suppose, for example, that firms make decisions about their production levels at the beginning of each quarter. Once their decisions are made, production cannot be adjusted for the rest of the quarter. If purchases by consumers are higher than production, firms draw down their inventories to satisfy the purchases. On the other hand, if purchases are lower than production, firms accumulate inventories.

■ Now suppose consumers decide to spend more, that they increase c_0. During the quarter in which this happens, demand increases, but production—because we assumed it was set at the beginning of the quarter—doesn't yet change. Therefore, income doesn't change either.

■ Having observed an increase in demand, firms are likely to set a higher level of production in the following quarter. This increase in production leads to a corresponding increase in income and a further increase in demand. If purchases still exceed production, firms further increase production in the following quarter, and so on.

■ In short, in response to an increase in consumer spending, output does not jump to the new equilibrium, but rather increases over time from Y to Y'.

    How long this adjustment takes depends on how and when firms revise their production schedule. If firms adjust their production schedules more frequently in response to past increases in purchases, the adjustment will occur faster.

We will often do in this book what I just did here. After we have looked at changes in equilibrium output, we will then describe informally how the economy moves from one equilibrium to the other. This will not only make the description of what happens in the economy feel more realistic, but it will often reinforce your intuition about why the equilibrium changes.

We have focused in this section on increases in demand. But the mechanism, of course, works both ways: Decreases in demand lead to decreases in output. The recent recession was the result of two of the four components of autonomous spending dropping

In the model we saw previously, we ruled out this possibility by assuming firms did not hold inventories, and so could not rely on drawing down inventories to satisfy an increase demand.

The Lehman Bankruptcy, Fears of Another Great Depression, and Shifts in the Consumption Function

Why would consumers decrease consumption if their disposable income has not changed? Or, in terms of equation (3.2), why might c_0 decrease—leading in turn to a decrease in demand, output, and so on?

One of the first reasons that come to mind is that, even if their current income has not changed, they start worrying about the future and decide to save more. This is precisely what happened at the start of the crisis, in late 2008 and early 2009. The basic facts are shown in Figure 1 below. The figure plots, from the first quarter of 2008 to the third quarter of 2009, the behavior of three variables, disposable income, total consumption, and consumption of durables—the part of consumption that falls on goods such as cars, computers, and so on (Appendix 1 at the end of the book gives a more precise definition). To make things visually simple, all three variables are normalized to equal 1 in the first quarter of 2008.

Note two things about the figure. First, despite the fact that the crisis led to a large fall in GDP, during that period, disposable income did not initially move much. It even increased in the first quarter of 2008. But consumption was unchanged from the first to the second quarter of 2008 and then fell before disposable income fell. It fell by 3 percentage points in 2009 relative to 2008, more than the decrease in disposable income. In terms of the Figure 1, the distance between the line for disposable income and the line for consumption increased. Second, during the third and especially the fourth quarters of 2008, the consumption of durables

dropped sharply. By the fourth quarter of 2008, it was down 10% relative to the first quarter, before recovering in early 2009 and decreasing again later.

Why did consumption, and especially, consumption of durables, decrease at the end of 2008 despite relatively small changes in disposable income? A number of factors were at play, but the main one was the psychological fallout of the financial crisis. Recall from Chapter 1, that, on September 15, 2008, Lehman Brothers, a very large bank, went bankrupt, and that, in the ensuing weeks, it appeared that many more banks might follow suit and the financial system might collapse. For most people, the main sign of trouble was what they read in newspapers: Even though they still had their job and received their monthly income checks, the events reminded them of the stories of the Great Depression and the pain that came with it. One way to see this is to look at the Google Trends series that gives the number of searches for "Great Depression," from January 2008 to September 2009, and is plotted in Figure 2. The series is normalized so its average value is 1 over the two years. Note how sharply the series peaked in October 2008 and then slowly decreased over the course of 2009, as it became clear that, while the crisis was a serious one, policy makers were going to do whatever they could do to avoid a repeat of the Great Depression.

If you felt that the economy might go into another Great Depression, what would you do? Worried that you might become unemployed or that your income might decline in the future, you would probably cut consumption, even if

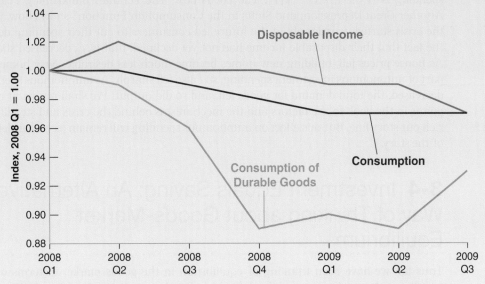

Figure 1 *Disposable Income, Consumption, and Consumption of Durables in the United States, 2008:1 to 2009:3*

Source: Calculated using series DPIC96, PCECC96, PCDGCC96: Federal Reserve Economic Data (FRED) http://research.stlouisfed.org/fred2/.

your disposable income had not yet changed. And, given the uncertainty about what was going on, you might also delay the purchases you could afford to delay; for example, the purchase of a new car or a new TV. As Figure 1 in this box shows, this is exactly what consumers did in late 2008: Total consumption decreased, and consumption of durables collapsed. In 2009, as the smoke slowly cleared and the worse scenarios became increasingly unlikely, consumption of durables picked up. But by then, many other factors were contributing to the crisis.

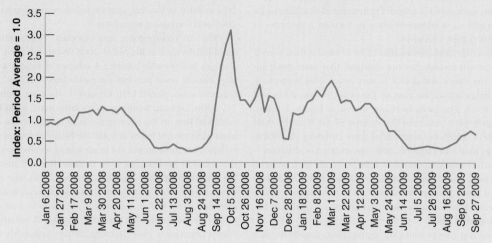

Figure 2 *Google Search Volume for "Great Depression," January 2008 to September 2009*

Source: Google Trends, "Great Depression."

by a large amount at the same time. To remind you, the expression for autonomous spending is $[c_0 + I + G - c_1 T]$. The Focus box "The Lehman Bankruptcy, Fears of Another Great Depression, and Shifts in the Consumption Function" shows how, when the crisis started, worries about the future led consumers to cut their spending despite the fact that their disposable income had not yet declined; that is, c_0 decreased sharply. As house prices fell, building new homes became much less desirable. New homes are part of autonomous investment spending, so I also fell sharply. As autonomous spending decreased, the total demand for goods fell, and so did output. We shall return at many points in the book to the factors and the mechanisms behind the crisis and steadily enrich our story line. But this effect on autonomous spending will remain a central element of the story.

3-4 Investment Equals Saving: An Alternative Way of Thinking about Goods-Market Equilibrium

Thus far, we have been thinking of equilibrium in the goods market in terms of the equality of the production and the demand for goods. An alternative—but, it turns out, equivalent—way of thinking about equilibrium focuses instead on investment and saving. This is how John Maynard Keynes first articulated this model in 1936, in *The General Theory of Employment, Interest and Money.*

Let's start by looking at saving. Saving is the sum of private saving and public saving.

- By definition, **private saving** (S), (i.e. saving by consumers) is equal to their disposable income minus their consumption:

$$S \equiv Y_D - C$$

Using the definition of disposable income, we can rewrite private saving as income minus taxes minus consumption:

$$S \equiv Y - T - C$$

Private saving is also done by firms, who do not distribute all of their profits and use those retained earnings to finance investment. For simplicity, we ignore saving by firms here. But the bottom line, namely the equality of investment and saving in equation (3.10), does not depend on this simplification.

- By definition, **public saving** ($T - G$) is equal to taxes (net of transfers) minus government spending. If taxes exceed government spending, the government is running a **budget surplus**, so public saving is positive. If taxes are less than government spending, the government is running a **budget deficit**, so public saving is negative.

Public saving > 0 $\Leftrightarrow$ Budget surplus

- Now return to the equation for equilibrium in the goods market that we derived previously. Production must be equal to demand, which, in turn, is the sum of consumption, investment, and government spending:

$$Y = C + I + G$$

Subtract taxes (T) from both sides and move consumption to the left side:

$$Y - T - C = I + G - T$$

The left side of this equation is simply private saving (S), so

$$S = I + G - T$$

Or, equivalently,

$$I = S + (T - G) \tag{3.10}$$

On the left is investment. On the right is saving, the sum of *private saving* and *public saving*.

Equation (3.10) gives us another way of thinking about equilibrium in the goods market: It says that equilibrium in the goods market requires that investment equal **saving**—the sum of private and public saving. This way of looking at equilibrium explains why the equilibrium condition for the goods market is called the **IS relation**, which stands for "**I**nvestment equals **S**aving": What firms want to invest must be equal to what people and the government want to save.

MyEconLab Video

To understand equation (3.10), imagine an economy with only one person who has to decide how much to consume, invest, and save—a "Robinson Crusoe" economy, for example. For Robinson Crusoe, the saving and the investment decisions are one and the same: What he invests (say, by keeping rabbits for breeding rather than having them for dinner), he automatically saves. In a modern economy, however, investment decisions are made by firms, whereas saving decisions are made by consumers and the government. In equilibrium, equation (3.10) tells us, all these decisions have to be consistent: Investment must equal saving.

To summarize: There are two equivalent ways of stating the condition for equilibrium in the goods market:

$$\text{Production} = \text{Demand}$$
$$\text{Investment} = \text{Saving}$$

We characterized the equilibrium using the first condition, equation (3.6). We now do the same using the second condition, equation (3.10). The results will be the same, but the derivation will give you another way of thinking about the equilibrium.

- Note first that *consumption and saving decisions are one and the same:* Given their disposable income, once consumers have chosen consumption, their saving is determined, and vice versa. The way we specified consumption behavior implies that private saving is given by:

$$S = Y - T - C$$
$$= Y - T - c_0 - c_1(Y - T)$$

Rearranging, we get

$$S = -c_0 + (1 - c_1)(Y - T) \tag{3.11}$$

- In the same way that we called c_1 the propensity to consume, we can call $(1 - c_1)$ the **propensity to save**. The propensity to save tells us how much of an additional unit of income people save. The assumption we made previously—that the propensity to consume (c_1) is between zero and one implies that the propensity to save $(1 - c_1)$ is also between zero and one. Private saving increases with disposable income, but by less than one dollar for each additional dollar of disposable income.

  In equilibrium, investment must be equal to saving, the sum of private and public saving. Replacing private saving in equation (3.10) by its expression,

$$I = -c_0 + (1 - c_1)(Y - T) + (T - G)$$

Solving for output,

$$Y = \frac{1}{1 - c_1} [c_0 + \bar{I} + G - c_1 T] \tag{3.12}$$

Equation (3.12) is exactly the same as equation (3.8). This should come as no surprise. We are looking at the same equilibrium condition, just in a different way. This alternative way will prove useful in various applications later in the book. The Focus box "The Paradox of Saving" looks at such an application, which was first emphasized by Keynes and is often called the paradox of saving.

3-5 Is the Government Omnipotent? A Warning

Equation (3.8) implies that the government, by choosing the level of spending (G) or the level of taxes (T), can choose the level of output it wants. If it wants output to be higher by, say, $1 billion, all it needs to do is to increase G by $\$(1 - c_1)$ billion. This increase in government spending, in theory, will lead to an output increase of $\$(1 - c_1)$ billion times the multiplier $1/(1 - c_1)$, or $1 billion.

Can governments really achieve the level of output they want? Obviously not: If they could, and it was as easy as it sounds in the previous paragraph, why would the U.S. government have allowed growth to stall in 2008 and output to actually fall in 2009? Why wouldn't the government increase the growth rate now, so as to decrease unemployment more rapidly? There are many aspects of reality that we have not yet incorporated in our model, and all of them complicate the government's task. We shall introduce them in due time. But it is useful to list them briefly here:

For a glimpse at the longer list, go to Section 22-1, "What We Have Learned," in Chapter 22.

- Changing government spending or taxes is not easy. Getting the U.S. Congress to pass bills always takes time, often becoming a president's nightmare (Chapters 21 and 22).

The Paradox of Saving

As we grow up, we are told about the virtues of thrift. Those who spend all their income are condemned to end up poor. Those who save are promised a happy life. Similarly, governments tell us, an economy that saves is an economy that will grow strong and prosper! The model we have seen in this chapter, however, tells a different and surprising story.

Suppose that, at a given level of disposable income, consumers decide to save more. In other words, suppose consumers decrease c_0, therefore decreasing consumption and increasing saving at a given level of disposable income. What happens to output and to saving?

Equation (3.12) makes it clear that equilibrium output decreases: As people save more at their initial level of income, they decrease their consumption. But this decreased consumption decreases demand, which decreases production.

Can we tell what happens to saving? Let's return to the equation for private saving, equation (3.11) (recall that we assume no change in public saving, so saving and private saving move together):

$$S = -c_0 + (1 - c_1)(Y - T)$$

On the one hand, $-c_0$ is higher (less negative): Consumers are saving more at any level of income; this tends to increase saving. But, on the other hand, their income Y is lower: This decreases saving. The net effect would seem to be ambiguous. In fact, we can tell which way it goes:

To see how, go back to equation (3.10), the equilibrium condition that investment and saving must be equal:

$$I = S + (T - G)$$

By assumption, investment does not change: $I = \bar{I}$. Nor do T or G. So the equilibrium condition tells us that in equilibrium, private saving S cannot change either. Although people want to save more at a given level of income, their income decreases by an amount such that their saving is unchanged.

This means that as people attempt to save more, the result is both a decline in output and unchanged saving. This surprising pair of results is known as the **paradox of saving** (or the *paradox of thrift*). Note that the same result would obtain if we looked at public rather than private saving: A decrease in the budget deficit would also lead to a lower output and unchanged overall (public and private) saving. And note that, if we extended our model to allow investment to decrease with output (we shall do this in Chapter 5) rather than assuming it is constant, the result would be even more dramatic: An attempt to save more, either by consumers or by the government, would lead to lower output, lower investment, and by implication lower saving!

So should you forget the old wisdom? Should the government tell people to be less thrifty? No. The results of this simple model are of much relevance in the short run. The desire of consumers to save more is an important factor in many of the U.S. recessions, including, as we saw in the previous Focus box, the recent crisis. But—as we will see later when we look at the medium run and the long run—other mechanisms come into play over time, and an increase in the saving rate is likely to lead over time to higher saving and higher income. A warning remains, however: Policies that encourage saving might be good in the medium run and in the long run, but they can lead to a reduction in demand and in output, and perhaps even a recession, in the short run.

- We have assumed that investment remained constant. But investment is also likely to respond in a variety of ways. So are imports: Some of the increased demand by consumers and firms will not be for domestic goods but for foreign goods. The exchange rate may change. All these responses are likely to be associated with complex, dynamic effects, making it hard for governments to assess the effects of their policies with much certainty (Chapters 5 and 9, and 18 to 20).

- Expectations are likely to matter. For example, the reaction of consumers to a tax cut is likely to depend on whether they think of the tax cut as transitory or permanent. The more they perceive the tax cut as permanent, the larger will be their consumption response. Similarly, the reaction of consumers to an increase in spending is likely to depend on when they think the government will raise taxes to pay for the spending (Chapters 14 to 16).

- Achieving a given level of output can come with unpleasant side effects. Trying to achieve too high a level of output can, for example, lead to increasing inflation and, for that reason, be unsustainable in the medium run (Chapter 9).

- Cutting taxes or increasing government spending, as attractive as it may seem in the short run, can lead to large budget deficits and an accumulation of public debt. A large debt has adverse effects in the long run. This is a hot issue in almost every advanced country in the world (Chapters 9, 11, 16, and 22).

In short, the proposition that, by using fiscal policy, the government can affect demand and output in the short run is an important and correct proposition. But as we refine our analysis, we will see that the role of the government in general, and the successful use of fiscal policy in particular, become increasingly difficult: Governments will never again have it so good as they have had in this chapter.

Summary

What you should remember about the components of GDP:

- GDP is the sum of consumption, investment, government spending, inventory investment, and exports minus imports.

- Consumption (C) is the purchase of goods and services by consumers. Consumption is the largest component of demand.

- Investment (I) is the sum of nonresidential investment—the purchase of new plants and new machines by firms—and of residential investment—the purchase of new houses or apartments by people.

- Government spending (G) is the purchase of goods and services by federal, state, and local governments.

- Exports (X) are purchases of U.S. goods by foreigners. Imports (IM) are purchases of foreign goods by U.S. consumers, U.S. firms, and the U.S. government.

- Inventory investment is the difference between production and purchases. It can be positive or negative.

What you should remember about our first model of output determination:

- In the short run, demand determines production. Production is equal to income. Income in turn affects demand.

- The consumption function shows how consumption depends on disposable income. The propensity to consume describes how much consumption increases for a given increase in disposable income.

- Equilibrium output is the level of output at which production equals demand. In equilibrium, output equals autonomous spending times the multiplier. Autonomous spending is that part of demand that does not depend on income. The multiplier is equal to $1/(1 - c_1)$, where c_1 is the propensity to consume.

- Increases in consumer confidence, investment demand, government spending, or decreases in taxes all increase equilibrium output in the short run.

- An alternative way of stating the goods-market equilibrium condition is that investment must be equal to saving—the sum of private and public saving. For this reason, the equilibrium condition is called the IS relation (I for investment, S for saving).

Key Terms

consumption (C), 68

investment (I), 68

fixed investment, 68

nonresidential investment, 68

residential investment, 68

government spending (G), 69

government transfers, 69

exports (X), 69

imports (IM), 69

net exports (X − IM), 69

trade balance, 69

trade surplus, 69

trade deficit, 69

inventory investment, 69

identity, 70

disposable income (Y_D), 70

consumption function, 70

behavioral equation, 70

linear relation, 71

parameter, 71

propensity to consume (c_1), 71

endogenous variables, 72

exogenous variables, 72

fiscal policy, 72

equilibrium, 73

equilibrium in the goods market, 73

equilibrium condition, 73

autonomous spending, 74

balanced budget, 74

multiplier, 74

geometric series, 77

econometrics, 77

dynamics, 78

private saving (S), 81

public saving (T − G), 81

budget surplus, 81

budget deficit, 81

saving, 81

IS relation, 81

propensity to save, 82

paradox of saving, 83

Questions and Problems

QUICK CHECK

MyEconLab Visit www.myeconlab.com to complete similar Quick Check problems and get instant feedback.

1. Using the information in this chapter, label each of the following statements true, false, or uncertain. Explain briefly.

  a. The largest component of GDP is consumption.

  b. Government spending, including transfers, was equal to 18.1% of GDP in 2014.

  c. The propensity to consume has to be positive, but otherwise it can take on any positive value.

  d. One factor in the 2009 recession was a drop in the value of the parameter c_0.

  e. Fiscal policy describes the choice of government spending and taxes and is treated as exogenous in our goods market model.

  f. The equilibrium condition for the goods market states that consumption equals output.

  g. An increase of one unit in government spending leads to an increase of one unit in equilibrium output.

  h. An increase in the propensity to consume leads to a decrease in output.

2. The following equations refer to the goods market of an economy in billions of euros:

$$C = 480 + 0.5Y_D$$

$$I = 110$$

$$T = 70$$

$$G = 250$$

  a. Solve for the goods market equilibrium.

  b. Find equilibrium disposable income (Y_D).

  c. Find equilibrium consumption (C).

3. Refer to the economy in Problem 2.

  a. Calculate the private savings, public savings, and investment spending.

  b. Calculate the multiplier and explain how it affects equilibrium output.

  c. Suppose that the government decides to increase its spending from €250 billion to €300 billion. Find the equilibrium output, consumption, and disposable income. Why would the government decide to expand fiscal spending?

DIG DEEPER

MyEconLab Visit www.myeconlab.com to complete all Dig Deeper problems and get instant feedback.

4. The balanced budget multiplier

  For both political and macroeconomic reasons, governments are often reluctant to run budget deficits. Here, we examine whether policy changes in G and T that maintain a balanced budget are macroeconomically neutral. Put another way, we examine whether it is possible to affect output through changes in G and T so that the government budget remains balanced.

Start from equation (3.8).

  a. By how much does Y increase when G increases by one unit?

  b. By how much does Y decrease when T increases by one unit?

  c. Why are your answers to parts and b different?

  Suppose that the economy starts with a balanced budget: G = T. If the increase in G is equal to the increase in T, then the budget remains in balance. Let us now compute the balanced budget multiplier.

  d. Suppose that G and T increase by one unit each. Using your answers to parts and b what is the change in equilibrium GDP? Are balanced budget changes in G and T macroeconomically neutral?

  e. How does the specific value of the propensity to consume affect your answer to part a? Why?

5. Automatic stabilizers

  In this chapter we have assumed that the fiscal policy variables G and T are independent of the level of income. In the real world, however, this is not the case. Taxes typically depend on the level of income and so tend to be higher when income is higher. In this problem, we examine how this automatic response of taxes can help reduce the impact of changes in autonomous spending on output.

  Consider the following behavioral equations:

$$C = c_0 + c_1 Y_D$$

$$T = t_0 + t_1 Y$$

$$Y_D = Y - T$$

G and I are both constant. Assume that t_1 is between 0 and 1.

  a. Solve for equilibrium output.

  b. What is the multiplier? Does the economy respond more to changes in autonomous spending when t_1 is 0 or when t_1 is positive? Explain.

  c. Why is fiscal policy in this case called an automatic stabilizer?

6. Balanced budget versus automatic stabilizers

  It is often argued that a balanced budget amendment would actually be destabilizing. To understand this argument, consider the economy in Problem 5.

  a. Solve for equilibrium output.

  b. Solve for taxes in equilibrium.

  Suppose that the government starts with a balanced budget and that there is a drop in c_0.

  c. What happens to Y? What happens to taxes?

  d. Suppose that the government cuts spending in order to keep the budget balanced. What will be the effect on Y? Does the cut in spending required to balance the budget counteract or reinforce the effect of the drop in c_0 on output? (Don't do the algebra. Use your intuition and give the answer in words.)

7. Taxes and transfers

  Recall that we define taxes, T, as net of transfers. In other words,

$$T = Taxes - Transfer\ Payments$$

  a. Suppose that the government increases transfer payments to private households, but these transfer payments are not financed by tax increases. Instead, the government borrows to pay for the transfer payments. Show in a diagram (similar to Figure 3-2) how this policy affects equilibrium output. Explain.

b. Suppose instead that the government pays for the increase in transfer payments with an equivalent increase in taxes. How does the increase in transfer payments affect equilibrium output in this case?

c. Now suppose that the population includes two kinds of people: those with high propensity to consume and those with low propensity to consume. Suppose the transfer policy increases taxes on those with low propensity to consume to pay for transfers to people with high propensity to consume. How does this policy affect equilibrium output?

d. How do you think the propensity to consume might vary across individuals according to income? In other words, how do you think the propensity to consume compares for people with high income and people with low income? Explain. Given your answer, do you think tax cuts will be more effective at stimulating output when they are directed toward high-income or toward low-income taxpayers?

8. Investment and income

This problem examines the implications of allowing investment to depend on output. Chapter 5 carries this analysis much further and introduces an essential relation—the effect of the interest rate on investment—not examined in this problem.

a. Suppose the economy is characterized by the following behavioral equations:

$$C = c_0 + c_1 Y_D$$
$$Y_D = Y - T$$
$$I = b_0 + b_1 Y$$

Government spending and taxes are constant. Note that investment now increases with output. (Chapter 5 discusses the reasons for this relation.) Solve for equilibrium output.

b. What is the value of the multiplier? How does the relation between investment and output affect the value of the multiplier? For the multiplier to be positive, what condition must $(c_1 + b_1)$ satisfy? Explain your answers.

c. What would happen if $(c_1 + b_1) > 1$? (Trick question. Think about what happens in each round of spending).

d. Suppose that the parameter b_0, sometimes called *business confidence*, increases. How will equilibrium output be affected? Will investment change by more or less than the change in b_0? Why? What will happen to national saving?

EXPLORE FURTHER

9. The paradox of saving revisited

You should be able to complete this question without doing any algebra, although you may find making a diagram helpful for part a. For this problem, you do not need to calculate the magnitudes of changes in economic variables—only the direction of change.

a. Consider the economy described in Problem 8. Suppose that consumers decide to consume less (and therefore to save more) for any given amount of disposable income.

Specifically, assume that consumer confidence (c_0) falls. What will happen to output?

b. As a result of the effect on output you determined in part a, what will happen to investment? What will happen to public saving? What will happen to private saving? Explain. (*Hint:* Consider the saving-equals-investment characterization of equilibrium.) What is the effect on consumption?

c. Suppose that consumers had decided to increase consumption expenditure, so that c_0 had increased. What would have been the effect on output, investment, and private saving in this case? Explain. What would have been the effect on consumption?

d. Comment on the following logic: "When output is too low, what is needed is an increase in demand for goods and services. Investment is one component of demand, and saving equals investment. Therefore, if the government could just convince households to attempt to save more, then investment, and output, would increase."

Output is not the only variable that affects investment. As we develop our model of the economy, we will revisit the paradox of saving in future chapter problems.

10. Greece's usage of fiscal policy to avoid the meltdown and the debt crisis

As a result of the combined effects of the global financial crisis and the sovereign debt crisis, the GDP of Greece declined from €281.44 billion in 2008 to €176.5 billion in 2015.

a. What is the percentage change of GDP during this period?

b. By how much should autonomous expenditure have risen in order to prevent the slide in the GDP of Greece, given that marginal propensity to consume is 0.6?

c. In reference to your reply to part (b), explain why the Greek Parliament refused the austerity measures that lender nations sanctioned for Greece.

d. The Greek reform program aimed to improve incentives to private investors. By how much do these incentives alone improve GDP if they have increased investment by €15.5 billion?

11. The "exit strategy" problem

In fighting the recession associated with the crisis, taxes were cut and government spending was increased. The result was a large government deficit. To reduce that deficit, taxes must be increased or government spending must be cut. This is the "exit strategy" from the large deficit.

a. How will reducing the deficit in either way affect the equilibrium level of output in the short run?

b. Which will change equilibrium output more: (i) cutting G by $100 billion (ii) raising T by $100 billion?

c. How does your answer to part (b) depend on the value of the marginal propensity to consume?

d. You hear the argument that a reduction in the deficit will increase consumer and business confidence and thus reduce the decline in output that would otherwise occur with deficit reduction. Is this argument valid?

Financial Markets I

Financial markets are intimidating. They involve a maze of institutions, from banks, to money market funds, mutual funds, investment funds, and hedge funds. Trading involves bonds, stocks, and other financial claims with exotic names, such as swaps and options. The financial pages of newspapers quote interest rates on many government bonds, on many corporate bonds, on short-term bonds, on long-term bonds, and it is easy to get confused. But financial markets play an essential role in the economy. They determine the cost of funds for firms, for households, for the government, and in turn affect their spending decisions. To understand their role we must proceed in steps.

In this chapter, we focus on the role of the central bank in affecting these interest rates. To do so, we drastically simplify reality and think of the economy as having only *two* financial assets, namely money, which does not pay interest, and bonds, which do. This will allow us to understand how the interest rate on bonds is determined, and the role of the central bank (in the United States, the **Fed**, short for **Federal Reserve Bank**) in this determination.

In the next chapter, Chapter 5, we shall combine the model of the goods market we developed in the previous chapter with the model of financial markets we develop in this chapter, and have another look at equilibrium output. Having done so however, we shall return to financial markets in Chapter 6, allowing for more financial assets and more interest rates, and focusing on the role of banks and other financial institutions. This will give us a richer model, and allow us to better understand what happened in the recent crisis.

The chapter has four sections:

Section 4-1 looks at the demand for money.

Section 4-2 assumes that the central bank directly controls the supply of money and shows how the interest rate is determined by the condition that the demand for money be equal to the supply of money.

Section 4-3 introduces banks as suppliers of money, revisits the determination of the interest rate, and describes the role of the central bank in that context.

Section 4-4 looks at the constraint on monetary policy coming from the fact that the interest rate on bonds cannot be negative, a constraint that has played an important role in the crisis.

4-1 The Demand for Money

This section looks at the determinants of *the demand for money*. A warning before we start: Words such as *money* or *wealth* have specific meanings in economics, often not the same meanings as in everyday conversation. The purpose of the Focus box "Semantic Traps: Money, Income, and Wealth" is to help you avoid some of these traps. Read it carefully, and refer back to it once in a while.

Suppose, as a result of having steadily saved part of your income in the past, your financial wealth today is $50,000. You may intend to keep saving in the future and increase your wealth further, but its value today is given. Suppose also that you only have the choice between two assets, money and bonds:

Make sure you see the difference between the decision about how much to save (a decision that determines how your wealth changes over time) and the decision about how to allocate a given stock of wealth between money and bonds.

- *Money*, which you can use for transactions, pays no interest. In the real world, as we already mentioned, there are two types of money: **currency**, coins and bills, and **checkable deposits**, the bank deposits on which you can write checks or use a debit card. The distinction between the two will be important when we look at the supply of money. For the moment, however, the distinction does not matter and we can ignore it. Just think currency.
- **Bonds** pay a positive interest rate, i, but they cannot be used for transactions. In the real world, there are many types of bonds and other financial assets, each associated with a specific interest rate. For the time being, we also ignore this aspect of reality and assume that there is just one type of bond and that it pays, i, *the* rate of interest.

Assume that buying or selling bonds implies some cost; for example, a phone call to your broker and the payment of a transaction fee. How much of your $50,000 should you hold in money, and how much in bonds? On the one hand, holding all your wealth in the form of money is clearly very convenient. You won't ever need to call a broker or pay transaction fees. But it also means you will receive no interest income. On the other hand, if you hold all your wealth in the form of bonds, you will earn interest on the full amount, but you will have to call your broker frequently—whenever you need money to take the subway, pay for a cup of coffee, and so on. This is a rather inconvenient way of going through life.

You may want to pay by credit card and avoid carrying currency. But you still have to have money in your checking account when you pay the credit card company.

Therefore, it is clear that you should hold both money and bonds. But in what proportions? This will depend mainly on two variables:

- Your *level of transactions*. You will want to have enough money on hand to avoid having to sell bonds whenever you need money. Say, for example, that you typically spend $3,000 a month. In this case, you might want to have, on average, say, two months worth of spending on hand, or $6,000 in money, and the rest, $50,000 − $6,000 = $44,000, in bonds. If, instead, you typically spend $4,000 a month, you might want to have, say, $8,000 in money and only $42,000 in bonds.
- *The interest rate on bonds.* The only reason to hold any of your wealth in bonds is that they pay interest. The higher the interest rate, the more you will be willing to deal with the hassle and costs associated with buying and selling bonds. If the interest rate is very high, you might even decide to squeeze your money holdings to an average of only two weeks' worth of spending, or $1,500 (assuming your monthly spending is $3,000). This way, you will be able to keep, on average, $48,500 in bonds and earn more interest as a result.

Let's make this last point more concrete. Most of you probably do not hold bonds; my guess is that few of you have a broker. However, some of you hold bonds indirectly if you have a money market account with a financial institution. **Money market funds** (the full name is *money market mutual funds*) pool together the funds of many people. The funds are then used to buy bonds—typically government bonds. Money market

Semantic Traps: Money, Income, and Wealth

In everyday conversation, we use "money" to denote many different things. We use it as a synonym for income: "making money." We use it as a synonym for wealth: "She has a lot of money." In economics, you must be more careful. Here is a basic guide to some terms and their precise meanings in economics.

Money is what can be used to pay for transactions. Money is currency and checkable deposits at banks. **Income** is what you earn from working plus what you receive in interest and dividends. It is a **flow**—something expressed in units of time: weekly income, monthly income, or yearly income, for example. J. Paul Getty was once asked what his income was. Getty answered: "$1,000." He meant but did not say: $1,000 per minute!

Saving is that part of after-tax income that you do not spend. It is also a flow. If you save 10% of your income, and your income is $3,000 per month, then you save $300 per month. **Savings** (plural) is sometimes used as a synonym for wealth—the value of what you have accumulated over time. To avoid confusion, I shall not use the term *savings* in this book.

Your **financial wealth**, or wealth for short, is the value of all your financial assets minus all your financial liabilities. In contrast to income or saving, which are flow variables, financial wealth is a **stock** variable. It is the value of wealth at a given moment in time.

At a given moment in time, you cannot change the total amount of your financial wealth. It can only change over time as you save or dissave, or as the value of your assets and liabilities change. But you can change the composition of your wealth; you can, for example, decide to repay part of your mortgage by writing a check against your checking account. This leads to a decrease in your liabilities (a smaller mortgage) and a corresponding decrease in your assets (a smaller checking account balance); but, at that moment, it does not change your wealth.

Financial assets that can be used directly to buy goods are called *money*. Money includes currency and checkable deposits—deposits against which you can write checks. Money is also a stock. Someone who is wealthy might have only small money holdings—say, $1,000,000 in stocks but only $500 in a checking account. It is also possible for a person to have a large income but only small money holdings—say, a monthly income of $10,000 but only $1,000 in his checking account.

Investment is a term economists reserve for the purchase of new capital goods, from machines to plants to office buildings. When you want to talk about the purchase of shares or other financial assets, you should refer them as a **financial investment**.

Learn how to be economically correct:

> Do not say "Mary is making a lot of money"; say "Mary has a high income."

> Do not say "Joe has a lot of money"; say "Joe is very wealthy."

---

funds pay an interest rate close to but slightly below the interest rate on the bonds they hold—the difference coming from the administrative costs of running the funds and from their profit margins.

When the interest rate on these funds reached 14% per year in the early 1980s (a very high interest rate by today's standards), people who had previously kept all of their wealth in their checking accounts (which paid little or no interest) realized how much interest they could earn by moving some of it into money market accounts instead. Now that interest rates are much lower, people are less careful about putting as much as they can in money market funds. Put another way, for a given level of transactions, people now keep more of their wealth in money than they did in the early 1980s.

Deriving the Demand for Money

Let's go from this discussion to an equation describing the demand for money.

Denote the amount of money people want to hold—their *demand for money*—by M^d (the superscript d stands for *demand*). The demand for money in the economy as a whole is just the sum of all the individual demands for money by the people and firms in the economy. Therefore, it depends on the overall level of transactions in the economy and on the interest rate. The overall level of transactions in the economy is hard to measure, but it is likely to be roughly proportional to nominal income (income

Revisit Chapter 2's example of an economy composed of a steel company and a car ▸ company. Calculate the total value of transactions in that economy. If the steel and the car companies doubled in size, what would happen to transactions and to GDP?

measured in dollars). If nominal income were to increase by 10%, it is reasonable to think that the dollar value of transactions in the economy would also increase by ▸ roughly 10%. So we can write the relation between the demand for money, nominal income, and the interest rate as:

$$M^d = \$Y \, L(i) \qquad (4.1)$$
$$(-)$$

where $\$Y$ denotes nominal income. Read this equation in the following way: *The demand for money M^d is equal to nominal income $\$Y$ times a decreasing function of the interest rate i, with the function denoted by $L(i)$.* The minus sign under i in $L(i)$ captures the fact that the interest rate has a negative effect on money demand: An increase in the interest rate *decreases* the demand for money, as people put more of their wealth into bonds.

Equation (4.1) summarizes what we have discussed so far:

What matters here is nominal income—income in dollars, not real income. If real income ▸ does not change but prices double, leading to a doubling of nominal income, people will need to hold twice as much money to buy the same consumption basket.

■ First, the demand for money increases in proportion to nominal income. If nominal income doubles, increasing from $\$Y$ to $\$2Y$, then the demand for money also doubles, increasing from $\$Y \, L(i)$ to $\$2Y \, L(i)$.

■ Second, the demand for money depends negatively on the interest rate. This is captured by the function $L(i)$ and the negative sign underneath: An increase in the interest rate decreases the demand for money.

The relation between the demand for money, nominal income, and the interest rate implied by equation (4.1) is shown in Figure 4-1. The interest rate, i, is measured on the vertical axis. Money, M, is measured on the horizontal axis.

The relation between the demand for money and the interest rate *for a given level of nominal income $\$Y$* is represented by the M^d curve. The curve is downward sloping: The lower the interest rate (the lower i), the higher the amount of money people want to hold (the higher M).

Figure 4-1

The Demand for Money

For a given level of nominal income, a lower interest rate increases the demand for money. At a given interest rate, an increase in nominal income shifts the demand for money to the right.

MyEconLab Animation

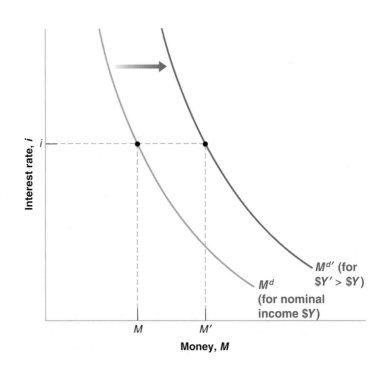

Who Holds U.S. Currency?

FOCUS

According to household surveys, in 2006, the average U.S. household held $1,600 in currency (dollar bills and coins). Multiplying by the number of households in the U.S. economy at the time (about 110 million), this implies that the total amount of currency held by U.S. households was around $170 billion.

According to the Federal Reserve Board, however—which issues the dollar bills and therefore knows how much is in circulation—the amount of currency in circulation was actually a much higher $750 billion. Here lies the puzzle: If it was not held by households, where was all this currency?

Clearly some currency was held by firms rather than by households. And some was held by those involved in the underground economy or in illegal activities. When dealing with drugs, dollar bills (and, in the future, bitcoin?), not checks, are the way to settle accounts. Surveys of firms and IRS estimates of the underground economy suggest, however, that this can only account for another $80 billion at the most. This leaves $500 billion, or 66% of the total, unaccounted for. So where was it? The answer: Abroad, held by foreigners.

A few countries, Ecuador and El Salvador among them, have actually adopted the dollar as their own currency. So people in these countries use dollar bills for transactions. But these countries are just too small to explain the puzzle.

In a number of countries that have suffered from high inflation in the past, people have learned that their domestic currency may quickly become worthless and they see dollars as a safe and convenient asset. This is, for example, the case of Argentina and of Russia. Estimates by the U.S. Treasury suggest that Argentina holds more than $50 billion in dollar bills, Russia more than $80 billion—so together, close to the holdings of U.S. households.

In yet other countries, people who have emigrated to the United States bring home U.S. dollar bills; or tourists pay some transactions in dollars, and the dollar bills stay in the country. This is, for example, the case for Mexico or Thailand.

The fact that foreigners hold such a high proportion of the dollar bills in circulation has two main macroeconomic implications. First, the rest of the world, by being willing to hold U.S. currency, is making in effect an interest-free loan to the United States of $500 billion. Second, while we shall think of money demand (which includes both currency and checkable deposits) as being determined by the interest rate and the level of transactions in the country, it is clear that U.S. money demand also depends on other factors. Can you guess, for example, what would happen to U.S. money demand if the degree of civil unrest increased in the rest of the world?

For a given interest rate, an increase in nominal income increases the demand for money. In other words, an increase in nominal income shifts the demand for money to the right, from M^d to $M^{d'}$. For example, at interest rate i, an increase in nominal income from $\$Y$ to $\$Y'$ increases the demand for money from M to M'.

4-2 Determining the Interest Rate: I

Having looked at the demand for money, we now look at the supply of money and then at the equilibrium.

In the real world, there are two types of money: checkable deposits, which are supplied by banks, and currency, which is supplied by the central bank. In this section, we shall assume that the only money in the economy is currency, central bank money. This is clearly not realistic, but it will make the basic mechanisms most transparent. We shall reintroduce checkable deposits, and look at the role banks play in the next section.

Money Demand, Money Supply, and the Equilibrium Interest Rate

Suppose the central bank decides to supply an amount of money equal to M, so

$$M^s = M$$

The superscript s stands for *supply*. (Let's disregard, for the moment, the issue of how exactly the central bank supplies this amount of money. We shall return to it in a few paragraphs.)

◀ Throughout this section, the term *money* means central bank money, or currency.

Figure 4-2

The Determination of the Interest Rate

The interest rate must be such that the supply of money (which is independent of the interest rate) is equal to the demand for money (which does depend on the interest rate).

MyEconLab Animation

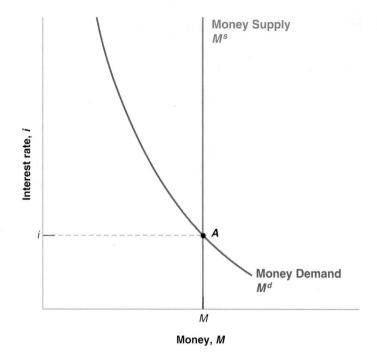

Equilibrium in financial markets requires that money supply be equal to money demand, that $M^s = M^d$. Then, using $M^s = M$, and equation (4.1) for money demand, the equilibrium condition is

$$\text{Money supply} = \text{Money demand}$$
$$M = \$Y\ L(i) \tag{4.2}$$

This equation tells us that the interest rate i must be such that, given their income $\$Y$, people are willing to hold an amount of money equal to the existing money supply M.

This equilibrium condition is represented graphically in Figure 4-2. As in Figure 4-1, money is measured on the horizontal axis, and the interest rate is measured on the vertical axis. The demand for money, M^d, drawn for a given level of nominal income, $\$Y$, is downward sloping: A higher interest rate implies a lower demand for money. The supply of money is drawn as the vertical line denoted M^s: The money supply equals M and is independent of the interest rate. Equilibrium occurs at point A, and the equilibrium interest rate is given by i.

Now that we have characterized the equilibrium, we can look at how changes in nominal income or changes in the money supply by the central bank affect the equilibrium interest rate.

■ Figure 4-3 shows the effects of an increase in nominal income on the interest rate.
   The figure replicates Figure 4-2, and the initial equilibrium is at point A. An increase in nominal income from $\$Y$ to Y' increases the level of transactions, which increases the demand for money at any interest rate. The money demand curve *shifts* to the right, from M^d to $M^{d'}$. The equilibrium moves from A up to A', and the equilibrium interest rate increases from i to i'.
   In words: For a given money supply, *an increase in nominal income leads to an increase in the interest rate.* The reason: At the initial interest rate, the demand for

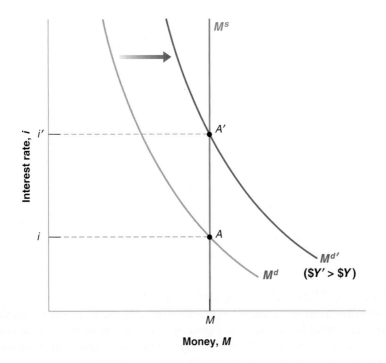

Figure 4-3

The Effects of an Increase in Nominal Income on the Interest Rate

Given the money supply, an increase in nominal income leads to an increase in the interest rate.

MyEconLab Animation

money exceeds the supply. The increase in the interest rate decreases the amount of money people want to hold and reestablishes equilibrium.

■ Figure 4-4 shows the effects of an increase in the money supply on the interest rate.

The initial equilibrium is at point A, with interest rate i. An increase in the money supply, from $M^s = M$ to $M^{s'} = M'$, leads to a shift of the money supply curve to the right, from M^s to $M^{s'}$. The equilibrium moves from A down to A'; the interest rate decreases from i to i'.

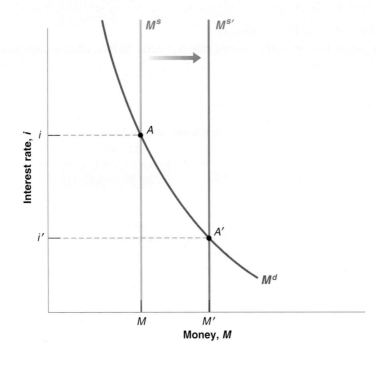

Figure 4-4

The Effects of an Increase in the Money Supply on the Interest Rate

An increase in the supply of money leads to a decrease in the interest rate.

MyEconLab Animation

In words: *an increase in the supply of money by the central bank leads to a decrease in the interest rate.* The decrease in the interest rate increases the demand for money so it equals the now larger money supply.

Monetary Policy and Open Market Operations

We can get a better understanding of the results in Figures 4-3 and 4-4 by looking more closely at how the central bank actually changes the money supply, and what happens when it does so.

In modern economies, the way central banks typically change the supply of money is by buying or selling bonds in the bond market. If a central bank wants to increase the amount of money in the economy, it buys bonds and pays for them by creating money. If it wants to decrease the amount of money in the economy, it sells bonds and removes from circulation the money it receives in exchange for the bonds. These actions are called **open market operations** because they take place in the "open market" for bonds.

The Balance Sheet of the Central Bank

The balance sheet of a bank (or firm, or individual) is a list of its assets and liabilities at a point in time. The assets are the sum of what the bank owns and what is owed to the bank by others. The liabilities are what the bank owes to others. It goes without saying that Figure 4-5 gives a much simplified version of an actual central bank balance sheet, but it will do for our purposes.

To understand what open market operations do, it is useful to start with the balance ▶ sheet of the central bank, given in Figure 4-5. The assets of the central bank are the bonds it holds in its portfolio. Its liabilities are the stock of money in the economy. Open market operations lead to equal changes in assets and liabilities.

If the central bank buys, say, $1 million worth of bonds, the amount of bonds it holds is higher by $1 million, and so is the amount of money in the economy. Such an operation is called an **expansionary open market operation**, because the central bank increases (*expands*) the supply of money.

If the central bank sells $1 million worth of bonds, both the amount of bonds held by the central bank and the amount of money in the economy are lower by $1 million. Such an operation is called a **contractionary open market operation**, because the central bank decreases (*contracts*) the supply of money.

Bond Prices and Bond Yields

We have focused so far on the interest rate on bonds. In fact, what is determined in bond markets are not interest rates, but bond *prices*. The two are however directly related. Understanding the relation between the two will prove useful both here and later in this book.

Figure 4-5

The Balance Sheet of the Central Bank and the Effects of an Expansionary Open Market Operation

The assets of the central bank are the bonds it holds. The liabilities are the stock of money in the economy. An open market operation in which the central bank buys bonds and issues money increases both assets and liabilities by the same amount.

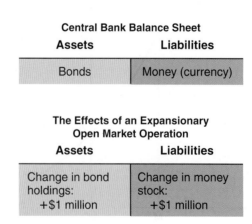

Central Bank Balance Sheet

Assets	Liabilities
Bonds	Money (currency)

The Effects of an Expansionary Open Market Operation

Assets	Liabilities
Change in bond holdings: +$1 million	Change in money stock: +$1 million

- Suppose the bonds in our economy are one-year bonds—bonds that promise a payment of a given number of dollars, say $100, a year from now. In the United States, bonds issued by the government promising payment in a year or less are called **Treasury bills** or **T-bills**. Let the price of a bond today be $\$P_B$, where the subscript B stands for "bond." If you buy the bond today and hold it for a year, the rate of return on holding the bond for a year is $(\$100 - \$P_B)/\$P_B$. Therefore, the interest rate on the bond is given by

$$i = \frac{\$100 - \$P_B}{\$P_B}$$

If $\$P_B$ is $99, the interest rate equals $\$1/\$99 = 0.010$, or 1.0% per year. If $\$P_B$ is $90, the interest rate is $\$1/\$90 = 11.1\%$ per year. *The higher the price of the bond, the lower the interest rate.*

The interest rate is what you get for the bond a year from now ($100) minus what you pay for the bond today ($\$P_B$), divided by the price of the bond today, ($\$P_B$).

- If we are given the interest rate, we can figure out the price of the bond using the same formula. Reorganizing the formula above, the price today of a one-year bond paying $100 a year from today is given by

$$\$P_B = \frac{100}{1 + i}$$

The price of the bond today is equal to the final payment divided by 1 plus the interest rate. If the interest rate is positive, the price of the bond is less than the final payment. *The higher the interest rate, the lower the price today.* You may read or hear that "bond markets went up today." This means that *the prices of bonds went up*, and therefore that *interest rates went down*.

Back to Open Market Operations

We are now ready to return to the effects of an open market operation and its effect on equilibrium in the money market.

Consider first an expansionary open market operation, in which the central bank buys bonds in the bond market and pays for them by creating money. As the central bank buys bonds, the demand for bonds goes up, increasing their price. Conversely, the interest rate on bonds goes down. Note that by buying the bonds in exchange for money that it created, the central bank has increased the money supply.

Consider instead a contractionary open market operation, in which the central bank decreases the supply of money. This leads to a decrease in their price. Conversely, the interest rate goes up. Note that by selling the bonds in exchange for money previously held by households, the central bank has reduced the money supply.

This way of describing how monetary policy affects interest rates is more intuitive. By buying or selling bonds in exchange for money, the central bank affects the price of bonds, and by implication, the interest rate on bonds.

Let's summarize what we have learned in the first two sections:

- The interest rate is determined by the equality of the supply of money and the demand for money.
- By changing the supply of money, the central bank can affect the interest rate.
- The central bank changes the supply of money through open market operations, which are purchases or sales of bonds for money.
- Open market operations in which the central bank increases the money supply by buying bonds lead to an increase in the price of bonds and a decrease in the interest rate. In Figure 4-2, the purchase of bonds by the central bank shifts the money supply to the right.

- Open market operations in which the central bank decreases the money supply by selling bonds lead to a decrease in the price of bonds and an increase in the interest rate. In Figure 4-2, the purchase of bonds by the central bank shifts the money supply to the left.

Choosing Money or Choosing the Interest Rate?

Let me take up one more issue before moving on. I have described the central bank as choosing the money supply and letting the interest rate be determined at the point where money supply equals money demand. Instead, I could have described the central bank as choosing the interest rate and then adjusting the money supply so as to achieve the interest rate it has chosen.

To see this, return to Figure 4-4. Figure 4-4 showed the effect of a decision by the central bank to increase the money supply from M^s to $M^{s'}$, causing the interest rate to fall from i to i'. However, we could have described the figure in terms of the central bank decision to lower the interest rate from i to i' by increasing the money supply from M^s to $M^{s'}$.

Suppose nominal income increases, as in Figure 4-3, and that the central bank wants to keep the interest rate unchanged. How does it need to adjust the money supply? ▶

Why is it useful to think about the central bank as choosing the interest rate? Because this is what modern central banks, including the Fed, typically do. They typically think about the interest rate they want to achieve, and then move the money supply so as to achieve it. This is why, when you listen to the news, you do not hear: "The Fed decided to decrease the money supply today." Instead you hear: "The Fed decided to increase the interest rate today." The way the Fed did it was by increasing the money supply appropriately.

4-3 Determining the Interest Rate: II

We took a shortcut in Section 4-2 in assuming that all money in the economy consisted of currency supplied by the central bank. In the real world, money includes not only currency but also checkable deposits. Checkable deposits are supplied not by the central bank but by (private) banks. In this section, we reintroduce checkable deposits and examine how this changes our conclusions. Let me give you the bottom line: Even, in this more complicated case, by changing the amount of central bank money, the central bank can and does control the interest rate.

To understand what determines the interest rate in an economy with both currency and checkable deposits, we must first look at what banks do.

What Banks Do

Modern economies are characterized by the existence of many types of **financial intermediaries**—institutions that receive funds from people and firms and use these funds to buy financial assets or to make loans to other people and firms. The assets of these institutions are the financial assets they own and the loans they have made. Their liabilities are what they owe to the people and firms from whom they have received funds.

Banks have other types of liabilities in addition to checkable deposits, and they are engaged in more activities than just holding bonds or making loans. Ignore these complications for the moment. We consider them in Chapter 6.

Banks are one type of financial intermediary. What makes banks special—and the reason we focus on banks here rather than on financial intermediaries in general—is that their liabilities are money: People can pay for transactions by writing checks up to the amount of their account balance. Let's look more closely at what they do.

The balance sheet of banks is shown in the bottom half of Figure 4-6, Figure 4-6b.

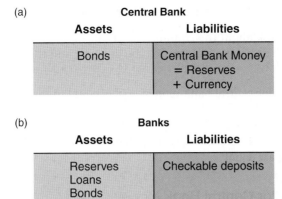

Figure 4-6

The Balance Sheet of Banks, and the Balance Sheet of the Central Bank Revisited

■ Banks receive funds from people and firms who either deposit funds directly or have funds sent to their checking accounts (via direct deposit of their paychecks, for example). At any point in time, people and firms can write checks, use a debit card, or withdraw funds, up to the full amount of their account balances. The liabilities of the banks are therefore equal to the value of these *checkable deposits*.

MyEconLab Video

■ Banks keep as **reserves** some of the funds they receive. They are held partly in cash and partly in an account the banks have at the central bank, which they can draw on when they need to. Banks hold reserves for three reasons:

On any given day, some depositors withdraw cash from their checking accounts, whereas others deposit cash into their accounts. There is no reason for the inflows and outflows of cash to be equal, so the bank must keep some cash on hand.

In the same way, on any given day, people with accounts at the bank write checks to people with accounts at other banks, and people with accounts at other banks write checks to people with accounts at the bank. What the bank, as a result of these transactions, owes the other banks can be larger or smaller than what the other banks owe to it. For this reason also, the bank needs to keep reserves.

The first two reasons imply that the banks would want to keep some reserves even if they were not required to do so. But, in addition, banks are typically subject to reserve requirements, which require them to hold reserves in some proportion of their checkable deposits. In the United States, reserve requirements are set by the Fed. In the U.S. banks are required to hold at least 10% of the value of the checkable deposits. They can use the rest to make loans or buy bonds.

■ Loans represent roughly 70% of banks' non reserve assets. Bonds account for the rest, 30%. The distinction between bonds and loans is unimportant for our purposes in this chapter—which is to understand how the money supply is determined. For this reason, to keep the discussion simple, we will assume in this chapter that banks do not make loans, that they hold only reserves and bonds as assets.

The distinction between loans and bonds is important for other purposes, from the possibility of "bank runs" to the role of federal deposit insurance. ◄ More on this in Chapter 6.

Figure 4-6a returns to the balance sheet of the central bank, in an economy in which there are banks. It is similar to the balance sheet of the central bank we saw in Figure 4-5. The asset side is the same as before: The assets of the central bank are the bonds it holds. The liabilities of the central bank are the money it has issued, **central bank money**. The new feature, relative to Figure 4-5, is that not all of central bank money is held as currency by the public. Some of it is held as reserves by banks.

The Demand and Supply for Central Bank Money

MyEconLab Video

So how do we think about the equilibrium in this more realistic setting? Very much in the same way as before, in terms of the demand and the supply of central bank money.

- The demand for central bank money is now equal to the demand for currency by people plus the demand for reserves by banks.
- The supply of central bank money is under the direct control of the central bank.
- The equilibrium interest rate is such that the demand and the supply for central bank money are equal.

The Demand for Central Bank Money

The demand for central bank money now has two components. The first is the demand for currency by people, the second is the demand for reserves by banks. To make the algebra simple, I shall assume in the text that people only want to hold money in the form of checkable deposits, and do not hold any currency. The more general case, where people hold both currency and checkable deposits, is treated in the appendix to this chapter. It involves more algebra but yields the same basic conclusions.

In this case, the demand for central bank money is simply the demand for reserves by banks. This demand in turn depends on the demand for checkable deposits by people. So let's start there. Under our assumption that people hold no currency, the demand for checkable deposits in turn is just equal to the demand for money by people. So, to describe the demand for checkable deposits, we can use the same equation as we used before (equation (4.1)):

$$M^d = \$Y \; L(i) \tag{4.3}$$
$$(-)$$

People want to hold more checkable deposits the higher their level of transactions and the lower the interest rate on bonds.

Now turn to the demand for reserves by banks. The larger the amount of checkable deposits, the larger the amount of reserves the banks must hold, both for precautionary and for regulatory reasons. Let θ (the Greek lowercase letter theta) be the **reserve ratio**, the amount of reserves banks hold per dollar of checkable deposits. Then, using equation (4.3), the demand for reserves by banks, call it H^d, is given by:

$$H^d = \theta M^d = \theta \$Y \; L(i) \tag{4.4}$$

The first equality reflects the fact that the demand for reserves is proportional to the demand for checkable deposits. The second equality reflects the fact that the demand for checkable deposits depends on nominal income and on the interest rate. So, the demand for central bank money, equivalent the demand for reserves by banks, is equal to θ times the demand for money by people.

The use of the letter H comes from the fact that central bank money is sometimes called **high-powered money**, to reflect its role in determining the equilibrium interest rate. Yet another name for central bank money is also the **monetary base**.

Equilibrium in the Market for Central Bank Money

Just as before, the supply of central bank money—equivalently the supply of reserves by the central bank—is under the control of the central bank. Let H denote the supply of central bank money. And just as before, the central bank can change the amount of H through open market operations. The equilibrium condition is that the supply of central bank money be equal to the demand for central bank money:

$$H = H^d \tag{4.5}$$

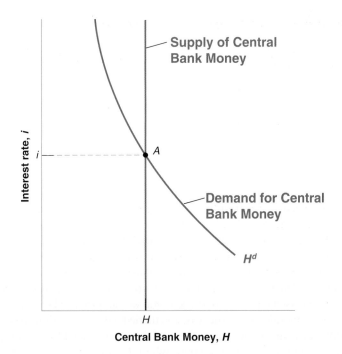

Figure 4-7

Equilibrium in the Market for Central Bank Money and the Determination of the Interest Rate

The equilibrium interest rate is such that the supply of central bank money is equal to the demand for central bank money.

MyEconLab Animation

Or, using equation (4.4):

$$H = \theta \$Y \, L(i) \qquad (4.6)$$

We can represent the equilibrium condition, equation (4.6), graphically, and we do this in Figure 4-7. The figure looks the same as Figure 4-2, but with central bank money rather than money on the horizontal axis. The interest rate is measured on the vertical axis. The demand for central bank money, H^d, is drawn for a given level of nominal income. A higher interest rate implies a lower demand for central bank money as demand for checkable deposits by people, and thus the demand for reserves by banks goes down. The supply of money is fixed and is represented by a vertical line at H. Equilibrium is at point A, with interest rate i.

The effects of either changes in nominal income or changes in the supply of central bank money are qualitatively the same as in the previous section. In particular, an increase in the supply of central bank money leads to a shift in the vertical supply line to the right. This leads to a lower interest rate. As before, an increase in central bank money leads to a decrease in the interest rate. Conversely, a decrease in central bank money leads to an increase in the interest rate. So, the basic conclusion is the same as in Section 4-2: By controlling the supply of central bank money, the central bank can determine the interest rate on bonds.

The Federal Funds Market and the Federal Funds Rate

You may wonder whether there is an actual market in which the demand and the supply of reserves determine the interest rate. And, indeed, in the United States, there is an actual market for bank reserves, where the interest rate adjusts to balance the supply and demand for reserves. This market is called the **federal funds market**. The interest rate determined in this market is called the **federal funds rate**. Because the Fed can in effect choose the federal funds rate it wants by changing the supply of central bank money, H, the federal funds rate is typically thought of as the main indicator of U.S. monetary policy. This is why so much attention is focused on it, and why changes in the federal funds rate typically make front page news.

4-4 The Liquidity Trap

The concept of a liquidity trap (i.e., a situation in which increasing the amount of money ["liquidity"] does not have an effect on the interest rate [the liquidity is "trapped"]), was developed by Keynes in the 1930s, although the expression itself came later.

The main conclusion from the first three sections was that the central bank can, by choosing the supply of central bank money, choose the interest rate that it wants. If it wants to increase the interest rate, it decreases the amount of central bank money. If it wants to decrease the interest rate, it increases the amount of central bank money. This section shows that this conclusion comes with an important caveat: The interest rate cannot go below zero, a constraint known as the **zero lower bound**. When the interest rate is down to zero, monetary policy cannot decrease it further. Monetary policy no longer works, and the economy is said to be in a **liquidity trap**.

Ten years ago, the zero lower bound was seen as a minor issue. Most economists believe that central banks would not want to have negative interest rates in any case, so the constraint would be unlikely to bind. The crisis however, has changed those perceptions. Many central banks decreased interest rates to zero and would have liked to go down even further. But the zero lower bound stood in the way, and turned out to be a serious constraint on policy.

If you look at Figure 4-1, you will see that I avoided the issue by not drawing the demand for money for interest rates close to zero.

Let's look at the argument more closely. When we derived the demand for money in Section 4-1, we did not ask what happens when the interest rate becomes equal to zero. Now we must ask the question. The answer: Once people hold enough money for transaction purposes, they are then indifferent between holding the rest of their financial wealth in the form of money or in the form of bonds. The reason they are indifferent is that both money and bonds pay the same interest rate, namely zero. Thus, the demand for money is as shown in Figure 4-8:

In fact, because of the inconvenience and the dangers of holding currency in very large amounts, people and firms are willing to hold some bonds even when the interest rate is a bit negative. We shall ignore this complication here.

- As the interest rate decreases, people want to hold more money (and thus fewer bonds): The demand for money increases.

Figure 4-8

Money Demand, Money Supply, and the Liquidity Trap

When the interest rate is equal to zero, and once people have enough money for transaction purposes, they become indifferent between holding money and holding bonds. The demand for money becomes horizontal. This implies that, when the interest rate is equal to zero, further increases in the money supply have no effect on the interest rate, which remains equal to zero.

MyEconLab Animation

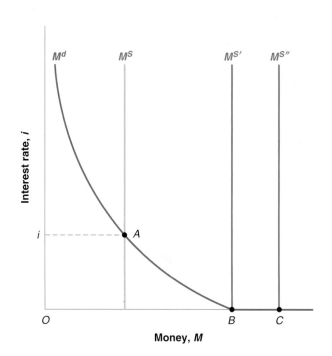

The Liquidity Trap in the United Kingdom

FOCUS

As we mentioned in Chapter 1, the global financial crisis prompted central banks in many countries to cut short-term policy rates to near zero levels. The Monetary Policy Committee of the Bank of England (BoE) cut the bank rate from 5% in mid-2008 to 0.5% in early 2009. In 2015–2016, the slowdown in the global economy, coupled with persistently low rates of inflation, has led several central banks across Europe, as well as in Japan, to cut interest rates below zero into negative territory. BoE was reluctant to cut interest rates below zero in the fear that negative rates could discourage depositors from keeping their savings in banks. The weaknesses of the recovery from the global financial crisis and the European sovereign crisis have led to a decline in household spending and business investment. The analysis in the text shows that uncertainty in the economic outlook would cause households to increase bank deposits and would prompt banks to increase their reserve holdings. As shown in Figure 1, this is precisely what happened. BoE has expanded cash and bank reserves substantially. Bank deposits increased more than ten-fold, from £23.6 billion in 2007 to £265.5 billion in mid-2016. This shows that the sharp expansion in money was absorbed by households and by banks as the bank rate remained at 0.5%. To boost the economy, BoE prefers to use expansionary monetary policy, through open market operations in which it buys government bonds in exchange for money. But negative interest rates remain an option for BoE.

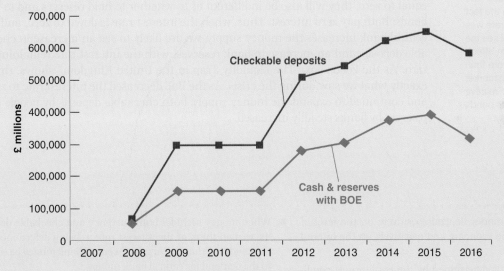

Figure 1   *Checkable Deposits, Cash, and Reserves with BoE, 2007–2016*

Source: Bank of England, Bankstats (Monetary & Financial Statistics).

■   As the interest rate becomes equal to zero, people want to hold an amount of money at least equal to the distance, OB. This is what they need for transaction purposes. But they are willing to hold even more money (and therefore hold fewer bonds) because they are indifferent between money and bonds. Therefore, the demand for money becomes horizontal beyond point B.

Now consider the effects of an increase in the money supply. (Let's ignore banks for the time being, and assume, as in Section 4-2, that all money is currency, so we can use the same diagram as in Figure 4-2 extended to allow for the horizontal portion of money demand. We shall come back to banks and bank money later.)

■   Consider the case where the money supply is M^s, so the interest rate consistent with financial market equilibrium is positive and equal to i. (This is the case we considered in Section 4-2.) Starting from that equilibrium, an increase in the money supply—a shift of the M^s line to the right—leads to a decrease in the interest rate.

■ Now consider the case where the money supply is $M^{s'}$, so the equilibrium is at point B; or the case where the money supply is $M^{s''}$, so the equilibrium is given by point C. In either case, the initial interest rate is zero. And, in either case, an increase in the money supply has no effect on the interest rate. Think of it this way:

Suppose the central bank increases the money supply. It does so through an open market operation in which it buys bonds and pays for them by creating money. As the interest rate is zero, people are indifferent to how much money or bonds they hold, so they are willing to hold fewer bonds and more money at the same interest rate, namely zero. The money supply increases, but with no effect on the interest rate—which remains equal to zero.

What happens when we reintroduce checkable deposits and a role for banks, along the lines of Section 4-3? Everything we just said still applies to the demand for money by people: If the interest rate is zero, they are indifferent to whether they hold money or bonds: Both pay zero interest. But, now a similar argument also applies to banks and their decision whether to hold reserves or buy bonds. If the interest rate is equal to zero, they will also be indifferent as to whether to hold reserves and to buy bonds: Both pay zero interest. Thus, when the interest rate is down to zero, and the central bank increases the money supply, we are likely to see an increase in checkable deposits and an increase in bank reserves, with the interest rate remaining at zero. As the Focus box "The Liquidity Trap in the United Kingdom" shows, this is exactly what we saw during the crisis. As the BoE decreased the interest rate to zero, and continued to expand the money supply, both checkable deposits by people and reserves by banks steadily increased.

In this context, you may ask why the Fed increased the money supply despite the fact that the federal funds rate was down to zero. We shall see the reason in Chapter 6: In effect, in an economy with more than one type of bond, open market operations can affect relative interest rates on other bonds and affect the economy. ▶

Summary

■ The demand for money depends positively on the level of transactions in the economy and negatively on the interest rate.

■ The interest rate is determined by the equilibrium condition that the supply of money be equal to the demand for money.

■ For a given supply of money, an increase in income leads to an increase in the demand for money and an increase in the interest rate. An increase in the supply of money for a given income leads to a decrease in the interest rate.

■ The way the central bank changes the supply of money is through open market operations.

■ Expansionary open market operations, in which the central bank increases the money supply by buying bonds, lead to an increase in the price of bonds and a decrease in the interest rate.

■ Contractionary open market operations, in which the central bank decreases the money supply by selling bonds, lead to a decrease in the price of bonds and an increase in the interest rate.

■ When money includes both currency and checkable deposits, we can think of the interest rate as being determined by the condition that the supply of central bank money be equal to the demand for central bank money.

■ The supply of central bank money is under the control of the central bank. In the special case where people hold only checkable deposits, the demand for central bank money is equal to the demand for reserves by banks, which is itself equal to the overall demand for money times the reserve ratio chosen by banks.

■ The market for bank reserves is called the *federal funds market*. The interest rate determined in that market is called the *federal funds rate*.

■ The interest rate chosen by the central bank cannot go below zero. When the interest rate is equal to zero, people and banks are indifferent to holding money or bonds. An increase in the money supply leads to an increase in money demand, an increase in reserves by banks, and no change in the interest rate. This case is known as the liquidity trap. In the liquidity trap monetary policy no longer affects the interest rate.

Key Terms

Federal Reserve Bank (Fed), 87

currency, 88

checkable deposits, 88

bonds, 88

money market funds, 88

money, 89

income, 89

flow, 89

saving, 89

savings, 89

financial wealth, 89

stock, 89

investment, 89

financial investment, 89

open market operation, 94

expansionary open market operation, 94

contractionary open market operation, 94

Treasury bill (T-bill), 95

financial intermediaries, 96

(bank) reserves, 97

central bank money, 97

reserve ratio, 98

high-powered money, 98

monetary base, 98

federal funds market, 99

federal funds rate, 99

zero lower bound, 100

liquidity trap, 100

Questions and Problems

QUICK CHECK

MyEconLab Visit www.myeconlab.com to complete similar Quick Check problems and get instant feedback.

1. Using the information in this chapter, label each of the following statements true, false, or uncertain. Explain briefly.

a. Income is a flow variable while financial wealth is a stock variable.

b. Economists distinguish between investors as those who produce goods and services, and traders as those who buy and sell financial instruments.

c. The demand for money is determined by income but not by interest rates.

d. Eurodollars comprise of the proportion of U.S. currency that is held in Europe only.

e. The central bank can contract money supply by selling Treasury bonds in the market for bonds.

f. Monetary policy determines money supply while interest policy determines interest rates

g. As the price of a bond rises, its interest rate also rises.

h. The central bank can either increase the money supply or raise interest rates to boost GDP growth in the economy.

2. Suppose that the household nominal income for an economy is £50,000 billion and the demand for money in this economy is given by

$$M^d = £Y(0.2 - 0.8i)$$

a. What is the demand for money when the interest rate is 1% and 5%?

b. What will be the impact on the demand for money if the nominal income declines by 20%?

c. What is the relationship between the demand for money and income? Money demand and the interest rate?

d. Explain what the central bank should do to interest rates if it needs to increase the demand for money.

3. Consider a bond that promises to pay $100 in one year.

a. What is the interest rate on the bond if its price today is $75? $85? $95?

b. What is the relation between the price of the bond and the interest rate?

c. If the interest rate is 8%, what is the price of the bond today?

4. The following are the money demand and money supply functions in an economy.

$$M^s = €8,000$$
$$M^d = €40,000(0.25 - i)$$

a. Calculate the equilibrium interest rate.

b. Suppose the central bank raises the equilibrium interest rate to 10%, will there be excess money supply or money demand? What monetary policy should be followed to reach the new equilibrium interest rate?

DIG DEEPER

MyEconLab Visit www.myeconlab.com to complete all Dig Deeper problems and get instant feedback.

5. Suppose that a person's wealth is $50,000 and that her yearly income is $60,000. Also suppose that her money demand function is given by

$$M^d = $Y(0.35 - i)$$

a. Derive the demand for bonds. Suppose the interest rate increases by 10 percentage points. What is the effect on her demand for bonds?

b. What are the effects of an increase in wealth on her demand for money and her demand for bonds? Explain in words.

c. What are the effects of an increase in income on her demand for money and her demand for bonds? Explain in words.

d. Consider the statement "When people earn more money, they obviously will hold more bonds." What is wrong with this statement?

6. The demand for money and bonds

You have learnt in this chapter that the interest rate affects both the prices of bonds and the demand for money. Explain each of these relationships.

Do these relationships hold when interest rates are negative? Why do you think central banks would choose to lower interest rates in their economies in the negative domain?

7. ATMs and credit cards

This problem examines the effect of the introduction of ATMs and credit cards on money demand. For simplicity, let's examine a person's demand for money over a period of four days.

Suppose that before ATMs and credit cards, this person goes to the bank once at the beginning of each four-day period and withdraws from her savings account all the money she needs for four days. Assume that she needs $4 per day.

a. How much does this person withdraw each time she goes to the bank? Compute this person's money holdings for days 1 through 4 (in the morning, before she needs any of the money she withdraws).

b. What is the amount of money this person holds, on average?

Suppose now that with the advent of ATMs, this person withdraws money once every two days.

c. Recompute your answer to part (a).

d. Recompute your answer to part (b).

Finally, with the advent of credit cards, this person pays for all her purchases using her card. She withdraws no money until the fourth day, when she withdraws the whole amount necessary to pay for her credit card purchases over the previous four days.

e. Recompute your answer to part a.

f. Recompute your answer to part b.

g. Based on your previous answers, what do you think has been the effect of ATMs and credit cards on money demand?

8. Money and the banking system

I described a monetary system that included simple banks in Section 4-3. Assume the following:

i. The public holds no currency.

ii. The ratio of reserves to deposits is 0.1.

iii. The demand for money is given by

$$M^d = \$Y(0.8 - 4i)$$

Initially, the monetary base is $100 billion, and nominal income is $5 trillion.

a. What is the demand for central bank money?

b. Find the equilibrium interest rate by setting the demand for central bank money equal to the supply of central bank money.

c. What is the overall supply of money? Is it equal to the overall demand for money at the interest rate you found in part (b)?

d. What is the effect on the interest rate if central bank money is increased to $300 billion?

e. If the overall money supply increases to $3,000 billion, what will be the effect on i? [Hint: Use what you discovered in part (c).]

9. Tools of monetary policy

Suppose that the household nominal income in an economy is £5,000 billion and the demand for money is given by

$$M^d = £Y(0.08 - 0.4i)$$

a. If the money demand is equal to £100 billion what is the interest rate?

b. What should the central bank do to interest rates if it wants to increase the money supply to £300 billion?

c. If the central bank decides to expand money supply to £300 billion, should it change the interest rate or implement open market operations?

10. Monetary policy in a liquidity trap

Suppose that money demand in problem 9 holds as long as interest rates are positive. Answer the following questions when the interest rate is equal to zero:

a. What is the demand for money when the central bank sets the interest rate at zero?

b. If the central bank cuts interest rate to −0.5%, what is the effect on the demand for money?

c. Which central banks have adopted a zero or a sub-zero interest rate policy?

d. Can you justify the reasons behind the negative interest rate policy? Do these reasons always hold in practice?

e. Bank of Japan has been using negative interest rates for a long period of time. Go to the Web site of the Bank of Japan and check the statistical database (https://www.stat-search.boj.or.jp) to trace the interest rates. Identify the periods when Bank of Japan followed a zero and sub-zero interest rate policy. Check from the same database how interest rates affect money stock.

EXPLORE FURTHER

11. Current monetary policy

The central bank of the Federal Republic of Germany is the Deutsche Bundesbank, also known as BUBA. BUBA is the most influential member of the European Central Bank and the European System of Central Bank. Go to the Web site of BUBA (www.bundesbank.de) and check the monetary policy tools of the Deutsche Bundesbank.

a. What is the mandate of the Deutsche Bundesbank and how is it defined? How does this mandate differ from that of the European Central Bank? What are the tools that BUBA uses in order to achieve price stability?

b. Find a press release explaining the monetary policy used by the Deutsche Bundesbank. What is the rationale explained by the BUBA to justify its need to adopt this policy?

c. By examining the most recent press releases of the Deutsche Bundesbank, which of the tools of monetary policy does BUBA use more frequently? Can you explain the reason why BUBA prefers to use this specific policy most often?

Finally you can visit the Fed's Web site and find various statements explaining the Fed's current policy on interest rates. These statements set the stage for the analysis in Chapter 5. Some parts of this statement should make more complete sense at the end Chapter 5.

Further Readings

- While we shall return to many aspects of the financial system throughout the book, you may want to dig deeper and read a textbook on money and banking. Here are four of them: *Money, Banking, and Financial Markets*, by Laurence Ball (Worth, 2011); *Money, Banking, and Financial Markets*, by Stephen Cecchetti and Kermit Schoenholtz (McGraw-Hill/Irwin, 2015); *Money, the Financial System and the Economy*, by R. Glenn Hubbard (Addison-Wesley, 2013); *The Economics of Money, Banking, and the Financial System*, by Frederic Mishkin, (Pearson, 2012).

- The Fed maintains a useful Web site, which contains not only data on financial markets but also information on what the Fed does, on recent testimonies by the Fed Chairperson, and so on (http://www.federalreserve.gov).

APPENDIX: The Determination of the Interest Rate When People Hold Both Currency and Checkable Deposits

In Section 4-3, we made the simplifying assumption that people only held checkable deposits and did not hold any currency. We now relax this assumption and derive the equilibrium interest rate under the assumption that people hold both checkable deposits and currency.

The easiest way to think about how the interest rate in this economy is determined is still by thinking in terms of the supply and the demand for *central bank money*:

- The demand for central bank money is equal to the demand for currency by people plus the demand for reserves by banks.
- The supply of central bank money is under the direct control of the central bank.
- The equilibrium interest rate is such that the demand and the supply for central bank money are equal.

Figure 4A-1 shows the structure of the demand and the supply of central bank money in more detail. (Ignore the equations for the time being. Just look at the boxes.) Start on the left side. The demand for money by people is for both checkable deposits and currency. Because banks have to hold reserves against checkable deposits, the demand for checkable deposits leads to a demand for reserves by banks. Consequently, the demand for central bank money is equal to the demand for reserves by banks plus the demand for currency. Go to the right side: The supply of central bank money is determined by the central bank. Look at the equal sign: The interest rate must be such that the demand and the supply of central bank money are equal.

We now go through each of the boxes in Figure 4-A1 and ask:

- What determines the demand for checkable deposits and the demand for currency?
- What determines the demand for reserves by banks?
- What determines the demand for central bank money?
- How does the condition that the demand for and the supply of central bank money be equal determine the interest rate?

The Demand for Money

When people can hold both currency and checkable deposits, the demand for money involves *two* decisions. First, people must decide how much money to hold. Second, they must decide how much of this money to hold in currency and how much to hold in checkable deposits.

It is reasonable to assume that the overall demand for money (currency plus checkable deposits) is given by the same factors as before. People will hold more money the higher the level of transactions and the lower the interest rate on bonds. So we can assume that overall money demand is given by the same equation as before (equation (4.1)):

$$M^d = \$Y \, L(i) \qquad (4.A1)$$
$$(-)$$

That brings us to the second decision. How do people decide how much to hold in currency, and how much in checkable deposits? Currency is more convenient for small transactions (it is also more convenient for illegal transactions). Checks are more convenient for large transactions. Holding money in your checking account is safer than holding cash.

Let's assume people hold a fixed proportion of their money in currency—call this proportion c—and, by implication, hold a fixed proportion $(1 - c)$ in checkable-deposits. Call the demand for currency CU^d (CU for currency, and d for demand). Call the demand for checkable deposits D^d (D for deposits, and d for demand). The two demands are given by

$$CU^d = cM^d \qquad (4.A2)$$
$$D^d = (1 - c)M^d \qquad (4.A3)$$

Equation (4.A2) shows the first component of the demand for central bank money—the demand for currency by the public. Equation (4.A3) shows the demand for checkable deposits.

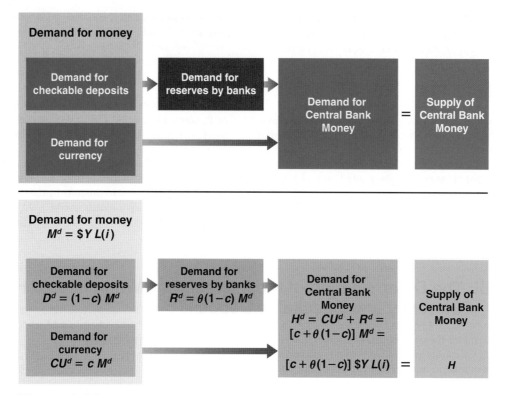

Figure 4-A1

Determinants of the Demand and the Supply of Central Bank Money

MyEconLab Animation

We now have a description of the first box, "Demand for Money," on the left side of Figure 4-A1: Equation (4.A1) shows the overall demand for money. Equations (4.A2) and (4.A3) show the demand for checkable deposits and the demand for currency, respectively.

The demand for checkable deposits leads to a demand by banks for reserves, the second component of the demand for central bank money. Let θ (the Greek lowercase letter theta) be the reserve ratio, the amount of reserves banks hold per dollar of checkable deposits. Let R denote the reserves of banks. Let D denote the dollar amount of checkable deposits. Then, by the definition of θ, the following relation holds between R and D:

$$R = \theta D \qquad (4.A4)$$

We saw previously that, in the United States today, the reserve ratio is roughly equal to 10%. Thus, θ is roughly equal to 0.1.

If people want to hold D^d in deposits, then, from equation (4.A4), banks must hold θD^d in reserves. Combining equations (4.A2) and (4.A4), the second component of the demand for central bank money—the demand for reserves by banks—is given by

$$R^d = \theta(1 - c)M^d \qquad (4.A5)$$

We now have the equation corresponding to the second box, "Demand for Reserves by Banks," on the left side of Figure 4-A1.

The Demand for Central Bank Money

Call H^d the demand for central bank money. This demand is equal to the sum of the demand for currency and the demand for reserves:

$$H^d = CU^d + R^d \qquad (4.A6)$$

Replace CU^d and R^d by their expressions from equations (4.A2) and (4.A5) to get

$$H^d = cM^d + \theta(1 - c)M^d = [c + \theta(1 - c)]M^d$$

Finally, replace the overall demand for money, M^d, by its expression from equation (4.A1) to get:

$$H^d = [c + \theta(1 - c)]\$Y L(i) \qquad (4.A7)$$

This gives us the equation corresponding to the third box, "Demand for Central Bank Money," on the left side of Figure 4-A1.

The Determination of the Interest Rate

We are now ready to characterize the equilibrium. Let H be the supply of central bank money; H is directly controlled by the central bank; just like in the previous section, the central bank can change the amount of H through open market operations. The equilibrium condition is that the supply of central bank money be equal to the demand for central bank money:

$$H = H^d \qquad (4.A8)$$

Or, using equation (4.9):

$$H = [c + \theta(1 - c)]\$YL(i) \qquad (4.A9)$$

The supply of central bank money (the left side of equation (4.A9)) is equal to the demand for central bank money (the right side of equation (4.A9)), which is equal to the term in brackets times the overall demand for money.

Look at the term in brackets more closely:

Suppose that people held only currency, so $c = 1$. Then, the term in brackets would be equal to 1, and the equation would be exactly the same as equation (4.2) in Section 4-2 (with the letter H replacing the letter M on the left side, but H and M both stand for the supply of central bank money). In this case, people would hold only currency, and banks would play no role in the supply of money. We would be back to the case we looked at in Section 4-2.

Assume instead that people did not hold currency at all, but held only checkable deposits, so $c = 0$. Then, the term in brackets would be equal to θ, and the equation would be exactly the same as equation (4.6) in Section 4-3.

Leaving aside these two extreme cases, note that the demand for central bank money is, as it was in Section 4-2, proportional to the overall demand for money, with the factor of proportionality being $[c + \theta(1 - c)]$ rather than just θ. Thus, the implications are very much the same as before. A decrease in central bank money leads to an increase in the interest rate, an increase in central bank money leads to a decrease in the interest rate.

Goods and Financial Markets; The *IS-LM* Model

I n Chapter 3, we looked at the goods market. In Chapter 4, we looked at financial markets. We now look at goods and financial markets together. By the end of this chapter you will have a framework to think about how output and the interest rate are determined in the short run.

In developing this framework, we follow a path first traced by two economists, John Hicks and Alvin Hansen in the late 1930s and the early 1940s. When the economist John Maynard Keynes published his *General Theory* in 1936, there was much agreement that his book was both fundamental and nearly impenetrable. (Try to read it, and you will agree.) There were (and still are) many debates about what Keynes "really meant." In 1937, John Hicks summarized what he saw as one of Keynes's main contributions: the joint description of goods and financial markets. His analysis was later extended by Alvin Hansen. Hicks and Hansen called their formalization the *IS-LM* model.

Macroeconomics has made substantial progress since the early 1940s. This is why the *IS-LM* model is treated in this and the next chapter rather than in Chapter 24 of this book. (If you had taken this course 40 years ago, you would be nearly done!) But to most economists, the *IS-LM* model still represents an essential building block—one that, despite its simplicity, captures much of what happens in the economy in *the short run.* This is why the *IS-LM* model is still taught and used today.

The version of the *IS-LM* presented in this book is a bit different (and, you will be happy to know, simpler) than the model developed by Hicks and Hansen. This reflects a change in the way central banks now conduct monetary policy, with a shift in focus from controlling the money stock in the past to controlling the interest rate today. More in ◀ Section 5-2.

This chapter develops the basic version of the *IS-LM* model. It has five sections:

Section 5-1 looks at equilibrium in the goods market and derives the *IS* relation.

Section 5-2 looks at equilibrium in financial markets and derives the *LM* relation.

Sections 5-3 and 5-4 put the *IS* and the *LM* relations together and use the resulting *IS-LM* model to study the effects of fiscal and monetary policy—first separately, then together.

Section 5-5 introduces dynamics and explores how the *IS-LM* model captures what happens in the economy in the short run.

5-1 The Goods Market and the *IS* Relation

Let's first summarize what we learned in Chapter 3:

- We characterized equilibrium in the goods market as the condition that production, *Y*, be equal to the demand for goods, *Z*. We called this condition the *IS* relation.
- We defined demand as the sum of consumption, investment, and government spending. We assumed that consumption was a function of disposable income (income minus taxes), and took investment spending, government spending, and taxes as given:

$$Z = C(Y - T) + \bar{I} + G$$

(In Chapter 3, we assumed, to simplify the algebra, that the relation between consumption, *C*, and disposable income, $Y - T$, was linear. Here, we shall not make this assumption but use the more general form $C = C(Y - T)$ instead.)

- The equilibrium condition was thus given by

$$Y = C(Y - T) + \bar{I} + G$$

- Using this equilibrium condition, we then looked at the factors that moved equilibrium output. We looked in particular at the effects of changes in government spending and of shifts in consumption demand.

Much more on the effects of interest rates on both consumption and investment in Chapter 15. ▶

The main simplification of this first model was that the interest rate did not affect the demand for goods. Our first task in this chapter is to abandon this simplification and introduce the interest rate in our model of equilibrium in the goods market. For the time being, we focus only on the effect of the interest rate on investment and leave a discussion of its effects on the other components of demand until later.

Investment, Sales, and the Interest Rate

In Chapter 3, investment was assumed to be constant. This was for simplicity. Investment is in fact far from constant and depends primarily on two factors:

- The level of sales. Consider a firm facing an increase in sales and needing to increase production. To do so, it may need to buy additional machines or build an additional plant. In other words, it needs to invest. A firm facing low sales will feel no such need and will spend little, if anything, on investment.

The argument still holds if the firm uses its own funds: The higher the interest rate, the ▶ more attractive it is to lend the funds rather than to use them to buy the new machine.

- The interest rate. Consider a firm deciding whether or not to buy a new machine. Suppose that to buy the new machine, the firm must borrow. The higher the interest rate, the less attractive it is to borrow and buy the machine. (For the moment, and to keep things simple, we make two simplifications. First, we assume that all firms can borrow at the same interest rate—namely, the interest rate on bonds as determined in Chapter 4. In fact, many firms borrow from banks, possibly at a different rate. We also leave aside the distinction between the nominal interest rate—the interest rate in terms of dollars—and the real interest rate—the interest rate in terms of goods. We return to both issues in Chapter 6.) At a high enough interest rate, the additional profits from using the new machine will not cover interest payments, and the new machine will not be worth buying.

To capture these two effects, we write the investment relation as follows:

$$I = I(Y, i)$$
$$(+, -) \tag{5.1}$$

Equation (5.1) states that investment I depends on production Y and the interest rate i. (We continue to assume that inventory investment is equal to zero, so sales and production are always equal. As a result, Y denotes both sales and production.) The positive sign under Y indicates that an increase in production (equivalently, an increase in sales) leads to an increase in investment. The negative sign under the interest rate i indicates that an increase in the interest rate leads to a decrease in investment.

◀ An increase in output leads to an increase in investment. An increase in the interest rate leads to a decrease in investment.

Determining Output

Taking into account the investment relation (5.1), the condition for equilibrium in the goods market becomes

$$Y = C(Y - T) + I(Y, i) + G \qquad (5.2)$$

Production (the left side of the equation) must be equal to the demand for goods (the right side). Equation (5.2) is our expanded *IS relation*. We can now look at what happens to output when the interest rate changes.

Start with Figure 5-1. Measure the demand for goods on the vertical axis. Measure output on the horizontal axis. For a given value of the interest rate i, demand is an increasing function of output, for two reasons:

■ An increase in output leads to an increase in income and thus to an increase in disposable income. The increase in disposable income leads to an increase in consumption. We studied this relation in Chapter 3.

■ An increase in output also leads to an increase in investment. This is the relation between investment and production that we have introduced in this chapter.

In short, an increase in output leads, through its effects on both consumption and investment, to an increase in the demand for goods. This relation between demand and output, for a given interest rate, is represented by the upward-sloping curve ZZ. Note two characteristics of ZZ in Figure 5-1:

■ Because we have not assumed that the consumption and investment relations in equation (5.2) are linear, ZZ is in general a curve rather than a line. Thus, we have drawn it as a curve in Figure 5-1. All the arguments that follow would apply if we

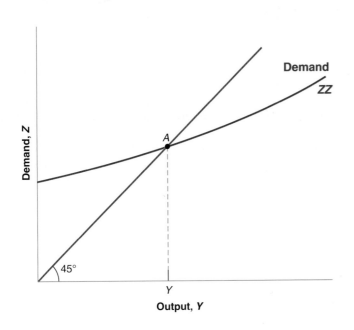

Figure 5-1

Equilibrium in the Goods Market

The demand for goods is an increasing function of output. Equilibrium requires that the demand for goods be equal to output.

MyEconLab Animation

Figure 5-2

The IS Curve

(a) An increase in the interest rate decreases the demand for goods at any level of output, leading to a decrease in the equilibrium level of output.

(b) Equilibrium in the goods market implies that an increase in the interest rate leads to a decrease in output. The *IS* curve is therefore downward sloping.

MyEconLab Animation

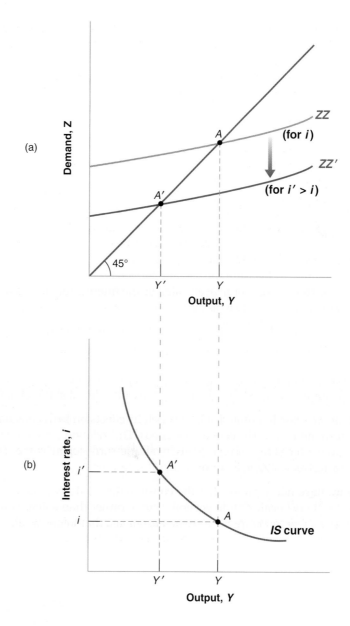

Make sure you understand ▶ why the two statements mean the same thing.

assumed that the consumption and investment relations were linear and that ZZ were a straight line.

■ We have drawn ZZ so that it is flatter than the 45-degree line. Put another way, we have assumed that an increase in output leads to a less than one-for-one increase in demand. In Chapter 3, where investment was constant, this restriction naturally followed from the assumption that consumers spend only part of their additional income on consumption. But now that we allow investment to respond to production, this restriction may no longer hold. When output increases, the sum of the increase in consumption and the increase in investment could exceed the initial increase in output. Although this is a theoretical possibility, the empirical evidence suggests that it is not the case in reality. That's why we shall assume the response of demand to output is less than one-for-one and draw ZZ flatter than the 45-degree line.

Equilibrium in the goods market is reached at the point where the demand for goods equals output; that is, at point A, the intersection of ZZ and the 45-degree line. The equilibrium level of output is given by Y.

So far, what we have done is extend, in straightforward fashion, the analysis of Chapter 3. But we are now ready to derive the IS curve.

Deriving the *IS* Curve

We have drawn the demand relation, ZZ, in Figure 5-1 for a given value of the interest rate. Let's now derive in Figure 5-2 what happens if the interest rate changes.

Suppose that, in Figure 5-2(a), the demand curve is given by ZZ, and the initial equilibrium is at point A. Suppose now that the interest rate increases from its initial value i to a new higher value i'. At any level of output, the higher interest rate leads to lower investment and lower demand. The demand curve ZZ shifts down to ZZ': At a given level of output, demand is lower. The new equilibrium is at the intersection of the lower demand curve ZZ' and the 45-degree line, at point A'. The equilibrium level of output is now equal to Y'.

In words: The increase in the interest rate decreases investment. The decrease in investment leads to a decrease in output, which further decreases consumption and investment, through the multiplier effect.

Using Figure 5-2(a), we can find the equilibrium value of output associated with *any* value of the interest rate. The resulting relation between equilibrium output and the interest rate is drawn in Figure 5-2(b).

Figure 5-2(b) plots equilibrium output Y on the horizontal axis against the interest rate on the vertical axis. Point A in Figure 5-2(b) corresponds to point A in Figure 5-2(a), and point A' in Figure 5-3(b) corresponds to A' in Figure 5-2(a). The higher interest rate is associated with a lower level of output.

This relation between the interest rate and output is represented by the downward–sloping curve in Figure 5-2(b). This curve is called the **IS curve**.

Shifts of the *IS* Curve

We have drawn the IS curve in Figure 5-2 taking as given the values of taxes, T, and government spending, G. Changes in either T or G will shift the IS curve.

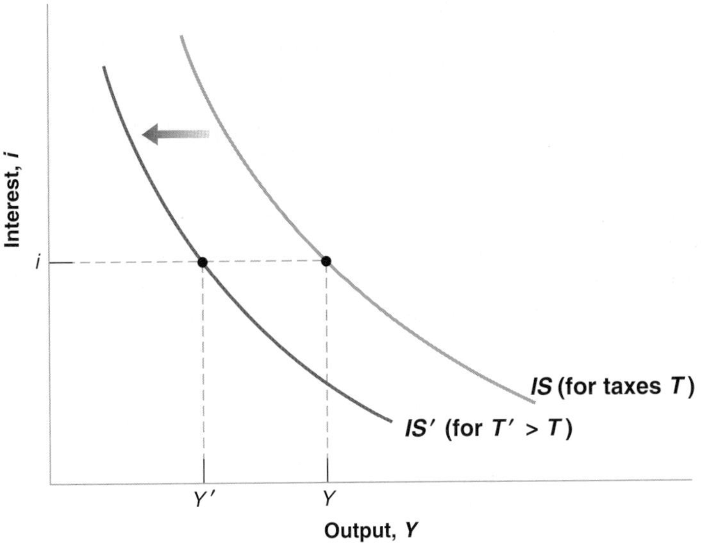

◀ Can you show graphically what the size of the multiplier is? (*Hint*: Look at the ratio of the decrease in equilibrium output to the initial decrease in investment.)

◀ Equilibrium in the goods market implies that an increase in the interest rate leads to a decrease in output. This relation is represented by the downward-sloping IS curve.

Figure 5-3

Shifts of the IS Curve

An increase in taxes shifts the IS curve to the left.

MyEconLab Animation

To see how, consider Figure 5-3. The *IS* curve gives the equilibrium level of output as a function of the interest rate. It is drawn for given values of taxes and spending. Now consider an increase in taxes, from T to T'. At a given interest rate, say i, disposable income decreases, leading to a decrease in consumption, leading in turn to a decrease in the demand for goods and a decrease in equilibrium output. The equilibrium level of output decreases from Y to Y'. Put another way, the *IS* curve shifts to the left: At a given interest rate, the equilibrium level of output is lower than it was before the increase in taxes.

For a given interest rate, an increase in taxes leads to a decrease in output. In graphic terms: An increase in taxes shifts the *IS* curve to the left. ▶

More generally, any factor that, for a given interest rate, decreases the equilibrium level of output causes the *IS* curve to shift to the left. We have looked at an increase in taxes. But the same would hold for a decrease in government spending, or a decrease in consumer confidence (which decreases consumption given disposable income). Symmetrically, any factor that, for a given interest rate, increases the equilibrium level of output—a decrease in taxes, an increase in government spending, an increase in consumer confidence—causes the *IS* curve to shift to the right.

Let's summarize:

Suppose that the government announces that the Social ▶ Security system is in trouble, and it may have to cut retirement benefits in the future. How are consumers likely to react? What is then likely to happen to demand and output today?

■ Equilibrium in the goods market implies that an increase in the interest rate leads to a decrease in output. This relation is represented by the downward-sloping *IS* curve.

■ Changes in factors that decrease the demand for goods given the interest rate shift the *IS* curve to the left. Changes in factors that increase the demand for goods given the interest rate shift the *IS* curve to the right.

5-2 Financial Markets and the *LM* Relation

Let's now turn to financial markets. We saw in Chapter 4 that the interest rate is determined by the equality of the supply of and the demand for money:

$$M = \$Y \, L(i)$$

The variable M on the left side is the nominal money stock. We shall ignore here the details of the money-supply process that we saw in Section 4-3, and simply think of the central bank as controlling M directly.

The right side gives the demand for money, which is a function of nominal income, $\$Y$, and of the nominal interest rate, i. As we saw in Section 4-1, an increase in nominal income increases the demand for money; an increase in the interest rate decreases the demand for money. Equilibrium requires that money supply (the left side of the equation) be equal to money demand (the right side of the equation).

Real Money, Real Income, and the Interest Rate

From Chapter 2:
Nominal GDP = Real GDP multiplied by the GDP deflator $\$Y = YP$.
Equivalently:
Real GDP = Nominal GDP divided by the GDP deflator $\$Y/P = Y$. ▶

The equation $M = \$Y \, L(i)$ gives a relation between money, nominal income, and the interest rate. It will be more convenient here to rewrite it as a relation among real money (that is, money in terms of goods), real income (that is, income in terms of goods), and the interest rate.

Recall that nominal income divided by the price level equals real income, Y. Dividing both sides of the equation by the price level P gives

$$\frac{M}{P} = Y \, L(i) \tag{5.3}$$

Hence, we can restate our equilibrium condition as the condition that the *real money supply*—that is, the money stock in terms of goods, not dollars—be equal to the *real money demand*, which depends on real income, Y, and the interest rate, i.

The notion of a "real" demand for money may feel a bit abstract, so an example will help. Think not of your demand for money in general but just of your demand for coins. Suppose you like to have coins in your pocket to buy two cups of coffee during the day. If a cup costs $1.20, you will want to keep about $2.40 in coins: This is your nominal demand for coins. Equivalently, you want to keep enough coins in your pocket to buy two cups of coffee. This is your demand for coins in terms of goods—here in terms of cups of coffee.

From now on, we shall refer to equation (5.3) as the *LM relation*. The advantage of writing things this way is that *real income*, Y, appears on the right side of the equation instead of *nominal income*, $Y. And real income (equivalently real output) is the variable we focus on when looking at equilibrium in the goods market. To make the reading lighter, we will refer to the left and right sides of equation (5.3) simply as "money supply" and "money demand" rather than the more accurate but heavier "real money supply" and "real money demand." Similarly, we will refer to income rather than "real income."

Deriving the *LM* Curve

In deriving the *IS* curve, we took the two policy variables as government spending, G, and taxes, T. In deriving the *LM* curve, we have to decide how we characterize monetary policy, as the choice of M, the money stock, or as the choice of i, the interest rate.

If we think of monetary policy as choosing the nominal money supply, M, and, by implication, given the price level which we shall take as fixed in the short run, choosing M/P, the real money stock, equation (5.3) tells us that real money demand, the right hand side of the equation, must be equal to the *given* real money supply, the left-hand side of the equation. Thus, if for example, real income increases, increasing money demand, the interest rate must increase so as money demand remains equal to the given money supply. In other words, for a given money supply, an increase in income automatically leads to an increase in the interest rate.

◀ Go back to Figure 4-3 in the previous chapter.

This is the traditional way of deriving the LM relation and the resulting LM curve. The assumption that the central bank chooses the money stock and then just lets the interest rate adjust is at odds however with reality today. Although, in the past, central banks thought of the money supply as the monetary policy variable, they now focus directly on the interest rate. They choose an interest rate, call it, $\bar{i}$, and adjust the money supply so as to achieve it. Thus, in the rest of the book, we shall think of the central bank as choosing the interest rate (and doing what it needs to do with the money supply to achieve this interest rate). This will make for an extremely simple **LM curve**, namely, a horizontal line in ◀ Figure 5-4, at the value of the interest rate, $\bar{i}$, chosen by the central bank.

LM curve is a bit of a misnomer, as, under our assumption, the LM relation is a simple horizontal line. But the use of the term *curve* is traditional, and I shall follow tradition.

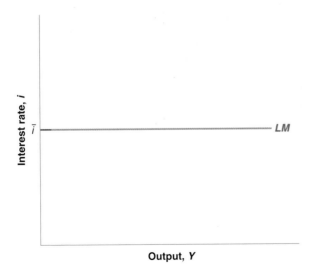

Figure 5-4

The *LM* Curve

The central bank chooses the interest rate (and adjusts the money supply so as to achieve it).

MyEconLab Animation

5-3 Putting the *IS* and the *LM* Relations Together

The *IS* relation follows from goods market equilibrium. The *LM* relation follows from financial market equilibrium. They must both hold.

$$IS\ relation: \quad Y = C(Y - T) + I(Y, i) + G$$
$$LM\ relation: \quad i = \bar{i}$$

Together they determine output. Figure 5-5 plots both the *IS* curve and the *LM* curve on one graph. Output—equivalently, production or income—is measured on the horizontal axis. The interest rate is measured on the vertical axis.

Any point on the downward-sloping *IS* curve corresponds to equilibrium in the goods market. *Any point* on the horizontal *LM* curve corresponds to equilibrium in financial markets. *Only at point A* are both equilibrium conditions satisfied. That means point *A*, with the associated level of output *Y* and interest rate $\bar{i}$ is the overall equilibrium—the point at which there is equilibrium in both the goods market and the financial markets.

The *IS* and *LM* relations that underlie Figure 5-5 contain a lot of information about consumption, investment, and equilibrium conditions. But you may ask: So what if the equilibrium is at point *A*? How does this fact translate into anything directly useful about the world? Don't despair: Figure 5-5 holds the answer to many questions in macroeconomics. Used properly, it allows us to study what happens to output when the central bank decides to decrease the interest rate, or when the government decides to increase taxes, or when consumers become more pessimistic about the future, and so on.

> In future chapters, you will see how we can extend it to think about the financial crisis, or about the role of expectations, or about the role of policy in an open economy.

Let's now see what the *IS-LM* model tells us, by looking separately at the effects of fiscal and monetary policy.

Fiscal Policy

> Decrease in G-T ⇔ fiscal contraction ⇔ fiscal consolidation

> Increase in G-T ⇔ fiscal expansion

Suppose the government decides to reduce the budget deficit and does so by increasing taxes while keeping government spending unchanged. Such a reduction in the budget deficit is often called a **fiscal contraction** or a **fiscal consolidation**. (An *increase* in the deficit, either due to an increase in government spending or to a decrease in taxes, is called a **fiscal expansion**.) What are the effects of this fiscal contraction on output, on its composition, and on the interest rate?

Figure 5-5

The IS-LM Model

Equilibrium in the goods market implies that an increase in the interest rate leads to a decrease in output. This is represented by the *IS* curve. Equilibrium in financial markets is represented by the horizontal *LM* curve. Only at point *A*, which is on both curves, are both goods and financial markets in equilibrium.

MyEconLab Animation

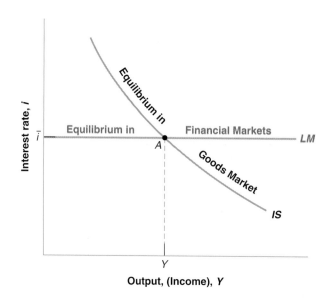

When you answer this or any question about the effects of changes in policy (or, more generally, changes in exogenous variables), always go through the following three steps:

1. Ask how the change affects equilibrium in the goods market and how it affects equilibrium in the financial markets. Put another way: Does it shift the *IS* curve and/or the *LM* curve, and, if so, how?

2. Characterize the effects of these shifts on the intersection of the *IS* and the *LM* curves. What does this do to equilibrium output and the equilibrium interest rate?

3. Describe the effects in words.

With time and experience, you will often be able to go directly to step 3. By then you will be ready to give an instant commentary on the economic events of the day. But until you get to that level of expertise, go step by step.

In this case, the three steps are easy. But going through them is good practice anyway:

◄ And when you feel really confident, put on a bow tie and go explain events on TV. (Why so many TV economists actually wear bow ties is a mystery.)

■ Start with step 1. The first question is how the increase in taxes affects equilibrium in the goods market—that is, how it affects the relation between output and the interest rate captured in the *IS* curve. We derived the answer in Figure 5-3 previously: At a given interest rate, the increase in taxes decreases output. The *IS* curve shifts to the left, from *IS* to *IS'*, in Figure 5-6.

Next, let's see if anything happens to the *LM* curve. By assumption, as we are looking at a change only in fiscal policy, the central bank does not change the interest rate. Thus, the *LM* curve, i.e. the horizontal line at $i = \bar{i}$ remains unchanged. The *LM* curve does not shift.

■ Now consider step 2, the determination of the equilibrium.

MyEconLab Video

Before the increase in taxes, the equilibrium is given by point *A*, at the intersection of the *IS* and *LM* curves. After the increase in taxes and the shift to the left of the *IS* curve from *IS* to *IS'*, the new equilibrium is given by point *A'*. Output decreases from *Y* to *Y'*. By assumption, the interest rate does not change. Thus, as the *IS* curve *shifts*, the economy *moves along* the *LM* curve, from *A* to *A'*. The reason these words are italicized is that it is important always to distinguish between the *shift of* a curve (here the shift of the *IS* curve) and the *movement along* a curve (here the movement along the *LM* curve). Many mistakes come from not distinguishing between the two.

◄ The increase in taxes shifts the *IS* curve. The *LM* curve does not shift. The economy moves along the *LM* curve.

Figure 5-6

The Effects of an Increase in Taxes

An increase in taxes shifts the *IS* curve to the left. This leads to a decrease in the equilibrium level of output.

MyEconLab Animation

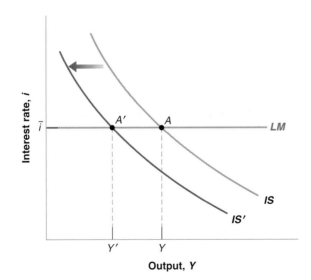

■ Step 3 is to tell the story in words:

The increase in taxes leads to lower disposable income, which causes people to decrease their consumption. This decrease in demand leads, in turn through a multiplier, to a decrease in output and income. At a given interest rate, the increase in taxes leads therefore to a decrease in output. Looking at the components of output: The decrease in income and the increase in taxes both contribute to the decrease in disposable income and, in turn, a decrease in consumption. The decrease in output leads to a decrease in investment. Thus, both consumption and investment decrease.

Note that we have just given a formal treatment of the informal discussion of the effects of an increase in public saving given in the Focus box on "The Paradox of Saving" in Chapter 3. ▶

Monetary Policy

Now turn to monetary policy. Suppose the central bank decreases the interest rate. Recall that, to do so, it increases the money supply, so such a change in monetary policy is called a **monetary expansion**. (Conversely, an increase in the interest rate, which is achieved through a decrease in the money supply, is called a **monetary contraction** or **monetary tightening**.)

Decrease in i ⟺ increase in ▶
M ⟺ monetary expansion.

Increase in i ⟺ decrease in
M ⟺ monetary contraction
⟺ monetary tightening.

■ Again, step 1 is to see whether and how the IS and the LM curves shift.

Let's look at the IS curve first. The change in the interest rate does not change the relation between output and the interest rate. It does not shift the IS curve.

The change in the interest rate however leads (trivially) to a shift in the LM curve. The LM curve shifts down, from the horizontal line at $i = \bar{i}$ to the horizontal line $i = \bar{i}'$.

■ Step 2 is to see how these shifts affect the equilibrium. The equilibrium is represented in Figure 5-7. The IS curve does not shift. The LM curve shifts down. The economy moves down along the IS curve, and the equilibrium moves from point A to point A'. Output increases from Y to Y', and the interest rate decreases from i to i'.

■ Step 3 is to say it in words: The lower interest rate leads to an increase in investment and, in turn, to an increase in demand and output. Looking at the components of output: The increase in output and the decrease in the interest rate both lead to an increase in investment. The increase in income leads to an increase in disposable income and, in turn, in consumption. So both consumption and investment increase.

Figure 5-7

The Effects of a Decrease in the Interest Rate

A monetary expansion shifts the LM curve down, and leads to higher output.

MyEconLab Animation

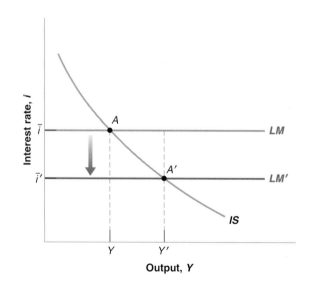

5-4 Using a Policy Mix

We have looked so far at fiscal policy and monetary policy in isolation. Our purpose was to show how each worked. In practice, the two are often used together. The combination of monetary and fiscal policies is known as the **monetary-fiscal policy mix**, or simply the *policy mix*.

MyEconLab Video

Sometimes, the right mix is to use fiscal and monetary policy in the same direction. Suppose for example that the economy is in a recession and output is too low. Then, both fiscal and monetary policies can be used to increase output. This combination is represented in Figure 5-8. The initial equilibrium is given by the intersection of IS and LM at point A, with corresponding output Y. Expansionary fiscal policy, say through a decrease in taxes, shifts the IS curve to the right, from IS to IS'. Expansionary monetary policy shifts the LM curve from LM to LM'. The new equilibrium is at A', with corresponding output Y'. Thus, both fiscal and monetary policies contribute to the increase in output. Higher income and lower taxes imply that consumption is also higher. Higher output and a lower interest rate imply that investment is also higher.

Such a combination of fiscal and monetary policy is typically used to fight recessions, and it was for example used during the 2001 recession. The story of how the German and French governments and central banks adopted unconventional policy mixes during the recessions are described in the Focus box "The German and French Recessions of 2001–2002." You might ask: Why use a policy mix when one on its own could achieve the desired increase in output? As we saw in the previous section, the increase in output could in principle be achieved just by using fiscal policy—say through a sufficiently large increase in government spending, or a sufficiently large decrease in taxes—or just by using monetary policy, through a sufficiently large decrease in the interest rate? The answer is that there are a number of reasons why policy makers may want to use a policy mix:

■ A fiscal expansion means either an increase in government spending, or an increase in taxes, or both. This means an increase in the budget deficit (or, if the budget was initially in surplus, a smaller surplus). As we shall see later, but you surely can guess why already, running a large deficit and increasing government debt may be dangerous. In this case, it is better to rely, at least in part, on monetary policy.

◀ More on this in Chapter 22.

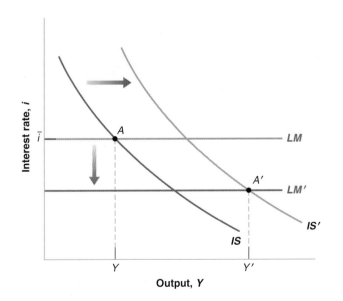

Figure 5-8

The Effects of a Combined Fiscal and Monetary Expansion

The fiscal expansion shifts the *IS* curve to the right. A monetary expansion shifts the *LM* curve down. Both lead to higher output.

MyEconLab Animation

The German and French Recessions of 2001–2002

At the turn of the millennium, several industrial nations suffered from a decline in economic activity. Germany and France are two of the developed economies of the European Union (EU) that were hit by the recession of 2001. A number of factors are blamed for this recession. First, after the prolonged economic boom and low inflation of the 1990s it was inevitable that a slump in economic activity and employment would follow suit. Second, the Asian financial crisis and the banking crises that hit many emerging market economies took their toll on international trade, hence reducing exports of industrial nations. Third, the collapse of the dot-com or information technology bubble in 2001 further impacted the economies of developed nations negatively. As a result of these combined factors, both manufacturing investments and consumption expenditures of private households declined, hence, weakening GDP growth throughout 2001 and 2002. The only sector that showed signs of stabilization in Europe was the construction sector.

The Organization of Economic Cooperation and Development (OECD), an international economic organization and a forum comprising 34 countries committed to democracy and to stimulate economic progress and world trade, concluded that the economies of Germany and France had suffered from a recession in 2001 starting in the second quarter of 2001 and ending after nine months. However, signs of slow recovery persisted till 2005.

As you observe from Figure 1, during the fourth quarter of 2001 France witnessed negative GDP growth of −0.2%. This macroeconomic contraction coincided with the lowest level of growth in consumption expenditure of 0.1% and −0.8% change in capital investment, according to OECD statistics. The ultimate result was that exports declined by 2.4%. Similarly, what triggered the recession in Q1 2002 in

Germany was a −0.7% slash of consumer spending accompanied by a sharp decline in investment demand equivalent to −1.9%. This was reflected by a massive decline in German exports for the first time in decades by −0.1%.

However, the 2001 recession in Germany and France was not that significant in comparison to previous worldwide recessions. In fact, many economists stipulate that this may not be a recession in its own right since neither Germany nor France witnessed two consecutive quarters of negative GDP growth. As it launched the euro in January 1999, the EU was in a state of cautious anticipation during the early 2000s after the recessions in both of these nations had led to a decline in the value of the euro. It was not till 2002 that the value of the euro began to increase, reaching parity with the US Dollar in mid-2002. The stronger euro hurt European exports.

While both France and Germany entered recession in late 2001, by mid-2002 both nations claimed that their recessions had ended. In reality, however, the economic slump persisted until the mid-2005. The slowdown was partly blamed on the weak macroeconomic policy responses. Let us try to evaluate these policies in both nations.

As shown in Figure 2, the response of the cut in fiscal spending was more marked in Germany in comparison to France. This could be explained by the fact that as a welfare state, France is committed to high social welfare spending. On the other hand, Germany's Social-Democrats/Greens ruling coalition at the time introduced the socially unpopular fiscal austerity and labor reform package, known as the Hartz concept. The German Chancellor Schröder implemented fiscal measures aiming to reduce the burdens and pressures on the fiscal budget exerted by the generous welfare system. The reforms that were to be phased out from 2003 throughout 2010 included gradual tax increases, phased rises in pension

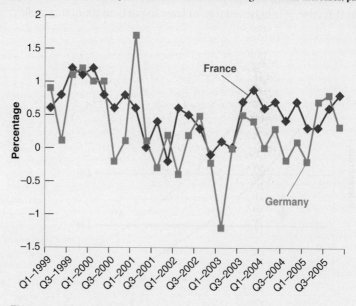

Figure 1 *France and Germany Quarterly GDP Growth Rates (1999–2005)*

Source: OECD.Stat. https://stats.oecd.org/index.aspx?queryid=350#.

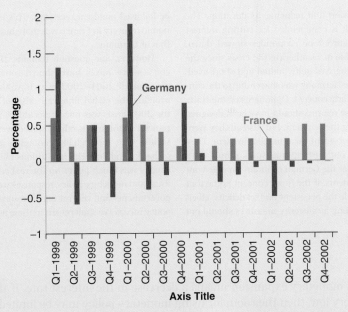

Figure 2 *Government Expenditure in France and Germany (1999–2002)*

Source: OECD.Stat, https://stats.oecd.org/index.aspx?queryid=350#.

contributions, cuts in pension benefits, reductions in the amounts allocated to medical treatment, and cutbacks in unemployment benefits.

The economic conditions of France and Germany are important because both these nations constitute more than 50% of the GDP of the EU. Sensing the potential impact of the recession on the rest of the Euro zone, the European Central Bank (ECB) adopted an expansionary monetary policy, increasing money supply and decreasing the interbank rate

aggressively. Figure 3 shows the gradual decline of the interbank rate from 2% in 1999 to 1% in 2004. The lower lending rate of the euro was most certainly very successful as it has effectively boosted consumption and investment expenditure.

From all of the above, it is obvious that the monetary and fiscal policy mix was used to reduce the impact of the recession in both France and Germany. Had economists been able to predict the imminent onset of the macroeconomic slump these policies would have been more effective in diluting

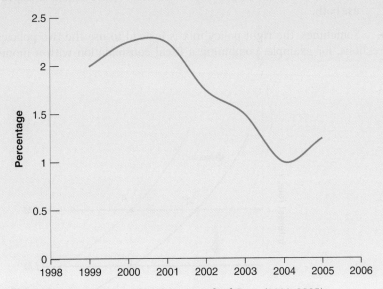

Figure 3 *European Central Bank Euro Interbank Rates (1999–2005)*

Source: European Central Bank; Key ECB Interest Rates, https://www.ecb.europa.eu/stats/monetary/rates/html/index.en.html.

the depth of the recession and reducing its duration. The European Central Bank is commended for cutting interest rates as soon as the Euro zone economies slowed down. France was more capable of weathering the crisis since the drop in its fiscal spending was quite limited and short-lived. However, the recovery in Germany was slower due to the contractive effects of the Hartz concept. Opponents of the Hartz concept argue that these reforms should have been designed to give room to boosting the economy, but instead they were geared to solving the persistent fiscal budget problem. They argue that the phased out austerity measures should have been discarded right after the German economy emerged out of the recession. Proponents of the Hartz concept argue that the reforms aim to tackle the persistent budget deficits, albeit that the timing was wrong as austerity measures should not be followed amidst a recession. This explains why the economic recovery in France was more marked in comparison to that of Germany.

However, one question remains. If the fiscal and monetary policy mixes have shown some success during the recession of 2001–2002, why have they been incapable of avoiding the global financial crisis of 2008? Quite simply, the 2008 crisis was not foreseeable since it started in the financial sector and its effects spilled over to various economic sectors with rapid global contagion impacts. As hundreds of banks and financial institutions failed, the impact of the shocks was much larger on the real economy. Conventional fiscal and monetary policy responses were ineffectual; hence, governments and central banks resorted to unconventional policy mixes. We shall return to these aspects in Chapter 6.

- A monetary expansion means a decrease in the interest rate. If the interest rate is very low, then the room for using monetary policy may be limited. In this case, fiscal policy has to do more of the job. If the interest rate is already equal to zero, the case of *the zero lower bound* we saw in the previous chapter, then fiscal policy has to do all the job.
- Fiscal and monetary policies have different effects on the composition of output. A decrease in income taxes for example will tend to increase consumption relative to investment. A decrease in the interest rate will affect investment more than consumption. Thus, depending on the initial composition of output, policy makers may want to rely more on fiscal or more on monetary policy.

MyEconLab Video
- Finally, neither fiscal policy nor monetary policy work perfectly. A decrease in taxes may fail to increase consumption. A decrease in the interest rate may fail to increase investment. Thus, in case one policy does not work as well as hoped for, it is better to use both.

Sometimes, the right policy mix is instead to use the two policies in opposite directions, for example, combining a fiscal consolidation with a monetary expansion.

Figure 5-9

The Effects of a Combined Fiscal Consolidation and a Monetary Expansion

The fiscal consolidation shifts the *IS* curve to the left. A monetary expansion shifts the *LM* curve down. Both lead to higher output.

MyEconLab Animation

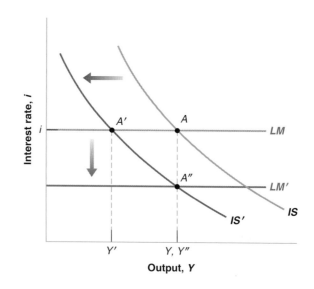

Deficit Reduction: Good or Bad for Investment?

You may have heard this argument in some form before: "Private saving goes either toward financing the budget deficit or financing investment. It does not take a genius to conclude that reducing the budget deficit leaves more saving available for investment, so investment increases."

This argument sounds convincing. But, as we have seen in the text, it must be wrong. If, for example, deficit reduction is not accompanied by a decrease in the interest rate, then we know that output decreases (see Figure 5-7), and by implication, so does investment—as it depends on output. So what is going on in this case?

To make progress, go back to Chapter 3, equation (3.10). There we learned that we can also think of the goods-market equilibrium condition as

$$\text{Investment} = \text{Private saving} \quad + \quad \text{Public saving}$$
$$I \quad = \quad S \quad + \quad (T - G)$$

In equilibrium, investment is indeed equal to private saving plus public saving. If public saving is positive, the government is said to be running a budget surplus; if public saving is negative, the government is said to be running a budget deficit. So it is true that *given private saving*, if the government reduces its deficit—either by increasing taxes or reducing government spending so that *T-G* goes up—investment must go up: Given *S*, *T-G* going up implies that *I* goes up.

The crucial part of this statement, however, is "given private saving." The point is that a fiscal contraction affects private saving as well: The contraction leads to lower output and therefore to lower income. As consumption goes down by less than income, private saving also goes down. It actually goes down by more than the reduction in the budget deficit, leading to a decrease in investment. In terms of the equation: *S* decreases by more than *T-G* increases, and so *I* decreases. (You may want to do the algebra and convince yourself that saving actually goes down by *more* than the increase in *T-G*. See problem 3 in the Questions and Problems section.)

Does this mean that deficit reduction always decreases investment? The answer is clearly *no*. We saw this in Figure 5-9. If when the deficit is reduced, the central bank also decreases the interest rate so as to keep output constant, then investment necessarily goes up. Although output is unchanged, the lower interest rate leads to higher investment.

The morale of this box is clear: Whether deficit reduction leads to an increase in investment is far from automatic. It may or it may not, depending on the response of monetary policy.

Suppose for example that the government is running a large budget deficit and would like to reduce it, but does not want to trigger a recession. In terms of Figure 5-9, the initial equilibrium is given by the intersection of the *IS* and *LM* curves at point *A*, with associated output *Y*. Output is thought to be at the right level, but the budget deficit, *T-G*, is too large.

If the government reduces the deficit, say by increasing *T* or by decreasing *G* (or both), the *IS* curve will shift to the left, from *IS* to *IS'*. The equilibrium will be at point *A'*, with level of output *Y'*. At a given interest rate, higher taxes or lower spending will decrease demand, and through the multiplier, decrease output. Thus, the reduction in the deficit will lead to a recession.

The recession can be avoided however if monetary policy is also used. If the central bank reduces the interest rate to $\bar{i}'$, the equilibrium is given by point *A'*, with corresponding output $Y'' = Y$. The combination of both policies thus allows for the reduction in the deficit, but without a recession.

What happens to consumption and investment in this case? What happens to consumption depends on how the deficit is reduced. If the reduction takes the form of a decrease in government spending rather than an increase in taxes, income is unchanged, disposable income is unchanged, and so consumption is unchanged. If the reduction takes the form of an increase in income taxes, then disposable income is lower, and so is consumption. What happens to investment is unambiguous: Unchanged output and a lower interest rate implies higher investment. The relation between deficit reduction and investment is discussed further in the Focus box "Deficit Reduction: Good or Bad for Investment?"

We have just seen a second example of a policy mix. Such a policy mix was used in the early 1990s in the United States. When Bill Clinton was elected President in 1992, one of his priorities was to reduce the budget deficit using a combination of cuts in spending and increases in taxes. Clinton was worried, however, that, by itself, such a fiscal contraction would lead to a decrease in demand and trigger another recession. The right strategy was to combine a fiscal contraction (so as to get rid of the deficit) with a monetary expansion (to make sure that demand and output remained high). This was the strategy adopted and carried out by Bill Clinton (who was in charge of fiscal policy) and Alan Greenspan (who was in charge of monetary policy). The result of this strategy—and a bit of economic luck—was a steady reduction of the budget deficit (which turned into a budget surplus at the end of the 1990s) and a steady increase in output throughout the rest of the decade.

5-5 How Does the *IS-LM* Model Fit the Facts?

We have so far ignored dynamics. For example, when looking at the effects of an increase in taxes in Figure 5-6—or the effects of a monetary expansion in Figure 5-7—we made it look as if the economy moved instantaneously from A to A', as if output went instantaneously from Y to Y'. This is clearly not realistic: The adjustment of output clearly takes time. To capture this time dimension, we need to reintroduce dynamics.

Introducing dynamics formally would be difficult. But, as we did in Chapter 3, we can describe the basic mechanisms in words. Some of the mechanisms will be familiar from Chapter 3, some are new:

■ Consumers are likely to take some time to adjust their consumption following a change in disposable income.
■ Firms are likely to take some time to adjust investment spending following a change in their sales.
■ Firms are likely to take some time to adjust investment spending following a change in the interest rate.
■ Firms are likely to take some time to adjust production following a change in their sales.

So, in response to an increase in taxes, it takes some time for consumption spending to respond to the decrease in disposable income, some more time for production to decrease in response to the decrease in consumption spending, yet more time for investment to decrease in response to lower sales, for consumption to decrease in response to the decrease in income, and so on.

In response to a decrease in the interest rate, it takes some time for investment spending to respond to the decrease in the interest rate, some more time for production to increase in response to the increase in demand, yet more time for consumption and investment to increase in response to the induced change in output, and so on.

Describing precisely the adjustment process implied by all these sources of dynamics is obviously complicated. But the basic implication is straightforward: Time is needed for output to adjust to changes in fiscal and monetary policy. How much time? This question can only be answered by looking at the data and using econometrics. Figure 5-10 shows the results of such an econometric study, which uses data from the United States from 1960 to 1990.

The study looks at the effects of a decision by the Fed to increase the federal funds rate by 1%. It traces the typical effects of such an increase on a number of macroeconomic variables.

Each panel in Figure 5-10 represents the effects of the change in the interest rate on a given variable. Each panel plots three lines. The solid line in the center of a band

We discussed the federal funds market and the federal funds rate in Chapter 4, Section 4-3. ▶

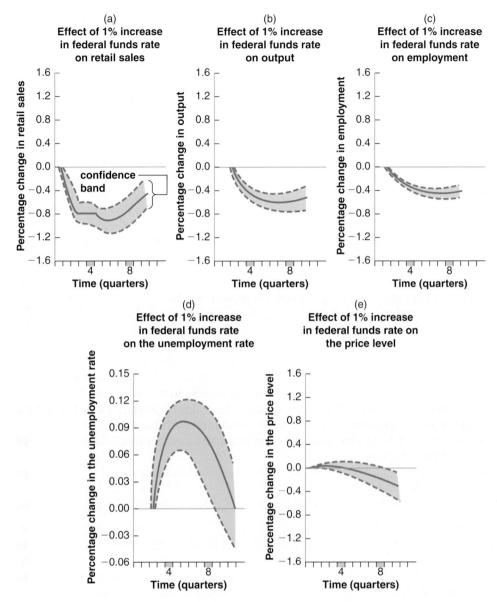

Figure 5-10

The Empirical Effects of an Increase in the Federal Funds Rate

In the short run, an increase in the federal funds rate leads to a decrease in output and to an increase in unemployment, but it has little effect on the price level.

Source: Lawrence Christiano, Martin Eichenbaum, and Charles Evans, "The Effects of Monetary Policy Shocks: Evidence From the Flow of Funds," *Review of Economics and Statistics.* 1996, 78 (February): pp. 16–34.

MyEconLab Animation

gives the best estimate of the effect of the change in the interest rate on the variable we look at in the panel. The two dashed lines and the tinted space between the dashed lines represents a **confidence band**, a band within which the true value of the effect lies with 60% probability.

■ Panel 5-10(a) shows the effects of an increase in the federal funds rate of 1% on retail sales over time. The percentage change in retail sales is plotted on the vertical axis; time, measured in quarters, is on the horizontal axis.

Focusing on the best estimate—the solid line—we see that the increase in the federal funds rate of 1% leads to a decline in retail sales. The largest decrease in retail sales, −0.9%, is achieved after five quarters.

■ Figure 5-10(b) shows how lower sales lead to lower output. In response to the decrease in sales, firms cut production, but by less than the decrease in sales. Put another way, firms accumulate inventories for some time. The adjustment of production is smoother and slower than the adjustment of sales. The largest decrease,

There is no such thing in econometrics as learning the exact value of a coefficient or ▶ the exact effect of one variable on another. Rather, what econometrics does is to provide us a best estimate—here, the thick line—and a measure of confidence we can have in the estimate—here, the confidence band.

−0.7%, is reached after eight quarters. In other words, monetary policy works, but it works with long lags. It takes nearly two years for monetary policy to have its full effect on output.

This explains why monetary ◄ policy could not prevent the 2001 recession. When at the start of 2001, the Fed starting decreasing the federal funds rate, it was already too late for these cuts to have much effect in 2001.

■ Panel 5-10(c) shows how lower output leads to lower employment: As firms cut production, they also cut employment. As with output, the decline in employment is slow and steady, reaching −0.5% after eight quarters. The decline in employment is reflected in an increase in the unemployment rate, shown in Panel 5-10(d).

■ Panel 5-10(e) looks at the behavior of the price level. Remember, one of the *assumptions* of the *IS-LM* model is that the price level is given, and so it does not change in response to changes in demand. Panel 5-10(b) shows that this assumption is not a bad approximation of reality in the short run. The price level is nearly unchanged for the first six quarters or so. Only after the first six quarters does the price level appear to decline. This gives us a strong hint as to why the *IS-LM* model becomes less reliable as we look at the medium run: In the medium run, we can no longer assume that the price level is given, and movements in the price level become important.

Figure 5-10 provides two important lessons. First, it gives us a sense of the dynamic adjustment of output and other variables to monetary policy.

Second, and more fundamentally, it shows that what we observe in the economy is consistent with the implications of the *IS-LM* model. This does not *prove* that the *IS-LM* model is the right model. It may be that what we observe in the economy is the result of a completely different mechanism, and the fact that the *IS-LM* model fits well is a coincidence. But this seems unlikely. The *IS-LM* model looks like a solid basis on which to build when looking at movements in activity in the short run. Later on, we shall extend the model to look at the role of expectations (Chapters 14 to 16) and the implications of openness in goods and financial markets (Chapters 17 to 20). But we must first understand what determines output in the medium run. This is the topic of the next four chapters.

Summary

■ The *IS-LM model* characterizes the implications of equilibrium in both the goods and the financial markets.

■ The *IS* relation and the *IS* curve show the combinations of the interest rate and the level of output that are consistent with equilibrium in the goods market. An increase in the interest rate leads to a decline in output. Consequently, the *IS* curve is downward sloping.

■ The *LM* relation and the *LM* curve show the combinations of the interest rate and the level of output consistent with equilibrium in financial markets. Under the assumption that the central bank chooses the interest rate, the *LM* curve is a horizontal line at the interest rate chosen by the central bank.

■ A fiscal expansion shifts the *IS* curve to the right, leading to an increase in output. A fiscal contraction shifts the *IS* curve to the left, leading to a decrease in output.

■ A monetary expansion shifts the *LM* curve down, leading to a decrease in the interest rate and an increase in output. A monetary contraction shifts the *LM* curve up, leading to an increase in the interest rate and a decrease in output.

■ The combination of monetary and fiscal policies is known as the monetary-fiscal policy mix, or simply the policy mix. Sometimes monetary and fiscal policy are used in the same direction. Sometimes, they are used in opposite directions. Together, fiscal contraction and monetary expansion can, for example, achieve a decrease in the budget deficit while avoiding a decrease in output.

■ The *IS-LM* model appears to describe well the behavior of the economy in the short run. In particular, the effects of monetary policy appear to be similar to those implied by the *IS-LM* model once dynamics are introduced in the model. An increase in the interest rate due to a monetary contraction leads to a steady decrease in output, with the maximum effect taking place after about eight quarters.

Key Terms

IS curve, 113
LM curve, 115
fiscal contraction, 116
fiscal consolidation, 116
fiscal expansion, 116

monetary expansion, 118
monetary contraction, 118
monetary tightening, 118
monetary-fiscal policy mix, 119
confidence band, 125

Questions and Problems

QUICK CHECK

MyEconLab Visit www.myeconlab.com to complete similar Quick Check problems and get instant feedback.

1. *Using the information in this chapter, label each of the following statements true, false, or uncertain. Explain briefly.*

 a. The main determinants of investment are the level of sales and the interest rate.

 b. If all the exogenous variables in the *IS* relation are constant, then a higher level of output can be achieved only by lowering the interest rate.

 c. The *IS* curve is downward sloping because goods market equilibrium implies that an increase in taxes leads to a lower level of output.

 d. If government spending and taxes increase by the same amount, the *IS* curve does not shift.

 e. The LM curve is horizontal at the central bank's policy choice of the interest rate.

 f. The real money supply is constant along the *LM* curve.

 g. If the nominal money supply is $400 billion and the price level rises from an index value of 100 to an index value of 103; the real money supply rises.

 h. If the nominal money supply rises from $400 billion to $420 billion and the price level rises from an index value of 100 to 102, the real money supply rises.

 i. An increase in government spending leads to a decrease in investment in the *IS-LM* model.

2. *Consider first the goods market model with constant investment that we saw in Chapter 3. Consumption is given by*

$$C = c_0 + c_1(Y - T)$$

 and I, G, *and* T *are given.*

 a. Solve for equilibrium output. What is the value of the multiplier for a change in autonomous spending?

 Now let investment depend on both sales and the interest rate:

$$I = b_0 + b_1 Y - b_2 i$$

 b. Solve for equilibrium output using the methods learned in Chapter 3. At a given interest rate, why is the effect of a change in autonomous spending bigger than what it was in part (a)? Why? (Assume $c_1 + b_1 < 1$.)

 c. Suppose the central bank chooses an interest rate of $\bar{i}$. Solve for equilibrium output at that interest rate.

 d. Draw the equilibrium of this economy using an *IS-LM* diagram.

3. *The response of the economy to fiscal policy*

 a. Use an *IS-LM* diagram, show the effects on output of a decrease in government spending. Can you tell what happens to investment? Why?

 Now consider the following IS-LM *model:*

$$C = c_0 + c_1(Y - T)$$
$$I = b_0 + b_1 Y - b_2 i$$
$$Z = C + I + G$$
$$i = \bar{i}$$

 b. Solve for equilibrium output when the interest rate is $\bar{i}$. Assume $c_1 + b_1 < 1$. (*Hint:* You may want to rework through Problem 2 if you are having trouble with this step.)

 c. Solve for equilibrium level of investment.

 d. Let's go behind the scene in the money market. Use the equilibrium in the money market $M/P = d_1 Y - d_2 i$ to solve for the equilibrium level of the real money supply when $i = \bar{i}$. How does the real money supply vary with government spending?

4. *Consider the money market to better understand the horizontal* LM *curve in this chapter.*

 The money market relation (equation 5.3) is $\dfrac{M}{P} = Y\,L(i)$

 a. What is on the left-hand side of equation (5.3)?

 b. What is on the right-hand side of equation (5.3)?

 c. Go back to Figure 4-3 in the previous chapter. How is the function $L(i)$ represented in that figure?

 d. You need to modify Figure 4-3 to represent equation (5.3) in two ways. How does the horizontal axis have to be relabeled? What is the variable that now shifts the money demand function? Draw a modified Figure 4-3 with the appropriate labels.

 e. Use your modified Figure 4-3 to show that (1) as output rises, to keep the interest rate constant, the central bank must increase the real money supply; (2) as output falls, to keep the interest rate constant, the central bank must decrease the real money supply.

5. *Consider the following numerical example of the IS-LM model:*

$$C = 100 + 0.3Y_D$$
$$I = 150 + 0.2Y - 1000i$$
$$T = 100$$
$$G = 200$$
$$\bar{i} = .01$$

$$(M/P)^s = 1200$$
$$(M/P)^d = 2Y - 4000i$$

a. Find the equation for aggregate demand (Y).
b. Derive the IS relation.
c. Derive the LM relation if the central bank sets an interest rate of 1%.
d. Solve for the equilibrium values of output, interest rate, C and I.
e. Expansionary monetary policy. Suppose that the central bank increases money supply to 1500. What is the impact of this expansionary monetary policy on the IS and LM curves? Find the new equilibrium values of output, interest rate, C and I.
f. Expansionary fiscal policy. Suppose that the government increases its spending G to 300. What is the impact of this expansionary fiscal policy on the IS and LM curves? Find the new equilibrium values of output, interest rate, C and I.

DIG DEEPER

MyEconLab Visit www.myeconlab.com to complete all Dig Deeper problems and get instant feedback.

6. Investment and the interest rate

The chapter argues that investment depends negatively on the interest rate because an increase in the cost of borrowing discourages investment. However, firms often finance their investment projects using their own funds.

If a firm is considering using its own funds (rather than borrowing) to finance investment projects, will higher interest rates discourage the firm from undertaking these projects? Explain. (*Hint*: Think of yourself as the owner of a firm that has earned profits and imagine that you are going to use the profits either to finance new investment projects or to buy bonds. Will your decision to invest in new projects in your firm be affected by the interest rate?)

7. The Fiscal-Monetary policy mix in the aftermath of the global financial crisis

The global financial crisis of 2008 left many nations with slow GDP growth rates and high levels of public debt. While most nations followed a unanimous monetary policy, some nations simply lowered income taxes while others massively expanded fiscal spending.

a. Compare and contrast the expected impact of each of these two policy mixes on output.
b. Why do you think nations followed different policy mixes in 2008?
c. Were these policy mixes successful in combatting the global meltdown?

8. What policy mix of monetary and fiscal policy is needed to meet the objectives given here?

a. Increase Y while keeping $\bar{i}$ constant. Would investment (I) change?
b. Decrease a fiscal deficit while keeping Y constant. Why must $\bar{i}$ also change?

9. The (less paradoxical) paradox of saving

A chapter problem at the end of Chapter 3 considered the effect of a drop in consumer confidence on private saving and investment, when investment depended on output but not on the interest rate. Here, we consider the same experiment in the context of the IS-LM framework, in which investment depends on the interest rate and output but the central bank moves interest rates to keep output constant.

a. Suppose households attempt to save more, so that consumer confidence falls. In an *IS-LM* diagram where the central bank moves interest rates to keep output constant, show the effect of the fall in consumer confidence on the equilibrium in the economy.
b. How will the fall in consumer confidence affect consumption, investment, and private saving? Will the attempt to save more necessarily lead to more saving? Will this attempt necessarily lead to less saving?

EXPLORE FURTHER

10. The Clinton-Greenspan policy mix

As described in this chapter, during the Clinton administration the policy mix changed toward more contractionary fiscal policy and more expansionary monetary policy. This question explores the implications of this change in the policy mix, both in theory and fact.

a. What must the Federal Reserve do to ensure that if G falls and T rises so that combination of policies has no effect on output. Show the effects of these policies in an *IS-LM* diagram. What happens to the interest rate? What happens to investment?
b. Go to the Web site of the *Economic Report of the President* (www.whitehouse.gov/administration/eop/cea/economic-report-of-the-President) Look at Table B-79 in the statistical appendix. What happened to federal receipts (tax revenues), federal outlays, and the budget deficit as a percentage of GDP over the period 1992 to 2000? (Note that federal outlays include transfer payments, which would be excluded from the variable G, as we define it in our *IS-LM* model. Ignore the difference.)
c. The Federal Reserve Board of Governors posts the recent history of the federal funds rate at http://www.federalreserve.gov/releases/h15/data.htm. You will have to choose to look at the rate on a daily, weekly, monthly, or annual interval. Look at the years between 1992 and 2000. When did monetary policy become more expansionary?
d. Go to Table B-2 of the *Economic Report of the President* and collect data on real GDP and real gross domestic investment for the period 1992 to 2000. Calculate investment as a percentage of GDP for each year. What happened to investment over the period?
e. Finally, go to Table B-31 and retrieve data on real GDP per capita (in chained 2005 dollars) for the period. Calculate the growth rate for each year. What was the average annual growth rate over the period 1992 to 2000? In Chapter 10 you will learn that the average annual growth rate of U.S. real GDP per capita was 2.6% between 1950 and 2004. How did growth between 1992 and 2000 compare to the Post World War II average?

11. *Consumption, investment, and GDP in China*

Along with other emerging market economies, China has been considered as the main driver of global growth especially during the global financial crisis. Since 1990, the Chinese economy has been able to sustain the highest levels of GDP growth, rendering it one of the largest economies in the world, second to USA. But why has the Chinese economy started to show slower GDP growth after the global financial crisis? To answer this question, you need to examine (1) the changes in the components of GDP over this period and (2) the movements of investment and consumption in China during the last two or three decades and its relative slowdown since the global financial crisis. Go to the Web site of the Bureau of Economic Analysis (www.stats.gov.cn). Find the annual National Accounts Tables and examine the Composition of Gross Domestic Product, which shows the percentage contribution of the components of GDP to the overall growth.

a. Track the change in GDP components since 1990. Which component changed most? How can these changes explain the pattern of changes in the Chinese economy? How has this pattern led to higher GDP growth from 1990 till 2010?

b. Why has this trend been reversed since the global financial crisis? To answer this question, you need to examine the levels of Chinese exports. Also, examine the exchange rate of the Yuan in order to study the policies adopted by the Chinese government to boost its exports. Explain whether these policies have been successful or unsuccessful.

c. Plot the changes in investment (gross capital formation) and final consumption expenditure since 1990. Which variable had the bigger percentage change since 1990?

d. Which region in China contributes most to investment expenditure, final consumption expenditure, and GDP growth? How can you explain these changes? Research the factors that have enabled each of these regions to achieve these levels of consumption and investment.

Further Reading

- A description of the U.S. economy, from the period of "irrational exuberance" to the 2001 recession and the role of fiscal and monetary policy, is given by Paul Krugman, in *The Great Unraveling*, W.W. Norton, 2003. New York. (Warning: Krugman did not like the Bush administration or its policies!)

Financial Markets II: The Extended *IS-LM* Model

Until now, we assumed that there were only two financial assets—money and bonds—and just one interest rate—the rate on bonds—determined by monetary policy. As you well know, the financial system is vastly more complex than that. There are many interest rates and many financial institutions. And the financial system plays a major role in the economy: In the United States, the financial system as a whole accounts for 7% of GDP, a large number.

Before the 2008 crisis, the importance of the financial system was downplayed in macroeconomics. All interest rates were often assumed to move together with the rate determined by monetary policy, so one could just focus on the rate determined by monetary policy and assume that other rates would move with it. The crisis made painfully clear that this assumption was too simplistic and that the financial system can be subject to crises with major macroeconomic implications. The purpose of this chapter is to look more closely at the role of the financial system and its macroeconomic implications, and having done so, give an account of what happened in the late 2000s.

However, be under no illusion. This chapter cannot replace a text in finance. But it will tell you enough to know why understanding the financial system is central to macroeconomics. ◄

Section 6-1 introduces the distinction between the nominal and the real interest rates.

Section 6-2 introduces the notion of risk and how this affects the interest rates charged to different borrowers.

Section 6-3 looks at the role of financial intermediaries.

Section 6-4 extends the IS-LM model to integrate what we have just learned.

Section 6-5 then uses this extended model to describe the recent financial crisis and its macroeconomic implications. ●

6-1 Nominal versus Real Interest Rates

At the time of this writing, the one-year T-bill rate is even lower and is close to zero. For our purposes, comparing 1981 with 2006 is the best way to convey this point. ▶

In January 1980, the one-year U.S. T-bill rate—the interest rate on one-year government bonds—was 10.9%. In January 2006, the one-year T-bill rate was only 4.2%. It was clearly much cheaper to borrow in 2006 than it was in 1981.

Or was it? In January 1980, expected inflation was around 9.5%. In January 2006, expected inflation was around 2.5%. This would seem relevant. The interest rate tells us how many dollars we shall have to pay in the future in exchange for having one more dollar today. But we do not consume dollars. We consume goods.

When we borrow, what we really want to know is how many goods we will have to give up in the future in exchange for the goods we get today. Likewise, when we lend, we want to know how many goods—not how many dollars—we will get in the future for the goods we give up today. The presence of inflation makes this distinction important. What is the point of receiving high interest payments in the future if inflation between now and then is so high that with what we shall receive then, we shall be unable to buy more goods?

This is where the distinction between nominal interest rates and real interest rates comes in.

Nominal interest rate is the ▶
interest rate in terms of dollars.

- Interest rates expressed in terms of dollars (or, more generally, in units of the national currency) are called **nominal interest rates**. The interest rates printed in the financial pages of newspapers are typically nominal interest rates. For example, when we say that the one-year T-bill rate is 4.2%, we mean that for every dollar the government borrows by issuing one-year T-bills, it promises to pay 1.042 dollars a year from now. More generally, if the nominal interest rate for year t is i_t, borrowing 1 dollar this year requires you to pay $1 + i_t$ dollars next year. (I shall use interchangeably "this year" for "today" and "next year" for "one year from today.")

Real interest rate is the interest rate in terms of a basket of goods.

- Interest rates expressed in terms of a basket of goods are called **real interest rates**. If we denote the real interest rate for year t by r_t, then, by definition, borrowing the equivalent of one basket of goods this year requires you to pay the equivalent of $1 + r_t$ baskets of goods next year.

What is the relation between nominal and real interest rates? How do we go from nominal interest rates—which we do observe—to real interest rates—which we typically do not observe? The intuitive answer: We must adjust the nominal interest rate to take into account expected inflation.

Let's go through the step-by-step derivation:

Assume there is only one good in the economy, bread (we shall add jam and other goods later). Denote the one-year nominal interest rate, in terms of dollars, by i_t, If you borrow one dollar this year, you will have to repay $1 + r_t$ dollars next year. But you are not interested in dollars. What you really want to know is: If you borrow enough to eat one more pound of bread this year, how much will you have to repay, in terms of pounds of bread, next year?

Figure 6-1 helps us derive the answer. The top part repeats the definition of the one-year real interest rate. The bottom part shows how we can derive the one-year real interest rate from information about the one-year nominal interest rate and the price of bread.

- Start with the downward pointing arrow in the lower left of Figure 6-1. Suppose you want to eat one more pound of bread this year. If the price of a pound of bread this year is P_t dollars, to eat one more pound of bread, you must borrow P_t dollars.

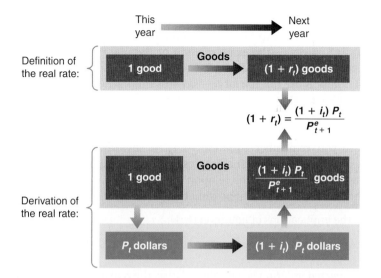

Figure 6-1

Definition and Derivation of the Real Interest Rate

MyEconLab Animation

- If i_t is the one-year nominal interest rate—the interest rate in terms of dollars—and if you borrow P_t dollars, you will have to repay $(1 + i_t)P_t$ dollars next year. This is represented by the arrow from left to right at the bottom of Figure 6-1.
- What you care about, however, is not dollars, but pounds of bread. Thus, the last step involves converting dollars back to pounds of bread next year. Let P_{t+1}^e be the price of bread you expect to pay next year. (The superscript e indicates that this is an expectation; you do not know yet what the price of bread will be next year.) How much you expect to repay next year, in terms of pounds of bread, is therefore equal to $(1 + i_t)P_t$ (the number of dollars you have to repay next year) divided by P_{t+1}^e (the price of bread in terms of dollars expected for next year), so $(1 + i_t)P_t/P_{t+1}^e$. This is represented by the arrow pointing up in the lower right of Figure 6-1.

> If you have to pay $10 next year and you expect the price of bread next year to be $2 a loaf, you expect to have to repay the equivalent of $10/2 = 5$ loaves of bread next year. This is why we divide the dollar amount $(1 + i_t)P_t$ by the expected price of bread next year, P_{t+1}^e.

Putting together what you see in both the top part and the bottom part of Figure 6-1, it follows that the one-year real interest rate, r_t is given by:

$$1 + r_t = (1 + i_t)\frac{P_t}{P_{t+1}^e} \tag{6.1}$$

This relation looks intimidating. Two simple manipulations make it look much friendlier:

- Denote expected inflation between t and $t + 1$ by π_{t+1}^e. Given that there is only one good—bread—the expected rate of inflation equals the expected change in the dollar price of bread between this year and next year, divided by the dollar price of bread this year:

$$\pi_{t+1}^e = \frac{(P_{t+1}^e - P_t)}{P_t} \tag{6.2}$$

> Add 1 to both sides in equation (6.2):
>
> $$1 + \pi_{t+1}^e = 1 + \frac{(P_{t+1}^e - P_t)}{P_t}$$
>
> Reorganize:
>
> $$1 + \pi_{t+1}^e = \frac{P_{t+1}^e}{P_t}$$
>
> Take the inverse on both sides:
>
> $$\frac{1}{1 + \pi_{t+1}^e} = \frac{P_t}{P_{t+1}^e}$$
>
> Replace in equation (6.1) and you get equation (6.3).

Using equation (6.2), rewrite P_t/P_{t+1}^e in equation (6.1) as $1/(1 + \pi_{t+1}^e)$. Replace in equation (6.1) to get

$$(1 + r_t) = \frac{1 + i_t}{1 + \pi_{t+1}^e} \tag{6.3}$$

See Proposition 6, Appendix 2 at the end of the text. Suppose $i = 10\%$ and $\pi^e = 5\%$. The exact relation in equation (6.3) gives $r_t = 4.8\%$. The approximation given by equation (6.4) gives 5%—close enough. The ▶ approximation can be quite bad, however, when i and π^e are high. If $i = 100\%$ and $\pi^e = 80\%$. the exact relation gives $r = 11\%$; but the approximation gives $r = 20\%$—a big difference.

One plus the real interest rate equals the ratio of one plus the nominal interest rate, divided by one plus the expected rate of inflation.

■ Equation (6.3) gives us the exact relation of the real interest rate to the nominal interest rate and expected inflation. However, when the nominal interest rate and expected inflation are not too large—say, less than 20% per year—a close approximation to this equation is given by a simpler relation.

$$r_t \approx i_t - \pi^e_{t+1} \tag{6.4}$$

Make sure you remember equation (6.4). It says that the real interest rate is (approximately) equal to the nominal interest rate minus expected inflation. (In the rest of the text, we shall often treat the relation in equation (6.4) as if it were an equality. Remember, however, it is only an approximation.)

Note some of the implications of equation (6.4):

■ When expected inflation equals zero, the nominal and the real interest rates are equal.

■ Because expected inflation is typically positive, the real interest rate is typically lower than the nominal interest rate.

■ For a given nominal interest rate, the higher the expected rate of inflation, the lower the real interest rate.

The case where expected inflation happens to be equal to the nominal interest rate is worth looking at more closely. Suppose the nominal interest rate and expected inflation both equal 10%, and you are the borrower. For every dollar you borrow this year, you will have to repay 1.10 dollars next year. This looks expensive. But dollars will be worth 10% less in terms of bread next year. So, if you borrow the equivalent of one pound of bread, you will have to repay the equivalent of one pound of bread next year. The real cost of borrowing—the real interest rate—is equal to zero. Now suppose you are the lender: For every dollar you lend this year, you will receive 1.10 dollars next year. This looks attractive, but dollars next year will be worth 10% less in terms of bread. If you lend the equivalent of one pound of bread this year, you will get the equivalent of one pound of bread next year: Despite the 10% nominal interest rate, the real interest rate is equal to zero.

We have assumed so far that there is only one good—bread. But what we have done generalizes easily to many goods. All we need to do is to substitute the price level—the price of a basket of goods—for the price of bread in equation (6.1) or (6.3). If we use the consumer price index (CPI) to measure the price level, the real interest rate tells us how much consumption we must give up next year to consume more today.

Nominal and Real Interest Rates in the United States since 1978

Let us return to the question at the start of this section. We can now restate it as follows: Was the real interest rate lower in 2006 than it was in 1981? More generally, what has happened to the real interest rate in the United States since the early 1980s?

The answer is shown in Figure 6-2, which plots both nominal and real interest rates since 1978. For each year, the nominal interest rate is the one-year T-bill rate at the beginning of the year. To construct the real interest rate, we need a measure of expected inflation—more precisely, the rate of inflation expected as of the beginning of each year. We use, for each year, the forecast of inflation, using the GDP deflator, for that year published at the end of the previous year by the OECD. For example, the forecast of inflation used to construct the real interest rate for 2006 is the forecast of inflation to occur over 2006 as published by the OECD in December 2005—2.5%.

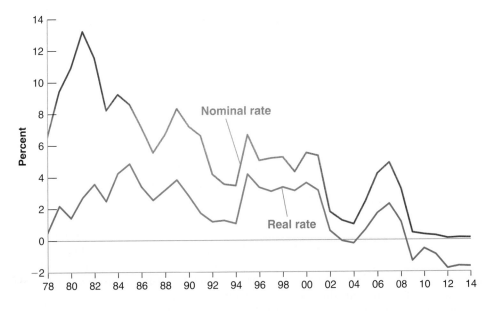

Figure 6-2

Nominal and Real One-Year T-Bill Rates in the United States since 1978

The nominal rate has declined considerably since the early 1980s, but because expected inflation has declined as well, the real rate has declined much less than the nominal rate.

Source: Nominal interest rate is the 1-year Treasury bill in December of the previous year: Series TB1YR, Federal Reserve Economic Data (FRED) http://research.stlouisfed.org/fred2/ (Series TB6MS in December 2001, 2002, 2003, and 2004.) Expected inflation is the 12-month forecast of inflation, using the GDP deflator, from the December OECD Economic Outlook from the previous year.

MyEconLab Real-time data

Note that the real interest rate $(i - \pi^e)$ is based on expected inflation. If actual inflation turns out to be different from expected inflation, the realized real interest rate $(i - \pi)$ will be different from the real interest rate. For this reason, the real interest rate is sometimes called the *ex-ante real interest rate* (*ex-ante* means "before the fact"; here, before inflation is known). The realized real interest rate is called the *ex-post real interest rate* (*ex-post* means "after the fact"; here, after inflation is known).

Figure 6-2 shows the importance of adjusting for inflation. Although the nominal interest was much lower in 2006 than it was in 1981, the real interest rate was actually higher in 2006 than it was in 1981. The real rate was about 1.7% in 2006 and about 1.4% in 1981. Put another way, despite the large decline in nominal interest rates, borrowing was actually more expensive in 2006 than it was 1981. This is due to the fact that inflation (and with it, expected inflation) has steadily declined since the early 1980s.

Nominal and Real Interest Rates: The Zero Lower Bound and Deflation

Which interest rate should enter the IS relation? Clearly, in thinking about consumption or investment decisions, what matters to people or to firms is the real interest rate, the rate in terms of goods. This has a straightforward implication for monetary policy. Although the central bank chooses the nominal rate (as we saw in Chapter 3), it cares about the real interest rate because this is the rate that affects spending decisions. To set the real interest rate it wants, it thus has to take into account expected inflation. If, for example, it wants to set the real interest rate equal to r, it must choose the nominal rate i so that, given expected inflation, π^e, the real interest rate, $r = i - \pi^e$, is at the level it desires. For example, if it wants the real interest rate to be 4%, and expected inflation is 2%, it will set the nominal interest rate, i, at 6%. So, we can think of the central bank as choosing the real interest rate.

This conclusion comes however with an important warning, one we discussed in Chapter 4 in the context of the liquidity trap. As we saw there, zero lower bound implies that the nominal interest rate cannot be negative; otherwise people would not want to hold bonds. This implies that the real interest rate cannot be lower than the negative of inflation. So, if expected inflation is 2% for example, then the lowest the real rate can be is $0\% - 2\% = -2\%$. So long as expected inflation is positive, this allows for negative real interest rates. But if expected inflation turns negative, if people anticipate deflation, then the lower bound on the real rate is positive and can turn out to be high. If, for example, expected deflation is 2%, the real rate cannot be less than 2%. This may not be low enough to increase the demand for goods by much, and the economy may remain in recession. As we shall see in Section 6-5, the zero lower bound turned out to be a serious concern during the 2008 crisis.

6-2 Risk and Risk Premia

Until now, we assumed there was only one type of bond. Bonds however differ in a number of ways. They differ in terms of maturity—i.e. the length of time over which they promise payments. For example, 1-year government bonds promise one payment a year hence. Ten-year government bonds promise instead a stream of payments over 10 years. They also differ in terms of risk. Some bonds are nearly riskless; the probability that the borrower will not repay is negligible. Some bonds instead are risky, with a non-negligible probability that the borrower will not be able or willing to repay. In this chapter, we shall ▶ focus on risk, leaving aside the issue of maturity.

We shall return to a discussion of maturity, and the relation between interest rates on bonds of different maturities once I have introduced a more formal treatment of expectations, in Chapter 14.

Neither you nor I can borrow at the federal funds rate set by the Fed. Nor can we borrow at the same rate as the U.S. government. There is a good reason for this. Whoever might be lending to us knows that there is a chance that we may not be able to repay. The same is true for firms that issue bonds. Some firms present little risk and others more. To compensate for the risk, bond holders require a **risk premium**.

What determines this risk premium?

- The first factor is the probability of default itself. The higher this probability, the higher the interest rate investors will ask for. More formally, let i be the nominal interest rate on a riskless bond, and $i + x$ be the nominal interest rate on a risky bond, which is a bond which has probability, p, of defaulting. Call x the risk premium. Then, to get the same expected return on the risky bonds as on the riskless bond, the following relation must hold:

$$(1 + i) = (1 - p)(1 + i + x) + (p)(0)$$

  The left-hand side gives the return on the riskless bond. The right-hand side gives the expected return on the risky bond. With probability $(1 - p)$, there is no default and the bond will pay $(1 + i + x)$. With probability p, there is default, and the bond will pay nothing. Reorganizing gives:

$$x = (1 + i)p/(1 - p)$$

MyEconLab Video

For small values of i and p, ▶ a good approximation to this formula is simply $x = p$.

  So for example, if the interest rate on a riskless bond is 4%, and the probability of default is 2%, then the risk premium required to give the same expected rate of return as on the riskless bond is equal to 2.1%.

- The second factor is the degree of **risk aversion** of the bond holders. Even if the expected return on the risky bond was the same as on a riskless bond, the risk itself will make them reluctant to hold the risky bond. Thus, they will ask for an even higher premium to compensate for the risk. How much more will depend on their degree of risk aversion. And, if they become more risk averse, the risk premium will go up even if the probability of default itself has not changed.

To show why this matters, Figure 6-3 plots the interest rates on three types of bonds since 2000. First, U.S. government bonds, which are considered nearly riskless. Second and third, corporate bonds rated respectively as safe (AAA) and less safe (BBB) by ratings

Figure 6-3

Yields on 10-Year U.S. Government Treasury, AAA, and BBB Corporate Bonds, since 2000

In September 2008, the financial crisis led to a sharp increase in the rates at which firms could borrow.

Source: For AAA and BBB corporate bonds, Bank of America Merrill Lynch; for 10-year U.S. treasury yield, Federal Reserve Board.

MyEconLab Real-time data

agencies. Note three things about the figure. First, the rate on even the most highly rated ◄ (AAA) corporate bonds is higher than the rate on U.S. government bonds, by a premium of about 2% on average. The U.S. government can borrow at cheaper rates than U.S. corporations. Second, the rate on lower rated (BBB) corporate bonds is higher than the rate on the most highly rated bonds by a premium often exceeding 5%. Third, note what happened during 2008 and 2009 as the financial crisis developed. Although the rate on government bonds decreased, reflecting the decision of the Fed to decrease the policy rate, the interest rate on lower-rated bonds increased sharply, reaching 10% at the height of the crisis. Put another way, despite the fact that the Fed was lowering the policy rate down to zero, the rate at which lower rated firms could borrow became much higher, making it extremely unattractive for these firms to invest. In terms of the IS-LM model, this shows why we have to relax our assumption that it is the policy rate that enters the IS relation. The rate at which many borrowers can borrow may be much higher than the policy rate.

> Different rating agencies use different rating systems. The rating scale used here is that of Standard and Poor's and ranges from AAA (nearly riskless) and BBB to C (bonds with a high probability of default).

To summarize: In the last two sections, I have introduced the concepts of real versus nominal rates and the concept of a risk premium. In Section 6-4, we shall extend the IS-LM model to take both concepts into account. Before we do, let's turn to the role of financial intermediaries.

6-3 The Role of Financial Intermediaries

Until now, we have looked at **direct finance**, that is, borrowing directly by the ultimate borrowers from the ultimate lenders. In fact, much of the borrowing and lending takes place through financial intermediaries, which are financial institutions that receive funds from some investors and then lend these funds to others. Among these institutions are banks, but also, and increasingly so, "non-banks," for example mortgage companies, money market funds, hedge funds, and such.

Financial intermediaries perform an important function. They develop expertise about specific borrowers and can tailor lending to their specific needs. In normal times, they function smoothly. They borrow and lend, charging a slightly higher interest rate than the rate at which they borrow so as to make a profit. Once in a while however, they run into trouble, and this is indeed what happened in the recent crisis. To

> Because it grew in the "shadow" ◄ of banks, the non-bank part of the financial system is called **shadow banking**. But it is now large and no longer in the shadows.

Figure 6-4

Bank Assets, Capital, and Liabilities

Bank Balance Sheet

Assets 100	Liabilities 80
	Capital 20

One wishes that the balance sheets of banks were that ▶ simple and transparent. Had it been the case, the crisis would have been much more limited.

understand why, let's first focus on banks and start, in Figure 6-4, with a much simplified bank balance sheet (the arguments apply to non-banks as well and we shall return to them later).

Consider a bank that has assets of 100, liabilities of 80, and capital of 20. You can think of the owners of the bank as having directly invested 20 of their own funds, then borrowed another 80 from other investors, and bought various assets for 100. The liabilities may be checkable deposits, interest-paying deposits, or borrowing from investors and other banks. The assets may be reserves (central bank money), loans to consumers, loans to firms, loans to other banks, mortgages, government bonds, or other forms of securities.

In drawing a bank balance sheet in Chapter 4, we ignored capital (and focused instead on the distinction between reserves and other assets). Ignoring capital was unimportant there. But it is important here. Let's see why.

The Choice of Leverage

Start with two definitions. The **capital ratio** of a bank is defined as the ratio of its capital to its assets, so, for the bank in Figure 6-4, $20/100 = 20\%$. The **leverage ratio** of a bank is defined as the ratio of assets to capital, so as the inverse of the capital ratio, in this case $100/20 = 5$. It is traditional to think in terms of leverage and to focus on the leverage ratio. I shall follow tradition. But given the simple relation between the two, the discussion could equivalently be in terms of the capital ratio.

In thinking what leverage ratio it should choose, the bank has to balance two factors. A higher leverage ratio implies a higher expected profit rate. But a higher leverage ratio also implies a higher risk of bankruptcy. Let's look at each factor in turn.

What would be the expected profit per unit of capital if the bank chose to have zero leverage? If the bank chose to have full leverage (no capital)? (The second question is a trick ▶ question.)

■ Suppose the expected rate of return on assets is 5%, and the expected rate of return on liabilities is 4%. Then, the expected profit of the bank is equal to $(100 \times 5\% - 80 \times 4\%) = 1.8$. Given that the owners of the bank have put 20 of their own funds, the expected profit per unit of capital is equal to $1.8/20 = 9\%$. Now suppose the owners of the bank decided instead to put only 10 of their own funds and borrowed 90. The capital ratio of the bank would then be equal to $10/100 = 10\%$, and its leverage would be 10. Its expected profit would be equal to $(100 \times 5\% - 90 \times 4\%) = 1.4$. Its expected profit per unit of capital would be $1.4/10 = 14\%$, so substantially higher. By increasing its leverage, and decreasing its own funds, the bank would increase its expected profit per unit of capital.

A bank is solvent if the value ▶ of its assets exceeds the value of its liabilities. It is insolvent otherwise.

■ So why shouldn't the bank choose a high leverage ratio? Because higher leverage also implies a higher risk that the value of the assets becomes less than the value of its liabilities, which, in turn, implies a higher risk of **insolvency**. For the bank in Figure 6-4, its assets can decrease in value down to 80 without the bank becoming insolvent and going bankrupt. But if it were to choose a leverage ratio of 10, any decrease in the value of the assets below 90 would lead the bank to become insolvent. The risk of bankruptcy would be much higher.

Thus, the bank must choose a leverage ratio that takes into account both factors. Too low a leverage ratio means less profit. Too high a leverage ratio means too high a risk of bankruptcy.

Leverage and Lending

Suppose a bank has chosen its preferred leverage ratio, and suppose that the value of its assets declines. For example, the assets of the bank in Figure 6-4 decrease in value from 100 to 90, say as a result of bad loans. The capital of the bank is now down to $90 - 80 = 10$. Its leverage ratio increases from 5 to 9. The bank is still solvent, but it is clearly more at risk than it was before. What will it want to do? It may want to increase capital, for example, by asking other investors to provide funds. But it is also likely to want to decrease the size of its balance sheet. For example, if it can call back some loans for an amount of 40 and thus reduce its assets down to $90 - 40 = 50$, and then use the 40 to decrease its liabilities to $80 - 40 = 40$, its capital ratio will be $10/50 = 20\%$, back to its original value. But although the capital ratio of the bank is back to its desired level, the effect is to lead to a sharp decrease in lending by the bank.

Let's go one step further. Suppose that, starting from the balance sheet in Figure 6-4, the decline in the value of the assets is large, say down from 100 to 70. Then the bank will become insolvent and go bankrupt. The borrowers that depended on the bank may have a hard time finding another lender.

MyEconLab Video

Why is this relevant to us? Because whether banks remain solvent but cut lending or become insolvent, the decrease in lending that this triggers may well have major adverse macroeconomic effects. Again, let's defer a discussion of macroeconomic implications to the next section. And before we get there, let's explore things further.

Liquidity

We looked at the case where bank assets declined in value and saw that this led banks to reduce lending. Now consider a case in which investors are unsure of the value of the assets of the bank, and believe, right or wrong, that the value of the assets may have come down. Then, leverage can have disastrous effects. Let's see why.

■ If investors have doubts about the value of the bank assets, the safe thing for them to do is to take their funds out of the bank. But this creates serious problems for the bank, which needs to find the funds to repay the investors. The loans it has made cannot easily be called back. Typically, the borrowers no longer have the funds at the ready; they have used them to pay bills, buy a car, purchase a machine, and such. Selling the loans to another bank is likely to be difficult as well. Assessing the value of the loans is difficult for the other banks, which do not have the specific knowledge about the borrowers the original bank has. In general, the harder it is for others to assess the value of the assets of the bank, the more likely the bank is to either be simply unable to sell them or to have to do it at **fire sale prices**, which are prices far below the true value of the loans. Such sales however only make matters worse for the bank. As the value of the assets decreases, the bank may well become insolvent and go bankrupt. In turn, as investors realize this may happen, this gives them even more reason to want to get their funds out, forcing more fire sales, and making the problem worse. Note that this can happen even if the initial doubts of investors were totally unfounded, even if the value of the bank assets had not decreased in the first place. The decision by investors to ask for their funds, and the fire sales this triggers, can make the bank insolvent even if it was fully solvent to start.

■ Note also that the problem is worse if investors can ask for their funds at short notice. This is clearly the case for checkable deposits at banks. Checkable deposits are also called **demand deposits**, precisely because people can ask for their funds on demand. The fact that banks' assets are largely composed of loans and their liabilities are largely composed of demand deposits makes them particularly

Bank Runs

Take a healthy bank, that is, a bank with a portfolio of good loans. Suppose rumors start that the bank is not doing well and some loans will not be repaid. Believing that the bank may fail, people with deposits at the bank will want to close their accounts and withdraw cash. If enough people do so, the bank will run out of funds. Given that the loans cannot easily be called back, the bank will not be able to satisfy the demand for cash, and it will have to close.

Conclusion: Fear that a bank will close can actually cause it to close—even if all its loans were good in the first place. The financial history of the United States up to the 1930s is full of such bank runs. One bank fails for the right reason (because it has made bad loans). This causes depositors at other banks to panic and withdraw money from their banks, forcing them to close. You have probably seen *It's a Wonderful Life*, a classic movie with James Stewart that runs on TV every year around Christmas. After another bank in Stewart's town fails, depositors at the savings and loan he manages get scared and want to withdraw their money, too. Stewart successfully persuades them this is not a good idea. *It's a Wonderful Life* has a happy ending. But in real life, most bank runs didn't end well. (For another famous movie bank run, and how it can start, watch *Mary Poppins*.)

What can be done to avoid bank runs?

One potential solution is called **narrow banking**. Narrow banking would restrict banks to holding liquid and safe government bonds, like T-bills. Loans would have to be made by financial intermediaries other than banks. This would likely eliminate bank runs. Some recent changes in U.S. regulation have gone in that direction, restricting banks that rely on deposits from engaging in some financial operations, but they stop far short of imposing narrow banking. One worry with narrow banking is that, although it might indeed eliminate runs on banks, the problem might migrate to shadow banking and create runs there.

In practice, the problem has been tackled in two ways. First, by trying to limit bank runs in the first place; second, if bank runs happen nevertheless, by having the central bank provide funds to banks so they do not have to engage in fire sales.

To limit bank runs, governments in most advanced countries have put in place a system of deposit insurance. The United States, for example, introduced **federal deposit insurance** in 1934. The U.S. government now insures each checkable deposit account up to a ceiling, which, since 2008, is $250,000. As a result, there is no reason for depositors to run and withdraw their money.

Deposit insurance leads, however, to problems of its own. Depositors, who do not have to worry about their deposits, no longer look at the activities of the banks in which they have their accounts. Banks may then misbehave, by making loans they wouldn't have made in the absence of deposit insurance. They may take too much risk, take too much leverage.

And as the crisis unfortunately showed, deposit insurance is no longer enough. First, banks rely on other sources of funds than deposits, often borrowing overnight from other financial institutions and investors. These other funds are not insured, and during the crisis, there was in effect a run on many banks, and this time, not from the traditional depositors but from wholesale funders. Second, financial institutions other than banks can be subject to the same problem, with investors wanting their funds back quickly and with assets difficult to dispose of or sell quickly.

So, to the extent that runs cannot be fully prevented, central banks have put in place programs to provide funds to banks in case they face a run. In such circumstances, the central bank will accept to lend to a bank against the value of the assets of the bank. This way, the bank does not have to sell the assets and fire sales can be avoided. Access to such provision was traditionally reserved for banks. But again, the recent crisis has shown that other financial institutions may be subject to runs and may also need access.

Just like deposit insurance, such **liquidity provision** (as it is called) by the central bank is not a perfect solution. In practice, central banks may face a difficult choice. Assessing which financial institutions beyond banks can have access to such liquidity provision is delicate. Assessing the value of the assets, and thus deciding how much can be lent to a financial institution, can also be difficult. The central bank would not want to provide funds to an institution that is actually insolvent; but, in the middle of a financial crisis, the difference between insolvency and illiquidity may be difficult to establish.

To watch the bank run in *It's a Wonderful Life*, go to *https://www.youtube.com/watch?v=lbwjS9iJ2Sw*

To watch the bank run in *Mary Poppins*, go to *https://www.youtube.com/watch?v=C6DGs3qjRwQ*

---

exposed to the risk of runs, and the history of the financial system is full of examples of **bank runs**, during which worries about the assets of the banks led to runs on banks, forcing them to close. Bank runs were a major feature of the Great Depression, and as discussed in the Focus box "Bank Runs," central banks have taken measures to limit them. As we shall see later in this chapter however, this has not fully taken care of the problem, and a modern form of runs—this time not on banks but on other financial intermediaries—again played a major role in the recent financial crisis.

We can summarize what we have just learned in terms of the **liquidity** of assets and liabilities. The lower the liquidity of the assets (i.e., the more difficult they are to sell), the higher the risk of fire sales, and the risk that the bank becomes insolvent and goes bankrupt. The higher the liquidity of the liabilities (i.e., the easier it is for investors to get their funds at short notice), the higher the risk of fire sales as well, and the risk that the bank becomes insolvent and goes bankrupt. Again, the reason this is relevant for us is that such bankruptcies, if they occur, may well have major macroeconomic consequences. This is the topic of the next section.

6-4 Extending the IS-LM

The IS-LM model we introduced in Chapter 5 had only one interest rate. This interest rate was determined by the central bank, and it entered spending decisions. It appeared both in the LM relation and the IS relation. The first three sections of this chapter should have convinced you that, although this was a useful first step, reality is substantially more complex, and we must extend our initial model.

First, we must distinguish between the nominal interest rate and the real interest rate. Second, we must distinguish the policy rate set by the central bank and the interest rates faced by borrowers. As we saw, these interest rates depend both on the risk associated with borrowers and on the state of health of financial intermediaries. The higher the risks, or the higher the leverage ratio of intermediaries, the higher the interest rate borrowers have to pay. We capture those two aspects by rewriting the IS-LM in the following way:

$$\text{IS relation: } Y = C(Y - T) + I(Y, i - \pi^e + x) + G$$
$$\text{LM relation: } i = \bar{i}$$

The LM relation remains the same. The central bank still controls the nominal interest rate. But there are two changes to the IS relation, the presence of expected inflation, π^e, and a new term that we shall call the *risk premium* and denote by x.

◀ The way in which the central bank controls the nominal interest rate is by adjusting the money supply. If you need a refresher, go back to Chapter 4.

- The expected inflation term reflects the fact that spending decisions depend, all other things equal, on the real interest rate, $r = i - \pi^e$ rather than on the nominal rate.
- The risk premium, x, captures, in a simplistic way, the factors we discussed previously. It may be high because lenders perceive a higher risk that borrowers will not repay or because they are more risk averse. Or it may be high because financial intermediaries are reducing lending, out either of solvency or liquidity worries.

The two equations make clear that the interest rate entering the LM equation, i is no longer the same as the interest rate entering the IS relation, $r + x$. Let's call the rate entering the LM equation the (nominal) **policy rate** (because it is determined by monetary policy), and the rate entering the IS equation the (real) **borrowing rate** (because it is the rate at which consumers and firms can borrow).

◀ Two important distinctions: Real versus nominal interest rate, and policy rate versus borrowing rate.

One simplification: As we discussed in Section 6-2, although the central bank formally chooses the nominal interest rate, it can choose it in such a way as to achieve the real interest rate it wants (this ignores the issue of the zero lower bound to which we shall come back). Thus, we can think of the central banks as choosing the real policy rate directly and rewrite the two equations as:

$$\text{IS relation: } Y = C(Y - T) + I(Y, r + x) + G \qquad (6.5)$$
$$\text{LM relation: } r = \bar{r} \qquad (6.6)$$

The central bank chooses the real policy rate, r. But the real interest rate relevant for spending decisions is the borrowing rate, $r + x$, which depends not only on the policy rate, but also on the risk premium.

Figure 6-5

Financial Shocks and Output

An increase in *x* leads to a shift of the IS curve to the left and a decrease in equilibrium output.

MyEconLab Animation

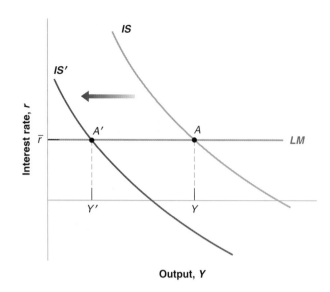

The two equations are represented in Figure 6-5. The policy rate is measured on the vertical axis and output on the horizontal axis. The IS curve is drawn for given values of G, T, and x. All other things equal, an increase in the real policy rate decreases spending and in turn output: The IS curve is downward sloping. The LM is just a horizontal line at the policy rate, the real interest rate implicitly chosen by the central bank. Equilibrium is given by point A, with associated level of output Y.

Financial Shocks and Policies

MyEconLab Video

For simplicity, we have looked at an exogenous increase in x. But x itself may well depend on output. A decrease in output, say a recession, increases the probability that some borrowers will be unable to repay; workers who become ► unemployed may not be able to repay the loans; firms that lose sales may go bankrupt. The increase in risk leads to a further increase in the risk premium, and thus to a further increase in the borrowing rate, which can further decrease output.

Suppose that, for some reason, *x*, increases. There are many potential scenarios here. This may be for example because investors have become more risk averse and require a higher risk premium, or it may be because one financial institution has gone bankrupt and investors have become worried about the health of other banks, starting a run, forcing these other banks to reduce lending. In terms of Figure 6-5, the IS curve shifts to the left. At the same policy rate *r*, the borrowing rate, *r* + *x*, increases, leading to a decrease in demand and a decrease in output. The new equilibrium is at point A'. Problems in the financial system lead to a recession. Put another way, a financial crisis becomes a macroeconomic crisis.

What can policy do? Just as in Chapter 5, fiscal policy, be it an increase in G, or a decrease in T can shift the IS curve to the right and increase output. But a large increase in spending or a cut in taxes may imply a large increase in the budget deficit, and the government may be reluctant to do so.

Given that the cause of the low output is that the interest rate facing borrowers is too high, monetary policy appears to be a better tool. Indeed, a sufficient decrease in the policy rate, as drawn in Figure 6-6, can in principle be enough to take the economy to point A″ and return output to its initial level. In effect, in the face of the increase in *x*, the central bank must decrease *r* so as to keep *r* + *x*, the rate relevant to spending decisions, unchanged.

Note that the policy rate that is needed to increase demand sufficiently and return output to its previous level may well be negative. This is indeed how I have drawn the equilibrium in Figure 6-6. Suppose that, for example, in the initial equilibrium, *r* was equal to 2% and *x* was equal to 1%. Suppose that *x* increases by 4%, from 1 to 5%. To maintain the same value of *r* + *x*, the central bank must decrease the policy rate from 2% to 2% − 4% = −2%. This raises an issue, which we have already discussed

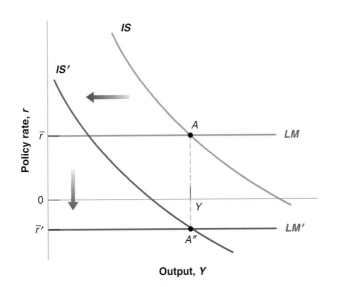

Figure 6-6

Financial Shocks, Monetary Policy, and Output

If sufficiently large, a decrease in the policy rate can in principle offset the increase in the risk premium. The zero lower bound may however put a limit on the decrease in the real policy rate.

MyEconLab Animation

in Chapter 4, namely the constraint arising from the zero lower bound on the nominal interest rate.

Given the zero lower bound on the nominal rate, the lowest real rate the central bank can achieve is given by $r = i - \pi^e = 0 - \pi^e = -\pi^e$. In words, the lowest real policy rate the central bank can achieve is the negative of inflation. If inflation is high enough, say for example 5%, then a zero nominal rate implies a real rate of -5%, which is likely to be low enough to offset the increase in x. But, if inflation is low or even negative, then the lowest real rate the central bank can achieve may not be enough to offset the increase in x. It may not be enough to return the economy to its initial equilibrium. As we shall see, two characteristics of the recent crisis were indeed a large increase in x and low actual and expected inflation, limiting how much central banks could use monetary policy to offset the increase in x.

We now have the elements we need to understand what triggered the financial crisis in 2008, and how it morphed into a major macroeconomic crisis. This is the topic of the next and last section of this chapter.

6-5 From a Housing Problem to a Financial Crisis

When housing prices started declining in the United States in 2006, most economists forecast that this would lead to a decrease in demand and a slowdown in growth. Few economists anticipated that it would lead to a major macroeconomic crisis. What most had not anticipated was the effect of the decline of housing prices on the financial system, and in turn, the effect on the economy. This is the focus of this section.

Housing Prices and Subprime Mortgages

Figure 6-7 shows the evolution of an index of U.S. housing prices since 2000. The index is known as the Case-Shiller index, named for the two economists who constructed it. The index is normalized to equal 100 in January 2000. You can see the large increase in prices in the early 2000s, followed by a large decrease later. From a value of 100 in 2000, the index increased to 226 in mid-2006. It then started to decline. By the end of

Look up *Case-Shiller* on the Internet if you want to find the index and see its recent evolution. You can also see what has happened to prices in the city in which you live.

Figure 6-7

U.S. Housing Prices since 2000

The increase in housing prices from 2000 to 2006 was followed by a sharp decline thereafter.

Source: Case-Shiller Home Price Indices, 10-city home price index, http://www.standardandpoors.com/indices/main/en/us

MyEconLab Real-time data

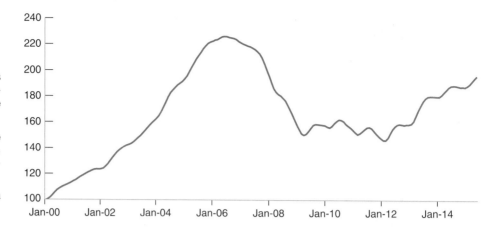

2008, at the start of the financial crisis, the index was down to 162. It reached a low of 146 in early 2012 and started recovering thereafter. At the time of this writing, it stands at 195, still below its 2006 peak.

Was the sharp price increase from 2000 to 2006 justified? In retrospect, and given the ensuing collapse, surely not. But at the time, when prices were increasing, economists were not so sure. Some increase in prices was clearly justified.

■ The 2000s were a period of unusually low interest rates. Mortgage rates were low, increasing the demand for housing and thus pushing up the price.

Even if people did not finance the purchase of a house by ▶ taking a mortgage, low interest rates would lead to an increase in the price of houses. More on this when we discuss present discounted values in Chapter 14.

■ Other factors were also at work. **Mortgage lenders** became increasingly willing to make loans to more risky borrowers. These mortgages, known as **subprime mortgages**, or **subprimes** for short, had existed since the mid-1990s but became more prevalent in the 2000s. By 2006, about 20% of all U.S. mortgages were subprimes. Was it necessarily bad? Again, at the time, this was seen by most economists as a positive development. It allowed more poor people to buy homes, and under the assumption that housing prices would continue to increase, so the value of the mortgage would decrease over time relative to the price of the house, it looked safe both for lenders and for borrowers. Judging from the past, the assumption that housing prices would not decrease also seemed reasonable. As you can see from Figure 6-7, housing prices had not decreased even during the 2000–2001 recession.

Some economists were worried even as prices were going up. Robert Shiller, one of the two economists behind the Case-Shiller index, was among them, warning that the ▶ price increase was a bubble that would most likely crash. Robert Shiller received the Nobel Prize in 2013 for his work on asset prices.

In retrospect, again, these developments were much less benign than most economists thought. First, housing prices *could* go down, as became evident from 2006 on. When this happened, many borrowers found themselves in a situation in which the mortgage they owed now exceeded the value of their house (when the value of the mortgage exceeds the value of the house, the mortgage is said to be **underwater**). Second, it became clear that, in many cases, the mortgages were in fact much riskier than either the lender pretended or the borrower understood. In many cases, borrowers had taken mortgages with low initial interest rates, known as "teaser rates," and thus low initial interest payments, probably not fully realizing that payments would increase sharply over time. Even if house prices had not declined, many of these borrowers would have been unable to meet their mortgage payments.

Some of these loans became known as NINJA loans (for no income, no job, no assets). ▶

Thus, as house prices turned around and many borrowers defaulted, lenders found themselves faced with large losses. In mid-2008, losses on mortgages were estimated to be around $300 billion. This is a large number, but, relative to the size of the U.S. economy, it is not a large one. Three hundred billion dollars is only about 2% of U.S. GDP. One might have thought that the U.S. financial system could absorb the shock and that the adverse effect on output would be limited. This was not to be. Although the trigger of the crisis was indeed the decline in housing prices, its effects were enormously amplified. Even those economists who had anticipated the housing price decline did not realize how strong the amplification mechanisms would be. To understand those, we must return to the role of financial intermediaries.

The Role of Financial Intermediaries

In the previous section, we saw that high leverage, illiquidity of assets, and liquidity of liabilities all increased the risk of trouble in the financial system. All three elements were present in 2008, creating a perfect storm.

Leverage

Banks were highly levered. Why was it so? For a number of reasons: First, banks probably underestimated the risk they were taking: Times were good, and in good times, banks, just like people, tend to underestimate the risk of bad times. Second, the compensation and bonus system gave incentives to managers to go for high expected returns without fully taking the risk of bankruptcy into account. Third, although financial regulation required banks to keep their capital ratio above some minimum, banks found new ways of avoiding the regulation, by creating new financial structures called **structured investment vehicles (SIVs)**.

On the liability side, SIVs borrowed from investors, typically in the form of short-term debt. On the asset side, SIVs held various forms of securities. To reassure the investors that they would get repaid, SIVs typically had a guarantee from the bank that had created them that, if needed, the bank would provide funds to the SIV. Although the first SIV was set up by Citigroup in 1988, SIVs rapidly grew in size in the 2000s. You may ask why banks did not simply do all these things on their own balance sheet rather than create a separate vehicle. The main reason was to be able to increase leverage. If the banks had done these operations themselves, the operations would have appeared on their balance sheet and been subject to regulatory capital requirements, forcing them to hold enough capital to limit the risk of bankruptcy. Doing these operations through an SIV did not require banks to put capital down. For that reason, through setting up an SIV, banks could increase leverage and increase expected profits, and they did.

When housing prices started declining and many mortgages turned out to be bad, the securities held by SIVs dropped in value. Questions arose about the solvency of the SIVs, and given the guarantee by banks to provide funds to the SIVs if needed, questions arose about the solvency of the banks themselves. Then, two other factors, securitization, and wholesale funding, came into play.

Securitization

An important financial development of the 1990s and the 2000s was the growth of **securitization**. Traditionally, the financial intermediaries that made loans or issued mortgages kept them on their own balance sheet. This had obvious drawbacks. A local bank, with local loans and mortgages on its books, was much exposed to the local economic situation. When, for example, oil prices had come down sharply in the mid-1980s and Texas was in recession, many local banks went bankrupt. Had they had a more diversified portfolio of mortgages, say mortgages from many parts of the country, these banks might have avoided bankruptcy.

This is the idea behind securitization. Securitization is the creation of securities based on a bundle of assets (e.g., a bundle of loans, or a bundle of mortgages). For instance, a **mortgage-based security (MBS)** for short, is a title to the returns from a bundle of mortgages, with the number of underlying mortgages often in the tens of thousands. The advantage is that many investors, who would not want to hold individual mortgages, will be willing to buy and hold these securities. This increase in the supply of funds from investors is, in turn, likely to decrease the cost of borrowing.

Securitization can go further. For example, instead of issuing identical claims to the returns on the underlying bundle of assets, one can issue different types of securities. For example, one can issue **senior securities**, which have first claims on the returns from the bundle, and **junior securities**, which come after and pay only if anything remains after the senior securities have been paid. Senior securities will appeal to investors who want little risk; junior securities will appeal to investors who are willing to take more risk. Such securities, known as **collateralized debt obligations (CDOs)**, were first issued in the late 1980s but, again, grew in importance in the 1990s and 2000s. Securitization went even further, with the creation of CDOs using previously created CDOs, or CDO^2.

One of the main obstacles to understanding the financial system is the alphabet soup of acronyms: SIVs, MBS, CDOs, etc.

Securitization would seem like a good idea, a way of diversifying risk and getting a larger group of investors involved in lending to households or firms. And, indeed, it is. But it also came with two large costs, which became clear during the crisis. The first was that if the bank sold the mortgage it had given as part of a securitization bundle and thus did not keep it on its balance sheet, it had fewer incentives to make sure that the borrower could repay. The second was the risk that **rating agencies**, those firms that assess the risk of various securities, had largely missed. When underlying mortgages went bad, assessing the value of the underlying bundles in the MBSs, or, even more so, of the underlying MBSs in the CDOs, was extremely hard to do. These assets came to be known as **toxic assets**. It led investors to assume the worst and be reluctant either to hold them or to continue lending to those institutions such as SIVs that did hold them. In terms of the discussion in the previous section, many of the assets held by banks, SIVs, and other financial intermediaries, were illiquid. They were extremely hard to assess and thus hard to sell, except at fire sale prices.

Wholesale Funding

Yet another development of the 1990s and 2000s was the development of other sources of finance than checkable deposits by banks. Increasingly, they relied on borrowing from other banks or other investors, in the form of short-term debt, to finance the purchase of their assets, a process known as **wholesale funding**. SIVs, the financial entities set up by banks, were entirely funded through such wholesale funding.

Wholesale funding again would seem like a good idea, giving banks more flexibility in the amount of funds they could use to make loans or buy assets. But it had a cost, and that cost again became clear during the crisis. Although holders of checkable deposits were protected by deposit insurance and did not have to worry about the value of their deposits, this was not the case for the other investors. Thus, when those investors worried about the value of the assets held by the banks or the SIVs, they asked for their funds back. In terms of the discussion in the previous section, banks and SIVs had liquid liabilities, much more liquid than their assets.

MyEconLab Video

The result of this combination of high leverage, illiquid assets, and liquid liabilities was a major financial crisis. As housing prices declined and some mortgages went bad, high leverage implied a sharp decline in the capital of banks and SIVs. This in turn forced them to sell some of their assets. Because these assets were often hard to value, they had to sell them at fire sale prices. This, in turn, decreased the value of similar assets remaining on their balance sheet, or on the balance sheet of other financial intermediaries, leading to a further decline in capital ratios and forcing further sales of assets and further declines in prices. The complexity of the securities held by banks and SIVs made it difficult to assess their solvency. Investors became reluctant to continue to lend to them, wholesale funding came to a stop, which forced further asset sales and

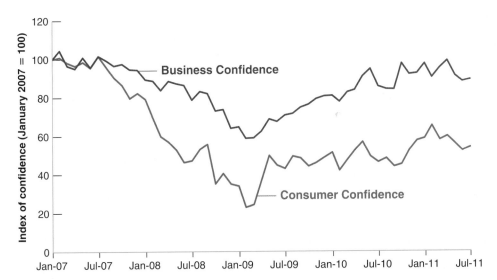

Figure 6-8

U.S. Consumer and Business Confidence, 2007–2011

The financial crisis led to a sharp drop in confidence, which bottomed in early 2009.

Source: Bloomberg L.P.

price declines. Even the banks became reluctant to lend to each other. On September 15, 2008, Lehman Brothers, a major bank with more than $600 billion in assets, declared bankruptcy, leading financial participants to conclude that many, if not most, other banks and financial institutions were indeed at risk. By mid-September 2008, the financial system had become paralyzed. Banks basically stopped lending to each other or to anyone else. Quickly, what had been largely a financial crisis turned into a macroeconomic crisis.

Macroeconomic Implications

The immediate effects of the financial crisis on the macroeconomy were twofold. First, a large increase in the interest rates at which people and firms could borrow, if they could borrow at all; second, a dramatic decrease in confidence.

We saw the effect on various interest rates in Figure 6-3. In late 2008, interest rates on highly rated (AAA) bonds increased to more than 8%, interest rates on lower rated (BBB) bonds increased to 10%. Suddenly, borrowing became extremely expensive for most firms. And for the many firms too small to issue bonds and thus depending on bank credit, it became nearly impossible to borrow at all.

The events of September 2008 also triggered wide anxiety among consumers and firms. Thoughts of another Great Depression and, more generally, confusion and fear about what was happening in the financial system, led to a large drop in confidence. The evolution of consumer confidence and business confidence indexes for the United States are shown in Figure 6-8. Both indexes are normalized to equal 100 in January 2007. Note how consumer confidence, which had started declining in mid-2007, took a sharp turn in the fall of 2008 and reached a low of 22 in early 2009, a level far below previous historical lows. The result of lower confidence and lower housing and stock prices was a sharp decrease in consumption.

See the Focus box "The Lehman Bankruptcy, Fears of Another Great Depression, and Shifts in the Consumption Function" in Chapter 3.

Policy Responses

The high cost of borrowing, lower stock prices, and lower confidence all combined to decrease the demand for goods. In terms of the IS-LM model, there was a sharp adverse shift of the IS curve, just as we drew in Figure 6-5. In the face of this large decrease in demand, policy makers did not remain passive.

Financial Policies

The most urgent measures were aimed at strengthening the financial system:

- To prevent a run by depositors, federal deposit insurance was increased from $100,000 to $250,000 per account. Recall, however, that much of banks' funding came not from deposits but from the issuance of short-term debt to investors. To allow the banks to continue to fund themselves through wholesale funding, the federal government offered a program guaranteeing new debt issues by banks.

- The Federal Reserve provided widespread liquidity to the financial system. We have seen that, if investors wanted to take their funds back, the banks had to sell some of their assets, often at fire sale prices. In many cases, this would have meant bankruptcy. To avoid this, the Fed put in place a number of **liquidity facilities** to make it easier to borrow from the Fed. It allowed not only banks, but also other financial intermediaries, to borrow from the Fed. Finally, it increased the set of assets that financial institutions could use as **collateral** when borrowing from the Fed (collateral refers to the asset a borrower pledges when borrowing from a lender. If the borrower defaults, the asset then goes to the lender). Together, these facilities allowed banks and financial intermediaries to pay back investors without having to sell their assets. It also decreased the incentives of investors to ask for their funds because these facilities decreased the risk that banks and financial intermediaries would go bankrupt.

- The government introduced a program, called the **Troubled Asset Relief Program (TARP)**, aimed at cleaning up banks. The initial goal of the $700 billion program, introduced in October 2008, was to remove the complex assets from the balance sheet of banks, thus decreasing uncertainty, reassuring investors, and making it easier to assess the health of each bank. The Treasury, however, faced the same problems as private investors. If these complex assets were going to be exchanged for, say, Treasury bills, at what price should the exchange be done? Within a few weeks, it became clear that the task of assessing the value of each of these assets was extremely hard and would take a long time, and the initial goal was abandoned. The new goal became to increase the capital of banks. This was done by the government acquiring shares and thus providing funds to most of the largest U.S. banks. By increasing their capital ratio, and thus decreasing their leverage, the goal of the program was to allow the banks to avoid bankruptcy and, over time, return to normal. As of the end of September 2009, total spending under the TARP was $360 billion, of which $200 billion was spent through the purchase of shares in banks.

Fiscal and monetary policies were used aggressively as well.

At the time of writing, all banks have bought back their shares and have reimbursed the government. Indeed, in the final estimation, TARP actually has made a small profit. ▶

Monetary Policy

Starting in the summer of 2007, the Fed began to worry about a slowdown in growth and had started decreasing the policy rate, slowly at first, faster later as evidence of the crisis mounted. The evolution of the federal funds rate from 2000 on was shown in Figure 1-4 in Chapter 1. By December 2008, the rate was down to zero. By then, however, monetary policy was constrained by the zero lower bound. The policy rate could not be decreased further. The Fed then turned to what has become known as **unconventional monetary policy**, buying other assets so as to directly affect the rate faced by borrowers. We shall explore the various dimensions of unconventional monetary policy at more length in Chapter 23. Suffice it to say that, although these measures were useful, the efficacy of monetary policy was nevertheless severely constrained by the zero lower bound.

Recall that the interest rate faced by borrowers is given by $r + x$. You can think of conventional monetary policy as the choice of r, and unconventional monetary policy as measures to reduce x. ▶

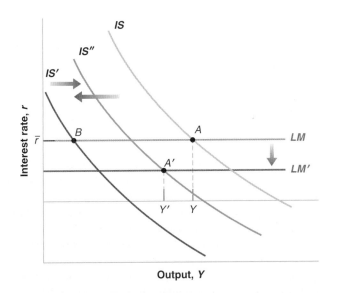

Figure 6-9

The Financial Crisis, and the Use of Financial, Fiscal, and Monetary Policies

The financial crisis led to a shift of the IS to the left. Financial and fiscal policies led to some shift back of the IS to the right. Monetary policy led to a shift of the LM curve down. Policies were not enough however to avoid a major recession.

MyEconLab Animation

Fiscal Policy

When the size of the adverse shock became clear, the U.S. government turned to fiscal policy. When the Obama administration assumed office in 2009, its first priority was to design a fiscal program that would increase demand and reduce the size of the recession. Such a fiscal program, called the **American Recovery and Reinvestment Act**, was passed in February 2009. It called for $780 billion in new measures, in the form of both tax reductions and spending increases, over 2009 and 2010. The U.S. budget deficit increased from 1.7% of GDP in 2007 to a high of 9.0% in 2010. The increase was largely the mechanical effect of the crisis because the decrease in output led automatically to a decrease in tax revenues and to an increase in transfer programs such as unemployment benefits. But it was also the result of the specific measures in the fiscal program aimed at increasing either private or public spending. Some economists argued that the increase in spending and the cuts in taxes should be even larger, given the seriousness of the situation. Others however worried that deficits were becoming too large, that it might lead to an explosion of public debt, and that they had to be reduced. From 2011, the deficit was indeed reduced, and it is much smaller today.

We can summarize our discussion by going back to the IS-LM model we developed in the previous section. This is done in Figure 6-9. The financial crisis led to a large shift of the IS curve to the left, from IS to IS′. In the absence of changes in policy, the equilibrium would have moved from point A to point B. Financial and fiscal policies offset some of the shift, so that, instead of shifting to IS′, the economy shifted to IS″. And monetary policy led to a shift of the LM down, from LM to LM′, so the resulting equilibrium was at point A′. At that point, the zero lower bound on the nominal policy rate implied that the real policy rate could not be decreased further. The result was a decrease in output from Y to Y′. The initial shock was so large that the combination of financial, fiscal, and monetary measures was just not enough to avoid a large decrease in output, with U.S. GDP falling by 3.5% in 2009 and recovering only slowly thereafter.

It is difficult to know what would have happened in the absence of those policies. It is reasonable to think, but impossible to prove, that the decrease in output would have been much larger, leading to a repeat of the Great ◄ Depression.

Summary

- The nominal interest rate tells you how many dollars you need to repay in the future in exchange for one dollar today.

- The real interest rate tells you how many goods you need to repay in the future in exchange for one good today.

- The real interest rate is approximately equal to the nominal rate minus expected inflation.

- The zero lower bound on the nominal interest rate implies that the real interest rate cannot be lower than minus expected inflation.

- The interest rate on a bond depends both on the probability that the issuer of the bond will default and on the degree of risk aversion of bond holders. A higher probability or a higher degree of risk aversion lead to a higher interest rate.

- Financial intermediaries receive funds from investors and then lend these funds to others. In choosing their leverage ratio, financial intermediaries trade off expected profit against the risk of insolvency.

- Because of leverage, the financial system is exposed to both solvency and illiquidity risks. Both may lead financial intermediaries to decrease lending.

- The higher the leverage ratio, or the more illiquid the assets, or the more liquid the liabilities, the higher the risk of a bank run, or more generally, a run on financial intermediaries.

- The IS-LM model must be extended to take into account the difference between the nominal and the real interest rate, and the difference between the policy rate chosen by the central bank and the interest rate at which firms and people can borrow.

- A shock to the financial system leads to an increase in the interest rate at which people and firms can borrow for a given policy rate. It leads to a decrease in output.

- The financial crisis of the late 2000s was triggered by a decrease in housing prices. It was amplified by the financial system.

- Financial intermediaries were highly leveraged. Because of securitization, their assets were hard to assess, and thus illiquid. Because of wholesale funding, their liabilities were liquid. Runs forced financial intermediaries to reduce lending, with strong adverse effects on output.

- Financial, fiscal, and monetary policies were used. They were not sufficient however to prevent a deep recession.

Key Terms

nominal interest rate, 132
real interest rate, 132
risk premium, 136
risk aversion, 136
direct finance, 137
shadow banking, 137
capital ratio, 138
leverage ratio, 138
insolvency, 138
fire sale prices, 139
demand deposits, 139
narrow banking, 140
federal deposit insurance, 140
liquidity provision, 140
bank runs, 140
liquidity, 141
policy rate, 141
borrowing rate, 141

mortgage lenders, 144
subprime mortgages, or subprimes, 144
underwater, 144
structured investment vehicles (SIVs), 145
securitization, 145
mortgage based security (MBS), 145
senior securities, 146
junior securities, 146
collateralized debt obligations (CDOs), 146
rating agencies, 146
toxic assets, 146
wholesale funding, 146
liquidity facilities, 148
collateral, 148
Troubled Asset Relief Program (TARP), 148
unconventional monetary policy, 148
American Recovery and Reinvestment
    Act, 149

Questions and Problems

QUICK CHECK

MyEconLab Visit www.myeconlab.com to complete similar Quick Check problems and get instant feedback.

1. Using the information in this chapter, label each of the following statements true, false, or uncertain. Explain briefly.

a. The nominal interest rate is measured in terms of goods; the real interest rate is measured in terms of money.

b. As long as expected inflation remains roughly constant, the movements in the real interest rate are roughly equal to the movements in the nominal interest rate.

c. The nominal policy interest rate was at the zero lower bound in the United States in 2013.

d. When expected inflation increases, the real rate of interest falls.

e. All bonds have equal risk of default and thus pay equal rates of interest.

f. The nominal policy interest rate is set by the central bank.

g. An increase in a bank's leverage ratio tends to increase both the expected profit of the bank and the risk of the bank going bankrupt.

h. The real borrowing rate and the real policy rate always move in the same direction.

i. It can be difficult to value assets of banks and other financial intermediaries, particularly in a financial crisis.

j. When a bank has high leverage and low liquidity, it may have to sell assets at fire sale prices.

k. Banks and other financial intermediaries have assets that are less liquid than their liabilities.

l. House prices have risen constantly since the year 2000.

m. The fiscal stimulus program adopted by the United States in response to the financial crisis helped offset the decline in aggregate demand and reduce the size of the recession.

n. The fiscal stimulus program adopted by the United States included a large increase in the deficit measured as a percent of GDP.

2. Suppose the interest rate in France is 1.7%, and the expected French inflation is 0.8%. The Swiss interest rate is also 1.7% and the expected Swiss inflation is 0.5%.

a. What are the exact real interest rates in France and Switzerland?

b. What are the approximate real interest rates in France and Switzerland?

c. How do you explain the difference in real rates between France and Switzerland?

3. Fill in the table below and answer the questions that relate to the data in the table

Situation	Nominal policy interest rate	Expected inflation	Real policy interest rate	Risk premium	Nominal borrowing interest rate	Real borrowing interest rate
A	3	0		0		
B	4		2	1		
C	0	2		4		
D				2	6	3
E	0	−2				5

a. Which situations correspond to a liquidity trap as defined in Chapter 4?

b. Which situations correspond to the case where the nominal policy interest rate is at the Zero Lower Bound?

c. Which situation has the highest risk premium? What two factors in bond markets lead to a positive risk premium?

d. Why is it so important when the nominal policy interest rate is at the Zero Lower Bound to maintain a positive expected rate of inflation?

4. Modern bank runs

Suppose that a European bank has customer deposits of €500 million and capital of €100 million and total assets of €600 million, divided as loans equal to €400 million and other assets equal to €200 million.

a. Prepare the balance sheet of the bank.

b. Suppose that some recent problems with the bank prompt customers to withdraw €100 million of their deposits. How can the bank preserve the same level of capital and assets on its balance sheet?

c. Prepare the new balance sheet of the bank.

d. If that the central bank does not insure customers' deposits, do you think that there will be a deposit run? How would the outcome change if the bank announces that it had recently approached a highly reputable and financially solid private insurance firm that has legally agreed to ensure customers' deposits?

e. Now suppose that it becomes known that the bank is facing serious solvency problems that do not allow it to borrow from depositors or financial institutions. What are the two options available to the bank to avoid bankruptcy?

Now consider a different sort of bank, still with assets of 100 and capital of 20, but now with short-term credit of 80 instead of checkable deposits. Short-term credit must be repaid or rolled over (borrowed again) when it comes due.

f. Set up this bank's balance sheet.

g. Again suppose the perceived value of the bank's assets falls. If lenders are nervous about the solvency of the bank, will they be willing to continue to provide short-term credit to the bank at low interest rates?

h. Assuming that the bank cannot raise additional capital, how can it raise the funds necessary to repay its debt coming due? If many banks are in this position at the same time (and if banks hold similar kinds of assets), what will likely happen to the value of the assets of these banks? How will this affect the willingness of lenders to provide short-term credit?

5. The IS-LM view of the world with more complex financial markets
Consider an economy described by Figure 6-6 in the text.

a. What are the units on the vertical axis of Figure 6-6?

b. If the nominal policy interest rate is 5% and the expected rate of inflation is 3%, what is the value for the vertical intercept of the LM curve?

c. Suppose the nominal policy interest rate is 5%. If expected inflation decreases from 3% to 2%, in order to keep the LM curve from shifting in Figure 6-6, what must the central bank do to the nominal policy rate of interest?

d. If the expected rate of inflation were to decrease from 3% to 2%, does the IS curve shift?

e. If the expected rate of inflation were to decrease from 3% to 2%, does the LM curve shift?

f. If the risk premium on risky bonds increases from 5% to 6%, does the LM curve shift?

g. If the risk premium on risky bonds increases from 5% to 6%, does the IS curve shift?

h. What are the fiscal policy options that prevent an increase in the risk premium on risky bonds from decreasing the level of output?

i. What are the monetary policy options that prevent an increase in the risk premium on risky bonds from decreasing the level of output?

DIG DEEPER

MyEconLab Visit www.myeconlab.com to complete all Dig Deeper problems and get instant feedback.

6. *Nominal and real interest rates around the world*

a. There are a few episodes of negative nominal interest rates around the world. Some may or may not be in play as you read this book. The Swiss nominal policy rate, the Swiss equivalent of the federal funds rate is series IRST-CI01CHM156N from the FRED database maintained at the Federal Reserve Bank of St. Louis. The Swiss nominal policy rate was negative in 2014 and 2015. If so, why not hold cash instead of bonds? In the United States, the Federal Reserve has not (yet) set the nominal policy rate below zero.

b. The real rate of interest is frequently negative, see Figure 6-2. Under what circumstances can it be negative? If so, why not just hold cash instead of bonds?

c. What are the effects of a negative real interest rate on borrowing and lending?

d. Find a recent issue of *The Economist* and look at the table in the back (titled "Economic and financial indicators"). Use the three-month money market rate as a proxy for the nominal policy interest rate, and the most recent three-month rate of change in consumer prices as a measure of the expected rate of inflation (both are expressed in annual terms). Which countries have the lowest nominal interest rates? Do any countries have a negative nominal policy rate? Which countries have the lowest real interest rates? Are some of these real interest rates negative?

7. *The Troubled Asset Relief Program (TARP)*

Consider a bank that has assets of 100, capital of 20, and short-term credit of 80. Among the bank's assets are securitized assets whose value depends on the price of houses. These assets have a value of 50.

a. Set up the bank's balance sheet.

Suppose that as a result of a housing price decline, the value of the bank's securitized assets falls by an uncertain amount, so that these assets are now worth somewhere between 25 and 45. Call the securitized assets "troubled assets." The value of the other assets remains at 50. As a result of the uncertainty about the value of the bank's assets, lenders are reluctant to provide any short-term credit to the bank.

b. Given the uncertainty about the value of the bank's assets, what is the range in the value of the bank's capital?

As a response to this problem, the government considers purchasing the troubled assets, with the intention of reselling them again when the markets stabilize. (This is the original version of the TARP.)

c. If the government pays 25 for the troubled assets, what will be the value of the bank's capital? How much would the government have to pay for the troubled assets to ensure that the bank's capital does not have a negative value? If the government pays 45 for the troubled assets, but the true value turns out to be much lower, who bears the cost of this mistaken valuation? Explain.

Suppose instead of buying the troubled assets, the government provides capital to the bank by buying ownership shares, with the intention of reselling the shares when the markets stabilize. (This is what the TARP ultimately became.) The government exchanges treasury bonds (which become assets for the bank) for ownership shares.

d. Suppose the government exchanges 25 of Treasury bonds for ownership shares. Assuming the worst-case scenario (so that the troubled assets are worth only 25), set up the new balance sheet of the bank. (Remember that the firm now has three assets: 50 of untroubled assets, 25 of troubled assets, and 25 of Treasury bonds.) What is the total value of the bank's capital? Will the bank be insolvent?

e. Given your answers and the material in the text, why might recapitalization be a better policy than buying the troubled assets?

8. *Calculating the risk premium on bonds*

The text presents a formula where

$$(1 + i) = (1 - p)(1 + i + x) + p(0)$$

p is the probability the bond does not pay at all (the bond issuer is bankrupt) and has a zero return.
i is the nominal policy interest rate.
x is the risk premium.

a. If the probability of bankruptcy is zero, what is the rate of interest on the risky bond?

b. Calculate the probability of bankruptcy when the nominal interest rate for a risky borrower is 8% and the nominal policy rate of interest is 3%.

c. Calculate the nominal interest rate for a borrower when the probability of bankruptcy is 1% and the nominal policy rate of interest is 4%.

d. Calculate the nominal interest rate for a borrower when the probability of bankruptcy is 5% and the nominal policy rate of interest is 4%.

e. The formula assumes that payment upon default is zero. In fact, it is often positive. How would you change the formula in this case?

9. *Unconventional monetary policy: financial policy and quantitative easing*

The IS curve represents the equilibrium in the goods market and the LM curve represents the equilibrium in the money market. As mentioned in the text, the following are the equations for the IS-LM curve:

IS relation: $Y = C(Y - T) + I(Y, r + x) + G$ (6.5)

LM relation: $r = \bar{r}$ (6.6)

Where the interest rate is the policy interest rate adjusted for expected inflation. Assume that the rate at which firms can borrow is much higher than the policy interest rate, hence the premium, x, in the IS equation is high.

a. After the global financial crisis several European economies adopted quantitative easing, better known as QE. Quantitative easing is an expansionary monetary policy used by the central bank, to buy financial assets from distressed commercial banks and large private institutions to facilitate the flow of credit in the financial markets. If QE proves to be successful, interest rates would decline, hence inducing increased investment and higher output. What is the effect on the IS-LM model?

b. Most emerging market economies did not have to resort to quantitative easing since their policy interest rates were quite high allowing for consecutive expansion of money supply and subsequent lower interest rates. However, it was the advanced economies with their interest rates approaching the zero level that were obliged to use this unconventional tool of monetary policy. Explain why QE was an imperative tool during the uncertainty and the low interest rates that prevailed during the global financial crisis.

c. One reason that quantitative easing was not successful is that it did not meet the outlook for higher expected inflation. What other reasons could explain why QE has not proved very effective?

EXPLORE FURTHER

10. The spread between riskless and risky bonds.

Immediately after the British voted for Brexit, two major credit rating agencies, Standard & Poor's and Fitch, downgraded the U.K.'s sovereign rating by two notches, from AAA to AA.

The spreads fluctuate between riskless rates on 5-year and 10-year U.K. Government bonds versus the 10-year AAA and BBB corporate bonds. Go to the Web site of the Bank of England (http://www.bankofengland.co.uk/) to extract the government bond yields.

a. What are the main requirements for a bond to be risk free? Does the downgrade of the U.K. sovereign rating imply that the U.K. government bonds would become riskier? Do you expect further credit rating downgrades for U.K. corporations? If so, what is most likely sector which you think is the most likely to be downgraded? Why?

b. Compare the yields and spreads of high-grade government and corporate bonds from any of the highly cited Web sites such as http://www.bloomberg.com/ - namely the U.K. Sovereign Bond Index (BRIT: IND) with the GBP High Yield Corporate Bond Index (BGBH: IND). Fill in the table below quoting the latest available yields with the yields on 20 June 2016 (just after the Brexit vote).

Date	BRIT: IND AAA/AA	BGBH: IND AAA/AA
Today		
20 June, 2016		

c. Explain and interpret the causes of the changes in the spreads and the in the risk premium for both categories of bonds since the Brexit vote.

11. Inflation-indexed bonds

Some bonds issued by the U.S. Treasury make payments indexed to inflation. These inflation-indexed bonds compensate investors for inflation. Therefore, the current interest rates on these bonds are real interest rates—interest rates in terms of goods. These interest rates can be used, together with nominal interest rates, to provide a measure of expected inflation. Let's see how.

Go to the Web site of the Federal Reserve Board and get the most recent statistical release listing interest rates (www.federalreserve.gov/releases/h15/Current). Find the current nominal interest rate on Treasury securities with a five-year maturity. Now find the current interest rate on "inflation-indexed" Treasury securities with a five-year maturity. What do you think participants in financial markets think the average inflation rate will be over the next five years?

Further Readings

■ There are many good books on the crisis, among them Michael Lewis's *The Big Short* (2010) and Gillian Tett's *Fool's Gold* (2009). Both books show how the financial system became increasingly risky until it finally collapsed. Both read like detective novels, with a lot of action and fascinating characters. *The Big Short* was made into a movie in 2015.

■ *In Fed We Trust* (2009), written by David Wessel, the economics editor of the *Wall Street Journal*, describes how the Fed reacted to the crisis. It also makes for fascinating reading. Read also the insider version, *The Courage to Act: A Memoir of a Crisis and Its Aftermath* (2015), by Ben Bernanke, who was Chairman of the Fed throughout the crisis.

The Medium Run

In the medium run, the economy returns to a level of output associated with the natural rate of unemployment.

Chapter 7

Chapter 7 looks at equilibrium in the labor market. It characterizes the natural rate of unemployment, which is the unemployment rate to which the economy tends to return in the medium run.

Chapter 8

Chapter 8 looks at the relation between inflation and unemployment, a relation known as the Phillips curve. In the short run, unemployment typically deviates from its natural rate. The behavior of inflation depends on the deviation of unemployment from its natural rate.

Chapter 9

Chapter 9 presents a model of the short run and the medium run. The model puts together the IS-LM model and the Phillips curve and thus is called the IS-LM-PC model. It describes the dynamics of output and unemployment, both in the short and the medium run.

7

The Labor Market

Think about what happens when firms respond to an increase in demand by increasing production. Higher production leads to higher employment. Higher employment leads to lower unemployment. Lower unemployment leads to higher wages. Higher wages increase production costs, leading firms to increase prices. Higher prices lead workers to ask for higher wages. Higher wages lead to further increases in prices, and so on.

So far, we have simply ignored this sequence of events. By assuming a constant price level in the IS-LM model, we in effect assumed that firms were able and willing to supply any amount of output at a given price level. So as long as our focus was on the *short run*, this assumption was fine. But, as our attention now turns to the *medium run*, we must now abandon this assumption, explore how prices and wages adjust over time, and how this, in turn, affects output. This will be our task in this and the next two chapters.

At the center of the sequence of events described in the first paragraph is *the labor market*, which is the market in which wages are determined. This chapter focuses on the labor market. It has six sections:

Section 7-1 provides an overview of the labor market.

Section 7-2 focuses on unemployment, how it moves over time, and how its movements affect individual workers.

Sections 7-3 and **7-4** look at wage and price determination.

Section 7-5 then looks at equilibrium in the labor market. It characterizes the *natural rate of unemployment*, which is the rate of unemployment to which the economy tends to return in the medium run.

Section 7-6 gives a map of where we will be going next.

7-1 A Tour of the Labor Market

The total U.S. population in 2014 was 318.9 million (Figure 7-1). Excluding those who were either younger than working age (under 16), in the armed forces, or behind bars, the number of people potentially available for civilian employment, the **non-institutional civilian population**, was 247.9 million.

The civilian **labor force**, which is the sum of those either working or looking for work, was only 155.9 million. The other 92.0 million people were **out of the labor force**, neither working in the market place nor looking for work. The **participation rate**, which is defined as the ratio of the labor force to the non-institutional civilian population, therefore was 155.9/247.9, or 62%. The participation rate has steadily increased over time, reflecting mostly the increasing participation rate of women. In 1950, one woman out of three was in the labor force; now the number is close to two out of three.

Of those in the labor force, 146.3 million were employed, and 9.5 million were unemployed—looking for work. The **unemployment rate**, which is defined as the ratio of the unemployed to the labor force, therefore was $9.5/155.9 = 6.1\%$.

> Work in the home, such as cooking or raising children, is not classified as work in the official statistics. This is a reflection of the difficulty of measuring these activities, not a value judgment about what constitutes work and what does not.

The Large Flows of Workers

To get a sense of what a given unemployment rate implies for individual workers, consider the following analogy.

Take an airport full of passengers. It may be crowded because many planes are coming and going, and many passengers are quickly moving in and out of the airport. Or it may be because bad weather is delaying flights and passengers are stranded, waiting for the weather to improve. The number of passengers in the airport will be high in both cases, but their plights are quite different. Passengers in the second scenario are likely to be much less happy.

In the same way, a given unemployment rate may reflect two different realities. It may reflect an active labor market, with many **separations** and many **hires**, and so with many workers entering and exiting unemployment, or it may reflect a sclerotic labor market, with few separations, few hires, and a stagnant unemployment pool.

> *Sclerosis*, a medical term, means "hardening of the arteries." By analogy, it is used in economics to describe markets that function poorly and have few transactions.

Finding out which reality hides behind the aggregate unemployment rate requires data on the movements of workers. In the United States, the data are available from

Figure 7-1

Population, Labor Force, Employment, and Unemployment in the United States (in Millions), 2014

Source: Current Population Survey
http://www.bls.gov/cps/.

MyEconLab Animation

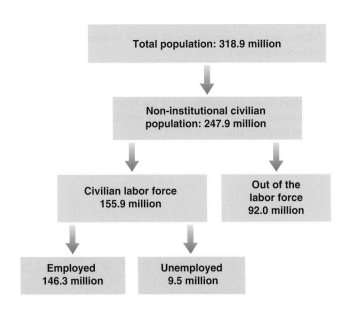

a monthly survey called the **Current Population Survey (CPS)**. Average monthly flows, computed from the CPS for the United States from 1996 to 2014, are reported in Figure 7-2. (See the Focus box "The Australian Monthly Population Survey" to understand how the Australian monthly population surveys work.")

Figure 7-2 has three striking features.

- The flows of workers in and out of employment are large.

  On average, there are 8.2 million separations each month in the United States (out of an employment pool of 139.0 million), 3.0 million change jobs (shown by the circular arrow at the top), 3.4 million move from employment to out of the labor force (shown by the arrow from employment to out of the labor force), and 1.8 million move from employment to unemployment (shown by the arrow from employment to unemployment).

  Why are there so many separations each month? About three-fourths of all separations are **quits**, which are workers leaving their jobs for what they perceive as a better alternative. The remaining one-fourth are **layoffs**. Layoffs come mostly from changes in employment levels across firms. The slowly changing aggregate employment numbers hide a reality of continual job destruction and job creation across firms. At any given time, some firms are suffering decreases in demand and decreasing their employment; other firms are enjoying increases in demand and increasing employment.

- The flows in and out of unemployment are large relative to the number of unemployed. The average monthly flow out of unemployment each month is 3.9 million: 2.0 million people get a job, and 1.9 million stop searching for a job and drop out of the labor force. Put another way, the proportion of unemployed leaving unemployment equals 3.9/8.8 or about 44% each month. Put yet another way, the average **duration of unemployment**, which is the average length of time people spend unemployed, is between two and three months.

  This fact has an important implication. You should not think of unemployment in the United States as a stagnant pool of workers waiting indefinitely for jobs. For most (but obviously not all) of the unemployed, being unemployed is more a quick transition than a long wait between jobs. One needs, however, to make two remarks at this point. First, the United States is unusual in this respect. In many European countries, the average duration is much longer than

The numbers for employment, unemployment, and those out ◄ of the labor force in Figure 7-1 referred to 2014. The numbers for the same variables in Figure 7-2 refer to averages from 1996 to 2014. This is why they are different.

Put another, and perhaps more dramatic way: On average, every day in the United States, about 60,000 workers ◄ become unemployed.

The average duration of unemployment equals the inverse of the proportion of unemployed leaving unemployment each month. To see why, consider an example. Suppose the number of unemployed is constant and equal to 100, and each unemployed person remains unemployed for two months. So, at any given time, there are 50 people who have been unemployed for one month and 50 who have been unemployed for two months. Each month, the 50 ◄ unemployed who have been unemployed for two months leave unemployment. In this example, the proportion of unemployed leaving unemployment each month is 50/100, or 50%. The duration of unemployment is two months, which is the inverse of 1/50%.

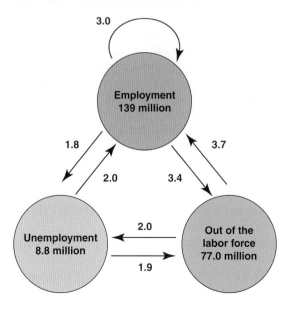

Figure 7-2

Average Monthly Flows between Employment, Unemployment, and Non-participation in the United States, 1996 to 2014 (Millions)

(1) The flows of workers in and out of employment are large. (2) The flows in and out of unemployment are large relative to the number of unemployment. (3) There are also large flows in and out of the labor force, much of it directly to and from employment.

Source: Calculated from the series constructed by Fleischman and Fallick, http://www.federalreserve.gov/econresdata/researchdata/feds200434.xls.

MyEconLab Animation

The Australian Monthly Population Survey

The Australia Bureau of Statistics' Monthly Population Surveys (MPS) gathers varied information about the country's labor force. One of the main objectives of the survey is to measure changes in the households over time. Since its inception in 1960, the MPS household sample size grew from 30,000 to over 300,000. To ensure that the sample provides a balanced representation of all Australian households, participation is compulsory. Each household is replaced every eight months. Around 43,000 permanent and temporary census staff members are employed to collect data, conducting all interviews either online or face-to-face. There are a set of standard questions asked in every monthly survey, while certain questions changed each month to help cover all characteristics of the household. In addition to employment-related data, the MPS collects information pertaining to cultural heritage, language spoken at home, country of birth, and ancestry including Aboriginal or Torres Strait Islander origin.

Census data are used in compiling the monthly national statistics on employment, unemployment, gender, size, and earnings of households. The MPS also counts the number of people in each geographic area in order to allocate Commonwealth funds to state and local governments. Economic analysts and policy makers use the data both in its static and continuous forms. In the case of static data forms, a snapshot of certain aspects at one point in time is collected and compared with other snapshots collected over previous years. An example is the change in the number of hours worked in each industry over the past 10 years. In the case of dynamic data forms, census workers compare the development of the situation of the same household over time. This is why census workers have the right to ask questions about changes in conditions of employment or the patterns of household spending on a wide range of goods and services, oftentimes triggering resentment of some of the households interviewed.

For more on the MPS, go to the homepage of the Australian Bureau of Statistics (http://www.abs.gov.au/websitedbs/D3310114.nsf/home/Current+Household+Surveys).

in the United States. Second, as we shall see, even in the United States, when unemployment is high, such as was the case in the crisis, the average duration of unemployment becomes much longer. Being unemployed becomes much more painful.

■ The flows in and out of the labor force are also surprisingly large. Each month, 5.3 million workers drop out of the labor force (3.4 plus 1.9), and a roughly equal slightly larger number, 5.7, join the labor force (3.7 plus 2.0). You might have expected these two flows to be composed, on one side, of those completing school and entering the labor force for the first time, and on the other side, of workers entering retirement. But each of these two groups actually represents a small fraction of the total flows. Each month only about 450,000 new people enter the labor force, and about 350,000 retire. But the actual flows in and out of the labor force are 11.2 million, so about 14 times larger.

What this fact implies is that many of those classified as "out of the labor force" are in fact willing to work and move back and forth between participation and non-participation. Indeed, among those classified as out of the labor force, a large proportion report that although they are not looking, they "want a job." What they really mean by this statement is unclear, but the evidence is that many do take jobs when offered them.

This fact has another important implication. The sharp focus on the unemployment rate by economists, policy makers, and news media is partly misdirected. Some of the people classified as out of the labor force are much like the unemployed. They are in effect **discouraged workers**. And although they are not actively looking for a job, they will take it if they find one.

This is why economists sometimes focus on the **employment rate**, which is the ratio of employment to the population available for work, rather than on the unemployment rate. The higher unemployment, or the higher the number of people out of the labor force, the lower the employment rate.

Working in the opposite direction: Some of the unemployed may be unwilling to accept any job offered to them and should probably not be counted as unemployed because they are not really looking for a job. ▷

In 2014, employment was 146.3 million and the population available for work was 247.9 million. The employment rate was 59.0%. The employment rate is sometimes called the *employment-to-population ratio*. ▷

I shall follow tradition in this text and focus on the unemployment rate as an indicator of the state of the labor market, but you should keep in mind that the unemployment rate is not the best estimate of the number of people available for work.

7-2 Movements in Unemployment

Let's now look at movements in unemployment. Figure 7-3 shows the average value of the U.S. unemployment rate over the year, for each year, all the way back to 1948. The shaded areas represent years during which there was a recession.

Figure 7-3 has two important features.

■ Until the mid-1980s, it looked as if the U.S. unemployment rate was on an upward trend, from an average of 4.5% in the 1950s to 4.7% in the 1960s, 6.2% in the 1970s, and 7.3% in the 1980s. From the 1980s on however, the unemployment rate steadily declined for more than two decades. By 2006, the unemployment rate was down to 4.6%. These decreases led a number of economists to conclude that the trend from 1950 to the 1980s had been reversed, and that the normal rate of unemployment in the United States had fallen. The unemployment rate increased sharply with the crisis, and then started coming down again. At the time of writing, it stands at 5.0%; whether it will go back to the low precrisis level is unclear.

■ Leaving aside these trend changes, year-to-year movements in the unemployment rate are closely associated with recessions and expansions. Look, for example, at the last four peaks in unemployment in Figure 7-3. The most recent peak, at 9.6% is in 2010, was the result of the crisis. The previous two peaks, associated with the recessions of 2001 and 1990–1991 recessions, had much lower unemployment rate peaks, around 7%. Only the recession of 1982, where the unemployment rate reached 9.7%, is comparable to the recent crisis. (Annual averages can mask larger values within the year. In the 1982 recession, although the average unemployment rate over the year was 9.7%, the unemployment rate actually reached 10.8% in November 1982. Similarly, ◄ the monthly unemployment rate in the crisis peaked at 10.0% in October 2009.)

Note also that the unemployment rate sometimes peaks in the year after the recession, not in the actual recession year. This occurred, for example, in the 2001 recession. The reason is that, although growth is positive, so the economy is technically no longer in recession, the additional output does not lead to enough new hires to reduce the unemployment rate.

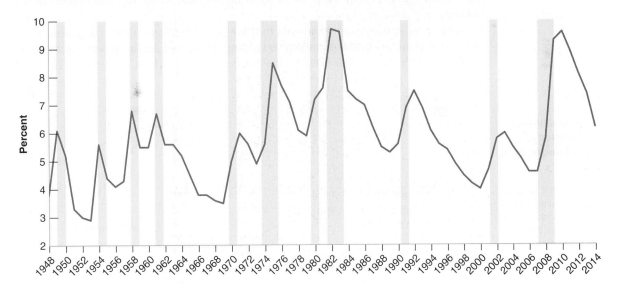

Figure 7-3 *Movements in the U.S. Unemployment Rate, 1948–2014*

MyEconLab Real-time data

Since 1948, the average yearly U.S. unemployment rate has fluctuated between 3 and 10%.

Source: Series UNRATE: Federal Reserve Economic Data (FRED) http://research.stlouisfed.org/fred2/.

How do these fluctuations in the aggregate unemployment rate affect individual workers? This is an important question because the answer determines both:

- The effect of movements in the aggregate unemployment rate on the welfare of individual workers, and
- The effect of the aggregate unemployment rate on wages.

Let's start by asking how firms can decrease their employment in response to a decrease in demand. They can hire fewer new workers, or they can lay off the workers they currently employ. Typically, firms prefer to slow or stop the hiring of new workers first, relying on quits and retirements to achieve a decrease in employment. But doing only this may not be enough if the decrease in demand is large, so firms may then have to lay off workers.

Now think about the implications for both employed and unemployed workers.

- If the adjustment takes place through fewer hires, the chance that an unemployed worker will find a job diminishes. Fewer hires means fewer job openings; higher unemployment means more job applicants. Fewer openings and more applicants combine to make it harder for the unemployed to find jobs.
- If the adjustment takes place instead through higher layoffs, then employed workers are at a higher risk of losing their job.

In general, as firms do both, higher unemployment is associated with both a lower chance of finding a job if one is unemployed and a higher chance of losing it if one is employed. Figures 7-4 and 7-5 show these two effects at work over the period 1996 to 2014.

Figure 7-4 plots two variables against time: the unemployment rate (measured on the left vertical axis) and the proportion of unemployed workers finding a job each month (measured on the right vertical axis). This proportion is constructed by dividing the flow from unemployment to employment during each month by the number of unemployed. To show the relation between the two variables more clearly, the proportion of unemployed finding jobs is plotted on an inverted scale. Be sure you see that on the right vertical scale, the proportion is lowest at the top and highest at the bottom.

The relation between movements in the proportion of unemployed workers finding jobs and the unemployment rate is striking. Periods of higher unemployment are associated with much lower proportions of unemployed workers finding jobs. In 2010,

Figure 7-4

***The Unemployment Rate
and the Proportion of
Unemployed Finding Jobs,
1996–2014***

When unemployment is higher, the proportion of unemployed finding jobs within one month is lower. Note that the scale on the right is an inverse scale.

Sources: Series UNRATE: Federal Reserve Economic Data (FRED) http://research.stlouisfed.org/fred2/. Series constructed by Fleischman and Fallick, http://www.federalreserve.gov/econresdata/researchdata/.

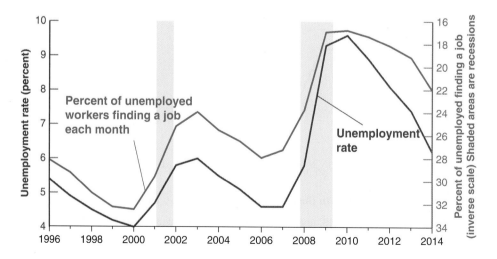

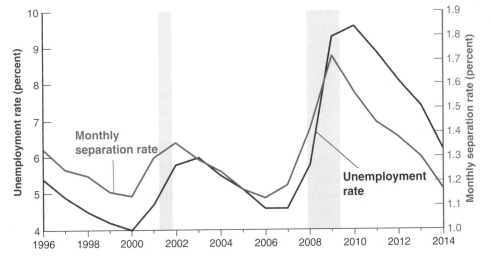

Figure 7-5

The Unemployment Rate and the Monthly Separation Rate from Employment, 1996–2014

When unemployment is higher, a higher proportion of workers lose their jobs.

Sources: Series UNRATE: Federal Reserve Economic Data (FRED) http://research.stlouisfed.org/fred2/.
Series constructed by Fleischman and Fallick, http://www.federalre serve.gov/econresdata/research data/feds200434.xls.

for example, with unemployment close to 10%, only about 17% of the unemployed found a job within a month, as opposed to 28% in 2007, when unemployment was much lower.

Similarly, Figure 7-5 plots two variables against time: the unemployment rate (measured on the left vertical axis) and the monthly separation rate from employment (measured on the right vertical axis). The monthly separation rate is constructed by dividing the flow from employment (to unemployment and to out of the labor force) during each month by the number of employed in the month. The relation between the separation rate and the unemployment rate plotted is quite strong. Higher unemployment implies a higher separation rate—that is, a higher chance of employed workers ◀ losing their jobs. The probability nearly doubles between times of low unemployment and times of high unemployment.

Let's summarize:

When unemployment is high, workers are worse off in two ways:

■ Employed workers face a higher probability of losing their job.
■ Unemployed workers face a lower probability of finding a job; equivalently, they can expect to remain unemployed for a longer time.

To be slightly more precise, we only learn from Figure 7-5 that, when unemployment is higher, separations into unemployment and out of the labor force are higher. Separations however include both quits and layoffs. We know from other sources that quits are lower when unemployment is high. It is more attractive to quit when there are plenty of jobs. So, if separations go up and quits go down, this implies that layoffs (which equal separations minus quits) go up even more than separations.

7-3 Wage Determination

Having looked at unemployment, let's turn to wage determination, and to the relation between wages and unemployment.

Wages are set in many ways. Sometimes they are set by **collective bargaining**, that is, bargaining between firms and unions. In the United States, however, collective ◀ bargaining plays a limited role, especially outside the manufacturing sector. Today, barely more than 10% of U.S. workers have their wages set by collective bargaining agreements. For the rest, wages are either set by employers or by bargaining between the employer and individual employees. The higher the skills needed to do the job, the more likely there is to be bargaining. Wages offered for entry-level jobs at McDonald's are on a take-it-or-leave-it basis. New college graduates, on the other hand, can typically negotiate a few aspects of their contracts. CEOs and baseball stars can negotiate a lot more.

Collective bargaining is bargaining between a union (or a set of unions) and a firm (or a set of firms).

There are also large differences across countries. Collective bargaining plays an important role in Japan and in most European countries. Negotiations may take place at the firm level, at the industry level, or at the national level. Sometimes contract agreements apply only to firms that have signed the agreement. Sometimes they are automatically extended to all firms and all workers in the sector or the economy.

Given these differences across workers and across countries, can we hope to formulate anything like a general theory of wage determination? Yes. Although institutional differences influence wage determination, there are common forces at work in all countries. Two sets of facts stand out:

- Workers are typically paid a wage that exceeds their **reservation wage**, which is the wage that would make them indifferent between working or being unemployed. In other words, most workers are paid a high enough wage that they prefer being employed to being unemployed.
- Wages typically depend on labor-market conditions. The lower the unemployment rate, the higher the wages. (I shall state this more precisely in the next section.)

To think about these facts, economists have focused on two broad lines of explanation. The first is that even in the absence of collective bargaining, most workers have some bargaining power, which they can and do use to obtain wages above their reservation wages. The second is that firms themselves may, for a number of reasons, want to pay wages higher than the reservation wage. Let's look at each explanation in turn.

Bargaining

How much **bargaining power** workers have depends on two factors. The first is how costly it would be for the firm to find other workers, were they to leave the firm. The second is how hard it would be for them to find another job, were they to leave the firm. The costlier it is for the firm to replace them, and the easier it is for them to find another job, the more bargaining power they will have. This has two implications:

- How much bargaining power a worker has depends first on the nature of the job. Replacing a worker at McDonald's is not costly. The required skills can be taught quickly, and typically a large number of willing applicants have already filled out job application forms. In this situation, the worker is unlikely to have much bargaining power. If he or she asks for a higher wage, the firm can lay him or her off and find a replacement at minimum cost. In contrast, a highly skilled worker who knows in detail how the firm operates may be difficult and costly to replace. This gives him or her more bargaining power. If he or she asks for a higher wage, the firm may decide that it is best to give it to him or her.
- How much bargaining power a worker has also depends on labor market conditions. When the unemployment rate is low, it is more difficult for firms to find acceptable replacement workers. At the same time, it is easier for workers to find other jobs. Under these conditions, workers are in a stronger bargaining position and may be able to obtain a higher wage. Conversely, when the unemployment rate is high, finding good replacement workers is easier for firms, whereas finding another job is harder for workers. Being in a weak bargaining position, workers may have no choice but to accept a lower wage.

Peter Diamond, Dale Mortensen, and Christopher Pissarides received the 2010 Nobel Prize in economics precisely for working out the characteristics of a labor market with large flows ▶ and wage bargaining.

Efficiency Wages

Regardless of workers' bargaining power, firms may want to pay more than the reservation wage. They may want their workers to be productive, and a higher wage can help them achieve that goal. If, for example, it takes a while for workers to learn how to do a

Henry Ford and Efficiency Wages

In 1914, Henry Ford the builder of the most popular car in the world at the time, the Model-T—made a stunning announcement. His company would pay all qualified employees a minimum of $5.00 a day for an eight-hour day. This was a large salary increase for most employees, who had been earning an average $2.30 for a nine-hour day. From the point of view of the Ford Company, this increase in pay was far from negligible; it represented about half of the company's profits at the time.

What Ford's motivations were is not entirely clear. Ford himself gave too many reasons for us to know which ones he actually believed. The reason was not that the company had a hard time finding workers at the previous wage. But the company clearly had a hard time retaining workers. There was a high turnover rate, as well as high dissatisfaction among workers.

Whatever the reasons behind Ford's decision, as Table 1 shows, the results of the wage increase were astounding, as the table shows.

Table 1	Annual Turnover and Layoff Rates (%) at Ford, 1913–1915		
	1913	**1914**	**1915**
Turnover rate (%)	370	54	16
Layoff rate (%)	62	7	0.1

The annual turnover rate (the ratio of separations to employment) plunged from a high of 370% in 1913 to a low of 16% in 1915. (An annual turnover rate of 370% means that on average 31% of the company's workers left each month, so that over the course of a year the ratio of separations to employment was $31\% \times 12 = 370\%$.) The layoff rate collapsed from 62% to nearly 0%. The average rate of absenteeism (not shown in the table), which ran at close to 10% in 1913, was down to 2.5% one year later. There is little question that higher wages were the main source of these changes.

Did productivity at the Ford plant increase enough to offset the cost of increased wages? The answer to this question is less clear. Productivity was much higher in 1914 than in 1913. Estimates of the productivity increases range from 30 to 50%. Despite higher wages, profits were also higher in 1914 than in 1913. But how much of this increase in profits was the result of changes in workers' behavior and how much was because of the increasing success of Model-T cars is harder to establish.

Although the effects support efficiency wage theories, it may be that the increase in wages to five dollars a day was excessive, at least from the point of view of profit maximization. But Henry Ford probably had other objectives as well, from keeping the unions out—which he did—to generating publicity for himself and the company—which he surely did.

Source: Dan Raff and Lawrence Summers, "Did Henry Ford Pay Efficiency Wages?" *Journal of Labor Economics* 1987, 5 (No. 4 Part 2): pp. S57–S87.

job correctly, firms will want their workers to stay for some time. But if workers are paid only their reservation wage, they will be indifferent between their staying or leaving. In this case, many of them will quit, and the turnover rate will be high. Paying a wage above the reservation wage makes it more attractive for workers to stay. It decreases turnover and increases productivity.

Behind this example lies a more general proposition. Most firms want their workers to feel good about their jobs. Feeling good promotes good work, which leads to higher productivity. Paying a high wage is one instrument the firm can use to achieve these goals. (See the Focus box "Henry Ford and Efficiency Wages.") Economists call the ◀ theories that link the productivity or the efficiency of workers to the wage they are paid **efficiency wage theories**.

Like theories based on bargaining, efficiency wage theories suggest that wages depend on both the nature of the job and on labor-market conditions.

■ Firms, such as high-tech firms, that see employee morale and commitment as essential to the quality of their work will pay more than firms in sectors where workers' activities are more routine.

■ Labor-market conditions will affect the wage. A low unemployment rate makes it more attractive for employed workers to quit. When unemployment is low, it is easy to find another job. That means, when unemployment decreases, a firm that wants to avoid an increase in quits will have to increase wages to induce workers to stay with the firm. When this happens, lower unemployment will again lead to higher wages. Conversely, higher unemployment will lead to lower wages.

MyEconLab Video

Before September 11, 2001, the approach to airport security was to hire workers at low wages and accept the resulting high turnover. Now that airport security has become a higher priority, the approach has been to make the jobs more attractive and increase pay, so as to get more motivated and more competent workers and reduce turnover. Turnover at the Transport Security Administration (TSA) is now roughly equal to the service industry average.

Wages, Prices, and Unemployment

We can capture our discussion of wage determination by using the following equation:

$$W = P^e \, F(u, z) \qquad\qquad (7.1)$$
$$(-,+)$$

The aggregate nominal wage W depends on three factors:

■ The expected price level, P^e
■ The unemployment rate, u
■ A catch-all variable, z, that stands for all other variables that may affect the outcome of wage setting.

Let's look at each factor.

The Expected Price Level

First, ignore the difference between the expected and the actual price level and ask: Why does the price level affect nominal wages? The answer: Because both workers and firms care about *real* wages, not nominal wages.

■ Workers do not care about how many dollars they receive but about how many goods they can buy with those dollars. In other words, they do not care about the nominal wages they receive, but about the nominal wages (W) they receive relative to the price of the goods they buy (P). They care about W/P.
■ In the same way, firms do not care about the nominal wages they pay but about the nominal wages (W) they pay relative to the price of the goods they sell (P). So they also care about W/P.

An increase in the expected price level leads to an increase ▶ in the nominal wage in the same proportion.

Think of it another way. If workers expect the price level—the price of the goods they buy—to double, they will ask for a doubling of their nominal wage. If firms expect the price level—the price of the goods they sell—to double, they will be willing to double the nominal wage. So, if both workers and firms expect the price level to double, they will agree to double the nominal wage, keeping the real wage constant. This is captured in equation (7.1): A doubling in the expected price level leads to a doubling of the nominal wage chosen when wages are set.

Return now to the distinction we set aside at the start of the paragraph: Why do wages depend on the *expected price level*, P^e, rather than the *actual price level, P*?

Because wages are set in nominal (dollar) terms, and when they are set, the relevant price level is not yet known.

For example, in some union contracts in the United States, nominal wages are set in advance for three years. Unions and firms have to decide what nominal wages will be over the following three years based on what they expect the price level to be over those three years. Even when wages are set by firms, or by bargaining between the firm and each worker, nominal wages are typically set for a year. If the price level goes up unexpectedly during the year, nominal wages are typically not readjusted. (How workers and firms form expectations of the price level will occupy us for much of the next two chapters; we will leave this issue aside for the moment.)

The Unemployment Rate

Also affecting the aggregate wage in equation (7.1) is the unemployment rate, u. The minus sign under u indicates that an increase in the unemployment rate *decreases* wages.

The fact that wages depend on the unemployment rate was one of the main conclusions of our previous discussion. If we think of wages as being determined by bargaining, then higher unemployment weakens workers' bargaining power, forcing them to accept lower wages. If we think of wages as being determined by efficiency wage considerations, then higher unemployment allows firms to pay lower wages and still keep workers willing to work.

◄ An increase in unemployment leads to a decrease in the nominal wage.

The Other Factors

The third variable in equation (7.1), z, is a catch-all variable that stands for all the factors that affect wages given the expected price level and the unemployment rate. By convention, we will define z so that an increase in z implies an increase in the wage (thus, the positive sign under z in the equation). Our previous discussion suggests a long list of potential factors here.

◄ By the definition of z, an increase in z leads to an increase in the nominal wage.

Take, for example, **unemployment insurance**, which is the payment of unemployment benefits to workers who lose their jobs. There are good reasons why society should provide some insurance to workers who lose their job and have a hard time finding another. But there is little question that, by making the prospects of unemployment less distressing, more generous unemployment benefits do increase wages at a given unemployment rate. To take an extreme example, suppose unemployment insurance did not exist. Some workers would have little to live on and would be willing to accept low wages to avoid remaining unemployed. But unemployment insurance does exist, and it allows unemployed workers to hold out for higher wages. In this case, we can think of z as representing the level of unemployment benefits. At a given unemployment rate, higher unemployment benefits increase the wage.

It is easy to think of other factors. An increase in the minimum wage may increase not only the minimum wage itself, but also wages just above the minimum wage, leading to an increase in the average wage, W, at a given unemployment rate. Or take an increase in **employment protection**, which makes it more expensive for firms to lay off workers. Such a change is likely to increase the bargaining power of workers covered by this protection (laying them off and hiring other workers is now costlier for firms), increasing the wage for a given unemployment rate.

We will explore some of these factors as we go along.

7-4 Price Determination

Having looked at wage determination, let's now turn to price determination.

The prices set by firms depend on the costs they face. These costs depend, in turn, on the nature of the **production function**, which is the relation between the inputs used in production and the quantity of output produced, and on the prices of these inputs.

For the moment, we will assume firms produce goods using labor as the only factor of production. We will write the production function as follows:

$$Y = AN$$

where Y is output, N is employment, and A is labor productivity. This way of writing the production function implies that **labor productivity**, which is output per worker, is constant and equal to A.

◄ Using a term from microeconomics, this assumption implies *constant returns to labor in production*. If firms double the number of workers they employ, they double the amount of output they produce.

It should be clear that this is a strong simplification. In reality, firms use other factors of production in addition to labor. They use capital—machines and factories. They use raw materials—oil, for example. Moreover, there is technological progress, so that labor productivity (A) is not constant but steadily increases over time. We shall introduce these complications later. We shall introduce raw materials in Chapter 9 when we discuss changes in the price of oil. We shall focus on the role of capital and technological progress when we turn to the determination of output in the *long run* in Chapter 10 through Chapter 13. For the moment, though, this simple relation between output and employment will make our lives easier and still serve our purposes.

Given the assumption that labor productivity, A, is constant, we can make one further simplification. We can choose the units of output so that one worker produces one unit of output—in other words, so that $A = 1$. (This way we do not have to carry the letter A around, and this will simplify notation.) With this assumption, the production function becomes:

$$Y = N \qquad (7.2)$$

The production function $Y = N$ implies that the cost of producing one more unit of output is the cost of employing one more worker, at wage W. Using the terminology introduced in your microeconomics course: The marginal cost of production—the cost of producing one more unit of output—is equal to W.

If there was perfect competition in the goods market, the price of a unit of output would be equal to marginal cost: P would be equal to W. But many goods markets are not competitive, and firms charge a price higher than their marginal cost. A simple way of capturing this fact is to assume that firms set their price according to

$$P = (1 + m)W \qquad (7.3)$$

where m is the **markup** of the price over the cost. If goods markets were perfectly competitive, m would be equal to zero, and the price, P, would simply equal the cost, W. To the extent they are not competitive and firms have market power, m is positive, and the price, P, will exceed the cost, W, by a factor equal to $(1 + m)$.

7-5 The Natural Rate of Unemployment

Let's now look at the implications of wage and price determination for unemployment.

For the rest of this chapter, we shall do so under the assumption that nominal wages depend on the actual price level, P, rather than on the expected price level, P^e (why we make this assumption will become clear soon). Under this additional assumption, wage setting and price setting determine the equilibrium (also called *natural*) rate of unemployment. Let's see how.

The rest of the chapter is based on the assumption that $P^e = P$. ▶

The Wage-Setting Relation

Given the assumption that nominal wages depend on the actual price level (P) rather than on the expected price level (P^e), equation (7.1), which characterizes wage determination, becomes:

$$W = PF(u, z)$$

Dividing both sides by the price level,

$$\frac{W}{P} = F(u, z) \qquad (7.4)$$

$$(-,+)$$

"Wage setters" are unions and firms if wages are set by collective bargaining; individual workers and firms if wages are set on a case-by-case basis; or firms if wages are set on a ▶ take-it-or-leave-it basis.

Wage determination implies a negative relation between the real wage, W/P, and the unemployment rate, u: *The higher the unemployment rate, the lower the real wage chosen by wage setters.* The intuition is straightforward. The higher the unemployment rate, the weaker the workers' bargaining position, and the lower the real wage will be.

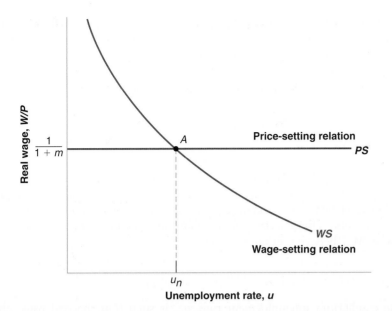

Figure 7-6

Wages, Prices, and the Natural Rate of Unemployment

The natural rate of unemployment is the unemployment rate such that the real wage chosen in wage setting is equal to the real wage implied by price setting.

MyEconLab Animation

This relation between the real wage and the rate of unemployment—let's call it the **wage-setting relation**—is drawn in Figure 7-6. The real wage is measured on the vertical axis. The unemployment rate is measured on the horizontal axis. The wage-setting relation is drawn as the downward–sloping curve *WS* (for wage setting). The higher the unemployment rate, the lower the real wage.

The Price-Setting Relation

Let's now look at the implications of price determination. If we divide both sides of the price-determination equation, (7.3), by the nominal wage, we get

$$\frac{P}{W} = 1 + m \tag{7.5}$$

The ratio of the price level to the wage implied by the price-setting behavior of firms equals 1 plus the markup. Now invert both sides of this equation to get the implied real wage:

$$\frac{W}{P} = \frac{1}{1 + m} \tag{7.6}$$

Note what this equation says: *Price-setting decisions determine the real wage paid by firms.* An increase in the markup leads firms to increase their prices given the wage they have to pay; equivalently, it leads to a decrease in the real wage.

The step from equation (7.5) to equation (7.6) is algebraically straightforward. But how price setting actually determines the real wage paid by firms may not be intuitively obvious. Think of it this way: Suppose the firm you work for increases its markup and therefore increases the price of its product. Your real wage does not change much; you are still paid the same nominal wage, and the product produced by the firm is at most a small part of your consumption basket. Now suppose that not only the firm you work for, but all the firms in the economy increase their markup. All the prices go up. Even if you are paid the same nominal wage, your real wage goes down. So, the higher the markup set by firms, the lower your (and everyone else's) real wage will be. This is what equation (7.6) says.

The **price-setting relation** in equation (7.6) is drawn as the horizontal line *PS* (for price setting) in Figure 7-6. The real wage implied by price setting is $1/(1 + m)$; it does not depend on the unemployment rate.

Equilibrium Real Wages and Unemployment

Equilibrium in the labor market requires that the real wage chosen in wage setting be equal to the real wage implied by price setting. (This way of stating equilibrium may sound strange if you learned to think in terms of labor supply and labor demand in your microeconomics course. The relation between wage setting and price setting, on the one hand, and labor supply and labor demand, on the other, is closer than it looks at first and is explored further in the appendix at the end of this chapter.) In Figure 7-6, equilibrium is therefore given by point *A*, and the equilibrium unemployment rate is given by u_n.

We can also characterize the equilibrium unemployment rate algebraically; eliminating W/P between equations (7.4) and (7.6) gives

$$F(u_n, z) = \frac{1}{1 + m} \tag{7.7}$$

The equilibrium unemployment rate, u_n, is such that the real wage chosen in wage setting—the left side of equation (7.7)—is equal to the real wage implied by price setting—the right side of equation (7.7).

The equilibrium unemployment rate u_n is called the **natural rate of unemployment** (which is why we have used the subscript *n* to denote it). The terminology has become standard, so we shall adopt it, but this is actually a bad choice of words. The word *natural* suggests a constant of nature, one that is unaffected by institutions and policy. As its derivation makes clear, however, the natural rate of unemployment is anything but natural. The positions of the wage-setting and price-setting curves, and thus the equilibrium unemployment rate, depend on both *z* and *m*. Consider two examples:

- ■ **An increase in unemployment benefits.** An increase in unemployment benefits can be represented by an increase in *z*. Because an increase in benefits makes the prospect of unemployment less painful, it increases the wage set by wage setters at a given unemployment rate. It shifts the wage-setting relation up, from *WS* to *WS'* in Figure 7-7. The economy moves along the *PS* line, from *A* to *A'*. The natural rate of unemployment increases from u_n to u_n'.

  In words: At a given unemployment rate, higher unemployment benefits lead to a higher real wage. A higher unemployment rate brings the real wage back to what firms are willing to pay.

- ■ **A less stringent enforcement of existing antitrust legislation.** To the extent that this allows firms to collude more easily and increase their market power, it will lead to an increase in their markup an increase in *m*. The increase in *m* implies a decrease in the real wage paid by firms, and so it shifts the price-setting relation down, from *PS* to *PS'* in Figure 7-8. The economy moves along *WS*. The equilibrium moves from *A* to *A'*, and the natural rate of unemployment increases from u_n to u_n'.

An increase in markups decreases the real wage and leads to an increase in the natural rate of unemployment. By letting firms increase their prices given the wage, less stringent enforcement of antitrust legislation leads to a decrease in the real wage. Higher unemployment is required to make workers accept this lower real wage, leading to an increase in the natural rate of unemployment.

Factors like the generosity of unemployment benefits or antitrust legislation can hardly be thought of as the result of nature. Rather, they reflect various characteristics

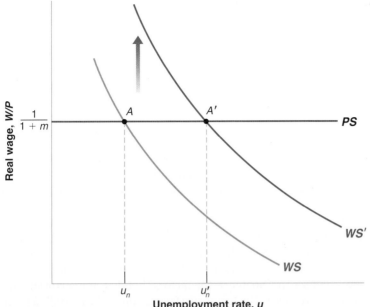

Figure 7-7

Unemployment Benefits and the Natural Rate of Unemployment

An increase in unemployment benefits leads to an increase in the natural rate of unemployment.

MyEconLab Animation

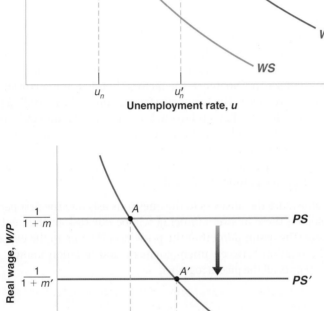

Figure 7-8

Markups and the Natural Rate of Unemployment

An increase in the markup leads to an increase in the natural rate of unemployment.

MyEconLab Animation

of the structure of the economy. For that reason, a better name for the equilibrium rate of unemployment would be the **structural rate of unemployment**, but so far the name has not caught on.

This name has been suggested by Edmund Phelps, from Columbia University. Phelps was awarded the Nobel Prize in 2006. For more on some of his contributions, see Chapters 8 and 24.

7-6 Where We Go from Here

We have just seen how equilibrium in the labor market determines the equilibrium unemployment rate (we have called it the *natural rate of unemployment*). Although we leave a precise derivation to Chapter 9, it is clear, for a given labor force, the unemployment rate determines the level of employment, and that, given the production function, the level of employment determines the level of output. Thus, associated with the natural rate of unemployment is a natural level of output.

So, you may (and, indeed, you should) ask, what did we do in the previous four chapters? If equilibrium in the labor market determines the unemployment rate and, by implication, determines the level of output, why did we spend so much time looking at the goods and financial markets? What about our previous conclusions that the level of output was determined by factors such as monetary policy, fiscal policy, consumer confidence, and so on—all factors that do not enter equation (7.8) and therefore do not affect the natural level of output?

The key to the answer lies in the difference between the *short run* and *the medium run*:

■ We have derived the natural rate of unemployment and, by implication, the associated level of output, under two assumptions. First, we have assumed equilibrium in the labor market. Second, we have assumed that the price level was equal to the expected price level.

In the short run, the factors that determine movements in output are the factors we focused on in the preceding four chapters: monetary policy, fiscal policy, and so on. ▷

MyEconLab Video

In the medium run, output tends to return to the natural level. The factors that determine unemployment and, by implication, output, are the factors we have focused on in this chapter.

■ However, there is no reason for the second assumption to be true in the *short run*. The price level may well turn out to be different from what was expected when nominal wages were set. Hence, in the short run, there is no reason for unemployment to be equal to the natural rate or for output to be equal to its natural level.

As we shall see in Chapter 9, the factors that determine movements in output *in the short run* are indeed the factors we focused on in the preceding three chapters: monetary policy, fiscal policy, and so on. Your time (and mine) was not wasted.

■ But expectations are unlikely to be systematically wrong (say, too high or too low) forever. That is why, in the medium run, output tends to return to its natural level. *In the medium run*, the factors that determine unemployment and output are the factors that appear in equations (7.7) and (7.8).

These, in short, are the answers to the questions asked in the first paragraph of this chapter. Developing these answers in detail will be our task in the next two chapters. Chapter 8 relaxes the assumption that the price level is equal to the expected price level and derives the relation between unemployment and inflation known as the Phillips curve. Chapter 9 puts all the pieces together.

Summary

■ The labor force consists of those who are working (employed) or looking for work (unemployed). The unemployment rate is equal to the ratio of the number of unemployed to the number in the labor force. The participation rate is equal to the ratio of the labor force to the working-age population.

■ The U.S. labor market is characterized by large flows between employment, unemployment, and "out of the labor force." On average, each month, about 44% of the unemployed move out of unemployment, either to take a job or to drop out of the labor force.

■ Unemployment is high in recessions and low in expansions. During periods of high unemployment, the probability of losing a job increases and the probability of finding a job decreases.

■ Wages are set unilaterally by firms or by bargaining between workers and firms. They depend negatively on the unemployment rate and positively on the expected price level. The reason why wages depend on the expected price level is that they are typically set in nominal terms for some period of time. During that time, even if the price level turns out to be different from what was expected, wages are typically not readjusted.

■ The price set by firms depends on the wage and on the markup of prices over wages. A higher markup implies a higher price given the wage, and thus a lower real wage.

■ Equilibrium in the labor market requires that the real wage chosen in wage setting be equal to the real wage implied by price setting. Under the additional assumption that the expected price level is equal to the actual price level, equilibrium in the labor market determines the unemployment rate. This unemployment rate is known as the *natural rate of unemployment*.

■ In general, the actual price level may turn out to be different from the price level expected by wage setters. Therefore, the unemployment rate need not be equal to the natural rate.

■ The coming chapters will show that, in the short run, unemployment and output are determined by the factors we focused on in the previous four chapters, but, in the medium run, unemployment tends to return to the natural rate, and output tends to return to its natural level.

Key Terms

non-institutional civilian population, 158
labor force, 158
out of the labor force, 158
participation rate, 158
unemployment rate, 158
separations, 158
hires, 158
Current Population Survey (CPS), 159
quits, 159
layoffs, 159
duration of unemployment, 159
discouraged workers, 160
employment rate, 160

collective bargaining, 163
reservation wage, 164
bargaining power, 164
efficiency wage theories, 165
unemployment insurance, 167
employment protection, 167
production function, 167
labor productivity, 167
markup, 168
wage-setting relation, 169
price-setting relation, 170
natural rate of unemployment, 170
structural rate of unemployment, 171

Questions and Problems

QUICK CHECK

MyEconLab Visit www.myeconlab.com to complete similar Quick Check problems and get instant feedback.

1. Using the information in this chapter, label each of the following statements true, false, or uncertain. Explain briefly.

a. Since 1950, the participation rate in the United States has remained roughly constant at 60%.

b. Each month, the flows into and out of employment are very small compared to the size of the labor force.

c. Fewer than 10% of all unemployed workers exit the unemployment pool each year.

d. The unemployment rate tends to be high in recessions and low in expansions.

e. Most workers are typically paid their reservation wage.

f. Workers who do not belong to unions have no bargaining power.

g. It may be in the best interest of employers to pay wages higher than their workers' reservation wage.

h. The natural rate of unemployment is unaffected by policy changes.

2. Answer the following questions using the information provided in this chapter.

a. As a percentage of employed workers, what is the size of the flows into and out of employment (i.e., hires and separations) each month?

b. As a percentage of unemployed workers, what is the size of the flows from unemployment into employment each month?

c. As a percentage of the unemployed, what is the size of total flows out of unemployment each month? What is the average duration of unemployment?

d. As a percentage of the labor force, what is the size of the total flows into and out of the labor force each month?

e. In the text we say that there is an average of 450,000 new workers entering the labor force each month. What percentage of total flows into the labor force do new workers entering the labor force constitute?

3. The natural rate of unemployment

   Suppose that the markup of the prices of products over wage cost, z, is 10%, and that the wage-setting equation is

$$W = P(1 - 2m + z)$$

   where m is the unemployment rate and z is the unemployment benefit/minimum wage.

a. What is the real wage, as determined by the price-setting equation?

b. Solve for the natural rate of unemployment

c. What happens to the natural rate of unemployment if z falls from 10% to 5%? Explain your answer.

DIG DEEPER

MyEconLab Visit www.myeconlab.com to complete all Dig Deeper problems and get instant feedback.

4. Reservation wages

   In the mid-1980s, a famous supermodel once said that she would not get out of bed for less than $10,000 (presumably per day).

a. What is your own reservation wage?

b. Did your first job pay more than your reservation wage at the time?

c. Relative to your reservation wage at the time you accept each job, which job pays more: your first one or the one you expect to have in 10 years?

d. Explain your answers to parts (a) through (c) in terms of the efficiency wage theory.

e. Part of the policy response to the crisis was to extend the length of time workers could receive unemployment benefits. How would this affect reservation wages if this change was made permanent?

5. *Bargaining power and wage determination*

Even in the absence of collective bargaining, workers do have some bargaining power that allows them to receive wages higher than their reservation wage. Each worker's bargaining power depends both on the nature of the job and on the economy-wide labor market conditions. Let's consider each factor in turn.

a. Compare the job of a delivery person and a computer network administrator. In which of these jobs does a worker have more bargaining power? Why?

b. For any given job, how do labor market conditions affect a worker's bargaining power? Which labor-market variable would you look at to assess labor-market conditions?

c. Suppose that for given labor-market conditions [the variable you identified in part (b)], worker bargaining power throughout the economy increases. What effect would this have on the real wage in the medium run? in the short run? What determines the real wage in the model described in this chapter?

6. *The existence of unemployment*

a. Consider Figure 7-6. Suppose the unemployment rate is very low. How does the low unemployment rate change the relative bargaining power of workers and firms? What do your answers imply about what happens to the wage as the unemployment rate gets very low?

b. Given your answer to part (a), why is there unemployment in the economy? (What would happen to real wages if the unemployment rate were equal to zero?)

7. *The informal labor market*

You learned in Chapter 2 that informal work at home (such as home-based unregistered cooks, baby sitters or garment workers working from home) is not counted as part of GDP. This constitutes the informal, shadow or the grey labor market. The World Bank reports that the size of the informal labor market varies from 4%–6% in the high-income countries to over 50%–75% in some low-income countries. Most developing nations and emerging market economies have a substantial informal or grey labor market comprising of subsistence agricultural jobs, street vendors, informally employed workers of formal enterprises, small-scale manufacturers or garbage recyclers. The informal sector does not usually count towards the official labor statistics. However, many attempts have been made to try to estimate the informal sector. This is because the reported formal employment and GDP figures would be substantially lower than the actual value of workers in the economy. This results in unreported earnings and tax evasion.

a. Go to the Web site of the International Labour Organization (ILO) (http://www.ilo.org) to define the informal economy and informal labor. What are the possible reasons behind the large informal employment levels in developing nations?

b. What are the main advantages and disadvantages of the informal labor sector? Why do you think some nations with high levels of informality endeavor to include the informal sector and informal employment in their official statistics?

c. Explain the method used by the ILO to estimate the level of informal employment. Detail all five steps used to produce the informal labor force.

d. Extract data from the database of the ILO on the informal employment (http://laborsta.ilo.org/informal_economy_E.html). Select a developing nation of your choice and compare against each of India and China. Prepare a table including the share of informal employment in total employment per economic activity. What is the economic sector with the highest level of informal employment for the three nations? What is the share of female workers in the total workforce and the informal work force for the three nations?

EXPLORE FURTHER

8. *Unemployment durations and long-term unemployment*

According to the data presented in this chapter, about 44% of unemployed workers leave unemployment each month.

a. Assume that the probability of leaving unemployment is the same for all unemployed, independent of how they have been unemployed. What is the probability that an unemployed worker will still be unemployed after one month? two months? six months?

Now consider the composition of the unemployment pool. We will use a simple experiment to determine the proportion of the unemployed who have been unemployed six months or more. Suppose the number of unemployed workers is constant and equal to x. Each month, 47% of the unemployed find jobs, and an equivalent number of previously employed workers become unemployed.

b. Consider the group of x workers who are unemployed this month. After a month, what percentage of this group will still be unemployed? (*Hint*: If 47% of unemployed workers find jobs every month, what percentage of the original x unemployed workers did not find jobs in the first month?)

c. After a second month, what percentage of the original x unemployed workers has been unemployed for at least two months? [*Hint*: Given your answer to part (b), what percentage of those unemployed for at least one month do not find jobs in the second month?] After the sixth month, what percentage of the original x unemployed workers has been unemployed for at least six months?

d. Using Table B-13 of the *Economic Report of the President* [this is the Table number as of the 2015 Report] you can compute the proportion of unemployed who have been unemployed six months or more (27 weeks or more) for each year between 2000 and 2014. How do the numbers between 2000 and 2008 (the pre-crisis years) compare with the answer you obtained in part (c)? Can you guess what may account for the difference between the actual numbers and the answer you obtained in this problem? (*Hint:* Suppose that the probability of exiting unemployment decreases the longer you are unemployed.)

e. What happens to the percentage of unemployed who have been unemployed 6 months or more during the crisis years 2009 to 2011?

f. Is there any evidence of the crisis ending when you look at the percentage of the unemployed who have been unemployed 6 months or more?

g. Part of the policy response to the crisis was an extension of the length of time that an unemployed worker could receive unemployment benefits. How do you predict this change would affect the proportion of those unemployed more than six months? Did this occur?

9. *Go to the Web site of the Office of National Statistics (https:// www.ons.gov.uk/), the United Kingdom's producer of official data and check the section "Employment and labor market."*

a. How does the Office of National Statistics define unemployment? How does this definition differ from that of the International Labour Organization?

b. What is the latest level of unemployment in the United Kingdom? What was the highest percentage change of unemployment in the United Kingdom during the last 10 years?

c. Does the sum of the level of employment and the level of unemployment in the United Kingdom add up to 100%? Explain your answer.

10. *The typical dynamics of unemployment over a recession*
   The table below shows the behavior of the annual growth rate of real GDP of the United Kingdom during four recession episodes:

the eighties, the nineties, the global financial crisis (2008–2010) and the European sovereign debt crisis (2010–2015).

Year	Real GDP Growth	Unemployment Rate
1982		
1984		
1992		
1993		
1994		
2008		
2009		
2011		
2012		

Download the time series from the Web site of the Office of National Statistics from the sections entitled "Gross Domestic Product: Quarter on Quarter growth: CVM SA %" and "Unemployment rate."

a. Explain whether the unemployment rate during each of these four recessions was higher during the year of declining output or the following year.

b. Go to the Web site of the U.K. government Services and Information (https://www.gov.uk/jobseekers-allowance/). What are terms and conditions of the unemployment benefits and the jobseeker's allowance in the United Kingdom?

c. How soon has the rate of unemployment started to decline after the each of the global financial crisis and the European Debt Crisis? Do you believe that these benefits could have discouraged workers from returning to the labor market as the economy started its recovery?

Further Reading

■ A further discussion of unemployment along the lines of this chapter is given by Richard Layard, Stephen Nickell, and Richard Jackman in *The Unemployment Crisis* (1994).

APPENDIX: Wage- and Price-Setting Relations versus Labor Supply and Labor Demand

If you have taken a microeconomics course, you probably saw a representation of labor-market equilibrium in terms of labor supply and labor demand. You may therefore be asking yourself: How does the representation in terms of wage setting and price setting relate to the representation of the labor market I saw in that course?

In an important sense, the two representations are similar.

To see why, let's redraw Figure 7-6 in terms of the real wage on the vertical axis, and the level of *employment* (rather

than the unemployment rate) on the horizontal axis. We do this in Figure 1.

Employment, N, is measured on the horizontal axis. The level of employment must be somewhere between zero and L, the labor force. Employment cannot exceed the number of people available for work (i.e., the labor force). For any employment level N, unemployment is given by $U = L - N$. Knowing this, we can measure unemployment by starting from L and *moving to the left* on the horizontal axis. Unemployment is given

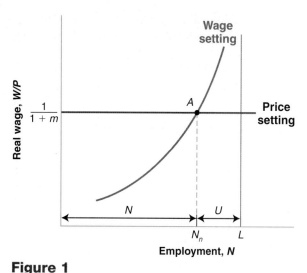

Figure 1

*Wage and Price Setting and the Natural Level
of Employment*

by the distance between L and N. The lower is employment, N, the higher is unemployment, and by implication the higher is the unemployment rate, U.

Let's now draw the wage-setting and price-setting relations and characterize the equilibrium.

- An increase in employment (a movement to the right along the horizontal axis) implies a decrease in unemployment and therefore an increase in the real wage chosen in wage setting. Thus, the wage-setting relation is now *upward sloping*. Higher employment implies a higher real wage.
- The price-setting relation is still a horizontal line at $W/P = 1/(1 + m)$.
- The equilibrium is given by point A, with "natural" employment level N_n (and an implied natural unemployment rate equal to $U_n = (L - N_n)/L$).

In this figure the wage-setting relation looks like a labor-supply relation. As the level of employment increases, the real wage paid to workers increases as well. For that reason, the wage-setting relation is sometimes called the "labor-supply" relation (in quotes).

What we have called the *price-setting relation* looks like a flat labor-demand relation. The reason it is flat rather than downward sloping has to do with our simplifying assumption of constant returns to labor in production. Had we assumed, more

conventionally, that there were decreasing returns to labor in production, our price-setting curve would, like the standard labor-demand curve, be downward sloping. As employment increased, the marginal cost of production would increase, forcing firms to increase their prices given the wages they pay. In other words, the real wage implied by price setting would decrease as employment increased.

But in a number of ways, the two approaches are different:

- The standard labor-supply relation gives the wage at which a given number of workers are willing to work. The higher the wage, the larger the number of workers who are willing to work.

  In contrast, the wage corresponding to a given level of employment in the wage-setting relation is the result of a process of bargaining between workers and firms or unilateral wage setting by firms. Factors like the structure of collective bargaining or the use of wages to deter quits affect the wage-setting relation. In the real world, they seem to play an important role. Yet they play no role in the standard labor-supply relation.

- The standard labor-demand relation gives the level of employment chosen by firms at a given real wage. It is derived under the assumption that firms operate in competitive goods and labor markets and therefore take wages and prices—and by implication the real wage—as given.

  In contrast, the price-setting relation takes into account the fact that in most markets firms actually set prices. Factors such as the degree of competition in the goods market affect the price-setting relation by affecting the markup. But these factors aren't considered in the standard labor-demand relation.

- In the labor supply-labor demand framework, those unemployed are *willingly unemployed*. At the equilibrium real wage, they prefer to be unemployed rather than work.

  In contrast, in the wage setting-price setting framework, unemployment is likely to be involuntary. For example, if firms pay an efficiency wage—a wage above the reservation wage—workers would rather be employed than unemployed. Yet, in equilibrium, there is still involuntary unemployment. This also seems to capture reality better than does the labor supply–labor demand framework.

These are the three reasons why we have relied on the wage-setting and the price-setting relations rather than on the labor supply–labor demand approach to characterize equilibrium in this chapter.

8

The Phillips Curve, the Natural Rate of Unemployment, and Inflation

I n 1958, A. W. Phillips drew a diagram plotting the rate of inflation against the rate of unemployment in the United Kingdom for each year from 1861 to 1957. He found clear evidence of a negative relation between inflation and unemployment. When unemployment was low, inflation was high, and when unemployment was high, inflation was low, often even negative.

Two years later, two U.S. economists, Paul Samuelson and Robert Solow replicated Phillips's exercise for the United States, using data from 1900 to 1960. Figure 8-1, on page 178, reproduces their findings using consumer price index (CPI) inflation as a measure of the inflation rate. Apart from the period of high unemployment during the 1930s (the years from 1931 to 1939 are denoted by triangles and are clearly to the right of the other points in the figure), there also appeared to be a negative relation between inflation and unemployment in the United States. This relation, which Samuelson and Solow labeled the **Phillips curve**, rapidly became central to macroeconomic thinking and policy. It appeared to imply that countries could choose between different combinations of unemployment and inflation. A country could achieve low unemployment if it were willing to tolerate higher inflation, or it could achieve price level stability—zero inflation—if it were willing to tolerate higher unemployment. Much of the discussion about macroeconomic policy became a discussion about which point to choose on the Phillips curve.

During the 1970s, however, this relation broke down. In the United States and most OECD countries, there was both high inflation *and* high unemployment, clearly contradicting the original Phillips curve. A relation reappeared, but it reappeared as a relation between the unemployment rate and the *change* in the inflation rate. The purpose of this chapter is to explore these mutations of the Phillips curve and, more generally, to understand the relation between inflation

◄ A. W. Phillips was a New Zealander who taught at the London School of Economics. He had, among other things, been a crocodile hunter in his youth. He also built a hydraulic machine to describe the behavior of the macroeconomy. A working version of the machine is still on display in Cambridge, England.

Figure 8-1

Inflation versus Unemployment in the United States, 1900–1960

During the period 1900–1960 in the United States, a low unemployment rate was typically associated with a high inflation rate, and a high unemployment rate was typically associated with a low or negative inflation rate.

Source: Historical Statistics of the United States. http://hsus.cambridge.org/HSUSWeb/index.do.

MyEconLab Animation

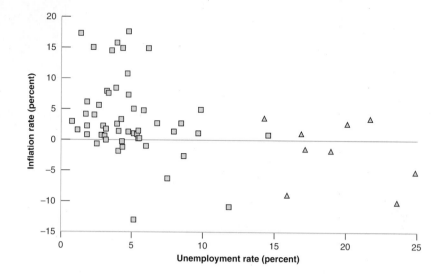

and unemployment. We shall derive the Phillips curve from the model of the labor market we saw in Chapter 7. And you will see how the mutations of the Phillips curve have come from changes in the way people and firms have formed expectations.

The chapter has four sections:

Section 8-1 shows how the model of the labor market we saw previously implies a relation between inflation, expected inflation, and unemployment.

Section 8-2 uses this relation to interpret the mutations of the Phillips curve over time.

Section 8-3 shows the relation between the Phillips curve and the natural rate of unemployment.

Section 8-4 further discusses the relation between unemployment and inflation across countries and over time. ●

8-1 Inflation, Expected Inflation, and Unemployment

In Chapter 7, we derived the following equation for wage determination (equation (7.1)):

$$W = P^e F(u, z)$$

The nominal wage W, set by wage setters, depends on the expected price level, P^e, on the unemployment rate, u, and on a variable, z, which captures all the other factors that affect wage determination, from unemployment benefits to the form of collective bargaining.

Also in Chapter 7, we derived the following equation for price determination (equation (6.3)):

$$P = (1 + m)W$$

The price, P, set by firms (equivalently, the price level) is equal to the nominal wage, W, times 1 plus the markup, m.

We then used these two relations together with the additional assumption that the actual price level was equal to the expected price level. Under this additional assumption, we then derived the natural rate of unemployment. We now explore what happens when we do not impose this additional assumption.

Replacing the nominal wage in the second equation by its expression from the first gives

$$P = P^e(1 + m) F(u, z)$$

An increase in the expected price level leads to an increase in nominal wages, which in turn leads firms to increase their prices, and thus leads to an increase in the price level. An increase in the unemployment rate leads to a decrease in nominal wages, which in turn leads to lower prices, and a decrease in the price level.

It will be convenient to assume a specific form for the function, F:

$$F(u, z) = 1 - \alpha u + z$$

This captures the notion that the higher the unemployment rate, the lower is the wage; and the higher z (e.g., the more generous unemployment benefits are), the higher is the wage. The parameter α (the Greek lowercase letter alpha) captures the strength of the effect of unemployment on the wage. Replacing the function, F, by this specific form in the equation above gives:

$$P = P^e(1 + m)(1 - \alpha u + z) \tag{8.1}$$

This gives us *a relation between the price level, the expected price level, and the unemployment rate.* Our next step is to derive *a relation between inflation, expected inflation, and the unemployment rate.* Let π denote the inflation rate, and π^e denote the expected inflation rate. Then equation (8.1) can be rewritten as:

◁ From now on, to lighten your reading, I shall often refer to the inflation rate simply as *inflation*, and to the unemployment rate simply as *unemployment*.

$$\pi = \pi^e + (m + z) - \alpha u \tag{8.2}$$

Deriving equation (8.2) from equation (8.1) is not difficult, but it is tedious; so it is left to an appendix at the end of this chapter. What is important is that you understand each of the effects at work in equation (8.2):

■ *An increase in expected inflation, π^e, leads to an increase in actual inflation, π.*

To see why, start from equation (8.1). An increase in the expected price level P^e leads, one for one, to an increase in the actual price level, P: If wage setters expect a higher price level, they set a higher nominal wage, which in turn to an increase in the price level.

Now note that, given last period's price level, a higher price level this period implies a higher rate of increase in the price level from last period to this period—that is, higher inflation. Similarly, given last period's price level, a higher expected price level this period implies a higher expected rate of increase in the price level from last period to this period—that is, higher expected inflation. Thus the fact that an increase in the expected price level leads to an increase in the actual price level can be restated as: An increase in expected inflation leads to an increase in inflation.

◁ Increase in $\pi^e \Rightarrow$ Increase in π.

■ *Given expected inflation, π^e, an increase in the markup, m, or an increase in the factors that affect wage determination—an increase in z—leads to an increase in actual inflation, π.*

From equation (8.1): Given the expected price level, P^e, an increase in either m or z increases the price level, P. Using the same argument as in the previous bullet to restate this proposition in terms of inflation and expected inflation: Given expected inflation, π^e, an increase in either m or z leads to an increase in inflation π.

◁ Increase in m or $z \rightarrow$ Increase in π.

■ *Given expected inflation, π^e, a decrease in the unemployment rate, u, leads to an increase in actual inflation π.*

From equation (8.1): Given the expected price level, P^e, a decrease in the unemployment rate, u, leads to a higher nominal wage, which leads to a higher price

Decrease in u → Increase in π. ▶

level, P. Restating this in terms of inflation and expected inflation: Given expected inflation, π^e, an increase in the unemployment rate, u, leads to an increase in inflation, π.

We need one more step before we return to a discussion of the Phillips curve. When we look at movements in inflation and unemployment in the rest of the chapter, it will often be convenient to use time indexes so that we can refer to variables such as inflation, expected inflation, or unemployment, in a specific year. So we rewrite equation (8.2) as:

$$\pi_t = \pi_t^e + (m + z) - \alpha u_t \qquad (8.3)$$

The variables π_t, π_t^e, and u_t refer to inflation, expected inflation, and unemployment in year t. Note that there are no time indexes on m and z. This is because although m and z may move over time, they are likely to move slowly, especially relative to movement in inflation and unemployment. Thus, for the moment, we shall treat them as constant.

Equipped with equation (8.3), we can now return to the Phillips curve, and its mutations.

8-2 The Phillips Curve and Its Mutations

Let's start with the relation between unemployment and inflation as it was first discovered by Phillips, Samuelson, and Solow.

The Early Incarnation

Assume that inflation varies from year to year around some value $\bar{\pi}$. Assume also that inflation is not persistent, so that inflation this year is not a good predictor of inflation next year. This happens to be a good characterization of the behavior of inflation over the period that Phillips, or Solow and Samuelson, were studying. In such an environment, it makes sense for wage setters to assume that, whatever inflation was last year, inflation this year will simply be equal to $\bar{\pi}$. In this case, $\pi_t^e = \bar{\pi}$ and equation (8.3) becomes:

$$\pi_t = \bar{\pi} + (m + z) - \alpha u_t \qquad (8.4)$$

In this case, we shall observe a negative relation between unemployment and inflation. This is precisely the negative relation between unemployment and inflation that Phillips found for the United Kingdom and Solow and Samuelson found for the United States. When unemployment was high, inflation was low, even sometimes negative. When unemployment was low, inflation was positive.

The Apparent Trade-Off and Its Disappearance

When these findings were published, they suggested that policy makers faced a trade-off between inflation and unemployment. If they were willing to accept more inflation, they could achieve lower unemployment. This looked like an attractive trade-off, and starting in the early 1960s, U.S. macroeconomic policy aimed at steadily decreasing unemployment. Figure 8-2 plots the combinations of the inflation rate and the unemployment rate in the United States for each year from 1961 to 1969. Note how well the relation between unemployment and inflation corresponding to equation (8.4) held during the long economic expansion that lasted throughout most of the 1960s. From 1961 to 1969, the unemployment rate declined steadily from 6.8 to 3.4%, and the inflation rate steadily increased, from 1.0 to 5.5%. Put informally, the U.S. economy moved up along the original Phillips curve. It indeed appeared that, if policy makers were willing to accept higher inflation, they could achieve lower unemployment.

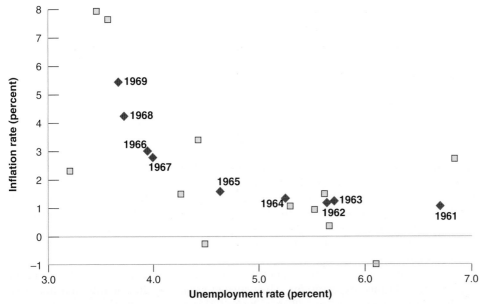

Figure 8-2

Inflation versus Unemployment in the United States, 1948–1969

The steady decline in the U.S. unemployment rate through-out the 1960s was associated with a steady increase in the inflation rate.

Source: Series UNRATE, CPIAUSCL Federal Reserve Economic Data (FRED) http://research.stlouisfed.org/fred2/.

MyEconLab Animation

Around 1970, however, the relation between the inflation rate and the unemployment rate, so visible in Figure 8-2, broke down. Figure 8-3 shows the combination of the inflation rate and the unemployment rate in the United States for each year from 1970 to today. The points are scattered in a roughly symmetric cloud. There is no longer any visible relation between the unemployment rate and the inflation rate.

Why did the original Phillips curve vanish? Because wage setters changed the way they formed their expectations about inflation.

MyEconLab Video

This change came, in turn, from a change in the behavior of inflation. The rate of inflation became more persistent. High inflation in one year became more likely to be followed by high inflation the next year. As a result, people, when forming expectations, started to take into account the persistence of inflation. In turn, this change in expectation formation changed the nature of the relation between unemployment and inflation.

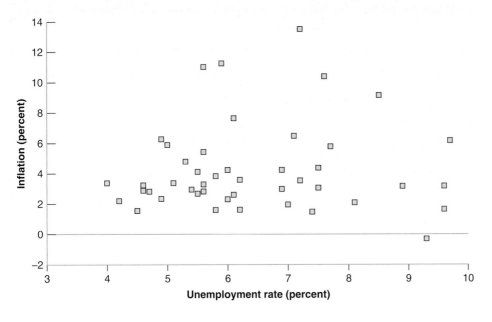

Figure 8-3

Inflation versus Unemployment in the United States, 1970–2014

Beginning in 1970 in the United States, the relation between the unemployment rate and the inflation rate disappeared.

Source: Series UNRATE, CPIAUSCL Federal Reserve Economic Data (FRED).

MyEconLab Animation
MyEconLab Real-time data

Let's look at the argument in the previous paragraph more closely. Suppose expectations of inflation are formed according to:

$$\pi_t^e = (1 - \theta)\bar{\pi} + \theta\pi_{t-1} \tag{8.5}$$

In words: Expected inflation this year depends partly on a constant value, $\bar{\pi}$, with weight, $1 - \theta$, and partly on inflation last year, which we denote by π_{t-1}, with weight, θ. The higher the value of θ, the more last year's inflation leads workers and firms to revise their expectations of what inflation will be this year, and so the higher is the expected inflation rate.

We can then think of what happened in the 1970s as an increase in the value of θ over time:

- So long as inflation was not persistent, it was reasonable for workers and firms to just ignore past inflation and to assume a constant value for inflation. For the period that Phillips and Samuelson and Solow had looked at, θ was close to zero, and expectations were roughly given by $\pi^e = \bar{\pi}$. The Phillips curve was given by equation (8.4).

- But as inflation became more persistent, workers and firms started changing the way they formed expectations. They started assuming that, if inflation had been high last year, inflation was likely to be high this year as well. The parameter θ, the effect of last year's inflation rate on this year's expected inflation rate, increased. The evidence suggests that, by the mid-1970s, people expected this year's inflation rate to be the same as last year's inflation rate—in other words, that θ was now equal to 1.

Now turn to the implications of different values of θ for the relation between inflation and unemployment. To do so, substitute equation (8.5) for the value of π_t^e into equation (8.2):

$$\pi_t = \overbrace{(1 - \theta)\bar{\pi} + \theta\pi_{t-1}}^{\pi^e} + (m + z) - \alpha u_t$$

- When θ equals zero, we get the original Phillips curve, a relation between the inflation rate and the unemployment rate:

$$\pi_t = \bar{\pi} + (m + z) - \alpha u_t$$

- When θ is positive, the inflation rate depends not only on the unemployment rate but also on last year's inflation rate:

$$\pi_t = [(1 - \theta)\bar{\pi} + (m + z)] + \theta\pi_{t-1} - \alpha u_t$$

- When θ equals 1, the relation becomes (moving last year's inflation rate to the left side of the equation)

$$\pi_t - \pi_{t-1} = (m + z) - \alpha u_t \tag{8.6}$$

So, when $\theta = 1$, the unemployment rate affects not *the inflation rate*, but rather the *change in the inflation rate*. High unemployment leads to decreasing inflation; low unemployment leads to increasing inflation.

This discussion is the key to what happened after 1970. As θ increased from 0 to 1, the simple relation between the unemployment rate and the inflation rate disappeared. This disappearance is what we saw in Figure 8-3. But a new relation emerged, this time between the unemployment rate and the change in the inflation rate, as predicted by equation (8.5). This relation is shown in Figure 8-4, which plots the change in the inflation rate versus the unemployment rate observed for each year since 1970, and shows a clear negative relation between the change in inflation and unemployment.

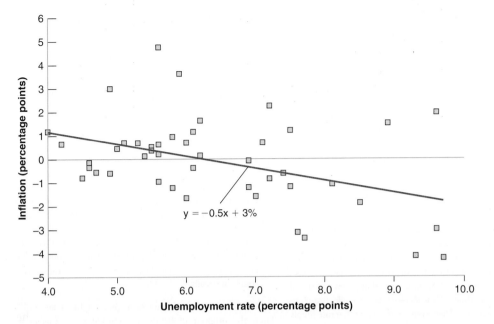

Since 1970, there has been a
negative relation between the
unemployment rate and the
change in the inflation rate in
the United States.

Series CPIAUCSL, UNRATE: Federal
Reserve Economic Data (FRED)
http://research.stlouisfed.org/fred2/.

MyEconLab Animation

MyEconLab Real-time data

The line that best fits the scatter of points for the period 1970–2014 is given by

$$\pi_t - \pi_{t-1} = 3.0\% - 0.5u_t \quad (8.7)$$

◀ This line, called a *regression
line*, is obtained using econometrics. (See Appendix 3 at
the end of the text.)

The line is drawn in Figure 8-4. For low unemployment, the change in inflation is positive. For high unemployment, the change in inflation is negative. To distinguish it from the original Phillips curve (equation (8.4)), equation (8.6)—or its empirical counterpart, equation (8.7)—is often called the **modified Phillips curve**, or the **expectations-augmented Phillips curve** (to indicate that π_{t-1} stands for expected inflation), or the **accelerationist Phillips curve** (to indicate that a low unemployment rate leads to an increase in the inflation rate and thus *an acceleration* of the price level). We shall simply call equation (8.7) the Phillips curve and refer to the previous incarnation, equation (8.4), as the *original* Phillips curve.

Original Phillips curve:
Increase in $u_t \Rightarrow$ Lower inflation.
(Modified) Phillips curve
◀ Increase in $u_t \Rightarrow$ Decreasing
inflation

Before we move on, one last observation. Although there is a clear negative relation between unemployment and the change in the inflation rate, you can see that the relation is far from tight. Some points are far from the regression line. The Phillips curve is both a crucial and a complex economic relation. It comes with plenty of warnings, which we shall discuss in Section 8-4. Before we do so, let's look at the relation of the Phillips curve to the concept of the natural rate of unemployment we derived in Chapter 7.

8-3 The Phillips Curve and the Natural Rate of Unemployment

The history of the Phillips curve is closely related to the discovery of the concept of the natural rate of unemployment that we introduced in Chapter 7.

The original Phillips curve implied that there was no such thing as a natural unemployment rate. If policy makers were willing to tolerate a higher inflation rate, they could maintain a lower unemployment rate forever. And, indeed, throughout the 1960s, it looked as though they were right.

Theory ahead of Facts: Milton Friedman and Edmund Phelps

Economists are usually not good at predicting major changes before they happen, and most of their insights are derived *after* the fact. Here is an exception.

In the late 1960s—precisely as the original Phillips curve relation was working like a charm—two economists, Milton Friedman and Edmund Phelps, argued that the appearance of a trade-off between inflation and unemployment was an illusion.

Here are a few quotes from Milton Friedman about the Phillips curve:

"Implicitly, Phillips wrote his article for a world in which everyone anticipated that nominal prices would be stable and in which this anticipation remained unshaken and immutable whatever happened to actual prices and wages. Suppose, by contrast, that everyone anticipates that prices will rise at a rate of more than 75% a year—as, for example, Brazilians did a few years ago. Then, wages must rise at that rate simply to keep real wages unchanged. An excess supply of labor [by this, Friedman means high unemployment] will be reflected in a less rapid rise in nominal wages than in anticipated prices, not in an absolute decline in wages."

He went on:

"To state [my] conclusion differently, there is always a temporary trade-off between inflation and unemployment; there is no permanent trade-off. The temporary trade-off comes not from inflation per se, but from a rising rate of inflation."

He then tried to guess how much longer the apparent trade-off between inflation and unemployment would last in the United States:

"But how long, you will say, is 'temporary'?... I can at most venture a personal judgment, based on some examination of the historical evidence, that the initial effect of a higher and unanticipated rate of inflation lasts for something like two to five years; that this initial effect then begins to be reversed; and that a full adjustment to the new rate of inflation takes as long for employment as for interest rates, say, a couple of decades."

Friedman could not have been more right. A few years later, the original Phillips curve started to disappear, in exactly the way Friedman had predicted.

Source: Milton Friedman, "The Role of Monetary Policy," *American Economic Review* 1968, 58(1): pp. 1–17. (The article by Phelps, "Money-Wage Dynamics and Labor-Market Equilibrium," *Journal of Political Economy* 1968, 76(4–part 2): pp. 678–711, made many of the same points more formally.)

Friedman was awarded the Nobel Prize in 1976. Phelps ▶ was awarded the Nobel Prize in 2006.

In the late 1960s however, although the original Phillips curve still gave a good description of the data, two economists, Milton Friedman and Edmund Phelps, questioned the existence of such a trade-off between unemployment and inflation. They questioned it on logical grounds, arguing that such a trade-off could exist only if wage setters systematically underpredicted inflation and that they were unlikely to make the same mistake forever. Friedman and Phelps also argued that if the government attempted to sustain lower unemployment by accepting higher inflation, the trade-off would ultimately disappear; the unemployment rate could not be sustained below a certain level, a level they called the *natural rate of unemployment*. Events proved them right, and the trade-off between the unemployment rate and the inflation rate indeed disappeared. (See the Focus box "Theory ahead of the Facts: Milton Friedman and Edmund Phelps.") Today, most economists accept the notion of a natural rate of unemployment, that is, subject to the many caveats we shall see in the next section.

Let's make explicit the connection between the Phillips curve and the natural rate of unemployment.

By definition (see Chapter 7), the natural rate of unemployment is the unemployment rate at which the actual price level is equal to the expected price level. Equivalently, and more conveniently here, the natural rate of unemployment is the unemployment rate such that the actual inflation rate is equal to the expected inflation rate. Denote the natural unemployment rate by u_n (the index n stands for "natural"). Then, imposing the condition that actual inflation and expected inflation be the same ($\pi = \pi^e$) in equation (8.3) gives:

$$0 = (m + z) - \alpha u_n$$

Solving for the natural rate u_n,

$$u_n = \frac{m + z}{\alpha} \qquad (8.8)$$

The higher the markup, m, or the higher the factors that affect wage setting, z, the higher the natural rate of unemployment.

Now rewrite equation (8.3) as

$$\pi_t - \pi_t^e = -\alpha \left(u_t - \frac{m + z}{\alpha} \right)$$

Note from equation (8.8) that the fraction on the right side is equal to u_n, so we can rewrite the equation as

$$\pi_t - \pi_t^e = -\alpha(u_t - u_n) \qquad (8.9)$$

If the expected rate of inflation, π^e, is well approximated by last year's inflation rate, π_{t-1}, the equation finally becomes

$$\pi_t - \pi_{t-1} = -\alpha(u_t - u_n) \qquad (8.10)$$

Equation (8.10) is an important relation, for two reasons:

- It gives us another way of thinking about the Phillips curve, as a relation between the actual unemployment rate u, the natural unemployment rate u_n, and the change in the inflation rate $\pi_t - \pi_{t-1}$.

  The change in the inflation rate depends on the difference between the actual and the natural unemployment rates. When the actual unemployment rate is higher than the natural unemployment rate, the inflation rate decreases; when the actual unemployment rate is lower than the natural unemployment rate, the inflation rate increases.

- It also gives us another way of thinking about the *natural rate of unemployment*:

  The natural rate of unemployment is the rate of unemployment required to keep the inflation rate constant. This is why the natural rate is also called the **nonaccelerating inflation rate of unemployment (NAIRU)**.

What has been the natural rate of unemployment in the United States since 1970? Put another way: What has been the unemployment rate that, on average, has led to constant inflation?

To answer this question, all we need to do is to return to equation (8.7), the estimated relation between the change in inflation and the unemployment rate since 1970. Setting the change in inflation equal to zero in the left of the equation implies a value for the natural unemployment rate of $3.0\%/0.5 = 6\%$. The evidence suggests that, since 1970 in the United States, the average rate of unemployment required to keep inflation constant has been equal to 6%.

Note that under our assumption that m and z are constant, the natural rate is also constant, so we can drop the time index. We shall return to a discussion of what happens if m and z change over time.

$u_t < u_n \Rightarrow \pi_t > \pi_{t-1}$
$u_t > u_n \Rightarrow \pi_t < \pi_{t-1}$

Calling the natural rate the *nonaccelerating inflation rate of unemployment* is actually wrong. It should be called the *nonincreasing inflation rate of unemployment*, or NIIRU. But NAIRU has now become so standard that it is too late to change it.

MyEconLab Video

8-4 A Summary and Many Warnings

Let's take stock of what we have learned:

- The relation between unemployment and inflation in the United States today is well captured by a relation between the change in the inflation rate and the deviation of the unemployment rate from the natural rate of unemployment (equation (8.10)).

- When the unemployment rate exceeds the natural rate of unemployment, the inflation rate typically decreases. When the unemployment rate is below the natural rate of unemployment, the inflation rate typically increases.

This relation has held quite well since 1970. But evidence from its earlier history, as well as the evidence from other countries, points to the need for a number of warnings. All of them are on the same theme. The relation between inflation and unemployment can and does vary across countries and time.

Variations in the Natural Rate across Countries

Recall from equation (8.8) that the natural rate of unemployment depends on all the factors that affect wage setting, represented by the catchall variable, z; the markup set by firms, m; and the response of inflation to unemployment, represented by α. If these factors differ across countries, there is no reason to expect all countries to have the same natural rate of unemployment. And natural rates indeed differ across countries, sometimes considerably.

Go back and look at Table ▶ 1-3 in Chapter 1.

Take, for example, the unemployment rate in the Euro area, which has averaged close to 9% since 1990. A high unemployment rate for a few years may well reflect a deviation of the unemployment rate from the natural rate. A high average unemployment rate for 25 years, together with no sustained decrease in inflation, surely reflects a high natural rate. This tells us where we should look for explanations, namely in the factors determining the wage-setting and the price-setting relations.

Is it easy to identify the relevant factors? One often hears the statement that one of the main problems of Europe is its **labor-market rigidities**. These rigidities, the argument goes, are responsible for its high unemployment. Although there is some truth to this statement, the reality is more complex. The Focus box, "What Explains European Unemployment?" discusses these issues further.

Variations in the Natural Rate over Time

In estimating equation (8.6), we implicitly treated $m + z$ as a constant. But there are good reasons to believe that m and z may vary over time. The degree of monopoly power of firms, the costs of inputs other than labor, the structure of wage bargaining, the system of unemployment benefits, and so on, are likely to change over time, leading to changes in either m or z and, by implication, changes in the natural rate of unemployment.

Changes in the natural unemployment rate over time are hard to measure. The reason is simply that we do not observe the natural rate, only the actual rate. But broad evolutions can be established by comparing average unemployment rates, say across decades. Using this approach, the Focus box "What Explains European Unemployment?" discusses how and why the natural rate of unemployment has increased in Europe since the 1960s. The U.S. natural rate has moved much less than that in Europe. Nevertheless, it is also far from constant. Go back and look at Figure 7-3. You can see that, from the 1950s to the 1980s, the unemployment rate fluctuated around a slowly increasing trend: Average unemployment was 4.5% in the 1950s, and 7.3% in the 1980s. Then, from 1990 on, and until the crisis, the trend was reversed, with an average unemployment rate of 5.8% in the 1990s, and an average unemployment rate of 5.0% from 2000 to 2007. In 2007, the unemployment rate was 4.6%, and inflation was roughly constant, suggesting that unemployment was

What Explains European Unemployment?

What do critics have in mind when they talk about the "labor-market rigidities" afflicting Europe? They have in mind in particular:

■ A generous system of unemployment insurance. The replacement rate—that is, the ratio of unemployment benefits to the after-tax wage—is often high in Europe, and the duration of benefits—the period of time for which the unemployed are entitled to receive benefits—often runs in years.

   Some unemployment insurance is clearly desirable. But generous benefits are likely to increase unemployment in at least two ways. They decrease the incentives the unemployed have to search for jobs. They may also increase the wage that firms have to pay. Recall our discussion of efficiency wages in Chapter 7. The higher unemployment benefits are, the higher the wages firms have to pay to motivate and keep workers.

■ A high degree of employment protection. By employment protection, economists have in mind the set of rules that increase the cost of layoffs for firms. These range from high severance payments, to the need for firms to justify layoffs, to the possibility for workers to appeal the decision and have it reversed.

   The purpose of employment protection is to decrease layoffs, and thus to protect workers from the risk of unemployment. It indeed does that. What it also does, however, is to increase the cost of labor for firms and thus to reduce hires and make it harder for the unemployed to get jobs. The evidence suggests that, although employment protection does not necessarily increase unemployment, it changes its nature. The flows in and out of unemployment decrease, but the average duration of unemployment increases. Such long durations increase the risk that the unemployed lose skills and morale, decreasing their employability.

■ Minimum wages. Most European countries have national minimum wages. And in some countries, the ratio of the minimum wage to the median wage can be quite high. High minimum wages clearly run the risk of limiting employment for the least-skilled workers, thus increasing their unemployment rate.

■ Bargaining rules. In most European countries, labor contracts are subject to **extension agreements**. A contract agreed to by a subset of firms and unions can be automatically extended to all firms in the sector. This considerably reinforces the bargaining power of unions because it reduces the scope for competition by nonunionized firms. As we saw in Chapter 7, stronger bargaining power on the part of the unions may result in higher unemployment. Higher unemployment is needed to reconcile the demands of workers with the wages paid by firms.

   Do these labor-market institutions really explain high unemployment in Europe? Is the case open and shut? Not quite. Here it is important to recall two important facts.

Fact 1: Unemployment was not always high in Europe. In the 1960s, the unemployment rate in the four major continental European countries was lower than that in the United States, around 2 to 3%. U.S. economists would cross the ocean to study the "European unemployment miracle"! The natural rate in these countries today is around 8 to 9%. How do we explain this increase?

One hypothesis is that institutions were different then, and that labor-market rigidities have only appeared in the last 40 years. This turns out not to be the case, however. It is true that, in response to the adverse shocks of the 1970s (in particular the two recessions following the increases in the price of oil), many European governments increased the generosity of unemployment insurance and the degree of employment protection. But even in the 1960s, European labor-market institutions looked nothing like U.S. labor-market institutions. Social protection was much higher in Europe; yet unemployment was lower.

A more convincing line of explanation focuses on the interaction between institutions and shocks. Some labor-market institutions may be benign in some environments, yet costly in others. Take employment protection. If competition between firms is limited, the need to adjust employment in each firm may be limited as well, and so the cost of employment protection may be low. But if competition, either from other domestic firms or from foreign firms, increases, the cost of employment protection may become high. Firms that cannot adjust their labor force quickly may simply be unable to compete and go out of business.

Fact 2: Prior to the start of the current crisis started, a number of European countries actually had low unemployment. This is shown in Figure 1, which gives the unemployment rate for 15 European countries (the 15 members of the European Union before the increase in membership to 27) in 2006. I chose 2006 because, in all these countries, inflation was stable, suggesting that the unemployment rate was roughly equal to the natural rate.

As you can see, the unemployment rate was indeed high in the four large continental countries: France, Spain, Germany, and Italy. But note how low the unemployment rate was in some of the other countries, in particular Denmark, Ireland, and the Netherlands.

Is it the case that these low unemployment countries had low benefits, low employment protection, and weak unions? Things are unfortunately not so simple. Countries such as Ireland or the United Kingdom indeed have labor-market institutions that resemble those of the United States: limited benefits, low employment protection, and weak unions. But countries such as Denmark or the Netherlands have a high degree of social protection (in particular high unemployment benefits) and strong unions.

So what is one to conclude? An emerging consensus among economists is that the devil is in the details. Generous social protection is consistent with low unemployment. But it has to be provided efficiently. For example, unemployment

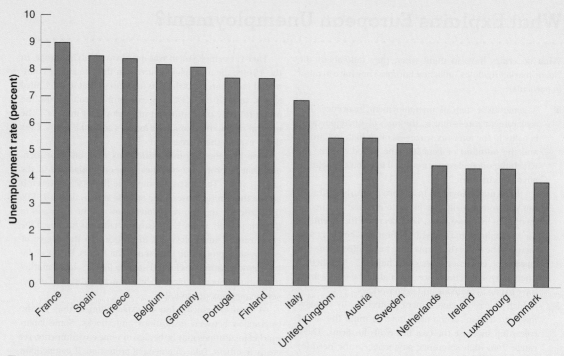

Figure 1   *Unemployment Rates in 15 European Countries, 2006*

benefits can be generous, so long as the unemployed are, at the same time, forced to take jobs if such jobs are available. Employment protection (e.g., in the form of generous severance payments) may be consistent with low unemployment, so long as firms do not face the prospect of long administrative or judicial uncertainty when they lay off workers. Countries such as Denmark appear to have been more successful in achieving these goals. Creating incentives for the unemployed to take jobs and simplifying the rules of employment protection are on the reform agenda of many European governments. One may hope they will lead to a decrease in the natural rate in the future.

For more on European unemployment, read Olivier Blanchard, "European Unemployment. The Evolution of Facts and Ideas," *Economic Policy*, 2006 (1): pp. 1–54.

More concretely, when inflation runs on average at 3% a year, wage setters can be reasonably confident inflation will be between 1 and 5%. When inflation runs on average at 30% a year, wage setters can be confident inflation will be between 20 and 40%. In the first case, the real wage may end up 2% higher or lower than they expected when they set the nominal wage. In the second case, it may end up 10% higher or lower than they ▶ expected. There is much more uncertainty in the second case.

close to the natural rate. In this context, the Focus box "Why Is the Natural Rate of Unemployment in Japan So Low?" looks at why Japan's official unemployment rate is much lower than those recorded in developed nations across the world.

High Inflation and the Phillips Curve Relation

Recall how, in the 1970s, the U.S. Phillips curve changed as inflation became more persistent and wage setters changed the way they formed inflation expectations. The lesson is a general one. The relation between unemployment and inflation is likely to change with the level and the persistence of inflation. Evidence from countries with high inflation confirms this lesson. Not only does the way workers and firms form their expectations change, but so do institutional arrangements.

When the inflation rate becomes high, inflation also tends to become more variable. As a result, workers and firms become more reluctant to enter into labor contracts that set nominal wages for a long period of time. If inflation turns out higher than expected, real wages may plunge and workers will suffer a large cut in their living standard. If

Why Is the Natural Rate of Unemployment in Japan So Low?

One of the questions puzzling economists is the fact that Japan's official unemployment rate is much lower than those recorded in its counterparts in developed nations. While the official unemployment rate in the 28 nations of the European Union (EU-28) was 8.9% in the first quarter of 2016, Japan's official unemployment rate was only 3.1% during the same period. Consequently the natural rate of unemployment in Japan is far below observed figures in other industrial nations. While the natural rate of unemployment in the United States was around 5.5% in 2015, Japan recorded a natural rate of unemployment of 2.25%. Yet, the low unemployment rate is not a sign of economic recovery from the long-lived Japanese economic contraction, but is reason for concern as it is indicative of a tight labor market. Labor shortages have prompted many Japanese housewives and retirees to enter the labor market, which raises questions about the capability of these re-entrants to keep up with technological advancements and managerial innovations. So why is Japan's unemployment rate so low when its growth rate has been so sluggish for the last two decades? Economic analysts and researchers have proposed a number of explanations.

- The bargaining power of Japanese trade unions is in decline. Every year the Japanese Trade Union Confederation (Rengo) and the independent Japanese trade unions engage in the *Shunto*, which is the springtime annual Japanese ritual of wage bargaining between business groups and labor unions. Higher wages are undoubtedly a means of boosting consumption expenditure and prompting the wage price spiral. Trade union membership in Japan has dropped substantially due to the rise in the number of temporary employees, who are ineligible to participate in labor unions. As we discussed earlier, weaker bargaining power on the part of the labor force would most likely cause lower unemployment. In the case of Japan, the inability of raising wages due to the weakening bargaining power of labor unions renders the expansionary fiscal and monetary policies less effectual.

- The Japanese seniority-based wage system (*nenkō joretsu*). This wage system has gone hand in hand with lifetime employment. While the seniority-based wage system underpays young workers, it rewards them well in later years awarding an increase in pay for each year of service. Accordingly, the seniority-based wage system offers workers a strong incentive to remain with their first employer, hence providing de facto lifetime employment. So that businesses could cut expenses, the seniority-wage system goes hand-in-hand with an early retirement age that forces Japanese employees to retire at the ages of 55 to 62. Early retirement allows younger generations the chance to acquire jobs, hence reducing unemployment levels.

- The shrinking population and high longevity in Japan. The childbearing level in Japan is among the lowest in the world, resulting in a decline of almost one million people of Japan's population every year. In addition, Japan has recorded the second highest longevity in the world. The combined effect is that for every retiree there are three working people in Japan.

- Japan's flexible remuneration system. The flexibility of the Japanese wage system partly explains the Japanese paradox of a recession and low unemployment. Unlike many other nations, the Japanese remuneration system is divided into low basic wages and high overtime pay and higher bonuses. This flexibility of the pay system allows Japanese businesses to retain workers as they further cut bonuses and overtime pay when the economy slumps. Yet, this is a double-edged sword. As workers take home a lower pay, it becomes more difficult for the Japanese economy to recover from its persistent deflationary slump.

- Sectoral factors. In addition to the high levels of employment provided by the manufacturing, technology, and service sectors Japan has a larger self-employed entrepreneurship sector. Moreover, employment in the agricultural sector makes up 3.7% of total employment which is much higher than the UK, Belgium, and Germany where employment in agriculture makes up only 1% of total employment in these nations. Certainly, this reduces the overall level of unemployment.

Since the aforementioned factors seem to be persistent, the low level of actual unemployment is apt to eventually translate into a lower natural unemployment rate. Therefore, it comes as no surprise that the expansionary fiscal and monetary policies during the last two decades were highly ineffective.

For more on the relationship between macroeconomic policies and natural unemployment rate, read: *Monetary Policy and Unemployment: The US, Euro-area and Japan* by Willi Semmler, Routledge International Studies in Money and Banking, 2005.

---

inflation turns out lower than expected, real wages may sharply increase. Firms may not be able to pay their workers. Some may go bankrupt.

For this reason, the terms of wage agreements change with the level of inflation. Nominal wages are set for shorter periods of time, down from a year to a month or even less. **Wage indexation**, which is a provision that automatically increases wages in line with inflation, becomes more prevalent.

These changes lead in turn to a stronger response of inflation to unemployment. To see this, an example based on wage indexation will help. Imagine an economy that has two types of labor contracts. A proportion λ (the Greek lowercase letter lambda) of labor contracts is indexed. Nominal wages in those contracts move one-for-one with variations in the actual price level. A proportion $1 - \lambda$ of labor contracts is not indexed. Nominal wages are set on the basis of expected inflation.

Under this assumption, equation (8.9) becomes

$$\pi_t = [\lambda \pi_t + (1 - \lambda)\pi_t^e] - \alpha(u_t - u_n)$$

The term in brackets on the right reflects the fact that a proportion λ of contracts is indexed and thus responds to actual inflation π_t, and a proportion, $1 - \lambda$, responds to expected inflation, π_t^e. If we assume that this year's expected inflation is equal to last year's actual inflation, $\pi_t^e = \pi_{t-1}$, we get

$$\pi_t = [\lambda \pi_t + (1 - \lambda)\pi_{t-1}] - \alpha(u_t - u_n) \qquad (8.11)$$

When $\lambda = 0$, all wages are set on the basis of expected inflation—which is equal to last year's inflation, π_{t-1}—and the equation reduces to equation (8.10):

$$\pi_t - \pi_{t-1} = -\alpha(u_t - u_n)$$

When λ is positive, however, a proportion λ of wages is set on the basis of actual inflation rather than expected inflation. To see what this implies, reorganize equation (8.11). Move the term in brackets to the left, factor $(1 - \lambda)$ on the left of the equation, and divide both sides by $1 - \lambda$ to get:

$$\pi_t - \pi_{t-1} = -\frac{\alpha}{(1 - \lambda)}(u_t - u_n)$$

Wage indexation increases the effect of unemployment on inflation. The higher the proportion of wage contracts that are indexed—the higher λ—the larger the effect the unemployment rate has on the change in inflation—the higher the coefficient $\alpha/(1 - \lambda)$.

The intuition is as follows: Without wage indexation, lower unemployment increases wages, which in turn increases prices. But because wages do not respond to prices right away, there is no further increase in prices within the year. With wage indexation, however, an increase in prices leads to a further increase in wages within the year, which leads to a further increase in prices, and so on, so that the effect of unemployment on inflation within the year is higher.

If, and when, λ gets close to 1—which is when most labor contracts allow for wage indexation—small changes in unemployment can lead to large changes in inflation. Put another way, there can be large changes in inflation with nearly no change in unemployment. This is what happens in countries where inflation is high. The relation between inflation and unemployment becomes more and more tenuous and eventually disappears altogether.

Deflation and the Phillips Curve Relation

We have just looked at what happens to the Phillips curve when inflation is high. Another issue is what happens when inflation is low, and possibly negative—when there is deflation.

The motivation for asking this question is given by an aspect of Figure 8-1 we mentioned at the start of the chapter but then left aside. In that figure, note how the points corresponding to the 1930s (they are denoted by triangles) lie to the right of the others. Not only is unemployment unusually high—this is no surprise because we are looking at the years corresponding to the Great Depression—but, *given the high unemployment rate*, the inflation rate is surprisingly high. In other words, given the high unemployment rate, we would have expected not merely deflation, but a large rate of deflation. In fact, deflation was limited, and from 1934 to 1937, despite still high unemployment, inflation actually turned positive.

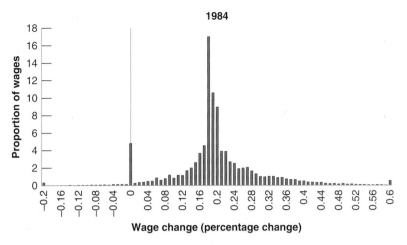

1984

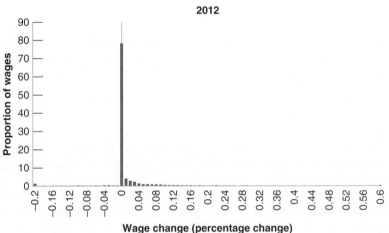

2012

Figure 8-5

Distribution of wage changes in Portugal, in times of high and low inflation

Source: Pedro Portugal, based on Portuguese household survey.

MyEconLab Animation

How do we interpret this fact? There are two potential explanations.

One is that the Great Depression was associated with an increase not only in the actual unemployment rate but also in the natural unemployment rate. This seems unlikely. Most economic historians see the Great Depression primarily as the result of a large adverse shift in aggregate demand leading to an increase in the actual unemployment rate over the natural rate of unemployment, rather than an increase in the natural rate of unemployment itself.

If u_n increases with u, then $u - u_n$ may remain small even if u is high.

The other is that, when the economy starts experiencing deflation, the Phillips curve relation breaks down. One possible reason is the reluctance of workers to accept decreases in their nominal wages. Workers will unwittingly accept a cut in their real wages that occurs when their nominal wages increase more slowly than inflation. However, they are likely to fight the same cut in their real wages if it results from an overt cut in their nominal wages. This mechanism is clearly at work in some countries. Figure 8-5 for example plots the distribution of wage changes in Portugal in two different years, 1984 when inflation rate was a high 27%, and in 2012, when the inflation rate was just 2.1%. Note how the distribution of wage changes is roughly symmetric in 1984, and how it is bunched at zero in 2012, with nearly no negative wage changes. To the extent that this mechanism is at work, this implies that the Phillips curve relation between the change in inflation and unemployment may disappear, or at least become weaker, when the economy is close to zero inflation.

Consider two scenarios. In one, inflation is 4%, and your nominal wage goes up by 2%. In the other, inflation is 0%, and your nominal wage is cut by 2%. Which do you dislike most? You should be indifferent between the two. In both cases, your real wage goes down by 2%. There is some evidence, however, that most people find the first scenario less painful, and thus suffer from *money illusion*, a term made more explicit in Chapter 24.

A decrease in θ would imply a return to a relation closer to equation (8.3), with a relation between the level of inflation and unemployment. This could explain why high unemployment has led to lower inflation, rather than steadily decreasing ▶ inflation.

When inflation is low, few workers accept a cut in nominal wages.

This issue is not just of historical interest. During the recent crisis, unemployment increased dramatically in many countries. One would have expected it to lead to a large decrease in inflation, indeed to substantial deflation. Yet, although a few countries experienced deflation, it has remained limited. In general, inflation has been higher than would have been predicted by estimated versions of equation (8.6) (estimated separately in each country). Whether this is due to the mechanism we just described, or whether it reflects a change in expectation formation (a decrease in θ) remains to be seen.

Summary

- Labor market equilibrium implies a relation between inflation, expected inflation, and unemployment. Given unemployment, higher expected inflation leads to higher inflation. Given expected inflation, higher unemployment leads to lower inflation.

- When inflation is not persistent, expected inflation does not depend on past inflation. Thus, the relation becomes a relation between inflation and unemployment. This is what Phillips in the United Kingdom and Solow and Samuelson in the United States discovered when they looked, in the late 1950s, at the joint behavior of unemployment and inflation.

- As inflation became more persistent starting in the 1960s, expectations of inflation became based more and more on past inflation. The relation became a relation between unemployment and the change in inflation. High unemployment led to decreasing inflation; low unemployment led to increasing inflation.

- The natural unemployment rate is the unemployment rate at which the inflation rate remains constant. When the actual unemployment rate exceeds the natural rate of unemployment, the inflation rate typically decreases; when the actual unemployment rate is less than the natural unemployment rate, the inflation rate typically increases.

- The natural rate of unemployment depends on many factors that differ across countries and can change over time. This is why the natural rate of unemployment varies across countries. It is higher in Europe than in the United States. Also, the natural unemployment rate varies over time. In Europe, the natural unemployment rate has greatly increased since the 1960s. In the United States, the natural unemployment rate increased from the 1960s to the 1980s and appears to have decreased since.

- Changes in the way the inflation rate varies over time affect the way wage setters form expectations and also affects how much they use wage indexation. When wage indexation is widespread, small changes in unemployment can lead to large changes in inflation. At high rates of inflation, the relation between inflation and unemployment disappears altogether.

- At very low or negative rates of inflation, the Phillips curve relation appears to become weaker. During the Great Depression even high unemployment led only to limited deflation. The issue is important because many countries have both high unemployment and low inflation today.

Key Terms

Phillips curve, 177
modified Phillips curve, 183
expectations-augmented Phillips curve, 183
accelerationist Phillips curve, 183

non-accelerating inflation rate of unemployment (NAIRU), 185
labor-market rigidities, 186
extension agreements, 187
wage indexation, 189

Questions and Problems   MyEconLab Real-time data exercises are marked 📊.

QUICK CHECK

MyEconLab Visit www.myeconlab.com to complete similar Quick Check problems and get instant feedback.

1. Using the information in this chapter, label each of the following statements true, false, or uncertain. Explain briefly.

a. The original Phillips curve is the negative relation between unemployment and inflation that was first observed in the United Kingdom.

b. The original Phillips curve relation has proven to be very stable across countries and over time.

c. For some periods of history, inflation has been very persistent between adjacent years. In other periods of history, this year's inflation has been a poor predictor of next year's inflation.

d. Policy makers can exploit the inflation–unemployment trade-off only temporarily.

e. Expected inflation always equals actual inflation.
f. In the late 1960s, the economists Milton Friedman and Edmund Phelps said that policy makers could achieve as low a rate of unemployment as they wanted.
g. If people assume that inflation will be the same as last year's inflation, the Phillips curve relation will be a relation between the change in the inflation rate and the unemployment rate.
h. The natural rate of unemployment is constant over time within a country.
i. The natural rate of unemployment is the same in all countries.
j. Deflation means that the rate of inflation is negative.

2. Discuss the following statements.
a. The Phillips curve implies that when an economy is operating below full capacity, a significant increase in aggregate demand is likely to cause a reduction in unemployment and an increase in inflation.
b. Monetary policy is quite important in determining the level of employment because the key connection or link between interest rate increases and lower price inflation is the pace at which wages are apt to increase during tight labor markets.
c. During the global financial crisis when the price level was negative, employers resisted cuts in wages and salaries.

3. The natural rate of unemployment
a. The Phillips curve is $\pi_t = \pi_t^e + (m + z) - \alpha u_t$.
Rewrite this relation as a relation between the deviation of the unemployment rate from the natural rate, inflation, and expected inflation.
b. In the previous chapter, we derived the natural rate of unemployment. What condition on the price level and the expected price level was imposed in that derivation? How does it relate to the condition imposed in part (a)?
c. How does the natural rate of unemployment vary with the markup?
d. How does the natural rate of unemployment vary with the catchall term z?
e. Identify two important sources of variation in the natural rate of unemployment across countries and across time.

4. The formation of expected inflation
The text proposes the following model of expected inflation
$$\pi_t^e = (1 - \theta)\pi + \theta\pi_t - 1$$
a. Describe the process of the formation of expected inflation when $\theta = 0$.
b. Describe the process of the formation of expected inflation when $\theta = 1$.
c. How do you form your own expectation of inflation? More like (a), or more like (b)?

5. Mutations of the Phillips curve
Suppose that the Phillips curve is given by
$$\pi_t = \pi_t^e + 0.1 - 2u_t$$

and expected inflation is given by
$$\pi_t^e = (1 - \theta)\bar{\pi} + \theta\pi_{t-1}$$
and suppose that θ is initially equal to 0 and $\bar{\pi}$ is given and does not change. It could be zero or any positive value. Suppose that the rate of unemployment is initially equal to the natural rate. In year t, the authorities decide to bring the unemployment rate down to 3% and hold it there forever.
a. Determine the rate of inflation in periods $t + 1, t + 2, t + 3, t + 4, t + 5$. How does $\bar{\pi}$ compare to pibar?
b. Do you believe the answer given in (a)? Why or why not? (Hint: Think about how people are more likely to form expectations of inflation.)
Now suppose that in year $t + 6$, θ increases from 0 to 1. Suppose that the government is still determined to keep u at 3% forever.
c. Why might θ increase in this way?
d. What will the inflation rate be in years $t + 6, t + 7$, and $t + 8$?
e. What happens to inflation when $\theta = 1$ and unemployment is kept below the natural rate of unemployment?
f. What happens to inflation when $\theta = 1$ and unemployment is kept at the natural rate of unemployment?

DIG DEEPER

MyEconLab Visit www.myeconlab.com to complete all Dig Deeper problems and get instant feedback.

6. The macroeconomic effects of the indexation of wages
Suppose that the Phillips curve is given by
$$\pi_t - \pi_t^e = 0.1 - 2u_t$$
where
$$\pi_t^e = \pi_{t-1}$$
Suppose that inflation in year $t - 1$ is zero. In year t, the central bank decides to keep the unemployment rate at 4% forever.
a. Compute the rate of inflation for years $t, t + 1, t + 2$, and $t + 3$.
Now suppose that half the workers have indexed labor contracts.
b. What is the new equation for the Phillips curve?
c. Based on your answer to part (b), recompute your answer to part (a).
d. What is the effect of wage indexation on the relation between π and u?

7. Estimating the natural rate of unemployment
To answer this question, you will need data on the annual French unemployment and inflation rates since 2000. Go to the English language Web site of the National Institute of Statistics and Economic Studies of France (http://www.insee.fr/en/default.asp) to retrieve and download the annual data for the unemployment rate and inflation rate for France under the title "statistical indices and series." Select the data for the consumer price index as a measure of the retail price levels.
a. Plot the unemployment and CPI data since 2000 to the present. Choose the unemployment on the horizontal axis

and the change in inflation on the vertical axis. What is the relationship between these two variables?

b. Draw a line of best fit for all points in the figure. Calculate the slope of the line and the intercept and then write down the equation for the line.

c. According to your analysis in (b), what has been the natural rate of unemployment since 2000?

8. *Changes in the natural rate of unemployment*

a. Repeat Problem 7, but now draw separate graphs for the period 2000 to 2008 and the period since 2008, which marks the global financial crisis.

b. Do you find that the relation between inflation and unemployment is different in the two periods? If so, how has the natural rate of unemployment changed after the global financial crisis?

EXPLORE FURTHER

9. *Using the natural rate of unemployment to predict changes in inflation*
   Suppose that the equation of the Phillips curve is

$$\pi_t - \pi_t - 1 = 4.0 - 0.32\theta t$$

Fill in the table below using the data collected in Question 7. You will need to use a spreadsheet.

a. Is the Phillips curve able to properly predict changes in the price level over the whole time period?

b. Was the Phillips curve able to predict changes in the price level during the global financial crisis years that lasted from 2007 till 2009? Explain your answer.

c. Assess the ability of the expectations augmented Phillips curve to predict inflation during each of the global financial crisis of 2007–2009 as well as the European sovereign crisis of 2010–2015.

Year	Inflation	Unemployment	Predicted change in inflation	Predicted change in inflation minus actual change in inflation
2000				
2001				
2002				
2003				
2004				
2005				
2006				
2007				
2008				
2009				
2010				
2011				
2012				
2013				
2014				
2015				
2016				
Future years				

10. *The rate of inflation and expected inflation in different decades*
    Fill in the values in the table below for inflation and expected inflation of your country during the 1980s. You need to use a spreadsheet once again.
    From the 1980's

Year	Actual inflation π_t	Lagged actual inflation π_{t-1}	Expected inflation under different assumptions π_t^e		Difference: expected minus actual inflation under different assumptions $\pi_t^e - \pi_t$	
Year			Assume $\theta = 0$ and $\pi = 0$	Assume $\theta = 0$	Assume $\theta = 0$ and $\pi = 0$	Assume $\theta = 0$
1980						
1981						
1982						
1983						
1984						
1985						
1986						
1987						
1988						
1989						

a. The textbook shows that the 1970s showed an inverse relationship between inflation and unemployment. Has this relationship between inflation and unemployment prevailed in the 1980s?

b. What is the best value for each of θ and π in the 1980s? Explain your answer.
   Fill in the values in the table below for inflation and expected inflation using the 1990s.

Year	Actual inflation π_t	Lagged actual inflation π_{t-1}	Expected inflation under different assumptions π_t^e		Difference: expected minus actual inflation under different assumptions $\pi_t^e - \pi_t$	
Year			Assume $\theta = 0$ and $\pi = 0$	Assume $\theta = 0$	Assume $\theta = 0$ and $\pi = 0$	Assume $\theta = 0$
1990						
1991						
1992						
1993						
1994						
1995						
1996						
1997						
1998						
1999						

c. Has the inverse relationship between inflation and unemployment relationship between inflation and unemployment prevailed in the 1990s??

d. What is the best value for each of θ and π in the 1990s? Explain your answer.

e. How do you compare the behavior of inflation, its average level and its persistence across the 1980s and 1990s?

APPENDIX: Derivation of the Relation to a Relation between Inflation, Expected Inflation, and Unemployment

This appendix shows how to go from the relation between the price level, the expected price level, and the unemployment rate given by equation (8.1),

$$P = P^e(1 + m)(1 - \alpha u + z)$$

to the relation between inflation, expected inflation, and the unemployment rate given by equation (8.2),

$$\pi = \pi^e + (m + z) - \alpha u$$

First, introduce time subscripts for the price level, the expected price level, and the unemployment rate, so P_t, P_t^e, and u_t refer to the price level, the expected price level, and the unemployment rate in year t. Equation (8.1) becomes

$$P_t = P_t^e(1 + m)(1 - \alpha u_t + z)$$

Next, go from an expression in terms of price levels to an expression in terms of inflation rates. Divide both sides by last year's price level, P_{t-1}:

$$\frac{P_t}{P_{t-1}} = \frac{P_t^e}{P_{t-1}}(1 + m)(1 - \alpha u_t + z) \qquad (8A.1)$$

Take the fraction P_t/P_{t-1} on the left side and rewrite it as

$$\frac{P_t}{P_{t-1}} = \frac{P_t - P_{t-1} + P_{t-1}}{P_{t-1}} = 1 + \frac{P_t - P_{t-1}}{P_{t-1}} = 1 + \pi_t$$

where the first equality follows from actually subtracting and adding P_{t-1} in the numerator of the fraction, the second equality follows from the fact that $P_{t-1}/P_{t-1} = 1$, and the third follows from the definition of the inflation rate ($\pi_t \equiv (P_t - P_{t-1})/P_{t-1}$).

Do the same for the fraction P_t^e/P_{t-1} on the right side, using the definition of the expected inflation rate ($\pi_t^e \equiv (P_t^e - P_{t-1})/P_{t-1}$):

$$\frac{P_t^e}{P_{t-1}} = \frac{P_t^e - P_{t-1} + P_{t-1}}{P_{t-1}} = 1 + \frac{P_t^e - P_{t-1}}{P_{t-1}} = 1 + \pi_t^e$$

Replacing P_t/P_{t-1} and P_t^e/P_{t-1} in equation (8A.1) by the expressions we have just derived,

$$(1 + \pi_t) = (1 + \pi_t^e)(1 + m)(1 - \alpha u_t + z)$$

This gives us a relation between inflation, π_t, expected inflation, π_t^e, and the unemployment rate, u_t. The remaining steps make the relation look more friendly.

Divide both sides by $(1 + \pi_t^e)(1 + m)$:

$$\frac{(1 + \pi_t)}{(1 + \pi_t^e)(1 + m)} = 1 - \alpha u_t + z$$

So long as inflation, expected inflation, and the markup are not too large, a good approximation to the left side of this equation is given by $1 + \pi_t - \pi_t^e - m$ (see Propositions 3 and 6 in Appendix 2 at the end of the book). Replacing in the previous equation and rearranging gives

$$\pi_t = \pi_t^e + (m + z) - \alpha u_t$$

Dropping the time indexes, this is equation (8.2) in the text. With the time indexes kept, this is equation (8.3) in the text.

The inflation rate, π_t, depends on the expected inflation rate π_t^e and the unemployment rate u_t. The relation also depends on the markup, m, on the factors that affect wage setting, z, and on the effect of the unemployment rate on wages, a.

9

From the Short to the Medium Run: The *IS-LM-PC* Model

I n Chapters 3 through 6, we looked at equilibrium in the goods and financial markets and saw how, in the short run, output is determined by demand. In Chapters 7 and 8, we looked at equilibrium in the labor market and derived how unemployment affects inflation. We now put the two parts together and use it to characterize the behavior of output, unemployment, and inflation, both in the short and the medium runs. When confronted with a macroeconomic question about a particular shock or a particular policy, this model, which we shall call the IS-LM-PC (PC for Phillips curve), is typically the model I use or I start from. I hope you find it as useful as I do.

The chapter is organized as follows.

Section 9-1 develops the IS-LM-PC model.

Section 9-2 looks at the dynamics of adjustment of output and inflation.

Section 9-3 looks at the dynamic effects of a fiscal consolidation.

Section 9-4 looks at the dynamic effects of an increase in the price of oil.

Section 9-5 concludes the chapter. ●

9-1 The IS-LM-PC model

In Chapter 6, we derived the following equation (equation 6.5) for the behavior of output in the short run:

$$Y = C(Y - T) + I(Y, r + x) + G \qquad (9.1)$$

In the short run, output is determined by demand. Demand is the sum of consumption, investment, and government spending. Consumption depends on disposable income, which is equal to income net of taxes. Investment depends on output and on the real borrowing rate; the real interest rate relevant to investment decisions is equal to the borrowing rate, the sum of real policy rate, r, chosen by the central bank, and a risk premium, x. Government spending is exogenous.

As we did in Chapter 6, we can draw the IS curve implied by equation (9.1) between output, Y, and the policy rate, r, for given taxes, T, risk premium x, and government spending G. This is done in the top half of Figure 9-1. The curve is downward sloping. The lower is real policy rate, r, given by the flat LM curve, the higher the equilibrium level of output. The mechanism behind the relation should be familiar by now: A lower policy rate increases investment. Higher investment leads to higher demand. Higher demand leads to higher output. The increase in output further increases consumption and investment, leading to a further increase in demand, and so on.

Now turn to the construction of the bottom half of Figure 9-1. In Chapter 8, we derived the following equation (equation 8.9) for the relation between inflation and unemployment, a relation we called the *Phillips curve*:

$$\pi - \pi^e = -\alpha(u - u_n) \qquad (9.2)$$

Figure 9-1

The IS-LM-PC Model

Top graph: A lower policy rate leads to higher output. Bottom graph: A higher output leads to a larger change in inflation.

MyEconLab Animation

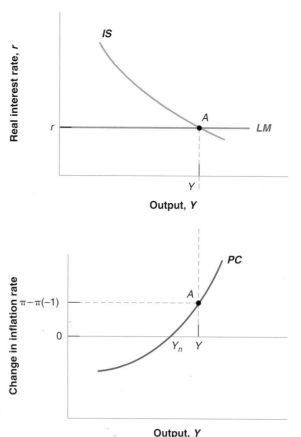

When the unemployment rate is lower than the natural rate, inflation turns out to be higher than expected. If the unemployment is higher than the natural rate, inflation turns out to be lower than expected.

Given that the first relation (equation (9.1)) is in terms of output, our first step must be to rewrite the Phillips curve in terms of output rather than unemployment. It is easy, but it takes a few steps. Start by looking at the relation between the unemployment rate and employment. By definition, the unemployment rate is equal to unemployment ◀ For a refresher, see Chapter 2. divided by the labor force:

$$u \equiv U/L = (L - N)/L = 1 - N/L$$

where N denotes employment and L denotes the labor force. The first equality is simply the definition of the unemployment rate. The second equality follows from the definition of unemployment, and the third equality is obtained through simplification. The unemployment rate is equal to one minus the ratio of employment to the labor force. Reorganizing to express N as a function of u gives:

$$N = L(1 - u)$$

Employment is equal to the labor force times one minus the unemployment rate. Turning to output, we shall maintain for the moment the simplifying assumption we made in Chapter 7, namely that output is simply equal to employment, so:

$$Y = N = L(1 - u)$$

where the second equality follows from the previous equation.

Thus, when the unemployment rate is equal to the natural rate, u_n, employment is given by $N_n = L(1 - u_n)$ and output is equal to $Y_n = L(1 - u_n)$. Call N_n the natural level of employment (natural employment for short), and Y_n the natural level of output (natural output for short). Y_n is also called **potential output** and I shall often use that expression in what follows.

It follows that we can express the deviation of employment from its natural level as:

$$Y - Y_n = L((1 - u) - (1 - u_n)) = -L(u - u_n)$$

This gives us a simple relation between the deviation of output from potential and the deviation of unemployment from its natural rate. The difference between output and potential output is called the **output gap**. If unemployment is equal to the natural rate, output is equal to potential, and the output gap is equal to zero; if unemployment is above the natural rate, output is below potential and the output gap is negative; and if unemployment is below the natural rate, output is above potential and the output gap is positive. (The relation of this equation to the actual relation between output and unemployment, known as Okun's law, is explored further in the Focus box, "Okun's Law across Time and Countries.")

Replacing $u - u_n$ in equation (9.2) gives:

$$\pi - \pi^e = (\alpha/L)(Y - Y_n) \tag{9.3}$$

We need to take one last step. We saw in Chapter 7 how the way wage setters form expectations has changed through time. We shall work in this chapter under the assumption that they assume inflation this year to be the same as last year. (I shall also discuss how results differ under alternative assumptions.) This assumption implies that ◀ the Phillips curve relation is given by:

To keep the notation light, instead of using time indexes in this chapter, I shall use (−1) to denote the value of a variable in the previous period. So, for example, $\pi(-1)$ denotes inflation last year.

$$\pi - \pi(-1) = (\alpha/L)(Y - Y_n) \tag{9.4}$$

In words: When output is above potential and therefore the output gap positive, inflation increases. When the output is below potential and therefore the output gap is

Okun's Law across Time and Countries

FOCUS

How does the relation between output and unemployment we have derived in the text relate to the empirical relation between the two, known as Okun's law, which we saw in Chapter 2?

To answer this question, we must first rewrite the relation in the text in a way which makes the comparison easy between the two. Before giving you the derivation, which takes a few steps, let me give you the bottom line. The relation between unemployment and output derived in the text can be rewritten as:

$$u - u(-1) \approx -g_Y \qquad (9B.1)$$

The change in the unemployment rate is approximately equal to the negative of the growth rate of output. (The symbol $\approx$ means approximately equal.)

Here is the derivation. Start from the relation between employment, the labor force, and the unemployment rate $N = L(1 - u)$. Write the same relation for the year before, assuming a constant labor force L, so $N(-1) = L(1 - u(-1))$. Put the two relations together to get:

$$N - N(-1) = L(1 - u) - L(1 - u(-1))$$
$$= -L(u - u(-1))$$

The change in employment is equal to minus the change in the unemployment rate, times the labor force. Divide both sides by $N(-1)$ to get

$$(N - N(-1))/N(-1) = -(L/N(-1))(u - u(-1))$$

Note that the expression on the left-hand side gives the rate of growth of employment, call it g_N. Given our assumption that output is proportional to employment, the rate of growth of output, call it g_Y, is simply equal to g_N. Note also that $L/N(-1)$ is a number close to one. If the unemployment rate is equal to 5% for example, then the ratio of the labor force to employment is 1.05. So, rounding it to one, we can rewrite the expression as:

$$g_Y \approx -(u - u(-1)),$$

Reorganizing gives us the equation we want:

$$u - u(-1) \approx -g_Y \qquad (9B.1)$$

Now turn to the actual relation between the change in the unemployment rate and output growth, which we saw in Figure 2-5 in Chapter 2, and is reproduced here as Figure 1. The regression line that fits the points best in Figure 1 is given by:

$$u - u(-1) = -0.4(g_Y - 3\%) \qquad (9B.2)$$

Like equation (9B.1), equation (9B.2) shows a negative relation between the change in unemployment and output growth. But it differs from equation (9B.1) in two ways.

- First, annual output growth has to be at least 3% to prevent the unemployment rate from rising. This is because of two factors we ignored in our derivation: Labor-force growth and labor-productivity growth. To maintain a constant unemployment rate, employment must grow at the same rate as the labor force. Suppose the labor force grows at 1.7% per year; then employment must grow at 1.7% per year. If, in addition, labor productivity

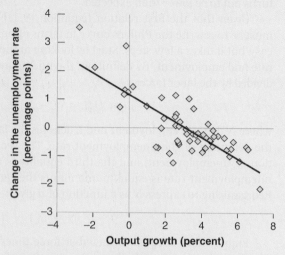

Figure 1 *Changes in the Unemployment Rate versus Output Growth in the United States, 1960–2014*

High output growth is associated with a reduction in the unemployment rate; low output growth is associated with an increase in the unemployment rate.

Source: Series GDPCA,GDPA: Federal Reserve Economic Data (FRED) http://research.stlouisfed.org/fred2/.

MyEconLab Real-time data

(i.e., output per worker) grows at 1.3% per year, this implies that output must grow at $1.7\% + 1.3\% = 3\%$ per year. In other words, just to maintain a constant unemployment rate, output growth must be equal to the sum of labor—force growth and labor—productivity growth. In the United States, the sum of the rate of labor—force growth and of labor—productivity growth has been equal to 3% per year on average since 1960, and this is why the number 3% appears on the right side of equation (9.2). (There is some evidence however, to which we shall come back to in later chapters, that productivity growth has declined in the last decade, and that the growth rate needed to maintain a constant unemployment rate is now closer to 2% than to 3%.)

- The coefficient on the right side of equation (9B.2) is -0.4, compared to -1.0 in equation (9B.1). Put another way, output growth 1% above normal leads only to a 0.4% reduction in the unemployment rate in equation (9B.2) rather than the 1% reduction in equation (9B.1). There are two reasons why:

    Firms adjust employment less than one for one in response to deviations of output growth from normal. More specifically, output growth 1% above normal for one year leads to only a 0.6% increase in the employment rate. One reason is that some workers are needed no matter what the level of output is. The accounting department of a firm, for example, needs roughly the same number of employees whether the firm is selling more or less than normal. Another reason is that training new employees is costly; for this reason, firms prefer to keep current workers rather than lay them off when output is lower than normal and ask them to work overtime rather than hire new employees when output is higher than normal. In bad times, firms in effect hoard labor, the labor they will need when times are better; this is why this behavior of firms is called **labor hoarding**.

An increase in the employment rate does not lead to a one-for-one decrease in the unemployment rate. More specifically, a 0.6% increase in the employment rate leads to only a 0.4% decrease in the unemployment rate. The reason is that labor force participation increases. When employment increases, not all the new jobs are filled by the unemployed. Some of the jobs go to people who were classified as *out of the labor force*, meaning they were not actively looking for a job.

Also, as labor-market prospects improve for the unemployed, some discouraged workers, who were previously classified as out of the labor force, decide to start actively looking for a job and become classified as unemployed. For both reasons, unemployment decreases less than employment increases.

Putting the two steps together: Unemployment responds less than one for one to movements in employment, which itself responds less than one for one to movements in output. The coefficient giving the effect of output growth on the change in the unemployment rate, here 0.4, is called the **Okun coefficient**. Given the factors which determine this coefficient, one would expect the coefficient to differ across countries and indeed it does. For example in Japan, which has a tradition of lifetime employment, firms to adjust employment much less in response to movements in output, leading to an Okun coefficient of only 0.1. Fluctuations in output are associated with much smaller fluctuations in unemployment in Japan than in the United States.

For more on Okun's law across countries and time, read "Okun's law: Fit at 50?" by Laurence Ball, Daniel Leigh, and Prakash Loungani, working paper 606, The Johns Hopkins University, 2012.

negative, inflation decreases. The positive relation between output and the change in inflation is drawn as the upward sloping curve in the bottom half of Figure 9-1. Output is measured on the horizontal axis, the change in inflation is measured on the vertical axis. When output is equal to potential, equivalently when the output gap is equal to zero, the change in inflation is equal to zero. Thus, the Phillips curve crosses the horizontal axis at the point where output is equal to potential.

We now have the two equations we need to describe what happens in the short and the medium run. This is what we do in the next section.

9-2 Dynamics and the Medium Run Equilibrium

Let's return to Figure 9-1. Suppose that the policy rate chosen by the central bank is equal to r. The top part of the figure tells us that, associated with this interest rate, the level of output is given by Y. The bottom part of the figure tells us that this level of output Y implies a change in inflation equal to $(\pi - \pi(-1))$. Given the way we have drawn the figure, Y is larger than Y_n, so output is above potential. This implies that inflation is increasing. Put less formally, the economy is overheating, putting pressure on inflation. This is the *short-run equilibrium*.

What happens over time if there is no change in the policy rate, nor in any of the variables which affect the position of the IS curve? Then output remains above potential, and inflation keeps increasing. At some point however, policy is likely to react to this increase in inflation. If we focus on the central bank, sooner or later the central bank will increase the policy rate so as to decrease output back to potential and there is no longer pressure on inflation. The adjustment process and the medium run equilibrium are represented in Figure 9-2. Let the initial equilibrium be denoted by point A in both the top and bottom graph. You can think of the central bank as increasing the policy rate over time, so the economy moves along the IS curve up from A to A'. Output decreases. Now turn to the bottom graph. As output decreases, the economy moves down the PC curve from A to A'. At point A', the policy rate is equal to r_n, output is equal to Y_n, and by implication, inflation is constant. This is the *medium-run equilibrium*. Output is equal to

PC curve is a bit repetitive because the *C* stands for *curve* already. But it will do.

Figure 9-2

Medium-Run Output and Inflation

Over the medium run, the economy converges to the natural level of output and stable inflation.

MyEconLab Animation

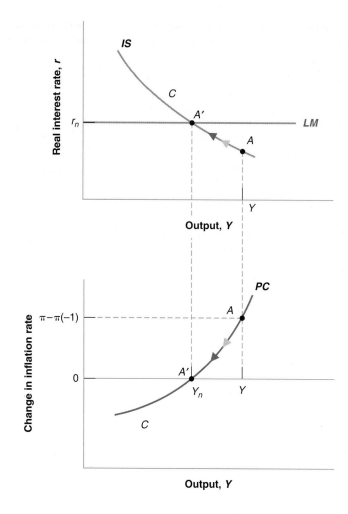

► potential, and, as a result, there is no longer any pressure on inflation. The interest rate r_n associated with Y_n is often the **natural rate of interest** (to reflect the fact that it is associated with the natural rate of unemployment, or the natural level of output); it is also sometimes called the **neutral rate of interest**, or the **Wicksellian rate of interest** (coming from the fact that the concept was first introduced by Wicksell, a Swedish economist who characterized it at the end of the 19th century).

Let's look at the dynamics and at the medium-run equilibrium more closely.

You may (and indeed you should) have the following reaction to the description of the dynamics. If the central bank wants to achieve stable inflation and keep output at Y_n, why doesn't it increase the policy rate to r_n right away, so that the medium run equilibrium is reached without delay? The answer is that the central bank would indeed like to keep the economy at Y_n. But, although it looks easy to do in Figure 9-2, reality is more complicated. The reasons parallel the discussion we had in Chapter 3 about the adjustment of the economy over time. First, it is often difficult for the central bank to know where potential output is exactly, and thus how far output is from potential. The change in inflation provides a signal of the output gap, the distance between actual and potential output, but in contrast to the simple equation (9.4), the signal is noisy. The central bank may thus want to adjust the policy rate slowly and see what happens. Second, it takes time for the economy to respond. Firms take time to adjust their investment decisions. As investment spending slows down in response to the higher policy rate, leading to lower demand, lower output, and lower income, it takes time for consumers to adjust

At the time of writing, this is an issue facing the Fed. The unemployment rate is down to 5.0%, and inflation is roughly constant. How close unemployment is to the natural rate is the subject of much discussion and disagreement.

to the decrease in income, and for firms to adjust to the decrease in sales. In short, so even if the central bank acts quickly, it takes time for the economy to go back to the natural level of output.

The fact that it takes time for output to go back to its natural level raises an issue about inflation. During the process of adjustment, output is consistently above potential, thus inflation is consistently increasing. Thus, when the economy reaches point A′, inflation is higher than it was at point A. If the central bank cares not only about stable inflation, but about the level of inflation, it may well decide that it has to not only stabilize but also reduce inflation. To do this, it needs to increase the policy rate beyond r_n to generate a decrease in inflation, until inflation is back to a level acceptable to the central bank. In this case, the adjustment is more complex. The economy moves up from A and passes A′, reaching for example point C, at which stage the central bank starts decreasing the policy rate back to r_n. In other words, if the central bank wants to achieve a constant level of inflation over the medium run, then the initial boom must be followed by a recession.

The Role of Expectations Revisited

The previous discussion depends on the way people form expectations, and on the specific form of the Phillips curve. To see this, return to our discussion of expectation formation in Chapter 8, and instead of assuming that expected inflation is equal to last year's inflation, $\pi(-1)$, assume instead that people think that inflation will be equal to some constant, $\bar{\pi}$, irrespective of what inflation was last year.

In this case, equation (9.3) becomes:

$$\pi - \bar{\pi} = (\alpha/L)(Y - Y_n) \qquad (9.5)$$

MyEconLab Video

To see what happens in this case, we can still use Figure 9-2, except for the fact that what is measured on the vertical axis of the bottom graph is $\pi - \bar{\pi}$ rather than $\pi - \pi(-1)$. A positive output gap generates *a higher level of inflation* rather than *an increase in inflation*. Now suppose that the economy is at point A, with associated level of output Y. Given that output is above potential, inflation is higher than expected inflation: $\pi - \bar{\pi} > 0$. As the central bank increases the policy rate to decrease output to its natural level, and the economy moves along the IS curve from A to A′. When the economy is at A′ and the policy rate is equal to r_n, output is back to potential, and inflation is back to $\bar{\pi}$. The difference with the previous case is clear. To return inflation to $\bar{\pi}$, there is no need in this case for the central bank to increase the rate beyond r_n for some time, as was the case before. Thus, the central bank has an easier job. So long as inflation **expectations** remain **anchored** (to use the term used by central banks), it does not need to compensate for the initial boom by a recession later.

The Zero Lower Bound and Debt Spirals

Our description of the adjustment has made the adjustment to the medium-run equilibrium look relatively easy. If output is too high, the central bank increases the policy rate until output is back up to potential. If output is too low, the central bank decreases the policy rate until output is back up to potential. This is however too optimistic a picture and things can go wrong. The reason is the combination of the zero lower bound and deflation.

In Figure 9-2, we considered the case where output was above potential, and inflation was increasing. Consider instead the case, represented in Figure 9-3, where the economy is in a recession. At the current policy rate r, output is equal to Y, which is far below Y_n. The output gap is negative, and inflation is decreasing. This initial equilibrium is represented by point A, in the top and the bottom graphs.

Figure 9-3

The Deflation Spiral

If the zero lower bound prevents monetary policy from increasing output back to potential, the result may be a deflation spiral. More deflation leads to a higher real policy rate, and the higher policy rate in turn leads to lower output and more deflation.

MyEconLab Animation

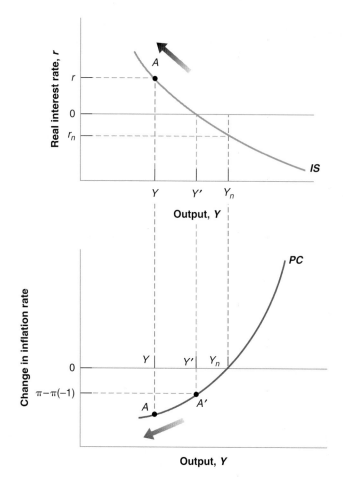

Recall that a negative real policy rate does not necessarily imply that people and firms, who borrow at a real rate equal to $r + x$ also face a ▶ negative real rate. If x is sufficiently large, the real rate at which they can borrow is positive even if the real policy rate is negative.

What the central bank should do in this case appears straightforward. It should decrease the policy rate until output has increased back to its natural level. In terms of Figure 9-3, it should decrease the policy rate from r down to r_n. At r_n, output is equal to Y_n, and inflation is stable again. Note that, if the economy is sufficiently depressed, the real policy rate, r_n, needed to return output to its natural level may be negative, and this is indeed how I have drawn it in the figure.

The zero lower bound constraint may however make it impossible to achieve this negative real policy rate. Suppose for example that initial inflation is zero. Because of the zero lower bound, the lowest the central bank can decrease the nominal policy rate is 0%, which, combined with zero inflation, implies a real policy rate of 0%. In terms of Figure 9-3, the central bank can decrease the real policy rate only down to 0%, with associated level of output Y'. At Y', output is still below potential, and thus inflation is still decreasing. This starts what economists call a **deflation spiral**, or a **deflation trap**. Let's continue to assume that inflation expectations are such that wage setters expect inflation to be the same as last year, so a negative output gap implies decreasing inflation. If inflation was equal to zero to start with, it becomes negative. Zero inflation turns into deflation. In turn, this implies that even if the nominal rate remains equal to zero, the real policy rate increases, leading to even lower demand and lower output. Deflation and low output feed on each other. Lower output leads to more deflation, and more deflation leads to a higher real interest rate and lower output. As indicated by the arrows in Figure 9-3, instead of converging to the medium-run equilibrium, the economy moves away from it, with output steadily decreasing and

Deflation in the Great Depression

FOCUS

After the collapse of the stock market in 1929, the U.S. economy plunged into an economic depression. As the first two columns of Table 1 show, the unemployment rate increased from 3.2% in 1929 to 24.9% in 1933, and output growth was strongly negative for four years in a row. From 1933 on, the economy recovered slowly, but by 1940, the unemployment rate was still a high 14.6%.

The Great Depression has many elements in common with the recent crisis. A large increase in asset prices before the crash—housing prices in the recent crisis, stock market prices in the Great Depression, and the amplification of the shock through the banking system. There are also important differences. As you can see by comparing the output growth and unemployment numbers in Table 1 to the numbers for the recent crisis in Chapter 1, the decrease in output and the increase in unemployment were much larger then than they have been in the recent crisis. In this box, we shall focus on just one aspect of the Great Depression: the evolution of the nominal and the real interest rates and the dangers of deflation.

As you can see in the third column of the table, monetary policy decreased the nominal rate, measured in the table by the one-year T-bill rate, although it did this slowly and did not quite go all the way to zero. The nominal rate decreased from 5.3% in 1929 to 2.6% in 1933. At the same time, as shown in the fourth column, the decline in output and the increase in unemployment led to a sharp decrease in inflation. Inflation, equal to zero 1929, turned negative in 1930, reaching −9.2% in 1931, and −10.8% in 1932. If we make the assumption that expected deflation was equal to actual deflation in each year, we can construct a series for the real rate. This is done in the last column of the table and gives a hint for why output continued to decline until 1933. The real rate reached 12.3% in 1931, 14.8% in 1932, and still a high 7.8% in 1933! It is no great surprise that, at those interest rates, both consumption and investment demand remained very low, and the depression worsened.

In 1933, the economy seemed to be in a deflation trap, with low activity leading to more deflation, a higher real interest rate, lower spending, and so on. Starting in 1934, however, deflation gave way to inflation, leading to a large decrease in the real interest rate, and the economy began to recover. Why, despite a high unemployment rate, the U.S. economy was able to avoid further deflation remains a hotly debated issue in economics. Some point to a change in monetary policy, a large increase in the money supply, leading to a change in inflation expectations. Others point to the policies of the New Deal, in particular the establishment of a minimum wage, thus limiting further wage decreases. Whatever the reason, this was the end of the deflation trap and the beginning of a long recovery.

For more on the Great Depression:

Lester Chandler, *America's Greatest Depression* (1970), gives the basic facts. So does the book by John A. Garraty, *The Great Depression* (1986).

Did Monetary Forces Cause the Great Depression? (1976), by Peter Temin, looks more specifically at the macroeconomic issues. So do the articles in a symposium on the Great Depression in the *Journal of Economic Perspectives*, Spring 1993.

For a look at the Great Depression in countries other than the United States, read Peter Temin's *Lessons from the Great Depression* (1989).

Table 1 The Nominal Interest Rate, Inflation, and the Real Interest Rate, 1929–1933

Year	Unemployment Rate (%)	Output Growth Rate (%)	One-Year Nominal Interest Rate (%), i	Inflation Rate (%), π	One-Year Real Interest Rate (%), r
1929	3.2	−9.8	5.3	0.0	5.3
1930	8.7	−7.6	4.4	−2.5	6.9
1931	15.9	−14.7	3.1	−9.2	12.3
1932	23.6	−1.8	4.0	−10.8	14.8
1933	24.9	9.1	2.6	−5.2	7.8

deflation steadily becoming larger. There is little the central bank can do, and the economy goes from bad to worse.

This scenario is not just a theoretical concern. This is very much the scenario which played out during the Great Depression. As shown in the Focus box "Deflation in the Great Depression," from 1929 to 1933, inflation turned into larger and larger deflation, steadily increasing the real policy rate and decreasing spending and output, until other measures were taken and the economy started turning around. The recent crisis gave rise to similar worries. With the policy rate down to zero in the major advanced countries, the worry was that inflation would turn negative and start a similar spiral. This did not happen. Inflation decreased and in some countries turned to deflation. As we saw in Chapter 6, this limited the ability of the central banks to decrease the real policy rate and increase output. But deflation remained limited, and the deflation spiral did not happen. One reason, which connects to our previous discussion of expectation formation, is that inflation expectations remained largely anchored. As a result, the Phillips curve relation took the form of equation (9.5) rather than (9.4). Low output led to low inflation, and in some cases, mild deflation, but not to steadily larger deflation, as had been the case during the Great Depression.

9-3 Fiscal Consolidation Revisited

We can now take the IS-LM-PC model through its paces. In this section, we go back to the fiscal consolidation we discussed in Chapter 5. We can now look not only at its short-run effects but at its medium-run effects as well.

Suppose that output is at potential, so the economy is at point A in both the top and the bottom graphs of Figure 9-4. Output Y is equal to Y_n, the policy rate is equal to r_n, and inflation is stable. Now, assume that the government, which was running a deficit, decides to reduce it by, say, increasing taxes. In terms of Figure 9-4, the increase in taxes shifts the IS curve to the left, from IS to IS'. The new short-run equilibrium is given by point A' in both the top and bottom graphs of Figure 9-4. At the given policy rate r_n, output decreases from Y_n to Y', and inflation starts decreasing. In other words, if output was at potential to start with, the fiscal consolidation, as desirable as it may be on other grounds, leads to a recession. This is the short-run equilibrium we characterized in Section 5-3 of Chapter 5. Note that, as income comes down and taxes increase, consumption decreases on both counts. Note also that, as output decreases, so does investment. In the short run, on macroeconomic grounds, fiscal consolidation looks rather unappealing: Both consumption and investment go down.

Let's however turn to the dynamics and to the medium run. As output is too low, and inflation is decreasing, the central bank is likely to react and decrease the policy rate until output is back to potential. In terms of Figure 9-4, the economy moves down the IS curve in the top graph, and output increases. As output increases, the economy moves up the PC curve in the bottom graph, until output is back to potential. Thus, the medium-run equilibrium is given by point A″ in both the top and bottom graph. Output is back at Y_n, and inflation is again stable. The policy rate needed to maintain output at potential is now lower than before, equal to r_n' rather than r_n. Now look at the composition of output in this new equilibrium. As income is the same as it was before fiscal consolidation but taxes are higher, consumption is lower, although not as low as it was in the short run. As output is the same as before but the interest rate is lower, investment is higher than before. In other words, the decrease in consumption is offset by an increase in investment, so demand, and by implication, is unchanged. This is in sharp contrast to what happened in the short run and makes fiscal consolidation look more attractive. Although consolidation may decrease investment in the short run, it increases investment in the medium run.

This discussion raises some of the same issues we discussed in the previous section. First, it looks as if fiscal consolidation could take place without a decrease in output in the short run. All that is needed is for the central bank and the government to coordinate carefully. As fiscal consolidation takes place, the central bank should decrease the policy rate so as to maintain output at the natural level. In other words, the proper combination

We have looked at a fiscal consolidation, equivalently at an increase in public saving. The same argument would apply to an increase in private saving. At a given policy rate, such an increase would lead to a decrease investment in the short run, but to an increase in investment in the medium run. ▶ (In the light of these results, you may want to go back to the Focus boxes on "The Paradox of Saving" in Chapter 3, and on "Deficit Reduction: Good or Bad for Investment," in Chapter 5.)

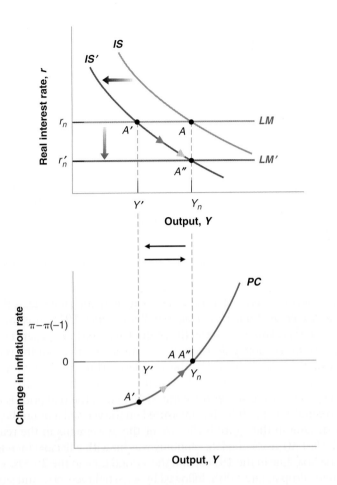

Figure 9-4

*Fiscal Consolidation
in the Short and the
Medium Run*

Fiscal consolidation leads to a
decrease in output in the short
run. In the medium run, output
returns to potential, and the
interest rate is lower.

MyEconLab Animation

of fiscal and monetary policy can achieve the medium-run equilibrium outcome in the
short run. Such coordination indeed happens sometimes; as we saw in Chapter 5, it
happened in the United States in the 1990s, when a fiscal consolidation was accompanied with a monetary expansion. But it does not always happen. One reason is that the
central bank may be unable to decrease the policy rate sufficiently. This takes us back to
another issue we discussed previously, the zero lower bound. The central bank may have
limited room to decrease the policy rate. This indeed has been the case in the Euro area in
the recent crisis. With the nominal policy rate at zero in the Euro area, monetary policy
was unable to offset the adverse effects of fiscal consolidation on output. The result was
a stronger and longer lasting adverse effect of fiscal consolidation on output than would
have been the case, had the European Central Bank been able to decrease the policy rate
further.

9-4 The Effects of an Increase in the Price of Oil

So far we have looked at shocks to demand, shocks that shifted the IS curve, but left
potential output and thus the position of the PC curve unaffected. There are other
shocks however that affect both demand and potential output and play an important
role in fluctuations. An obvious candidate is movements in the price of oil. To see why,
turn to Figure 9-5.

Figure 9-5

The Nominal and the Real Price of Oil, 1970–2015

Over the last 40 years, there have been two sharp increases in the real price of oil, the first in the 1970s and the second in the 2000s.

Source: Series OILPRICE, CPIAUSCL Federal Reserve Economic Data (FRED) http://research.stlouisfed.org/fred2/. The value of the index is set equal to 100 in 1970.

MyEconLab Real-time data

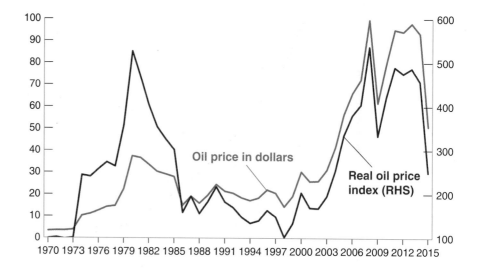

Figure 9-5 plots two series. The first, represented by the blue line, is the dollar price of oil—that is, the price of a barrel of oil in dollars—since 1970. It is measured on the vertical axis on the left. This is the series that is quoted in the newspapers every day. What matters, however, for economic decisions is not the dollar price, but the real price of oil; that is, the dollar price of oil divided by the price level. Thus, the second series in the figure, represented by the red line, shows the real price of oil, constructed as the dollar price of oil divided by the U.S. consumer price index. Note that the real price is an index; it is normalized to equal 100 in 1970. It is measured on the vertical axis on the right.

What is striking in the figure is the size of the movements in the real price of oil. Twice over the last 40 years, the U.S. economy was hit with a fivefold increase in the real price of oil, the first time in the 1970s, and the second time in the 2000s. The crisis then led to a dramatic drop in late 2008, followed by a partial recovery. And since 2014, the price has again dropped to pre-2000 levels.

What was behind the two large increases? In the 1970s, the main factors were the formation of **OPEC** (the **Organization of Petroleum Exporting Countries**), a cartel of oil producers that was able to act as a monopoly and increase prices, and disruptions because of wars and revolutions in the Middle East. In the 2000s, the main factor was quite different, namely the fast growth of emerging economies, in particular China, which led to a rapid increase in the world demand for oil and, by implication, a steady increase in real oil prices.

What was behind the two large decreases? The sudden drop in the price at the end of the 2008 was as a result of the crisis, which led to a large recession, and in turn to a large and sudden decrease in the demand for oil. The causes of the more recent drop since 2014 are still being debated. Most observers believe that it is a combination of increased supply because of the increase in shale oil production in the United States and the partial breakdown of the OPEC cartel.

Let's focus on the two large increases. Although the causes were different, the implication for U.S. firms and consumers was the same: more expensive oil. The question is: What would we expect the short- and medium-run effects of such increases to be? It is clear however that, in answering the question, we face a problem. The price of oil appears nowhere in the model we have developed so far! The reason is that, until now, we have assumed that output was produced using only labor. One way to extend our model would be to recognize explicitly that output is produced using labor *and* other inputs (including energy), and then figure out what effect an increase in the price of oil has on the price set by firms and on the relation between output and employment. An easier

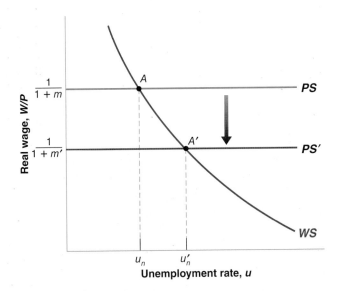

Figure 9-6

The Effects of an Increase in the Price of Oil on the Natural Rate of Unemployment

An increase in the price of oil is equivalent to an increase in the markup. It leads to lower real wages and a higher natural rate of unemployment.

MyEconLab Animation

way, and the way we shall go here, is simply to capture the increase in the price of oil by an increase in m—the markup of the price over the nominal wage. The justification is straightforward. Given wages, an increase in the price of oil increases the cost of production, forcing firms to increase prices to maintain the same profit rate.

Having made this assumption, we can then track the dynamic effects of an *increase in the markup* on output and inflation.

Effects on the Natural Rate of Unemployment

Let's start by asking what happens to the natural rate of unemployment when the real price of oil increases (for simplicity, I shall drop "real" in what follows). Figure 9-6 reproduces the characterization of labor-market equilibrium from Figure 7-8 in Chapter 7.

The wage-setting relation is downward sloping; a higher unemployment rate leads to lower real wages. The price-setting relation is represented by the horizontal line at $W/P = 1/(1 + m)$. The initial equilibrium is at point A, and the initial natural unemployment rate is u_n. An increase in the markup leads to a downward shift of the price-setting line, from PS to PS'. The higher the markup, the lower the real wage implied by price setting. The equilibrium moves from A to A'. The real wage is lower and the natural unemployment rate is higher. Think of it this way: Because firms have to pay more for the oil, the wage they can pay is lower. Getting workers to accept the lower real wage requires an increase in unemployment.

The increase in the natural rate of unemployment leads in turn to a decrease in the natural level of employment. If we assume that the relation between employment and output is unchanged—that is, that each unit of output still requires one worker in addition to the energy input—then the decrease in the natural level of employment leads to an identical decrease in potential output. Putting things together: An increase in the price of oil leads to a decrease in potential output.

We can now go back to the IS-LM-PC model, and this is done in Figure 9-7. Assume the initial equilibrium is at point A in both the top and bottom panels, with output at potential, so Y is equal to Y_n, inflation is stable, and the policy rate is equal to r_n. As the price of oil increases, the natural level of output decreases (this is what we just saw), say from Y_n to Y'_n. The PC curve shifts up, from PC to PC'. If the IS curve does not shift (we return to this assumption later) and the central bank does not change the policy rate, output does not change, but the same level of output is now associated with higher

This assumes that the increase in the price of oil is permanent. ◄ If, in the medium run, the price of oil goes back to its initial value, then the natural rate of unemployment is clearly unaffected.

Figure 9-7

Short and Medium Run Effects of an Increase in the Price of Oil

MyEconLab Animation

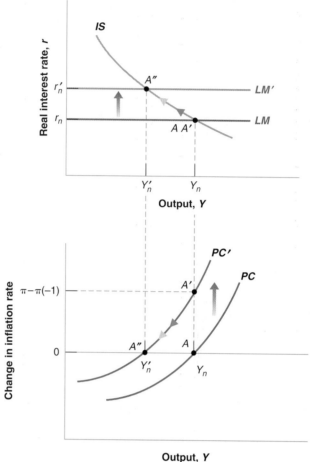

inflation. For given wages, the price of oil leads firms to increase their prices, so inflation is higher. The short-run equilibrium is given by point A′ in the top and bottom panels. In the short run, output does not change, but inflation is higher.

Turn to the dynamics. If the central bank were to leave the policy rate unchanged, output would continue to exceed the now lower level of potential output, and inflation would keep increasing. Thus, at some point, the central bank will increase the policy rate to stabilize inflation. As it does so, the economy moves up from A′ to A″ along the IS curve in the top panel, and down from A′ to A″ along the PC curve in the bottom panel. As output decreases to its lower level, inflation continues to increase, although more and more slowly until eventually it becomes stable again. Once the economy is at point A″, the economy is in its medium-run equilibrium. Because potential output is lower, the increase in the price of oil is reflected in a permanently lower level of output. Note that along the way, lower output is associated with higher inflation, a combination that economists call **stagflation** (stag for stagnation, and flation for inflation).

As in the previous sections, this description raises a number of issues. The first is our assumption that the IS curve does not shift. In fact, there are many channels through which the increase in the price of oil may affect demand and shift the IS curve. The higher price of oil may lead firms to change their investment plans, canceling some investment projects, shifting to less energy-intensive equipment. The increase in the price of oil also redistributes income from oil buyers to oil producers. Oil producers may spend less than oil buyers, leading to a decrease in demand. So it may well be that the IS

This is especially true if the oil producers are located in other countries than the oil buyers (which is the case when the United States buys oil from the Middle East for example). As the price increases and their income increases, the oil producers are likely to spend most of it on their own goods, not on the goods produced by the oil buyers. Thus, demand for domestic goods is likely to go down.

Plummeting Oil Price and Consumer Price Expectations

FOCUS

During the last 40 years, episodes of oil price fluctuations have coincided with substantial instabilities in economic activity, inflation, and employment levels. The plunge in oil prices from over $100 per barrel to less than $50 per barrel since mid-2014 has been driven by a number of factors: weakening global demand; OPEC's renouncement of support of oil prices; and the expansion of oil supply from unconventional sources such as shale oil in the United States. Some may conclude that this oil price decline would cause consumer prices to fall, unemployment to ease and economic growth to rise. However, the long-term impact of oil price fluctuations on macroeconomic activity has substantially declined. As shown in Figure 1, inflation expectations appear to correlate with oil prices more in the short-run than in the long-run. So why is it that oil price fluctuations now show some short-term macroeconomic impact but have little effect on the economy in the long run?

The first explanation is that oil-related products are increasingly making up a smaller share of production and consumption. Many advanced and emerging economies have launched a number of supply-side initiatives by expanding investments in alternative and renewable energy, improving the efficiency of energy use, enhancing the energy performance of buildings, reducing the energy usage of vehicles and appliances, and increasing the effectiveness of power and heat generation. Moreover, awareness campaigns and energy labeling for domestic appliances and vehicles have rendered consumers energy savvy. This has led to a substantial decline in the usage of oil for production, consumption, and transportation, which are the three major end-users of oil. Substantial energy savings were made in most Eastern European economies, whereby the amount of energy required to produce a unit of economic output (as measured by GDP) was reduced by around 25.0 %.

Secondly, in tandem with supply-side policies and the reduction in energy demand, various economies are attempting to decouple oil prices from economic growth. Central banks are using monetary policy and inflation rate targeting to offset oil shocks on CPI and macroeconomic growth. On the other hand, governments dilute the deflationary impacts of falling oil prices by adjusting currencies, taxes, and subsidies as well as by regulating prices.

A third reason behind the low correlation between oil prices and consumer prices is the downward real wage rigidity. A key reason behind wage rigidities is the reluctance of employers to cut salaries and wages during periods of deflation or recessions, especially for talented labor.

As much as the impact of oil is declining, tumbling oil prices are apt to have mixed implications on the global economy. Even though declining oil prices would support global consumer prices and macroeconomic activity, oil-exporting countries may come under stress as falling oil revenues could put fiscal budgets and exchange rates under pressure and deteriorate growth prospects. Moreover, fluctuating oil prices may increase the volatility in financial and currency markets, hence affecting capital flows. Investment in the oil industry may fall sharply, impacting growth in oil exporting and extracting countries. On the flipside, falling oil prices would likely reduce the prices of the energy-intensive agricultural products, therefore benefiting the poor.

Global economies should take advantage of lower oil prices to introduce structural reforms. Oil-importing economies could release fuel subsidies to rebuild fiscal space and to strengthen infrastructure and human capital investments. Oil-exporting economies need to intensify efforts to diversify economic activity away from oil-extraction.

Figure 1 *Inflation Expectations*

Source: Zsolt Darvas and Pia Hüttl "Oil Prices and Inflation Expectations," *Bruegel | The Brussels-Based Economic Think Tank*, January 21, 2016.

curve shifts to the left, leading to a decrease in output not only in the medium run, but in the short run as well.

A second issue has to do with the evolution of inflation. Note that, until output decreases to its new lower potential level, inflation continues to increase. Thus, when the economy reaches point A″, inflation is higher than it was before the increase in the price of oil. If the central bank wants to return inflation to its initial level, it must decrease output below potential for some time to decrease inflation. In this case, the decrease in output along the adjustment process will exceed the medium-run decrease for some time. Put more simply, the economy may go through a large recession, with only a partial recovery.

MyEconLab Video

The third issue is related to the second and again has to do with the formation of inflation expectations. Suppose that instead of assuming that inflation will be equal to last year's inflation, wage setters expect inflation to be constant. In this case, as we have seen, output above potential leads to high rather than increasing inflation. Then, as output declines to its lower potential level, inflation declines as well. When the economy reaches point A″, inflation is back to where it was before the increase in the price of oil. There is no need for the central bank to further decrease output to decrease inflation. This again shows the importance of expectation formation on the dynamic effects of shocks. It also helps explain the difference between the effect of the price of oil in the 1970s, which led to high inflation and a large recession, with the effects of the price of oil in the 2000s, which was much more benign. The Focus box "Plummeting Oil Price and Consumer Price Expectations" explores fluctuations in oil prices in relation to consumer expectations.

9-5 Conclusions

This chapter has covered a lot of ground. Let us repeat some key ideas and develop some of the conclusions.

The Short Run versus the Medium Run

One key message of this chapter is that shocks or changes in policy typically have different effects in the short run and in the medium run. Disagreements among economists about the effects of various policies often come from differences in the time frame they have in mind. If you are worried about output and investment in the short run, you might be reluctant to proceed with fiscal consolidation. But if your focus is on the medium and long run, you will see the consolidation as helping investment and eventually, through higher investment and thus capital accumulation, increasing output. One implication is that where you stand depends in particular on how fast you think the economy adjusts to shocks. If you believe that it takes a long time for output to return to potential you will naturally focus more on the short run and be willing to use policies that increase output in the short run, even if medium-run effects are nil or negative. If you believe instead that output returns to potential quickly, you will put more emphasis on the medium-run implications and will, by implication, be more reluctant to use those policies.

Shocks and Propagation Mechanisms

This chapter also gives you a general way of thinking about **output fluctuations** (sometimes called **business cycles**)—movements in output around its trend (a trend that we have ignored so far but on which we will focus in Chapters 10 through 13).

You can think of the economy as being constantly hit by **shocks**. These shocks may be shifts in consumption coming from changes in consumer confidence, shifts in investment, and so on. Or they may come from changes in policy—from the introduction of a new tax law, to a new program of infrastructure investment, to a decision by the ▶ central bank to fight inflation.

Each shock has dynamic effects on output and its components. These dynamic effects are called the **propagation mechanism** of the shock. Propagation mechanisms are different for different shocks. The effects of a shock on activity may build up over time, affecting output in the medium run. Or the effects may build up for a while and then decrease and disappear. At times, some shocks are sufficiently large or come in sufficiently bad combinations that they create a recession. The two recessions of the 1970s were due largely to increases in the price of oil; the recession of the early 1980s was due to a sharp contraction in money; the recession of the early 1990s was due primarily to a sudden decline in consumer confidence; the recession of 2001 was due to a sharp drop in investment spending. The recent crisis and the sharp decrease in output in 2009 had its origins in the problems of the housing market, which then led to a major financial shock, and in turn to a sharp reduction in output. What we call *economic fluctuations* are the result of these shocks and their dynamic effects on output. Typically, the economy returns over time to its medium-run equilibrium. But, as we have seen when discussing for example the interaction between the zero lower bound and deflation, things can get quite bad for some time.

How to define *shocks* is harder than it looks. Suppose a failed economic program in an Eastern European country leads to political chaos in that country, which leads to increased risk of nuclear war in the region, which leads to a fall in consumer confidence in the United States, which leads to a recession in the United States. What is the "shock"? The failed program? The fall of democracy? The increased risk of nuclear war? Or the decrease in consumer confidence? In practice, we have to cut the chain of causation somewhere. Thus, we may refer to the drop in consumer confidence as the shock and ignore its underlying causes.

Summary

- In the short run, output is determined by demand. The output gap, defined as the difference between output and potential output, affects inflation.

- A positive output gap leads to higher inflation. Higher inflation leads the central bank to increase the policy rate. The increase in the policy rate leads to a decrease in output and thus to a decrease in the output gap. Symmetrically, a negative output gap leads to lower inflation. Lower inflation leads to the central bank to decrease the policy rate. The decrease in the policy rate increases output and thus decreases the output gap.

- In the medium run, output is equal to potential output. The output gap is equal to zero, and inflation is stable. The interest rate associated with output equal to potential is called the *natural interest rate*.

- When the output gap is negative, the combination of the zero lower bound and deflation may lead to a *deflation spiral*. Lower output leads to lower inflation. Lower inflation leads to a higher real interest rate. The higher real interest rate further decreases output, further lowering inflation.

- In the short run, a fiscal consolidation through higher taxes leads, at an unchanged policy rate, to a decrease in output, a decrease in consumption, and a decrease in investment. In the medium run, output returns to potential. Consumption is lower, and investment is higher.

- An increase in the price of oil leads in the short run to higher inflation. Depending on the effect of the price of oil on demand, it may also lead to a decrease in output. The combination of higher inflation and lower output is called *stagflation*. In the medium run, the increase in the price of oil leads to leads to lower potential output and thus lower actual output.

- The difference between short-run effects and medium-run effects of policies is one of the reasons economists disagree in their policy recommendations. Some economists believe the economy adjusts quickly to its medium-run equilibrium, so they emphasize medium-run implications of policy. Others believe the adjustment mechanism through which output returns to the natural level of output is a slow process at best, and so they put more emphasis on the short-run effects of policy.

- Economic fluctuations are the result of a continual stream of shocks to aggregate supply or to aggregate demand and of the dynamic effects of each of these shocks on output. Sometimes the shocks are sufficiently adverse, alone or in combination, that they lead to a recession.

Key Terms

potential output, 199
output gap, 199
labor hoarding, 201
Okun coefficient, 201
natural rate of interest, 202
neutral rate of interest, 202
Wicksellian rate of interest, 202
anchored (expectations), 203

deflation spiral, 204
deflation trap, 204
Organization of Petroleum Exporting Countries (OPEC), 208
stagflation, 210
output fluctuations, 212
business cycles, 212
shocks, 212
propagation mechanism, 213

Questions and Problems

QUICK CHECK

MyEconLab Visit www.myeconlab.com to complete similar Quick Check problems and get instant feedback.

1. *Using the information in this chapter, label each of the following statements true, false, or uncertain. Explain briefly.*

a. The *IS* curve shifts up with an increase in G, up with an increase in T, and up with an increase in x.

b. If $(u - u_n)$ is greater than zero, then $(Y - Y_n)$ is greater than zero.

c. If $(u - u_n)$ is equal to zero, the output is at potential.

d. If $(u - u_n)$ is less than zero, the output gap is negative.

e. If the output gap is positive, inflation is higher than expected inflation.

f. Okun's law says that if output growth increases by one percentage point, the rate of unemployment drops by one percentage point.

g. At the natural rate of unemployment, inflation is neither rising nor falling.

h. In a medium-run equilibrium, the rate of inflation is stable.

i. The central bank can always act to keep output equal to potential output.

j. It is easier for the central bank to keep output at potential output if expectations of inflation are anchored.

k. A large increase in the price of oil increases the natural rate of unemployment.

2. *The medium-run equilibrium is characterized by four conditions:*

Output is equal to potential output $Y = Y_n$.
The unemployment rate is equal to the natural rate $u = u_n$.
The real policy interest rate is equal to the natural rate of interest r_n where aggregate demand equals Y_n.
The expected rate of inflation π^e is equal to the actual rate of inflation π.

a. If the level of expected inflation is formed so π^e equals $\pi(-1)$, characterize the behavior of inflation in a medium-run equilibrium.

b. If the level of expected inflation is $\bar{\pi}$, what is the level of actual inflation in the medium-run equilibrium?

c. Write the *IS* relation as $Y = C(Y - T) + I(Y, r + x) + G$. Suppose r_n is 2%. If x increases from 3 to 5%, how must the central bank change r_n to maintain the existing medium-run equilibrium. Explain in words.

d. Suppose G increases. How must the central bank change r_n to maintain the existing medium-run equilibrium? Explain in words.

e. Suppose T decreases. How must the central bank change r_n to maintain the existing medium-run equilibrium? Explain in words.

f. Discuss: In the medium run, a fiscal expansion leads to an increase in the natural rate of interest.

3. *The two paths to the medium-run equilibrium explored in this chapter make two different assumptions about the formation of the level of expected inflation. One path assumes the level of expected inflation equals lagged inflation. The level of expected inflation changes over time. The other path assumes the level of expected inflation is anchored to a specific value and never changes. Begin in medium-run equilibrium where actual and expected inflation equals 2% in period t.*

a. Suppose there is an increase in consumer confidence in period $t + 1$. How does the *IS* curve shift? Assume that the central bank does not change the real policy rate. How will the short-run equilibrium in period $t + 1$ compare to the equilibrium in period t?

b. Consider the period $t + 2$ equilibrium under the assumption that $\pi^e_{t+2} = \pi_{t+1}$. If the central bank leaves the real policy rate unchanged, how does actual inflation in period $t + 2$ compare to inflation in period $t + 1$? How must the central bank change the nominal policy rate to keep the real policy rate unchanged? Continue to period $t + 3$. Making the same assumption about the level of expected inflation and the real policy rate, how does actual inflation in period $t + 3$ compare to inflation in period $t + 2$.

c. Consider the period $t + 2$ equilibrium making the assumption that $\pi^e_{t+2} = \bar{\pi}$. If the central bank leaves the real policy rate unchanged, how does actual inflation in period $t + 2$ compare to inflation in period $t + 1$? How must the central bank change the nominal policy rate to keep the real policy rate unchanged? Continue to period $t + 3$. Making the same assumption about the level of expected inflation and the real policy rate, how does actual inflation in period $t + 3$ compare to inflation in period $t + 2$?

d. Compare the inflation and output outcomes in part b to that in part c.

e. Which scenario, part b or part c, do you think is more realistic. Discuss.

f. Suppose in period $t + 4$, the central bank decides to raise the real policy rate high enough to return the economy immediately to potential output and to the period t rate of inflation. Explain the difference between central bank policies using the two assumptions about expected inflation in part b and part c.

4. *A shock to aggregate supply will also have different outcomes when there are different assumptions about the formation of the level of expected inflation. As in Question 3, one path assumes that the level of expected inflation equals lagged inflation. The level of expected inflation changes over time. The second path assumes the level of expected inflation is anchored to a specific value and never changes. Begin in medium-run equilibrium where actual and expected inflation equal 2% in period t.*

a. Suppose there is a permanent increase in the price of oil in period $t + 1$. How does the PC curve shift? Assume that the central bank does not change the real policy rate. How will the short-run equilibrium in period $t + 1$ compare to the equilibrium in period t? What happens to output? What happens to inflation?

b. Consider the period $t + 2$ equilibrium under the assumption that $\pi^e_{t+2} = \pi_{t+1}$. If the central bank leaves the real policy rate unchanged, how does actual inflation in period $t + 2$ compare to inflation in period $t + 1$? Continue to period $t + 3$. Making the same assumption about the level of expected inflation and the real policy rate, how does actual inflation in period $t + 3$ compare to inflation in period $t + 2$?

c. Consider the period $t + 2$ equilibrium under the assumption that $\pi^e_{t+2} = \bar{\pi}$. If the central bank leaves the real policy rate unchanged, how does actual inflation in period $t + 2$ compare to inflation in period $t + 1$? Continue to period $t + 3$. Making the same assumption about the level of expected inflation and the real policy rate, how does actual inflation in period $t + 3$ compare to inflation in period $t + 2$.

d. Compare the inflation and output outcomes in part b to that in part c.

e. In period $t + 4$, the central bank decides to change the real policy rate to return the economy as quickly as possible to potential output and to the inflation rate of period t. Under which path for the formation of expected inflation is the nominal policy rate of interest higher in period $t + 4$, the path from b or the path from c. Explain why, when inflation expectations are anchored as in part c, the central bank can change the policy rate to immediately reach the new level of potential output and the period t level of inflation in period $t + 4$. Make the argument that is not possible for the central bank to immediately hit both the new level of potential output and the period t level of inflation in period $t + 4$ when expected inflation is equal to its lagged value.

DIG DEEPER

MyEconLab Visit www.myeconlab.com to complete all Dig Deeper problems and get instant feedback.

5. *Okun's Law is written as* $u - u(-1) = -0.4(g_Y - 3\%)$

a. What is the sign of $u - u(-1)$ in a recession? What is the sign of $u - u(-1)$ in a recovery?

b. Explain where the 3% number comes from?

c. Explain why the coefficient on the term $(g_Y - 3\%)$ is -0.4 and not -1.

d. Suppose the number of immigrants per year allowed to enter the United States is sharply increased. How would Okun's law change?

6. *Fiscal consolidation at the Zero Lower Bound*

Suppose the economy is operating at the zero lower bound for the nominal policy rate; there is a large government deficit and the economy is operating at potential output in period t. A newly elected government vows to cut spending and reduces the deficit in period $t + 1$, period $t + 2$ and subsequent periods.

a. Show the effects of the policy on output in period $t + 1$.

b. Show the effects of the policy on the change in inflation in period $t + 1$.

c. If expected inflation depends on past inflation, then what happens to the real policy rate in period $t + 2$? How will this affect output in period $t + 3$?

d. How does the zero lower bound on nominal interest rates make a fiscal consolidation more difficult?

EXPLORE FURTHER

7. *Consider the data in the Focus box, "Deflation in the Great Depression."*

a. Do you believe that output had returned to its potential level in 1933?

b. Which years suggest a deflation spiral as described in Figure 9-3?

c. Make the argument that if the expected level of inflation had remained anchored at the actual value of inflation in 1929, the Great Depression would have been less severe.

d. Make the argument that a substantial fiscal stimulus in 1930 would have made the Great Depression less severe.

8. *Consider the data in the Focus box, "Deflation in the Great Depression."*

a. Calculate real interest rates in each year making the assumption that the expected level of inflation is last year's rate of inflation. The rate of inflation in 1928 was -1.7%. Do the changes in real interest rates explain the data on real output growth and unemployment better than when you make the assumption the expected rate of inflation is the current year's rate of inflation?

b. Calculate the Okun's law coefficient for each year from 1930 to 1933. To do so, assume potential output is not growing. Speculate on why firms did not take on additional workers in 1933 even though output growth was 9.1%. Hint: If potential output is not growing, Okun's law is $u - u(-1) = -\alpha g_Y$.

9. *The Great Depression in the United Kingdom*
    Answer the following questions based on information found in the table below

a. Is there evidence of the deflation spiral from 1929 to 1933 in the United Kingdom?

b. Is there evidence of the effect of high real interest rates on output?

c. Is there evidence of a poor choice of the real policy interest rate by the central bank?

The Nominal Interest Rate, Inflation, and the Real Interest Rate in the United Kingdom, 1929–1933					
Year	Unemployment Rate (%)	Output Growth Rate (%)	One-Year Nominal Interest Rate (%), i	Inflation Rate (%), π	One-Year Real Interest Rate (%), r
1929	10.4	3.0	5.0	−0.90	5.9
1930	21.3	−1.0	3.0	−2.8	5.8
1931	22.1	−5.0	6.0	−4.3	10.3
1932	19.9	0.4	2.0	−2.6	4.6
1933	16.7	3.3	2.0	−2.1	4.1

The Long Run

The next four chapters focus on the long run. In the long run, what dominates is not fluctuations, but growth. So now we need to ask: What determines growth?

Chapter 10

Chapter 10 looks at the facts of growth. It first documents the large increase in output that has taken place in rich countries over the past 50 years. Then, taking a wider look, it shows that on the scale of human history, such growth is a recent phenomenon. And it is not a universal phenomenon: Some countries are catching up, but some poor countries are suffering from no or low growth.

Chapter 11

Chapter 11 focuses on the role of capital accumulation in growth. It shows that capital accumulation cannot by itself sustain growth, but that it does affect the level of output. A higher saving rate typically leads to lower consumption initially, but to more consumption in the long run.

Chapter 12

Chapter 12 turns to technological progress. It shows how, in the long run, the growth rate of an economy is determined by the rate of technological progress. It then looks at the role of research and development in generating such progress. It returns to the facts of growth presented in Chapter 10 and shows how to interpret these facts in the light of the theories developed in Chapters 11 and 12.

Chapter 13

Chapter 13 looks at a number of issues raised by technological progress in the short, the medium, and the long run. Focusing on the short and the medium run, it discusses the relation between technological progress, unemployment, and wage inequality. Focusing on the long run, it discusses the role of institutions in sustaining technological progress and growth.

The Facts of Growth

Our perceptions of how the economy is doing are often dominated by year-to-year fluctuations in economic activity. A recession leads to gloom, and an expansion to optimism. But if we step back to get a look at activity over longer periods—say over many decades—the picture changes. Fluctuations fade. **Growth**, which is the steady increase in aggregate output over time, dominates the picture.

Figure 10-1, panels (a) and (b), shows the evolution of U.S. GDP and the evolution of U.S. GDP per person (both in 2009 dollars), respectively, since 1890. (The scale used to measure GDP on the vertical axis in Figure 10-1 is called a **logarithmic scale**. The defining characteristic of a logarithmic scale is that the same proportional increase in a variable is represented by the same distance on the vertical axis.)

◄ For more on log scales, see Appendix 2 at the end of the book.

The shaded years from 1929 to 1933 correspond to the large decrease in output during the Great Depression, and the other two shaded ranges correspond to the 1980–1982 recession, which is the largest post-war recession before the recent crisis, and 2008–2010, the most recent crisis and the subject of much of the analysis in the rest of this text. Note how small these three episodes appear compared to the steady increase in output per person over the last 100 years. The cartoon makes the same point about growth and fluctuations, in an even more obvious way.

With this in mind, we now shift our focus from fluctuations to growth. Put another way, we turn from the study of the determination of output in the *short and medium run*—where fluctuations dominate—to the determination of output in the *long run*—where growth dominates. Our goal is to understand what determines growth, why some countries are growing while others are not, and why some countries are rich while many others are still poor.

Section 10-1 discusses a central measurement issue; namely how to measure the standard of living.

Section 10-2 looks at growth in the United States and other rich countries over the last 50 years.

Section 10-3 takes a broader look, across both time and space.

Section 10-4 then gives a primer on growth and introduces the framework that will be developed in the next three chapters. ●

Figure 10-1

U.S. GDP since 1890 and U.S. GDP per Person since 1890

Panel *A* shows the enormous increase in U.S. output since 1890, by a factor of 46. Panel *B* shows that the increase in output is not simply the result of the large increase in U.S. population from 63 million to more than 300 million over this period. Output per person has risen by a factor of 9.

Source: 1890–1947: *Historical Statistics of the United States.* http://hsus.cambridge.org/HSUSWeb/toc/hsusHome.do. 1948 to 2014: *National Income and Product Accounts.* Population estimates 1890 to 2014, from Louis Johnston and Samuel H. Williamson, "What Was the U.S. GDP Then?" Measuring Worth, 2015, https://www.measuringworth.com/datasets/usgdp/

MyEconLab Real-time data

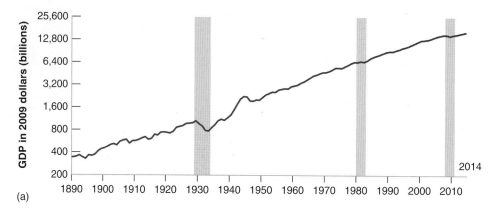

(a)

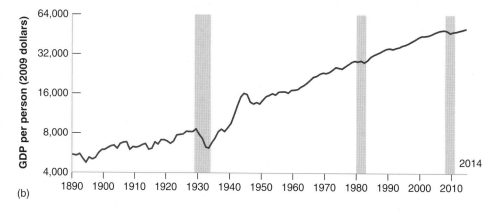

(b)

10-1 Measuring the Standard of Living

Output per person is also called *output per capita* (*capita* means "head" in Latin). And given that output and income ▶ are always equal, it is also called *income per person*, or *income per capita*.

The reason we care about growth is that we care about the **standard of living**. Looking across time, we want to know by how much the standard of living has increased. Looking across countries, we want to know how much higher the standard of living is in one country relative to another. Thus, the variable we want to focus on, and compare either over time or across countries, is **output per person**, rather than *output* itself.

A practical problem then arises: How do we compare output per person across countries? Countries use different currencies; thus output in each country is expressed in terms of its own currency. A natural solution is to use exchange rates. When comparing, say, the output per person of India to the output per person of the United States, we can compute Indian GDP per person in rupees, use the exchange rate to get Indian GDP per person in dollars, and compare it to the U.S. GDP per person in dollars. This simple approach will not do, however, for two reasons.

■ First, exchange rates can vary a lot (more on this in Chapters 17 to 20). For example, the dollar increased and then decreased in the 1980s by roughly 50% vis-à-vis the currencies of the trading partners of the United States. But surely the standard of living in the United States did not increase by 50% and then decrease by 50% compared to the standard of living of its trading partners during the decade. Yet this is the conclusion we would reach if we were to compare GDP per person using exchange rates.

*"It's true, Caesar. Rome is declining, but I expect it
to pick up in the next quarter."*

■ The second reason goes beyond fluctuations in exchange rates. In 2011, GDP per
person in India, using the current exchange rate, was $1,529 compared to $47,880
in the United States. Surely no one could live on $1,529 a year in the United States.
But people live on it—admittedly, not very well—in India, where the prices of basic
goods, which are those goods needed for subsistence, are much lower than in the
United States. The level of consumption of the average person in India, who consumes mostly basic goods, is not 31.3 (47,880 divided by 1,529) times smaller than
that of the average person in the United States. This point applies to other countries
besides the United States and India. In general, the lower a country's output per
person, the lower the prices of food and basic services in that country.

MyEconLab Video

Recall a similar discussion in
Chapter 1 where we looked at
output per person in China.

So, when we focus on comparing standards of living, we get more meaningful comparisons by correcting for the two effects we just discussed—variations in exchange rates
and systematic differences in prices across countries. The details of constructing these
differences are complicated, but the principle is simple. The numbers for GDP—and
hence for GDP per person—are constructed using a common set of prices for all countries. Such adjusted real GDP numbers, which you can think of as measures of **purchasing power** across time or across countries, are called **purchasing power parity
(PPP)** numbers. Further discussion is given in the Focus box "The Construction of PPP
Numbers."

When comparing rich versus poor countries, the differences between PPP numbers and the numbers based on current exchange rates can be large. Return to the
comparison between India and the United States. We saw that, at current exchange
rates, the ratio of GDP per person in the United States to GDP per person in India was
31.3. Using PPP numbers, the ratio is "only" 11. Although this is still a large difference, it is much smaller than the ratio we obtained using current exchange rates.
Differences between PPP numbers and numbers based on current exchange rates
are typically smaller when making comparisons among rich countries. For example,

The Construction of PPP Numbers

FOCUS

Consider two countries—let's call them the United States and Russia, although we are not attempting to fit the characteristics of those two countries very closely.

In the United States, annual consumption per person equals $20,000. People in the United States each buy two goods. Every year, they buy a new car for $10,000 and spend the rest on food. The price of a yearly bundle of food in the United States is $10,000.

In Russia, annual consumption per person equals 60,000 rubles. People there keep their cars for 15 years. The price of a car is 300,000 rubles, so individuals spend on average 20,000 rubles—300,000/15—a year on cars. They buy the same yearly bundle of food as their U.S. counterparts, at a price of 40,000 rubles.

Russian and U.S. cars are of identical quality, and so are Russian and U.S. food. (You may dispute the realism of these assumptions. Whether a car in country X is the same as a car in country Y is the type of problem confronting economists when constructing PPP measures.) The exchange rate is such that one dollar is equal to 30 rubles. What is consumption per person in Russia relative to consumption per person in the United States?

One way to answer is by taking consumption per person in Russia and converting it into dollars using the exchange rate. Using this method, Russian consumption per person in dollars is $2,000 (60,000 rubles divided by the exchange rate, 30 rubles to the dollar). According to these numbers, consumption per person in Russia is only 10% of U.S. consumption per person.

Does this answer make sense? True, Russians are poorer, but food is much cheaper in Russia. A U.S. consumer spending all of his 20,000 dollars on food would buy 2 bundles of food ($20,000/$10,000). A Russian consumer spending all of his 60,000 rubles on food would buy 1.5 bundles of food (60,000 rubles/40,000 rubles). In terms of food bundles, the difference looks much smaller between U.S. and Russian consumption per person. And given that one-half of consumption in the United States and two-thirds of consumption in Russia go to spending on food, this seems like a relevant computation.

Can we improve on our initial answer? Yes. One way is to use the same set of prices for both countries and then measure the quantities of each good consumed in each country using this common set of prices. Suppose we use U.S. prices. In terms of U.S. prices, annual consumption per person in the United States is obviously still $20,000. What is it in Russia? Every year, the average Russian buys approximately 0.07 car (one car every fifteen years) and one bundle of food. Using U.S. prices—specifically, $10,000 for a car and $10,000 for a bundle of food—gives Russian consumption per person as $[(0.07 \times \$10,000) + (1 \times \$10,000)] = [\$700 + \$10,000] = \$10,700$. So, using U.S. prices to compute consumption in both countries puts annual Russian consumption per person at $\$10,700/\$20,000 = 53.5\%$ of annual U.S. consumption per person, a better estimate of relative standards of living than we obtained using our first method (which put the number at only 10%).

This type of computation, namely the construction of variables across countries using a common set of prices, underlies PPP estimates. Rather than using U.S. dollar prices as in our example (why use U.S. rather than Russian or, for that matter, French prices?), these estimates use average prices across countries. These average prices are called *international dollar prices*. Many of the estimates we use in this chapter are the result of an ambitious project known as the "Penn World Tables." (Penn stands for the University of Pennsylvania, where the project was initially located.) Led by three economists—Irving Kravis, Robert Summers, and Alan Heston—over the course of more than 40 years, researchers working on the project have constructed PPP series not only for consumption (as we just did in our example), but more generally for GDP and its components, going back to 1950, for most countries in the world. Recently the Penn World Tables project, while keeping the same name, has been taken over by the University of California–Davis and the University of Groningen in the Netherlands, with continued input from Alan Heston at the University of Pennsylvania. The most recent data (version 8.1 of the Tables) are available at http://cid.econ.ucdavis.edu/instead of internationaldata.org (See Feenstra, Robert C., Robert Inklaar, and Marcel P. Timmer (2015), "The Next Generation of the Penn World Tables" published in the *American Economic Review*.)

The bottom line: When comparing the standard of living across countries, make sure to use PPP numbers.

using current exchange rates, GDP per person in the United States in 2011 was equal to 109% of GDP per person in Germany; based on PPP numbers, GDP per person in the United States was equal to 123% of GDP per person in Germany. More generally, PPP numbers suggest that the United States still has the highest GDP per person among the world's major countries.

Let me end this section with three remarks before we move on and look at growth.

■ What matters for people's welfare is their consumption rather than their income. One might therefore want to use *consumption per person* rather than output per person as a measure of the standard of living. (This is indeed what we did in the Focus

box, "The Construction of PPP Numbers.") Because the ratio of consumption to output is rather similar across countries, the ranking of countries is roughly the same, whether we use consumption per person or output per person.

■ Thinking about the production side, we may be interested in differences in productivity rather than in differences in the standard of living across countries. In this case, the right measure is *output per worker*—or, even better, *output per hour worked* if the information about total hours worked is available—rather than output per person. Output per person and output per worker (or per hour) will differ to the extent that the ratio of the number of workers (or hours) to population differs across countries. Most of the difference we saw between output per person in the United States and in Germany comes, for example, from differences in hours worked per person rather than from differences in productivity. Put another way, German workers are about as productive as their U.S. counterparts. However, they work fewer hours, so their standard of living, measured by output per person, is lower. In exchange, however, they enjoy more leisure time.

■ The reason we ultimately care about the standard of living is presumably that we care about happiness. We may therefore ask the obvious question: Does a higher standard of living lead to greater happiness? The answer is given in the Focus box "Does Money Buy Happiness?". The answer: a qualified yes.

10-2 Growth in Rich Countries since 1950

Let's start by looking, in this section, at growth in rich countries since 1950. In the next section, we shall look further back in time and across a wider range of countries.

Table 10-1 shows the evolution of output per person (GDP divided by population, measured at PPP prices) for France, Japan, the United Kingdom, and the United States, since 1950. We have chosen these four countries not only because they are some of the world's major economic powers, but also because what has happened to them is broadly representative of what has happened in other advanced countries over the last half-century or so.

Table 10-1 yields two main conclusions:

■ There has been a large increase in output per person.
■ There has been a convergence of output per person across countries.

Let's look at each of these points in turn.

Table 10-1 The Evolution of Output per Person in Four Rich Countries since 1950				
	Annual Growth Rate Output per Person (%)	Real Output per Person (2005 dollars)		
	1950–2011	1950	2011	2011/1950
France	2.5	6,499	29,586	4.6
Japan	4.1	2,832	31,867	11.3
United Kingdom	2.0	9,673	32,093	3.3
United States	2.0	12,725	42,244	3.3
Average	2.4	7,933	33,947	4.3

Notes: The data stop in 2011, the latest year (at this point) available in the Penn tables.
The average in the last line is a simple unweighted average.

Source: Penn Tables, http://cid.econ.ucdavis.edu/pwt.html.

Does Money Lead to Happiness?

Does money lead to happiness? Or, put more accurately, does higher income per person lead to more happiness? The implicit assumption, when economists assess the performance of an economy by looking at its level of income per person or at its growth rate, is that this is indeed the case. Early examinations of data on the relation between income and self-reported measures of happiness suggested that this assumption may not be right. They yielded what is now known as the **Easterlin paradox** (so named for Richard Easterlin, who was one of the first economists to look systematically at the evidence):

- Looking across countries, happiness in a country appeared to be higher, the higher the level of income per person. The relation, however, appeared to hold only in relatively poor countries. Looking at rich countries, say the set of Organisation for Economic Co-operation and Development (OECD) countries (look at Chapter 1 for the list), there appeared to be little relation between income per person and happiness.

- Looking at individual countries over time, average happiness in rich countries did not seem to increase much, if at all, with income. (There were no reliable data for poor countries.) In other words, in rich countries, higher income per person did not appear to increase happiness.

- Looking across people within a given country, happiness appeared to be strongly correlated with income.

Rich people were consistently happier than poor people. This was true in both poor and rich countries.

The first two facts suggested that, once basic needs are satisfied, higher income per person does not increase happiness. The third fact suggested that what was important was not the absolute level of income but the level of income relative to others.

If this interpretation is right, it has major implications for the way we think about the world and about economic policies. In rich countries, policies aimed at increasing income per person might be misdirected because what matters is the distribution of income rather than its average level. Globalization and the diffusion of information, to the extent that it makes people in poor countries compare themselves not to rich people in the same country but to people in richer countries, may actually decrease rather than increase happiness. So, as you can guess, these findings have led to an intense debate and further research. As new data sets have become available, better evidence has accumulated. The state of knowledge and the remaining controversies are analyzed in a recent article by Betsey Stevenson and Justin Wolfers. Their conclusions are well summarized in Figure 1.

The figure contains a lot of information. Let's go through it step by step.

The horizontal axis measures PPP GDP per person for 131 countries. The scale is a logarithmic scale, so a given size interval represents a given percentage increase in GDP per

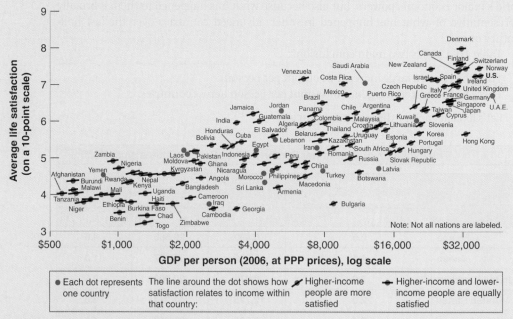

Figure 1 *Life Satisfaction and Income per Person*

Source: Betsey Stevenson and Justin Wolfers, Wharton School at the University of Pennsylvania.

FOCUS

person. The vertical axis measures average life satisfaction in each country. The source for this variable is a 2006 Gallup World Poll survey, which asked about a thousand individuals in each country the following question:

> "Here is a ladder representing the 'ladder of life.' Let's suppose the top of the ladder represents the best possible life for you; and the bottom, the worst possible life for you. On which step of the ladder do you feel you personally stand at the present time?"

The ladder went from 0 to 10. The variable measured on the vertical axis is the average of the individual answers in each country.

Focus first on the dots representing each country, ignoring for the moment the lines that cross each dot. The visual impression is clear. There is a strong relation across countries between average income and average happiness. The index is around 4 in the poorest countries, around 8 in the richest. And, more importantly in view of the early Easterlin paradox, this relation appears to hold both for poor and rich countries; if anything, life satisfaction appears to increase faster, as GDP per person increases, in rich than in poor countries.

Focus now on the lines through each dot. The slope of each line reflects the estimated relation between life satisfaction and income across individuals *within* each country. Note first that all the lines slope upward. This confirms the third leg of the Easterlin paradox. In each country, rich people are happier than poor people. Note also that the slopes of most of these lines are roughly similar to the slope of the relation across countries. This goes against the Easterlin paradox. Individual happiness increases with income, whether this is because the country is getting richer or because the individual becomes relatively richer within the country.

Stevenson and Wolfers draw a strong conclusion from their findings. Although individual happiness surely depends on much more than income, it definitely increases with income. While the idea that there is some critical level of income beyond which income no longer impacts well-being is intuitively appealing, it is at odds with the data. Thus, it is not a crime for economists to focus first on levels and growth rates of GDP per person.

So, is the debate over? The answer is no. Even if we accept this interpretation of the evidence, clearly, many other aspects of the economy matter for welfare, income distribution surely being one of them. And not everyone is convinced by the evidence. In particular, the evidence on the relation between happiness and income per person over time within a country is not as clear as the evidence across countries or across individuals presented in Figure 1.

Given the importance of the question, the debate will continue for some time. One aspect which has become clear, for example from the work of Nobel Prize winners Angus Deaton and Daniel Kahneman is that, when thinking about "happiness," it is important to distinguish between two ways in which a person may assess her or his well-being. The first one is *emotional well-being*—the frequency and intensity of experiences such as joy, stress, sadness, anger, and affection that make one's life pleasant or unpleasant. Emotional well-being appears to rise with income because low income exacerbates the emotional pain associated with such misfortunes as divorce, ill health, and being alone. But only up to a threshold; there is no further progress beyond an annual income of about $75,000 (the experiment was run in 2009). The second is *life satisfaction*, a person's assessment of her or his life when they think about it. Life satisfaction appears more closely correlated with income. Deaton and Kahneman conclude that high income buys life satisfaction but does not necessarily buy happiness. If measures of well-being are to be used to guide policy, their findings raise the question of whether life evaluation or emotional well-being is better suited to these aims.

Sources: Betsey Stevenson and Justin Wolfers, "Economic Growth and Subjective Well-Being: Reassessing the Easterlin Paradox," Brookings Papers on Economic Activity, Vol. 2008 (Spring 2008): 1–87 and "Subjective Well-Being and Income: Is There Any Evidence of Satiation?" *American Economic Review: Papers & Proceedings* 2013, 103(3): 598–604; Daniel Kahneman and Angus Deaton, "High Income Improves Evaluation of Life but Not Emotional Well-Being," *Proceedings of the National Academy of Sciences* 2010, 107(38): 16489–16493. For a view closer to the Easterlin paradox and a fascinating discussion of policy implications, read Richard Layard, *Happiness: Lessons from a New Science* (2005).

The Large Increase in the Standard of Living since 1950

Look at the column on the far right of Table 10-1. Output per person has increased by a factor of 3.3 since 1950 in the United States, by a factor of 4.6 in France, and by a factor of 11.3 in Japan. These numbers show what is sometimes called the **force of compounding**. In a different context, you probably have heard how saving even a little while you are young will build to a large amount by the time you retire. For example, if the interest rate is 4.0% a year, an investment of one dollar, with the proceeds reinvested every year, will grow to about 11 dollars 61 years later. The same logic applies to growth rates. The average annual growth rate in Japan over the period 1950 to 2011 (which is 61 years) was equal to 4.0%. This high growth rate has led to an 11-fold increase in real ◀ output per person in Japan over the period.

Most of the increase in Japan took place before 1990. Since then, Japan has been in a prolonged economic slump, with much lower growth.

$1.01^{40} - 1 = 1.48 - 1 = 48\%$

Unfortunately, policy measures with such magic results have proven difficult to discover!

Clearly, a better understanding of growth, if it leads to the design of policies that ▶ stimulate growth, can have a large effect on the standard of living. Suppose we could find a policy measure that permanently increased the growth rate by 1% per year. This ▶ would lead, after 40 years, to a standard of living 48% higher than it would have been without the policy—a substantial difference.

The Convergence of Output per Person

The second and third columns of Table 10-1 show that the levels of output per person have converged (become closer) over time. The numbers for output per person are much more similar in 2011 than they were in 1950. Put another way, those countries that were behind have grown faster, reducing the gap between them and the United States.

As a child in France in the 1950s, I thought of the United States as the land of sky-scrapers, big automobiles, and Hollywood movies.

In 1950, output per person in the United States was roughly twice the level of output per person in France and more than four times the level of output per person in Japan. From the perspective of Europe or Japan, the United States was seen as the land of ▶ plenty, where everything was bigger and better.

Today these perceptions have faded, and the numbers explain why. Using PPP numbers, U.S. output per person is still the highest, but in 2011, it was only 7% above average output per person in the other three countries, a much smaller difference than in the 1950s.

This **convergence** of levels of output per person across countries is not specific to the four countries we are looking at. It extends to the set of OECD countries. This is shown in Figure 10-2, which plots the average annual growth rate of output per person since 1950 against the initial level of output per person in 1950 for the set of countries

For the list of countries, see the appendix to Chapter 1. The figure includes only those OECD members for which we have a reliable estimate of the level of output per person in 1950.

▶ that are members of the OECD today. There is a clear negative relation between the initial level of output per person and the growth rate since 1950. Countries that were behind in 1950 have typically grown faster. The relation is not perfect. Turkey, which had roughly the same low level of output per person as Japan in 1950, has had a growth rate equal to only about one-half that of Japan. But the relation is clearly there.

Some economists have pointed to a problem in graphs like Figure 10-2. By looking at the subset of countries that are members of the OECD today, what we have done in effect is to look at a club of economic winners. OECD membership is not officially based on economic success, but economic success is surely an important determinant of membership. But when you look at a club whose membership is based on economic success, you will find that those who came from behind had the fastest growth. This is precisely why they made it to the club! The finding of convergence could come in part from the way we selected the countries in the first place.

Figure 10-2

Growth Rate of GDP per Person since 1950 versus GDP per Person in 1950; OECD Countries

Countries with lower levels of output per person in 1950 have typically grown faster.

Source: Penn World Table Version 8.1./Feenstra, Robert C., Robert Inklaar and Marcel P. Timmer (2015), "The Next Generation of the Penn World Table" forthcoming American Economic Review, available for download at www.ggdc.net/pwt.

MyEconLab Animation

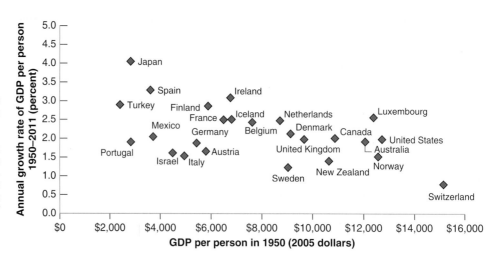

So a better way of looking at convergence is to define the set of countries we look at not on the basis of where they are today—as we did in Figure 10-2 by taking today's OECD members—but on the basis of where they were in, say, 1950. For example, we can look at all countries that had an output per person of at least one-fourth of U.S. output per person in 1950, and then look for convergence within that group. It turns out that most of the countries in that group have indeed converged, and therefore convergence is not solely an OECD phenomenon. However, a few countries—Uruguay, Argentina, and Venezuela among them—have not converged. In 1950, those three countries had roughly the same output per person as France. In 2009, they had fallen far behind; their level of output per person stood only between one-fourth and one-half of the French level.

10-3 A Broader Look across Time and Space

In the previous section, we focused on growth over the last 50 years in rich countries. Let's now put this in context by looking at the evidence both over a much longer time span and a wider set of countries.

Looking across Two Millennia

Has output per person in the currently rich economies always grown at rates similar to the growth rates in Table 10-1? The answer is no. Estimates of growth are clearly harder to construct as we look further back in time. But there is agreement among economic historians about the main evolutions over the last 2,000 years.

From the end of the Roman Empire to roughly year 1500, there was essentially no growth of output per person in Europe. Most workers were employed in agriculture in which there was little technological progress. Because agriculture's share of output was so large, inventions with applications outside agriculture could only contribute little to overall production and output. Although there was some output growth, a roughly proportional increase in population led to roughly constant output per person.

This period of stagnation of output per person is often called the *Malthusian era*. Thomas Robert Malthus, an English economist at the end of the 18th century, argued that this proportional increase in output and population was not a coincidence. Any increase in output, he argued, would lead to a decrease in mortality, leading to an increase in population until output per person was back to its initial level. Europe was in a **Malthusian trap**, unable to increase its output per person.

Eventually, Europe was able to escape this trap. From about 1500 to 1700, growth of output per person turned positive, but it was still small—only around 0.1% per year. It then increased to just 0.2% per year from 1700 to 1820. Starting with the Industrial Revolution, growth rates increased, but from 1820 to 1950 the growth rate of output per person in the United States was still only 1.5% per year. On the scale of human history, therefore, sustained growth of output per person—especially the high growth rates we have seen since 1950—is definitely a recent phenomenon.

Looking across Countries

We have seen how output per person has converged among OECD countries. But what about the other countries? Are the poorest countries also growing faster? Are they converging toward the United States, even if they are still far behind?

The answer is given in Figure 10-3 on page 228, which plots the average annual growth rate of output per person since 1960 against output per person for the year 1960, for the 85 countries for which we have data.

◄ The numbers for 1950 are missing for too many countries to use 1950 as the initial year, as we did in Figure 10-2.

Figure 10-3

Growth Rate of GDP per Person since 1960, versus GDP per Person in 1960 (2005 dollars); 85 Countries

There is no clear relation between the growth rate of output since 1960 and the level of output per person in 1960.

Source: Penn World Table Version 8.1./Feenstra, Robert C., Robert Inklaar and Marcel P. Timmer (2015), "The Next Generation of the Penn World Table" forthcoming American Economic Review, available for download at www.ggdc.net/pwt.

MyEconLab Animation

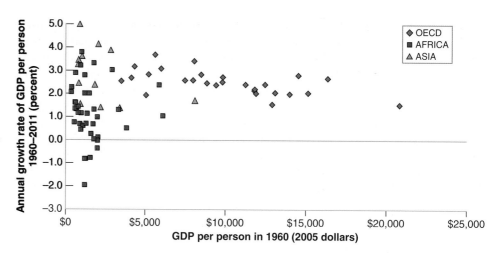

The striking feature of Figure 10-3 is that there is no clear pattern. It is not the case that, in general, countries that were behind in 1960 have grown faster. Some have, but many have clearly not.

The cloud of points in Figure 10-3 hides, however, a number of interesting patterns that appear when we put countries into different groups. Note that we have used different symbols in the figure. The diamonds represent OECD countries; the squares represent African countries; the triangles represent Asian countries. Looking at patterns by groups yields three main conclusions.

1. The picture for the OECD countries (for the rich countries) is much the same as in Figure 10-2, which looked at a slightly longer period of time (from 1950 onward, rather than from 1960). Nearly all start at high levels of output per person (say, at least one-third of the U.S. level in 1960), and there is clear evidence of convergence.

2. Convergence is also visible for many Asian countries: Most of the countries with high growth rates over the period are in Asia. Japan was the first country to take off. Starting a decade later, in the 1960s, four countries—Singapore, Taiwan, Hong Kong, and South Korea, a group of countries sometimes called the **four tigers**—started catching up as well. In 1960, their average output per person was about 18% of the United States; by 2011, it had increased to 85% of U.S. output. More recently, the major story has been China—both because of its very high growth rates and because of its sheer size. Over the period 1960–2011, growth of output per person in China has been 5.2% per year on average. But, because it started low, its output per person is still only about one-sixth of the United States.

MyEconLab Video

3. The picture is different, however, for African countries. Most African countries (represented by squares) were very poor in 1960, and most have not done well over the period. Many have suffered from either internal or external conflicts. Eight of them have had negative growth of output per person—an absolute decline in their standard of living between 1960 and 2011. Growth averaged –0.83% in the Central African Republic as it did in Niger. As a result, output per person in the Central African Republic in 2011 is only 63% of its level in 1960. Hope for Africa, however, comes from more recent numbers. Growth of output per person in sub-Saharan Africa, which averaged only 1.3% in the 1990s, has been close to 5.5% since 2000.

Paradoxically, two of the fastest growing countries in Figure 10.3 are Botswana and Equatorial Guinea, both in Africa. In both cases, however, high ▶ growth reflects primarily favorable natural resources—diamonds in Botswana and oil in Guinea.

Looking further back in time, the following picture emerges. For much of the first millennium, and until the 15th century, China probably had the world's highest level of output per person. For a couple of centuries, leadership moved to the cities of northern Italy. But until the 19th century, differences across countries were typically much smaller than they are today. Starting in the 19th century, a number of countries, first in Western Europe, then in North and South America, started growing faster than others. Since then, a number of other countries, most notably in Asia, have started growing fast and are converging. Many others, mainly in Africa, are not.

Our main focus, in this and the next chapter, will primarily be on growth in rich and emerging countries. We shall not take on some of the wider challenges raised by the facts we have just seen, such as why growth of output per person started in earnest in the 19th century or why Africa has remained so poor. Doing so would take us too far into economic history and development economics. But these facts put into perspective ◄ the two basic facts we discussed previously when looking at the OECD. Neither growth nor convergence is a historical necessity.

The distinction between *growth theory* and *development economics* is fuzzy. A rough distinction: Growth theory takes many of the institutions of a country (e.g., its legal system and its form of government) as given. Development economics asks what institutions are needed to sustain steady growth, and how they can be put in place.

10-4 Thinking about Growth: A Primer

To think about growth, economists use a framework developed originally by Robert Solow, from the Massachusetts Institute of Technology (MIT) in the late 1950s. The ◄ framework has proven sturdy and useful, and we will use it here. This section provides an introduction. Chapters 11 and 12 will provide a more detailed analysis, first of the role of capital accumulation and then of the role of technological progress in the process of growth.

See Robert M. Solow's article, "A Contribution to the Theory of Economic Growth," *The Quarterly Journal of Economics*, Vol. 70, No. 1. (Feb., 1956), pp. 65–94. Solow was awarded the Nobel Prize in 1987 for his work on growth.

The Aggregate Production Function

The starting point for any theory of growth must be an **aggregate production function**, which is a specification of the relation between aggregate output and the inputs in production.

The aggregate production function we introduced in Chapter 7 to study the determination of output in the short run and the medium run took a particularly simple form. Output was simply proportional to the amount of labor used by firms; more specifically, proportional to the number of workers employed by firms (equation (7.2)). So long as our focus was on fluctuations in output and employment, the assumption was acceptable. But now that our focus has shifted to growth this assumption will no longer do. It implies that output per worker is constant, ruling out growth (or at least growth of output per worker) altogether. It is time to relax it. From now on, we will assume that there are two inputs—capital and labor—and that the relation between aggregate output and the two inputs is given by:

$$Y = F(K, N) \tag{10.1}$$

As before, Y is aggregate output. K is capital—the sum of all the machines, plants, and office buildings in the economy. N is labor—the number of workers in the economy. The function F, which tells us how much output is produced for given quantities of capital and labor, is the *aggregate production function*.

This way of thinking about aggregate production is an improvement on our treatment in Chapter 7. But it should be clear that it is still a dramatic simplification of reality. Surely, machines and office buildings play different roles in production and should be treated as separate inputs. Surely, workers with doctorate degrees are different from high-school dropouts; yet, by constructing the labor input as simply the *number* of workers in the economy, we treat all workers as identical. We will relax some of these simplifications later. For the time being, equation (10.1), which emphasizes the role of both labor and capital in production, will do.

The aggregate production function is

$$Y = F(K, N)$$

Aggregate output (Y) depends ◄ on the aggregate capital stock (K) and aggregate employment (N).

The next step must be to think about where the aggregate production function F, which relates output to the two inputs, comes from. In other words, what determines how much output can be produced for given quantities of capital and labor? The answer: the **state of technology**. A country with a more advanced technology will produce more output from the same quantities of capital and labor than will an economy with a primitive technology.

The function F depends on the state of technology. The higher the state of technology, the higher $F(K, N)$ for a given K ▶ and a given N.

How should we define the *state of technology*? Should we think of it as the list of blueprints defining both the range of products that can be produced in the economy as well as the techniques available to produce them? Or should we think of it more broadly, including not only the list of blueprints, but also the way the economy is organized—from the internal organization of firms, to the system of laws and the quality of their enforcement, to the political system, and so on? In the next two chapters we will have in mind the narrower definition—the set of blueprints. In Chapter 13, however, we will consider the broader definition and return to what we know about the role of the other factors, from legal institutions to the quality of government.

Returns to Scale and Returns to Factors

Now that we have introduced the aggregate production function, the next question is: What restrictions can we reasonably impose on this function?

Consider first a thought experiment in which we double both the number of workers and the amount of capital in the economy. What do you expect will happen to output? A reasonable answer is that output will double as well. In effect, we have cloned the original economy, and the clone economy can produce output in the same way as the original economy. This property is called **constant returns to scale**. If the scale of operation is doubled—that is, if the quantities of capital and labor are doubled—then output will also double.

Constant returns to scale: $F(xK, xN) = xY$.

$$2Y = F(2K, 2N)$$

Or, more generally, for any number x (this will be useful later)

$$xY = F(xK, xN) \tag{10.2}$$

We have just looked at what happens to production when *both* capital and labor are increased. Let's now ask a different question. What should we expect to happen if *only one* of the two inputs in the economy—say capital—is increased?

Output here is secretarial services. The two inputs are secretaries and computers. The production function relates ▶ secretarial services to the number of secretaries and the number of computers.

Surely output will increase. That part is clear. But it is also reasonable to assume that the same increase in capital will lead to smaller and smaller increases in output as the level of capital increases. In other words, if there is little capital to start with, a little more capital will help a lot. If there is a lot of capital to start with, a little more capital may make little difference. Why? Think, for example, of a secretarial pool, composed of a given number of secretaries. Think of capital as computers. The introduction of the first computer will substantially increase the pool's production because some of the more time-consuming tasks can now be done automatically by the computer. As the number of computers increases and more secretaries in the pool get their own computers, production will further increase, although by less per additional computer than was the case when the first one was introduced. Once each and every secretary has a computer, increasing the number of computers further is unlikely to increase production much, if at all. Additional computers might simply remain unused and left in their shipping boxes and lead to no increase in output.

We shall refer to the property that increases in capital lead to smaller and smaller increases in output as **decreasing returns to capital** (a property that will be familiar to those who have taken a course in microeconomics).

A similar argument applies to the other input, labor. Increases in labor, given capital, lead to smaller and smaller increases in output. (Return to our example, and think of what happens as you increase the number of secretaries for a given number of computers.) There are **decreasing returns to labor** as well.

Even under constant returns to scale, there are decreasing returns to each factor, keeping the other factor constant.

There are decreasing returns to capital. Given labor, increases in capital lead to smaller and smaller increases in output.

There are decreasing returns to labor. Given capital, increases in labor lead to smaller and smaller increases in output.

Output per Worker and Capital per Worker

The production function we have written down, together with the assumption of constant returns to scale, implies that there is a simple relation between *output per worker* and *capital per worker.*

To see this, set $x = 1/N$ in equation (10.2), so that

$$\frac{Y}{N} = F\left(\frac{K}{N}, \frac{N}{N}\right) = F\left(\frac{K}{N}, 1\right) \tag{10.3}$$

Note that Y/N is output per worker, K/N is capital per worker. So equation (10.3) tells us that the amount of output per worker depends on the amount of capital per worker. This relation between output per worker and capital per worker will play a central role in what follows, so let's look at it more closely.

Make sure you understand what is behind the algebra. Suppose capital and the number of workers both double. What happens to output per worker?

This relation is drawn in Figure 10-4. Output per worker *(Y/N)* is measured on the vertical axis, and capital per worker *(K/N)* is measured on the horizontal axis. The relation between the two is given by the upward-sloping curve. As capital per worker increases, so does output per worker. Note that the curve is drawn so that increases in capital lead to smaller and smaller increases in output. This follows from the property that there are *decreasing returns to capital*: At point *A*, where capital per worker is low, an increase in capital per worker, represented by the horizontal distance *AB*, leads to an increase in output per worker equal to the vertical distance *A'B'*. At point *C*, where capital per worker is larger, the same increase in capital per worker, represented by the horizontal distance *CD* (where the distance *CD* is equal to the distance *AB*), leads to a much smaller increase in output per worker, only the distance *C'D'*. This is just like our secretarial pool example, in which additional computers had less and less impact on total output.

Increases in capital per worker lead to smaller and smaller increases in output per worker as the level of capital per worker increases.

The Sources of Growth

We are now ready to return to our basic question. Where does growth come from? Why does output per worker—or output per person, if we assume the ratio of workers to the population as a whole remains constant over time—go up over time? Equation (10.3) gives a first answer:

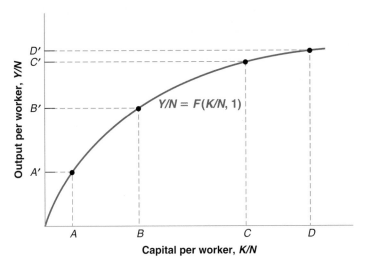

Figure 10-4

Output and Capital per Worker

Increases in capital per worker lead to smaller and smaller increases in output per worker.

MyEconLab Animation

- Increases in output per worker (Y/N) can come from increases in capital per worker (K/N). This is the relation we just looked at in Figure 10-4. As (K/N) increases—that is, as we move to the right on the horizontal axis—(Y/N) increases.

- Or they can come from improvements in the state of technology that shift the production function, F, and lead to more output per worker *given* capital per worker. This is shown in Figure 10-5. An improvement in the state of technology shifts the production function up, from $F(K/N, 1)$ to $F(K/N, 1)'$. For a given level of capital per worker, the improvement in technology leads to an increase in output per worker. For example, for the level of capital per worker corresponding to point A, output per worker increases from A' to B'. (To go back to our secretarial pool example, a reallocation of tasks within the pool may lead to a better division of labor and an increase in the output per secretary.)

Increases in capital per worker: Movements along the production function.

Improvements in the state of technology: Shifts (up) of the production function. ▷

Hence, we can think of growth as coming from **capital accumulation** and from **technological progress**—the improvement in the state of technology. We will see, however, that these two factors play different roles in the growth process.

- Capital accumulation *by itself* cannot sustain growth. A formal argument will have to wait until Chapter 11. But you can already see the intuition behind this from Figure 10-5. Because of decreasing returns to capital, sustaining a steady increase in output per worker will require larger and larger increases in the level of capital per worker. At some stage, the economy will be unwilling or unable to save and invest enough to further increase capital. At that stage, output per worker will stop growing.

  Does this mean that an economy's **saving rate**, which is the proportion of income that is saved, is irrelevant? No. It is true that a higher saving rate cannot permanently increase the *growth rate* of output. But a higher saving rate can sustain a higher *level* of output. Let me state this in a slightly different way. Take two economies that differ only in their saving rates. The two economies will grow at the same rate, but at any point in time, the economy with the higher saving rate will have a higher level of output per person than the other. How this happens, how much the saving rate affects the level of output, and whether or not a country like the United States (which has a low saving rate) should try to increase its saving rate will be one of the topics we take up in Chapter 11.

- Sustained growth requires sustained technological progress. This really follows from the previous proposition. Given that the two factors that can lead to an increase in output are capital accumulation and technological progress, if capital

Figure 10-5

The Effects of an Improvement in the State of Technology

An improvement in technology shifts the production function up, leading to an increase in output per worker for a given level of capital per worker.

MyEconLab Animation

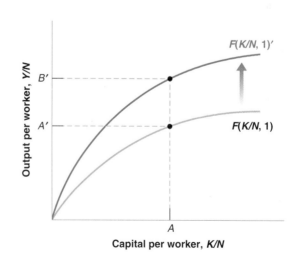

accumulation cannot sustain growth forever, then technological progress must be the key to growth. And it is. We will see in Chapter 12 that the economy's rate of growth of output per person is eventually determined by its rate of technological progress.

This is important. It means that in the long run, an economy that sustains a higher rate of technological progress will eventually overtake all other economies. This, of course, raises the next question. What determines the rate of technological progress? Recall the two definitions of the state of technology we discussed previously: a narrow definition, namely the set of blueprints available to the economy, and a broader definition, which captures how the economy is organized, from the nature of institutions to the role of the government. What we know about the determinants of technological progress narrowly defined—the role of fundamental and applied research, the role of patent laws, the role of education and training—will be taken up in Chapter 12. The role of broader factors will be discussed in Chapter 13. ◄

Following up on the distinction introduced previously between growth theory and development economics: Chapter 12 will deal with technological progress from the viewpoint of growth theory; Chapter 13 will come closer to development economics.

Summary

- Over long periods, fluctuations in output are dwarfed by growth, which is the steady increase of aggregate output over time.

- Looking at growth in four rich countries (France, Japan, the United Kingdom, and the United States) since 1950, two main facts emerge.
  1. All four countries have experienced strong growth and a large increase in the standard of living. Growth from 1950 to 2011 increased real output per person by a factor of 3.3 in the United States and by a factor of 11.3 in Japan.
  2. The levels of output per person across the four countries have converged over time. Put another way, those countries that were behind have grown faster, reducing the gap between them and the current leader, the United States.

- Looking at the evidence across a broader set of countries and a longer period, the following facts emerge.
  1. On the scale of human history, sustained output growth is a recent phenomenon.

  2. The convergence of levels of output per person is not a worldwide phenomenon. Many Asian countries are rapidly catching up, while most African countries have both low levels of output per person and low growth rates.

- To think about growth, economists start from an aggregate production function relating aggregate output to two factors of production: capital and labor. How much output is produced given these inputs depends on the state of technology.

- Under the assumption of constant returns, the aggregate production function implies that increases in output per worker can come either from increases in capital per worker or from improvements in the state of technology.

- Capital accumulation by itself cannot permanently sustain growth of output per person. Nevertheless, how much a country saves is important because the saving rate determines the *level* of output per person, if not its growth rate.

- Sustained growth of output per person is ultimately due to technological progress. Perhaps the most important question in growth theory is what the determinants of technological progress are.

Key Terms

growth, 219
logarithmic scale, 219
standard of living, 220
output per person, 220
purchasing power, 221
purchasing power parity (PPP), 221
Easterlin paradox, 224
force of compounding, 225
convergence, 226
Malthusian trap, 227

four tigers, 228
aggregate production function, 229
state of technology, 230
constant returns to scale, 230
decreasing returns to capital, 230
decreasing returns to labor, 231
capital accumulation, 232
technological progress, 232
saving rate, 232

Questions and Problems

QUICK CHECK

MyEconLab Visit www.myeconlab.com to complete similar Quick Check problems and get instant feedback.

1. *Using the information in this chapter, label each of the following statements true, false, or uncertain. Explain briefly.*

   a. On a logarithmic scale, a variable that increases at 5% per year will move along an upward-sloping line with a slope of 0.05.

   b. The price of food is higher in poor countries than it is in rich countries.

   c. Evidence suggests that happiness in rich countries increases with output per person.

   d. In virtually all the countries of the world, output per person is converging to the level of output per person in the United States.

   e. For about 1,000 years after the fall of the Roman Empire, there was essentially no growth in output per person in Europe because any increase in output led to a proportional increase in population.

   f. Capital accumulation does not affect the level of output in the long run, only technological progress does.

   g. The aggregate production function is a relation between output on one hand and labor and capital on the other.

2. *Suppose that every month the average student in Tokyo, Japan, and the average student in Beijing, China, consume the following quantities of food and transportation services at the following prices:*

	Food		Transportation Services	
	Price	Quantity (meals)	Price	Quantity (rides)
Tokyo	¥600	60	¥170	80
Beijing	RMB15	50	RMB3	100

   a. Compute the average expenditure of the Japanese student for food and transportation services (in Yen).

   b. Compute the average expenditure of the Chinese student for food and transportation services (in Yuan).

   c. Suppose that 1 Yuan is worth 17 Yen. Compute the average expenditure of the Chinese student in Yen.

   d. Using the purchasing power parity method, compute the average expenditure of the Chinese student in Yen.

   e. Compare the standards of living of the Chinese and Japanese students. Which one is lower? What difference does the choice of method make?

3. *Consider the following production function:*

$$Y = K + 2N$$

   a. Suppose that $K = 10$ and $N = 20$. What is the value of Y?

   b. Suppose that K and N triple. What happens to Y?

   c. How would you qualify the returns to scale for this function?

   d. Write this function as a relation between output per worker and capital per worker.

   e. Suppose $K/N = 2$. What is the value of Y/N? What happens to Y/N if K/N is doubled?

   f. Does the relation between output per worker and capital per worker exhibit the same returns to scale as the above production function?

   g. What is the difference between the two functions?

   h. Plot the relation between output per worker and capital per worker. How does the shape of the relationship between the two compare with Figure 10.4?

DIG DEEPER

MyEconLab Visit www.myeconlab.com to complete all Dig Deeper problems and get instant feedback.

4. *The growth rates of capital and output*

   Consider the production function given in problem 3. Assume that N is constant and equal to 1. Note that if $z = x^a$, then $g_z \approx ag_x$, where g_z and g_x are the growth rates of z and x.

   a. Given the growth approximation here, derive the relation between the growth rate of output and the growth rate of capital.

   b. Suppose we want to achieve output growth equal to 2% per year. What is the required rate of growth of capital?

   c. In (b), what happens to the ratio of capital to output over time?

   d. Is it possible to sustain output growth of 2% forever in this economy? Why or why not?

5. *Between 1950 and 1973, France, Germany, and Japan all experienced growth rates that were at least two percentage points higher than those in the United States. Yet the most important technological advances of that period were made in the United States. How can this be?*

EXPLORE FURTHER

6. *On the World Bank's Web site (http://data.worldbank.org/indicator/NY.GDP.PCAP.KD), find the data on GDP per capita (in constant 2005 US$) for China and for the Euro area (which includes Austria, Belgium, Cyprus, Estonia, Finland, France, Germany, Greece, Ireland, Italy, Latvia, Lithuania, Luxembourg, Malta, the Netherlands, Portugal, Slovakia, Slovenia, and Spain), for the years 1960, 1980, 2000, and the latest year available.*

   a. Compare the levels of GDP per capita in China and the Euro area at these four periods. Do you observe any convergence?

   b. Calculate the average annual growth rate of GDP per capita in China and the Euro area for three periods: 1960–1980, 1980–2000, and 2000–last year available. Do growth rates actually confirm your finding of convergence/non-convergence between the GDP per capita of the two countries/areas?

   c. Suppose that the Euro area's GDP per capita were to increase by 1% each year during the next 20 years, while China's GDP per capita were to rise by 6% per year during the same period. How would the distance between the two economies' GDP per capita change after 20 years?

7. *Convergence in two sets of countries*

   Go to the Web site containing the Penn World Table and collect data on real GDP per person (chained series) from 1950 to 2011 (or the most recent year available) for the United States, France,

Belgium, Italy, Ethiopia, Kenya, Nigeria, and Uganda. You will need to download total real GDP in chained 2005 US dollars and population. Define for each country for each year the ratio of its real GDP per person to that of the United States for that year (so that this ratio will be equal to 1 for the United States for all years).

a. Plot these ratios for France, Belgium, and Italy over the period for which you have data. Does your data support the notion of convergence among France, Belgium, and Italy with the United States?

b. Plot these ratios for Ethiopia, Kenya, Nigeria, and Uganda. Does this data support the notion of convergence among Ethiopia, Kenya, Nigeria, and Uganda with the United States?

8. Growth successes and failures

Go to the Web site containing the Penn World Table and collect data on real GDP per capita (chained series) for 1970 for all available countries. Do the same for a recent year of data, say one year before the most recent year available in the Penn World Table. (If you choose the most recent year available, the Penn World Table may not have the data for some countries relevant to this question.)

a. Rank the countries according to GDP per person in 1970. List the countries with the 10 highest levels of GDP per person in 1970. Are there any surprises?

b. Carry out the analysis in part (a) for the most recent year for which you collected data. Has the composition of the 10 richest countries changed since 1970?

c. Use all the countries for which there are data in both 1970 and the latest year. Which five countries have the highest proportional increase in real GDP per capita?

d. Use all the countries for which there are data in both 1970 and the latest year. Which five countries have the lowest proportional increase in real GDP per capita?

e. Do a brief Internet search on either the country from part (c) with the greatest increase in GDP per capita or the country from part (d) with the smallest increase. Can you ascertain any reasons for the economic success, or lack of it, for this country?

Further Readings

■ Brad deLong has a number of fascinating articles on growth (http://web.efzg.hr/dok/MGR/vcavrak//Berkeley%20Faculty%20Lunch%20Talk.pdf). Read in particular "Berkeley Faculty Lunch Talk: Main Themes of Twentieth Century Economic History," which covers many of the themes of this chapter.

■ A broad presentation of facts about growth is given by Angus Maddison in *The World Economy. A Millenium Perspective* (2001). The associated site, www.theworldeconomy.org, has a large number of facts and data on growth over the last two millenia.

■ Chapter 3 in *Productivity and American Leadership*, by William Baumol, Sue Anne Batey Blackman, and Edward Wolff (1989), gives a vivid description of how life has been transformed by growth in the United States since the mid-1880s.

Saving, Capital Accumulation, and Output

Since 1970, the U.S. **saving rate**—the ratio of saving to gross domestic product (GDP)—has averaged only 17%, compared to 22% in Germany and 30% in Japan. Can this explain why the U.S. growth rate has been lower than in most OECD countries in the last 40 years? Would increasing the U.S. saving rate lead to sustained higher U.S. growth in the future?

We have already given the basic answer to these questions at the end of Chapter 10. The answer is no. Over long periods—an important qualification to which we will return—an economy's growth rate does not depend on its saving rate. It does not appear that lower U.S. growth in the last 50 years comes primarily from a low saving rate. Nor should we expect that an increase in the saving rate will lead to sustained higher U.S. growth.

This conclusion does not mean, however, that we should not be concerned about the low U.S. saving rate. Even if the saving rate does not permanently affect the growth rate, it does affect the level of output and the standard of living. An increase in the saving rate would lead to higher growth for some time and eventually to a higher standard of living in the United States.

This chapter focuses on the effects of the saving rate on the level and the growth rate of output.

Sections 11-1 and **11-2** look at the interactions between output and capital accumulation and the effects of the saving rate.

Section 11-3 plugs in numbers to give a better sense of the magnitudes involved.

Section 11-4 extends our discussion to take into account not only physical but also human capital.

11-1 Interactions between Output and Capital

At the center of the determination of output in the long run are two relations between output and capital:

- The amount of capital determines the amount of output being produced.
- The amount of output being produced determines the amount of saving and, in turn, the amount of capital being accumulated over time.

Together, these two relations, which are represented in Figure 11-1, determine the evolution of output and capital over time. The green arrow captures the first relation, from capital to output. The blue and purple arrows capture the two parts of the second relation, from output to saving and investment, and from investment to the change in the capital stock. Let's look at each relation in turn.

The Effects of Capital on Output

We started discussing the first of these two relations, the effect of capital on output, in Section 10-3. There we introduced the aggregate production function and you saw that, under the assumption of constant returns to scale, we can write the following relation between output and capital per worker:

$$\frac{Y}{N} = F\left(\frac{K}{N}, 1\right)$$

Output per worker (Y/N) is an increasing function of capital per worker (K/N). Under the assumption of decreasing returns to capital, the effect of a given increase in capital per worker on output per worker decreases as the ratio of capital per worker gets larger. When capital per worker is already high, further increases in capital per worker have only a small effect on output per worker.

To simplify notation, we will rewrite this relation between output and capital per worker simply as

$$\frac{Y}{N} = f\left(\frac{K}{N}\right)$$

where the function f represents the same relation between output and capital per worker as the function F:

$$f\left(\frac{K}{N}\right) \equiv F\left(\frac{K}{N}, 1\right)$$

In this chapter, we shall make two further assumptions:

- The first is that the size of the population, the participation rate, and the unemployment rate are all constant. This implies that employment, N, is also constant. To see why, go back to the relations we saw in Chapter 2 and again in Chapter 7, between population, the labor force, unemployment, and employment.

Suppose, for example, the function F has the "double square_root" form $F(K,N) = \sqrt{K}\sqrt{N}$, so

$$Y = \sqrt{K}\sqrt{N}$$

Divide both sides by N, so

$$Y/N = \sqrt{K}\sqrt{N}/N$$

Note $\sqrt{N}/N = \sqrt{N}/(\sqrt{N}\sqrt{N})$ Using this result in the preceding equation leads to a model of income per person:

$$Y/N = \sqrt{K}/\sqrt{N} = \sqrt{K/N} \blacktriangleright$$

So, in this case, the function f giving the relation between output per worker and capital per worker is simply the square root function

$$f(K/N) = \sqrt{K/N}$$

Figure 11-1

Capital, Output, and Saving/Investment

MyEconLab Animation

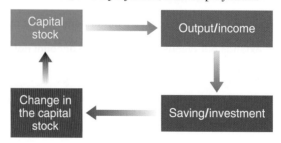

- The labor force is equal to population multiplied by the participation rate. So if population is constant and the participation rate is constant, the labor force is also constant.
- Employment, in turn, is equal to the labor force multiplied by 1 minus the unemployment rate. If, for example, the size of the labor force is 100 million and the unemployment rate is 5%, then employment is equal to 95 million (100 million times $(1 - 0.05)$). So, if the labor force is constant and the unemployment rate is constant, employment is also constant.

Under these assumptions, output per worker, output per person, and output itself all move proportionately. Although we will usually refer to movements in output or capital *per worker*, to lighten the text we shall sometimes just talk about movements in output or capital, leaving out the "per worker" or "per person" qualification.

◄ In the United States in 2014, output per person (in 2005 PPP dollars) was $46,400; output per worker was much higher, at $100,790. (From these two numbers, can you derive the ratio of employment to population?)

The reason for assuming that N is constant is to make it easier to focus on how capital accumulation affects growth. If N is constant, the only factor of production that changes over time is capital. The assumption is not realistic, however, so we will relax it in the next two chapters. In Chapter 12, we will allow for steady population and employment growth. In Chapter 13, we shall see how we can integrate our analysis of the long run—which ignores fluctuations in employment—with our earlier analysis of the short and medium runs—which focused precisely on these fluctuations in employment (and the associated fluctuations in output and unemployment). Both steps are better left to later.

- The second assumption is that there is no technological progress, so the production function f (or, equivalently, F) does not change over time.

Again, the reason for making this assumption—which is obviously contrary to reality—is to focus just on the role of capital accumulation. In Chapter 12, we shall introduce technological progress and see that the basic conclusions we derive here about the role of capital in growth also hold when there is technological progress. Again, this step is better left to later.

With these two assumptions, our first relation between output and capital per worker, from the production side, can be written as

$$\frac{Y_t}{N} = f\left(\frac{K_t}{N}\right) \tag{11.1}$$

where we have introduced time indexes for output and capital—but not for labor, N, which we assume to be constant and so does not need a time index.

In words: Higher capital per worker leads to higher output per worker.

From the production side: The level of capital per worker determines the level of output ◄ per worker.

The Effects of Output on Capital Accumulation

To derive the second relation between output and capital accumulation, we proceed in two steps.

First, we derive the relation between output and investment.

Then we derive the relation between investment and capital accumulation.

Output and Investment

To derive the relation between output and investment, we make three assumptions:

- We continue to assume that the economy is closed. As we saw in Chapter 3 (equation (3.10)), this means that investment, I, is equal to saving—the sum of private saving, S, and public saving, $T - G$.

$$I = S + (T - G)$$

As we shall see in Chapter 17, saving and investment need not be equal in an open economy. A country can save less ◄ than it invests, and borrow the difference from the rest of the world. This is indeed the case for the United States today.

- To focus on the behavior of private saving, we assume that public saving, $T - G$, is equal to zero. (We shall later relax this assumption when we focus on the effects of fiscal policy on growth.) With this assumption, the previous equation becomes

$$I = S$$

Investment is equal to private saving.

- We assume that private saving is proportional to income, so

$$S = sY$$

You have now seen two specifications of saving behavior (equivalently consumption behavior): one for the short run in Chapter 3, and one for the long run in this chapter. You may wonder how the two specifications relate to each other and whether they are consistent. The answer is yes. A full discussion is given in Chapter 15.

The parameter s is the saving rate. It has a value between zero and 1. This assumption captures two basic facts about saving. First, the saving rate does not appear to systematically increase or decrease as a country becomes richer. Second, richer countries do not appear to have systematically higher or lower saving rates than poorer ones.

Combining these two relations and introducing time indexes gives a simple relation between investment and output:

$$I_t = sY_t$$

Investment is proportional to output; the higher output is, the higher is saving and so the higher is investment.

Investment and Capital Accumulation

Recall: Flows are variables that have a time dimension (that is, they are defined per unit of time); stocks are variables that do not have a time dimension (they are defined at a point in time). Output, saving, and investment are flows. Employment and capital are stocks.

The second step relates investment, which is a flow (the new machines produced and new plants built during a given period), to capital, which is a stock (the existing machines and plants in the economy at a point in time).

Think of time as measured in years, so t denotes year $t, t + 1$ denotes year $t + 1$, and so on. Think of the capital stock as being measured at the beginning of each year, so K_t refers to the capital stock at the beginning of year t, K_{t+1} to the capital stock at the beginning of year $t + 1$ and so on.

Assume that capital depreciates at rate δ (the lowercase Greek letter delta) per year. That is, from one year to the next, a proportion δ of the capital stock breaks down and becomes useless. Equivalently, a proportion $(1 - \delta)$ of the capital stock remains intact from one year to the next.

The evolution of the capital stock is then given by

$$K_{t+1} = (1 - \delta)K_t + I_t$$

The capital stock at the beginning of year $t + 1$, K_{t+1}, is equal to the capital stock at the beginning of year t, which is still intact in year $t + 1, (1 - \delta)K_t$, plus the new capital stock put in place during year t (i.e., investment during year t, I_t).

We can now combine the relation between output and investment and the relation between investment and capital accumulation to obtain the second relation we need to think about growth: the relation from output to capital accumulation.

Replacing investment by its expression from above and dividing both sides by N (the number of workers in the economy) gives

$$\frac{K_{t+1}}{N} = (1 - \delta)\frac{K_t}{N} + s\frac{Y_t}{N}$$

In words: Capital per worker at the beginning of year $t + 1$ is equal to capital per worker at the beginning of year t, adjusted for depreciation, plus investment per worker during year t, which is equal to the saving rate times output per worker during year t.

Expanding the term $(1 - \delta)K_t/N$ to $K_t/N - \delta K_t/N$, moving K_t/N to the left, and reorganizing the right side,

$$\frac{K_{t+1}}{N} - \frac{K_t}{N} = s\frac{Y_t}{N} - \delta\frac{K_t}{N} \tag{11.2}$$

In words: The change in the capital stock per worker, represented by the difference between the two terms on the left, is equal to saving per worker, represented by the first term on the right, minus depreciation, represented by the second term on the right. This equation gives us the second relation between output and capital per worker.

From the saving side: The level of output per worker determines the change in the level of capital per worker over time.

11-2 The Implications of Alternative Saving Rates

We have derived two relations:

- From the production side, we have seen in equation (11.1) how capital determines output.
- From the saving side, we have seen in equation (11.2) how output in turn determines capital accumulation.

We can now put the two relations together and see how they determine the behavior of output and capital over time.

Dynamics of Capital and Output

Replacing output per worker (Y_t/N) in equation (11.2) by its expression in terms of capital per worker from equation (11.1) gives

$$\underset{\substack{\text{change in capital}\\ \text{from year } t \text{ to year } t+1}}{\frac{K_{t+1}}{N} - \frac{K_t}{N}} = \underset{\substack{\text{Invesment}\\ \text{during year } t}}{sf\left(\frac{K_t}{N}\right)} - \underset{\substack{\text{depreciation}\\ \text{during year } t}}{\delta\left(\frac{K_t}{N}\right)} \tag{11.3}$$

This relation describes what happens to capital per worker. The change in capital per worker from this year to next year depends on the difference between two terms:

- Investment per worker, the first term on the right: The level of capital per worker this year determines output per worker this year. Given the saving rate, output per worker determines the amount of saving per worker and thus the investment per worker this year.
- Depreciation per worker, the second term on the right: The capital stock per worker determines the amount of depreciation per worker this year.

$K_t/N \Rightarrow f(K_t/N) \Rightarrow sf(K_t/N)$

$K_t/N \Rightarrow \delta K_t/N$

If investment per worker exceeds depreciation per worker, the change in capital per worker is positive. Capital per worker increases.

If investment per worker is less than depreciation per worker, the change in capital per worker is negative. Capital per worker decreases.

Given capital per worker, output per worker is then given by equation (11.1):

$$\frac{Y_t}{N} = f\left(\frac{K_t}{N}\right)$$

Equations (11.3) and (11.1) contain all the information we need to understand the dynamics of capital and output over time. The easiest way to interpret them is to use a

Figure 11-2

Capital and Output Dynamics

When capital and output are low, investment exceeds depreciation and capital increases. When capital and output are high, investment is less than depreciation and capital decreases.

MyEconLab Animation

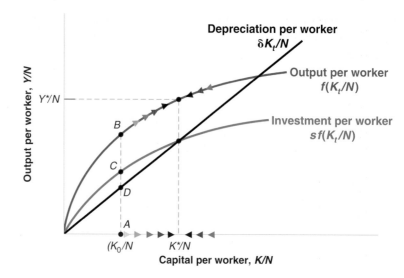

graph. We do this in Figure 11-2: Output per worker is measured on the vertical axis, and capital per worker is measured on the horizontal axis.

In Figure 11-2, look first at the curve representing output per worker, $f(K_t/N)$, as a function of capital per worker. The relation is the same as in Figure 10-4: Output per worker increases with capital per worker, but, because of decreasing returns to capital, the effect is smaller the higher the level of capital per worker.

Now look at the two curves representing the two components on the right of equation (11.3):

■ The relation representing investment per worker, $sf(K_t/N)$, has the same shape as
To make the graph easier to ▶ read, I have assumed an unrealistically high saving rate. (Can you tell roughly what value we have assumed for s? What would be a plausible value for s?)
the production function except that it is lower by a factor s (the saving rate). Suppose the level of capital per worker is equal to K_0/N in Figure 11-2. Output per worker is then given by the distance AB, and investment per worker is given by the vertical distance AC, which is equal to s times the vertical distance AB. Thus, just like output per worker, investment per worker increases with capital per worker, but by less and less as capital per worker increases. When capital per worker is already high, the effect of a further increase in capital per worker on output per worker, and by implication on investment per worker, is small.

■ The relation representing depreciation per worker, $\delta K_t/N$, is represented by a straight line. Depreciation per worker increases in proportion to capital per worker so the relation is represented by a straight line with slope equal to δ. At the level of capital per worker K_0/N, depreciation per worker is given by the vertical distance AD.

The change in capital per worker is given by the difference between investment per worker and depreciation per worker. At K_0/N, the difference is positive; investment per worker exceeds depreciation per worker by an amount represented by the vertical distance $CD = AC - AD$, so capital per worker increases. As we move to the right along the horizontal axis and look at higher and higher levels of capital per worker, investment increases by less and less, while depreciation keeps increasing in proportion to capital. For some level of capital per worker, K^*/N in Figure 11-2, investment is just enough to

When capital per worker is low, capital per worker and output per worker increase over time. When capital per worker is high, capital per worker and output per worker ▶ decrease over time.
cover depreciation, and capital per worker remains constant. To the left of K^*/N, investment exceeds depreciation and capital per worker increases. This is indicated by the arrows pointing to the right along the curve representing the production function. To the right of K^*/N, depreciation exceeds investment, and capital per worker decreases. This is indicated by the arrows pointing to the left along the curve representing the production function.

Characterizing the evolution of capital per worker and output per worker over time now is easy. Consider an economy that starts with a low level of capital per worker—say, K^*/N in Figure 11-2. Because investment exceeds depreciation at this point, capital per worker increases. And because output moves with capital, output per worker increases as well. Capital per worker eventually reaches K^*/N, the level at which investment is equal to depreciation. Once the economy has reached the level of capital per worker K^*N, output per worker and capital per worker remain constant at Y^*/N and K^*/N, their long-run equilibrium levels.

Think, for example, of a country that loses part of its capital stock, say as a result of bombing during a war. The mechanism we have just seen suggests that, if the country has suffered larger capital losses than population losses, it will come out of the war with a low level of capital per worker; that is, at a point to the left of K^*/N. The country will then experience a large increase in both capital per worker and output per worker for some time. This describes well what happened after World War II to countries that had proportionately larger destructions of capital than losses of human lives (see the Focus box "Capital Accumulation and Growth in France in the Aftermath of World War II").

What does the model predict for postwar growth if a country suffers proportional losses in population and in capital? Do you find this answer convincing? What elements may be missing from the model?

If a country starts instead from a high level of capital per worker—that is, from a point to the right of K^*/N—then depreciation will exceed investment, and capital per worker and output per worker will decrease. The initial level of capital per worker is too high to be sustained given the saving rate. This decrease in capital per worker will continue until the economy again reaches the point where investment is equal to depreciation and capital per worker is equal to K^*/N. From then on, capital per worker and output per worker will remain constant.

Let's look more closely at the levels of output per worker and capital per worker to which the economy converges in the long run. The state in which output per worker and capital per worker are no longer changing is called the **steady state** of the economy. Setting the left side of equation (11.3) equal to zero (in steady state, by definition, the change in capital per worker is zero), the steady-state value of capital per worker, K^*/N, is given by

$$s f\left(\frac{K^*}{N}\right) = \delta \frac{K^*}{N} \tag{11.4}$$

The steady-state value of capital per worker is such that the amount of saving per worker (the left side) is just sufficient to cover depreciation of the capital stock per worker (the right side of the equation).

◄ K^*/N is the long-run level of capital per worker.

Given steady-state capital per worker (K^*/N), the steady-state value of output per worker (Y^*/N) is given by the production function

$$\frac{Y^*}{N} = f\left(\frac{K^*}{N}\right) \tag{11.5}$$

We now have all the elements we need to discuss the effects of the saving rate on output per worker, both over time and in steady state.

The Saving Rate and Output

Let's return to the question we posed at the beginning of the chapter: How does the saving rate affect the growth rate of output per worker? Our analysis leads to a three-part answer:

1. *The saving rate has no effect on the long-run growth rate of output per worker, which is equal to zero.*

Capital Accumulation and Growth in France in the Aftermath of World War II

FOCUS

When World War II ended in 1945, France had suffered some of the heaviest losses of all European countries. The losses in lives were large. Out of a population of 42 million, more than 550,000 people died. Relatively speaking, though, the losses in capital were much larger. It is estimated that the French capital stock in 1945 was about 30% below its prewar value. A vivid picture of the destruction of capital is provided by the numbers in Table 1.

The model of growth we have just seen makes a clear prediction about what will happen to a country that loses a large part of its capital stock. The country will experience high capital accumulation and output growth for some time. In terms of Figure 11-2, a country with capital per worker initially far below K^*/N will grow rapidly as it converges to K^*/N and output per worker converges to Y^*/N.

This prediction fares well in the case of postwar France. There is plenty of anecdotal evidence that small increases in capital led to large increases in output. Minor repairs to a major bridge would lead to the reopening of the bridge. Reopening the bridge would significantly shorten the travel time between two cities, leading to much lower transport

costs. The lower transport costs would then enable a plant to get much needed inputs, increase its production, and so on.

More convincing evidence, however, comes directly from actual aggregate output numbers. From 1946 to 1950, the annual growth rate of French real GDP was a high 9.6% per year. This led to an increase in real GDP of about 60% over the course of 5 years.

Was all of the increase in French GDP the result of capital accumulation? The answer is no. There were other forces at work in addition to the mechanism in our model. Much of the remaining capital stock in 1945 was old. Investment had been low in the 1930s (a decade dominated by the Great Depression) and nearly nonexistent during the war. A good portion of the postwar capital accumulation was associated with the introduction of more modern capital and the use of more modern production techniques. This was another reason for the high growth rates of the postwar period.

Source: Gilles Saint-Paul, "Economic Reconstruction in France, 1945–1958," in Rudiger Dornbusch, Willem Nolling, and Richard Layard, eds. *Postwar Economic Reconstruction and Lessons for the East Today* (Cambridge, MA: MIT Press, 1993).

Table 1	Proportion of the French Capital Stock Destroyed by the End of World War II				
Railways	Tracks	6%	Rivers	Waterways	86%
	Stations	38%		Canal locks	11%
	Engines	21%		Barges	80%
	Hardware	60%	Buildings	(numbers)	
Roads	Cars	31%		Dwellings	1,229,000
	Trucks	40%		Industrial	246,000

This conclusion is rather obvious; we have seen that, eventually, the economy converges to a constant level of output per worker. In other words, in the long run, the growth rate of output is equal to zero, no matter what the saving rate is.

There is, however, a way of thinking about this conclusion that will be useful when we introduce technological progress in Chapter 12. Think of what would be needed to sustain a constant positive growth rate of output per worker in the long run. Capital per worker would have to increase. Not only that, but, because of decreasing returns to capital, it would have to increase faster than output per worker. This implies that each year the economy would have to save a larger and larger fraction of its output and dedicate it to capital accumulation. At some point, the fraction of output it would need to save would be greater than 1—something clearly impossible. This is why it is impossible, absent technological progress, to sustain a constant positive growth rate forever. In the long run, capital per worker must be constant, and so output per worker must also be constant.

Some economists argue that the high output growth achieved by the Soviet Union from 1950 to 1990 was the result of such a steady increase in the saving rate over time, which could not be sustained forever. Paul Krugman ▶ has used the term *Stalinist growth* to denote this type of growth, which is growth resulting from a higher and higher saving rate over time.

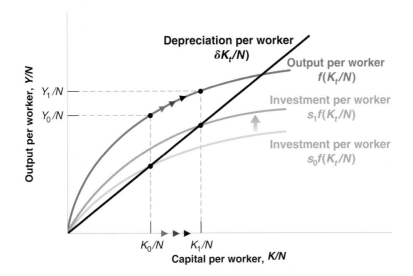

Figure 11-3

The Effects of Different Saving Rates

A country with a higher saving rate achieves a higher steady-state level of output per worker.

MyEconLab Animation

2. Nonetheless, *the saving rate determines the level of output per worker in the long run.* Other things being equal, countries with a higher saving rate will achieve higher output per worker in the long run.

Note that the first proposition ◀ is a statement about the growth rate of output per worker. The second proposition is a statement about the level of output per worker.

   Figure 11-3 illustrates this point. Consider two countries with the same production function, the same level of employment, and the same depreciation rate, but with different saving rates, say s_0 and $s_1 > s_0$. Figure 11-3 draws their common production function, $f(K_t/N)$, and the functions showing saving/investment per worker as a function of capital per worker for each of the two countries, $s_0 f(K_t/N)$ and $s_1 f(K_t/N)$. In the long run, the country with saving rate s_0 will reach the level of capital per worker K_0/N and output per worker Y_0/N. The country with saving rate s_1 will reach the higher levels K_1/N and Y_1/N.

3. *An increase in the saving rate will lead to higher growth of output per worker for some time, but not forever.*

   This conclusion follows from the two propositions we just discussed. From the first, we know that an increase in the saving rate does not affect the long-run *growth rate of output per worker*, which remains equal to zero. From the second, we know that an increase in the saving rate leads to an increase in the long-run *level of output per worker*. It follows that, as output per worker increases to its new higher level in response to the increase in the saving rate, the economy will go through a period of positive growth. This period of growth will come to an end when the economy reaches its new steady state.

   We can use Figure 11-3 again to illustrate this point. Consider a country that has an initial saving rate of s_0. Assume that capital per worker is initially equal to K_0/N, with associated output per worker Y_0/N. Now consider the effects of an increase in the saving rate from s_0 to s_1. The function giving saving/investment per worker as a function of capital per worker shifts upward from $s_0 f(K_t/N)$ to $s_1 f(K_t/N)$.

   At the initial level of capital per worker, K_0/N, investment exceeds depreciation, so capital per worker increases. As capital per worker increases, so does output per worker, and the economy goes through a period of positive growth. When capital per worker eventually reaches K_1/N, however, investment is again equal to depreciation, and growth ends. From then on, the economy remains at K_1/N, with associated output per worker Y_1/N. The movement of output per worker is plotted against

Figure 11-4

The Effects of an Increase in the Saving Rate on Output per Worker in an Economy without Technological Progress

An increase in the saving rate leads to a period of higher growth until output reaches its new higher steady-state level.

MyEconLab Animation

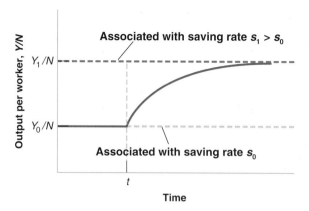

See the discussion of logarithmic scales in Appendix 2 at the end of the book.

time in Figure 11-4. Output per worker is initially constant at level Y_0/N. After the increase in the saving rate, say, at time t, output per worker increases for some time until it reaches the higher level of output per worker Y_1/N and the growth rate returns to zero.

We have derived these three results under the assumption that there was no technological progress, and therefore, no growth of output per worker in the long run. But, as we will see in Chapter 12, the three results extend to an economy in which there is technological progress. Let us briefly indicate how.

An economy in which there is technological progress has a positive growth rate of output per worker, even in the long run. This long-run growth rate is independent of the saving rate—the extension of the first result just discussed. The saving rate affects the level of output per worker, however—the extension of the second result. An increase in the saving rate leads to growth greater than steady-state growth for some time until the economy reaches its new higher path—the extension of our third result.

These three results are illustrated in Figure 11-5, which extends Figure 11-4 by plotting the effect an increase in the saving rate has on an economy with positive technological progress. The figure uses a logarithmic scale to measure output per worker. It follows that an economy in which output per worker grows at a constant rate is represented by a line with slope equal to that growth rate. At the initial saving rate, s_0, the economy moves along AA. If, at time t, the saving rate increases to s_1, the economy experiences higher growth for some time until it reaches its new, higher path, BB. On path BB, the growth rate is again the same as before the increase in the saving rate (that is, the slope of BB is the same as the slope of AA).

Figure 11-5

The Effects of an Increase in the Saving Rate on Output per Worker in an Economy with Technological Progress

An increase in the saving rate leads to a period of higher growth until output reaches a new, higher path.

MyEconLab Animation

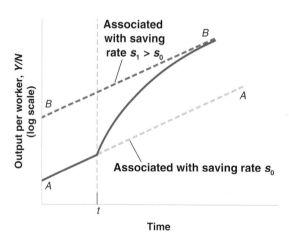

The Saving Rate and Consumption

Governments can affect the saving rate in various ways. First, they can vary public saving. Given private saving, positive public saving—a budget surplus, in other words—leads to higher overall saving. Conversely, negative public saving—a budget deficit—leads to lower overall saving. Second, governments can use taxes to affect private saving. For example, they can give tax breaks to people who save, making it more attractive to save and thus increasing private saving.

Recall: Saving is the sum of private plus public saving. Recall also, that
  Public saving ⟺ Budget surplus;
  Public dissaving ⟺ Budget deficit.

What saving rate should governments aim for? To think about the answer, we must shift our focus from the behavior of *output* to the behavior of *consumption*. The reason: What matters to people is not how much is produced, but how much they consume.

It is clear that an increase in saving must come initially at the expense of lower consumption (except when we think it helpful, we drop "per worker" in this subsection and just refer to consumption rather than consumption per worker, capital rather than capital per worker, and so on). A change in the saving rate this year has no effect on capital this year, and consequently no effect on output and income *this year*. So an increase in saving comes initially with an equal decrease in consumption.

Does an increase in saving lead to an increase in consumption in the long run? Not necessarily. Consumption may decrease, not only initially, but also in the long run. You may find this surprising. After all, we know from Figure 11-3 that an increase in the saving rate always leads to an increase in the level of *output* per worker. But output is not the same as consumption. To see why not, consider what happens for two extreme values of the saving rate.

Because we assume that employment is constant, we are ignoring the short-run effect of an increase in the saving rate on output we focused on in Chapters 3, 5, and 9. In the short run, not only does an increase in the saving rate reduce consumption given income, but it may also create a recession and decrease income further. We shall return to a discussion of short-run and long-run effects of changes in saving in Chapters 16 and 22.

- An economy in which the saving rate is (and has always been) zero is an economy in which capital is equal to zero. In this case, output is also equal to zero, and so is consumption. A saving rate equal to zero implies zero consumption in the long run.
- Now consider an economy in which the saving rate is equal to one. People save all their income. The level of capital, and thus output, in this economy will be high. But because people save all of their income, consumption is equal to zero. What happens is that the economy is carrying an excessive amount of capital. Simply maintaining that level of output requires that all output be devoted to replacing depreciation! A saving rate equal to one also implies zero consumption in the long run.

These two extreme cases mean that there must be some value of the saving rate between zero and one that maximizes the steady-state level of consumption. Increases in the saving rate below this value lead to a decrease in consumption initially, but lead to an increase in consumption in the long run. Increases in the saving rate beyond this value decrease consumption not only initially but also in the long run. This happens because the increase in capital associated with the increase in the saving rate leads to only a small increase in output—an increase that is too small to cover the increased depreciation. In other words, the economy carries too much capital. The level of capital associated with the value of the saving rate that yields the highest level of consumption in steady state is known as the **golden-rule level of capital**. Increases in capital beyond the golden-rule level reduce steady-state consumption.

This argument is illustrated in Figure 11-6, which plots consumption per worker in steady state (on the vertical axis) against the saving rate (on the horizontal axis). A saving rate equal to zero implies a capital stock per worker equal to zero, a level of output per worker equal to zero, and, by implication, a level of consumption per worker equal to zero. For s between zero and s_G (G for golden rule), a higher saving rate leads to higher capital per worker, higher output per worker, and higher consumption per worker. For s larger than s_G, increases in the saving rate still lead to higher values of capital per worker and output per worker; but they now lead to lower values of consumption per worker.

Figure 11-6

The Effects of the Saving Rate on Steady-State Consumption per Worker

An increase in the saving rate leads to an increase, then to a decrease in steady-state consumption per worker.

MyEconLab Animation

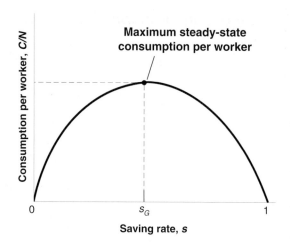

MyEconLab Video

This is because the increase in output is more than offset by the increase in depreciation as a result of the larger capital stock. For $s = 1$, consumption per worker is equal to zero. Capital per worker and output per worker are high, but all of the output is used just to replace depreciation, leaving nothing for consumption.

If an economy already has so much capital that it is operating beyond the golden rule, then increasing saving further will decrease consumption not only now, but also later. Is this a relevant worry? Do some countries actually have too much capital? The empirical evidence indicates that most OECD countries are actually far below their golden-rule level of capital. If they were to increase the saving rate, it would lead to higher consumption in the future—not lower consumption.

This means that, in practice, governments face a trade-off: An increase in the saving rate leads to lower consumption for some time but higher consumption later. So what should governments do? How close to the golden rule should they try to get? That depends on how much weight they put on the welfare of current generations—who are more likely to lose from policies aimed at increasing the saving rate—versus the welfare of future generations—who are more likely to gain. Enter politics; future generations do not vote. This means that governments are unlikely to ask current generations to make large sacrifices, which, in turn, means that capital is likely to stay far below its golden-rule level. These intergenerational issues are at the forefront of the current debate on Social Security reform in the United States. The Focus box "Ageing, Contractual Mandatory Retirement, and Slow Growth in Japan" explores this further.

11-3 Getting a Sense of Magnitudes

How big an impact does a change in the saving rate have on output in the long run? For how long and by how much does an increase in the saving rate affect growth? How far is the United States from the golden-rule level of capital? To get a better sense of the answers to these questions, let's now make more specific assumptions, plug in some numbers, and see what we get.

Assume the production function is

$$Y = \sqrt{K}\sqrt{N} \tag{11.6}$$

▶ Check that this production function exhibits both constant returns to scale and decreasing returns to either capital or labor.

Output equals the product of the square root of capital and the square root of labor. (A more general specification of the production function known as the Cobb-Douglas production function, and its implications for growth, is given in the appendix to this chapter.)

Ageing, Contractual Mandatory Retirement, and Slow Growth in Japan

FOCUS

The very sluggish growth Japan started to experience in the early 1990s was, at first, attributed to a combination of financial troubles and insufficient effective demand. Financial troubles, epitomized by the high proportion of problem loans at Japanese banks, were similarly overcome at the dawn of the 2000s. But GDP continued to grow at a slow pace.

Another explanation was offered on the basis of demographic trends, aggregate household behavior and the specific structure of the Welfare State in Japan. The Japanese population is among the fastest ageing populations in the world. As a result of low fertility rates and high life expectancy, the proportion of the elderly (persons aged 65 and more) has continuously increased over the past decades, to reach a peak of 25.9% of total population in 2014. While the Japanese population is ageing fast, the practice of contractual mandatory retirement is widespread—as in several other high-income countries, particularly Continental European ones. However, Japan is unique among other advanced economies in the low mandatory retirement age it sets for many of its workers—often years before the age required to benefit from state or national pensions.

What effect, then, could this particular combination of ageing and contractual mandatory retirement may have on the savings rate and the growth rate? It is very straightforward: these two factors are likely to reduce the savings rate. Early retirees with no access to state or national pensions must draw on their savings to maintain spending and, more generally, their standard of living. Indeed, this is exactly what has happened in Japan. The Japanese household savings rate was among the highest in high-income countries at the outset of the "lost decade:" in 1994, according to OECD data, Japanese households saved, on average, 11.56% of their disposable income—a little less than twice the average savings rate of U.S. households (6.53%). Since then, however, household savings has dropped dramatically, reaching an all-time low of –0.47% in 2014 (meaning that 2014 aggregate household spending was slightly more than aggregate household disposable income).

Dividing both sides by N (because we are interested in output per worker),

$$\frac{Y}{N} = \frac{\sqrt{K}\sqrt{N}}{N} = \frac{\sqrt{K}}{\sqrt{N}} = \sqrt{\frac{K}{N}}$$

The second equality follows ▶ from: $\sqrt{N}/N = \sqrt{N}/(\sqrt{N}\sqrt{N})$ $= 1/\sqrt{N}$.
Output per worker equals the square root of capital per worker. Put another way, the production function f relating output per worker to capital per worker is given by

$$f\left(\frac{K_t}{N}\right) = \sqrt{\frac{K_t}{N}}$$

Replacing $f(K_t/N)$ by $\sqrt{K_t/N}$ in equation (11.3),

$$\frac{K_{t+1}}{N} - \frac{K_t}{N} = s\sqrt{\frac{K_t}{N}} - \delta\frac{K_t}{N} \qquad (11.7)$$

This equation describes the evolution of capital per worker over time. Let's look at what it implies.

The Effects of the Saving Rate on Steady-State Output

How big an impact does an increase in the saving rate have on the steady-state level of output per worker?

Start with equation (11.7). In steady state the amount of capital per worker is constant, so the left side of the equation equals zero. This implies

$$s\sqrt{\frac{K^*}{N}} = \delta\frac{K^*}{N}$$

(We have dropped time indexes, which are no longer needed because in steady state K/N is constant. The star is to remind you that we are looking at the steady-state value of capital.) Square both sides:

$$s^2\frac{K^*}{N} = \delta^2\left(\frac{K^*}{N}\right)^2$$

Divide both sides by (K/N) and reorganize:

$$\frac{K^*}{N} = \left(\frac{s}{\delta}\right)^2 \tag{11.8}$$

Steady-state capital per worker is equal to the square of the ratio of the saving rate to the depreciation rate.

From equations (11.6) and (11.8), steady-state output per worker is given by

$$\frac{Y^*}{N} = \sqrt{\frac{K^*}{N}} = \sqrt{\left(\frac{s}{\delta}\right)^2} = \frac{s}{\delta} \tag{11.9}$$

Steady-state output per worker is equal to the ratio of the saving rate to the depreciation rate.

A higher saving rate and a lower depreciation rate both lead to higher steady-state capital per worker (equation (11.8)) and higher steady-state output per worker (equation (11.9)). To see what this means, let's take a numerical example. Suppose the depreciation rate is 10% per year, and suppose the saving rate is also 10%. Then, from equations (11.8) and (11.9), steady-state capital per worker and output per worker are both equal to 1. Now suppose that the saving rate doubles, from 10% to 20%. It follows from equation (11.8) that in the new steady state, capital per worker increases from 1 to 4. And, from equation (11.9), output per worker doubles, from 1 to 2. Thus, doubling the saving rate leads, in the long run, to doubling the output per worker; this is a large effect.

The Dynamic Effects of an Increase in the Saving Rate

We have just seen that an increase in the saving rate leads to an increase in the steady-state level of output. But how long does it take for output to reach its new steady-state level? Put another way, by how much and for how long does an increase in the saving rate affect the growth rate?

To answer these questions, we must use equation (11.7) and solve it for capital per worker in year 0, in year 1, and so on.

Suppose that the saving rate, which had always been equal to 10%, increases in year 0 from 10% to 20% and remains at this higher value forever. In year 0, nothing happens to the capital stock (recall that it takes one year for higher saving and higher investment to show up in higher capital). So, capital per worker remains equal to the steady-state value associated with a saving rate of 0.1. From equation (11.8),

$$\frac{K_0}{N} = (0.1/0.1)^2 = 1^2 = 1$$

In year 1, equation (11.7) gives

$$\frac{K_1}{N} - \frac{K_0}{N} = s\sqrt{\frac{K_0}{N}} - \delta\frac{K_0}{N}$$

With a depreciation rate equal to 0.1 and a saving rate now equal to 0.2, this equation implies

$$\frac{K_1}{N} - 1 = [(0.2)(\sqrt{1})] - [(0.1)1]$$

so

$$\frac{K_1}{N} = 1.1$$

In the same way, we can solve for K_2/N, and so on. Once we have determined the values of capital per worker in year 0, year 1, and so on, we can then use equation (11.6) to solve for output per worker in year 0, year 1, and so on. The results of this computation are presented in Figure 11-7. Panel (a) plots the *level* of output per worker against time. (Y/N) increases over time from its initial value of 1 in year 0 to its steady-state value of 2 in the long run. Panel (b) gives the same information in a different way, plotting instead the *growth rate* of output per worker against time. As panel (b) shows, growth of output per worker is highest at the beginning and then decreases over time. As the economy reaches its new steady state, growth of output per worker returns to zero.

The difference between investment and depreciation is ▶ greatest at the beginning. This is why capital accumulation, and in turn, output growth, is highest at the beginning.

Figure 11-7 clearly shows that the adjustment to the new, higher, long-run equilibrium takes a long time. It is only 40% complete after 10 years, and 63% complete after 20 years. Put another way, the increase in the saving rate increases the growth rate of output per worker for a long time. The average annual growth rate is 3.1% for the first 10 years, and 1.5% for the next 10. Although the changes in the saving rate have no effect on growth in the long run, they do lead to higher growth for a long time.

To go back to the question raised at the beginning of the chapter, can the low saving/investment rate in the United States explain why the U.S. growth rate has been so low—relative to other OECD countries—since 1950? The answer would be yes if the United States had had a higher saving rate in the past, and if *this saving rate had fallen*

Figure 11-7

The Dynamic Effects of an Increase in the Saving Rate from 10% to 20% on the Level and the Growth Rate of Output per Worker

It takes a long time for output to adjust to its new higher level after an increase in the saving rate. Put another way, an increase in the saving rate leads to a long period of higher growth.

MyEconLab Animation

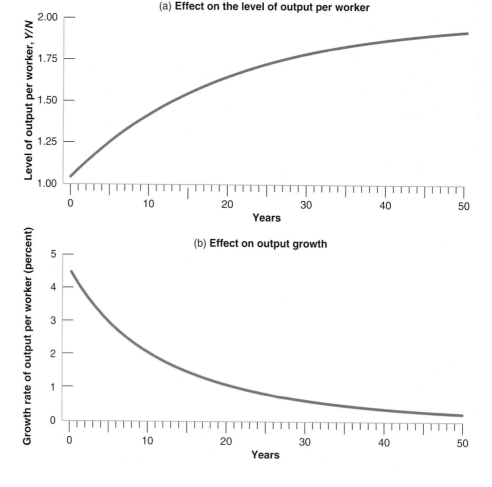

substantially in the last 50 years. If this were the case, it could explain the period of lower growth in the United States in the last 50 years along the lines of the mechanism in Figure 11-7 (with the sign reversed, as we would be looking at a decrease—not an increase—in the saving rate). But this is not the case. The U.S. saving rate has been low for a long time. Low saving cannot explain the relative poor U.S. growth performance over the last 50 years.

The U.S. Saving Rate and the Golden Rule

What is the saving rate that would maximize steady-state consumption per worker? Recall that, in steady state, consumption is equal to what is left after enough is put aside to maintain a constant level of capital. More formally, in steady state, consumption per worker is equal to output per worker minus depreciation per worker:

$$\frac{C}{N} = \frac{Y}{N} - \delta \frac{K}{N}$$

Using equations (11.8) and (11.9) for the steady-state values of output per worker and capital per worker, consumption per worker is thus given by

$$\frac{C}{N} = \frac{s}{\delta} - \delta \left(\frac{s}{\delta} \right)^2 = \frac{s(1-s)}{\delta}$$

Using this equation, together with equations (11.8) and (11.9), Table 11-1 gives the steady-state values of capital per worker, output per worker, and consumption per worker for different values of the saving rate (and for a depreciation rate equal to 10%).

Steady-state consumption per worker is largest when *s* equals 1/2. In other words, the golden-rule level of capital is associated with a saving rate of 50%. Below that level, increases in the saving rate lead to an increase in long-run consumption per worker. We saw previously that the average U.S. saving rate since 1970 has been only 17%. So we can be quite confident that, at least in the United States, an increase in the saving rate would increase both output per worker and consumption per worker in the long run.

Check your understanding of the issues: Using the equations in this section, argue the pros and cons of policy measures aimed at increasing the ◄ U.S. saving rate.

Table 11-1	The Saving Rate and the Steady-State Levels of Capital, Output, and Consumption per Worker		
Saving Rate *s*	Capital per Worker *K/N*	Output per Worker *Y/N*	Consumption per Worker *C/N*
0.0	0.0	0.0	0.0
0.1	1.0	1.0	0.9
0.2	4.0	2.0	1.6
0.3	9.0	3.0	2.1
0.4	16.0	4.0	2.4
0.5	25.0	5.0	2.5
0.6	36.0	6.0	2.4
...	...	...	...
1.0	100.0	10.0	0.0

11-4 Physical versus Human Capital

We have concentrated so far on physical capital—machines, plants, office buildings, and so on. But economies have another type of capital: the set of skills of the workers in the economy, or what economists call **human capital**. An economy with many highly skilled workers is likely to be much more productive than an economy in which most workers cannot read or write.

The increase in human capital has been as large as the increase in physical capital over the last two centuries. At the beginning of the Industrial Revolution, only 30% of the population of the countries that constitute the OECD today knew how to read. Today, the literacy rate in OECD countries is above 95%. Schooling was not compulsory prior to the Industrial Revolution. Today it is compulsory, usually until the age of 16. Still, there are large differences across countries. Today, in OECD countries, nearly 100% of children get a primary education, 90% get a secondary education, and 38% get a higher education. The corresponding numbers in poor countries, countries with GDP per person below $400, are 95%, 32%, and 4% respectively.

Even this comparison may be misleading because the quality of education can be quite different across countries. ▶

How should we think about the effect of human capital on output? How does the introduction of human capital change our earlier conclusions? These are the questions we take up in this last section.

Extending the Production Function

The most natural way of extending our analysis to allow for human capital is to modify the production function relation (11.1) to read

$$\frac{Y}{N} = f\left(\frac{K}{N}, \frac{H}{N}\right) \qquad (11.10)$$
$$(+,+)$$

Note that we are using the same ▶ symbol, H, to denote central bank money in Chapter 4, and human capital in this chapter. Both uses are traditional. Do not be confused.

The level of output per worker depends on both the level of physical capital per worker, K/N, and the level of human capital per worker, H/N. As before, an increase in capital per worker (K/N) leads to an increase in output per worker. And an increase in the average level of skill (H/N) also leads to more output per worker. More skilled workers can do more complex tasks; they can deal more easily with unexpected complications. All of this leads to higher output per worker.

We assumed previously that increases in physical capital per worker increased output per worker, but that the effect became smaller as the level of capital per worker increased. We can make the same assumption for human capital per worker: Think of increases in H/N as coming from increases in the number of years of education. The evidence is that the returns to increasing the proportion of children acquiring a primary education are large. At the very least, the ability to read and write allows people to use equipment that is more complicated but more productive. For rich countries, however, primary education—and, for that matter, secondary education—are no longer the relevant margin. Most children now get both. The relevant margin is now higher education. We are sure it will come as good news to you that the evidence shows that higher education increases people's skills, at least as measured by the increase in the wages of those who acquire it. But to take an extreme example, it is not clear that forcing everyone to acquire an advanced college degree would increase aggregate output much. Many people would end up overqualified and probably more frustrated rather than more productive.

We look at this evidence in Chapter 13. ▶

How should we construct the measure for human capital, H? The answer is very much the same way we construct the measure for physical capital, K. To construct K, we just add the values of the different pieces of capital, so that a machine that costs $2,000 gets twice the weight of a machine that costs $1,000. Similarly, we construct the measure of H such that workers who are paid twice as much get twice the weight. Take, for example, an economy with 100 workers, half of them unskilled and half of them skilled. Suppose the relative wage of the skilled workers is twice that of the unskilled workers. We can then construct H as $[(50 \times 1) + (50 \times 2)] = 150$. Human capital per worker, H/N is then equal to $150/100 = 1.5$.

The rationale for using relative wages as weights is that they reflect relative marginal products. A worker who is paid three times as much as another is assumed to have a marginal product that is three times higher.
An issue, however, is whether or not relative wages accurately reflect relative marginal products. To take a controversial example, in the same job, with the same seniority, women still often earn less than men. Is it because their marginal product is lower? Should they be given a lower weight than men in the construction of human capital?

Human Capital, Physical Capital, and Output

How does the introduction of human capital change the analysis of the previous sections?

Our conclusions about *physical capital accumulation* remain valid. An increase in the saving rate increases steady-state physical capital per worker and therefore increases output per worker. But our conclusions now extend to *human capital accumulation* as well. An increase in how much society "saves" in the form of human capital—through education and on-the-job training—increases steady-state human capital per worker, which leads to an increase in output per worker. Our extended model gives us a richer picture of how output per worker is determined. In the long run, it tells us that output per worker depends on both how much society saves and how much it spends on education.

What is the relative importance of human capital and of physical capital in the determination of output per worker? A place to start is to compare how much is spent on formal education to how much is invested in physical capital. In the United States, spending on formal education is about 6.5% of GDP. This number includes both government expenditures on education and private expenditures by people on education. It is between one-third and one-half of the gross investment rate for physical capital (which is around 16%). But this comparison is only a first pass. Consider the following complications:

- Education, especially higher education, is partly consumption—done for its own sake—and partly investment. We should include only the investment part for our purposes. However, the 6.5% number in the preceding paragraph includes both.
- At least for post-secondary education, the opportunity cost of a person's education is his or her forgone wages while acquiring the education. Spending on education should include not only the actual cost of education but also this opportunity cost. The 6.5% number does not include this opportunity cost.

How large is your opportunity cost relative to your tuition?

- Formal education is only a part of education. Much of what we learn comes from on-the-job training, formal or informal. Both the actual costs and the opportunity costs of on-the-job training should also be included. The 6.5% number does not include the costs associated with on-the-job training.
- We should compare investment rates net of depreciation. Depreciation of physical capital, especially of machines, is likely to be higher than depreciation of human capital. Skills deteriorate, but do so only slowly. And unlike physical capital, they deteriorate less quickly the more they are used.

For all these reasons, it is difficult to come up with reliable numbers for investment in human capital. Recent studies conclude that investment in physical capital and in education play roughly similar roles in the determination of output. This implies that output per worker depends roughly equally on the amount of physical capital and the amount of human capital in the economy. Countries that save more or spend more on education can achieve substantially higher steady-state levels of output per worker.

Endogenous Growth

Note what the conclusion we just reached did say and did not say. It did say that a country that saves more or spends more on education will achieve a *higher level* of output per worker in steady state. It did not say that by saving or spending more on education a country can sustain permanently *higher growth* of output per worker.

Robert Lucas was awarded the Nobel Prize in 1995. He teaches at the University of Chicago. Paul Romer teaches at New York University.

This conclusion, however, has been challenged. Following the lead of Robert Lucas and Paul Romer, researchers have explored the possibility that the joint accumulation of physical capital and human capital might actually be enough to sustain growth. Given human capital, increases in physical capital will run into decreasing returns. And given physical capital, increases in human capital will also run into decreasing returns. But these researchers have asked, what if both physical and human capital increase in tandem? Can't an economy grow forever just by steadily having more capital and more skilled workers?

Models that generate steady growth even without technological progress are called **models of endogenous growth** to reflect the fact that in those models—in contrast to the model we saw in previous sections of this chapter—the growth rate depends, even in the long run, on variables such as the saving rate and the rate of spending on education. The jury on this class of models is still out, but the indications so far are that the conclusions we drew earlier need to be qualified and not abandoned. The current consensus is as follows:

- Output per worker depends on the level of both physical capital per worker and human capital per worker. Both forms of capital can be accumulated, one through physical investment, the other through education and training. Increasing either the saving rate or the fraction of output spent on education and training can lead to much higher levels of output per worker in the long run. However, given the rate of technological progress, such measures do not lead to a permanently higher growth rate.

- Note the qualifier in the last proposition: *given the rate of technological progress*. But is technological progress unrelated to the level of human capital in the economy? Can't a better educated labor force lead to a higher rate of technological progress? These questions take us to the topic of the next chapter, the sources and the effects of technological progress.

Summary

MEL
Video

- In the long run, the evolution of output is determined by two relations. (To make the reading of this summary easier, we shall omit "per worker" in what follows.) First, the level of output depends on the amount of capital. Second, capital accumulation depends on the level of output, which determines saving and investment.

- These interactions between capital and output imply that, starting from any level of capital (and ignoring technological progress, the topic of Chapter 12), an economy converges in the long run to a *steady-state* (constant) level of capital. Associated with this level of capital is a steady-state level of output.

- The steady-state level of capital, and thus the steady-state level of output, depends positively on the saving rate. A higher saving rate leads to a higher steady-state level of output; during the transition to the new steady state, a higher saving rate leads to positive output growth. But (again ignoring technological progress) in the long run, the growth rate of output is equal to zero and so does not depend on the saving rate.

- An increase in the saving rate requires an initial decrease in consumption. In the long run, the increase in the saving rate may lead to an increase or a decrease in consumption, depending on whether the economy is below or above the *golden-rule level of capital*, which is the level of capital at which steady-state consumption is highest.

- Most countries have a level of capital below the golden-rule level. Thus, an increase in the saving rate leads to an initial decrease in consumption followed by an increase in consumption in the long run. When considering whether or not to adopt policy measures aimed at changing a country's saving rate, policy makers must decide how much weight to put on the welfare of current generations versus the welfare of future generations.

- Although most of the analysis of this chapter focuses on the effects of physical capital accumulation, output depends on the levels of both physical *and* human capital. Both forms of capital can be accumulated, one through investment, the other through education and training. Increasing the saving rate or the fraction of output spent on education and training can lead to large increases in output in the long run.

Key Terms

saving rate, 237
steady state, 243
golden-rule level of capital, 247

human capital, 254
models of endogenous growth, 256

Questions and Problems

QUICK CHECK

MyEconLab Visit www.myeconlab.com to complete similar Quick Check problems and get instant feedback.

1. Using the information in this chapter, label each of the following statements true, false, or uncertain. Explain briefly.
  a. The saving rate is always equal to the investment rate.
  b. A higher investment rate can sustain higher growth of output forever.
  c. If capital never depreciated, growth could go on forever.
  d. The higher the saving rate, the higher consumption in steady state.
  e. A lower depreciation rate leads to an upward shift in the golden-rule level of capital.
  f. Slower growth in the United States in the past 50 years could be attributed to a low savings rate only if the United States had started off with a much higher savings rate than today and there had been a substantial decline in the savings rate over time.
  g. According to endogenous growth theory, higher levels of education lead to higher output growth rates.

2. Suppose that the head of the Finance Ministry in your country were to go on the record advocating an effort to restrain current consumption, arguing that "lower consumption now means higher savings; and higher savings now means a permanent higher level of consumption in the future." What would you make of such statement?

3. In Chapter 3 we saw that an increase in the saving rate can lead to a recession in the short run (i.e., the paradox of saving). We examined the issue in the medium run in Problem 5 at at the end of Chapter 7. We can now examine the long-run effects of an increase in saving.

Using the model presented in this chapter, what is the effect of an increase in the saving rate on output per worker likely to be after one decade? After five decades?

DIG DEEPER

MyEconLab Visit www.myeconlab.com to complete all Dig Deeper problems and get instant feedback.

4. Discuss how the level of output per person in the long run would likely be affected by each of the following changes:
  a. The right to exclude saving from income when paying income taxes.
  b. A higher rate of female participation in the labor market (but constant population).

5. Suppose that in a given economy, both the savings rate and the depreciation rate increase. What would the effect of this dual movement be on the economy's capital per worker and output per worker, in the short and the long run?

6. Suppose that an economy is characterized by the following production function:

$$Y = 3\sqrt{K}\sqrt{N}$$

  a. Derive the steady-state level of output per worker, and the steady-state level of capital per worker as a function of the savings rate, s, and the depreciation rate, δ.
  b. Derive the equation for the steady-state level of consumption per worker as a function of the savings rate, s, and the depreciation rate, δ.
  c. Suppose that δ = 0.02. Calculate the steady-state level of consumption per worker and output per worker when s = 0; s = 0.1; s = 0.2; s = 1. What do you observe?
  d. Using spreadsheets, plot your results on a graph showing the relationship between the savings rate (on the X axis) and consumption per worker (on the Y axis). Is there a savings rate that maximizes consumption per worker? Explain.

7. The Cobb-Douglas production function and the steady state

This problem is based on the material in the chapter appendix. Suppose that the economy's production function is given by

$$Y = K^\alpha N^{1-\alpha}$$

and assume that $\alpha = 1/3$.

a. Is this production function characterized by constant returns to scale? Explain.

b. Are there decreasing returns to capital?

c. Are there decreasing returns to labor?

d. Transform the production function into a relation between output per worker and capital per worker.

e. For a given saving rate, s, and depreciation rate, δ, give an expression for capital per worker in the steady state.

f. Give an expression for output per worker in the steady state.

g. Solve for the steady-state level of output per worker when $s = 0.32$ and $\delta = 0.08$.

h. Suppose that the depreciation rate remains constant at $\delta = 0.08$, while the saving rate is reduced by half, to $s = 0.16$. What is the new steady-state output per worker?

8. Continuing with the logic from Problem 7, suppose that the economy's production function is given by $Y = K^{1/3}N^{2/3}$ and that both the saving rate, s, and the depreciation rate, δ are equal to 0.10.

a. What is the steady-state level of capital per worker?

b. What is the steady-state level of output per worker?

   Suppose that the economy is in steady state and that, in period t, the depreciation rate increases permanently from 0.10 to 0.20.

c. What will be the new steady-state levels of capital per worker and output per worker?

d. Compute the path of capital per worker and output per worker over the first three periods after the change in the depreciation rate.

9. The savings rate and changes in the capital stock

   Suppose that in country X, the savings rate slowly declines from 12% in year t to 11% in year $t + 1$ and 10% in year $t + 2$. Suppose, moreover, that the depreciation rate, δ, is 10%.

a. Using the production function (11.9) given in the chapter, what happens to the steady-state levels of capital per worker and of output per worker overtime?

b. Due to technological progress, suppose that the depreciation rate were to increase to 12% at time t (remaining stable afterwards). How would that affect the results of part (a)?

EXPLORE FURTHER

10. Savings and government deficits.

a. The World Bank has a database on gross domestic savings (as % of GDP) available on its Web site. Using the data (for 2014), find the savings rates for France, Germany, and Italy, for the latest year available. With a depreciation rate of 10%, and using equation (11.8), calculate the steady-state levels of output and capital per worker for each of the three countries.

b. The OECD regularly publishes detailed data on government finances on its Web site, https://data.oecd.org/gga/general-government-deficit.htm. Find the data on government deficits as percentage of GDP for France, Germany, and Italy for the year used in part (a). Assume the two worst-performing countries permanently reduce their deficit to the level of the best performing country. Moreover, the private savings remain unchanged. How would these changes affect the long-run levels of capital per worker and output per worker for the two worst performers?

c. In terms of output per worker, how do the performance of the two worst-performing countries compare to that of the best performer after the deficit reduction?

Further Readings

- The classic treatment of the relation between the saving rate and output is by Robert Solow, *Growth Theory: An Exposition* (1970).
- An easy-to-read discussion of whether and how to increase saving and improve education in the United States

is given in Memoranda 23 to 27 in *Memos to the President: A Guide through Macroeconomics for the Busy Policymaker*, by Charles Schultze, who was the Chairman of the Council of Economic Advisers during the Carter administration (1992).

APPENDIX: The Cobb-Douglas Production Function and the Steady State

In 1928, Charles Cobb (a mathematician) and Paul Douglas (an economist, who went on to become a U.S. senator) concluded that the following production function gave a good description of the relation between output, physical capital, and labor in the United States from 1899 to 1922:

$$Y = K^\alpha N^{1-\alpha} \qquad (11.A1)$$

with α being a number between zero and one. Their findings proved surprisingly robust. Even today, the production function (11.A1), now known as the **Cobb-Douglas production function**, still gives a good description of the relation between output, capital, and labor in the United States, and it has become a standard tool in the economist's toolbox. (Verify for yourself that it satisfies the two properties we discussed in the text: constant returns to scale and decreasing returns to capital and to labor.)

The purpose of this appendix is to characterize the steady state of an economy when the production function is given by (11.A1). (All you need to follow the steps is a knowledge of the properties of exponents.)

Recall that, in steady state, saving per worker must be equal to depreciation per worker. Let's see what this implies.

- To derive saving per worker, we must first derive the relation between output per worker and capital per worker implied by equation (11.A1). Divide both sides of equation (11.A1) by N:

$$Y/N = K^\alpha N^{1-\alpha}/N$$

Using the properties of exponents,

$$N^{1-\alpha}/N = N^{1-\alpha}N^{-1} = N^{-\alpha}$$

so, replacing the terms in N in the preceding equation, we get:

$$Y/N = K^\alpha N^{-\alpha} = (K/N)^\alpha$$

Output per worker, Y/N, is equal to the ratio of capital per worker, K/N, raised to the power α.

Saving per worker is equal to the saving rate times output per worker, so, using the previous equation, it is equal to

$$s(K^*/N)^\alpha$$

- Depreciation per worker is equal to the depreciation rate times capital per worker:

$$\delta(K^*/N)$$

- The steady-state level of capital, K^*, is determined by the condition that saving per worker be equal to depreciation per worker, so:

$$s(K^*/N)^\alpha = \delta(K^*/N)$$

To solve this expression for the steady-state level of capital per worker K^*/N, divide both sides by $(K^*/N)^\alpha$:

$$s = \delta(K^*/N)^{1-\alpha}$$

Divide both sides by δ, and change the order of the equality:

$$(K^*/N)^{1-\alpha} = s/\delta$$

Finally, raise both sides to the power $1/(1-\alpha)$:

$$(K^*/N) = (s/\delta)^{1/(1-\alpha)}$$

This gives us the steady-state level of capital per worker.

From the production function, the steady-state level of output per worker is then equal to

$$(Y^*/N) = K/N^\alpha = (s/\delta)^{\alpha/(1-\alpha)}$$

Let's see what this last equation implies.

- In the text, we actually worked with a special case of an equation (11.A1), the case where $\alpha = 0.5$. (Taking a variable to the power 0.5 is the same as taking the square root of this variable.) If $\alpha = 0.5$, the preceding equation means

$$Y^*/N = s/\delta$$

Output per worker is equal to the ratio of the saving rate to the depreciation rate. This is the equation we discussed in the text. A doubling of the saving rate leads to a doubling in steady-state output per worker.

- The empirical evidence suggests, however, that, if we think of K as physical capital, α is closer to one-third than to one-half. Assuming $\alpha = 1/3$, then $\alpha(1-\alpha) = (1/3)/(1-(1/3)) = (1/3)/(2/3) = 1/2$, and the equation for output per worker yields

$$Y^*/N = (s/\delta)^{1/2} = \sqrt{s/\delta}$$

This implies smaller effects of the saving rate on output per worker than was suggested by the computations in the text. A doubling of the saving rate, for example, means that output per worker increases by a factor of $\sqrt{2}$, or only about 1.4 (put another way, a 40% increase in output per worker).

- There is, however, an interpretation of our model in which the appropriate value of α is close to 1/2, so the computations in the text are applicable. If, along the lines of Section 11-4, we take human capital into account as well as physical capital, then a value of α around 1/2 for the contribution of this broader definition of capital to output is, indeed, roughly appropriate. Thus, one interpretation of the numerical results in Section 11-3 is that they show the effects of a given saving rate, but that saving must be interpreted to include saving in both physical capital and in human capital (more machines and more education).

Key Term

Cobb-Douglas production function, 259

Technological Progress and Growth

The conclusion in Chapter 11 that capital accumulation cannot by itself sustain growth has a straight-forward implication: Sustained growth *requires* technological progress. This chapter looks at the role of technological progress in growth.

Section 12-1 looks at the respective role of technological progress and capital accumulation in growth. It shows how, in steady state, the rate of growth of output per person is simply equal to the rate of technological progress. This does not mean, however, that the saving rate is irrelevant. The saving rate affects the level of output per person but not its steady state rate of growth.

Section 12-2 turns to the determinants of technological progress, the role of research and development (R&D), and the role of innovation versus imitation.

Section 12-3 discusses why some countries are able to achieve steady technological progress while others do not. In so doing, it looks at the role of institutions in sustaining growth.

Section 12-4 returns to the facts of growth presented in Chapter 10 and interprets them in the light of what we have learned in this and the previous chapter. ⬤

12-1 Technological Progress and the Rate of Growth

In an economy in which there is both capital accumulation and technological progress, at what rate will output grow? To answer this question, we need to extend the model developed in Chapter 11 to allow for technological progress. To introduce technological progress into the picture, we must first revisit the aggregate production function.

Technological Progress and the Production Function

Technological progress has many dimensions:

- It can lead to larger quantities of output for given quantities of capital and labor. Think of a new type of lubricant that allows a machine to run at a higher speed and to increase production.
- It can lead to better products. Think of the steady improvement in automobile safety and comfort over time.
- It can lead to new products. Think of the introduction of the iPad, wireless communication technology, flat screen monitors, and high-definition television.
- It can lead to a larger variety of products. Think of the steady increase in the number of breakfast cereals available at your local supermarket.

The average number of items carried by a supermarket increased from 2,200 in 1950 to 38,700 in 2010. To get a sense of what this means, see Robin ▶ Williams (who plays an immigrant from the Soviet Union) in the supermarket scene in the movie *Moscow on the Hudson*.

These dimensions are more similar than they appear. If we think of consumers as caring not about the goods themselves but about the services these goods provide, then they all have something in common. In each case, consumers receive more services. A better car provides more safety, a new product such as an iPad or faster communication technology provides more communication services, and so on. If we think of output as the set of underlying services provided by the goods produced in the economy, we can think of technological progress as leading to increases in output for given amounts of capital and labor. We can then think of the **state of technology** as a variable that tells us how much output can be produced from given amounts of capital and labor at any time. If we denote the state of technology by A, we can rewrite the production function as

As you saw in the Focus box "Real GDP, Technological Progress, and the Price of Computers" in Chapter 2, thinking of ▶ products as providing a number of underlying services is the method used to construct the price index for computers.

$$Y = F(K, N, A)$$
$$(+,+,+)$$

This is our extended production function. Output depends on both capital and labor (K and N) and on the state of technology (A). Given capital and labor, an improvement in the state of technology, A, leads to an increase in output.

For simplicity, we shall ignore human capital here. We return ▶ to it later in the chapter.

It will be convenient to use a more restrictive form of the preceding equation, namely

$$Y = F(K, AN) \tag{12.1}$$

This equation states that production depends on capital and on labor multiplied by the state of technology. Introducing the state of technology in this way makes it easier to think about the effect of technological progress on the relation between output, capital, and labor. Equation (12.1) implies that we can think of technological progress in two equivalent ways:

- Technological progress *reduces* the number of workers needed to produce a given amount of output. Doubling A produces the same quantity of output with only half the original number of workers, N.
- Technological progress *increases* the output that can be produced with a given number of workers. We can think of AN as the amount of **effective labor** in the

economy. If the state of technology A doubles, it is as if the economy had twice as many workers. In other words, we can think of output being produced by two factors: capital (K), and effective labor (AN).

AN is also sometimes called **labor in efficiency units**. The use of *efficiency* for "efficiency units" here and for "efficiency wages" in Chapter 6 is a coincidence; the two notions are unrelated.

What restrictions should we impose on the extended production function (12.1)? We can build directly here on our discussion in Chapter 11.

Again, it is reasonable to assume constant returns to scale. *For a given state of technology (A), doubling both the amount of capital (K) and the amount of labor (N) is likely to lead to a doubling of output*

$$2Y = F(2K, 2AN)$$

More generally, for any number x,

$$xY = F(xK, xAN)$$

It is also reasonable to assume decreasing returns to each of the two factors—capital and effective labor. Given effective labor, an increase in capital is likely to increase output but at a decreasing rate. Symmetrically, given capital, an increase in effective labor is likely to increase output, but at a decreasing rate.

It was convenient in Chapter 11 to think in terms of output *per worker* and capital *per worker*. That was because the steady state of the economy was a state where output *per worker* and capital *per worker* were constant. It is convenient here to look at output *per effective worker* and capital *per effective worker*. The reason is the same; as we shall soon see, in steady state, output *per effective worker* and capital *per effective worker* are constant.

Per worker: divided by the number of workers (N).
Per effective worker: divided by the number of effective workers (AN)—the number of workers, N, times the state of technology, A.

To get a relation between output per effective worker and capital per effective worker, take $x = 1/AN$ in the preceding equation. This gives

$$\frac{Y}{AN} = F\left(\frac{K}{AN}, 1\right)$$

Or, if we define the function f so that $f(K/AN) = F(K/AN, 1)$:

$$\frac{Y}{AN} = f\left(\frac{K}{AN}\right) \qquad (12.2)$$

Suppose that F has the "double square root" form:

$$Y = F(K, AN) = \sqrt{K}\sqrt{AN}$$

Then

$$\frac{Y}{AN} = \frac{\sqrt{K}\sqrt{AN}}{AN} = \frac{\sqrt{K}}{\sqrt{AN}}$$

So the function f is simply the square root function:

$$f\left(\frac{K}{AN}\right) = \sqrt{\frac{K}{AN}}$$

In words: *Output per effective worker* (the left side) is a function of *capital per effective worker* (the expression in the function on the right side).

The relation between output per effective worker and capital per effective worker is drawn in Figure 12-1. It looks much the same as the relation we drew in Figure 11-2

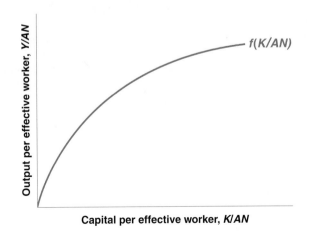

Capital per effective worker, *K/AN*

(vertical axis label) Output per effective worker, *Y/AN*

f(K/AN)

Figure 12-1

Output per Effective Worker versus Capital per Effective Worker

Because of decreasing returns to capital, increases in capital per effective worker lead to smaller and smaller increases in output per effective worker.

MyEconLab Animation

between output per worker and capital per worker in the absence of technological progress. There, increases in K/N led to increases in Y/N, but at a decreasing rate. Here, increases in K/AN lead to increases in Y/AN, but at a decreasing rate.

Interactions between Output and Capital

A simple key to understanding the results in this section: The results we derived for *output per worker* in Chapter 11 still hold in this chapter, but now for *output per effective worker*. For example, in Chapter 11, we saw that output per worker was constant in steady state. In this chapter, we shall see that output per effective worker is constant in steady state. And so on.

We now have the elements we need to think about the determinants of growth. Our analysis will parallel the analysis of Chapter 11. There we looked at the dynamics of *output per worker* and *capital per worker*. Here we look at the dynamics of *output per effective worker* and *capital per effective worker*.

In Chapter 11, we characterized the dynamics of output and capital per worker using Figure 11-2. In that figure, we drew three relations:

■ The relation between output per worker and capital per worker.
■ The relation between investment per worker and capital per worker.
■ The relation between depreciation per worker—equivalently, the investment per worker needed to maintain a constant level of capital per worker—and capital per worker.

The dynamics of capital per worker and, by implication output per worker, were determined by the relation between investment per worker and depreciation per worker. Depending on whether investment per worker was greater or smaller than depreciation per worker, capital per worker increased or decreased over time, as did output per worker.

We shall follow the same approach in building Figure 12-2. The difference is that we focus on output, capital, and investment *per effective worker*, rather than per worker.

■ The relation between output per effective worker and capital per effective worker was derived in Figure 12-1. This relation is repeated in Figure 12-2; output per effective worker increases with capital per effective worker, but at a decreasing rate.
■ Under the same assumptions as in Chapter 11—that investment is equal to private saving, and the private saving rate is constant—investment is given by

$$I = S = sY$$

Divide both sides by the number of effective workers, AN, to get

$$\frac{I}{AN} = s\frac{Y}{AN}$$

Figure 12-2

The Dynamics of Capital per Effective Worker and Output per Effective Worker

Capital per effective worker and output per effective worker converge to constant values in the long run.

MyEconLab Animation

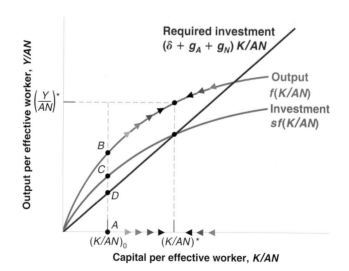

Replacing output per effective worker, Y/AN, by its expression from equation (12.2) gives

$$\frac{I}{AN} = sf\left(\frac{K}{AN}\right)$$

The relation between investment per effective worker and capital per effective worker is drawn in Figure 12-2. It is equal to the upper curve—the relation between output per effective worker and capital per effective worker—multiplied by the saving rate, s. This gives us the lower curve.

■ Finally, we need to ask what level of investment per effective worker is needed to maintain a given level of capital per effective worker.

In Chapter 11, the answer was: For capital to be constant, investment had to be equal to the depreciation of the existing capital stock. Here, the answer is slightly more complicated. The reason is as follows: Now that we allow for technological progress (so A increases over time), the number of effective workers (AN) increases over time. Thus, maintaining the same ratio of capital to effective workers (K/AN) requires an increase in the capital stock (K) proportional to the increase in the number of effective workers (AN). Let's look at this condition more closely.

In Chapter 11, we assumed $g_A = 0$ and $g_N = 0$. Our focus in this chapter is on the implications of technological progress, $g_A > 0$. But, once we allow for technological progress, introducing population growth $g_N > 0$ is straightforward. Thus, we allow for both ◄ $g_A > 0$ and $g_N > 0$.

Let δ be the depreciation rate of capital. Let the rate of technological progress be equal to g_A. Let the rate of population growth be equal to g_N. If we assume that the ratio of employment to the total population remains constant, the number of workers (N) also grows at annual rate g_N. Together, these assumptions imply that the growth rate of effective labor (AN) equals $g_A + g_N$. For example, if the number of workers is growing at 1% per year and the rate of technological progress is 2% per year, then the growth rate of effective labor is equal to 3% per year.

These assumptions imply that the level of investment needed to maintain a given level of capital per effective worker is therefore given by

$$I = \delta K + (g_A + g_N)K$$

The growth rate of the product ◄ of two variables is the sum of the growth rates of the two variables. See Proposition 7 in Appendix 2 at the end of the book.

Or, equivalently,

$$I = (\delta + g_A + g_N)K \tag{12.3}$$

An amount δK is needed just to keep the capital stock constant. If the depreciation rate is 10%, then investment must be equal to 10% of the capital stock just to maintain the same level of capital. And an additional amount $(g_A + g_N)K$ is needed to ensure that the capital stock increases at the same rate as effective labor. If effective labor increases at 3% per year, for example, then capital must increase by 3% per year to maintain the same level of capital per effective worker. Putting δK and $(g_A + g_N)K$ together in this example: If the depreciation rate is 10% and the growth rate of effective labor is 3%, then investment must equal 13% of the capital stock to maintain a constant level of capital per effective worker.

Dividing the previous expression by the number of effective workers to get the amount of investment per effective worker needed to maintain a constant level of capital per effective worker gives

$$\frac{I}{AN} = (\delta + g_A + g_N)\frac{K}{AN}$$

The level of investment per effective worker needed to maintain a given level of capital per effective worker is represented by the upward-sloping line, "Required investment" in Figure 12-2. The slope of the line equals $(\delta + g_A + g_N)$.

Dynamics of Capital and Output

We can now give a graphical description of the dynamics of capital per effective worker and output per effective worker.

Consider a given level of capital per effective worker, say $(K/AN)_0$ in Figure 12-2. At that level, output per effective worker equals the vertical distance AB. Investment per effective worker is equal to AC. The amount of investment required to maintain that level of capital per effective worker is equal to AD. Because actual investment exceeds the investment level required to maintain the existing level of capital per effective worker, K/AN increases.

Hence, starting from $(K/AN)_0$, the economy moves to the right, with the level of capital per effective worker increasing over time. This goes on until investment per effective worker is just sufficient to maintain the existing level of capital per effective worker, until capital per effective worker equals $(K/AN)^*$.

In the long run, capital per effective worker reaches a constant level, and so does output per effective worker. Put another way, the steady state of this economy is such that *capital per effective worker and output per effective worker are constant and equal to* $(K/AN)^*$ *and* $(Y/AN)^*$, *respectively.*

If *Y/AN* is constant, *Y* must grow at the same rate as *AN*. So, it must grow at rate $g_A + g_N$.

This implies that, in steady state, output (Y) is growing at the same rate as effective labor (AN), so that the ratio of the two is constant. Because effective labor grows at rate $(g_A + g_N)$, output growth in steady state must also equal $(g_A + g_N)$. The same reasoning applies to capital. Because capital per effective worker is constant in steady state, ▶ capital is also growing at rate $(g_A + g_N)$.

Stated in terms of capital or output per effective worker, these results seem rather abstract. But it is straightforward to state them in a more intuitive way, and this gives us our first important conclusion:

In steady state, the growth rate of output equals the rate of population growth (g_N) plus the rate of technological progress (g_A). By implication, the growth rate of output is independent of the saving rate.

To strengthen your intuition, let's go back to the argument we used in Chapter 11 to show that, in the absence of technological progress and population growth, the economy could not sustain positive growth forever.

- The argument went as follows: Suppose the economy tried to sustain positive output growth. Because of decreasing returns to capital, capital would have to grow faster than output. The economy would have to devote a larger and larger proportion of output to capital accumulation. At some point there would be no more output to devote to capital accumulation. Growth would come to an end.
- Exactly the same logic is at work here. Effective labor grows at rate $(g_A + g_N)$. Suppose the economy tried to sustain output growth in excess of $(g_A + g_N)$. Because of decreasing returns to capital, capital would have to increase faster than output. The economy would have to devote a larger and larger proportion of output to capital accumulation. At some point this would prove impossible. Thus, the economy cannot permanently grow faster than $(g_A + g_N)$.

The growth rate of *Y/N* is equal to the growth rate of *Y* minus the growth rate of *N* (see Proposition 8 in Appendix 2 at the end of the book). So the growth rate of *Y/N* is given by $(g_Y - g_N) = (g_A + g_N) - g_N = g_A$.

We have focused on the behavior of aggregate output. To get a sense of what happens not to aggregate output, but rather to the standard of living over time, we must look instead at the behavior of output per worker (not output per *effective* worker). Because output grows at rate $(g_A + g_N)$ and the number of workers grows at rate g_N, output per ▶ worker grows at rate g_A. In other words, *when the economy is in steady state, output per worker grows at the rate of technological progress.*

Because output, capital, and effective labor all grow at the same rate $(g_A + g_N)$ in steady state, the steady state of this economy is also called a state of **balanced growth**.

Table 12-1 The Characteristics of Balanced Growth		Growth Rate:
1	Capital per effective worker	0
2	Output per effective worker	0
3	Capital per worker	g_A
4	Output per worker	g_A
5	Labor	g_N
6	Capital	$g_A + g_N$
7	Output	$g_A + g_N$

In steady state, output and the two inputs, capital and effective labor, grow "in balance" at the same rate. The characteristics of balanced growth will be helpful later in the chapter and are summarized in Table 12-1.

On the balanced growth path (equivalently: in steady state; equivalently: in the long run):

■ *Capital per effective worker* and *output per effective worker* are constant; this is the result we derived in Figure 12-2.
■ Equivalently, *capital per worker* and *output per worker* are growing at the rate of technological progress, g_A.
■ Or in terms of labor, capital, and output: *Labor* is growing at the rate of population growth, g_N; *capital* and *output* are growing at a rate equal to the sum of population growth and the rate of technological progress, $(g_A + g_N)$.

The Effects of the Saving Rate

In steady state, the growth rate of output depends *only* on the rate of population growth and the rate of technological progress. Changes in the saving rate do not affect the steady-state growth rate. But changes in the saving rate do increase the steady-state level of output per effective worker.

This result is best seen in Figure 12-3, which shows the effect of an increase in the saving rate from s_0 to s_1. The increase in the saving rate shifts the investment relation up, from $s_0 f(K/AN)$ to $s_1 f(K/AN)$. It follows that the steady-state level of capital per

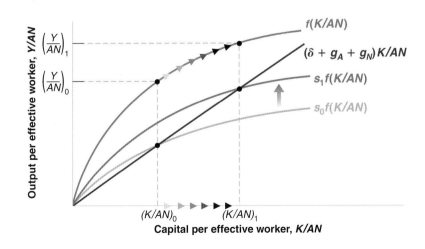

Capital per effective worker, *K/AN*

Figure 12-3

The Effects of an Increase in the Saving Rate: I

An increase in the saving rate leads to an increase in the steady-state levels of output per effective worker and capital per effective worker.

MyEconLab Animation

Figure 12-4

The Effects of an Increase in the Saving Rate: II

The increase in the saving rate leads to higher growth until the economy reaches its new, higher, balanced growth path.

MyEconLab Animation

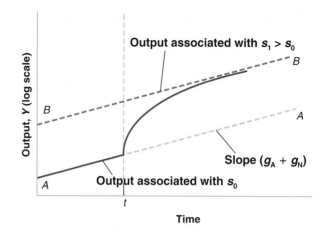

Output associated with $s_1 > s_0$

Slope $(g_A + g_N)$

Output associated with s_0

Time

Figure 12-4 is the same as Figure 11-5, which anticipated the derivation presented here.

For a description of logarithmic scales, see Appendix 2 at the end of the book. When a logarithmic scale is used, a variable growing at a constant rate moves along a straight line. The slope of the line is equal to the rate of growth of the variable.

effective worker increases from $(K/AN)_0$ to $(K/AN)_1$, with a corresponding increase in the level of output per effective worker from $(Y/AN)_0$ to $(Y/AN)_1$.

Following the increase in the saving rate, capital per effective worker and output per effective worker increase for some time as they converge to their new higher level. Figure 12-4 plots output against time. Output is measured on a logarithmic scale. The economy is initially on the balanced growth path AA. Output is growing at rate $(g_A + g_N)$—so the slope of AA is equal to $(g_A + g_N)$. After the increase in the saving rate at time t, output grows faster for some period of time. Eventually, output ends up at a higher level than it would have been without the increase in saving. But its growth rate returns to $g_A + g_N$. In the new steady state, the economy grows at the same rate, but on a higher growth path BB. BB, which is parallel to AA, also has a slope equal to $(g_A + g_N)$.

Let's summarize: In an economy with technological progress and population growth, output grows over time. In steady state, output *per effective worker* and capital *per effective worker* are constant. Put another way, output *per worker* and capital *per worker* grow at the rate of technological progress. Put yet another way, output and capital grow at the same rate as effective labor, and therefore at a rate equal to the growth rate of the number of workers plus the rate of technological progress. When the economy is in steady state, it is said to be on a balanced growth path.

The rate of output growth in steady state is independent of the saving rate. However, the saving rate affects the steady-state level of output per effective worker. And increases in the saving rate lead, for some time, to an increase in the growth rate above the steady-state growth rate.

12-2 The Determinants of Technological Progress

We have just seen that the growth rate of output per worker is ultimately determined by the rate of technological progress. This leads naturally to the next question: What determines the rate of technological progress? This is the question we take up in this section.

The term *technological progress* brings to mind images of major discoveries: the invention of the microchip, the discovery of the structure of DNA, and so on. These discoveries suggest a process driven largely by scientific research and chance rather than by economic forces. But the truth is that most technological progress in modern advanced economies is the result of a humdrum process: the outcome of firms' **research and development (R&D)** activities. Industrial R&D expenditures account for between

2% and 3% of GDP in each of the four major rich countries we looked at in Chapter 10 (the United States, France, Japan, and the United Kingdom). About 75% of the roughly one million U.S. scientists and researchers working in R&D are employed by firms. U.S. firms' R&D spending equals more than 20% of their spending on gross investment, and more than 60% of their spending on net investment—gross investment less depreciation.

Firms spend on R&D for the same reason they buy new machines or build new plants: to increase profits. By increasing spending on R&D, a firm increases the probability that it will discover and develop a new product. (We shall use *product* as a generic term to denote new goods or new techniques of production.) If the new product is successful, the firm's profits will increase. There is, however, an important difference between purchasing a machine and spending more on R&D. The difference is that the outcome of R&D is fundamentally *ideas*. And unlike a machine, an idea can potentially be used by many firms at the same time. A firm that has just acquired a new machine does not have to worry that another firm will use that particular machine. A firm that has discovered and developed a new product can make no such assumption.

This last point implies that the level of R&D spending depends not only on the **fertility of research**—how spending on R&D translates into new ideas and new products—but also on the **appropriability** of research results, which is the extent to which firms can benefit from the results of their own R&D. Let's look at each aspect in turn.

The Fertility of the Research Process

If research is fertile—that is, if R&D spending leads to many new products—then, other things being equal, firms will have strong incentives to spend on R&D; R&D spending and, by implication, technological progress will be high. The determinants of the fertility of research lie largely outside the realm of economics. Many factors interact here.

The fertility of research depends on the successful interaction between basic research (the search for general principles and results) and applied research and development (the application of these results to specific uses, and the development of new products). Basic research does not by itself lead to technological progress. But the success of applied research and development depends ultimately on basic research. Much of the computer industry's development can be traced to a few breakthroughs, from the invention of the transistor to the invention of the microchip. On the software side, much of the progress comes from progress in mathematics. For example, progress in encryption comes from progress in the theory of prime numbers.

Some countries appear more successful at basic research; other countries are more successful at applied research and development. Studies point to differences in the education system as one of the reasons why. For example, it is often argued that the French higher education system, with its strong emphasis on abstract thinking, produces researchers who are better at basic research than at applied research and development. Studies also point to the importance of a "culture of entrepreneurship," in which a big part of technological progress comes from the ability of entrepreneurs to organize the successful development and marketing of new products—a dimension in which the United States appears better than most other countries.

In Chapter 11, we looked at the role of human capital as an input in production. People with more education can use more complex machines, or handle more complex tasks. Here, we see a second role for human capital: better researchers and scientists and, by implication, a higher rate of technological progress.

It takes many years, and often many decades, for the full potential of major discoveries to be realized. The usual sequence is one in which a major discovery leads to the exploration of potential applications, then to the development of new products, and finally, to the adoption of these new products. The Focus box "Foreign Direct Investment, Technological Change, and Economic Growth" shows, this is exactly what we saw

Foreign Direct Investment, Technological Change, and Economic Growth

Among the characteristics of the current economic period is the rapid increase in international capital flows, particularly the flows of Foreign Direct Investment (FDI). The availability of capital is clearly one key economic benefit brought forward by FDI to the host economy. However, FDI may contribute differently to economic growth, through the diffusion and assimilation of technologies and technological know-how across borders.

Looking at multinational companies, it has been noted that such companies may spread technological change through the acquisition of foreign firms and, thus, not through "Greenfield" projects only. In a paper published in 1997, Barrel and Pain found such positive effect of FDI on total factor productivity on Germany and the United Kingdom.

Moreover, FDI may affect technological change through productivity spillovers. In a 2000 paper, Liu, Siler, Wang, and Wei have shown that the mere presence of foreign firms in British manufacturing industries have had a positive effect on domestic firms' productivity during the same period (1991–1995).

Sources: Ray Barrel and Nigel Plain, "Foreign Direct Investment, Technological Change, and Economic Growth within Europe," *The Economic Journal*, 1997, 107 (No. 445): 1770–1786; Xiaming Liu, Pamela Siler, Chengqi Wang, and Yingqi Wei, "Productivity Spillovers from Foreign Direct Investment: Evidence from UK Industry Level Panel Data," *Journal of International Business Studies*, 2000, 31 (No. 3): 407–425.

during the crisis. As the BoE decreased the interest rate to zero, and continued to expand the money supply, the checkable deposits by people and reserves by banks steadily increased. Closer to us is the example of personal computers. Twenty-five years after the commercial introduction of personal computers, it often seems as if we have just begun discovering their uses.

An age-old worry is that research will become less and less fertile, that most major discoveries have already taken place and that technological progress will begin to slow down. This fear may come from thinking about mining, where higher-grade mines were exploited first, and where we have had to exploit increasingly lower-grade mines. But this is only an analogy, and so far there is no evidence that it is correct.

The Appropriability of Research Results

The second determinant of the level of R&D and of technological progress is the degree of *appropriability* of research results. If firms cannot appropriate the profits from the development of new products, they will not engage in R&D and technological progress will be slow. Many factors are also at work here:

The nature of the research process itself is important. For example, if it is widely believed that the discovery of a new product by one firm will quickly lead to the discovery of an even better product by another firm, there may be little advantage to being first. In other words, a highly fertile field of research may not generate high levels of R&D because no company will find the investment worthwhile. This example is extreme, but revealing.

Even more important is the legal protection given to new products. Without such legal protection, profits from developing a new product are likely to be small. Except in rare cases where the product is based on a trade secret (such as Coca Cola), it will generally not take long for other firms to produce the same product, eliminating any advantage the innovating firm may have initially had. This is why countries have patent laws. **Patents** give a firm that has discovered a new product—usually a new technique or device—the right to exclude anyone else from the production or use of the new product for some time.

How should governments design patent laws? On the one hand, protection is needed to provide firms with the incentives to spend on R&D. On the other, once firms ◄ This type of dilemma is known have discovered new products, it would be best for society if the knowledge embodied as *time inconsistency*. We shall in those new products were made available to other firms and to people without restrictions. Take, for example, biogenetic research. Only the prospect of large profits is leading bioengineering firms to embark on expensive research projects. Once a firm has found a new product, and the product can save many lives, it would clearly be best to make it available at cost to all potential users. But if such a policy was systematically followed, it would eliminate incentives for firms to do research in the first place. So patent law must strike a difficult balance. Too little protection will lead to little R&D. Too much protection will make it difficult for new R&D to build on the results of past R&D and may also lead to little R&D. (The difficulty of designing good patent or copyright laws is illustrated in the ◄ cartoon about cloning.)

see other examples and discuss it at length in Chapter 22.

These issues go beyond patent laws. To take two controversial examples: What is the role of open-source software? Should students download music, movies, and even texts without making payments to the creators?

© Chappatte in "L'Hebdo," Lausanne, www.globecartoon.com

Management Practices: Another Dimension of Technological Progress

For a given technology and a given human capital of its workers, the way a firm is managed also affects its performance. Some researchers actually believe that management practices might be stronger than many of the other factors that determine a firm's performance, including technological innovations. In a project that examined management practices and performance of more than 4,000 medium-sized manufacturing operations in Europe, the U.S. and Asia, Nick Bloom of Stanford University and John Van Reenen of the London School of Economics found that firms across the globe that use the same technology but apply good management practices perform significantly better than those that do not. This suggests that improved management practices is one of the most effective ways for a firm to outperform its peers. ("Why do management practices differ across firms and countries, by Nick Bloom and John Van Reenen, *Journal of Economic Perspectives*, Spring 2010).

A fascinating piece of evidence of the importance of management practices comes from an experimental study conducted by Nick Bloom on a set of 20 Indian textile plants. To investigate the role of good management practices Bloom provided free consulting on management practices to a randomly chosen group of the 20 plants. Then he compared the performance of the firms that received management advice with that of the control plants—those that did not receive advice. He found that adopting good management practices raised productivity by 18 percent through improved quality and efficiency and reduced inventory ("Does management matter? Evidence from India" by Nick Bloom, Ben Eifert, Abrijit Mahajan, David McKenzie and John Roberts, *Quarterly Journal of Economics*, Vol. 128, No. 1, pp 1–51.)

Management, Innovation, and Imitation

Although R&D is clearly central to technological progress, it would be wrong to focus exclusively on it because other dimensions are relevant. Existing technologies can be used more or less efficiently. Strong competition among firms forces them to be more efficient. Also, as shown in the Focus box "Management Practices: Another Dimension of Technological Progress," good management makes a substantial difference to the productivity of firms. And for some countries, R&D may be less important than for others. In this context, recent research on growth has emphasized the distinction between growth by innovation and growth by imitation. To sustain growth, advanced countries, which are at the **technology frontier**, must innovate. This requires substantial spending on R&D. Poorer countries, which are further from the technology frontier, can instead grow largely by imitating rather than innovating, by importing and adapting existing technologies instead of developing new ones. Importation and adaptation of existing technologies has clearly played a central role in generating high growth in China over the last three decades. This difference between innovation and imitation also explains why countries that are less technologically advanced often have poorer patent protection. China, for example, is a country with poor enforcement of patent rights. Our discussion helps explain why. These countries are typically users rather than producers of new technologies. Much of their improvement in productivity comes not from inventions within the country but from the adaptation of foreign technologies. In this case, the costs of weak patent protection are small because there would be few domestic inventions anyway. But the benefits of low patent protection are clear. They allow domestic firms to use and adapt foreign technology without having to pay high royalties to the foreign firms that developed the technology, which is good for the country.

At this stage, you might have the following question: If in poor countries technological progress is more a process of imitation rather than a process of innovation, why are some countries, such as China and other Asian countries, good at doing this, whereas others, for example many African countries, are not? This question takes us from macroeconomics to development economics, and it would take a text in development economics to do it justice. But it is too important a question to leave aside entirely here; we will discuss this issue in the next section.

12-3 Institutions, Technological Progress, and Growth

To get a sense of why some countries are good at imitating existing technologies, whereas others are not, compare Kenya and the United States. PPP GDP per person in Kenya is about 1/20th of PPP GDP per person in the United States. Part of the difference is due to a much lower level of capital per worker in Kenya. The other part of the difference is due to a much lower technological level in Kenya. It is estimated that A, the state of technology in Kenya, is about 1/13th of the U.S. level. Why is the state of technology in Kenya so low? Kenya potentially has access to most of the technological knowledge in the world. What prevents it from simply adopting much of the advanced countries' technology and quickly closing much of its technological gap with the United States?

One can think of a number of potential answers, ranging from Kenya's geography and climate to its culture. Most economists believe, however, that the main source of the problem, for poor countries in general and for Kenya in particular, lies in their poor institutions.

What institutions do economists have in mind? At a broad level, the protection of **property rights** may well be the most important. Few individuals are going to create firms, introduce new technologies, and invest in R&D if they expect that profits will be either appropriated by the state, extracted in bribes by corrupt bureaucrats, or stolen by other people in the economy. Figure 12-5 plots PPP GDP per person in 1995 (using a logarithmic scale) for 90 countries against an index measuring the degree of protection from expropriation; the index was constructed for each of these countries by an international business organization. The positive correlation between the two is striking (the figure also plots the regression line). Low protection is associated with a low GDP per person (at the extreme left of the figure are Zaire and Haiti); high protection is associated with a high GDP per person (at the extreme right are the United States, Luxembourg, Norway, Switzerland, and the Netherlands).

MyEconLab Video

Kenya's index is 6. Kenya is below the regression line, which means that Kenya has lower GDP per person than would be predicted based just on the index.

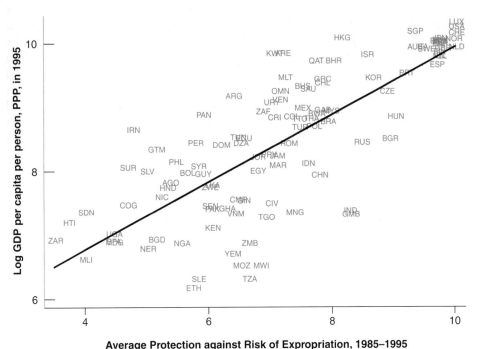

Average Protection against Risk of Expropriation, 1985–1995

Figure 12-5

Protection from Expropriation and GDP per Person

There is a strong positive relation between the degree of protection from expropriation and the level of GDP per person.

Source: Daron Acemoglu, "Understanding Institutions," Lionel Robbins Lectures, 2004. London School of Economics. http://economics.mit.edu/files/1353.

MyEconLab Animation

FOCUS

The Importance of Institutions: North Korea and South Korea

Following the surrender of Japan in 1945, Korea formally acquired its independence but became divided at the 38th parallel into two zones of occupation, with Soviet armed forces occupying the North and U.S. armed forces occupying the South. Attempts by both sides to claim jurisdiction over all of Korea triggered the Korean War, which lasted from 1950 to 1953. At the armistice in 1953, Korea became formally divided into two countries, the Democratic People's Republic of North Korea in the North, and the Republic of Korea in the South.

An interesting feature of Korea before separation was its ethnic and linguistic homogeneity. The North and the South were inhabited by essentially the same people, with the same culture and the same religion. Economically, the two regions were also highly similar at the time of separation. PPP GDP per person, in 1996 dollars, was roughly the same, about $700 in both the North and South.

Yet, 50 years later, as shown in Figure 1, GDP per person was 10 times higher in South Korea than in North Korea—$12,000 versus $1,100! On the one hand, South Korea had joined the OECD, the club of rich countries. On the other, North Korea had seen its GDP per person decrease by nearly two-thirds from its peak of $3,000 in the mid-1970s and was facing famine on a large scale. (The graph, taken from the work of Daron Acemoglu, stops in 1998. But, if anything, the difference between the two Koreas has become larger since then.)

What happened? Institutions and the organization of the economy were dramatically different during that period in the South and in the North. South Korea relied on a capitalist organization of the economy, with strong state intervention but also private ownership and legal protection of private producers. North Korea relied on central planning. Industries were quickly nationalized. Small firms and farms were forced to join large cooperatives so they could be supervised by the state. There were no private property rights for individuals. The result was the decline of the industrial sector and the collapse of agriculture. The lesson is sad, but transparent; institutions matter very much for growth.

Source: Daron Acemoglu, "Understanding Institutions," Lionel Robbins Lectures, 2004. London School of Economics. http://economics.mit.edu/files/1353.

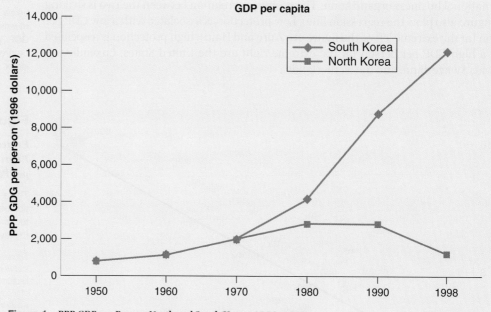

GDP per capita

Figure 1 *PPP GDP per Person: North and South Korea, 1950–1998*

What does "protection of property rights" mean in practice? It means a good political system, in which those in charge cannot expropriate or seize the property of the citizens. It means a good judicial system, where disagreements can be resolved efficiently, rapidly, and fairly. Looking at an even finer degree of detail, it means laws against insider trading in the stock market, so people are willing to buy stocks and so provide

What Is behind Chinese Growth?

From 1949—the year in which the People's Republic of China was established—to the late 1970s, China's economic system was based on central planning. Two major politico-economic reforms, the Great Leap Forward in 1958 and the Cultural Revolution in 1966, ended up as human and economic catastrophes. Output decreased by 20% from 1959 to 1962, and it is estimated that 25 million people died of famine during the same period. Output again decreased by more than 10% from 1966 to 1968.

After Chairman Mao's death in 1976, the new leaders decided to progressively introduce market mechanisms in the economy. In 1978, an agricultural reform was put in place, allowing farmers, after satisfying a quota due to the state, to sell their production in rural markets. Over time, farmers obtained increasing rights to the land, and today, state farms produce less than 1% of agricultural output. Outside of agriculture, and also starting in the late 1970s, state firms were given increasing autonomy over their production decisions, and market mechanisms and prices were introduced for an increasing number of goods. Private entrepreneurship was encouraged, often taking the form of "Town and Village Enterprises," collective ventures guided by a profit motive. Tax advantages and special agreements were used to attract foreign investors.

The economic effects of these cumulative reforms have been dramatic. Average growth of output per worker has increased from 2.5% between 1952 and 1977, to more than 9% since then.

Is such high growth surprising? One could argue that it is not. Looking at the 10-fold difference in productivity between North Korea and South Korea we saw in the previous Focus box, it is clear that central planning is a poor economic system. Thus, it would seem that, by moving from central planning to a market economy, countries could easily experience large increases in productivity. The answer is not so obvious, however, when one looks at the experience of the many countries that, since the late 1980s, have indeed moved away from central planning. In most Central European countries, this transition was typically associated with an initial 10% to 20% drop in GDP, and it took five years or more for output to exceed its pretransition level. In Russia and in the new countries carved out of the Soviet Union, the drop was even larger and longer lasting. (Many transition countries now have strong growth, although their growth rates are far below that of China.)

In Central and Eastern Europe, the initial effect of transition was a collapse of the state sector, only partially compensated by slow growth of the new private sector. In China, the state sector has declined more slowly, and its decline has been more than compensated by strong private sector growth. This gives a proximate explanation for the difference between China and the other transition countries. But it still begs the question: How was China able to achieve this smoother transition?

Some observers offer a cultural explanation. They point to the Confucian tradition, based on the teachings of Confucius, which still dominates Chinese values and emphasizes hard work, respect of one's commitments, and trustworthiness among friends. All these traits, they argue, are the foundations of institutions that allow a market economy to perform well.

Some observers offer an historical explanation. They point to the fact that, in contrast to Russia, central planning in China lasted only for a few decades. Thus, when the shift back to a market economy took place, people still knew how such an economy functioned and adapted easily to the new economic environment.

Most observers point to the strong rule of the communist party in the process. They point out that, in contrast to Central and Eastern Europe, the political system did not change, and the government was able to control the pace of transition. It was able to experiment along the way, to allow state firms to continue production while the private sector grew and to guarantee property rights to foreign investors (in Figure 12-5, China has an index of property rights of 7.7, not far from its value in rich countries). With foreign investors has come the technology from rich countries, and in time, the transfer of this knowledge to domestic firms. For political reasons, such a strategy was simply not open to governments in Central and Eastern Europe.

The limits of the Chinese strategy are clear. Property rights are still not well established. The banking system is still inefficient. So far, however, these problems have not stood in the way of growth.

For more on China's economy, read Gregory Chow, *China's Economic Transformation*, 3rd ed. (2014).

For a comparison between transition in Eastern Europe and China, read Jan Svejnar, "China in Light of the Performance of Central and East European Economies," IZA Discussion Paper 2791, May 2007.

financing to firms; it means clearly written and well-enforced patent laws, so firms have an incentive to do research and develop new products. It means good antitrust laws, so competitive markets do not turn into monopolies with few incentives to introduce new methods of production and new products. And the list obviously goes on. (A particularly dramatic example of the role of institutions is given in the Focus box, on page 274 "The Importance of Institutions: North Korea and South Korea.")

A quote from Gordon Brown, a former U.K. prime minister, "In establishing the rule of law, the first five centuries are always the hardest!"

This still leaves one essential question: Why don't poor countries adopt these good institutions? The answer is that it is hard! Good institutions are complex and difficult for poor countries to put in place. Surely, causality runs both ways in Figure 12-5: Low protection against expropriation leads to low GDP per person. But it is also the case that low GDP per person leads to worse protection against expropriation. Poor countries are often too poor to afford a good judicial system and to maintain a good police force, for example. Thus, improving institutions and starting a virtuous cycle of higher GDP per person and better institutions is often difficult. The fast growing countries of Asia have succeeded. (The Focus box, on page 275 "What Is behind Chinese Growth?" explores the case of China in more detail.) Some African countries appear also to be succeeding; others are still struggling.

12-4 The Facts of Growth Revisited

We can now use the theory we have developed in this and the previous chapter to interpret some of the facts we saw in Chapter 10.

Capital Accumulation versus Technological Progress in Rich Countries since 1985

Suppose we observe an economy with a high growth rate of output per worker over some period of time. Our theory implies this fast growth may come from two sources:

- It may reflect a high rate of technological progress under balanced growth.
- It may reflect instead the adjustment of capital per effective worker, K/AN, to a higher level. As we saw in Figure 12-4, such an adjustment leads to a period of higher growth, even if the rate of technological progress has not increased.

Can we tell how much of the growth comes from one source and how much comes from the other? Yes. If high growth reflects high balanced growth, output per worker should be growing at a rate *equal* to the rate of technological progress (see Table 10-1, line 4). If high growth reflects instead the adjustment to a higher level of capital per effective worker, this adjustment should be reflected in a growth rate of output per worker that *exceeds* the rate of technological progress.

Let's apply this approach to interpret the facts about growth in rich countries we saw in Table 10-1. This is done in Table 12-2, which gives, in column 1, the average rate of growth of output per worker $(g_Y - g_N)$ for 1985 to 2014 and, in column 2, the average rate of technological progress g_A, for 1985 to 2013 for each of four countries—France, Japan, the United Kingdom, and the United States—we looked at in Table 10-1. Note two differences between Tables 10-1 and 12-2: First, as suggested by the theory, Table 12-2

Table 12-2	Average Annual Rates of Growth of Output per Worker and Technological Progress in Four Rich Countries since 1985	
	Rate of Growth of Output per Worker (%) 1985–2014	Rate of Technological Progress (%) 1985–2013
France	1.3	1.4
Japan	1.6	1.7
United Kingdom	1.9	1.4
United States	1.7	1.4
Average	1.6	1.5

Source: Calculations from the OECD Productivity Statistics.

looks at the growth rate of output per worker, where Table 10-1, which was focusing on the standard of living, looked at the growth rate of output per person; the differences however are rather small. Second, because of data limitations, Table 12-2 starts in 1985 rather than in 1950. The rate of technological progress, g_A, is constructed using a method introduced by Robert Solow; the method and the details of construction are given in the appendix to this chapter.

In the United States, for example, the ratio of employment to population decreased slightly from 60.1% in 1985 to 59% in 2014. Thus, output per person and output per worker grew at virtually the same rate over this period.

Table 12-2 leads to two conclusions. First, over the period 1985–2014, output per worker has grown at rather similar rates across the five countries. In particular, there was little or no catchup of the United States by the other four countries. This is in contrast to the numbers in Table 10-1 which looked at the period 1950–2014, and showed substantial convergence to the United States. Put another way, much of the convergence happened between 1950 and 1985, and appears to have slowed down or even stopped since then.

Second, growth since 1985 has mostly come from technological progress, not from unusually high capital accumulation. This conclusion follows from the fact that the growth rate of output per worker (column 1) has been roughly equal to the rate of technological progress (column 2). This is what we would expect when countries are growing along their balanced growth path.

Note what this conclusion does not say. It does not say that capital accumulation was irrelevant. Capital accumulation was such as to allow these countries to maintain a roughly constant ratio of output to capital and achieve balanced growth. What it says is that, over the period, growth did not come from an unusual increase in capital accumulation (i.e., from an increase in the ratio of capital to output).

What would have happened to the growth rate of output per worker if these countries had had the same rate of technological progress, but no capital accumulation, during the period?

Capital Accumulation versus Technological Progress in China

Going beyond growth in OECD countries, one of the striking facts of Chapter 10 was the high growth rates achieved by a number of Asian countries in the last three decades. This raises again the same questions as those we just discussed: Do these high growth rates reflect fast technological progress, or do they reflect unusually high capital accumulation?

To answer these questions, we shall focus on China, because of its size and because of the astonishingly high output growth rate, nearly 10% since the late 1970s. Table 12-3 gives the average rate of growth, g_Y, the average rate of growth of output per worker, $g_Y - g_N$, and the average rate of technological progress, g_A, for two periods, 1978 to 1995 and 1996 to 2011.

Table 12-3 yields two conclusions. From the late 1970s to the mid-1990s, the rate of technological progress was close to the rate of growth of output per worker. China was roughly on a (rapid) balanced growth path. Since 1996, however, although growth of output per worker has remained high, the contribution of technological progress has decreased. Put another way, more recently, growth in China has come partly from unusually high capital accumulation—from an increase in the ratio of capital to output.

Warning: Chinese data for output, employment, and the capital stock (the latter is needed to construct g_A) are not as reliable as similar data for OECD countries. Thus, the numbers in the table should be seen as more tentative than the numbers in Table 12-2.

Table 12-3	Average Annual Rate of Growth of Output per Worker and Technological Progress in China, 1978–2011		
Period	Rate of Growth of Output (%)	Rate of Growth of Output per Worker (%)	Rate of Technological Progress (%)
1978–1995	10.1	7.4	7.9
1996–2011	9.8	8.8	5.9
Source: Penn World Table version 8.1.			

We can look at it another way. Recall, from Table 12-1, that under balanced growth, $g_K = g_Y = g_A + g_N$. To see what investment rate would be required if China had balanced growth, go back to equation (12.3) and divide both sides by output, Y, to get

$$\frac{I}{Y} = (\delta + g_A + g_N)\frac{K}{Y}$$

Let's plug in numbers for China for the period 1996–2011. The estimate of δ, the depreciation rate of capital in China, is 5% a year. As we just saw, the average value of g_A for the period was 5.9%. The average value of g_N, the rate of growth of employment, was 0.9%. The average value of the ratio of capital to output was 2.9. This implies a ratio of investment of output required to achieve balanced growth of $(5\% + 5.9\% + 0.9\%) \times 2.9 = 34.2\%$.

The actual average ratio of investment to output for 1995–2011 was a much higher 47%. Thus, both rapid technological progress and unusually high capital accumulation explain high Chinese growth. If the rate of technological progress were to remain the same, this suggests that, as the ratio of capital to output stabilizes, the Chinese growth rate will decrease, closer to 6% than to 9.8%.

Where does technological progress in China come from? A closer look at the data suggests two main channels. First, China has transferred labor from the countryside, where productivity is low, to industry and services in the cities, where productivity is much higher. Second, China has imported the technology of more technologically advanced countries. It has, for example, encouraged the development of joint ventures between Chinese firms and foreign firms. Foreign firms have come with better technologies, and over time, Chinese firms have learned how to use them. To relate to our discussion, growth has come largely through imitation, the importation and adaptation of modern technologies from more advanced countries. As China catches up and gets closer to the technology frontier, it will have to shift from imitation to innovation, and thus modify its growth model.

Summary

■ When we think about the implications of technological progress for growth, it is useful to think of technological progress as increasing the amount of effective labor available in the economy (that is, labor multiplied by the state of technology). We can then think of output as being produced with capital and effective labor.

■ In steady state, output *per effective worker* and capital *per effective worker* are constant. Put another way, output *per worker* and capital *per worker* grow at the rate of technological progress. Put yet another way, output and capital grow at the same rate as effective labor, thus at a rate equal to the growth rate of the number of workers plus the rate of technological progress.

■ When the economy is in steady state, it is said to be on a balanced growth path. Output, capital, and effective labor are all growing "in balance," that is, at the same rate.

MEL ■ The rate of output growth in steady state is independent of
Video   the saving rate. However, the saving rate affects the steady-state level of output per effective worker. And increases in the saving rate will lead, for some time, to an increase in the growth rate above the steady-state growth rate.

■ Technological progress depends on both (1) the fertility of research and development, how spending on R&D translates into new ideas and new products, and (2) the appropriability of the results of R&D, which is the extent to which firms benefit from the results of their R&D.

■ When designing patent laws, governments must balance their desire to protect future discoveries and provide incentives for firms to do R&D with their desire to make existing discoveries available to potential users without restrictions.

■ Sustained technological progress requires that the right institutions are in place. In particular, it requires well-established and well-protected property rights. Without good property rights, a country is likely to remain poor. But in turn, a poor country may find it difficult to put in place good property rights.

■ France, Japan, the United Kingdom, and the United States have experienced roughly balanced growth since 1950. Growth of output per worker has been roughly equal to the rate of technological progress. Growth in China is a combination of a high rate of technological progress and unusually high investment, leading to an increase in the ratio of capital to output.

Key Terms

state of technology, 262
effective labor, 262
labor in efficiency units, 263
balanced growth, 266
research and development (R&D), 268

fertility of research, 269
appropriability, 269
patents, 271
technology frontier, 272
property rights, 273

Questions and Problems

QUICK CHECK

MyEconLab Visit www.myeconlab.com to complete similar Quick Check problems and get instant feedback.

1. Using the information in this chapter, label each of the following statements true, false, or uncertain. Explain briefly.

a. Writing the production function in terms of capital and effective labor implies that as the level of technology increases by 10%, the number of workers required to achieve the same level of output decreases by 10%.

b. If the rate of technological progress increases, the investment rate (the ratio of investment to output) must increase to keep capital per effective worker constant.

c. In steady state, output per effective worker grows at the rate of population growth.

d. In steady state, output per worker grows at the rate of technological progress.

e. A higher saving rate implies a higher level of capital per effective worker in the steady state and thus a higher rate of growth of output per effective worker.

f. Even if the potential returns from research and development (R&D) spending are identical to the potential returns from investing in a new machine, R&D spending is much riskier for firms than investing in new machines.

g. The fact that one cannot patent a theorem implies that private firms will not engage in basic research.

h. Because eventually we will know everything, growth will have to come to an end.

i. Technology has not played an important part in Chinese economic growth.

2. R&D and growth

a. Why is the amount of R&D spending important for growth? How do the appropriability and fertility of research affect the amount of R&D spending?

How do each of the policy proposals listed in (b) through (e) affect the appropriability and fertility of research, R&D spending in the long run, and output in the long run?

b. An international treaty ensuring that each country's patents are legally protected all over the world. This may be a part of the proposed Trans-Pacific Partnership.

c. Tax credits for each dollar of R&D spending.

d. A decrease in funding of government-sponsored conferences between universities and corporations.

e. The elimination of patents on breakthrough drugs, so the drugs can be sold at a low cost as soon as they become available.

3. Sources of technological progress: Leaders versus followers

a. Where does technological progress come from for the economic leaders of the world?

b. Do developing countries have other alternatives to the sources of technological progress you mentioned in part (a)?

c. Do you see any reasons developing countries may choose to have poor patent protection? Are there any dangers in such a policy (for developing countries)?

DIG DEEPER

MyEconLab Visit www.myeconlab.com to complete all Dig Deeper problems and get instant feedback.

4. For the following changes in economic policy, explain how the growth rate and the level of output in the future would be affected. Distinguish between short-run effects and long-term effects.

a. The government announces a policy aimed at balancing the government budget that amounts to a permanent reduction in public deficits (see Chapter 7 for a more extensive treatment of fiscal policy).

b. The government decides a massive investment in fundamental research that increases AN. However, during the same period, the country experiences a 1% drop in the labor force.

5. Measurement error, inflation, and productivity growth

   Suppose that there are only two goods produced in an economy: haircuts and banking services. Prices, quantities, and the number of workers occupied in the production of each good for year 1 and for year 2 are given in the table:

	Year 1			Year 2		
	P_1	Q_1	W_1	P_2	Q_2	W_2
Haircuts	10	100	50	12	100	50
Banking	10	200	50	12	230	60

a. What is nominal GDP in each year?

b. Using year 1 prices, what is real GDP in year 2? What is the growth rate of real GDP?

c. What is the rate of inflation using the GDP deflator?

d. Using year 1 prices, what is real GDP per worker in year 1 and year 2? What is labor productivity growth between year 1 and year 2 for the whole economy?

   Now suppose that banking services in year 2 are not the same as banking services in year 1. Year 2 banking services include telebanking, which year 1 banking services did not include. The technology for telebanking was available in year 1, but the price of banking services with telebanking in year 1 was $13, and no one chose to purchase this package. However, in year 2, the price of banking services with telebanking was $12, and everyone chose to have this package (i.e., in year 2 no one chose to have the year 1 banking services package without telebanking). (Hint: Assume that there are now two types of banking services: those with telebanking and those without. Rewrite the preceding table but now with three goods: haircuts and the two types of banking services.)

e. Using year 1 prices, what is real GDP for year 2? What is the growth rate of real GDP?

f. What is the rate of inflation using the GDP deflator?

g. What is labor productivity growth between year 1 and year 2 for the whole economy?

h. Consider this statement: "If banking services are mismeasured—for example, by not taking into account the introduction of telebanking—we will overestimate inflation and underestimate productivity growth." Discuss this statement in light of your answers to parts (a) through (g).

6. Suppose that a country's production function is

$$Y = 2\sqrt{K} \sqrt{AN}$$

and that the savings rate, s, is equal to 20% and the depreciation rate, δ, is 10%. Suppose further that the labor force grows by 1% each year and that the rate of technological progress is 6% per year.

a. Calculate the values of
   i. the steady-state level of capital per effective worker
   ii. the steady-state level of output per effective worker
   iii. the growth rate of output per effective worker
   iv. the growth rate of output per worker
   v. the growth rate of output

b. Suppose that the labor force now grows at 5% per year. Calculate the changes in the values obtained in part (a). Compare parts (a) and (b) and comment.

c. Suppose that the country experiences a technological setback, and now grows at 2% a year while the labor force continues to grow at 5%. Recompute the answers to part (b). Compare and comment with respect to (a).

7. Discuss the potential role of each of the factors listed in (a) through (g) on the steady-state level of output per worker. In each case, indicate whether the effect is through A, through K, through H, or through some combination of A, K, and H. A is the level of technology, K is the level of capital stock, and H is the level of the human capital stock.

a. Geographic location
b. Education
c. Protection of property rights
d. Openness to trade
e. Low tax rates
f. Good public infrastructure
g. Low population growth

EXPLORE FURTHER

8. Growth accounting

The appendix to this chapter shows how data on output, capital, and labor can be used to construct estimates of the rate of growth of technological progress. We modify that approach in this problem to examine the growth of capital per worker.

$$Y = K^{1/3} (AN)^{2/3}$$

The function gives a good description of production in rich countries. Following the same steps as in the appendix, you can show that

$$(2/3)g_A = g_Y - (2/3)g_N - (1/3)g_K$$
$$= (g_Y - g_N) - (1/3)(g_K - g_N)$$

where g_y denotes the growth rate of Y.

a. What does the quantity $g_Y - g_N$ represent? What does the quantity $g_K - g_N$ represent?

b. Rearrange the preceding equation to solve for the growth rate of capital per worker.

c. Look at Table 12-2 in the chapter. Using your answer to part (b), substitute in the average annual growth rate of output per worker and the average annual rate of technological progress for the United States for the period 1985 to 2013 to obtain a crude measure of the average annual growth of capital per worker. (Strictly speaking, we should construct these measures individually for every year, but we limit ourselves to readily available data in this problem.) Do the same for the other countries listed in Table 12-2 (where data goes to 2014). How does the average growth of capital per worker compare across the countries in Table 12-2? Do the results make sense to you? Explain.

Further Readings

- For more on growth, both theory and evidence, read Charles Jones, *Introduction to Economic Growth*, 3rd ed. (2013). Jones's Web page, http://web.stanford.edu/~chadj/ is a useful portal to the research on growth.

- For more on patents, see *The Economist*, Special Report: Patents and Technology, October 20th, 2005.

- For more on growth in two large, fast growing countries, read Barry Bosworth and Susan M. Collins, "Accounting for Growth: Comparing China and India," *Journal of Economic Perspectives*, 2008, Vol. 22, No. 1: 45–66.

- For the role of institutions in growth, read "Growth Theory Through the Lens of Development Economics," by Abhijit Banerjee and Esther Duflo, Chapter 7, *Handbook of Economic Growth* (2005), read sections 1 to 4.

- For more on institutions and growth, you can read the slides from the 2004 Lionel Robbins lectures "Understanding Institutions" given by Daron Acemoglu. These are found at http://economics.mit.edu/files/1353.

On two issues we have not explored in the text:

- Growth and global warming. Read the *Stern Review on the Economics of Climate Change* (2006). You can find it at www.wwf.se/source.php/1169157 (The report is long. Read just the executive summary.)

- Growth and the environment. Read the Economist Survey on *The Global Environment: The Great Race*, July 4, 2002, and the update titled "The Anthropocene: A Man-made World," May 26, 2011.

APPENDIX: Constructing a Measure of Technological Progress

In 1957, Robert Solow devised a way of constructing an estimate of technological progress. The method, which is still in use today, relies on one important assumption: that each factor of production is paid its marginal product.

Under this assumption, it is easy to compute the contribution of an increase in any factor of production to the increase in output. For example, if a worker is paid $30,000 a year, the assumption implies that her contribution to output is equal to $30,000. Now suppose that this worker increases the amount of hours she works by 10%. The increase in output coming from the increase in her hours will therefore be equal to $30,000 × 10%, or $3,000.

Let us write this more formally. Denote output by Y, labor by N, and the real wage by W/P. The symbol, Δ, means change in. Then, as we just established, the change in output is equal to the real wage multiplied by the change in labor.

$$\Delta Y = \frac{W}{P} \Delta N$$

Divide both sides of the equation by Y, divide and multiply the right side by N, and reorganize:

$$\frac{\Delta Y}{Y} = \frac{WN}{PY} \frac{\Delta N}{N}$$

Note that the first term on the right (WN/PY) is equal to the share of labor in output—the total wage bill in dollars divided by the value of output in dollars. Denote this share by α. Note that $\Delta Y/Y$ is the rate of growth of output, and denote it by g_Y. Note similarly that $\Delta N/N$ is the rate of change of the labor input, and denote it by g_N. Then the previous relation can be written as

$$g_Y = \alpha g_N$$

More generally, this reasoning implies that the part of output growth attributable to growth of the labor input is equal to α times g_N. If, for example, employment grows by 2% and the share of labor is 0.7, then the output growth due to the growth in employment is equal to 1.4% (0.7 times 2%).

Similarly, we can compute the part of output growth attributable to growth of the capital stock. Because there are only two factors of production, labor and capital, and because the share of labor is equal to α, the share of capital in income must be equal to $(1 - \alpha)$. If the growth rate of capital is equal to g_K, then the part of output growth attributable to growth of capital is equal to $(1 - \alpha)$ times g_K. If, for example, capital grows by 5%, and the share of capital is 0.3, then the output growth due to the growth of the capital stock is equal to 1.5% (0.3 times 5%).

Putting the contributions of labor and capital together, the growth in output attributable to growth in both labor and capital is equal to $(\alpha g_N + (1 - \alpha)g_K)$.

We can then measure the effects of technological progress by computing what Solow called the *residual*, the excess of actual growth of output g_Y over the growth attributable to growth of labor and the growth of capital $(\alpha g_N + (1 - \alpha)g_K)$.

$$\text{residual} \equiv g_Y - [\alpha g_N + (1 - \alpha)g_K]$$

This measure is called the **Solow residual**. It is easy to compute. All we need to know to compute it are the growth rate of output, g_Y, the growth rate of labor, g_N, and the growth rate of capital, g_K, together with the shares of labor, α, and capital, $(1 - \alpha)$.

To continue with our previous numerical examples: Suppose employment grows by 4%, the capital stock grows by 5%, and the share of labor is 0.7 (and so the share of capital is 0.3). Then the part of output growth attributable to growth of labor and growth of capital is equal to 2.9% (0.7 × 2% + 0.3 × 5%). If output growth is equal, for example, to 4%, then the Solow residual is equal to 1.1% (4% − 2.9%).

The Solow residual is sometimes called the **rate of growth of total factor productivity** (or the **rate of TFP growth**, for short). The use of "total factor productivity" is to distinguish it from the *rate of growth of labor productivity*, which is defined as $(g_Y - g_N)$, the rate of output growth minus the rate of labor growth.

The Solow residual is related to the rate of technological progress in a simple way. The residual is equal to the share of labor times the rate of technological progress:

$$\text{residual} = \alpha g_A$$

We shall not derive this result here. But the intuition for this relation comes from the fact that what matters in the production function $Y = F(K, AN)$ (equation (12.1)) is the product of the state of technology and labor, AN. We saw that to get the contribution of labor growth to output growth, we must multiply the growth rate of labor by its share. Because N and A enter the production function in the same way, it is clear that to get the contribution of technological progress to output growth, we must also multiply it by the share of labor.

If the Solow residual is equal to zero, so is technological progress. To construct an estimate of g_A, we must construct the Solow residual and then divide it by the share of labor. This is how the estimates of g_A presented in the text are constructed.

In the numerical example we saw previously: The Solow residual is equal to 1.1%, and the share of labor is equal to 0.7. So, the rate of technological progress is equal to 1.6% (1.1% divided by 0.7).

Keep straight the definitions of productivity growth you have seen in this chapter:

■ Labor productivity growth (equivalently, the rate of growth of output per worker): $g_Y - g_N$
■ The rate of technological progress: g_A

In steady state, labor productivity growth $(g_Y - g_N)$ equals the rate of technological progress g_A. Outside of steady state, they need not be equal. An increase in the ratio of capital per effective worker due, for example, to an increase in the saving rate, will cause $g_Y - g_N$ to be higher than g_A for some time.

The original presentation of the ideas discussed in this appendix is found in Robert Solow, "Technical Change and the Aggregate Production Function," *Review of Economics and Statistics*, 1957, 312–320.

Key Terms

Solow residual, 281
rate of growth of total factor productivity, 281
rate of TFP growth, 281

Technological Progress: The Short, the Medium, and the Long Run

We spent much of Chapter 12 celebrating the merits of technological progress. In the long run, technological progress, we argued, is the key to increases in the standard of living. Popular discussions of technological progress are often more ambivalent. Technological progress is often blamed for higher unemployment, and for higher income inequality. Are these fears groundless? This is the set of issues we take up in this chapter.

Section 13-1 looks at the short-run response of output and unemployment to increases in productivity.

Even if, in the long run, the adjustment to technological progress is through increases in output rather than increases in unemployment, the question remains: How long will this adjustment take? The section concludes that the answer is ambiguous. In the short run, increases in productivity sometimes decrease unemployment and sometimes increase it.

Section 13-2 looks at the medium-run response of output and unemployment to increases in productivity.

It concludes that neither the theory nor the evidence supports the fear that faster technological progress leads to higher unemployment. If anything, the effect seems to go the other way. In the medium run, increases in productivity growth appear to be associated with lower unemployment.

Section 13-3 returns to the long run and discusses the effects of technological progress on income inequality.

Along with technological progress comes a complex process of job creation and job destruc- MyEconLab Video tion. For those who lose their jobs, or for those who have skills that are no longer in demand, technological progress can indeed be a curse, not a blessing. As consumers, they benefit from the availability of new and cheaper goods. As workers, they may suffer from prolonged unemployment and have to settle for lower wages when taking a new job. As a result of these effects technological progress is often associated with changes in income inequality. Section 13-3 discusses these various effects and looks at the evidence.

13-1 Productivity, Output, and Unemployment in the Short Run

In Chapter 12, we represented technological progress as an increase in A, the *state of technology*, in the production function

$$Y = F(K, AN)$$

What matters for the issues we shall be discussing in this chapter is technological progress, not capital accumulation. So, for simplicity, we shall ignore capital for now and assume that output is produced according to the following production function:

$$Y = AN \tag{13.1}$$

Under this assumption, output is produced using only labor, N, and each worker produces A units of output. Increases in A represent technological progress.

"Output per worker" (Y/N) and "the state of technology" (A) are in general not the same. Recall from Chapter 12 that an increase in output per worker may come from an increase in capital per worker, even if the state of technology has not changed. They are the same here because, in writing the production function as equation (13.1), we ignore the role of capital in production.

A has two interpretations here. One is indeed as the state of technology. The other is as labor productivity (output per worker), which follows from the fact that $Y/N = A$. So, when referring to increases in A, we shall use *technological progress* or (labor) *productivity growth* interchangeably. Let's rewrite equation (13.1) as

$$N = Y/A \tag{13.2}$$

Employment is equal to output divided by productivity. Given output, the higher the level of productivity, the lower the level of employment. This naturally leads to the question: When productivity increases, does output increase enough to avoid a decrease in employment? In this section we look at the short-run responses of output, employment, and unemployment. Then, in the next two sections, we look at their medium-run responses and, in particular, at the relation between the natural rate of unemployment and the rate of technological progress.

In the *short run*, the level of output is determined by the IS and the LM relations

$$Y = Y(C - T) + I(r + x, Y) + G$$
$$r = \bar{r} \tag{13.3}$$

For a refresher, go back to Chapter 6

Output depends on demand, which is the sum of consumption, investment and government spending. Consumption depends on disposable income. Investment depends on the borrowing rate, equal to the policy rate plus a risk premium, and on sales. Government spending is given. The central bank determines the policy rate.

What is the effect of an increase in productivity, A, on demand? Does an increase in productivity increase or decrease the demand for goods at a given real policy rate? There is no general answer because productivity increases do not appear in a vacuum; what happens to the demand for goods depends on what triggered the increase in productivity in the first place:

Recall our discussion of such major inventions in Chapter 12. This argument points to the role of expectations in affecting consumption and investment, something we have not yet studied formally, but shall do in Chapter 16.

■ Take the case where productivity increases come from the widespread implementation of a major invention. It is easy to see how such a change may be associated with an increase in demand. The prospect of higher growth in the future leads consumers to feel more optimistic about the future, so they increase their consumption given their current disposable income. The prospect of higher profits in the future, as well as the need to put the new technology in place, may also lead to a boom in investment given current sales and given the current policy rate. In this case, the demand for goods increases; the IS curve shifts to the right, from *IS* to *IS''* in Figure 13-1. The economy moves from A to A''. The short run level of output increases from Y to Y''.

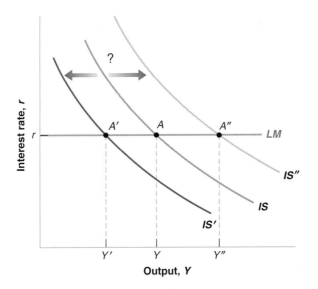

Figure 13-1

The Demand for Goods in the Short Run following an Increase in Productivity

An increase in productivity may increase or decrease the demand for goods. Thus, it may shift the *IS* to the left or to the right. What happens depends on what triggered the increase in productivity in the first place.

MyEconLab Animation

■ Now take the case where productivity growth comes not from the introduction of new technologies but from the more efficient use of existing technologies. One of the implications of increased international trade has been an increase in foreign competition. This competition has forced many firms to cut costs by reorganizing production and eliminating jobs (this is often called *downsizing*). When such reorganizations are the source of productivity growth, there is no presumption that aggregate demand will increase. Reorganization of production may require little or no new investment. Increased uncertainty and job security worries faced by workers might cause them to want to save more, and so to reduce consumption spending given their current income. In this case, the demand for goods falls at a given real policy rate; the *IS* curve shifts to the left and the short run level of output falls from *Y* to *Y'* as in Figure 13-1.

Let's assume the more favorable case (more favorable from the point of view of output and employment), namely the case where the *IS* shifts to the right from *IS* to *IS''* as in Figure 13-1. Equilibrium output rises, from *Y* to *Y''*. In this case, the increase in productivity, by raising expected output growth and expected profits, unambiguously leads to an increase in demand and thus to a higher equilibrium output.

Even in this favorable case, however, we cannot tell what happens to employment ◀ without having more information. To see why, note that equation (13.2) implies the following relation:

% change in employment = % change in output − % change in productivity

Thus, what happens to employment depends on whether output increases proportionately more or less than productivity. If productivity increases by 2%, it takes an increase in output of at least 2% to avoid a decrease in employment—that is, an increase in unemployment. And without a lot more information about the slope and the size of the shift of the *IS* curve, we cannot tell whether this condition is satisfied even in the more favorable case in Figure 13-1, that is when the IS shifts to the right and output rises to *Y'*. In the short run, an increase in productivity may or may not lead to an increase in unemployment. Theory alone cannot settle the issue.

Start from the production function $Y = A/N$. From Proposition 7 in Appendix 2 implies, this relation at the end of the book, This relation implies that $g_Y = g_A + g_N$. Or equivalently: $g_N = g_Y - g_A$.

The discussion has assumed that macroeconomic policy was given. But both fiscal policy and monetary policy can clearly affect the outcome. Suppose you were in charge of monetary policy in this economy, and there appeared to be an increase in the rate of productivity growth. What would you do? This was one of the questions the Fed faced in the 1990s at the height of the IT revolution.

Figure 13-2

Labor Productivity and Output Growth in the United States since 1960

There is a strong positive relation between output growth and productivity growth. But the causality runs from output growth to productivity growth, not the other way around.

Source: Real GDP growth rate; Series A191RL1A225NBEA Federal Reserve Economic Data (FRED); Productivity growth; Series PRS84006092, U.S. Bureau of Labor Statistics.

MyEconLab Real-time data

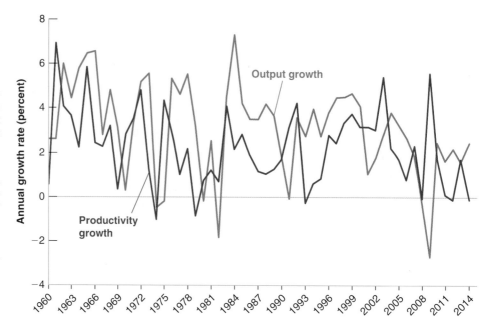

Correlation versus causality: If we see a positive correlation between output growth and productivity growth, should we conclude that high productivity growth leads to high output growth, or that high output growth leads to high productivity growth?

This discussion is directly related to our discussion of the Focus box on "Okun's Law" in Chapter 9. There, we saw that a change in output leads to a smaller proportional change in employment. This is the same as saying that a change in output is associated with a change in labor productivity in the same direction. (Make sure you understand why.)

The Empirical Evidence

Can empirical evidence help us decide whether, in practice, productivity growth increases or decreases employment? At first glance, it would seem to. Look at Figure 13-2, which plots the behavior of labor productivity and the behavior of output for the U.S. business sector from 1960 to 2014.

The figure shows a strong positive relation between year-to-year movements in output growth and productivity growth. Furthermore, the movements in output are typically larger than the movements in productivity. This would seem to imply that, when productivity growth is high, output increases by more than enough to avoid any adverse effect on employment. But this conclusion would be wrong. The reason is that, *in the short run*, the causal relation runs mostly the other way, from output growth to productivity growth. That is, in the short run, higher output growth leads to higher productivity growth, not the other way around. The reason is that, in bad times, firms hoard labor; they keep more workers than is necessary for current production. So when demand and output decrease, employment decreases by less than output; equivalently labor productivity decreases. This was particularly clear in 2008, at the beginning of the crisis when firms didn't immediately realize that it would last so long When instead demand and output increase, firms increase employment by less than output, and labor productivity increases. This is what we see in Figure 13-2, but this is not the relation we are after. Rather, we want to know what happens to output and unemployment when there is an *exogenous* change in productivity—a change in productivity that comes from a change in technology, not from the response of firms to movements in output. Figure 13-2 does not help us much here. And the conclusion from the research that has looked at the effects of exogenous movements in productivity growth on output is that the data give an answer just as ambiguous as the answer given by the theory:

- Sometimes increases in productivity lead to increases in output sufficient to maintain or even increase employment in the short run.
- Sometimes they do not, and unemployment increases in the short run.

13-2 Productivity and the Natural Rate of Unemployment

We have looked so far at *short-run* effects of a change in productivity on output and, by implication, on employment and unemployment. In the *medium run*, the economy tends to return to the natural level of unemployment. Now we must ask: Is the natural rate of unemployment itself affected by changes in productivity?

Since the beginning of the Industrial Revolution, workers have worried that technological progress would eliminate jobs and increase unemployment. In early 19th-century England, groups of workers in the textile industry, known as the *Luddites*, destroyed the new machines that they saw as a direct threat to their jobs. Similar movements took place in other countries. *"Saboteur"* comes from one of the ways French workers destroyed machines: by putting their sabots (their heavy wooden shoes) into the machines.

The theme of **technological unemployment** typically resurfaces whenever unemployment is high. During the Great Depression, a movement called the *technocracy movement* argued that high unemployment came from the introduction of machinery, and that things would only get worse if technological progress were allowed to continue. In the late 1990s, France passed a law reducing the normal workweek from 39 to 35 hours. One of the reasons invoked was that, because of technological progress, there was no longer enough work for all workers to have full-time jobs. Thus the proposed solution: Have each worker work fewer hours (at the same hourly wage) so that more of them could be employed.

In its crudest form, the argument that technological progress must lead to unemployment is obviously false. The large improvements in the standard of living that advanced countries have enjoyed during the 20th century have come with large *increases* in employment and no systematic increase in the unemployment rate. In the United States, output per person has increased by a factor of 9 since 1890 and, far from declining, employment has increased by a factor of 6 (reflecting a parallel increase in the size of the U.S. population). Nor, looking across countries, is there any evidence of a systematic positive relation between the unemployment rate and the level of productivity.

A more sophisticated version of the argument cannot, however, be dismissed so easily. Perhaps periods of unusually fast technological progress are associated with a higher natural rate of unemployment, periods of unusually slow progress associated with a lower natural rate of unemployment. To think about these issues, we can use the model we developed in Chapter 7.

Recall from Chapter 7 that we can think of the natural rate of unemployment (the natural rate, for short, in what follows) as being determined by two relations, the price-setting relation and the wage-setting relation. Our first step must be to think about how changes in productivity affect each of these two relations.

> In Chapter 7, we assumed that A was constant (and we conveniently set it equal to 1). ◄ We now relax this assumption.

Price Setting and Wage Setting Revisited

Consider price setting first.

■ From equation (13.1), each worker produces A units of output; put another way, producing 1 unit of output requires $1/A$ workers.

■ If the nominal wage is equal to W, the nominal cost of producing 1 unit of output is therefore equal to $(1/A)W = W/A$.

■ If firms set their price equal to $1 + m$ times cost (where m is the markup), the price level is given by:

$$\text{Price setting } P = (1 + m)\frac{W}{A} \qquad (13.3)$$

The only difference between this equation and equation (7.3) is the presence of the productivity term, A (which we had implicitly set to 1 in Chapter 7). An increase in productivity decreases costs, which decreases the price level given the nominal wage.

Turn to wage setting. The evidence suggests that, other things being equal, wages are typically set to reflect the increase in productivity over time. If productivity has been growing at 2% per year on average for some time, then wage contracts will build in a wage increase of 2% per year. This suggests the following extension of our previous wage-setting equation (7.1):

$$\text{Wage setting} \qquad W = A^e P^e F(u, z) \qquad (13.4)$$

Look at the three terms on the right of equation (13.4).

Think of workers and firms setting the wage so as to divide (expected) output between workers and firms according to their relative bargaining power. If both sides expect higher productivity and therefore higher output, this will be reflected in the bargained wage. ▶

■ Two of them, P^e and $F(u, z)$, should be familiar from equation (7.1). Workers care about real wages, not nominal wages, so wages depend on the (expected) price level, P^e. Wages depend (negatively) on the unemployment rate, u, and on institutional factors captured by the variable z.

■ The new term is A^e: Wages now also depend on the expected level of productivity, A^e. If workers and firms both expect productivity to increase, they will incorporate those expectations into the wages set in bargaining.

The Natural Rate of Unemployment

We can now characterize the natural rate. Recall that the natural rate is determined by the price-setting and wage-setting relations, and the additional condition that expectations be correct. In this case, this condition requires that expectations of *both* prices *and* productivity be correct, so $P^e = P$ and $A^e = A$.

The price-setting equation determines the real wage paid by firms. Reorganizing equation (13.3), we can write

$$\frac{W}{P} = \frac{A}{1 + m} \qquad (13.5)$$

The real wage paid by firms, W/P, increases one-for-one with productivity A. The higher the level of productivity, the lower the price set by firms given the nominal wage, and therefore the higher the real wage paid by firms.

This equation is represented in Figure 13-3. The real wage is measured on the vertical axis. The unemployment rate is measured on the horizontal axis. Equation (13.5) is represented by the lower horizontal line at $W/P = A/(1 + m)$: The real wage implied by price setting is independent of the unemployment rate.

Turn to the wage-setting equation. Under the condition that expectations are correct—so both $P^e = P$ and $A^e = A$—the wage-setting equation (13.4) becomes

$$\frac{W}{P} = A F(u, z) \qquad (13.6)$$

The reason for using B rather than A to denote the equilibrium is that we are already using the letter A to denote the level of productivity. ▶

The real wage W/P implied by wage bargaining depends on both the level of productivity and the unemployment rate. For a given level of productivity, equation (13.6) is represented by the lower downward-sloping curve in Figure 13-3: The real wage implied by wage setting is a decreasing function of the unemployment rate.

Equilibrium in the labor market is given by point B, and the natural rate is equal to u_n. Let's now ask what happens to the natural rate in response to an increase in productivity. Suppose that A increases by 3%, so the new level of productivity A' equals 1.03 times A.

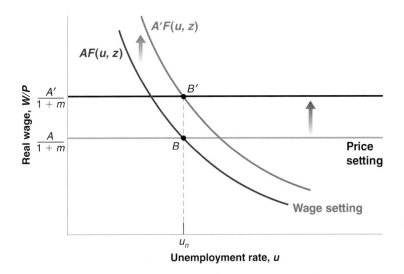

Figure 13-3

The Effects of an Increase in Productivity on the Natural Rate of Unemployment

An increase in productivity shifts both the wage and the price-setting curves by the same proportion and thus has no effect on the natural rate.

MyEconLab Animation

- From equation (13.5) we see that the real wage implied by price setting is now higher by 3%: The price setting line shifts up.
- From equation (13.6), we see that at a given unemployment rate, the real wage implied by wage setting is also higher by 3%: The wage-setting curve shifts up.
- Note that, at the initial unemployment rate u_n, both curves shift up by the same amount, namely 3% of the initial real wage. That is why the new equilibrium is at B' directly above B. The real wage is higher by 3%, and the natural rate remains the same.

The intuition for this result is straightforward. A 3% increase in productivity leads firms to reduce prices by 3% given wages, leading to a 3% increase in real wages. This increase exactly matches the increase in real wages from wage bargaining at the initial unemployment rate. Real wages increase by 3%, and the natural rate remains the same.

We have looked at a one-time increase in productivity, but the argument we have developed also applies to productivity growth. Suppose that productivity steadily increases, so that each year A increases by 3%. Then, each year, real wages will increase by 3%, and the natural rate will remain unchanged.

The Empirical Evidence

We have just derived two strong results. The natural rate should depend neither on the level of productivity nor on the rate of productivity growth. How do these two results fit the facts?

An obvious problem in answering this question is one we discussed in Chapter 8 before, namely that we do not observe the natural rate. Because the actual unemployment rate moves around the natural rate, looking at the average unemployment rate over a decade should give us however a good estimate of the natural rate for that decade. Looking at average productivity growth over a decade also takes care of another problem we discussed previously. Although changes in labor hoarding can have a large effect on year-to-year changes in labor productivity, these changes in labor hoarding are unlikely to make much difference when we look at average productivity growth over a decade.

Figure 13-4 plots average U.S. labor productivity growth and the average unemployment rate during each decade since 1890. At first glance, there seems to be little relation

Figure 13-4

Productivity Growth and Unemployment. Averages by Decade, 1890–2014

There is little relation between the 10-year averages of productivity growth and the 10-year averages of the unemployment rate. If anything, higher productivity growth is associated with lower unemployment.

Source: Data prior to 1960: Historical Statistics of the United States. Data after 1960: Bureau of Labor Statistics.

MyEconLab Animation

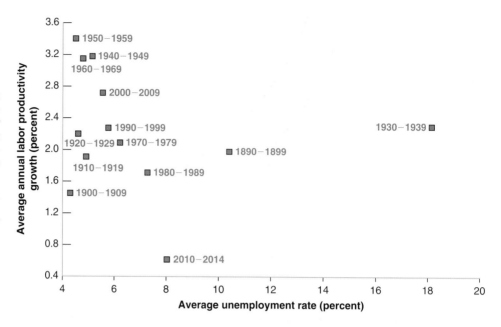

between the two. But it is possible to argue that the decade of the Great Depression is so different that it should be left aside. If we ignore the 1930s (the decade of the Great Depression), then a relation—although not a strong one—emerges between productivity growth and the unemployment rate. But it is the *opposite* of the relation predicted by those who believe in technological unemployment. Periods of *high productivity growth*, like the 1940s to the 1960s, have been associated with *a lower unemployment rate*. Periods of *low productivity growth*, such as the United States saw during 2010–2014, have been associated with *a higher unemployment rate*.

Can the theory we have developed be extended to explain this inverse relation in the medium run between productivity growth and unemployment? The answer is yes. To see why, we must look more closely at how expectations of productivity are formed.

Up to this point, we have looked at the rate of unemployment that prevails when *both* price expectations *and* expectations of productivity are correct. However, the evidence suggests that it takes a long time for expectations of productivity to adjust to the reality of lower or higher productivity growth. When, for example, productivity growth slows down for any reason, it takes a long time for society, in general, and for workers, in particular, to adjust their expectations. In the meantime, workers keep asking for wage increases that are no longer consistent with the new lower rate of productivity growth.

To see what this implies, let's look at what happens to the unemployment rate when price expectations are correct (that is, $P^e = P$) but expectations of productivity (A^e) may not be (that is, A^e may not be equal to A). In this case, the relations implied by price setting and wage setting are

$$\text{Price setting} \quad \frac{W}{P} = \frac{A}{1 + m}$$

$$\text{Wage setting} \quad \frac{W}{P} = A^e F(u, z)$$

Suppose productivity growth declines. A increases more slowly than before. If expectations of productivity growth adjust slowly, then A^e will increase for some time by more than A does. What will then happen to unemployment is shown in Figure 13-5.

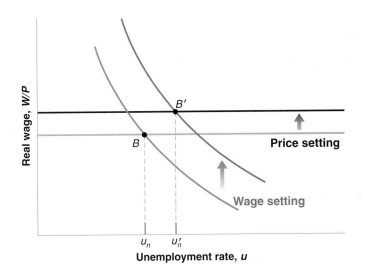

Figure 13-5

The Effects of a Decrease in Productivity Growth on the Unemployment Rate When Expectations of Productivity Growth Adjust Slowly

If it takes time for workers to adjust their expectations of productivity growth, a slow-down in productivity growth will lead to an increase in the natural rate for some time.

MyEconLab Animation

If A^e increases by more than A, the wage-setting relation will shift up by more than the price-setting relation. The equilibrium will move from B to B', and the natural rate will increase from u_n to u'_n. The natural rate will remain higher until expectations of productivity have adjusted to the new reality—that is, until A^e and A are again equal. In words: After the slowdown in productivity growth, workers will ask for larger wage increases than firms are able to give. This will lead to a rise in unemployment. As workers eventually adjust their expectations, unemployment will fall back to its original level.

Let's summarize what we have seen in this and the preceding section.

There is not much support, either in theory or in the data, for the idea that faster productivity growth leads to higher unemployment.

- In the short run, there is no reason to expect, nor does there appear to be, a systematic relation between movements in productivity growth and movements in unemployment.
- In the medium run, if there is a relation between productivity growth and unemployment, it appears to be, if anything, an inverse relation. Lower productivity growth leads to higher unemployment. Higher productivity growth leads to lower unemployment.

Given this evidence, where do fears of technological unemployment come from? They probably come from the dimension of technological progress we have neglected so far, **structural change**—the change in the structure of the economy induced by technological progress. For some workers—those with skills no longer in demand—structural change may indeed mean unemployment, or lower wages, or both. Let's now turn to that.

13-3 Technological Progress, Churning, and Inequality

Technological progress is a process of structural change. This theme was central to the work of Joseph Schumpeter, a Harvard economist who, in the 1930s, emphasized that the process of growth was fundamentally a process of **creative destruction**. New goods are developed, making old ones obsolete. New techniques of production are introduced, requiring new skills and making some old skills less useful. The essence of this

The Churn: The Paradox of Progress (1993).

churning process is nicely reflected in the following quote from a past president of the
▶ Federal Reserve Bank of Dallas in his introduction to a report titled *The Churn:*

> "My grandfather was a blacksmith, as was his father. My dad, however, was part of the
> evolutionary process of the churn. After quitting school in the seventh grade to work
> for the sawmill, he got the entrepreneurial itch. He rented a shed and opened a filling
> station to service the cars that had put his dad out of business. My dad was success-
> ful, so he bought some land on the top of a hill, and built a truck stop. Our truck stop
> was extremely successful until a new interstate went through 20 miles to the west.
> The churn replaced US 411 with Interstate 75, and my visions of the good life faded."

Many professions, from those of blacksmiths to harness makers, have vanished forever. For example, there were more than 11 million farm workers in the United States at
the beginning of the last century; because of high productivity growth in agriculture,
there are less than a million today. By contrast, there are now more than 3 million truck,
bus, and taxi drivers in the United States; there were none in 1900. Similarly, today,
there are more than 1 million computer programmers; there were practically none in
1960. Even for those with the right skills, higher technological change increases uncertainty and the risk of unemployment. The firm in which they work may be replaced by a
more efficient firm, the product their firm was selling may be replaced by another product. This tension between the benefits of technological progress for consumers (and, by
implication, for firms and their shareholders) and the risks for workers is well captured
in the cartoon. The tension between the large gains for all of society from technological
change and the large costs of that technological change for the workers who lose their
jobs is explored in the Focus box "Job Destruction, Churning, and Earnings Losses."

The Increase in Wage Inequality

For those in growing sectors, or those with the right skills, technological progress leads
to new opportunities and higher wages. But for those in declining sectors, or those with
skills that are no longer in demand, technological progress can mean the loss of their

Job Destruction, Churning, and Earnings Losses

Technological progress may be good for the economy, but it is tough on the workers who lose their jobs. This is documented in a study by Steve Davis and Till von Wachter (2011), who use records from the Social Security Administration between 1974 and 2008 to look at what happens to workers who lose their job as a result of a mass layoff.

Davis and von Wachter first identify all the firms with more than 50 workers where at least 30% of the workforce was laid off during one quarter, an event they call a mass layoff. Then they identify the laid-off workers who had been employed at that firm for at least three years. These are long-term employees. They compare the labor market experience of long-term employees who were laid off in a mass layoff to similar workers in the labor force who did not separate in the layoff year or in the next two years. Finally, they compare the workers who experience a mass layoff in a recession to those who experience a mass layoff in an expansion.

Figure 1 summarizes their results. The year 0 is the year of the mass layoff. Years 1, 2, 3, and so on are the years after the mass layoff event. The negative years are the years prior to the layoff. If you have a job and are a long-term employee, your earnings rise relative to the rest of society prior to the mass layoff event. Having a long-term job at the same firm is good for an individual's wage growth. This is true in both recessions and expansions.

Look at what happens in the first year after the layoff. If you experience a mass layoff in a recession, your earnings fall by 40 percentage points relative to a worker who does not experience a mass layoff. If you are less unfortunate and you experience your mass layoff in an expansion, then the fall

in your relative earnings is only 25 percentage points. The conclusion: Mass layoffs cause enormous relative earnings declines whether they occur in a recession or an expansion.

Figure 1 makes another important point. The decline in relative earnings of workers who are part of a mass layoff persists for years after the layoff. Beyond 5 years or even up to 20 years after the mass layoff, workers who experienced a mass layoff suffer a relative earnings decline of about 20 percentage points if the mass layoff took place in a recession and about 10 percentage points in the mass layoff took place in an expansion. Thus, the evidence is strong that a mass layoff is associated with a very substantial decline in lifetime earnings.

It is not hard to explain why such earnings losses are likely, even if the size of the loss is surprising. The workers who have spent a considerable part of their career at the same firm have specific skills, skills that are most useful in that firm or industry. The mass layoff, if due to technological change, renders those skills much less valuable than they were.

Other studies have found that in families that experience a mass layoff, the worker has a less stable employment path (more periods of unemployment), poorer health outcomes, and children who have a lower level of educational achievement and higher mortality when compared to the workers who have not experienced a mass layoff. These are additional personal costs associated with mass layoffs.

So, although technological change is the main source of growth in the long run, and clearly enables a higher standard of living for the average person in society, the workers who experience mass layoffs are the clear losers. It is not surprising that technological change can and does generate anxiety.

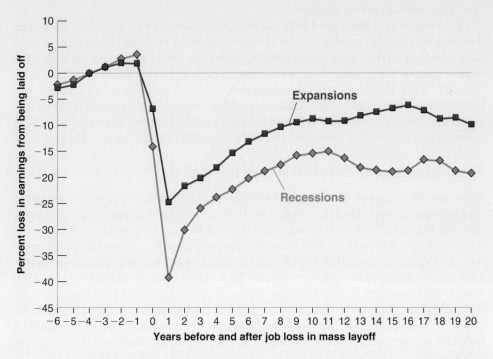

Figure 1

Earnings Losses of Workers Who Experience a Mass Layoff

Source: Steven J. Davis and Till M. von Wachter, "Recessions and the Cost of Job Loss," National Bureau of Economics Working Paper No. 17638.

Figure 13-6

Evolution of Relative Wages by Education Level, 1973–2012

Since the early 1980s, the relative wages of workers with a low education level have fallen; the relative wages of workers with a high education level have risen.

Source: Economic Policy Institute Data Zone. www.epi.org/types/data-zone/.

MyEconLab Real-time data

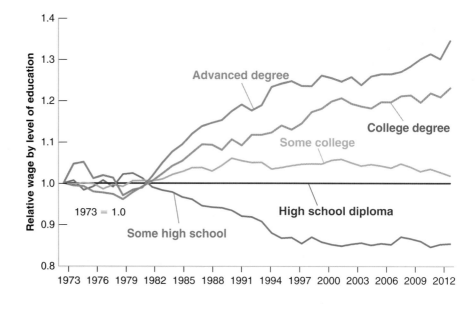

We described the Current ▶ Population Survey and some of its uses in Chapter 7.

job, a period of unemployment, and possibly much lower wages. The last 25 years in the United States have seen a large increase in wage inequality. Most economists believe that one of the main culprits behind this increase is technological change.

Figure 13-6 shows the evolution of relative wages for various groups of workers, by education level, from 1973 to 2012. The figure is based on information about individual workers from the Current Population Survey. Each of the lines in the figure shows the evolution of the wage of workers with a given level of education—"some high school," "high school diploma," "some college," "college degree," "advanced degree"—*relative to* the wage of workers who only have high school diplomas. All relative wages are further divided by their value in 1973, so the resulting wage series are all equal to one in 1973. The figure yields a striking conclusion:

Starting around the early 1980s, workers with low levels of education have seen their relative wage fall steadily over time, whereas workers with high levels of education have seen their relative wage rise steadily. At the bottom end of the education ladder, the relative wage of workers who have not completed high school has declined by 15% since the early 1980s. This implies that, in many cases, these workers have seen a drop not only in their relative wage, but in their absolute real wages as well. At the top end of the education ladder, the relative wage of those with an advanced degree has increased by 34%. In short, wage inequality has increased a lot in the United States over the last 30 years.

The Causes of Increased Wage Inequality

What are the causes of this increase in wage inequality? There is general agreement that the main factor behind the increase in the wage of high-skill relative to the wage of low-skill workers is a steady increase in the demand for high-skill workers relative to the demand for low-skill workers. This trend in relative demand is not new, but it appears to have increased. Also, until the 1980s it was largely offset by a steady increase in the relative supply of high-skill workers. A steadily larger proportion of children finished high school, went to college, finished college, and so on. Since the early 1980s however, relative supply has continued to increase, but not fast enough to match the continuing increase in relative demand. The result has been a steady increase in the relative wage of high-skill workers versus low-skill workers. In this context see the Focus box "The Role of Technology in the Decrease in Income Inequality in Latin America in the 2000s."

The Role of Technology in the Decrease in Income Inequality in Latin America in the 2000s

One of the most topical issues in advanced industrial economies today is the increase in income inequality, especially (but not only) income inequalities. As shown in this chapter, technology has to do with it: by increasing the value put on skilled labor, technological progress pushes up the demand for such labor; if supply is not perfectly elastic there will be a rise in relative wages earned by skilled workers, with respect to other workers. This is sometimes called the "skill premium," that is, the relative returns to workers with higher education respective to workers with lower education.

In other parts of the world, however, the trends are different. In Central and South America, for instance, income inequality has actually declined across most countries in the first decade of the 21st century. In some cases, the decline in inequality in the 2000s was steeper than the increase in inequality in the 1990s. In a 2013 study on three Latin American middle-income countries (namely, Argentina, Brazil, and Mexico), Nora Lustig, Luis F. Lopez-Calva, and Eduardo Ortiz-Juarez investigate the causes of such a decline in income inequality – and especially labor income inequality.

There are, the authors of the study find, two major causal factors behind this decline in income inequality. A first factor has to do with public policies and in particular higher and more progressive government transfers across the region. The second factor is the decline in the skill premium (see figures below). Part of this fall in the skill premium can be attributed to "institutional factors" such as rising minimum wages and unionization. The other part is the result of changes in the demand and supply of skilled and unskilled labor, where technological progress plays a role. This role, however, varied across countries.

In Argentina, the decline in the skill premium is generally attributed to a decreasing upward pressures on skilled workers' wages, following a decline in relative demand for skilled workers (more than an increase the relative supply of those workers) and a corresponding increase in the relative demand for unskilled workers; both trends are linked to a petering out of the technological upgrading that had taken place in the previous decades. In Brazil, by contrast, the decline in labor income inequality is attributed to the combination of a drop in the inequality of education and in the steepness of returns to education. In other words, the expansion of schooling has sustained the relative supply of skilled workers while making low-skilled and unskilled labor less abundant. While technological progress has not slowed down as soon as in Argentina, other factors (especially public policies) have changed the composition of the labor force and reduced the skill premium. In Mexico, where the skill premium has declined, too, the relative supply of skilled workers has declined while the relative returns have declined.

Technological change, therefore, does not have an unambiguous net effect on labor income inequality. Whereas, in Argentina, a lower demand for skilled labor driven by a slowdown in technological change clearly drove the decline in the skill premium, such was not the case in Brazil and Mexico, where supply-side factors dominated (in particular relating to education). Furthermore, in all three countries, the effects of technological change on labor income inequality are either mitigated or complemented by public policies affecting income, labor, and education.

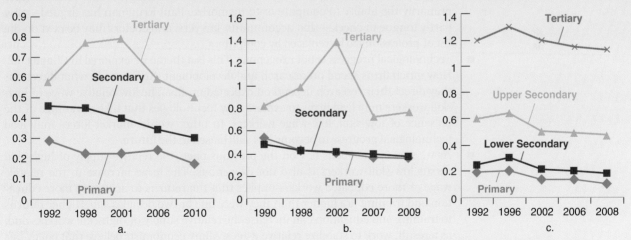

Figure 1 a. *Returns to Education in Argentina, 1992–2010;* b. *Returns to Education in Brazil, 1990–2009;* c. *Returns to Education in Mexico, 1992–2008.*

Source: Nora Lustig, Luis F. Lopez-Calva, and Eduardo Ortiz-Juarez, "Declining Inequality in Latin America in the 2000s: The Cases of Argentina, Brazil, and Mexico," *World Development* 44 (2013): pp. 129–141.

The next question: What is behind this steady shift in relative demand?

Pursuing the effects of inter-national trade would take us too far afield. For a more thor-ough discussion of who gains and who loses from trade, ▶ look at the text by Paul Krug-man and Maurice Obstfeld, *International Economics*, 9th ed. (2012).

- One line of argument focuses on the role of international trade. Those U.S. firms that employ higher proportions of low-skill workers, the argument goes, are increas-ingly driven out of markets by imports from similar firms in low-wage countries. Alternatively, to remain competitive, firms must relocate some of their production to low-wage countries. In both cases, the result is a steady decrease in the relative de-mand for low-skill workers in the United States. There are clear similarities between the effects of trade and the effects of technological progress. Although both trade and technological progress are good for the economy as a whole, they lead none-the-less to structural change and make some workers worse off.

    There is no question that trade is partly responsible for increased wage inequal-ity. But a closer examination shows that trade accounts for only part of the shift in relative demand. The most telling fact countering explanations based solely on trade is that the shift in relative demand toward high-skill workers appears to be present even in those sectors that are not exposed to foreign competition.

- The other line of argument focuses on **skill-biased technological progress**. New machines and new methods of production, the argument goes, require more and more high-skill workers. The development of computers requires workers to be increasingly computer literate. The new methods of production require workers to be more flexible and better able to adapt to new tasks. Greater flexibility in turn requires more skills and more education. Unlike explanations based on trade, skill-biased technological progress can explain why the shift in relative demand appears to be present in nearly all sectors of the economy. At this point, most economists believe it is the dominant factor in explaining the increase in wage inequality.

Does all this imply that the United States is condemned to steadily increasing wage inequality? Not necessarily. There are at least three reasons to think that the future may be different from the recent past:

- The trend in relative demand may simply slow down. For example, it is likely that computers will become steadily easier to use in the future, even by low-skill workers. Computers may even replace high-skill workers, those workers whose skills involve primarily the ability to compute or to memorize. Paul Krugman has argued—only partly tongue in cheek—that accountants, lawyers, and doctors may be next on the list of professions to be replaced by computers.

- Technological progress is not exogenous. This is a theme we explored in Chapter 12. How much firms spend on research and development (R&D) and in what directions they direct their research depend on expected profits. The low relative wage of low-skill workers may lead firms to explore new technologies that take advantage of the presence of low-skill, low-wage workers. In other words, market forces may lead technological progress to become less skill biased in the future.

- As we saw in the Focus box on the previous page, the relative supply of high-skill versus low-skill workers is also not exogenous. The large increase in the relative wage of more educated workers implies that the returns to acquiring more educa-tion and training are higher than they were one or two decades ago. Higher returns to training and education can increase the relative supply of high-skill workers and, as a result, work to stabilize relative wages. Many economists believe that policy has an important role to play here. It should ensure that the quality of primary and sec-ondary education for the children of low-wage workers does not further deteriorate, and that those who want to acquire more education can borrow to pay for it.

Figure 13-7

The Evolution of the Top 1% Income Share in the United States since 1913

Top 1% refers to the top percentile. In 2014, these were families with annual income (including capital gains) above $387,000. Top 1% to 5% is the next 4%, with annual income between $167,000 and $387,000 dollars. Top 5% to 10% is the bottom half of the top decile; families with annual income between $118,000 and $167,000 dollars. Income is defined as annual gross income reported on tax returns excluding all government transfers.

Source: The World Top Income Database. http://topincomes.parisschoolofeconomics.eu/#Database.

Inequality and the Top 1%

We have focused on wage inequality, the distribution of wages across all wage earners. Another dimension of inequality however is the proportion of income that accrues to the richest households (e.g. those in the top 1% of the income distribution). When we consider inequality at very high levels of income, wages are not a good measure of income because entrepreneurs derive a large fraction of their income (sometimes almost all of it) not from wages but from capital income and capital gains. This is because they are typically not paid with wages but with company shares that they can then sell (with some limitations) at a profit.

The evolution of the top 1% share, shown in Figure 13-7, is striking. Although the share of total income going to households in the top 1% was around 10% in the late 1970s, it now stands at more than 20% today. And while the graph stops in 2008, inequality appears to have gotten worse since then, with the top 1% capturing 95% of income growth from 2009 to 2014, if capital gains are included. Inequality in the United ◄ States, measured this way is "probably higher than in any other society at any time in the past, anywhere in the world," writes Thomas Piketty whose book, *Capital in the XXI Century*, when it was published in 2014, topped the list of best-selling books worldwide.

Why is this going on? Piketty attributes it in part to unjustifiably large salaries for people he calls "supermanagers." By his calculations, about 70% of the top 0.1% of earners are corporate executives. Piketty points to bad corporate governance; company boards who grant CEOs exorbitant pay packages. Above a certain level, he argues, it is hard to find in the data any link between pay and performance. Although there is plenty of anecdotal evidence for such excesses, Figure 13-7 suggests that perhaps another factor is at play. Note that the two periods during which the share of the top 1% has jumped up are periods of rapid technological innovation: the 1920s, when electric power was brought into U.S. factories, revolutionizing production; and the years since the early 1980s when personal computers and the Internet became widely available. This suggests that innovation and the share of the top 1% are correlated. Indeed, Figure 13-8, which plots the evolution of patents and the top 1% income share in the United States since 1960, shows that the two have moved very much together.

MyEconLab Video

Note that the sharp increase is limited to the 1%. The shares of the other groups in the top 10% have increased, but by much less. This suggests that there is more than skill bias at work.

Figure 13-8

The Top Income Share and Patenting in the United States, 1963–2013

The figure plots the number of patent applications per 1,000 inhabitants against the top 1% income share. Observations span the years between 1963 and 2013.

Source: Aghion, P., U. Akcigit, A. Bergeaud, R. Blundell, and D. Hemous. (2015) "Innovation and Top Income Inequality," CEPR Discussion Paper No 10659.

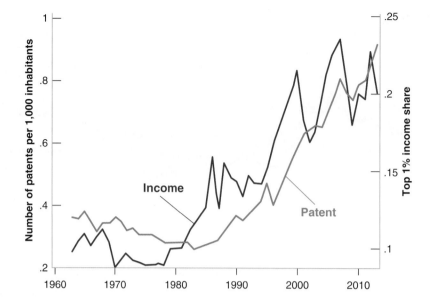

Philippe Aghion and co-authors, in the article from which Figure 13-8 is taken, make the point that a technological innovation allows the innovator to get ahead of competing producers. Often it also allows him to produce with fewer workers. Both of these, the new technology and the lower labor input, contribute to increasing the innovator's share of income at the expense of the workers' share of income, at least until other entrepreneurs catch up with the new technology. Through this mechanism, innovation raises top income inequality, the more so, the higher the number of innovations, and this can explain the rise in the share of the top 1% in the 1920s and since the early 1980s. However, even if the benefits of innovation may initially be captured by those who generate it, eventually it is shared broadly as the innovation diffuses through the economy. Moreover, innovation also appears to foster social mobility; for example, the most innovative state in the United States, California, has both top 1% incomes shares and a level of social mobility that are much higher than those in the least innovative state, Alabama. This happens, Aghion argues, as a result of "creative destruction." As older firms are replaced by firms employing the new technology, older entrepreneurs are replaced by newer ones, thus enhancing social mobility.

In our discussion of wage inequality, and of the top 1% income share, we have focused on the United States. Interestingly, other advanced countries, which are presumably exposed to the same forces of globalization and skill-biased technological progress have typically seen less of an increase in wage inequality, and much less of an increase in the top 1% income share. This suggests that institutions and policy do play an important role in shaping these evolutions. Given the economic and political importance of the question, the debate about the sources of inequality, and whether governments have tools to deal with it, is likely to remain one of the central debates in macroeconomics for some time to come.

Summary

- People often fear that technological progress destroys jobs and leads to higher unemployment. This fear was present during the Great Depression. Theory and evidence suggest these fears are largely unfounded. There is not much support, either in theory or in the data, for the idea that faster technological progress leads to higher unemployment.

- In the short run, there is no reason to expect, nor does there appear to be, a systematic relation between changes in productivity and movements in unemployment.

- If there is a relation between changes in productivity and movements in unemployment in the medium run, it appears to be an inverse relation. Lower productivity growth appears to lead to higher unemployment; higher productivity growth appears to lead to lower unemployment. An explanation is that it takes higher unemployment for some time to reconcile workers' wage expectations with lower productivity growth.

- Technological progress is not a smooth process in which all workers are winners. Rather, it is a process of structural change. Even if most people benefit from the increase in the average standard of living, there are losers as well. As new goods and new techniques of production are developed, old goods and old techniques of production become obsolete. Some workers find their skills in higher demand and benefit from technological progress. Others find their skills in lower demand and suffer unemployment or reductions in relative wages.

- Wage inequality has increased in the past 30 years in the United States. The real wage of low-skill workers has declined not only relative to the real wage of high-skill workers but also in absolute terms. The two main causes are international trade and skill-biased technological progress.

- The income share going to the top 1% has dramatically increased in the United States since the early 1980s. How much of this is explained by poor governance of firms or by high returns to innovation, is hotly disputed.

Key Terms

technological unemployment, 287

structural change, 291

creative destruction, 291

churning, 292

skill-biased technological progress, 296

Questions and Problems

QUICK CHECK

MyEconLab Visit www.myeconlab.com to complete similar Quick Check problems and get instant feedback.

1. *Using the information in this chapter, label each of the following statements true, false, or uncertain. Explain briefly.*

a. The change in employment and output per person in the United States since 1900 lends support to the argument that technological progress leads to a steady increase in employment.

b. Workers benefit equally from the process of creative destruction.

c. In the past two decades, the real wages of low-skill U.S. workers have declined relative to the real wages of high-skill workers.

d. Technological progress leads to a decrease in employment if, and only if, the increase in output is smaller than the increase in productivity.

e. The apparent decrease in the natural rate of unemployment in the United States in the second-half of the 1990s can be explained by the fact that productivity growth was unexpectedly high during that period.

f. If we could stop technological progress, doing so would lead to a decrease in the natural rate of unemployment.

2. *Suppose an economy is characterized by the following equations:*

$$\text{Price setting: } P = (1 + m)(W/A)$$
$$\text{Wage setting: } W = A^e P^e (1 - u)$$

a. Solve for the unemployment rate if $P^e = P$ but A^e does not necessarily equal A. Explain the effects of (A^e/A) on the unemployment rate.

   Now suppose that expectations of both prices and productivity are accurate.

b. Solve for the natural rate of unemployment if the markup (m) is equal to 5%.

c. Does the natural rate of unemployment depend on productivity? Explain.

3. Discuss the following statement: *"Higher labor productivity allows firms to produce more goods with the same number of workers and thus to sell the goods at the same or even lower prices. That's why increases in labor productivity can permanently reduce the rate of unemployment without causing inflation."*

4. Discuss the potential impact of the following policies on wage inequalities.
   a. New fiscal incentives for corporate spending on on-the-job training for low-skilled employees.
   b. Trade barriers erected to protect one country's low-tech textile industry.
   c. Tax breaks on research and development expenditures in agriculture.
   d. Sustained efforts to support the financial services industry at the cost of steel and car manufacturing.

DIG DEEPER

MyEconLab Visit www.myeconlab.com to complete all Dig Deeper problems and get instant feedback.

5. Technological progress, agriculture, and employment
   Discuss the following statement: *"Those who argue that technological progress does not reduce employment should look at agriculture. At the start of the last century, there were more than 11 million farm workers. Today, there are fewer than 1 million. If all sectors start having the productivity growth that took place in agriculture during the 20th century, no one will be employed a century from now."*

6. Productivity and the aggregate supply curve
   Consider an economy in which production is given by

   $$Y = AN$$

   Assume that price setting and wage setting are described in the following equations:

   Price setting: $P = (1 + m)(W/A)$
   Wage setting: $W = A^e P^e (1 - u)$

   Recall that the relation between employment, N, the labor force, L, and the unemployment rate, u, is given by

   $$N = (1 - u)L$$

   a. Derive the aggregate supply curve (that is, the relation between the price level and the level of output, given the markup, the actual and expected levels of productivity, the labor force, and the expected price level). Explain the role of each variable.
   b. Show the effect of an equiproportional increase in A and A^e (so that A/A^e remains unchanged) on the position of the aggregate supply curve. Explain.
   c. Suppose instead that actual productivity, A, increases, but expected productivity, A^e, does not change. Compare the results in this case to your conclusions in (b). Explain the difference.

7. Technology and the labor market
   In the appendix to Chapter 7, we learned how the wage-setting and price-setting equations could be expressed in terms of labor demand and labor supply. In this problem, we extend the analysis to account for technological change.
   Consider the wage-setting equation

   $$W/P = F(u, z)$$

as the equation corresponding to labor supply. Recall that for a given labor force, L, the unemployment rate, u, can be written as

$$u = 1 - N/L$$

where N is employment.
   a. Substitute the expression for u into the wage-setting equation.
   b. Using the relation you derived in (a), graph the labor supply curve in a diagram with N on the horizontal axis and W/P the real wage, on the vertical axis.
   Now write the price setting equation as

   $$P = (1 + m)MC$$

where MC is the marginal cost of production. To generalize somewhat our discussion in the text, we shall write

   $$MC = W/MPL$$

   where W is the wage and MPL is the marginal product of labor.
   c. Substitute the expression for MC into the price-setting equation and solve for the real wage, W/P. The result is the labor demand relation, with W/P as a function of the MPL and the markup, m.
   In the text, we assumed for simplicity that the MPL was constant for a given level of technology. Here, we assume that the MPL decreases with employment (again for a given level of technology), a more realistic assumption.
   d. Assuming that the MPL decreases with employment, graph the labor demand relation you derived in (c). Use the same diagram you drew for (b).
   e. What happens to the labor demand curve if the level of technology improves? (*Hint*: What happens to MPL when technology improves?) Explain. How is the real wage affected by an increase in the level of technology?

EXPLORE FURTHER

8. The churn
   In 2014, the European Commission (EC) published a "European Vacancy and Recruitment Report" on its Web site, which contains data on the occupations with the sharpest declines and increases in employment in European Union (EU) member states in previous years.
   a. Find the data concerning the 10 occupations with the strongest employee growth in Germany (for the period 2008–2010). How many of these occupations and how much of this growth can be attributed to technological change?
   b. Find the data concerning the 10 occupations with the strongest decline in number of employees in Germany. How many of these occupations, and how much of this decline, can be attributed to technological change? To trade?

9. Real wages
   According to the International Labour Office's (ILO) latest Global Wage Report's appendix on Asia and the Pacific, available on its Web site, real wage growth has been very strong in the Asia and Pacific region in the past 10 years.
   a. Find data concerning real wage growth in various parts of Asia since 1999 (table 1). Compare the following:

i. The pace of real wage growth of Asia with that experienced in the "Developed economies" since 1999.
ii. The growth of real wages across various sub-regions within Asia.
What do you observe?

b. A good chunk of real wage growth in Asia has to do with growth in output. How much of it can be related to technological progress, and why?

c. While this chapter seems to indicate that low-skilled workers may suffer the most in times of technological progress, what does the example of the Asian garment industry, illustrated in Box 1 of the ILO report, tell you about the relationship between real wages and low-skill work in fast growing economies?

d. This chapter seems to indicate that low-skilled workers may suffer the most in times of technological progress. The ILO's report quoted above dedicates one page to the case of the Asian garment industry, which has undergone rapid change over the past few years. This fast-growing industry is notoriously characterized by low wages and poor working conditions. However, according to the ILO, "Global garment buyers increasingly prioritize productivity and reliability of supply, and they are adverse to the reputational risks of poor working conditions." What does this case tell you about the relationship between real wages and low-skill work in fast growing economies?

10. Income Inequality
Use the World Income Database (at http://www.wid.world/#Database) to find data about income inequality in France and the United Kingdom.

a. Find data about the top 1% income earners' share of total income for the two countries between 1945 and 2012. What do you see? Can you find trends similar to what Figure 13-7 shows about the United States?

b. How would you explain cross-country differences in both the level and the evolution of income inequality over time, in terms of relative demand and supply of unskilled?

c. How would you explain cross-country differences in both the level and the evolution of income inequality over time, in terms of relative demand and supply of skilled workers?

d. Technological progress has been comparable in the two countries over the past six decades. What other factors may explain observable differences in income inequality in the two countries during that period?

Further Readings

- For more on the process of reallocation that characterizes modern economies, read *The Churn: The Paradox of Progress*, a report by the Federal Reserve Bank of Dallas (1993).

- For a fascinating account on how computers are transforming the labor market, read *The New Division of Labor: How Computers Are Creating the Next Job Market*, by Frank Levy and Richard Murnane (2004).

- For more statistics on various dimensions of inequality in the United States, a useful site is "The State of Working America," published by the Economic Policy Institute, at http://www.stateofworkingamerica.org/.

- For more on innovation and income inequality you can read, beyond Thomas Piketty's *Capital in the XXI Century* (2014), another piece by Thomas Piketty and Emmanuel Saez, "Income Inequality in the United States, 1913–1998." *The Quarterly Journal of Economics*, 118 (1): 1–41, and Emmanuel Saez (2013) "Striking it Richer: The Evolution of Top Incomes in the United States," mimeo UC Berkeley.

- For a more general view on technology and inequality, and one that comes from a slightly different perspective, you can also read "Technology and Inequality" by David Rotman, *MIT Technology Review*, October 21, 2014, available at http://www.technologyreview.com/featuredstory/531726/technology-and-inequality/.

Expectations

The next three chapters cover the first extension of the core. They look at the role of expectations in output fluctuations.

Chapter 14

Chapter 14 focuses on the role of expectations in financial markets. It introduces the concept of expected present discounted value, which plays a central role in the determination of asset prices and in consumption and investment decisions. Using this concept, it studies the determination of bond prices and bond yields. It shows how we can learn about the course of expected future interest rates by looking at the yield curve. It then turns to stock prices and shows how they depend on expected future dividends and interest rates. Finally, it discusses whether stock prices always reflect fundamentals or may instead reflect bubbles or fads.

Chapter 15

Chapter 15 focuses on the role of expectations in consumption and investment decisions. It shows how consumption depends partly on current income, partly on human wealth, and partly on financial wealth. It shows how investment depends partly on current cash flow and partly on the expected present value of future profits.

Chapter 16

Chapter 16 looks at the role of expectations in output fluctuations. Starting from the *IS-LM* model, it extends the description of goods-market equilibrium (the *IS* relation) to reflect the effect of expectations on spending. It revisits the effects of monetary and fiscal policy on output, taking into account their effect through expectations.

14

Financial Markets and Expectations

Our focus throughout this chapter will be on the role expectations play in the determination of asset prices, from bonds, to stocks, to houses. We discussed the role of expectations informally at various points in the core. It is now time to do it more formally. As you will see, not only are these asset prices affected by current and expected future activity, but they in turn affect decisions that influence current economic activity. Understanding their determination is thus central to understanding fluctuations.

Section 14-1 introduces the concept of expected present discounted value, which plays a central role in the determination of asset prices and in consumption and investment decisions.

Section 14-2 looks at the determination of bond prices and bond yields. It shows how bond prices and yields depend on current and expected future short-term interest rates. It then shows how we can use the yield curve to learn about the expected course of future short-term interest rates.

Section 14-3 looks at the determination of stock prices. It shows how stock prices depend on current and expected future profits, as well as on current and expected future interest rates. It then discusses how movements in economic activity affect stock prices.

Section 14-4 looks more closely at the relevance of fads and bubbles—episodes in which asset prices (stock or house prices, in particular) appear to move for reasons unrelated to either current and expected future payments or interest rates.

14-1 Expected Present Discounted Values

To understand why present discounted values are important, consider the problem facing a manager who is deciding whether or not to buy a new machine. On the one hand, buying and installing the machine involves a cost today. On the other, the machine allows for higher production, higher sales, and higher profits in the future. The question facing the manager is whether the value of these expected profits is higher than the cost of buying and installing the machine. This is where the concept of expected present discounted value comes in handy. The **expected present discounted value** of a sequence of future payments is the value today of this expected sequence of payments. Once the manager has computed the expected present discounted value of the sequence of profits, her problem becomes simpler. She compares two numbers, the expected present discounted value and the initial cost. If the value exceeds the cost, she should go ahead and buy the machine. If it does not, she should not.

The practical problem is that expected present discounted values are not directly observable. They must be constructed from information on the sequence of expected payments and expected interest rates. Let's first look at the mechanics of construction.

Computing Expected Present Discounted Values

In this section, to keep things simple, we ignore an issue ► we discussed at length in Chapter 6, the issue of risk. We return to it in the next section.

Denote the one-year nominal interest rate by i_t, so lending one dollar this year implies getting back $1 + i_t$ dollars next year. Equivalently, borrowing one dollar this year implies paying back $1 + i_t$ dollars next year. In this sense, one dollar this year is worth $1 + i_t$ dollars next year. This relation is represented graphically in the first line of Figure 14-1.

Turn the argument around and ask: How much is one dollar *next year* worth this year? The answer, shown in the second line of Figure 14-1, is $1/(1 + i_t)$ dollars. Think of it this way: If you lend $1/(1 + i_t)$ dollars this year, you will receive $1/(1 + i_t)$ times $(1 + i_t) = 1$ dollar next year. Equivalently, if you borrow $1/(1 + i_t)$ dollars this year, you will have to repay exactly one dollar next year. So, one dollar next year is worth $1/(1 + i_t)$ dollars this year.

i_t: discount rate.
$1/(1 + i_t)$: discount factor. If the discount rate goes up, the discount factor goes down.

More formally, we say that $1/(1 + i_t)$ is the *present discounted value* of one dollar next year. The word *present* comes from the fact that we are looking at the value of a payment next year in terms of dollars *today*. The word *discounted* comes from the fact that the value next year is discounted, with $1/(1 + i_t)$ being the **discount factor**. (The rate at which you discount, in this case the nominal interest rate, i_t, is sometimes called the ► **discount rate**.)

The higher the nominal interest rate, the lower the value today of a dollar received next year. If $i = 5\%$, the value this year of a dollar next year is $1/1.05 \approx 95$ cents. If $i = 10\%$ the value today of a dollar next year is $1/1.10 \approx 91$ cents.

Now apply the same logic to the value today of a dollar received *two years from now*. For the moment, assume that current and future one-year nominal interest rates are known with certainty. Let i_t be the nominal interest rate for this year, and i_{t+1} be the one-year nominal interest rate next year.

Figure 14-1

Computing Present Discounted Values

MyEconLab Animation

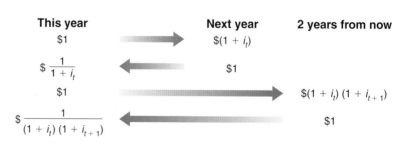

If, today, you lend one dollar for two years, you will get $(1 + i_t)(1 + i_{t+1})$ dollars two years from now. Put another way, one dollar today is worth $(1 + i_t)(1 + i_{t+1})$ dollars two years from now. This relation is represented in the third line of Figure 14-1.

What is one dollar two years from now worth today? By the same logic as before, the answer is $1/(1 + i_t)(1 + i_{t+1})$ dollars. If you lend $1/(1 + i_t)(1 + i_{t+1})$ dollars this year, you will get exactly one dollar in two years. So, the *present discounted value of a dollar two years from now* is equal to $1/(1 + i_t)(1 + i_{t+1})$ dollars. This relation is shown in the last line of Figure 14-1. If, for example, the one-year nominal interest rate is the same this year and next and equal to 5%, so $i_t = i_{t+1} = 5\%$ then the present discounted value of a dollar in two years is equal to $1/(1.05)^2$ or about 91 cents today.

A General Formula

Having gone through these steps, it is easy to derive the present discounted value for the case where both payments and interest rates can change over time.

Consider a sequence of payments in dollars, starting today and continuing into the future. Assume for the moment that both future payments and future interest rates are known with certainty. Denote today's payment by $\$z_t$, the payment next year by $\$z_{t+1}$, the payment two years from today by $\$z_{t+2}$, and so on.

The present discounted value of this sequence of payments—that is, the value in today's dollars of the sequence of payments—which we shall call $\$V_t$ is given by

$$\$V_t = \$z_t + \frac{1}{(1 + i_t)}\$z_{t+1} + \frac{1}{(1 + i_t)(1 + i_{t+1})}\$z_{t+2} + \cdots$$

Each payment in the future is multiplied by its respective discount factor. The more distant the payment, the smaller the discount factor, and thus the smaller today's value of that distant payment. In other words, future payments are discounted more heavily, so their present discounted value is lower.

We have assumed that future payments and future interest rates were known with certainty. Actual decisions, however, have to be based on expectations of future payments rather than on actual values for these payments. In our previous example, the manager cannot be sure of how much profit the new machine will actually bring, nor does she know what interest rates will be in the future. The best she can do is get the most accurate forecasts she can and then compute the *expected present discounted value* of profits based on these forecasts.

How do we compute the expected present discounted value when future payments and interest rates are uncertain? Basically in the same way as before, but by replacing the *known* future payments and *known* interest rates with *expected* future payments and *expected* interest rates. Formally: Denote expected payments next year by $\$z_{t+1}^e$, expected payments two years from now by $\$z_{t+2}^e$, and so on. Similarly, denote the expected one-year nominal interest rate next year by i_{t+1}^e, and so on (the one-year nominal interest rate this year, i_t, is known today, so it does not need a superscript e. The expected present discounted value of this expected sequence of payments is given by

$$\$V_t = \$z_t + \frac{1}{(1 + i_t)}\$z_{t+1}^e + \frac{1}{(1 + i_t)(1 + i_{t+1}^e)}\$z_{t+2}^e + \cdots \qquad (14.1)$$

"Expected present discounted value" is a heavy expression to carry; instead, for short, we will often just use **present discounted value**, or even just **present value**. Also, it will be convenient to have a shorthand way of writing expressions like equation (14.1). To denote the present value of an expected sequence for $\$z$, we shall write $V(\$z_t)$, or just $V(\$z)$.

Using Present Values: Examples

Equation (14.1) has two important implications:

$z or future $z^e increase ⇒ $V increases.

■ The present value depends positively on today's actual payment and expected future payments. An increase in either today's $z or any future $z^e leads to an increase in the present value.

i or future i^e increase ⇒ $V decreases.

■ The present value depends negatively on current and expected future interest rates. An increase in either current i or in any future i^e leads to a decrease in the present value.

Equation (14.1) is not simple, however, and so it will help to go through some examples.

Constant Interest Rates

To focus on the effects of the sequence of payments on the present value, assume that interest rates are expected to be constant over time, so that $i_t = i^e_{t+1} = \ldots$, and denote their common value by i. The present value formula—equation (14.1)—becomes:

$$\$V_t = \$z_t + \frac{1}{(1+i)}\$z^e_{t+1} + \frac{1}{(1+i)^2}\$z^e_{t+2} + \cdots \tag{14.2}$$

The weights correspond to the terms of a geometric series. See the discussion of geometric series in Appendix 2 at the end of the book.

In this case, the present value is a *weighted sum* of current and expected future payments, with weights that decline *geometrically* through time. The weight on a payment this year is 1, the weight on the payment n years from now is $(1/(1+i))^n$. With a positive interest rate, the weights get closer and closer to zero as we look further and further into the future. For example, with an interest rate equal to 10%, the weight on a payment 10 years from today is equal to $1/(1+0.10)^{10} = 0.386$, so that a payment of $1,000 in 10 years is worth $386 today. The weight on a payment in 30 years is $1/(1+0.10)^{30} = 0.057$, so that a payment of $1,000 thirty years from today is worth only $57 today!

Constant Interest Rates and Payments

In some cases, the sequence of payments for which we want to compute the present value is simple. For example, a typical fixed-rate, 30-year mortgage requires constant dollar payments over 30 years. Consider a sequence of equal payments—call them $z without a time index—over n years, including this year. In this case, the present value formula in equation (14.2) simplifies to

$$\$V_t = \$z\left[1 + \frac{1}{(1+i)} + \cdots + \frac{1}{(1+i)^{n-1}}\right]$$

By now, geometric series should not hold any secret, and you should have no problem deriving this relation. But if you do, see Appendix 2 at the end of the book.

Because the terms in the expression in brackets represent a geometric series, we can compute the sum of the series and get

$$\$V_t = \$z\frac{1 - [1/(1+i)^n]}{1 - [1/(1+i)]}$$

Suppose you have just won one million dollars from your state lottery and have been presented with a 6-foot $1,000,000 check on TV. Afterward, you are told that, to protect you from your worst spending instincts as well as from your many new "friends," the state will pay you the million dollars in equal yearly installments of $50,000 over the next 20 years. What is the present value of your prize today?

What is the present value if i equals 4%? 8%? (Answers: $706,000, $530,000)

Taking, for example, an interest rate of 6% per year, the preceding equation gives $V = \$50,000(0.688)/(0.057) =$ or about $608,000. Not bad, but winning the prize did not make you a millionaire.

Constant Interest Rates and Payments Forever

Let's go one step further and assume that payments are not only constant, but go on forever. Real-world examples are harder to come by for this case, but one example comes from 19th-century England, when the government issued *consols*, bonds paying a fixed yearly amount forever. Let $\$z$ be the constant payment. Assume that payments start next year, rather than right away as in the previous example (this makes for simpler algebra). From equation (14.2), we have

Most consols were bought back by the British government at the end of the 19th century and early 20th century. ◀ A few are still out there!

$$\$V_t = \frac{1}{(1 + i)} \$z + \frac{1}{(1 + i)^2} \$z + \cdots$$

$$= \frac{1}{(1 + i)} \left[1 + \frac{1}{(1 + i)} + \cdots \right] \$z$$

where the second line follows by factoring out $1/(1 + i)$. The reason for factoring out $1/(1 + i)$ should be clear from looking at the term in brackets. It is an infinite geometric sum, so we can use the property of geometric sums to rewrite the present value as

$$\$V_t = \frac{1}{1 + i} \frac{1}{(1 - (1/(1 + i)))} \$z$$

Or, simplifying (the steps are given in the application of Proposition 2 in Appendix 2 at the end of the book),

$$\$V_t = \frac{\$z}{i}$$

The present value of a constant sequence of payments $\$z$ is simply equal to the ratio of $\$z$ to the interest rate i. If, for example, the interest rate is expected to be 5% per year forever, the present value of a consol that promises $10 per year forever equals $10/0.05 = \$200$. If the interest rate increases and is now expected to be 10% per year forever, the present value of the consol decreases to $10/0.10 = \$100$.

Zero Interest Rates

Because of discounting, computing present discounted values typically requires the use of a calculator. There is, however, a case where computations simplify. This is the case where the interest rate is equal to zero. If $i = 0$, then $1/(1 + i)$ equals 1, and so does $(1/(1 + i)^n)$ for any power n. For that reason, the present discounted value of a sequence of expected payments is just the *sum* of those expected payments. Because the interest rate is in fact typically positive, assuming the interest rate is zero is only an approximation. But it can be a useful one for back-of-the-envelope computations.

Nominal versus Real Interest Rates and Present Values

So far, we have computed the present value of a sequence of dollar payments by using interest rates in terms of dollars—nominal interest rates. Specifically, we have written equation (14.1):

$$\$V_t = \$z_t + \frac{1}{(1 + i_t)} \$z_{t+1}^e + \frac{1}{(1 + i_t)(1 + i_{t+1}^e)} \$z_{t+2}^e + \cdots$$

where $i_t, i_{t+1}^e, \ldots$ is the sequence of current and expected future nominal interest rates and $\$z_t, \$z_{t+1}^e, \$z_{t+2}^e, \ldots$ is the sequence of current and expected future dollar payments.

Suppose we want to compute instead the present value of a sequence of *real* payments—that is, payments in terms of a basket of goods rather than in terms of dollars. Following the same logic as before, we need to use the right interest rates for this case, namely interest rates in terms of the basket of goods—*real interest rates*. Specifically, we can write the present value of a sequence of real payments as

$$V_t = z_t + \frac{1}{(1 + r_t)}z^e_{t+1} + \frac{1}{(1 + r_t)(1 + r^e_{t+1})}z^e_{t+2} + \cdots \qquad (14.3)$$

where $r_t, r^e_{t+1}, \ldots$ is the sequence of current and expected future real interest rates, $z_t, z^e_{t+1}, z^e_{t+2}, \ldots$ is the sequence of current and expected future real payments, and V_t is the real present value of future payments.

The proof is given in the appendix to this chapter. Although it may not be fun, go through it to test your understanding of the two concepts, real interest rate versus nominal interest rate and expected present value.

These two ways of writing the present value turn out to be equivalent. That is, the real value obtained by constructing $\$V_t$ using equation (14.1) and dividing by P_t, the price level, is equal to the real value V_t obtained from equation (14.3), so

$$\$V_t/P_t = V_t$$

In words: We can compute the present value of a sequence of payments in two ways. One way is to compute it as the present value of the sequence of payments expressed in dollars, discounted using nominal interest rates, and then divided by the price level today. The other way is to compute it as the present value of the sequence of payments expressed in real terms, discounted using real interest rates. The two ways give the same answer.

Do we need both formulas? Yes. Which one is more helpful depends on the context:

Take bonds, for example. Bonds typically are claims to a sequence of nominal payments over a period of years. For example, a 10-year bond might promise to pay $50 each year for 10 years, plus a final payment of $1,000 in the last year. So when we look at the pricing of bonds in the next section, we shall rely on equation (14.1) (which is expressed in terms of dollar payments) rather than on equation (14.3) (which is expressed in real terms).

But sometimes, we have a better sense of future expected real values than of future expected dollar values. You might not have a good idea of what your dollar income will be in 20 years. Its value depends very much on what happens to inflation between now and then. But you might be confident that your nominal income will increase by at least as much as inflation—in other words, that your real income will not decrease. In this case, using equation (14.1), which requires you to form expectations of future dollar income, will be difficult. However, using equation (14.3), which requires you to form expectations of future real income, may be easier. For this reason, when we discuss consumption and investment decisions in Chapter 15, we shall rely on equation (14.3) rather than equation (14.1).

14-2 Bond Prices and Bond Yields

Bonds differ in two basic dimensions:

■ *Maturity*: The **maturity** of a bond is the length of time over which the bond promises to make payments to the holder of the bond. A bond that promises to make one payment of $1,000 in six months has a maturity of six months; a bond that promises to pay $100 per year for the next 20 years and a final payment of $1,000 at the end of those 20 years has a maturity of 20 years.

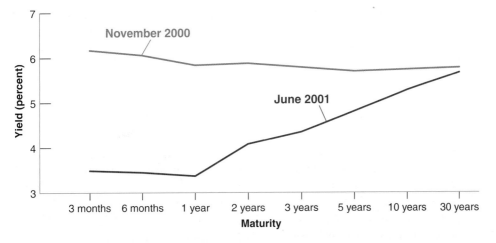

Figure 14-2

U.S. Yield Curves: November 1, 2000 and June 1, 2001

The yield curve, which was slightly downward sloping in November 2000, was sharply upward sloping seven months later.

Source: Series DGS1MO, DGS3MO, DGS6MO, DGS1, DGS2, DGS3, DGS5, DGS7, DGS10, DGS20, DGS30. Federal Reserve Economic Data (FRED) http://research.stlouis-fed.org/fred2/.

MyEconLab Animation

■ *Risk*: This may be default risk, the risk that the issuer of the bond (it could be a government or a company) will not pay back the full amount promised by the bond. Or it may be price risk, the uncertainty about the price you can sell the bond for if you want to sell it in the future before maturity.

Both risk and maturity matter in the determination of interest rates. As I want to focus here on the role of maturity and, by implication, the role of expectations, I shall ignore risk to start and reintroduce it later.

Bonds of different maturities each have a price and an associated interest rate called the **yield to maturity**, or simply the **yield**. Yields on bonds with a short maturity, typically a year or less, are called **short-term interest rates**. Yields on bonds with a longer maturity are called **long-term interest rates**. On any given day, we observe the yields on bonds of different maturities, and so we can trace graphically how the yield depends on the maturity of a bond. This relation between maturity and yield is called the **yield curve**, or the **term structure of interest rates** (the word *term* is synonymous with maturity).

◀ We had introduced earlier two distinctions between different interest rates, real versus nominal interest rates, and policy rate versus borrowing rate (we are leaving this second distinction aside for the moment). We are now introducing a third one, short versus long rates. Note that this makes for six combinations....

Figure 14-2 gives, for example, the term structure of U.S. government bonds on November 1, 2000, and the term structure of U.S. government bonds on June 1, 2001. The choice of the two dates is not accidental; why I chose them will become clear later.

◀ To find out what the yield curve for U.S bonds is at the time you read this chapter, go to yieldcurve.com and click on "yield curves." You will see the yield curves for both U.K. and U.S. bonds.

Note that in Figure 14-2, on November 1, 2000, the yield curve was slightly downward sloping, declining from a three-month interest rate of 6.2% to a 30-year interest rate of 5.8%. In other words, long-term interest rates were slightly lower than short-term interest rates. Note how, seven months later, on June 1, 2001, the yield curve was sharply upward sloping, increasing from a three-month interest rate of 3.5% to a 30-year interest rate of 5.7%. In other words, long-term interest rates were much higher than short-term interest rates.

Why was the yield curve downward sloping in November 2000 but upward sloping in June 2001? Put another way, why were long-term interest rates slightly lower than short-term interest rates in November 2000, but substantially higher than short-term interest rates in June 2001? What were financial market participants thinking at each date? To answer these questions, and more generally to think about the determination of the yield curve and the relation between short-term interest rates and long-term interest rates, we proceed in two steps:

1. First, we derive *bond prices* for bonds of different maturities.

2. Second, we go from bond prices to *bond yields* and examine the determinants of the yield curve and the relation between short- and long-term interest rates.

The Vocabulary of Bond Markets

Understanding the basic vocabulary of financial markets will help make them (a bit) less mysterious. Here is a basic vocabulary review.

- Bonds are issued by governments or by firms. If issued by the government or government agencies, the bonds are called **government bonds**. If issued by firms (corporations), they are called **corporate bonds**.

- Bonds are rated for their default risk (the risk that they will not be repaid) by rating agencies. The two major rating agencies are the Standard and Poor's Corporation (S&P) and Moody's Investors Service. Moody's **bond ratings** range from Aaa for bonds with nearly no risk of default, to C for bonds where the default risk is high. In August 2011, Standard and Poor's downgraded U.S. government bonds from Aaa to AA+, reflecting its worry about the large budget deficits. This downgrade created a strong controversy. A lower rating typically implies that the bond has to pay a higher interest rate or else investors will not buy it. The difference between the interest rate paid on a given bond and the interest rate paid on the bond with the highest (best) rating is called the **risk premium** associated with the given bond. Bonds with high default risk are sometimes called **junk bonds**.

- Bonds that promise a single payment at maturity are called **discount bonds**. The single payment is called the **face value** of the bond.

- Bonds that promise multiple payments before maturity and one payment at maturity are called **coupon bonds**. The payments before maturity are called **coupon payments**. The final payment is called the face value of the bond. The ratio of coupon payments to the face value is called the **coupon rate**. The **current yield** is the ratio of the coupon payment to the price of the bond.

    For example, a bond with coupon payments of $5 each year, a face value of $100, and a price of $80 has a coupon rate of 5% and a current yield of $5/80 = 0.0625 = 6.25\%$. From an economic viewpoint, neither the coupon rate nor the current yield are interesting measures. The correct measure of the interest rate on a bond is its yield to maturity, or simply yield; you can think of it as roughly the average interest rate paid by the bond over its **life** (the life of a bond is the amount of time left until the bond matures). We shall define the *yield to maturity* more precisely later in this section.

- The maturity of government bonds may vary widely, from a few days to dozens of years. Usually, short-term bonds are called "bills" (such as the US Treasury bills, which have a maturity of up to a year). In Germany, 6- to 12-month maturity government bonds are called "Bubills" (or *Unverzinsliche Schatzanweisungen*). Bills are pure discount, or zero-coupon bonds. Long-term government bonds, by contrast, often carry coupons. In Germany, federal government bonds with a maturity of more than 10 years are called "Bunds" (or Bundesanleihen). There is also a typology of government bonds that are perpetual and redeemable by governments at will: such is the case of the British consols, which were first issued in 1751.

- Bonds are typically nominal bonds. They promise a sequence of fixed nominal payments—payments in terms of domestic currency. There are, however, other types of bonds. Among them are **indexed bonds**, bonds that promise payments adjusted for inflation rather than fixed nominal payments. Instead of promising to pay, say, $100 in a year, a one-year indexed bond promises to pay $100 (1 + \pi)$ dollars, whatever π, the rate of inflation that will take place over the coming year, turns out to be. Because they protect bondholders against the risk of inflation, indexed bonds are popular in many countries. They play a particularly important role in the United Kingdom, where, over the last 30 years, people have increasingly used them to save for retirement. By holding long-term indexed bonds, people can make sure that the payments they receive when they retire will be protected from inflation. Indexed bonds (called **Treasury Inflation Protected Securities (TIPS)**) were introduced in the United States in 1997.

Bond Prices as Present Values

In much of this section, we shall look at just two types of bonds, a bond that promises one payment of $100 in one year—a one-year bond—and a bond that promises one payment of $100 in two years—a two-year bond. Once you understand how their prices and yields are determined, it will be easy to generalize our results to bonds of any maturity. We shall do so later.

Note that both bonds are *discount bonds* (see the Focus box "The Vocabulary of Bond Markets").

Let's start by deriving the prices of the two bonds.

- Given that the one-year bond promises to pay $100 next year, it follows, from the previous section, that its price, call it $\$P_{1t}$, must be equal to the present value of a payment of $100 next year. Let the current one-year nominal interest rate be i_{1t}.

Note that we now denote the one-year interest rate in year t by i_{1t} rather than simply by i_t as we did in previous chapters. This is to make it easier for you to remember that it is the *one-year* interest rate. So,

$$\$P_{1t} = \frac{\$100}{1 + i_{1t}} \tag{14.4}$$

The price of the one-year bond varies inversely with the current one-year nominal interest rate.

◄ We already saw this relation in Chapter 4, Section 4-2.

- Given that the two-year bond promises to pay $100 in two years, its price, call it $\$P_{2t}$, must be equal to the present value of $100 two years from now:

$$\$P_{2t} = \frac{\$100}{(1 + i_{1t})(1 + i_{1t+1}^{e})} \tag{14.5}$$

where i_{1t} denotes the one-year interest rate this year and i_{1t+1}^{e} denotes the one-year rate expected by financial markets for next year. The price of the two-year bond depends inversely on both the current one-year rate and the one-year rate expected for next year.

Arbitrage and Bond Prices

Before further exploring the implications of equations (14.4) and (14.5), let us look at an alternative derivation of equation (14.5). This alternative derivation will introduce you to the important concept of **arbitrage**.

Suppose you have the choice between holding one-year bonds or two-year bonds and what you care about is how much you will have *one year from today*. Which bonds should you hold?

- Suppose you hold one-year bonds. For every dollar you put in one-year bonds, you will get $(1 + i_{1t})$ dollars next year. This relation is represented in the first line of Figure 14-3.
- Suppose you hold two-year bonds. Because the price of a two-year bond is $\$P_{2t}$, every dollar you put in two-year bonds buys you $\$1/\$P_{2t}$ bonds today. When next year comes, the bond will have one more year before maturity. Thus, one year from today, the two-year bond will now be a one-year bond. Therefore, the price at which you can expect to sell it next year is $\$P_{1t+1}^{e}$, the expected price of a one-year bond next year.

    So for every dollar you put in two-year bonds, you can expect to receive $\$1/\$P_{2t}$ multiplied by $\$P_{1t+1}^{e}$, or, equivalently, $\$P_{1t+1}^{e}/\$P_{2t}$ dollars next year. This is represented in the second line of Figure 14-3.

Which bonds should you hold? Suppose you, and other financial investors, care *only* about the expected return and do not care about risk. This assumption is known as the **expectations hypothesis**. It is a simplification. You and other investors are likely to care not only about the expected return but also about the risk associated with holding each bond. If you hold a one-year bond, you know with certainty what you will get next year. If you hold a two-year bond, the price at which you will sell it next year is uncertain;

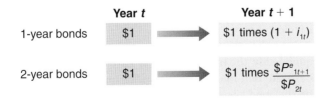

	Year *t*	Year *t* + 1
1-year bonds	$1	$1 times $(1 + i_{1t})$
2-year bonds	$1	$1 times $\dfrac{\$P_{1t+1}^{e}}{\$P_{2t}}$

Figure 14-3

Returns from Holding One-Year and Two-Year Bonds for One Year

MyEconLab Animation

holding the two-year bond for one year is risky. As we indicated previously, we are disregarding this for now but shall come back to it later.

Under the assumption that you and other financial investors care only about expected return, it follows that the two bonds must offer the same expected one-year return. Suppose this condition was not satisfied. Suppose that, for example, the one-year return on one-year bonds was lower than the expected one-year return on two-year bonds. In this case, no one would want to hold the existing supply of one-year bonds, and the market for one-year bonds could not be in equilibrium. Only if the expected one-year return is the same on both bonds will you and other financial investors be willing to hold both one-year bonds and two-year bonds.

If the two bonds offer the same expected one-year return, it follows from Figure 14-3 that

$$1 + i_{1t} = \frac{\$P^e_{1t+1}}{\$P_{2t}} \tag{14.6}$$

We use *arbitrage* to denote the proposition that *expected* returns on two assets must be equal. Some finance economists reserve *arbitrage* for the narrower proposition that *riskless* profit opportunities do not go unexploited.

The left side of the equation gives the return per dollar from holding a one-year bond for one year; the right side gives the expected return per dollar from holding a two-year bond for one year. We shall call equations such as (14.6)—equations that state that the expected returns on two assets must be equal—*arbitrage* relations. Rewrite equation (14.6) as

$$\$P_{2t} = \frac{\$P^e_{1t+1}}{1 + i_{1t}} \tag{14.7}$$

Arbitrage implies that the price of a two-year bond today is the present value of the expected price of the bond next year. This naturally raises the next question. What does the expected price of one-year bonds next year ($\$P^e_{1t+1}$) depend on?

The answer is straightforward. Just as the price of a one-year bond this year depends on this year's one-year interest rate, the price of a one-year bond next year will depend on the one-year interest rate next year. Writing equation (14.4) for next year (year $t + 1$) and denoting expectations in the usual way, we get

$$\$P^e_{1t+1} = \frac{\$100}{(1 + i^e_{1t+1})} \tag{14.8}$$

The price of the bond next year is expected to equal the final payment, $\$100$, discounted by the one-year interest rate expected for next year.

Replacing $\$P^e_{1t+1}$ from equation (14.8) in equation (14.7) gives

The relation between arbitrage and present values: Arbitrage between bonds of different maturities implies that bond prices are equal to the expected present values of payments on these bonds.

$$\$P_{2t} = \frac{\$100}{(1 + i_{1t})(1 + i^e_{1t+1})} \tag{14.9}$$

This expression is the same as equation (14.5). What we have shown is that *arbitrage* between one- and two-year bonds implies that the price of two-year bonds is the *present value* of the payment in two years, namely $\$100$, discounted using current and next year's expected one-year interest rates.

From Bond Prices to Bond Yields

Having looked at bond prices, we now go on to bond yields. The basic point: Bond yields contain the same information about future expected interest rates as bond prices. They just do so in a much clearer way.

To begin, we need a definition of the yield to maturity. The *yield to maturity* on an n-year bond, or equivalently, the **n-year interest rate**, is defined is defined as that constant annual interest rate that makes the bond price today equal to the present value of future payments on the bond.

This definition is simpler than it sounds. Take, for example, the two-year bond we introduced previously. Denote its yield by i_{2t}, where the subscript 2 is there to remind us that this is the *yield to maturity* on a two-year bond, or, equivalently, the two-year interest rate. Following the definition of the yield to maturity, this yield is the constant annual interest rate that would make the present value of $100 in two years equal to the price of the bond today. So, it satisfies the following relation:

$$\$P_{2t} = \frac{\$100}{(1 + i_{2t})^2} \qquad (14.10)$$

Suppose the bond sells for $90 today. Then, the two-year interest rate i_{2t} is given by $\sqrt{100/90} - 1$, or 5.4%. In other words, holding the bond for two years—until maturity—yields an interest rate of 5.4% per year.

What is the relation of the two-year interest rate to the current one-year interest rate and the expected one-year interest rate? To answer that question, look at equation (14.10) and equation (14.9). Eliminating $\$P_{2t}$ between the two gives

$$\frac{\$100}{(1 + i_{2t})^2} = \frac{\$100}{(1 + i_{1t})(1 + i^e_{1t+1})}$$

Rearranging,

$$(1 + i_{2t})^2 = (1 + i_{1t})(1 + i^e_{1t+1})$$

This gives us the relation between the two-year interest rate i_{2t}, the current one-year interest rate i_{1t}, and next year's expected one-year interest rate i^e_{t+1}. A useful approximation to this relation is given by

$$i_{2t} \approx \frac{1}{2}(i_{1t} + i^e_{1t+1}) \qquad (14.11)$$

Equation (14.11) simply says that *the two-year interest rate is (approximately) the average of the current one-year interest rate and next year's expected one-year interest rate*.

We have focused on the relation between the prices and yields of one-year and two-year bonds. But our results generalize to bonds of any maturity. For instance, we could have looked at bonds with maturities of less than a year. To take an example, the yield on a bond with a maturity of six months is (approximately) equal to the average of the current three-month interest rate and next quarter's expected three-month interest rate. Or we could have looked instead at bonds with maturities longer than two years. For example, the yield on a 10-year bond is (approximately) equal to the average of the current one-year interest rate and the one-year interest rates expected for the next nine years.

The general principle is clear: Long-term interest rates reflect current and future expected short-term interest rates. Before we return to an interpretation of the yield curves in Figure 14-2, we need to take one last step, reintroduce risk.

Reintroducing Risk

We have assumed so far that investors did not care about risk. But they do care. Go back to the choice between holding a one-year bond for one year or holding a two-year bond for one year. The first option is riskless. The second is risky as you do not know the price at which you will sell the bond in a year. You are thus likely to ask for a risk premium to hold the two-year bond, and the arbitrage equation takes the form:

$$1 + i_{1t} + x = \frac{\$P^e_{1t+1}}{\$P_{2t}}$$

$90 = \$100/(1 + i_{2t})^2 \Rightarrow$
$(1 + i_{2t})^2 = \$100/\$90 \Rightarrow$
$(1 + i_{2t}) = \sqrt{\$100/\$90} \Rightarrow$
◀ $i_{2t} = 5.4\%$

We used a similar approximation when we looked at the relation between the nominal interest rate and the real interest rate in Chapter 6. See Proposition 4 in Appendix 2 at the end of this book.

The expected return on the two-year bond (the right-hand side) must exceed the return on the one-year bond by some risk premium x. Reorganizing gives:

$$\$P_{2t} = \frac{\$P^e_{1t+1}}{1 + i_{1t} + x}$$

The price of the two-year bond is the discounted value of the expected price of a one-year bond next year, with the discount rate now reflecting the risk premium. As one-year bonds have a known return and are therefore not risky, the expected price of a one-year bond next year is still given by equation (14.8). So replacing in the previous equation gives:

$$\$P_{2t} = \frac{\$100}{(1 + i_{1t})(1 + i^e_{1t+1} + x)} \qquad (14.12)$$

Now, to go from prices to yields, let's go through the same steps as before. Using the two expressions for the price of the two-year bond, equation (14.10) and equation (14.12), gives:

$$\frac{\$100}{(1 + i_{2t})^2} = \frac{\$100}{(1 + i_{1t})(1 + i_{1t+1} + x)}$$

Manipulating the equation gives:

$$(1 + i_{2t})^2 = (1 + i_{1t})(1 + i^e_{1t+1} + x)$$

Finally, using the same approximation as before gives:

$$i_{2t} \approx \frac{1}{2}(i_{1t} + i^e_{1t+1} + x) \qquad (14.13)$$

The two-year rate is the average of the current and expected one-year rate plus a risk premium. Take the case where the one-year rate is expected to be the same next year as this year. Then the two-year rate will exceed the one-year rate by a term reflecting the risk in holding two-year bonds. As the price risk increases with the maturity of the bonds, the risk premium typically increases with maturity, typically reaching 1%-2% for long-term bonds. This implies that, on average, the yield curve is slightly upward sloping, reflecting the higher risk involved in holding longer maturity bonds.

Interpreting the Yield Curve

We now have what we need to interpret Figure 14-2.

Consider the yield curve for November 1, 2000. Recall that when investors expect interest rates to be constant over time, the yield curve should be slightly upward sloping, reflecting the fact that the risk premium increases with maturity. Thus, the fact that the yield curve was downward sloping, something relatively rare, tells us that investors expected interest rates to go down slightly over time, with the expected decrease in rates more than compensating for a rising term premium. And if we look at the macroeconomic situation at the time, they had good reasons to hold this view. At the end of November 2000, the U.S. economy was slowing down. Investors expected what they called a *smooth landing*. They thought that to maintain growth, the Fed would slowly decrease the policy rate, and these expectations were what laid behind the downward-sloping yield curve. By June 2001, however, growth had declined much more than was expected in November 2000, and by then, the Fed had decreased the interest rate much more than investors had expected previously. Investors now expected that, as

The Yield Curves for AAA-rated Central Government Bonds

Figure 1, which accompanies this case, represents the yield curves for AAA rated Euro-area central government bonds in two different periods—November 2014 and April 2015. In this figure, the horizontal axis shows maturities by number of months and highlights three features.

First, in both cases the short-term government bonds carry negative yields; these became positive in the first period (November 2014), for bonds with maturities over 24 months, and in the second period (April 2015), for bonds with maturities over 42 months. Negative yields may result from different causes. In Europe, the negative yields on short-term government bonds in recent years would indicate a "flight to safety" of investors in light of slow growth and financial market uncertainties.

Second, the yield curve for April 2015 is below that for November 2014. The third is the shape of the two curves,

which is significantly different in the left-hand segments—a U shape for November 2014 and a more complex shape for April 2015, first an inverted U shape (positive, then negative yield-maturity relationship), then a flattening of the curve, and finally an upward slope. What happened within the few months separating these two periods that could explain these shifts?

Monetary policy. In March 2015, the European Central Bank and Euro-area central banks launched a massive government bond purchase program designed to boost a sluggish overall growth. These resulted in a further reduction in already negative yields on short-term bonds while encouraging investors seeking non-negative yields to shift demand to long-term bonds, whose yields consequently declined, thus flattening the yield curve.

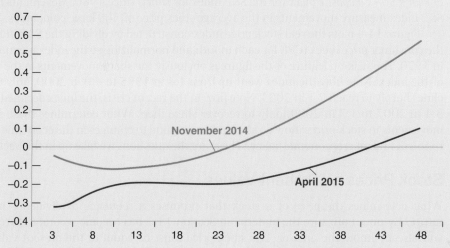

Figure 1   *Yield Curves for AAA Rated Euro-Area Central Government Bonds, November 2014 and April 2015*

Source: European Central Bank.

---

the economy recovered, the Fed would start increasing the policy rate. As a result, the yield curve was upward sloping. Note however that the yield curve was nearly flat for maturities up to one year. This tells us that financial markets did not expect interest rates to start rising until a year hence; that is, before June 2002. Did they turn out to be right? Not quite. In fact, the recovery was much weaker than had been expected, and the Fed did not increase the policy rate until June 2004—fully two years later than financial markets had anticipated.

Another example of how to learn from the yield curve is given in the Focus box, "The Yield Curves for AAA-rated Central Government Bonds."

Let's summarize what you have learned in this section. You have seen how arbitrage determines the price of bonds. You have seen how bond prices and bond yields depend on current and future expected interest rates and risk premiums and what can be learned by looking at the yield curve.

14-3 The Stock Market and Movements in Stock Prices

So far, we have focused on bonds. But although governments finance themselves by issuing bonds, the same is not true of firms. Firms finance themselves in four ways. First, they rely on **internal finance**, that is they use some of the earnings; second, and this is the main channel of **external finance** for small firms, through bank loans. As we saw in Chapter 6, this channel has played a central role in the crisis; third, through **debt finance**—bonds and loans; and fourth, through **equity finance**, issuing **stocks**—or **shares**, as stocks are also called. Instead of paying predetermined amounts as bonds do, stocks pay **dividends** in an amount decided by the firm. Dividends are paid from the firm's profits. Typically, dividends are less than profits because firms retain some of their profits to finance their investment. But dividends move with profits. When profits increase, so do dividends.

Our focus in this section is on the determination of stock prices. As a way of introducing the issues, let's look at the behavior of an index of U.S. stock prices, the *Standard & Poor's 500 Composite Index* (or the S&P index for short) since 1980. Movements in the S&P index measure movements in the average stock price of 500 large companies.

Figure 14-4 plots the real stock price index constructed by dividing the S&P index by the consumer price index (CPI) for each month and normalizing so the index is equal to 1 in 1970. The striking feature of the figure is obviously the sharp movements in the value of the index. Note how the index went up from 1.4 in 1995 to 4.0 in 2000, only to decline sharply to reach 2.1 in 2003. Note how in the recent crisis, the index declined from 3.4 in 2007 to 1.7 in 2009, only to recover since then. What determines these sharp movements in stock prices; how do stock prices respond to changes in the economic environment and macroeconomic policy? These are the questions we take up in this section.

Stock Prices as Present Values

What determines the price of a stock that promises a sequence of dividends in the future? By now, I am sure the material in Section 14-1 has become second nature, and you already know the answer. The stock price must be equal to the present value of future expected dividends.

Another and better-known index is the *Dow Jones Industrial Index*, an index of stocks of primarily industrial firms only and therefore less representative of the average price of stocks than is the S&P index. Similar indexes exist for other countries. The *Nikkei Index* reflects movements in stock prices in Tokyo, and the *FT* and *CAC40* indexes reflect stock price movements in London and Paris, respectively.

Figure 14-4

Standard and Poor's Stock Price Index in Real Terms since 1970

Note the sharp fluctuations in stock prices since the mid-1990s.

Source: Calculated from Haver Analytics using series SP500@ USECON.

MyEconLab Real-time data

Expectations   **Extensions**

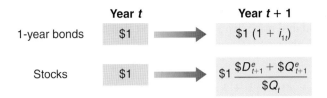

Just as we did for bonds, let's derive this result from looking at the implications of arbitrage between one-year bonds and stocks. Suppose you face the choice of investing either in one-year bonds or in stocks for a year. What should you choose?

- Suppose you decide to hold one-year bonds. Then for every dollar you put in one-year bonds, you will get $(1 + i_{1t})$ dollars next year. This payoff is represented in the upper line of Figure 14-5.
- Suppose you decide instead to hold stocks for a year. Let $\$Q_t$ be the price of the stock. Let $\$D_t$ denote the dividend this year, $\$D_{t+1}^e$ the expected dividend next year. Suppose we look at the price of the stock after the dividend has been paid this year; this price is known as the **ex-dividend price**—so that the first dividend to be paid after the purchase of the stock is next year's dividend. (This is just a matter of convention; we could alternatively look at the price before this year's dividend has been paid. What term would we have to add?)

Holding the stock for a year implies buying a stock today, receiving a dividend next year, and then selling the stock. As the price of a stock is $\$Q_t$, every dollar you put in stocks buys you $\$1/\$Q_t$ stocks. And for each stock you buy, you expect to receive $(\$D_{t+1}^e + \$Q_{t+1}^e)$, the sum of the expected dividend and the stock price next year. Therefore, for every dollar you put in stocks, you expect to receive $(\$D_{t+1}^e + \$Q_{t+1}^e)/\$Q_t$. This payoff is represented in the lower line of Figure 14-5.

Let's use the same arbitrage argument we used for bonds. It is clear that holding a stock for one year is risky, much riskier than holding a one-year bond for a year (which is riskless). Rather than proceeding in two steps as we did for bonds (first leaving risk considerations out and then introducing a risk premium), let's take risk into account from the start and assume that financial investors require a risk premium to hold stocks.

In the case of stocks, the risk premium is called the **equity premium**. Equilibrium then requires that the expected rate of return from holding stocks for one year be the same as the rate of return on one-year bonds plus the equity premium:

$$\frac{\$D_{t+1}^e + \$Q_{t+1}^e}{\$Q_t} = 1 + i_{1t} + x$$

Where x denotes the equity premium. Rewrite this equation as

$$\$Q_t = \frac{\$D_{t+1}^e}{(1 + i_{1t} + x)} + \frac{\$Q_{t+1}^e}{(1 + i_{1t} + x)} \tag{14.14}$$

Arbitrage implies that the price of the stock today must be equal to the present value of the expected dividend plus the present value of the expected stock price next year.

The next step is to think about what determines $\$Q_{t+1}^e$, the expected stock price next year. Next year, financial investors will again face the choice between stocks and one-year bonds. Thus, the same arbitrage relation will hold. Writing the previous equation, but now for time $t + 1$ and taking expectations into account gives

$$\$Q_{t+1}^e = \frac{\$D_{t+2}^e}{(1 + i_{1t+1}^e + x)} + \frac{\$Q_{t+2}^e}{(1 + i_{1t+1}^e + x)}$$

The expected price next year is simply the present value next year of the sum of the expected dividend and price two years from now. Replacing the expected price $\$Q^e_{t+1}$ in equation (14.14) gives

$$\$Q_t = \frac{\$D^e_{t+1}}{(1 + i_{1t} + x)} + \frac{\$D^e_{t+2}}{(1 + i_{1t} + x)(1 + i^e_{1t+1} + x)} + \frac{\$Q^e_{t+2}}{(1 + i_{1t} + \theta)(1 + i^e_{1t+1} + x)}$$

The stock price is the present value of the expected dividend next year, plus the present value of the expected dividend two years from now, plus the expected price two years from now.

If we replace the expected price in two years as the present value of the expected price and dividends in three years, and so on for n years, we get

$$\$Q_t = \frac{\$D^e_{t+1}}{(1 + i_{1t} + x)} + \frac{\$D^e_{t+2}}{(1 + i_{1t} + x)(1 + i^e_{1t+1} + x)} + \cdots$$

$$+ \frac{\$D^e_{t+n}}{(1 + i_{1t} + x)\cdots(1 + i^e_{1t+n-1} + x)} + \frac{\$Q^e_{t+n}}{(1 + i_{1t} + x)\cdots(1 + i^e_{1t+n-1} + x)}$$

$$(14.15)$$

A subtle point: The condition that people expect the price of the stock to converge to some value over time seems reasonable. Indeed, most of the time it is likely to be satisfied. When, however, prices are subject to rational bubbles (Section 14-4), this is when people are expecting large increases in the stock price in the future and this is when the condition that the expected stock price does not explode ▶ is not satisfied. This is why, when there are bubbles, this argument fails, and the stock price is no longer equal to the present value of expected dividends.

Look at the last term in equation (14.15), the present value of the expected price in n years. As long as people do not expect the stock price to explode in the future, then as we keep replacing Q^e_{t+n} and n increases, this term will go to zero. To see why, suppose the interest rate is constant and equal to i. The last term becomes

$$\frac{\$Q^e_{t+n}}{(1 + i_{1t} + x)\cdots(1 + i^e_{1t+n-1} + x)} = \frac{\$Q^e_{t+n}}{(1 + i + x)^n}$$

Suppose further that people expect the price of the stock to converge to some value, call it $\$\bar{Q}$, in the far future. Then, the last term becomes

$$\frac{\$Q^e_{t+n}}{(1 + i + x)^n} = \frac{\$\bar{Q}}{(1 + i + x)^n}$$

If the interest rate is positive, this expression goes to zero as n becomes large. Equation (14.15) reduces to

$$\$Q_t = \frac{\$D^e_{t+1}}{(1 + i_{1t} + x)} + \frac{\$D^e_{t+2}}{(1 + i_{1t} + x)(1 + i^e_{1t+1} + x)} + \cdots$$

$$+ \frac{\$D^e_{t+n}}{(1 + i_{1t} + x)\cdots(1 + i^e_{1t+n-1} + x)} \qquad (14.16)$$

Two equivalent ways of writing the stock price: The—nominal—stock price equals the expected present discounted value of future nominal dividends, discounted by current and future nominal interest rates.

The—real—stock price equals the expected present discounted value of future real dividends, discounted by current and future real interest rates.

The price of the stock is equal to the present value of the dividend next year, discounted using the current one-year interest rate plus the equity premium, plus the present value of the dividend two years from now, discounted using both this year's one-year interest rate and the next-year's expected one-year interest rate, plus the equity premium, and so on.

Equation (14.16) gives the stock price as the present value of *nominal* dividends, discounted by *nominal* interest rates. From Section 14-1, we know we can rewrite this equation to express the *real* stock price as the present value of *real* dividends, discounted by *real* interest rates. So we can rewrite the real stock price as:

$$Q_t = \frac{D^e_{t+1}}{(1 + r_{1t} + x)} + \frac{D^e_{t+2}}{(1 + r_{1t} + x)(1 + r^e_{1t+1} + x)} + \cdots \qquad (14.17)$$

Q_t and D_t, without a dollar sign, denote the real price and real dividends at time t. The real stock price is the present value of future real dividends, discounted by the sequence of one-year real interest rates plus the equity premium.

This relation has three important implications:

■ Higher expected future real dividends lead to a higher real stock price.
■ Higher current and expected future one-year real interest rates lead to a lower real stock price.
■ A higher equity premium leads to a lower stock price.

Let's now see what light this relation sheds on movements in the stock market.

The Stock Market and Economic Activity

Figure 14-4 showed the large movements in stock prices over the last two decades. It is not unusual for the index to go up or down by 15% within a year. In 1997, the stock market went up by 24% (in real terms); in 2008, it went down by 46%. Daily movements of 2% or more are not unusual. What causes these movements?

The first point to be made is that these movements should be, and they are for the most part, unpredictable. The reason why is best understood by thinking in terms of the choice people have between stocks and bonds. If it were widely believed that, a year from now, the price of a stock was going to be 20% higher than today's price, holding the stock for a year would be unusually attractive, much more attractive than holding short-term bonds. There would be a very large demand for the stock. Its price would increase *today* to the point where the expected return from holding the stock was back in line with the expected return on other assets. In other words, the expectation of a high stock price next year would lead to a high stock price today.

There is indeed a saying in economics that it is a sign of a *well-functioning stock market* that movements in stock prices are unpredictable. The saying is too strong. At any moment, a few financial investors will have better information or simply be better at reading the future. If they are only a few, they may not buy enough of the stock to bid its price all the way up today. Thus, they may get large expected returns. But the basic idea is nevertheless correct. The financial market gurus who regularly predict large imminent movements in the stock market are quacks. Major movements in stock prices cannot be predicted.

If movements in the stock market cannot be predicted, if they are the result of news, where does this leave us? We can still do two things:

■ We can do Monday-morning quarterbacking, looking back and identifying the news to which the market reacted.
■ We can ask "what if" questions. For example: What would happen to the stock market if the Fed were to embark on a more expansionary policy, or if consumers were to become more optimistic and increase spending?

Let us look at two "what if" questions using the *IS-LM* model we developed (we shall extend it in the next chapter to take explicit account of expectations; for the moment the old model will do). To simplify, let's assume, as we did earlier, that expected inflation equals zero, so that the real interest rate and the nominal interest rate are equal.

A Monetary Expansion and the Stock Market

Suppose the economy is in a recession and the Fed decides to decrease the policy rate. The *LM* curve shifts down to *LM'* in Figure 14-6, and equilibrium output moves from point A to point A'. How will the stock market react?

You may have heard the proposition that stock prices follow a **random walk**. This is a technical term, but with a simple interpretation. Something—it can be a molecule, or the price of an asset—follows a random walk if each step it takes is as likely to be up as it is to be down. Its movements are therefore unpredictable.

This assumes that the policy rate is positive to start with, so the economy is not in a liquidity trap.

Figure 14-6

An Expansionary Monetary Policy and the Stock Market

A monetary expansion decreases the interest rate and increases output. What it does to the stock market depends on whether or not financial markets anticipated the monetary expansion.

MyEconLab Animation

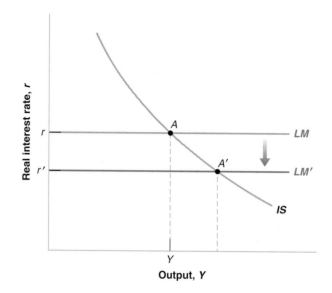

The answer depends on what participants in the stock market expected monetary policy to be before the Fed's move.

If they fully anticipated the expansionary policy, then the stock market will not react. Neither its expectations of future dividends nor its expectations of future interest rates are affected by a move it had already anticipated. Thus, in equation (14.17), nothing changes, and stock prices will remain the same.

Suppose instead that the Fed's move is at least partly unexpected. In this case, stock prices will increase. They increase for two reasons: First, a more expansionary monetary policy implies lower interest rates for some time. Second, it also implies higher output for some time (until the economy returns to the natural level of output), and therefore higher dividends. As equation (14.17) tells us, both lower interest rates and higher dividends—current and expected—will lead to an increase in stock prices.

An Increase in Consumer Spending and the Stock Market

Now consider an unexpected shift of the *IS* curve to the right, resulting, for example, from stronger-than-expected consumer spending. As a result of the shift, output in Figure 14-7 on page 324 increases from *A* to *A'*.

Will stock prices go up? You might be tempted to say yes. A stronger economy means higher profits and higher dividends for some time. But this answer is not necessarily right.

The reason is that it ignores the response of the Fed. If the market expects that the Fed will not respond and will keep the real policy rate unchanged at *r*, output will increase a lot, as the economy moves to *A'*. With unchanged interest rates and higher output, stock prices go up. The Fed's behavior is what financial investors often care about the most. After receiving the news of unexpectedly strong economic activity, the main question on Wall Street is: How will the Fed react?

What will happen if the market expects that the Fed might worry that an increase in output above Y_A may lead to an increase in inflation? This will be the case if Y_A was already close to the natural level of output. In this case, a further increase in output would lead to an increase in inflation, something that the Fed wants to avoid. A decision by the Fed to counteract the rightward shift of the *IS* curve with an increase in the policy rate, causes the *LM* curve to shift up, from *LM* to *LM'* so the economy goes from *A* to *A''* and output does not change. In that case, stock prices will surely go down: There is no change in expected profits, but the interest rate is now higher.

On September 30, 1998, the Fed lowered the target federal funds rate by 0.5%. This decrease was expected by financial markets, though, so the Dow Jones index remained roughly unchanged (actually, going down 28 points for the day). Less than a month later, on October 15, 1998, the Fed lowered the target federal funds rate again, this time by 0.25%. In contrast to the September cut, this move by the Fed came as a complete surprise to financial markets. As a result, the Dow Jones index increased by 330 points on that day, an increase of more than 3%. (Go to a Web site which gives the history of the yield curve, and look at what happened to the yield curve on each of those two days.)

Making (Some) Sense of (Apparent) Nonsense: Why the Stock Market Moved Yesterday and Other Stories

MEL Video

Here are some quotes from *The Wall Street Journal* from April 1997 to August 2001. Try to make sense of them, using what you've just learned. (And if you have time, find your own quotes.)

■ April 1997. Good news on the economy, leading to an increase in stock prices:

"Bullish investors celebrated the release of market-friendly economic data by stampeding back into stock and bond markets, pushing the Dow Jones Industrial Average to its second-largest point gain ever and putting the blue-chip index within shooting distance of a record just weeks after it was reeling."

■ December 1999. Good news on the economy, leading to a decrease in stock prices:

"Good economic news was bad news for stocks and worse news for bonds. . . . The announcement of stronger-than-expected November retail-sales numbers wasn't welcome. Economic strength creates inflation fears and sharpens the risk that the Federal Reserve will raise interest rates again."

■ September 1998. Bad news on the economy, leading to an decrease in stock prices:

"Nasdaq stocks plummeted as worries about the strength of the U.S. economy and the profitability of U.S. corporations prompted widespread selling."

■ August 2001. Bad news on the economy, leading to an increase in stock prices:

"Investors shrugged off more gloomy economic news, and focused instead on their hope that the worst is now over for both the economy and the stock market. The optimism translated into another 2% gain for the Nasdaq Composite Index."

Let's summarize: Stock prices depend on current and future movements in activity. But this does not imply any simple relation between stock prices and output. How stock prices respond to a change in output depends on: (1) what the market expected in the first place, (2) the source of the shocks behind the change in output, and (3) how the market expects the central bank to react to the output change. Test your newly acquired understanding by reading the Focus box "Making (Some) Sense of (Apparent) Nonsense: Why the Stock Market Moved Yesterday, and Other Stories."

Figure 14-7

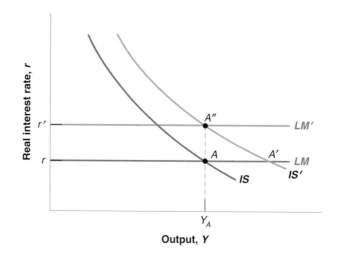

An Increase in Consumption Spending and the Stock Market

The increase in consumption leads to a higher level of output. What happens to the stock market depends on what investors expect the Fed will do.

If investors expect that the Fed will not respond and will keep the policy rate unchanged, output will increase, as the economy moves to A'. With an unchanged policy rate and higher output, stock prices will go up.

If instead investors expect that the Fed will respond by raising the policy rate, output may remain unchanged as the economy moves to A''. With unchanged output, and a higher policy rate, stock prices will go down.

MyEconLab Animation

14-4 Risk, Bubbles, Fads, and Asset Prices

Do all movements in stock and other asset prices come from news about future dividends or interest rates? The answer is no, for two different reasons: The first is that there is variation over time in perceptions of risk. The second is deviations of prices from their fundamental value, namely bubbles or fads. Let's look at each one in turn.

Stock Prices and Risk

In the previous section, I assumed that the equity premium x was constant. It is not. After the Great Depression, the equity premium was very high, perhaps reflecting the fact that investors, remembering the collapse of the stock market in 1929, were reluctant to hold stocks unless the premium was high enough. It started to decrease in the early 1950s, from around 7% to less than 3% today. And it can also change quickly. Part of the large stock market fall in 2008 was due not only to more pessimistic expectations of future dividends, but also to the large increase in uncertainty and the perception of higher risk by stock market participants. Thus, a lot of the movement in stock prices comes not just from expectations of future dividends and interest rates, but also from shifts in the equity premium.

Asset Prices, Fundamentals, and Bubbles

In the previous section, we assumed that stock prices were always equal to their *fundamental value*, defined as the present value of expected dividends given in equation (14.17). Do stock prices always correspond to their fundamental value? Most economists doubt it. They point to Black October in 1929, when the U.S. stock market fell by 23% in two days and to October 19, 1987, when the Dow Jones index fell by 22.6% in a single day. They point to the amazing rise in the Nikkei index (an index of Japanese stock prices) from around 13,000 in 1985 to around 35,000 in 1989, followed by a decline back to 16,000 in 1992. In each of these cases, they point to a lack of obvious news or at least of news important enough to cause such enormous movements.

MyEconLab Video

Instead, they argue that stock prices are not always equal to their **fundamental value**, defined as the present value of expected dividends given in equation (14.17) and that stocks are sometimes underpriced or overpriced. Overpricing eventually comes to an end, sometimes with a crash, as in October 1929, or with a long slide, as in the case of the Nikkei index.

Famous Bubbles: From Tulipmania in 17th-Century Holland to Russia in 1994

Tulipmania in Holland

In the 17th century, tulips became increasingly popular in Western European gardens. A market developed in Holland for both rare and common forms of tulip bulbs.

An episode called the "tulip bubble" took place from 1634 to 1637. In 1634, the price of rare bulbs started increasing. The market went into a frenzy, with speculators buying tulip bulbs in anticipation of even higher prices later. For example, the price of a bulb called "Admiral Van de Eyck" increased from 1,500 guineas in 1634 to 7,500 guineas in 1637, equal to the price of a house at the time. There are stories about a sailor mistakenly eating bulbs, only to realize the cost of his "meal" later. In early 1637, prices increased faster. Even the price of some common bulbs exploded, rising by a factor of up to 20 in January. But in February 1637, prices collapsed. A few years later, bulbs were trading for roughly 10% of their value at the peak of the bubble.

This account is taken from Peter Garber, "Tulipmania," *Journal of Political Economy* 1989, 97 (3): pp. 535–560.

The MMM Pyramid in Russia

In 1994 a Russian "financier," Sergei Mavrodi, created a company called MMM and proceeded to sell shares, promising shareholders a rate of return of at least 3,000% per year!

The company was an instant success. The price of MMM shares increased from 1,600 rubles (then worth $1) in February to 105,000 rubles (then worth $51) in July. And by July, according to the company claims, the number of shareholders had increased to 10 million.

The trouble was that the company was not involved in any type of production and held no assets, except for its 140 offices in Russia. The shares were intrinsically worthless. The company's initial success was based on a standard pyramid scheme, with MMM using the funds from the sale of new shares to pay the promised returns on the old shares. Despite repeated warnings by government officials, including Boris Yeltsin, the then President of the Russian Federation, that MMM was a scam and that the increase in the price of shares was a bubble, the promised returns were just too attractive to many Russian people, especially in the midst of a deep economic recession.

The scheme could work only as long as the number of new shareholders—and thus new funds to be distributed to existing shareholders—increased fast enough. By the end of July 1994, the company could no longer make good on its promises and the scheme collapsed. The company closed. Mavrodi tried to blackmail the government into paying the shareholders, claiming that not doing so would trigger a revolution or a civil war. The government refused, leading many shareholders to be angry at the government rather than at Mavrodi. Later on in the year, Mavrodi actually ran for Parliament, as a self-appointed defender of the shareholders who had lost their savings. He won!

Under what conditions can such mispricing occur? The surprising answer is that it can occur even when investors are rational and when arbitrage holds. To see why, consider the case of a truly worthless stock (that is, the stock of a company that all financial investors know will never make profits and will never pay dividends). Putting D_{t+1}^e, D_{t+2}^e, and so on equal to zero in equation (14.17) yields a simple and unsurprising answer: The fundamental value of such a stock is equal to zero.

Might you nevertheless be willing to pay a positive price for this stock? Maybe. You might if you expect the price at which you can sell the stock next year to be higher than this year's price. And the same applies to a buyer next year. He may well be willing to buy at a high price if he expects to sell at an even higher price in the following year. This process suggests that stock prices may increase just because investors expect them to. Such movements in stock prices are called **rational speculative bubbles**. Financial investors might well be behaving rationally as the bubble inflates. Even those investors who hold the stock at the time of the crash, and therefore sustain a large loss, may have been rational. They may have realized there was a chance of a crash but also a chance that the bubble would continue and they could sell at an even higher price.

To make things simple, our example assumed the stock to be fundamentally worthless. But the argument is general and applies to stocks with a positive fundamental value as well. People might be willing to pay more than the fundamental value of a stock if they expect its price to further increase in the future. And the same argument

The Increase in U.S. Housing Prices: Fundamentals or Bubble?

Recall from Chapter 6 that the trigger behind the current crisis was a decline in housing prices starting in 2006 (see Figure 6-7 for the evolution of the housing price index). In retrospect, the large increase from 2000 on that preceded the decline is now widely interpreted as a bubble. But, in real time as prices went up, there was little agreement as to what lay behind this increase.

Economists belonged to three camps:

The pessimists argued that the price increases could not be justified by fundamentals. In 2005, Robert Shiller said: "The home-price bubble feels like the stock-market mania in the fall of 1999, just before the stock bubble burst in early 2000, with all the hype, herd investing and absolute confidence in the inevitability of continuing price appreciation."

To understand his position, go back to the derivation of stock prices in the text. We saw that, absent bubbles, we can think of stock prices as depending on current and expected future interest rates, current and expected future dividends, and a risk premium. The same applies to house prices. Absent bubbles, we can think of house prices as depending on current and expected future interest rates, current and expected rents, and a risk premium. In that context, pessimists pointed out that the increase in house prices was not matched by a parallel increase in rents. You can see this in Figure 1, which plots the price-to-rent ratio (i.e., the ratio of an index of house prices to an index of rents) from 1985

to today (the index is set so its average value from 1987 to 1995 is 100). After remaining roughly constant from 1987 to 1995, the ratio then increased by nearly 60%, reaching a peak in 2006 and declining since then. Furthermore, Shiller pointed out, surveys of house buyers suggested extremely high expectations of continuing large increases in housing prices, often in excess of 10% a year, and thus of large capital gains. As we saw previously, if assets are valued at their fundamental value, investors should not be expecting large capital gains in the future.

The optimists argued that there were good reasons for the price-to-rent ratio to go up. First, as we saw in Figure 6-2, the real interest rate was decreasing, increasing the present value of rents. Second, the mortgage market was changing. More people were able to borrow and buy a house; people who borrowed were able to borrow a larger proportion of the value of the house. Both of these factors contributed to an increase in demand, and thus an increase in house prices. The optimists also pointed out that, every year since 2000, the pessimists had kept predicting the end of the bubble, and prices continued to increase. The pessimists were losing credibility.

The third group was by far the largest and remained agnostic. (Harry Truman is reported to have said: "Give me a one-handed economist! All my economists say, On the one hand, on the other.") They concluded that the increase in house prices reflected both improved fundamentals and bubbles and that it was difficult to identify their relative importance.

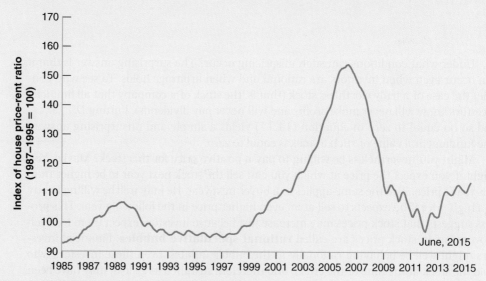

Figure 1   *The U.S. Housing Price-to-Rent Ratio since 1985*

Source: Calculated using Case-Shiller Home Price Indices, http://us.spindices.com/index-family/real-estate/sp-case-shiller. Rental component of the Consumer Price Index: CUSR0000SEHA, Rent of Primary Residence, Bureau of Labor Statistics.

MyEconLab Real-time data

What conclusions should you draw? The pessimists were clearly largely right. But bubbles and fads are clearer to see in retrospect than while they are taking place. This makes the task of policy makers much harder. If they were sure it was a bubble, they should try to stop it before it gets too large and then bursts. But they can rarely be sure until it is too late.

Source: "Reasonable People Did Disagree: Optimism and Pessimism about the U.S. Housing Market before the Crash," Kristopher S. Gerardi, Christopher Foote, and Paul Willen, Federal Reserve Bank of Boston, Discussion Paper No. 10-5, September 10, 2010, available at http://www.bostonfed.org/economic/ppdp/2010/ppdp1005.pdf.

applies to other assets, such as housing, gold, and paintings. Two such bubbles are described in the Focus box "Famous Bubbles: From Tulipmania in 17th-Century Holland to Russia in 1994."

Are all deviations from fundamental values in financial markets rational bubbles? Probably not. The fact is that many investors are not rational. An increase in stock prices in the past, say due to a succession of good news, often creates excessive optimism. If investors simply extrapolate from past returns to predict future returns, a stock may become "hot" (high priced) for no reason other than its price has increased in the past. This is true not only of stocks, but also of houses. (See the Focus box "The Increase in U.S. Housing Prices in the United States in the 2000s: Fundamentals or Bubble?") Such deviations of stock prices from their fundamental value are sometimes called **fads**. We are all aware of fads outside of the stock market; there are good reasons to believe they exist in the stock market as well.

We have focused in this chapter on the determination of asset prices. The reason why this belongs to a macroeconomic text is that asset prices are more than just a sideshow. They affect economic activity by influencing consumption and investment spending. There is little question, for example, that the decline in the stock market was one of the factors behind the 2001 recession. Most economists also believe that the stock market crash of 1929 was one of the sources of the Great Depression. And as we saw in Chapter 6, the decline in housing prices was the trigger for the recent crisis. These interactions among asset prices, expectations, and economic activity are the topics of the next two chapters.

Summary

- The expected present discounted value of a sequence of payments equals the value this year of the expected sequence of payments. It depends positively on current and future expected payments and negatively on current and future expected interest rates.

- When discounting a sequence of current and expected future nominal payments, one should use current and expected future nominal interest rates. In discounting a sequence of current and expected future real payments, one should use current and expected future real interest rates.

- Arbitrage between bonds of different maturities implies that the price of a bond is the present value of the payments on the bond, discounted using current and expected short-term interest rates over the life of the bond, plus a risk premium. Higher current or expected short-term interest rates lead to lower bond prices.

- The yield to maturity on a bond is (approximately) equal to the average of current and expected short-term interest rates over the life of a bond, plus a risk premium.

- The slope of the yield curve—equivalently, the term structure—tells us what financial markets expect to happen to short-term interest rates in the future.

- The fundamental value of a stock is the present value of expected future real dividends, discounted using current and future expected one-year real interest rates plus the equity premium. In the absence of bubbles or fads, the price of a stock is equal to its fundamental value.

- An increase in expected dividends leads to an increase in the fundamental value of stocks; an increase in current and expected one-year interest rates leads to a decrease in their fundamental value.

- Changes in output may or may not be associated with changes in stock prices in the same direction. Whether they are or not depends on (1) what the market expected in the first place, (2) the source of the shocks, and (3) how the market expects the central bank to react to the output change.

- Asset prices can be subject to bubbles and fads that cause the price to differ from its fundamental value. Bubbles are episodes in which financial investors buy an asset for a price higher than its fundamental value, anticipating to resell it at an even higher price. Fads are episodes in which, because of excessive optimism, financial investors are willing to pay more for an asset than its fundamental value.

Key Terms

expected present discounted value, 306

discount factor, 306

discount rate, 306

present discounted value, 307

present value, 307

maturity, 310

yield to maturity, 311

yield, 311

short-term interest rate, 311

long-term interest rate, 311

yield curve, 311

term structure of interest rates, 311

government bonds, 312

corporate bonds, 312

bond ratings, 312

risk premium, 312

junk bonds, 312

discount bonds, 312

face value, 312

coupon bonds, 312

coupon payments, 312

coupon rate, 312

current yield, 312

life (of a bond), 312

Treasury bills (T-bills), 312

indexed bonds, 312

Treasury Inflation Protected Securities (TIPS), 312

arbitrage, 313

expectations hypothesis, 313

n-year interest rate, 314

internal finance, 318

external finance, 318

debt finance, 318

equity finance, 318

stocks or shares, 318

dividends, 318

ex-dividend price, 319

equity premium, 319

random walk, 321

fundamental value, 324

rational speculative bubbles, 325

fads, 327

Questions and Problems

QUICK CHECK

MyEconLab Visit www.myeconlab.com to complete similar Quick Check problems and get instant feedback.

1. *Using the information in this chapter, label each of the following statements true, false, or uncertain. Explain briefly.*

   a. The present discounted value of a stream of returns can be calculated in real or nominal terms.

   b. The higher the one-year interest rate, the lower the present discounted value of a payment next year.

   c. One-year interest rates are normally expected to be constant over time.

   d. Bonds are a claim to a sequence of constant payments over a number of years.

   e. Stocks are a claim to a sequence of dividend payments over a number of years.

   f. House prices are a claim to a sequence of expected future rents over a number of years.

   g. The yield curve normally slopes up.

   h. All assets held for one year should have the same expected rate of return.

   i. In a bubble, the value of the asset is the expected present value of its future returns.

   j. The overall real value of the stock market does not fluctuate very much over a year.

   k. Indexed bonds protect the holder against unexpected inflation.

2. *Suppose that an investor buys a three-year bond with the expectations of constant interest rates during the bond's lifetime. According to her calculations, the bond price is now $100. The real interest rate expected by the investor is 5%.*

   a. What happens to the bond price if, following an economic shock, the investor's expectations about the state of the economy worsen, and she now expects a decline in the interest rate next year, for instance to 3%?

   b. What happens to the bond price if the investor expects next year's change in the interest rate to be cancelled out in the third year, that is, the expected interest rate returns to an expected value of 5%?

3. *A famous example of future value calculations using compounding is the acquisition of Manhattan Island by Peter Minuit in 1626. Minuit, who was appointed by the Dutch West India Company Director General of the "New Netherlands" colony on Manhattan, apparently negotiated with and acquired the entire island of Manhattan from a local Indian tribe in exchange for a bundle of goods valued 60 guilders—by some estimates the equivalent of 1.160 of today's U.S. dollars.*

   a. Assuming a constant interest rate of 8% a year, what would be the 2016 value of Manhattan?

b. Do you reckon the value computed is a good approximation of the actual real estate value of Manhattan today? Why or why not?

4. *The equity premium and the value of stocks*

a. Explain why, in equation (14.14), it is important that the stock is ex-dividend, that is, it has just paid its dividend and expects to pay its next dividend in one year.

b. Using equation (14.14), explain the contribution of each component to today's stock price.

c. If the risk premium is larger, all else equal, what happens to the price of the stock today?

d. If the one-period interest rate increases, what happens to the price of the stock today?

e. If the expected value of the stock at the beginning of period $t + 1$ increases, what happens to the value of the stock today?

f. Now look carefully at equation (14.15). Set $i_{1t} = i_{1t+n} = 0.05$ for all n. Set $x = 0.03$. Compute the coefficients on $\$D^e_{t+3}$ and $\$D^e_{t+10}$. Compare the effect of a $1 expected increase in a dividend 3 years from now and 10 years from now.

g. Repeat the computation in (f) with $i_{1t} = i_{1t+n} = 0.08$ for all n and $x = 0.05$.

5. *Arbitrage and bond pricing*

Suppose that a one-year bond with a face value of $1,000 and a two-year bond with a face value of $1,060 are exchanged in the market. Suppose that the two bonds have the exact same risk characteristics. Suppose further that the current interest rate is 5%, and that market participants expect the interest rate to be 6% next year.

a. If investors want to hold the two bonds for one year only, what is the present value of the two bonds?

b. Explain whether arbitrage work in this case or not.

c. Suppose that the two bonds had the same face value. How should the expected one-year interest rate change to make arbitrage work?

6. *Monetary policy and the stock market*

Assume all policy rates, current and expected into the future had been 2%. Suppose the Fed decides to tighten monetary policy and increase the short-term policy rate (r_{1t}) from 2% to 3%.

a. What happens to stock prices if the change in r_{1t} is expected to be temporary, that is, last for only one period? Assume expected real dividends do not change. Use equation (14.17).

b. What happens to stock prices if the change in r_{1t} is expected to be permanent, that is, is expected to persist? Assume expected real dividends do not change. Use equation (14.17).

c. What happens to stock prices today if the change in r_{1t} is expected to be permanent and that change increases expected future output and expected future dividends? Use equation (14.17).

DIG DEEPER

MyEconLab Visit www.myeconlab.com to complete all Dig Deeper problems and get instant feedback.

7. *Risk premium*

Suppose that an investor has a choice between buying a three-year bond with a face value of $60 and a stock paying a constant dividend of $20 per year, which the investor plans to hold for three years. The real interest rate on the stock and the bond is the same,

5%. In addition, the risk premium on the stock is constant at 10%; on the bond, the risk premium is 5%.

a. Compare the present value of the two investments. Which one should the investor chose?

b. Imagine that the risk premia on the stock and the bond were to be equalized at 5%. How would that affect the choice made in part (a)?

c. Suppose, now, that the risk premium is set back at its initial value, which is 10% for the stock, and 5% for the bond. The interest rate changes each year for both securities: 5% in the first year, 8% in the second, and 12% in the third. How would that affect the investor's valuation of the two investments? How do you explain your result?

8. *House prices and bubbles*

Houses can be thought of as assets with a fundamental value equal to the expected present discounted value of their future real rents.

a. Would you prefer to use real payments and real interest rates to value a house or nominal payments and nominal interest rates?

b. The rent on a house, whether you live in the house yourself and thus save paying the rent to an owner, or whether you own the house and rent it, is like the dividend on a stock. Write the equivalent of equation (14.17) for a house.

c. Why would low interest rates help explain an increase in the price-to-rent ratio?

d. If housing is perceived as a safer investment, what will happen to the price-to-rent ratio?

e. The Focus box "The Increase in U.S. Housing Prices: Fundamental or Bubble?" has a graph of the price-to-rent ratio. You should be able to find the value of the Case-Shiller home price index and the rental component of the consumer price index in the FRED economic database maintained at the Federal Reserve Bank of St. Louis (variables *SPCS2ORSA* and *CUSR0000SEHA* respectively). The graph in Figure 1 in this Focus box ends in June 2015. Calculate the percentage increase in the home price index between June and the latest date available. Calculate the percentage increase in the rent price index from June 2015 to the latest date available. Has the price-to-rent ratio increased or decreased since June 2015?

EXPLORE FURTHER

9. *House prices around the world*

The Economist *annually publishes* The Economist House Price Index. *It attempts to assess which housing markets, by country, are the most overvalued or undervalued relative to fundamentals. Find the most recent version of this data on the Web.*

a. One index of overvaluation is the ratio of house prices to rents. Why might this index help detect a housing price bubble? Using the data you are studying, in which country are house prices most overvalued by the ratio of prices to rents? Would this measure have helped predict the U.S. housing market crash?

b. A second index is the ratio of house prices to income. Why might this index help detect a housing price bubble? Using this data, in which country are houses most overvalued by the ratio of prices to rents? Would this measure have helped predict the U.S. housing market crash?

10. Bond prices and the yield curve
   Go to the Japanese Ministry of Finance Web site and get the historical data about government bond yields. The data divides government bonds according to their maturity.
   a. Construct the yield curve for the latest available data. What do you observe? Does the slope of the yield curve correspond to the relationship between bond maturity and yields as explained in the chapter?
   b. Pick another period, preferably a year before the date chosen for part (a). Construct the yield curve again. What has happened to the yield curve during the period? How can you explain it?

Further Readings

- There are many bad books written about the stock market. A good one and one that is fun to read, is Burton Malkiel, *A Random Walk Down Wall Street*, 10th ed. (2011).

- An account of some historical bubbles is given by Peter Garber in "Famous First Bubbles," *Journal of Economic Perspectives*, Spring 1990, 4(2): pp. 35–54.

APPENDIX: Deriving the Expected Present Discounted Value Using Real or Nominal Interest Rates

This appendix shows that the two ways of expressing present discounted values, equations (14.1) and (14.3), are equivalent.

Equation (14.1) gives the present value as the sum of current and future expected *nominal payments*, discounted using current and future expected *nominal interest rates*:

$$\$ V_t = \$ z_t + \frac{1}{1 + i_t} \$ z_{t+1}^e$$
$$+ \frac{1}{(1 + i_t)(1 + i_{t+1}^e)} \$ z_{t+2}^e + \cdots \quad (14.1)$$

Equation (14.3) gives the present value as the sum of current and future expected *real payments*, discounted using current and future expected *real interest rates*:

$$V_t = z_t + \frac{1}{1 + r_t} z_{t+1}^e + \frac{1}{(1 + r_t)(1 + r_{t+1}^e)} z_{t+2}^e + \cdots \quad (14.3)$$

Divide both sides of equation (14.1) by the current price level, P_t, so:

$$\frac{\$ V_t}{P_t} = \frac{\$ z_t}{P_t} + \frac{1}{1 + i_t} \frac{\$ z_{t+1}^e}{P_t} + \frac{1}{(1 + i_t)(1 + i_{t+1}^e)} \frac{\$ z_{t+2}^e}{P_t} + \cdots$$
$$(14.A1)$$

Let's look at each term on the right side of equation (14.3) and show that it is equal to the corresponding term in equation (14.A1):

- Take the first term, $\$ z_t / P_t$. Note $\$ z_t / P_t = z_t$, the real value of the current payment. So, this term is the same as the first term on the right of equation (14.3).
- Take the second term:

$$\frac{1}{1 + i_t} \frac{\$ z_{t+1}^e}{P_t}$$

Multiply the numerator and the denominator by P_{t+1}^e, the price level expected for next year, to get:

$$\frac{1}{1 + i_t} \frac{P_{t+1}^e}{P_t} \frac{\$ z_{t+1}^e}{P_{t+1}^e}$$

Note that the fraction on the right, $\$ z_{t+1}^e / P_{t+1}^e$, is equal to z_{t+1}^e, the expected real payment at time $t + 1$. Note that the fraction in the middle, P_{t+1}^e / P_t, can be rewritten as $1 + [(P_{t+1}^e - P_t)/P_t]$. Using the definition of expected inflation as $(1 + \pi_{t+1}^e)$ and the rewriting of the middle term, we arrive at:

$$\frac{(1 + \pi_{t+1}^e)}{(1 + i_t)} z_{t+1}^e$$

Recall the relation among the real interest rate, the nominal interest rate, and expected inflation in equation (14.3) $(1 + r_t) = (1 + i_t)/(1 + \pi_{t+1}^e)$. Using this relation in the previous equation gives:

$$\frac{1}{(1 + r_t)} z_{t+1}^e$$

This term is the same as the second term on the right side of equation (14.3).

- The same method can be used to rewrite the other terms; make sure that you can derive the next one.

We have shown that the right sides of equations (14.3) and (14.A1) are equal to each other. It follows that the terms on the left side are equal, so:

$$V_t = \frac{\$ V_t}{P_t}$$

This says that the present value of current and future expected *real payments*, discounted using current and future expected *real interest rates* (the term on the left side), is equal to the present value of current and future expected *nominal payments*, discounted using current and future expected *nominal interest rates*, divided by the current price level (the term on the left side).

15

Expectations, Consumption, and Investment

H aving looked at the role of expectations in financial markets, we now turn to the role expecta- MyEconLab Video
tions play in determining the two main components of spending—consumption and investment.
This description of consumption and investment will be the main building block of the expanded
IS–LM model we develop in Chapter 16.

Section 15-1 looks at consumption and shows how consumption decisions depend not only
on a person's current income but also on his or her expected future income and on financial
wealth.

Section 15-2 turns to investment and shows how investment decisions depend on current
and expected profits and on current and expected real interest rates.

Section 15-3 looks at the movements in consumption and investment over time and shows
how to interpret those movements in light of what you learned in this chapter.

15-1 Consumption

How do people decide how much to consume and how much to save? In Chapter 3, we assumed that consumption depended only on current income. But even then, it was clear that consumption depended on much more, particularly on expectations about the future. We now explore how those expectations affect the consumption decision.

Friedman received the Nobel Prize in economics in 1976; Modigliani received the Nobel Prize in economics in 1985.

The modern theory of consumption, on which this section is based, was developed independently in the 1950s by Milton Friedman of the University of Chicago, who called it the **permanent income theory of consumption**, and by Franco Modigliani of MIT, who called it the **life cycle theory of consumption**. Each chose his label carefully. Friedman's "permanent income" emphasized that consumers look beyond current income. Modigliani's "life cycle" emphasized that consumers' natural planning horizon is their entire lifetime.

From Chapter 3: Consumption spending accounts for 68% of total spending in the United States.

The behavior of aggregate consumption has remained a hot area of research ever since, for two reasons: One is simply the sheer size of consumption as a component of GDP and therefore the need to understand movements in consumption. The other is the increasing availability of large surveys of individual consumers, such as the Panel Study of Income Dynamics (PSID). These surveys, which were not available when Friedman and Modigliani developed their theories, have allowed economists to steadily improve their understanding of how consumers actually behave. This section summarizes what we know today. The Focus box "Understanding Aggregate Consumption Patterns" looks at the Eurosystem Household Finance and Consumption Survey.

The Very Foresighted Consumer

Let's start with an assumption that will surely—and rightly—strike you as extreme, but will serve as a convenient benchmark. We'll call it the theory of the *very foresighted consumer*. How would a very foresighted consumer decide how much to consume? He would proceed in two steps:

With a slight abuse of language, we shall use *housing wealth* to refer not only to housing, but also to the other goods that the consumer may own, from cars to paintings and so on.

MyEconLab Video

■ First, he would add up the value of the stocks and bonds he owns, the value of his checking and savings accounts, the value of the house he owns minus the mortgage still due, and so on. This would give him an idea of his **financial wealth** and his **housing wealth**.

He would also estimate what his after-tax labor income was likely to be over his working life and compute the present value of expected after-tax labor income. This would give him an estimate of what economists call his **human wealth**—to contrast it with his **nonhuman wealth**, defined as the sum of financial wealth and housing wealth.

Human wealth + Nonhuman wealth = Total wealth

■ Adding his human wealth and nonhuman wealth, he would have an estimate of his **total wealth**. He would then decide how much to spend out of this total wealth. A reasonable assumption is that he would decide to spend a proportion of his total wealth such as to maintain roughly the same level of consumption each year throughout his life. If that level of consumption were higher than his current income, he would then borrow the difference. If it were lower than his current income, he would instead save the difference.

Let's write this formally. What we have described is a consumption decision of the form

$$C_t = C(\text{total wealth}_t) \tag{15.1}$$

where C_t is consumption at time t, and (total wealth$_t$) is the sum of nonhuman wealth (financial plus housing wealth) and human wealth at time t (the expected present value, as of time t, of current and future after-tax labor income).

This description contains much truth. Like the foresighted consumer, we surely do think about our wealth and our expected future labor income when deciding how much

Understanding Aggregate Consumption Patterns: The Eurosystem Household Finance and Consumption Survey

In 2010, the first Eurosystem Household Finance and Consumption Survey (HFCS) was performed in Euro-area countries, under the supervision of the European Central Bank, national central banks and statistical offices. The HFCS collects household-level data on European households' financial assets and liabilities, wealth, and consumption patterns. The first wave of the HFCS covered 62,000 households in the 15 Euro-area member countries.

The survey's questions cover a wide range of issues relating to households' finances and consumption patterns, which then allow policy makers, statisticians and economists (and others) to draw important indications in terms of aggregate economic behavior. For instance, the survey enables researchers to study the relationship between changing patterns of financial investment and savings among households, on the one hand, and aggregate spending decisions on the other hand. Since the survey contains detailed information about household debt and access to credit, economists may also use the HFCS to probe the effects of changes in mortgage lending rates on patterns of house acquisition.

Source: The HFCS homepage, http://www.ecb.europa.eu/pub/economic-research/research-networks/html/researcher_hfcn.en.html.

to consume today. But one cannot help thinking that it assumes too much computation and foresight on the part of the typical consumer.

To get a better sense of what this description implies and what is wrong with it, let's apply this decision process to a problem facing a typical U.S. college student.

An Example

Let's assume you are 19 years old, with three more years of college before you start your first job. You may be in debt today, having taken out a loan to go to college. You may own a car and a few other worldly possessions. For simplicity, let's assume your debt and your possessions roughly offset each other, so that your nonhuman wealth is equal to zero. Your only wealth therefore is your human wealth, the present value of your expected after-tax labor income.

You expect your starting annual salary in three years to be around $40,000 (in 2015 dollars) and to increase by an average of 3% per year in real terms, until your retirement at age 60. About 25% of your income will go to taxes.

Building on what we saw in Chapter 14, let's compute the present value of your labor income as the value of *real* expected after-tax labor income, discounted using *real* interest rates. Let Y_{Lt} denote real labor income in year t. Let T_t denote real taxes in year t. Let $V(Y_{Lt}^e - T_t^e)$ denote your human wealth; that is, the expected present value of your after-tax labor income—expected as of year t.

To make the computation simple, assume the rate at which you can borrow is equal to zero—so the expected present value is simply the sum of expected labor income over your working life and is therefore given by

$$V(Y_{Lt}^e - T_t^e) = (\$40{,}000)(0.75)[1 + (1.03) + (1.03)^2 + \cdots + (1.03)^{38}]$$

The first term ($40,000) is your initial level of labor income, in year 2015 dollars.

The second term (0.75) comes from the fact that, because of taxes, you keep only 75% of what you earn.

The third term $[1 + (1.03) + (1.03)^2 + \cdots + (1.03)^{38}]$ reflects the fact that you expect your real income to increase by 3% a year for 39 years (you will start earning income at age 22, and work until age 60).

You are welcome to use your own numbers and see where ◀ the computation takes you.

The computation of the consumption level you can sustain is made much easier by our assumption that the real interest rate you face equals zero, which is why I made it! In this case, if you consume one less good today, you can consume exactly one more good next year, and the condition you must satisfy is simply that the sum of consumption over ▶ your lifetime is equal to your wealth. So, if you want to consume a constant amount each year, you just need to divide your wealth by the remaining number of years you expect to live.

Using the properties of geometric series to solve for the sum in brackets gives

$$V(Y_{Lt}^e - T_t^e) = (\$40,000)(0.75)(72.2) = \$2,166,000$$

Your wealth today, the expected value of your lifetime after-tax labor income, is around $2 million.

How much should you consume? You can expect to live about 20 years after you retire, so that your expected remaining life today is 62 years. If you want to consume the same amount every year, the constant level of consumption that you can afford equals your total wealth divided by your expected remaining life, or $2,166,000/62 = $34,935 a year. Given that your income until you get your first job is equal to zero, this implies you will have to borrow $34,935 a year for the next three years, and begin to save when you get your first job.

Toward a More Realistic Description

Your first reaction to this computation may be that this is a stark and slightly sinister way of summarizing your life prospects. You might find yourself more in agreement with the retirement plans described in the cartoon on the next page.

Your second reaction may be that although you agree with most of the ingredients that went into the computation, you surely do not intend to borrow $34,935 × 3 = $104,805 over the next three years. For example:

1. You might not want to plan for constant consumption over your lifetime. Instead you may be quite happy to defer higher consumption until later. Student life usually does not leave much time for expensive activities. You may want to defer trips to the Galapagos Islands to later in life. You also have to think about the additional expenses that will come with having children, sending them to nursery school, summer camp, college, and so on.

2. You might find that the amount of computation and foresight involved in the computation we just went through far exceeds the amount you use in your own decisions. You may never have thought until now about exactly how much income you are going to earn, and for how many years. You might feel that most consumption decisions are made in a simpler, less forward-looking fashion.

3. The computation of total wealth is based on forecasts of what is expected to happen. But things can turn out better or worse. What happens if you are unlucky and you become unemployed or sick? How will you pay back what you borrowed? You might want to be prudent, making sure that you can adequately survive even the worst outcomes, and thus decide to borrow much less than $104,805.

4. Even if you decide to borrow $104,805, you might have a hard time finding a bank willing to lend it to you. Why? The bank may worry that you are taking on a commitment you will not be able to afford if times turn bad and that you may not be able or willing to repay the loan. In other words, if you want to borrow this much money, the borrowing rate you face may be much higher than assumed in the computation.

These reasons, all good ones, suggest that to characterize consumers' actual behavior, we must modify the description we gave previously. The last three reasons in particular suggest that consumption depends not only on total wealth but also on current income.

Take the second reason: You may, because it is a simple rule, decide to let your consumption follow your income and not think about what your wealth might be. In that case your consumption will depend on your current income, not on your wealth.

Now take the third reason: It implies that a safe rule may be to consume no more than your current income. This way, you do not run the risk of accumulating debt that you cannot repay if times were to turn bad.

UNUSUAL RETIREMENT PLANS

1000-F.A.I.

I'll take a thousand bucks, stick it in a bank, "forget about it," and in thirty years I'll be pleasantly surprised.

M.K. Plan

"My Kids" will take care of me. I'm virtually certain of that.

Jackpot Account

I'm not going to need one, because I'm going to be RICH, yessirree Bob.

The ? Plan

Who can plan, like, next week? Because an asteroid could smash into the Earth tomorrow, so what's the point?

Or take the fourth reason: It implies that you may have little choice anyway. Even if you wanted to consume more than your current income, you might be unable to do so because no bank will give you a loan.

If we want to allow for a direct effect of current income on consumption, what measure of current income should we use? A convenient measure is after-tax labor income, which we introduced when we defined human wealth. This leads to a consumption function of the form

$$C_t = C(\text{Total wealth}_t, \ Y_{Lt} - T_t) \tag{15.2}$$
$$(\quad + \quad , \quad + \quad)$$

In words, consumption is an increasing function of total wealth and also an increasing function of current after-tax labor income. Total wealth is the sum of nonhuman

How Much Do Expectations Matter in Estonia?

FOCUS

The theoretical model linking current consumption to expectations about future earnings or total human wealth can be tested in different ways. One possibility is to examine whether household consumption reacts differently to income changes that have different impacts on a household's total human wealth (e.g., permanent or transitory income changes). The study of Kukk, Kulikov, and Staehr (2012) investigates this hypothesis in Estonia by using a Household Budget Survey. The survey observes monthly income and consumption of a household twice yearly, so it is possible to compare the consumption change to income change. Additionally, the database enables us to distinguish temporary income fluctuation from income changes that last longer. The study covers the period of 2002–2007—when the Estonian economy experienced rapid growth.

The study reveals that households use expectations when formulating consumption, but also relate their consumption to current income. More precisely, the results indicate that households' consumption reacts stronger to more persistent income changes than to transitory income changes: An increase in more persistent income by 10% increases consumption by 3.3%, while a transitory income change of the same magnitude increases consumption by 2%. The evidence that households also react to transitory income indicates a relationship between current income and consumption.

However, the changes in current income capture only a fraction of possible changes in total lifetime human wealth. It is more challenging to test whether current consumption is affected by households' expectations regarding their long-term lifetime human wealth. Nevertheless, the Estonian case gives several hints about the presence of the relationship.

Figure 1 illustrates that Estonia has experienced, in addition to volatile GDP growth, the most volatile household consumption-to-disposable-income rate in Europe since 2000. During 2003–2007, households were even spending more than they earned; household spending reached its peak in 2006, when consumption exceeded current income by 6.3%. At the same time the real GDP growth reached 10.1%. Three years later in 2009, when the economy was experiencing the sharp recession and GDP fell by 14.3%, household consumption was only 88.4% of household disposable income.

The increasing consumption-to-income rate until 2006 can be explained by expectations of households about their increasing long-term income and wealth. Estonia, as other Central and Eastern European countries, has undergone a rapid economic transformation since the beginning of the 1990s, when Estonia regained independence and introduced a market economy. The economy has expanded rapidly since; the EU accession in 2004 supported optimistic expectations about a fast convergence of the economy and wages to the Eurozone countries. The vigorous economic growth was accompanied by promises from politicians about remarkable wage increases that were also witnessed in 2006–2007—when real wages increased by 12%–13%. Still consumption was increasing faster than income, as seen from the increasing consumption-to-income ratio. It can be explained by the optimistic assessment of consumers' continuous future wealth increases. Consequently, households started to consume bravely based on their expected future wealth.

The recession that reached Estonia at the end of 2007 and hit bottom in 2009, bringing a real wage decrease by 5%, forced consumers to adjust their expectations. The understanding that the economy and wages were not going to grow in double-digit numbers forever and that convergence can take several decades compelled households to reevaluate their expectations about future wealth and therefore revise their consumption habits. As a result, households contracted their consumption more than their income decreased.

It can be debated whether households voluntarily decreased their consumption because of falling expectations or whether the reason lies behind more strict credit conditions that constrained the consumption. However, according to the survey of household financial behavior in Estonia, the demand for borrowing diminished in 2009, indicating that the decrease in borrowing and consuming was mainly decided by consumers.

Sources: Merike Kukk, Dmitry Kulikov, and Karsten Staehr (2012). "Consumption Sensitivities in Estonia: Income Shocks of Different Persistence," Bank of Estonia Working Papers, No. 3. Jaanika Meriküll (2012). "Households Borrowing during Creditless Recovery," Bank of Estonia Working Papers, No. 2. Dmitry Kulikov, Annika Paabut, and Karsten Staehr (2009). "A Microeconometric Analysis of Household Saving in Estonia: Income, Wealth and Financial Exposure." In Mayes, D. (ed.), Microfoundations of Economic Success: Lessons from Estonia, Edward Elgar, Ch. 6, pp. 190–241, Edward Elgar Publishing, Cheltenham, UK, 2009.

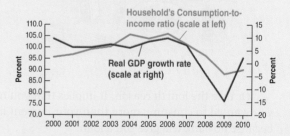

Figure 1 *Real GDP Growth Rate and Households' Consumption-to-Income Rate in Estonia*

Note: Households' consumption-to-income ratio is reverse of households' saving ratio computed by national statistics.

Source: Eurostat. Statistics database. Available at: http://epp.eurostat.ec.europa.eu/portal/page/portal/eurostat/home.

wealth—financial wealth plus housing wealth—and human wealth—the present value of expected after-tax labor income.

How much does consumption depend on total wealth (and therefore on expectations of future income) and how much does it depend on current income? The evidence is that most consumers look forward in the spirit of the theory developed by Modigliani and Friedman. (See the Focus box "How Much Do Expectations Matter in Estonia?") But some consumers, especially those who have temporarily low income and poor access to credit, are likely to consume their current income, regardless of what they expect will happen to them in the future. A worker who becomes unemployed and has no financial wealth may have a hard time borrowing to maintain her level of consumption, even if she is fairly confident that she will soon find another job. Consumers who are richer and have easier access to credit are more likely to give more weight to the expected future and to try to maintain roughly constant consumption over time.

Putting Things Together: Current Income, Expectations, and Consumption

Let's go back to what motivates this chapter—the importance of expectations in the determination of spending. Note first that, with consumption behavior described by equation (15.2), expectations affect consumption in two ways:

■ Expectations affect consumption directly through *human wealth*: To compute their human wealth, consumers have to form their own expectations about future labor income, real interest rates, and taxes.

■ Expectations affect consumption indirectly, through *nonhuman wealth*—stocks, bonds, and housing. Consumers do not need to do any computation here and can just take the value of these assets as given. As you saw in Chapter 14, the computation is in effect done for them by participants in financial markets. The price of their stocks, for example, itself depends on expectations of future dividends and interest rates.

This dependence of consumption on expectations has in turn two main implications for the relation between consumption and income:

■ *Consumption is likely to respond less than one-for-one to fluctuations in current income.* When deciding how much to consume, a consumer looks at more than her current income. If she concludes that the decrease in her income is permanent, she is likely to decrease consumption one-for-one with the decrease in income. But if she concludes that the decrease in her current income is transitory, she will adjust her consumption by less. In a recession, consumption adjusts less than one-for-one to decreases in income. This is because consumers know that recessions typically do not last for more than a few quarters and that the economy will eventually return to the natural level of output. The same is true in expansions. Faced with an unusually rapid increase in income, consumers are unlikely to increase consumption by as much as income. They are likely to assume that the boom is transitory and that things will return to normal.

■ *Consumption may move even if current income does not change.* The election of a charismatic president who articulates the vision of an exciting future may lead people to become more optimistic about the future in general, and about their own future income in particular, leading them to increase consumption even if their current income does not change. Other events may have the opposite effect.

The effects of the recent crisis are particularly striking in this respect. Figure 15-1 shows, using data from a survey of consumers, the evolution of expectations about family income growth over the following year, for each year since 1990. Note how

How expectations of higher output in the future affect consumption today:

Expected future output increases
⇒ Expected future labor income increases
⇒ Human wealth increases
⇒ Consumption increases

Expected future output increases
⇒ Expected future dividends increase
⇒ Stock prices increase
⇒ Nonhuman wealth increases
◀ ⇒ Consumption increases

◀ Looking at the short run (Chapter 3), we assumed $C = c_0 + c_1 Y$ (ignoring taxes here). This implied that, when income increased, consumption increased less than proportionately with income (C/Y went down). This was appropriate because our focus was on fluctuations, on transitory movements in income.
Looking at the long run (Chapter 10), we assumed that $S = sY$, or equivalently $C = (1 - s)Y$. This implied that, when income increased, consumption increased proportionately with income (C/Y remained the same). This was appropriate because our focus was on permanent—long run—movements in income.

Figure 15-1

Expected Change in Family Income since 1990

After falling sharply in 2008, expectations of income growth remained low for a long time.

Source: Surveys of Consumers, Thomson Reuters and University of Michigan, https://data.sca.isr.umich.edu.

The shaded areas represent recessions.

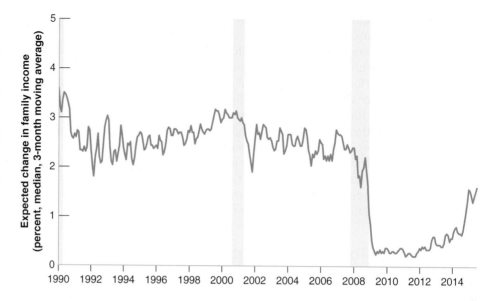

expectations remained relatively stable until 2008, how sharply they dropped in 2009, and how long they remained low after that. Only since 2014 have they started to recover. The drop at the start of the crisis is not surprising. As consumers saw output falling, it was normal for them to expect a drop in income over the following year. Both previous recessions, in 1991 and in 2000, also had a drop in expected income growth. What is different about the recent crisis is how long it has taken for expectations of income growth to recover, and so far, only partially. Low expectations of income growth have led consumers to limit their consumption, and this in turn has led to a slow and painful recovery.

15-2 Investment

How do firms make investment decisions? In our first pass at the answer in the core (Chapter 5), we took investment to depend on the current interest rate and the current level of sales. We refined that answer in Chapter 6 by pointing out that what mattered was the real interest rate, not the nominal interest rate. It should now be clear that investment decisions, just as consumption decisions, depend on more than current sales and the current real interest rate. They also depend very much on expectations of the future. We now explore how those expectations affect investment decisions.

Just like the basic theory of consumption, the basic theory of investment is straightforward. A firm deciding whether to invest—say, whether to buy a new machine—must make a simple comparison. The firm must first compute the present value of profits it can expect from having this additional machine. It must then compare the present value of profits to the cost of buying the machine. If the present value exceeds the cost, the firm should buy the machine—invest; if the present value is less than the cost, then the firm should not buy the machine—not invest. This, in a nutshell, is the theory of investment. Let's look at it in more detail.

Investment and Expectations of Profit

Let's go through the steps a firm must take to determine whether to buy a new machine. (Although we refer to a machine, the same reasoning applies to the other components of investment—the building of a new factory, the renovation of an office complex, and so on.)

Depreciation

To compute the present value of expected profits, the firm must first estimate how long the machine will last. Most machines are like cars. They can last nearly forever, but as time passes, they become more and more expensive to maintain and less and less reliable. ◀ Look at cars in Cuba.

Assume a machine loses its usefulness at rate δ (the Greek lowercase letter delta) per year. A machine that is new this year is worth only $(1 - \delta)$ machines next year, $(1 - \delta)^2$ machines in two years, and so on. The *depreciation rate*, δ, measures how much usefulness the machine loses from one year to the next. What are reasonable values for δ? This is a question that the statisticians in charge of measuring the U.S. capital stock have had to answer. Based on their studies of depreciation of specific machines and buildings, U.S. statisticians use numbers from 2.5% for office buildings, to 15% for communication equipment, to 55% for pre-packaged software.

If the firm has a large number of machines, we can think of δ as the proportion of machines that die every year (think of light bulbs, which work perfectly until they die). If the firm starts the year with K working machines and does not buy new ones, it will have only $K(1 - \delta)$ machines left one year later, and so on.

The Present Value of Expected Profits

The firm must then compute the present value of expected profits.

To capture the fact that it takes some time to put machines in place (and even more time to build a factory or an office building), let's assume that a machine bought in year t becomes operational—and starts depreciating—only one year later, in year $t + 1$. Denote profit per machine in real terms by Π.

This is an uppercase Greek pi as opposed to the lowercase Greek pi, which we use to denote inflation. ◀

If the firm buys a machine in year t, the machine will generate its first profit in year $t + 1$; denote this expected profit by Π^e_{t+1}. The present value, in year t, of this expected profit in year $t + 1$, is given by

For simplicity, and to focus on the role of expectations as opposed to risk, let me assume again that the risk premium is equal to zero, so we do not have to carry it along in the formulas below. ◀

$$\frac{1}{1 + r_t} \Pi^e_{t+1}$$

This term is represented by the arrow pointing left in the upper line of Figure 15-2. Because we are measuring profit in real terms, we are using real interest rates to discount future profits.

Denote expected profit per machine in year $t + 2$ by Π^e_{t+2}. Because of depreciation, only $(1 - \delta)$ of the machine is left in year $t + 2$, so the expected profit from the machine is equal to $(1 + \delta)\Pi^e_{t+2}$. The present value of this expected profit as of year t is equal to

$$\frac{1}{(1 + r_t)(1 + r^e_{t+1})}(1 - \delta)\Pi^e_{t+2}$$

This computation is represented by the arrow pointing left in the lower line of Figure 15-2.

The same reasoning applies to expected profits in the following years. Putting the pieces together gives us *the present value of expected profits* from buying the machine in year t, which we shall call $V(\Pi^e_t)$:

$$V(\Pi^e_t) = \frac{1}{1 + r_t} \Pi^e_{t+1} + \frac{1}{(1 + r_t)(1 + r^e_{t+1})}(1 - \delta)\Pi^e_{t+2} + \cdots \quad (15.3)$$

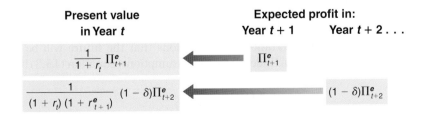

Present value in Year t	Expected profit in:	
	Year $t + 1$	Year $t + 2 \ldots$
$\frac{1}{1 + r_t} \Pi^e_{t+1}$	Π^e_{t+1}	
$\frac{1}{(1 + r_t)(1 + r^e_{t+1})}(1 - \delta)\Pi^e_{t+2}$		$(1 - \delta)\Pi^e_{t+2}$

Figure 15-2

Computing the Present Value of Expected Profits

MyEconLab Animation

The expected present value is equal to the discounted value of expected profit next year, plus the discounted value of expected profit two years from now (taking into account the depreciation of the machine), and so on.

The Investment Decision

The firm must then decide whether or not to buy the machine. This decision depends on the relation between the present value of expected profits and the price of the machine. To simplify notation, let's assume the real price of a machine—that is, the machine's price in terms of the basket of goods produced in the economy—equals 1. What the firm must then do is to compare the present value of profits to 1.

If the present value is less than 1, the firm should not buy the machine. If it did, it would be paying more for the machine than it expects to get back in profits later. If the present value exceeds 1, the firm has an incentive to buy the new machine.

Let's now go from this one-firm one-machine example to investment in the economy as a whole.

Let I_t denote aggregate investment.

Denote profit per machine, or, more generally, profit per unit of capital (where capital includes machines, factories, office buildings, and so on) for the economy as a whole by Π_t.

Denote the expected present value of profit per unit of capital by $V(\Pi_t^e)$, as defined in equation (15.3).

Our discussion suggests an investment function of the form

$$I_t = I[V(\Pi_t^e)] \qquad (15.4)$$
$$(\quad + \quad)$$

In words: Investment depends positively on the expected present value of future profits (per unit of capital). The higher the expected profits, the higher the expected present value and the higher the level of investment. The higher expected real interest rates, the lower the expected present value, and thus the lower the level of investment.

If the present value computation the firm has to make strikes you as quite similar to the present value computation we saw in Chapter 14 for the fundamental value of a

Tobin received the Nobel Prize in economics in 1981 for this and many other contributions.

stock, you are right. This relation was first explored by James Tobin, from Yale University, who argued that, for this reason, there should indeed be a tight relation between investment and the value of the stock market. See the Focus box "Investment and the Stock Market."

A Convenient Special Case

Before exploring further implications and extensions of equation (15.4), it is useful to go through a special case where the relation among investment, profit, and interest rates becomes simple.

Suppose firms expect both future profits (per unit of capital) and future interest rates to remain at the same level as today, so that

$$\Pi_{t+1}^e = \Pi_{t+2}^e = \cdots = \Pi_t$$

and

$$r_{t+1}^e = r_{t+2}^e = \cdots = r_t$$

Economists call such expectations—expectations that the future will be like the present—**static expectations**. Under these two assumptions, equation (15.3) becomes

$$V(\Pi_t^e) = \frac{\Pi_t}{r_t + \delta} \qquad (15.5)$$

Investment and the Stock Market

Suppose a firm has 100 machines and 100 shares outstanding—one share per machine. Suppose the price per share is $2, and the purchase price of a machine is only $1. Obviously the firm should invest—buy a new machine—and finance it by issuing a share. Each machine costs the firm $1 to purchase, but stock market participants are willing to pay $2 for a share corresponding to this machine when it is installed in the firm.

This is an example of a more general argument made by Tobin that there should be a tight relation between the stock market and investment. When deciding whether or not to invest, he argued firms might not need to go through the type of complicated computation you saw in the text. In effect, the stock price tells firms how much the stock market values each unit of capital already in place. The firm then has a simple problem. Compare the purchase price of an additional unit of capital to the price the stock market is willing to pay

for it. *If the stock market value exceeds the purchase price, the firm should buy the machine; otherwise, it should not.*

Tobin then constructed a variable corresponding to the value of a unit of capital in place relative to its purchase price and looked at how closely it moved with investment. He used the symbol *q* to denote the variable, and the variable has become known as **Tobin's *q***. Its construction is as follows:

1. Take the total value of U.S. corporations, as assessed by financial markets. That is, compute the sum of their stock market value (the price of a share times the number of shares). Compute also the total value of their bonds outstanding (firms finance themselves not only through stocks but also through bonds). Add together the value of stocks and bonds. Subtract the firms' financial assets, the value of the cash, bank accounts, and any bonds the firms might hold.

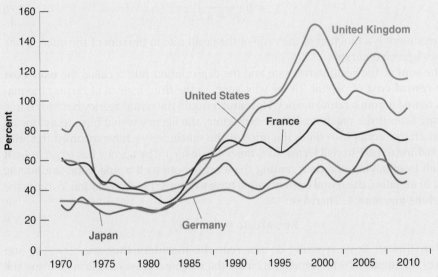

Figure 1 *Estimated Tobin's q for Selected Countries, 1970–2010*

Source: Piketty (2014).

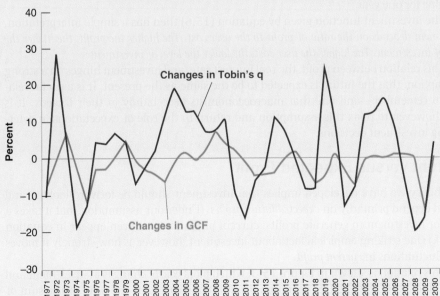

Figure 2 *Changes in Tobin's q and in Gross Capital Formation as % of GDP for Japan, 1971–2010.*

Source: Piketty (2014) and the World Bank; Thomas Piketty, *Capital in the 21st Century*, Harvard University Press 2014, Cambridge, MA.

2. Divide this total value by the value of the capital stock of U.S. corporations at replacement cost (the price firms would have to pay to replace their machines, their plants, and so on).

The ratio gives us, in effect, the value of a unit of capital in place relative to its current purchase price. This ratio is *Tobin's q*. Intuitively, the higher *q*, the higher the value of capital relative to its current purchase price, and the higher investment should be. (In the example at the start of the box, Tobin's *q* is equal to 2, so the firm should definitely invest.)

How tight is the relation between Tobin's *q* and investment? One way to approach the question is by comparing changes in Tobin's q and changes in investment over time. This is done in the two figures below. The first figure shows estimates for aggregate Tobin's q for five advanced industrial countries, from 1970 until 2010. They are taken from Thomas Piketty's best-selling book on "the Capital in the 21st century" (Piketty, 2014). You can observe a steady increase in Tobin's q for all five countries, starting in the mid-1970s (and after a slight decline in the early 1970s). The fluctuations around 2000 and 2007–2008 represent financial markets booms and busts.

If one plots the annual changes in Tobin's q and in Gross Capital Formation (GCF), the relationship appears much more clearly. As shown in Figure 2, despite much sharper fluctuations, the changes in Tobin's q appear correlated to changes in GCF. This illustrates the fact that investment decisions and stock market prices depend on the same factors: expected future profits and expected changes in the interest rate.

The present value of expected profits is simply the ratio of the profit rate—that is, profit per unit of capital—to the sum of the real interest rate and the depreciation rate. (The derivation is given in the appendix to this chapter.)

Replacing (15.5) in equation (15.4), investment is given by:

$$I_t = I\left(\frac{\Pi_t}{r_t + \delta}\right) \tag{15.6}$$

Investment is a function of the ratio of the profit rate to the sum of the interest rate and the depreciation rate.

The sum of the real interest rate and the depreciation rate is called the **user cost** or the **rental cost** of capital. To see why, suppose the firm, instead of buying the machine, rented it from a rental agency. How much would the rental agency have to charge per year? Even if the machine did not depreciate, the agency would have to ask for an interest charge equal to r_t times the price of the machine (we have assumed the price of a machine to be 1 in real terms, so r_t times 1 is just r_t). The agency has to get at least as much from buying and then renting the machine out as it would from, say, buying bonds. In addition, the rental agency would have to charge for depreciation, δ, times the price of the machine, 1. Therefore:

> Such arrangements exist. For example, many firms lease cars and trucks from leasing companies.

$$\text{Rental cost} = (r_t + \delta)$$

Even though firms typically do not rent the machines they use, $(r_t + \delta)$ still captures the implicit cost—sometimes called the *shadow cost*—to the firm of using the machine for one year.

The investment function given by equation (15.6) then has a simple interpretation. *Investment depends on the ratio of profit to the user cost. The higher the profit, the higher the level of investment. The higher the user cost, the lower the level of investment.*

This relation between profit, the real interest rate, and investment hinges on a strong assumption: that the future is expected to be the same as the present. It is a useful relation to remember—and one that macroeconomists keep handy in their toolbox. It is time, however, to relax this assumption and return to the role of expectations in determining investment decisions.

Current versus Expected Profit

The theory we have developed implies that investment should be forward looking and should depend primarily on *expected future profits*. (Under our assumption that it takes a year for investment to generate profits, current profit does not even appear in equation (15.3).) One striking empirical fact about investment, however, is how strongly it moves with fluctuations in *current profit*.

This relation is shown in Figure 15-3, which plots yearly changes in investment and profit since 1960 for the U.S. economy. Profit is constructed as the ratio of the sum of

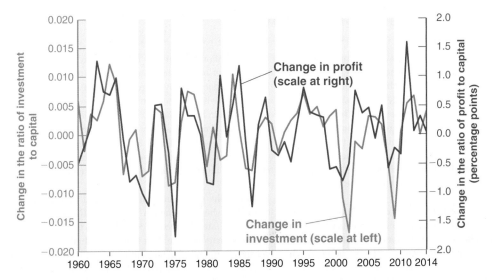

Figure 15-3

Changes in Investment and Changes in Profit in the United States since 1960

Investment and profit move very much together.

Source: Haver Analytics. Original source: Gross investment, Flow of funds variable FA105013005.A; Capital stock measured by Nonfinancial assets; Profit is constructed from Net operating surplus, taxes, and transfers, Bureau of Economic Analysis.

after-tax profits plus interest payments paid by U.S. nonfinancial corporations, divided by their capital stock. Investment is constructed as the ratio of investment by U.S. nonfinancial corporations to their capital stock. Profit is lagged once. For 2000, for example, the figure shows the change in investment for 2000, and the change in profit for 1999—that is, a year earlier. The reason for presenting the two variables this way is that the strongest relation in the data appears to be between investment in a given year and profit the year before—a lag plausibly due to the fact that it takes time for firms to decide on new investment projects in response to higher profit. The shaded areas in the figure represent years in which there was a recession—a decline in output for at least two consecutive quarters of the year.

There is a clear positive relation between changes in investment and changes in current profit in Figure 15-3. Is this relation inconsistent with the theory we have just developed, which holds that investment should be related to the present value of expected future profits rather than to current profit? Not necessarily. If firms expect future profits to move very much like current profit, then the present value of those future profits will move very much like current profit, and so will investment.

Economists who have looked at the question more closely have concluded, however, that the effect of current profit on investment is stronger than would be predicted by the theory we have developed so far. How they have gathered some of the evidence is described in the Focus box on page 344 "Profitability versus Cash Flow." On the one hand some firms with highly profitable investment projects but low current profits appear to be investing too little. On the other hand, some firms that have high current profit appear sometimes to invest in projects of doubtful profitability. In short, current profit appears to affect investment, even after controlling for the expected present value of profits.

Why does current profit play a role in the investment decision? The answer parallels our discussion of consumption in Section 15-1, where we discussed why consumption depends directly on current income; some of the reasons we used to explain the behavior of consumers also apply to firms:

- If its current profit is low, a firm that wants to buy new machines can get the funds it needs only by borrowing. It may be reluctant to borrow. Although expected profits might look good, things may turn bad, leaving the firm unable to repay the debt. But if current profit is high, the firm might be able to finance its investment just by

MyEconLab Video

Profitability versus Cash Flow

How much does investment depend on the expected present value of future profits, and how much does it depend on current profit? In other words: Which is more important for investment decisions: **Profitability** (the expected present discounted value of future profits) or **cash flow** (current profit, the net flow of cash the firm is receiving now)?

The difficulty in answering this question is that, most of the time, cash flow and profitability move together. Firms that do well typically have both large cash flows and good future prospects. Firms that suffer losses often have poor future prospects.

The best way to isolate the effects of cash flow and profitability on investment is to identify times or events when cash flow and profitability move in different directions, and then look at what happens to investment. This is the approach taken by Owen Lamont, an economist at Harvard University. An example will help you understand Lamont's strategy.

Think of two firms, A and B. Both firms are involved in steel production. Firm B is also involved in oil exploration.

Suppose there is a sharp drop in the price of oil, leading to losses in oil exploration. This shock decreases firm B's cash flow. If the losses in oil exploration are large enough to offset the profits from steel production, firm B might even show an overall loss.

The question we can now ask is: As a result of the drop in the price of oil, will firm B invest less in its steel operation than firm A does? If only the profitability of steel production matters, there is no reason for firm B to invest less in its steel operation than firm A. But if current cash flow also matters, the fact that firm B has a lower cash flow may prevent it from investing as much as firm A in its steel operation. Looking at investment in the steel operations of the two firms can tell us how much investment depends on cash flow versus profitability.

This is the empirical strategy followed by Lamont. He focused on what happened in 1986 when the price of oil in the United States dropped by 50%, leading to large losses in oil-related activities. He then looked at whether firms that had substantial oil activities cut investment in their nonoil activities relatively more than other firms in the same non-oil activities. He concluded that they did. He found that for every $1 decrease in cash flow as a result of the decrease in the price of oil, investment spending in nonoil activities was reduced by 10 to 20 cents. In short: Current cash flow matters.

Source: Owen Lamont, "Cash Flow and Investment: Evidence from Internal Capital Markets," *Journal of Finance* 1997, Vol. 52 (1): pp. 83–109.

retaining some of its earnings and without having to borrow. The bottom line is that higher current profit may lead the firm to invest more.

- Even if the firm wants to invest, it might have difficulty borrowing. Potential lenders may not be convinced the project is as good as the firm says it is, and they may worry the firm will be unable to repay. If the firm has large current profits, it does not have to borrow and so does not need to convince potential lenders. It can proceed and invest as it pleases and is more likely to do so.

In summary, to fit the investment behavior we observe in practice, the investment equation is better specified as

$$I_t = I[V(\Pi_t^e), \Pi_t] \qquad (15.7)$$
$$(\ +\ ,\ +)$$

In words: *Investment depends both on the expected present value of future profits and on the current level of profit.*

Profit and Sales

Let's take stock of where we are. We have argued that investment depends both on current profit and on expected profit or, more specifically, current and expected profit per unit of capital. We need to take one last step. What determines profit per unit of capital? Answer: Primarily two factors: (1) the level of sales, and (2) the existing capital stock. If sales are low relative to the capital stock, profits per unit of capital are likely to be low as well.

Let's write this more formally. Ignore the distinction between sales and output, and let Y_t denote output—equivalently, sales. Let K_t denote the capital stock at time t. Our discussion suggests the following relation:

$$\Pi_t = \Pi\left(\frac{Y_t}{K_t}\right) \qquad (15.8)$$
$$(+)$$

Profit per unit of capital is an increasing function of the ratio of sales to the capital stock. For a given capital stock, the higher the sales, the higher the profit per unit of capital. For given sales, the higher the capital stock, the lower the profit per unit of capital.

How well does this relation hold in practice? Figure 15-4 plots yearly changes in profit per unit of capital (measured on the right vertical axis) and changes in the ratio of output to capital (measured on the left vertical axis) for the United States since 1960. As in Figure 15-3, profit per unit of capital is defined as the sum of after-tax profits plus interest payments by U.S. nonfinancial corporations, divided by their capital stock measured at replacement cost. The ratio of output to capital is constructed as the ratio of gross domestic product (GDP) to the aggregate capital stock.

Figure 15-4 shows that there is a strong relation between changes in profit per unit of capital and changes in the ratio of output to capital. Given that most of the year-to-year changes in the ratio of output to capital come from movements in output, and most of the year-to-year changes in profit per unit of capital come from movements in profit (capital moves slowly over time; the reason is that capital is large compared to yearly investment, so even large movements in investment lead to small changes in the capital stock), we can state the relation as follows: Profit decreases in recessions (shaded areas are periods of recession), and increases in expansions.

Why is this relation between output and profit relevant here? Because it implies a link between *current output and expected future output,* on the one hand, and *investment,* on the other. Current output affects current profit, expected future output affects expected future profit, and current and expected future profits affect investment. For example, the anticipation of a long, sustained economic expansion leads firms to expect high profits, now and for some time in the future. These expectations in turn lead to higher investment. The effect of current and expected output on investment, together with the effect of investment back on demand and output, will play a crucial role when we return to the ◀ determination of output in Chapter 16.

High expected output ⇒ High expected profit ⇒ High investment today.

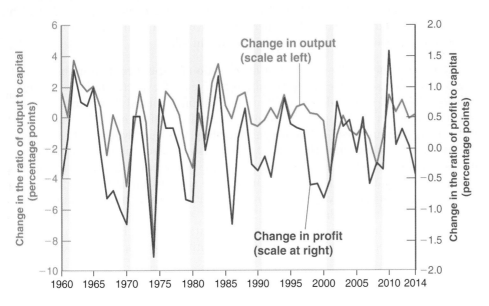

Figure 15-4

Changes in Profit per Unit of Capital versus Changes in the Ratio of Output to Capital in the United States since 1960

Profit per unit of capital and the ratio of output to capital move largely together.

Source: Haver Analytics. Original source: Capital stock measured by Nonfinancial assets, Financial accounts; profit is constructed from net operating surplus, taxes, and transfers, Bureau of Economic Analysis; output of nonfinancial corporate sector is measured by gross value added, Bureau of Economic Analysis.

15-3 The Volatility of Consumption and Investment

You will surely have noticed the similarities between our treatment of consumption and of investment behavior in Sections 15-1 and 15-2:

- Whether consumers perceive current movements in income to be transitory or permanent affects their consumption decision. The more transitory they expect a current increase in income to be, the less they will increase their consumption.

- In the same way, whether firms perceive current movements in sales to be transitory or permanent affects their investment decisions. The more transitory they expect a current increase in sales to be, the less they revise their assessment of the present value of profits, and thus the less likely they are to buy new machines or build new factories. This is why, for example, the boom in sales that happens every year between Thanksgiving and Christmas does not lead to a boom in investment every December. Firms understand that this boom is transitory.

But there are also important differences between consumption decisions and investment decisions:

- The theory of consumption we developed previously implies that when faced with an increase in income consumers perceive as permanent, they respond with, *at most*, an equal increase in consumption. The permanent nature of the increase in income implies that they can afford to increase consumption now and in the future by the same amount as the increase in income. Increasing consumption more than one-for-one would require cuts in consumption later, and there is no reason for consumers to want to plan consumption this way.

- Now consider the behavior of firms faced with an increase in sales they believe to be permanent. The present value of expected profits increases, leading to an increase in investment. In contrast to consumption, however, this does not imply that the increase in investment should be at most equal to the increase in sales. Rather, once a firm has decided that an increase in sales justifies the purchase of a new machine or the building of a new factory, it may want to proceed quickly, leading to a large but short-lived increase in investment spending. This increase in investment spending may exceed the increase in sales.

More concretely, take a firm that has a ratio of capital to its annual sales of, say, 3. An increase in sales of $10 million this year, if expected to be permanent, requires the firm to spend $30 million on additional capital if it wants to maintain the same ratio of capital to output. If the firm buys the additional capital right away, the increase in investment spending this year will equal *three times* the increase in sales. Once the capital stock has adjusted, the firm will return to its normal pattern of investment. This example is extreme because firms do not adjust their capital stock right away. But even if they do adjust their capital stock more slowly, say over a few years, the increase in investment might still exceed the increase in sales for a while.

We can tell the same story in terms of equation (15.8). Because we make no distinction here between output and sales, the initial increase in sales leads to an

In the United States, retail sales are 24% higher on average in December than in other months. In France and Italy, sales are 60% higher in ▶ December.

Expectations   Extensions

equal increase in output, Y, so that Y/K—the ratio of the firm's output to its existing capital stock—also increases. The result is higher profit, which leads the firm to undertake more investment. Over time, the higher level of investment leads to a higher capital stock, K, so that Y/K decreases back to normal. Profit per unit of capital returns to normal and so does investment. Thus, in response to a permanent increase in sales, investment may increase a lot initially, and then return to normal over time.

These differences suggest that investment should be more volatile than consumption. How much more? The answer is given in Figure 15-5, which plots yearly rates of change in U.S. consumption and investment since 1960. The shaded areas are years during which the U.S. economy was in recession. To make the figure easier to interpret, both rates of change are plotted as deviations from the average rate of change over the period, so that they are, on average, equal to zero.

Figure 15-5 yields three conclusions:

■ Consumption and investment usually move together. Recessions, for example, are typically associated with decreases in *both* investment and consumption. Given our discussion, which has emphasized that consumption and investment depend largely on the same determinants, this should not come as a surprise.

■ Investment is much more volatile than consumption. Relative movements in investment range from -29% to $+26\%$, whereas relative movements in consumption range only from -5% to $+3\%$.

■ Because, however, the level of investment is much smaller than the level of consumption (recall that investment accounts for about 15% of GDP, versus 70% for consumption), changes in investment from one year to the next end up being of the same overall magnitude as changes in consumption. In other words, both components contribute roughly equally to fluctuations in output over time.

MyEconLab Video

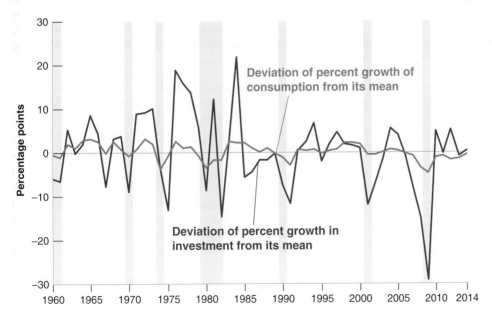

Figure 15-5

Rates of Change of Consumption and Investment in the United States since 1960

Relative movements in investment are much larger than relative movements in consumption.

Source: Series PCECC96, GPDI Federal Reserve Economic Data (FRED) http://research.stlouisfed.org/fred2/.

MyEconLab Real-time data

Summary

- Consumption depends on both wealth and current income. Wealth is the sum of nonhuman wealth (financial wealth and housing wealth) and human wealth (the present value of expected after-tax labor income).

- The response of consumption to changes in income depends on whether consumers perceive these changes as transitory or permanent.

- Consumption is likely to respond less than one-for-one to movements in income. Consumption might move even if current income does not change.

- Investment depends on both current profit and the present value of expected future profits.

- Under the simplifying assumption that firms expect profits and interest rates to be the same in the future as they are today, we can think of investment as depending on the ratio of profit to the user cost of capital, where the user cost is the sum of the real interest rate and the depreciation rate.

- Movements in profit are closely related to movements in output. Hence, we can think of investment as depending indirectly on current and expected future output movements. Firms that anticipate a long output expansion, and thus a long sequence of high profits, will invest. Movements in output that are not expected to last will have a small effect on investment.

- Investment is much more volatile than consumption. But because investment accounts only for 15% of GDP and consumption accounts for 70%, movements in investment and consumption are of roughly equal importance in accounting for movements in aggregate output.

Key Terms

permanent income theory of consumption, 332
life cycle theory of consumption, 332
financial wealth, 332
housing wealth, 332
human wealth, 332
nonhuman wealth, 332
total wealth, 332

static expectations, 340
Tobin's q, 341
user cost, 342
rental cost, 342
profitability, 344
cash flow, 344

Questions and Problems

QUICK CHECK

MyEconLab Visit www.myeconlab.com to complete similar Quick Check problems and get instant feedback.

1. Using the information in this chapter, label each of the following statements true, false, or uncertain. Explain briefly.

a. For a typical college student, human wealth and nonhuman wealth are approximately equal.

b. Natural experiments, such as retirement, do not suggest that expectations of future income are a major factor affecting consumption.

c. Following the financial crisis, expected future income growth fell.

d. Buildings and factories depreciate much faster than machines.

e. A high value for Tobin's q indicates that the stock market believes that capital is overvalued, and thus investment should be lower.

f. Unless current profit affects expectations of future profit, it should have no impact on investment.

g. Data from the past three decades in the United States suggest that corporate profits are closely tied to the business cycle.

h. Changes in consumption and investment typically occur in the same direction and are roughly of the same magnitude.

2. Two friends, Lucy and Adam, start working at the same time, right after graduating from university. Lucy works as a computer programmer for an annual salary of $70,000; Adam as a teacher for an annual salary of $45,000. Both friends expect their annual salary to increase by 2% in real terms each year for the next 3 years. The real interest rate is 0% and the tax rate on labor income is 30% for both friends. Lucy has no nonhuman wealth, while Adam was just bequeathed $50,000 worth of bonds from an old aunt who passed away.

a. Calculate the human wealth and the total wealth of the two friends over the next three years (assume there is uncertainty about the future beyond during these three years).

b. If both friends wanted to maintain a constant consumption level over this period, what would that consumption level be?

c. How would an increase in taxation (to, for instance, 40%) affect the relative wealth positions of Lucy and Adam? How would that affect their permanent consumption levels?

d. Suppose that Lucy works for a firm whose stock market value jumps after being bought by a multinational, and that as a result, Lucy, along with all her colleagues, sees her salary increase by 10% instead of 2% in real terms in the next 3 years. How does that change Lucy's human wealth?

e. If the increase in salary were to be made permanent, how would that affect Lucy's consumption levels?

3. *Suppose that a private hospital is pondering its next investment—the buying of costly medical equipment for $1 million. The new equipment should bring in real net profits of $150,000 per year. The real interest rate is 8% this year and expected to be constant; the depreciation rate is 10% for this kind of machinery.*

a. Should the hospital make the investment? Compare the cost of the equipment and its expected profits.

b. Suppose that the rate of interest were to decrease permanently, due to an improvement of the general conditions of the economy, to 5%. How would that affect the hospital's investment decision?

4. *Suppose that at age 22, you have just finished college and have been offered a job with a starting salary of $40,000. Your salary will remain constant in real terms. However, you have also been admitted to a professional school. The school can be completed in two years. Upon graduation, you expect your starting salary to be 10% higher in real terms and to remain constant in real terms thereafter. The tax rate on labor income is 40%.*

a. If the real interest rate is zero and you expect to retire at age 60 (i.e., if you do not go to professional school, you expect to work for 38 years total), what is the maximum you should be willing to pay in tuition to attend this professional school?

b. What is your answer to part (a) if you expect to pay 30% in taxes?

DIG DEEPER

MyEconLab Visit www.myeconlab.com to complete all Dig Deeper problems and get instant feedback.

5. *Individual saving and aggregate capital accumulation*

Suppose that every consumer is born with zero financial wealth and lives for three periods: youth, middle age, and old age. Consumers work in the first two periods and retire in the last one. Their income is $5 in the first period, $25 in the second, and $0 in the last one. Inflation and expected inflation are equal to zero, and so is the real interest rate.

a. What is the present discounted value of labor income at the beginning of the first period of life? What is the highest sustainable level of consumption such that consumption is equal in all three periods?

b. For each age group, what is the amount of saving that allows consumers to maintain the constant level of consumption you found in part (a)? (*Hint*: Saving can be a negative number if the consumer needs to borrow to maintain a certain level of consumption.)

c. Suppose there are *n* people born each period. What is total saving in the economy? (*Hint*: Add up the saving of each age group. Remember that some age groups may have negative saving.) Explain.

d. What is total financial wealth in the economy? (*Hint*: Compute the financial wealth of people at the beginning of the first period of life, the beginning of the second period, and the beginning of the third period. Add the three numbers. Remember that people can be in debt, so financial wealth can be negative.)

6. *Borrowing constraints and aggregate capital accumulation*

Continue with the setup from Problem 5, but suppose now that borrowing restrictions do not allow young consumers to borrow. If we call the sum of income and total financial wealth "cash on hand," then the borrowing restriction means that consumers cannot consume more than their cash on hand. In each age group, consumers compute their total wealth and then determine their desired level of consumption as the highest level that allows their consumption to be equal in all three periods. However, if at any time, desired consumption exceeds cash on hand, then consumers are constrained to consume exactly their cash on hand.

a. Calculate consumption in each period of life. Compare this answer to your answer to part (a) of Problem 5, and explain any differences.

b. Calculate total saving for the economy. Compare this answer to your answer to part (c) of Problem 5, and explain any differences.

c. Derive total financial wealth for the economy. Compare this answer to your answer to part (d) of Problem 5, and explain any differences.

d. Consider the following statement: "Financial liberalization may be good for individual consumers, but it is bad for overall capital accumulation." Discuss.

7. *Saving with uncertain future income*

Consider a consumer who lives for three periods: youth, middle age, and old age. When young, the consumer earns $20,000 in labor income. Earnings during middle age are uncertain; there is a 50% chance that the consumer will earn $40,000 and a 50% chance that the consumer will earn $100,000. When old, the consumer spends savings accumulated during the previous periods. Assume that inflation, expected inflation, and the real interest rate equal zero. Ignore taxes for this problem.

a. What is the expected value of earnings in the middle period of life? Given this number, what is the present discounted value of expected lifetime labor earnings? If the consumer wishes to maintain constant expected consumption over her lifetime, how much will she consume in each period? How much will she save in each period?

b. Now suppose the consumer wishes, above all else, to maintain a minimum consumption level of $20,000 in each period of her life. To do so, she must consider the worst outcome. If earnings during middle age turn out to be $40,000, how much should the consumer spend when she is young to guarantee consumption of at least $20,000 in each period? How does this level of consumption compare to the level you obtained for the young period in part (a)?

c. Given your answer in part (b), suppose that the consumer's earnings during middle age turn out to be $100,000. How much will she spend in each period of life? Will consumption be constant over the consumer's lifetime? (*Hint*: When the consumer reaches middle age, she will try to maintain constant consumption for the last two periods of life, as long as she can consume at least $20,000 in each period.)

d. What effect does uncertainty about future labor income have on saving (or borrowing) by young consumers?

EXPLORE FURTHER

8. Investment, output, and sales

The United Kingdom's Office for National Statistics (ONS) periodically releases series of data on various subjects. On the ONS Web site you can find the time series related to: quarter-to-quarter growth in GDP, business investment, and retail sales. For the latter, make sure you select the non-seasonally adjusted value for total retail sales (available on a quarterly-basis for the last three years only).

a. Compute the percentage quarterly change in investment and sales for the last years available (for investment: since 1997; for sales: since 2013).

b. Compare the three series. Which indicator is more volatile? Why? How does it fit with the arguments made in this chapter?

9. Consumer and business confidence

The European Commission (EC) measures consumer and business confidence throughout the European Union (EU) through periodic Business and Consumer Surveys. Find the non-seasonally adjusted data for consumer confidence in EU member states on the Commission's Web site (http://ec.europa.eu/). The EC also compiles macroeconomic data accessible through the AMECO database. Find the values of final consumption expenditure at current prices.

a. Compute the average value of the consumer confidence index for the EU as a whole. Calculate the annual change in consumer confidence since 1985. What do you see?

b. Calculate the correlation between the level of consumer confidence and consumption growth at EU level since 1995. What do you observe?

c. Compare the two time series. Do you observe any correlation? In other words, does the EU data show a strong relationship between consumer confidence and actual consumption over time?

APPENDIX: Derivation of the Expected Present Value of Profits under Static Expectations

You saw in the text (equation (15.3)) that the expected present value of profits is given by

$$V(\Pi_t^e) = \frac{1}{1 + r_t} \Pi_{t+1}^e + \frac{1}{(1 + r_t)(1 + r_{t+1}^e)} (1 - \delta) \Pi_{t+2}^e + \cdots$$

If firms expect both future profits (per unit of capital) and future interest rates to remain at the same level as today, so that $\Pi_{t+1}^e = \Pi_{t+2}^e = \cdots = \Pi_t$ and $r_{t+1}^e = r_{t+2}^e = \cdots = r_t$, the equation becomes

$$V(\Pi_t^e) = \frac{1}{1 + r_t} \Pi_t + \frac{1}{(1 + r_t)^2} (1 - \delta) \Pi_t + \cdots$$

Factoring out $[1/(1 + r_t)] \Pi_t$,

$$V(\Pi_t^e) = \frac{1}{1 + r_t} \Pi_t \left(1 + \frac{1 - \delta}{1 + r_t} + \cdots \right) \qquad (15.A1)$$

The term in parentheses in this equation is a geometric series, a series of the form $1 + x + x^2 + \cdots$. So, from Proposition 2 in Appendix 2 at the end of the book,

$$(1 + x + x^2 + \cdots) = \frac{1}{1 - x}$$

Here x equals $(1 - \delta)/(1 + r_t)$, so

$$\left(1 + \frac{1 - \delta}{1 + r_t} + \left(\frac{1 - \delta}{1 + r_t} \right)^2 + \cdots \right)$$

$$= \frac{1}{1 - (1 - \delta)/(1 + r_t)} = \frac{1 + r_t}{r_t + \delta}$$

Replacing the term in parentheses in equation (15.A1) with the expression above and manipulating gives:

$$V(\Pi_t^e) = \frac{1}{1 + r_t} \frac{1 + r_t}{r_t + \delta} \Pi_t$$

Simplifying gives equation (15.5) in the text:

$$V(\Pi_t^e) = \frac{\Pi_t}{(r_t + \delta)}$$

16

Expectations, Output, and Policy

In Chapter 14, we saw how expectations affected asset prices, from bonds to stocks to houses. In Chapter 15, we saw how expectations affected consumption decisions and investment decisions. In this chapter we put the pieces together and take another look at the effects of monetary and fiscal policy.

Section 16-1 draws the major implication of what we have learned, namely that expectations of both future output and future interest rates affect current spending, and therefore current output.

Section 16-2 looks at monetary policy. It shows that the effects of monetary policy depend crucially on how changes in the policy rate lead people and firms to change their expectations of future interest rates and future income, and by implication, to change their spending decisions.

Section 16-3 turns to fiscal policy. It shows how, in contrast to the simple model you saw back in the core, a fiscal contraction can sometimes lead to an increase in output, even in the short run. Again, how expectations respond to policy is at the center of the story.

16-1 Expectations and Decisions: Taking Stock

Let's start by reviewing what we have learned, and then discuss how we should modify the characterization of goods and financial markets—the *IS-LM* model—we developed in the core.

Expectations, Consumption, and Investment Decisions

The theme of Chapter 15 was that both consumption and investment decisions depend very much on expectations of future income and interest rates. The channels through which expectations affect consumption and investment spending are summarized in Figure 16-1.

Note the many channels through which expected future variables affect current decisions, both directly and through asset prices:

- An increase in current and expected future after-tax real labor income or a decrease in current and expected future real interest rates increase human wealth (the expected present discounted value of after-tax real labor income), which in turn leads to an increase in consumption.
- An increase in current and expected future real dividends or a decrease in current and expected future real interest rates increase stock prices, which leads to an increase in non-human wealth, and in turn, to an increase in consumption.

Note that in the case of bonds, it is nominal rather than real ▶ interest rates that matter because bonds are claims to future dollars rather than to future goods.

- A decrease in current and expected future nominal interest rates leads to an increase in bond prices, which leads to an increase in nonhuman wealth, and in turn, to an increase in consumption.
- An increase in current and expected future real after-tax profits or a decrease in current and expected future real interest rates increase the present value of real after-tax profits, which leads in turn to an increase in investment.

Expectations and the *IS* Relation

A model that gave a detailed treatment of consumption and investment along the lines suggested in Figure 16-1 would be complicated. It can be done, and indeed it is done in

Figure 16-1

Expectations and Private Spending: The Channels

Expectations affect consumption and investment decisions both directly and through asset prices.

MyEconLab Animation

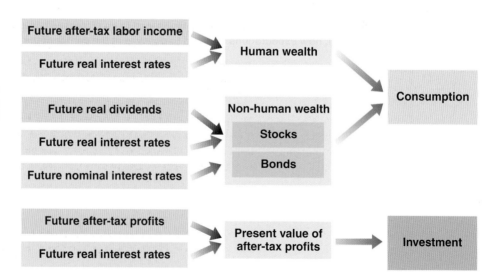

the large empirical models that macroeconomists build to understand the economy and analyze policy; but this is not the place for such complications. We want to capture the essence of what you have learned so far, how consumption and investment depend on expectations of the future—without getting lost in the details.

This way of dividing time between "today" and "later" is the way many of us organize our own lives. Think of "things to do today" versus "things that can wait."

To do so, let's make a major simplification. Let's reduce the present and the future to only two periods: (1) a *current* period, which you can think of as the current year, and (2) a *future* period, which you can think of as all future years lumped together. This way we do not have to keep track of expectations about each future year.

Having made this assumption, the question becomes: How should we write the *IS* relation for the current period? In Chapter 6, we wrote the following equation for the *IS* relation:

$$Y = C(Y - T) + I(Y, r + x) + G$$

We assumed that consumption depended only on current income, and that investment depended only on current output and the current borrowing rate, equal to the policy rate plus a risk premium. We now want to modify this to take into account how expectations affect both consumption and investment. We proceed in two steps:

The reason for doing so is to group together the two components of demand, C and I, which both depend on expectations.

First, we simply rewrite the equation in more compact form but without changing its content. For that purpose, let's define aggregate private spending as the sum of consumption and investment spending.

$$A(Y, T, r, x) \equiv C(Y - T) + I(Y, r + x)$$

where *A* stands for **aggregate private spending**, or simply, **private spending**. With this notation we can rewrite the *IS* relation as

$$Y = A(Y, T, r, x) + G \qquad (16.1)$$
$$(+,-,-,-)$$

The properties of aggregate private spending, *A*, follow from the properties of consumption and investment that we derived in previous chapters:

- Aggregate private spending is an increasing function of income *Y*: Higher income (equivalently, output) increases both consumption and investment.
- Aggregate private spending is a decreasing function of taxes *T*: Higher taxes decrease consumption.
- Aggregate private spending is a decreasing function of the real policy rate *r*: A higher real policy rate decreases investment.
- Aggregate private spending is a decreasing function of the risk premium *x*: A higher risk premium increases the borrowing rate and decreases investment.

The first step only simplified notation. The second step is to modify equation (16.1) to take into account the role of expectations. Because the focus in this chapter is on expectations rather than on the risk premium, I shall assume that it is constant, and so to save on notation, I shall ignore it for the rest of the chapter. With the focus on expectations, the natural extension of equation (16.1) is to allow spending to depend not only on current variables but also on their expected values in the future period.

$$Y = A(Y, T, r, Y'^e, T'^e, r'^e) + G \qquad (16.2)$$
$$(+,-,-, +, -, -)$$

Primes denote future values and the superscript e denotes an expectation, so Y'^e, T'^e, and r'^e denote future expected income, future expected taxes, and the future expected real interest rate, respectively. The notation is a bit heavy, but what it captures is straightforward.

Notation: Primes stand for values of the variables in the future period. The superscript e stands for *expected*.

Increases in either current or expected future income increase private spending.
Increases in either current or expected future taxes decrease private spending.
Increases in either the current or expected future real policy rate decrease private spending.

With the goods market equilibrium now given by equation (16.2), Figure 16-2 shows the new *IS* curve for the current period. As usual, to draw the curve we take all variables other than current output, Y, and the current real policy rate, r, as given. Thus, the *IS* curve is drawn for given values of current and future expected taxes, T and T'^e, for given values of expected future output, Y'^e, and for given values of the expected future real policy rate, r'^e.

The new *IS* curve, based on equation (16.2), is still downward sloping, for the same reason as in Chapter 6: A decrease in the current policy rate leads to an increase in private spending. This increase in private spending leads, through a multiplier effect, to an increase in output. We can say more, however. The new *IS* curve is much steeper than the *IS* curve we drew in previous chapters. Put another way, *everything else the same*, a large decrease in the current policy rate is likely to have only a small effect on equilibrium output.

> For purposes of this discussion, think of the policy rate as the real interest rate relevant to the current period, for example, ▶ the one-year rate.

To see why the effect is small, take point A on the *IS* curve in Figure 16-2, and consider the effects of a decrease in the real policy rate, from r_A to r_B. The effect of the decrease in the real interest rate on output depends on the strength of two effects: the effect of the real policy rate on spending given income and on the size of the multiplier. Let's examine each one:

> Suppose you have a 30-year loan, and the 1-year interest rate goes down from 5% to 2%. All future 1-year rates remain the same. By how much will the 30-year interest rate come down? (Answer: from 5% to 4.9%. To see why, extend equation (14.11) to the ▶ 30-year yield: The 30-year yield is the average of the 30 one-year rates.)

■ A decrease in the current real policy rate, *given unchanged expectations of the future real policy rate*, does not have much effect on private spending. We saw why in the previous chapters: A change in only the current real interest rate does not lead to large changes in present values, and therefore does not lead to large changes in spending. For example, firms are not likely to change their investment plans very much in response to a decrease in the current real interest rate if they do not expect future real interest rates to be lower as well.

Figure 16-2

The New IS Curve

Given expectations, a decrease in the real policy rate leads to a small increase in output. The *IS* curve is steeply downward sloping. Increases in government spending, or in expected future output, shift the *IS* curve to the right. Increases in taxes, in expected future taxes, or in the expected future real policy rate shift the *IS* curve to the left.

MyEconLab Animation

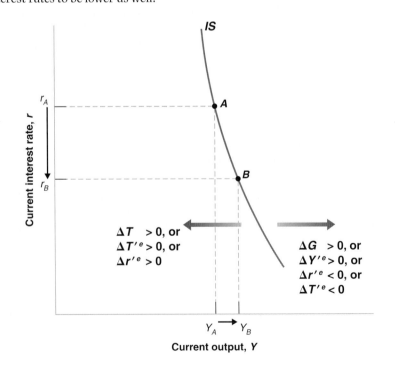

- The multiplier is likely to be small. Recall that the size of the multiplier depends on the size of the effect a change in current income (output) has on spending. But a change in current income, *given unchanged expectations of future income*, is unlikely to have a large effect on spending. The reason: Changes in income that are not expected to last have only a limited effect on either consumption or investment. Consumers who expect their income to be higher only for a year will increase consumption, but by much less than the increase in their income. Firms that expect sales to be higher only for a year are unlikely to change their investment plans much, if at all.

Suppose the firm where you work decides to give all employees a one-time bonus of $10,000. You do not expect it to happen again. By how much will you increase your consumption this year? (If you need to, look at the discussion of consumption behavior in Chapter 15.)

Putting things together, a large decrease in the current real policy rate—from r_A to r_B in Figure 16-2—leads to only a small increase in output, from Y_A to Y_B. Put another way: The *IS* curve, which goes through points *A* and *B*, is steeply downward sloping.

A change in any variable in equation (16.2) other than *Y* and *r* shifts the *IS* curve.

- Changes in current taxes (T) or in current government spending (G) shift the *IS* curve.

  An increase in current government spending increases spending at a given interest rate, shifting the *IS* curve to the right; an increase in taxes shifts the *IS* curve to the left. These shifts are represented in Figure 16-2.

- Changes in expected future variables (Y'^e, T'^e, r'^e), also shift the *IS* curve.

  An increase in expected future output, Y'^e, shifts the *IS* curve to the right. Higher expected future income leads consumers to feel wealthier and spend more; higher expected future output implies higher expected profits, leading firms to invest more. Higher spending by consumers and firms leads, through the multiplier effect, to higher output. By a similar argument, an increase in expected future taxes leads consumers to decrease their current spending and shifts the *IS* curve to the left. And an increase in the expected future real policy rate decreases current spending, also leading to a decrease in output, and shifting the *IS* curve to the left. These shifts are also represented in Figure 16-2.

16-2 Monetary Policy, Expectations, and Output

The interest rate that the Fed affects directly is the *current real interest rate, r*. So, the *LM* curve is still given by a horizontal line at the real policy rate chosen by the Fed, call it $\bar{r}$. The *IS* and *LM* relations are thus given by:

$$IS: \quad Y = A(Y, T, r, Y'^e, T'^e, r'^e) + G \tag{16.3}$$

$$LM: \quad r = \bar{r} \tag{16.4}$$

The corresponding *IS* and *LM* curves are drawn in Figure 16-3. Equilibrium in goods and financial markets implies that the economy is at point *A*.

Monetary Policy Revisited

Now suppose the economy is in recession, and the Fed decides to lower the real policy rate.

Assume first that this expansionary monetary policy does not change expectations of either the future real policy rate or future output. In Figure 16-4, the *LM* shifts down, from *LM* to *LM''*. (Because I have already used primes to denote future values of the variables, I have to use double primes, such as in *LM''*, to denote shifts in curves in this chapter.) The equilibrium moves from point *A* to point *B*, with higher output and a lower real interest rate. The steep *IS* curve, however, implies that the decrease in the current interest rate has only a small effect on output. Changes in the current interest rate, if not

Figure 16-3

The New IS-LM

The *IS* curve is steeply downward sloping. Other things being equal, a change in the current interest rate has a small effect on output. Given the current real interest set by the central bank, $\bar{r}$, the equilibrium is at point *A*.

MyEconLab Animation

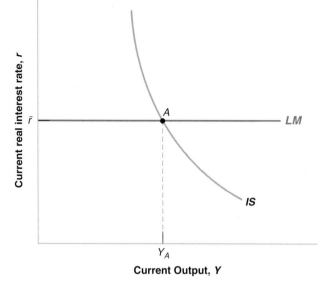

accompanied by changes in expectations, have only a small effect on spending, and in turn a small effect on output.

Is it reasonable, however, to assume that expectations are unaffected by an expansionary monetary policy? Isn't it likely that, as the Fed lowers the current real policy rate, financial markets now anticipate lower real interest rates in the future as well, along with higher future output stimulated by this lower future interest rate? What happens if they do? At a given current real policy rate, prospects of a lower future real policy rate and of higher future output both increase spending and output; they shift the *IS* curve to the right, from *IS* to *IS″*. The new equilibrium is given by point *C*. Thus, although the direct effect of the monetary expansion on output is limited, the full effect, once changes in expectations are taken into account, is much larger.

This is why central banks often argue that their task is not only to adjust the policy rate but also to "manage expectations," so as to lead to predictable effects of changes in this policy rate on the economy. More on this in Chapters 21 ▶ and 23.

You have just learned an important lesson. The effects of monetary policy—the effects of any type of macroeconomic policy, for that matter—depend crucially on its effect on expectations:

Figure 16-4

The Effects of an Expansionary Monetary Policy

The effects of monetary policy on output depend very much on whether and how monetary policy affects expectations.

MyEconLab Animation

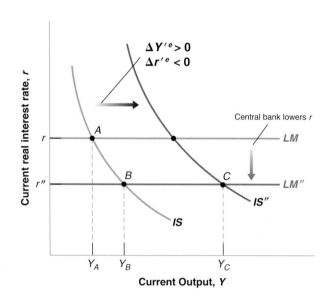

Rational Expectations

MEL
Video

Most macroeconomist modelers today routinely solve their models under the assumption of rational expectations. This was not always the case. The last 40 years in macroeconomic research are often called the *"rational expectations revolution"*.

The importance of expectations is an old theme in macroeconomics. But until the early 1970s, macroeconomists thought of expectations in one of two ways:

■ One was as **animal spirits** (from an expression Keynes introduced in the *General Theory* to refer to movements in investment that could not be explained by movements in current variables). In other words, shifts in expectations were considered important but were left largely unexplained.

■ The other was as the result of simple, backward-looking rules. For example, people were assumed to have **static expectations**; that is, to expect the future to be like the present (we used this assumption when discussing the Phillips curve in Chapter 8 and when exploring investment decisions in Chapter 15). Or people were assumed to have **adaptive expectations**. If, for example, their forecast of a given variable in a given period turned out to be too low, people were assumed to "adapt" by raising their expectation for the value of the variable for the following period. For example, seeing an inflation rate higher than they had expected led people to revise upward their forecast of inflation in the future.

In the early 1970s, a group of macroeconomists led by Robert Lucas (at Chicago) and Thomas Sargent (at Minnesota) argued that these assumptions did not reflect the way people form expectations. (Robert Lucas received the Nobel Prize in 1995; Thomas Sargent received the Nobel Prize in 2011.) They argued that, in thinking about the effects of alternative policies, economists should assume that people have rational expectations, that people look into the future and do the best job they can in predicting it. This is not the same as assuming that people know the future, but rather that they use the information they have in the best possible way.

Using the popular macroeconomic models of the time, Lucas and Sargent showed how replacing traditional assumptions about expectations formation by the assumption of rational expectations could fundamentally alter the results. For example, Lucas challenged the notion that disinflation necessarily required an increase in unemployment for some time. Under rational expectations, he argued, a credible disinflation policy might be able to decrease inflation without any increase in unemployment. More generally, Lucas and Sargent's research showed the need for a complete rethinking of macroeconomic models under the assumption of rational expectations, and this is what happened over the next two decades.

Most macroeconomists today use rational expectations as a working assumption in their models and analyses of policy. This is not because they believe that people always have rational expectations. Surely there are times when adaptive expectations may be a better description of reality; there are also times when people, firms, or financial market participants lose sight of reality and become too optimistic or too pessimistic. (Recall our discussion of bubbles and fads in Chapter 14.) But, when thinking about the likely effects of a particular economic policy, the best assumption to make seems to be that financial markets, people, and firms will do the best they can to work out the implications of that policy. Designing a policy on the assumption that people will make systematic mistakes in responding to it is unwise.

Why did it take until the 1970s for rational expectations to become a standard assumption in macroeconomics? The answer: Largely because of technical problems. Under rational expectations, what happens today depends on expectations of what will happen in the future. But what happens in the future also depends on what happens today. Solving such models is hard. The success of Lucas and Sargent in convincing most macroeconomists to use rational expectations came not only from the strength of the case, but also from showing how it could actually be done. Much progress has been made since in developing solution methods for larger and larger models. Today, a number of large macro-econometric models are solved under the assumption of rational expectations.

■ If a monetary expansion leads financial investors, firms, and consumers to revise their expectations of future interest rates and output, then the effects of the monetary expansion on output may be large.

■ But if expectations remain unchanged, the effects of the monetary expansion on output will be limited.

We can link this to our previous discussion in Chapter 14 about the effects of changes in monetary policy on the stock market. Many of the same issues were present there. If, when the change in monetary policy takes place, it comes as no surprise to investors, firms, and consumers, then expectations will not change. The stock market will react only a little, if at all. And thus, demand and output will change only a little, if at all. But if the change comes as a surprise and is expected to last, expectations of future output will go up, expectations of future interest rates will come down, the stock market will boom, and output will increase.

At this stage, you may have become skeptical that macroeconomists can say much about the effects of policy or the effects of other shocks. If the effects depend so much on what happens to expectations, can macroeconomists have any hope of predicting what will happen? The answer is yes.

MyEconLab Video

Saying that the effect of a particular policy depends on its effect on expectations is not the same as saying that anything can happen. Expectations are not arbitrary. The manager of a mutual fund who must decide whether to invest in stocks or bonds, the firm thinking about whether or not to build a new plant, the consumer thinking about how much she should save for retirement, all give a lot of thought to what might happen in the future. We can think of each of them as forming expectations about the future by assessing the likely course of future expected policy and then working out the implications for future activity. If they do not do it themselves (surely most of us do not spend our time solving macroeconomic models before making decisions), they do so indirectly by watching TV and reading newsletters and newspapers or finding public information on the Web, all of which in turn rely on the forecasts of public and private forecasters. Economists refer to expectations formed in this forward-looking manner as **rational expectations**. The introduction of the assumption of rational expectations, starting in the 1970s, has largely shaped the way macroeconomists think about policy. It is discussed further in the Focus box "Rational Expectations."

We could go back and think about the implications of rational expectations in the case of the monetary expansion we have just studied. It will be more fun to do this in the context of a change in fiscal policy, and this is what we now turn to.

16-3 Deficit Reduction, Expectations, and Output

We discussed the short- and ▶ medium-run effects of changes in fiscal policy in Section 9-3. We discussed the long-run effects of changes in fiscal policy in Section 11-2.

Recall the conclusions we reached in the core about the effects of a budget deficit reduction:

- In the short run, a reduction in the budget deficit, unless it is offset by a monetary expansion, leads to lower private spending and to a contraction in output.
- In the medium run, a lower budget deficit implies higher saving and higher investment.
- In the long run, higher investment translates into higher capital and thus higher output.

It is this adverse short-run effect that—in addition to the unpopularity of increases in taxes or reductions in government programs in the first place—often deters governments from tackling their budget deficits. Why take the risk of a recession now for benefits that will accrue only in the future?

A number of economists have argued however that, under some conditions, a deficit reduction might actually increase output even in the *short run*. Their argument is that if people take into account the future beneficial effects of deficit reduction, their expectations about the future might improve enough so as to lead to an increase—rather than a decrease—in current spending, thereby increasing current output. This section explores their argument. The Focus box on page 361 "Can a Budget Deficit Reduction Lead to an Output Expansion? Ireland in the 1980s" reviews some of the supporting evidence.

Assume the economy is described by equation (16.3) for the *IS* relation and equation (16.4) for the *LM* relation. Now suppose the government announces a program to reduce the deficit, through decreases both in current spending G and in future spending, G'^e. What will happen to output *this period?*

The Role of Expectations about the Future

Suppose first that expectations of future output (Y'^e) and of the future interest rate (r'^e) do not change. Then we get the standard answer: The decrease in government spending in the current period leads to a shift of the *IS* curve to the left, and so to a decrease in output.

The crucial question therefore is what happens to expectations. To answer, let us go back to what we learned in the core about the effects of a deficit reduction in the medium run and the long run.

- In the medium run, a deficit reduction has no effect on output. It leads, however, to a lower interest rate and to higher investment. These were two of the main lessons of Chapter 9.

    Let's review the logic behind each.

    Recall that, when we look at the medium run, we ignore the effects of capital accumulation on output. So in the medium run, the natural level of output depends on the level of productivity (taken as given) and on the natural level of employment. The natural level of employment depends in turn on the natural rate of unemployment. If spending by the government on goods and services does not affect the natural rate of unemployment—and there is no obvious reason why it should—then changes in spending will not affect the natural level of output. Therefore, a deficit reduction has no effect on the level of output in the medium run.

    Now recall that output must be equal to spending, and that spending is the sum of public spending and private spending. Given that output is unchanged and that public spending is lower, private spending must therefore be higher. Higher private spending requires a lower equilibrium interest rate. The lower interest rate leads to higher investment, and thus to higher private spending, which offsets the decrease in public spending and output is unchanged. ◀ In the medium run: Output, Y, does not change; investment, I, is higher.

- In the long run—that is, taking into account the effects of capital accumulation on output—higher investment leads to a higher capital stock, and therefore, a higher ◀ In the long run: I increases $\Rightarrow K$ increases $\Rightarrow Y$ increases. level of output.

This was the main lesson of Chapter 11. The higher the proportion of output saved (or invested; investment and saving must be equal for the goods market to be in equilibrium in a closed economy), the higher the capital stock, and thus the higher the level of output in the long run.

We can think of our *future period* as including both the medium and the long run. If people, firms, and financial market participants have *rational expectations*, then, in response to the announcement of a deficit reduction, they will expect these developments to take place in the future. Thus, they will revise their expectation of future output (Y'^e) ◀ up, and their expectation of the future interest rate (r'^e) down.

The way this is likely to happen: Forecasts by economists will show that these lower deficits are likely to lead to higher output and lower interest rates in the future. In response to these forecasts, long-term interest rates will decrease and the stock market will increase. People and firms, reading these forecasts and looking at bond and stock prices, will revise their spending plans and increase spending.

Back to the Current Period

We can now return to the question of what happens *this period* in response to the announcement and start of the deficit reduction program. Figure 16-5 draws the *IS* and *LM* curves for the current period. In response to the announcement of the deficit reduction, there are now three factors shifting the *IS* curve:

- Current government spending (G) goes down, leading the *IS* curve to shift to the left. At a given interest rate, the decrease in government spending leads to a decrease in

Figure 16-5

When account is taken of its effect on expectations, the decrease in government spending need not lead to a decrease in output.

MyEconLab Animation

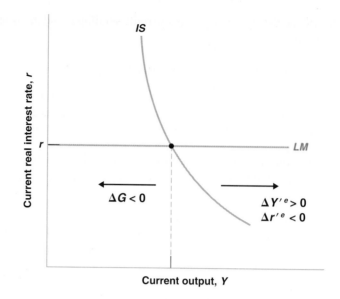

total spending and so a decrease in output. This is the standard effect of a reduction in government spending, and the only one taken into account in the basic *IS-LM* model.

■ Expected future output (Y'^e) goes up, leading the *IS* curve to shift to the right. At a given interest rate, the increase in expected future output leads to an increase in private spending, increasing output.

■ The expected future interest rate (r'^e) goes down, leading the *IS* curve to shift to the right. At a given current interest rate, a decrease in the future interest rate stimulates spending and increases output.

What is the net effect of these three shifts in the *IS* curve? Can the effect of expectations on consumption and investment spending offset the decrease in government spending? Without much more information about the exact form of the *IS* relation and about the details of the deficit reduction program, we cannot tell which shifts will dominate and whether output will go up or down. But our analysis suggests that both cases are possible, that output may go up in response to the deficit reduction. And it gives us a few hints as to when this might happen:

MyEconLab Video   ■ Timing matters. Note that the smaller the decrease in current government spending (G), the smaller the adverse effect on spending today. Note also that the larger the decrease in expected future government spending (G'^e), the larger the effect on expected future output and interest rates, thus the larger the favorable effect on spending today. This suggests that credibly **backloading** the deficit reduction program toward the future, with small cuts today and larger cuts in the future is more likely to lead to an increase in output. On the other hand, backloading raises an obvious issue. Announcing the need for painful cuts in spending, and then leaving them to the future, is likely to decrease the program's **credibility**— the perceived probability that the government will do what it has promised when the time comes to do it. The government must play a delicate balancing act; enough cuts in the current period to show a commitment to deficit reduction; enough cuts left to the future to reduce the adverse effects on the economy in the short run.

Can a Budget Deficit Reduction Lead to an Output Expansion? Ireland in the 1980s

Ireland went through two major deficit reduction programs in the 1980s.

1. The first program was started in 1982. In 1981, the budget deficit had reached a high 13% of gross domestic product (GDP). Government debt, the result of the accumulation of current and past deficits, was 77% of GDP, also a high level. The Irish government clearly had to regain control of its finances. Over the next three years, it embarked on a program of deficit reduction, based mostly on tax increases. This was an ambitious program. Had output continued to grow at its normal growth rate, the program would have reduced the deficit by 5% of GDP.

    The results, however, were dismal. As shown in line 2 of Table 1, output growth was low in 1982, and negative in 1983. Low output growth was associated with a major increase in unemployment, from 9.5% in 1981 to 15% in 1984 (line 3). Because of low output growth, tax revenues—which depend on the level of economic activity—were lower than anticipated. The actual deficit reduction from 1981 to 1984, shown in line 1, was only 3.5% of GDP. And the result of continuing high deficits and low GDP growth was a further increase in the ratio of debt to GDP to 97% in 1984.

2. A second attempt to reduce budget deficits was made starting in February 1987. At the time, things were still very bad. The 1986 deficit was 10.7% of GDP; debt stood at 11.6% of GDP, a record high in Europe at the time. This new program of deficit reduction was different from the first. It was focused more on reducing the role of government and cutting government spending than on increasing taxes. The tax increases in the program were achieved through a tax reform widening the tax base—increasing the number of households paying taxes—rather than through an increase in the marginal tax rate. The program was again ambitious. Had output grown at its normal rate, the reduction in the deficit would have been 6.4% of GDP.

    The results of the second program could not have been more different from the results of the first.

The years 1987 to 1989 were years of strong growth, with average GDP growth exceeding 5%. The unemployment rate was reduced by almost 2%. Because of strong output growth, tax revenues were higher than anticipated, and the deficit was reduced by nearly 9% of GDP.

A number of economists have argued that the striking difference between the results of the two programs can be traced to the different reaction of expectations in each case. The first program, they argue, focused on tax increases and did not change what many people saw as too large a role of government in the economy. The second program, with its focus on cuts in spending and on tax reform, had a much more positive impact on expectations, and so a positive impact on spending and output.

Are these economists right? One variable, the household saving rate—defined as disposable income minus consumption, divided by disposable income—strongly suggests that expectations are an important part of the story. To interpret the behavior of the saving rate, recall the lessons from Chapter 15 about consumption behavior. When disposable income grows unusually slowly or falls—as it does in a recession—consumption typically slows down or declines by less than disposable income because people expect things to improve in the future. Put another way, when the growth of disposable income is unusually low, the saving rate typically comes down. Now look (in line 4) at what happened from 1981 to 1984. Despite low growth throughout the period and a recession in 1983, the household saving rate actually increased slightly during the period. Put another way, people reduced their consumption by more than the reduction in their disposable income: The reason must be that they were pessimistic about the future.

Now turn to the period 1986 to 1989. During that period, economic growth was unusually strong. By the same argument as in the previous paragraph, we would have expected consumption to increase less strongly, and thus the saving rate to increase. Instead, the saving rate dropped sharply, from 15.7% in 1986 to 12.6% in 1989. Consumers must have become much more optimistic about the future

Table 1 Fiscal and Other Macroeconomic Indicators in Ireland, 1981 to 1984, and 1986 to 1989

		1981	1982	1983	1984	1986	1987	1988	1989
1	Budget deficit (% of GDP)	−13.0	−13.4	−11.4	−9.5	−10.7	−8.6	−4.5	−1.8
2	Output growth rate (%)	3.3	2.3	−0.2	4.4	−0.4	4.7	5.2	5.8
3	Unemployment rate (%)	9.5	11.0	13.5	15.0	16.1	16.9	16.3	15.1
4	Household saving rate (% of disposable income)	17.9	19.6	18.1	18.4	15.7	12.9	11.0	12.6

Source: OECD Economic Outlook, June 1998.

to increase their consumption by more than the increase in their disposable income.

The next question is whether this difference in the adjustment of expectations over the two episodes can be attributed fully to the differences in the two fiscal programs. The answer is surely no. Ireland was changing in many ways at the time of the second fiscal program. Productivity was increasing much faster than real wages, reducing the cost of labor for firms. Attracted by tax breaks, low labor costs, and an educated labor force, many foreign firms were relocating to Ireland and building new plants. These factors played a major role in the expansion of the late 1980s. Irish growth was then very strong, usually more than 5% per year from 1990 to the time of the crisis in 2007. Surely, this long expansion is due to many factors. Nevertheless, the change in fiscal policy in 1987 probably played an important role in convincing people,

firms—including foreign firms—and financial markets, that the government was regaining control of its finances. And the fact remains that the substantial deficit reduction of 1987–1989 was accompanied by a strong output expansion, not by the recession predicted by the basic *IS-LM* model.

For a more detailed discussion, look at Francesco Giavazzi and Marco Pagano, "Can Severe Fiscal Contractions Be Expansionary? Tales of Two Small European Countries," NBER Macroeconomics Annual (MIT Press, 1990), Olivier Jean Blanchard and Stanley Fischer, editors.

For a more systematic look at whether and when fiscal consolidations have been expansionary (and a mostly negative answer), see "Will It Hurt? Macroeconomic Effects of Fiscal Consolidation," Chapter 3, World Economic Outlook, International Monetary Fund, October 2010.

■ Composition matters. How much of the reduction in the deficit is achieved by raising taxes and how much by cutting spending, may be important. If some government spending programs are perceived as "wasteful," cutting these programs today will allow the government to cut taxes in the future. Expectations of lower future taxes and lower distortions could induce firms to invest today, thus raising output in the short run.

■ The initial situation matters. Take an economy where the government appears to have, in effect, lost control of its budget. Government spending is high, tax revenues are low, and the deficit is large. Government debt is increasing fast. In such an environment, a credible deficit reduction program is also more likely to increase output in the short run. Before the announcement of the program, people may have expected major political and economic troubles in the future. The announcement of a program of deficit reduction may well reassure them that the government has regained control, and that the future is less bleak than they anticipated. This decrease in pessimism about the future may lead to an increase in spending and output, even if taxes are increased as part of the deficit reduction program. Investors who thought that the government might default on the debt and were asking for a large risk premium may conclude that the risk of default is much lower and ask for much lower interest rates. Lower interest rates for the government are likely to translate into lower interest rates for firms and people.

■ Monetary policy matters. The three previous arguments focused on the direction of the shift in the *IS* curve, with no change in monetary policy. But as we have discussed before, even if it cannot fully offset the effect of an adverse shift in the *IS* curve, monetary policy can, by decreasing the policy rate, help reduce the adverse effects of the shift on output.

Let's summarize.

Note how far we have moved from the results of Chapter 3, ▶ where, by choosing spending and taxes wisely, the government could achieve any level of output it wanted. Here, even the sign of the effect of a deficit reduction on output is ambiguous. More on current fiscal policy issues in Chapter 22.

A program of deficit reduction may increase output even in the short run. Whether it does or does not depends on many factors:

■ The credibility of the program: Will spending be cut or taxes increased in the future as announced?
■ The composition of the program: Does the program remove some of the distortions in the economy?
■ The state of government finances in the first place: How large is the initial deficit? Is this a "last chance" program? What will happen if it fails?

■ Monetary and other policies: Will they help offset the direct adverse effect on demand in the short run?

This gives you a sense of both the importance of expectations in determining the outcome and of the complexities involved in the use of fiscal policy in such a context. And it is far more than an illustrative example. This has been a major bone of contention in the Euro area since the beginning of 2010.

By 2010, the sharp economic downturn, together with the fiscal measures taken to limit the fall in demand during 2009, had led large budget deficits and large increases in government debt. There was little question that the large deficits could not go on forever, and debt had to be eventually stabilized. The question was when and at what pace?

Some economists, and most of the policy makers in the Euro area, believed that fiscal consolidation had to start immediately and be strong. They argued that this was essential to convince investors that the fiscal situation was under control. They argued that, if coupled with structural reforms to increase future output, the effect through anticipations of higher output later would dominate the direct adverse effects of consolidation. For example, the president of the European Central Bank, Jean Claude Trichet, said in September 2010:

> "[Fiscal consolidation] is a prerequisite for maintaining confidence in the credibility of governments' fiscal targets. Positive effects on confidence can compensate for the reduction in demand stemming from fiscal consolidation, when fiscal adjustment strategies are perceived as credible, ambitious and focused on the expenditure side. The conditions for such positive effects are particularly favourable in the current environment of macroeconomic uncertainty."

Others were more skeptical. They were skeptical that, in a depressed environment, the positive expectation effects would be strong. They pointed out that the policy rate was already at the zero bound, and so monetary policy could not help much, if at all. They argued for a slow and steady fiscal consolidation, even if it were to lead to higher levels of debt until debt stabilized.

The debate became known as the **fiscal multipliers** debate. Those in favor of strong consolidation argued that the fiscal multipliers, that is, the net effects of fiscal consolidation once direct and expectation effects were taken into account, were likely to be *negative*. Smaller deficits would lead, other things equal, to *an increase* in output. Those against it argued that fiscal multipliers were likely to be *positive* and possibly large. Smaller deficits would lead to a decrease in output, or at least slowdown the recovery.

The skeptics turned out, unfortunately, to be right. As evidence accumulated, it became clear that the net effect of fiscal consolidation was contractionary. The strongest piece of evidence was the relation between forecast errors and the size of fiscal consolidation across countries. In most Euro countries, growth in 2010 and 2011 turned out to be much lower than had been forecast. Looking across countries, these negative forecast errors were closely correlated with the size of fiscal consolidation. As shown in Figure 16-6 on page 364, which plots growth forecast errors against a measure of fiscal consolidation, countries with larger fiscal consolidations showed a larger (negative) forecast error. This was particularly striking in the case of Greece, but was true of other countries as well. Given that the forecasts had been constructed using models which implied small positive multipliers, this evidence implied that the fiscal multipliers were in fact not only positive, but larger than had been assumed. Expectation effects did not offset the adverse direct effects of lower spending and higher taxes.

MyEconLab Video

Figure 16-6

**Growth Forecast Errors
and Fiscal Consolidation
in Europe, 2010–2011**

European countries with stronger fiscal consolidations in 2010 and 2011 had larger negative growth forecast errors.

MyEconLab Animation

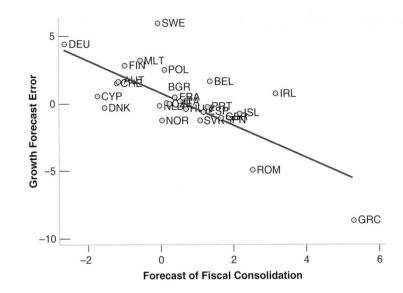

Summary

- Private spending in the goods market depends on current and expected future output and on current and expected future real interest rates.

- Expectations affect demand and, in turn, affect output. Changes in expected future output or in the expected future real interest rate lead to changes in spending and in output today.

- By implication, the effects of fiscal and monetary policy on spending and output depend on how the policy affects expectations of future output and real interest rates.

- Rational expectations is the assumption that people, firms, and participants in financial markets form expectations of the future by assessing the course of future expected policy and then working out the implications for future output, future interest rates, and so on. Although it is clear that most people do not go through this exercise themselves, we can think of them as doing so indirectly by relying on the predictions of public and private forecasters.

- Although there are surely cases in which people, firms, or financial investors do not have rational expectations, the assumption of rational expectations seems to be the best benchmark to evaluate the potential effects of alternative policies. Designing a policy on the assumption that people will make systematic mistakes in responding to it would be unwise.

- The central bank controls the short-term nominal interest rate. Spending, however, depends instead on current and expected future real interest rates. Thus, the effect of monetary policy on activity depends crucially on whether and how changes in the short-term nominal interest rate lead to changes in current and expected future real interest rates.

- A budget deficit reduction may lead to an increase rather than a decrease in output. This is because expectations of higher output and lower interest rates in the future may lead to an increase in spending that more than offsets the reduction in spending coming from the direct effect of the deficit reduction on total spending. Whether it does depends on the pace, the credibility, the nature of the deficit reduction, and the ability of monetary policy to accommodate and to sustain demand. These conditions were not satisfied in the Europe in the 2010s.

Key Terms

aggregate private spending, or private spending, 353

animal spirits, 357

static expectations, 357

adaptive expectations, 357

rational expectations, 358

backloading, 360

credibility, 360

fiscal multipliers, 363

Questions and Problems

QUICK CHECK

MyEconLab Visit www.myeconlab.com to complete similar Quick Check problems and get instant feedback.

1. *Using the information in this chapter, label each of the following statements true, false, or uncertain. Explain briefly.*

a. Changes in the current one-year real interest rate are likely to have a much larger effect on spending than changes in expected future one-year real interest rates.

b. The introduction of expectations in the goods market model makes the *IS* curve flatter, although it is still downward sloping.

c. Investment depends on current and expected future interest rates.

d. The rational expectations assumption implies that consumers take into account the effects of future fiscal policy on output.

e. Expected future fiscal policy affects expected future economic activity but not current economic activity.

f. Depending on its effect on expectations, a fiscal contraction may actually lead to an economic expansion.

g. Ireland's experience with deficit reduction programs in 1982 and 1987 provides strong evidence against the hypothesis that deficit reduction can lead to an output expansion.

h. The Euro area experience in 2010 and 2011 suggests that fiscal consolidations, through expectations, lead to substantial increases in output growth.

2. *Consider these two quotes concerning recent Federal Reserve policy*

On December 12, 2012 the Federal Reserve issued the following statement:

"In particular, the Committee decided to keep the target range for the federal funds rate at 0 to 1/4 percent and currently anticipates that this exceptionally low range for the federal funds rate will be appropriate at least as long as the unemployment rate remains above 6.5 percent."

On July 10, 2013, Ben Bernanke, Chairman of the Federal Reserve said:

"There will not be an automatic increase in interest rate when unemployment hits 6.5%."

a. Why do both quotes focus on what policy will be in the future, rather than just explain what the Fed is doing in the present?

b. Why do you think the Fed Chair made the second statement?

c. On January 25, 2012, while the nominal policy interest rate was at the zero lower bound, the Federal Reserve announced an inflation target of 2%. What was the goal of this announcement?

3. *For each of the changes in expectations in parts (a) through (d), determine whether there is a shift in the IS curve, the LM curve, both curves, or neither. In each case assume that no other exogenou variable is changing.*

a. a decrease in the expected future real interest rate.

b. an increase in the current real policy interest rate.

c. an increase in expected future taxes.

d. a decrease in expected future income.

4. *Consider the following statement: "The rational expectations assumption is unrealistic because, essentially, it amounts to the assumption that every consumer has perfect knowledge of the economy." Discuss.*

5. *A new president, who promised during the campaign that she would cut taxes, has just been elected. People trust that she will keep her promise, but expect that the tax cuts will be implemented only in the future. Determine the impact of the election on current output, the current interest rate, and current private spending under each of the assumptions in parts (a) through (c). In each case, indicate what you think will happen to Y'^e, r'^e, and T'^e, and then how these changes in expectations affect output today.*

a. The Fed will not change its current real policy interest rate.

b. The Fed will act to prevent any change in current and future output.

c. The Fed will not change either the current real policy interest rate or the future real policy interest rate.

6. *The Irish deficit reduction packages*

The Focus box "Can a Budget Deficit Reduction Lead to an Output Expansion? Ireland in the 1980s" provides an example of fiscal consolidation. Ireland had a large budget deficit in 1981 and 1982.

a. What does a deficit reduction imply for the medium run and the long run? What are the advantages of reducing the deficit?

b. The box discusses two deficit reduction programs. How did they differ?

c. The box presents evidence that the two deficit reduction programs had different effects on household expectations. What is that evidence?

d. Although the data show strong output growth from 1987 to 1989, there is some evidence of continued macroeconomic weakness in Ireland during the second fiscal consolidation. What is that evidence?

DIG DEEPER

MyEconLab Visit www.myeconlab.com to complete all Dig Deeper problems and get instant feedback.

7. *Role of expectations*

Given the increasing role expectations play in shaping the effectiveness of economic policy, it is not surprising that a great deal of central bankers' job is to manage expectations, especially through careful communication strategies. In recent years, a new instrument has been increasingly used to that effect. The instrument is known as "forward guidance," that is, the public signaling by central banks, of future policy intents in the area of monetary policy. However, this tool can be tricky as central bankers may well have to retract previous announcements.

a. Suppose that the central bank in your country just announced, at time t, that it would implement a rapid expansionary policy at a time when the output is not growing. What would happen to current output and interest rates, if markets participants were taken completely by surprise, but did not believe that the expansionary policy would last?

b. Now consider the same situation a year later: output growth is sluggish, and the central bank has, again, adopted expansionary measures. How would the markets react? Describe both the behavior of the yield curve as a result, and the *IS-LM* curves.

c. Suppose that, after a long period of sustained expansion, the central bank were to announce one last expansionary package, commenting that since output has resumed growing, it would be much more vigilant on inflationary pressures in the forthcoming period. What would the impact be on current output and interest rates?

EXPLORE FURTHER

8. Fiscal consolidation

Canada in the 1990s and early 2000s seemed to embody the paradox encapsulated by the expression "expansionary austerity." This means while the Liberals, who gained power after the 1993 federal elections, pursued a policy of drastic public spending cuts, the economy seemed to thrive well into the 2007–2008 global financial crises.

a. Go to The Canadian national statistical office's Web site (http://www5.statcan.gc.ca/) and retrieve annual data on GDP and government spending. Calculate real GDP growth rates and government expenditure as percentage of GDP for the period 1994–2008, and 2008 till present. What do you see?

b. Some economists have argued that the "expansionary austerity" apparently experienced by Canada in the late 1990s to early 2000s was the outcome of luck and expansionary monetary policy. Luck consisted in a period of fast growth in the United States, Canada's main trading partner, resulting on a good performance of Canadian exports, which partly drove demand for Canadian goods. Go to the Canadian central bank's Web site and retrieve historical data on bank's discount rates. How does that modify the "expansionary austerity" argument?

c. Compare Canada's economic situation of the early 1990s with the current global situation. In particular, compare the monetary policy. If "austerity" policies were to be adopted today, would they be likely to be as successful as they seemed in the 1990s? Why? Explain using expectations.

The Open Economy

The next four chapters cover the second extension of the core. They look at the implications of openness—the fact that most economies trade both goods and assets with the rest of the world.

Chapter 17

Chapter 17 discusses the implications of openness in goods markets and financial markets. Openness in goods markets allows people to choose between domestic goods and foreign goods. An important determinant of their decisions is the real exchange rate—the relative price of domestic goods in terms of foreign goods. Openness in financial markets allows people to choose between domestic assets and foreign assets. This imposes a tight relation between the exchange rate, both current and expected, and domestic and foreign interest rates—a relation known as the *interest parity condition*.

Chapter 18

Chapter 18 focuses on equilibrium in the goods market in an open economy. It shows how the demand for domestic goods now depends also on the real exchange rate. It shows how fiscal policy affects both output and the trade balance. It discusses the conditions under which a real depreciation improves the trade balance and increases output.

Chapter 19

Chapter 19 characterizes goods and financial markets' equilibrium in an open economy. In other words, it gives an open economy version of the *IS-LM* model we saw in the core. It shows how, under flexible exchange rates, monetary policy affects output not only through its effect on the interest rate but also through its effect on the exchange rate. It shows how fixing the exchange rate also implies giving up the ability to change the interest rate.

Chapter **20**

Chapter 20 looks at the properties of different exchange rate regimes. It first shows how, in the medium run, the real exchange rate can adjust even under a fixed exchange rate regime. It then looks at exchange rate crises under fixed exchange rates, and at movements in exchange rates under flexible exchange rates. It ends by discussing the pros and cons of various exchange rate regimes, including the adoption of a common currency such as the euro.

Openness in Goods and Financial Markets

e have assumed until now that the economy we looked at was *closed*—that it did not interact with the rest of the world. We had to start this way to keep things simple and to build up intuition for the basic macroeconomic mechanisms. Figure 17-1, which repeats for convenience the first figure in the text, Figure 1-1, shows how bad, in fact, this assumption is. The figure plots the growth rates for advanced and emerging economies since 2005. What is striking is how the growth rates have moved together. Despite the fact that the crisis originated in the United States, the outcome was a worldwide recession with negative growth both in advanced and emerging economies. It is therefore time to relax our closed economy assumption. Understanding the macroeconomic implications of openness will occupy us for this and the next three chapters.

Openness has three distinct dimensions:

1. **Openness in goods markets**—the ability of consumers and firms to choose between domestic goods and foreign goods. In no country is this choice completely free of restrictions. Even the countries most committed to free trade have **tariffs**—taxes on imported goods—and **quotas**—restrictions on the quantity of goods that can be imported—on at least some foreign goods. At the same time, in most countries, average tariffs are low and getting lower.

2. **Openness in financial markets**—the ability of financial investors to choose between domestic assets and foreign assets. Until recently, even some of the richest countries in the world, such as France and Italy, had **capital controls**—restrictions on the foreign assets their domestic residents could hold and the domestic assets foreigners could hold. These restrictions have largely disappeared. As a result, world financial markets are becoming more closely integrated.

3. **Openness in factor markets**—the ability of firms to choose where to locate production, and of workers to choose where to work. Here also trends are clear. Multinational companies operate plants in many countries and move their operations around the world to take advantage of low costs. Much of the debate about the **North American Free Trade Agreement (NAFTA)** signed in 1993 by the United States, Canada, and Mexico centered on how it would affect the relocation of U.S. firms to Mexico. Similar fears now center on China. And immigration from low-wage countries is a hot political issue throughout Europe and in the United States.

Figure 17-1

Growth in Advanced and Emerging Economies since 2005

The crisis started in the United States, but it affected nearly every country in the world.

Source: IMF, World Economic Outlook, Oct 2015. Used courtesy of IMF.

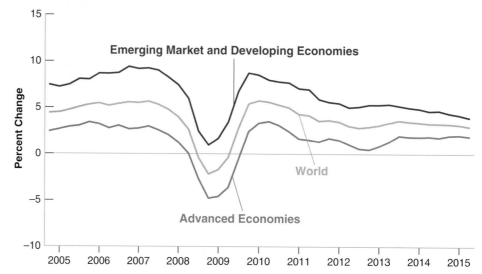

MyEconLab Video

In the short run and in the medium run—the focus of this and the next three chapters—openness in factor markets plays much less of a role than openness in either goods markets or financial markets. Thus, we shall ignore openness in factor markets and focus on the implications of the first two dimensions of openness here.

Section 17-1 looks at openness in the goods market, the determinants of the choice between domestic goods and foreign goods, and the role of the real exchange rate.

Section 17-2 looks at openness in financial markets, the determinants of the choice between domestic assets and foreign assets, and the role of interest rates and exchange rates.

Section 17-3 gives a map to the next three chapters.

17-1 Openness in Goods Markets

Let's start by looking at how much the United States sells to and buys from the rest of the world. Then we shall be better able to think about the choice between domestic goods and foreign goods, and the role of the relative price of domestic goods in terms of foreign goods—the real exchange rate.

Exports and Imports

Figure 17-2 plots the evolution of U.S. exports and U.S. imports, as ratios to GDP, since 1960 ("U.S. exports" means exports *from* the United States; "U.S. imports" means imports *to* the United States). The figure suggests two main conclusions:

From Chapter 3: The trade balance is the difference between exports and imports:
 If exports exceed imports, there is a trade surplus (equivalently, a positive trade balance).
 If imports exceed exports, there is a trade deficit (equivalently, a negative trade balance). ▶

■ The U.S. economy is becoming more open over time. Exports and imports, which were equal to 5% of GDP in the early 1960s, are now equal to about 15% of GDP (13.5% for exports, 16.5% for imports). In other words, the United States trades three times as much (relative to its GDP) with the rest of the world than it did 50 years ago.

■ Although imports and exports have followed the same upward trend, since the early 1980s imports have consistently exceeded exports. Put another way, for the last 30 years, the United States has consistently run a trade deficit. For four years in

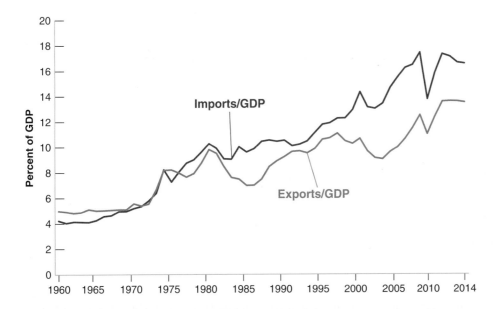

Figure 17-2

U.S. Exports and Imports as Ratios to GDP since 1960

Since 1960, exports and imports have more than tripled in relation to GDP. The United States has become a much more open economy.

Source: Series GDP, EXPGS, IMPGS. Federal Reserve Economic Data (FRED) https://research.stlouisfed.org/fred2/.

MyEconLab Real-time data

a row in the mid-2000s, the ratio of the trade deficit to GDP exceeded 5% of GDP. Although it has decreased since the beginning of the crisis, it remains large today. Understanding the sources and implications of this large deficit is an important issue and one to which we shall return later.

Given all the talk in the media about *globalization*, a volume of trade (measured by the average of the ratios of exports and imports to GDP) around 15% of GDP might strike you as small. However, the volume of trade is not necessarily a good measure of openness. Many firms are exposed to foreign competition, but by being competitive and keeping their prices low enough, these firms are able to retain their domestic market share and limit imports. This suggests that a better index of openness than export or import ratios is the proportion of aggregate output composed of **tradable goods**—goods that compete ◀ with foreign goods in either domestic markets or foreign markets. Estimates are that tradable goods represent about 60% of aggregate output in the United States today.

Tradable goods: cars, computers, etc. Nontradable goods: housing, most medical services, haircuts, etc.

With exports around 13.5% of GDP, it is true that the United States has one of the smallest ratios of exports to GDP among the rich countries of the world. Table 17-1 gives ◀ ratios for a number of OECD countries.

For more on the OECD and for the list of member countries, see Chapter 1.

The United States is at the low end of the range of export ratios. Japan's ratio is a bit higher, the United Kingdom's twice as large, Germany's three times as large. And the smaller European countries have large ratios, from 64.1% in Switzerland to 82.9% in the Netherlands. (The Netherlands's 82.9% ratio of exports to GDP raises an odd possibility: Can a country have exports larger than its GDP; in other words, can a country have an

Table 17-1	Ratios of Exports to GDP for Selected OECD Countries, 2014		
Country	**Export Ratio**	**Country**	**Export Ratio**
United States	13.5%	Germany	45.7%
Japan	17.7%	Austria	53.2%
United Kingdom	28.3%	Switzerland	64.1%
Chile	33.8%	Netherlands	82.9%
Source: IMF, *World Economic Outlook.*			

Can Exports Exceed GDP?

Can a country have exports larger than its GDP—that is, can it have an export ratio greater than one?

It would seem that the answer must be no. A country cannot export more than it produces, so that the export ratio must be less than one. Not so. The key to the answer is to realize that exports and imports may include exports and imports of intermediate goods.

Take, for example, a country that imports intermediate goods for $1 billion. Suppose it then transforms them into final goods using only labor. Say labor is paid $200 million and that there are no profits. The value of these final goods is thus equal to $1,200 million. Assume that $1 billion worth of final goods is exported and the rest, $200 million, is consumed domestically.

Exports and imports therefore both equal $1 billion. What is GDP in this economy? Remember that GDP is value added in the economy (see Chapter 2). So in this example, GDP equals $200 million, and the ratio of exports to GDP equals $1000/$200 = 5.

Hence, exports can exceed GDP. This is actually the case for a number of small countries where most economic activity is organized around a harbor and import-export activities. This is even the case for small countries such as Singapore, where manufacturing plays an important role. In 2014, the ratio of exports to GDP in Singapore was 188%!

export ratio greater than one? The answer is yes. The reason why is given in the Focus box "Can Exports Exceed GDP?")

Do these numbers indicate that the United States has more trade barriers than, say, the United Kingdom or the Netherlands? No. The main factors behind these differences are geography and size. Distance from other markets explains a part of the lower Japanese ratio. Size also matters; the smaller the country, the more it must specialize in producing and exporting only a few products and rely on imports for the other products. The Netherlands can hardly afford to produce the range of goods produced by the United States, a country roughly 20 times its economic size.

Iceland is both isolated and small. What would you expect its export ratio to be? (Answer: 56%.) ▶

The Choice between Domestic Goods and Foreign Goods

How does openness in goods markets force us to rethink the way we look at equilibrium in the *goods market*?

In a closed economy, people face one spending decision:
Save or buy (consume).
In an open economy, they face two spending decisions:
Save or buy.
And buy domestic or buy foreign. ▶

Until now, when we were thinking about consumers' decisions in the goods market, we focused on their decision to save or to consume. When goods markets are open, domestic consumers face a second decision: whether to buy domestic or foreign goods. Indeed, all buyers—including domestic and foreign firms and governments—face the same decision. This decision has a direct effect on domestic output. If buyers decide to buy more domestic goods, the demand for domestic goods increases, and so does domestic output. If they decide to buy more foreign goods, then foreign output increases instead of domestic output.

Central to this second decision (to buy domestic goods or foreign goods) is the price of domestic goods relative to foreign goods. We call this relative price the **real exchange rate**. The real exchange rate is not directly observable, and you will not find it in the newspapers. What you will find in newspapers are *nominal exchange rates*, the relative prices of currencies. So we start by looking at nominal exchange rates and then see how we can use them to construct real exchange rates.

Nominal Exchange Rates

Nominal exchange rates between two currencies can be quoted in one of two ways:

■ As the price of the domestic currency in terms of the foreign currency. If, for example, we look at the United States and the United Kingdom, and think of the dollar as the domestic currency and the pound as the foreign currency, we can express the nominal exchange rate as the price of a dollar in terms of pounds. In October 2015, the exchange rate defined this way was 0.65. In other words, one dollar was worth 0.65 pounds.

■ As the price of the foreign currency in terms of the domestic currency. Continuing with the same example, we can express the nominal exchange rate as the price of a pound in terms of dollars. In October 2015, the exchange rate defined this way was 1.55. In other words, one pound was worth 1.55 dollars.

Warning: There is unfortunately no agreed-upon rule among economists or among newspapers as to which of the two definitions to use. You will encounter both. Always check which definition is used.

Either definition is fine; the important thing is to remain consistent. In this text, we shall adopt the first definition; we shall define the **nominal exchange rate** as *the price of the domestic currency in terms of foreign currency*, and denote it by E. When looking, for example, at the exchange rate between the United States and the United Kingdom (from the viewpoint of the United States, so the dollar is the domestic currency), E will denote the price of a dollar in terms of pounds (so, for example, E was 0.65 in October 2015).

E: Nominal exchange rate— Price of domestic currency in terms of foreign currency. (From the point of view of the United States looking at the United Kingdom, the price of a dollar in terms of pounds.)

Exchange rates between the dollar and most foreign currencies are determined in foreign exchange markets, and change every day—indeed every minute of the day. These changes are called *nominal appreciations* or *nominal depreciations*—appreciations or depreciations for short.

■ An **appreciation** of the domestic currency is an increase in the price of the domestic currency in terms of a foreign currency. Given our definition of the exchange rate, an appreciation corresponds to an *increase* in the exchange rate.

Appreciation of the domestic currency ⇔ Increase in the price of the domestic currency in terms of foreign currency ⇔ Increase in the exchange rate.

■ A **depreciation** of the domestic currency is a decrease in the price of the domestic currency in terms of a foreign currency. So given our definition of the exchange rate, a depreciation of the domestic currency corresponds to a decrease in the exchange rate, E.

Depreciation of the domestic currency ⇔ Decrease in the price of the domestic currency in terms of foreign currency ⇔ Decrease in the exchange rate.

You may have encountered two other words to denote movements in exchange rates: "revaluations" and "devaluations." These two terms are used when countries operate under **fixed exchange rates**—a system in which two or more countries maintain a constant exchange rate between their currencies. Under such a system, increases in the exchange rate—which are infrequent by definition—are called **revaluations** (rather than appreciations). Decreases in the exchange rate are called **devaluations** (rather than depreciations).

We shall discuss fixed exchange rates in Chapter 20.

Figure 17-3 on page 374 plots the nominal exchange rate between the dollar and the pound since 1971. Note the two main characteristics of the figure:

■ *The trend increase in the exchange rate.* In 1971, a dollar was worth only 0.41 pounds. In 2015, a dollar was worth 0.65 pounds. Put another way, there was an appreciation of the dollar relative to the pound over the period.

■ *The large fluctuations in the exchange rate.* In the 1980s, a sharp appreciation, in which the dollar more than doubled in value relative to the pound, was followed by a nearly equally sharp depreciation. In the 2000s, a large depreciation was followed by a large appreciation as the crisis started, and a smaller depreciation since then.

If we are interested, however, in the choice between domestic goods and foreign goods, the nominal exchange rate gives us only part of the information we need. Figure 17-3, for example, tells us only about movements in the relative price of the two currencies, the dollar and the pound. To U.S. tourists thinking of visiting the United Kingdom, the question is not only how many pounds they will get in exchange for their dollars but how much goods will cost in the United Kingdom relative to how much they cost in the United States. This takes us to our next step—the construction of real exchange rates.

Figure 17-3

The Nominal Exchange Rate between the Dollar and the Pound since 1971

Although the dollar has appreciated relative to the pound over the past four decades, this appreciation has come with large swings in the nominal exchange rate between the two currencies.

Source: Series XUMAGBD. Bank of England.

MyEconLab Real-time data

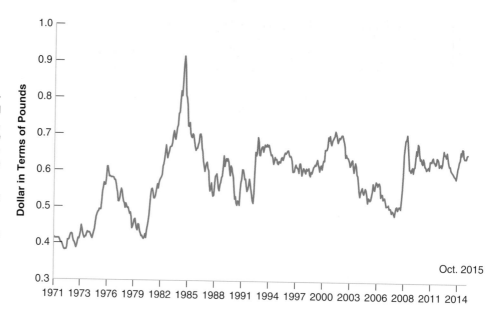

From Nominal to Real Exchange Rates

How can we construct the real exchange rate between the United States and the United Kingdom—the price of U.S. goods in terms of British goods?

Suppose the United States produced only one good, a Cadillac luxury sedan, and the United Kingdom also produced only one good, a Jaguar luxury sedan. (This is one of those "suppose" statements that run completely against the facts, but we shall become more realistic shortly.) Constructing the real exchange rate, the price of the U.S. goods (Cadillacs) in terms of British goods (Jaguars) would be straightforward. We would express both goods in terms of the same currency and then compute their relative price.

▷ *Check that if we expressed both goods in terms of dollars instead, we would get the same result for the real exchange rate.*

Suppose, for example, we expressed both goods in terms of pounds.

■ The first step would be to take the price of a Cadillac in dollars and convert it to a price in pounds. The price of a Cadillac in the United States is, say, $40,000. The dollar is worth, say, £0.65, so the price of a Cadillac in pounds is $40,000 multiplied by 0.65 = £26,000.

■ The second step would be to compute the ratio of the price of the Cadillac in pounds to the price of the Jaguar in pounds. The price of a Jaguar in the United Kingdom is, say, £30,000. So the price of a Cadillac in terms of Jaguars—that is, the real exchange rate between the United States and the United Kingdom—would be $26,000/£30,000 = £0.87. A Cadillac would be 13% cheaper than a Jaguar.

This example is straightforward, but how do we generalize it? The United States and the United Kingdom produce more than Cadillacs and Jaguars, and we want to construct a real exchange rate that reflects the relative price of *all* the goods produced in the United States in terms of *all* the goods produced in the United Kingdom.

The computation we just went through tells us how to proceed. Rather than using the price of a Jaguar and the price of a Cadillac, we must use a price index for all goods produced in the United Kingdom and a price index for all goods produced in the United States. This is exactly what the GDP deflators we introduced in Chapter 2 do. They are, by definition, price indexes for the set of final goods and services produced in the economy.

Figure 17-4

The Construction of the Real Exchange Rate

MyEconLab Animation

Let P be the GDP deflator for the United States, P^* be the GDP deflator for the United Kingdom (as a rule, we shall denote foreign variables by a star), and E be the dollar–pound nominal exchange rate. Figure 17-4 goes through the steps needed to construct the real exchange rate.

- The price of U.S. goods in dollars is P. Multiplying it by the exchange rate, E—the price of dollars in terms of pounds—gives us the price of U.S. goods in pounds, EP.
- The price of British goods in pounds is P^*. The *real exchange rate*, the price of U.S. goods in terms of British goods, which we shall call ε (the Greek lowercase epsilon), is thus given by

$$\varepsilon = \frac{EP}{P^*} \tag{17.1}$$

◀ ε: Real exchange rate is the price of domestic goods in terms of foreign goods. (For example, from the point of view of the United States looking at the United Kingdom, the price of U.S. goods in terms of British goods.)

The real exchange rate is constructed by multiplying the domestic price level by the nominal exchange rate and then dividing by the foreign price level—a straightforward extension of the computation we made in our Cadillac/Jaguar example.

Note, however, an important difference between our Cadillac/Jaguar example and this more general computation.

Unlike the price of Cadillacs in terms of Jaguars, the real exchange rate is an index number; that is, its level is arbitrary, and therefore uninformative. It is uninformative because the GDP deflators used to construct the real exchange rate are themselves index numbers. As we saw in Chapter 2, they are equal to 1 (or 100) in whatever year is chosen as the base year.

But all is not lost. Although the level of the real exchange rate is uninformative, the rate of change of the real exchange rate is informative. If, for example, the real exchange rate between the United States and the United Kingdom increases by 10%, this tells us U.S. goods are now 10% more expensive relative to British goods than they were before.

Like nominal exchange rates, real exchange rates move over time. These changes are called *real appreciations* or *real depreciations*.

- An increase in the real exchange rate—that is, an increase in the relative price of domestic goods in terms of foreign goods—is called a **real appreciation**.
- A decrease in the real exchange rate—that is, a decrease in the relative price of domestic goods in terms of foreign goods—is called a **real depreciation**.

Real appreciation ⇔ Increase in the price of the domestic goods in terms of foreign goods ⇔ Increase in the real ◀ exchange rate.

◀ Real depreciation ⇔ Decrease in the price of the domestic goods in terms of foreign goods ⇔ Decrease in the real exchange rate.

Figure 17-5 on page 376, plots the evolution of the real exchange rate between the United States and the United Kingdom since 1971, constructed using equation (17.1). For convenience, it also reproduces the evolution of the *nominal* exchange rate from Figure 17-3. The GDP deflators have both been set equal to 1 in the year 2000, so the nominal exchange rate and the real exchange rate are equal in that year by construction.

Figure 17-5

Real and Nominal Exchange Rates between the United States and the United Kingdom since 1971

Except for the difference in trend reflecting higher average inflation in the United Kingdom than in the United States until the early 1990s, the nominal and the real exchange rates have moved largely together.

Source: Series GDPDEF, GBRGDPDEFAISMEI, EXUSUK. Federal Reserve Economic Data (FRED). https://research.stlouisfed.org/fred2.

MyEconLab Real-time data

You should draw two lessons from Figure 17-5.

■ The nominal and the real exchange rate can move in opposite directions. Note for example how, from 1971 to 1976, whereas the nominal exchange rate went up, the real exchange rate actually went down.

How do we reconcile the fact that there was both a nominal appreciation (of the dollar relative to the pound) and a real depreciation (of U.S. goods relative to British goods) during the period? To see why, return to the definition of the real exchange rate in equation (17.1), and rewrite it as:

$$\varepsilon = E\,\frac{P}{P^*}$$

Two things happened in the 1970s:

First, E increased. The dollar went up in terms of pounds—this is the nominal appreciation we saw previously.

Second, P/P^* decreased. The price level increased less in the United States than in the United Kingdom. Put another way, over the period, average inflation was lower in the United States than in the United Kingdom.

The resulting decrease in P/P^* was larger than the increase in E, leading to a decrease in ε a real depreciation—a decrease in the relative price of domestic goods in terms of foreign goods.

To get a better understanding of what happened, let's go back to our U.S tourists thinking about visiting the United Kingdom, circa 1976. They would find that they could buy more pounds per dollar than in 1971 (E had increased). Did this imply their trip would be cheaper? No. When they arrived in the United Kingdom, they would discover that the prices of goods in the United Kingdom had increased much more than the prices of goods in the United States (P^* has increased more than P, so P/P^* has declined), and this more than canceled the increase in the value of the dollar in terms of pounds. They would find that their trip was actually more expensive (in terms of U.S. goods) than it would have been 5 years earlier.

Can there be a real appreciation with no nominal appreciation?
Can there be a nominal appreciation with no real appreciation? (The answers to ▶ both questions: yes.)

There is a general lesson here. Over long periods of time, differences in inflation rates across countries can lead to very different movements in nominal exchange rates and real exchange rates. We shall return to this issue in Chapter 20.

■ The large fluctuations in the nominal exchange rate we saw in Figure 17-3 also show up in the real exchange rate.

This not surprising. Price levels move slowly. So year-to-year movements in the price ratio P/P^* are typically small compared to the often sharp movements in the nominal exchange rate E. Thus, from year to year, or even over the course of a few years, movements in the real exchange rate ε tend to be driven largely by movements in the nominal exchange rate E. Note that since the early 1990s, the nominal exchange rate and the real exchange rate have moved nearly together. This reflects the fact that, since the early 1990s, inflation rates have been similar—and low—in both countries.

> If inflation rates were exactly equal, P/P^* would be constant, and ε and E would move exactly together.

From Bilateral to Multilateral Exchange Rates

We need to take one last step. So far we have concentrated on the exchange rate between the United States and the United Kingdom. But the United Kingdom is just one of many countries the United States trades with. Table 17-2 shows the geographic composition of U.S. trade for both exports and imports.

The main message of the table is that the United States does most of its trading with three sets of countries. The first includes its neighbors to the North and to the South, Canada and Mexico. Trade with Canada and Mexico accounts for 28% of both U.S. exports and imports. The second includes the countries of Western Europe, which account for 15% of U.S. exports and 18% of U.S. imports. The third includes the Asian countries, including Japan and China, which together account for 11% of U.S. exports and 26% of U.S. imports.

How do we go from **bilateral exchange rates**, like the real exchange rate between the United States and the United Kingdom we focused on previously, to **multilateral exchange rates** that reflect this composition of trade? The principle we want to use is simple, even if the details of construction are complicated. We want the weight of a given country to incorporate not only how much the country trades with the United States but also how much it competes with the United States in other countries. (Why not just look at trade shares between the United States and each individual country? Take two countries, the United States and country A. Suppose the United States and country A do not trade with each other—so trade shares are equal to zero—but they are both exporting to another country, call it country B. The real exchange rate between the United States and country A will matter very much for how much the United States exports to country B and thus to the U.S. export performance.) The variable constructed in this way is called the **multilateral real U.S. exchange rate**, or the U.S. real exchange rate for short.

> *Bi* means "two." *Multi* means "many."

> These are all equivalent names for the relative price of U.S. goods in terms of foreign goods: the multilateral real U.S. exchange rate, the U.S. **trade-weighted real exchange rate**, the U.S. **effective real exchange rate**.

Table 17-2	The Country Composition of U.S. Exports and Imports, 2014	
	Percent of Exports to	Percent of Imports from
Canada	16	15
Mexico	12	13
European Union	15	18
China	7	20
Japan	4	6
Rest of Asia and Pacific	11	10
Others	35	18

Source: US Census, Related Party Trade, May 2015.

Figure 17-6

The U.S. Multilateral Real Exchange Rate, since 1973

Since 1973 there have been two large real appreciations of the U.S. dollar and two large real depreciations.

Source: Price-adjusted Broad Dollar Index, Monthly Index. Federal Reserve Board. www.federalreserve. gov/releases/h10/summary.

MyEconLab Real-time data

The figure begins in 1973 because this multilateral real exchange rate, which is constructed by the Federal Reserve Board, is only available back as far as 1973.

Figure 17-6 shows the evolution of this multilateral real exchange rate, the price of U.S goods in terms of foreign goods since 1973. Like the bilateral real exchange rates we saw a few pages earlier, it is an index number and its level is arbitrary. You should note two things about Figure 17-6. First, a trend real depreciation since 1973 (in contrast to the trend nominal appreciation vis-à-vis the pound in Figure 17-3). Second, and more strikingly, the large swings in the multilateral real exchange rate in the 1980s and, to a lesser extent, in the 2000s. These swings are so striking that they have been given various names, from the "dollar cycle" to the more graphic "dance of the dollar." In the coming chapters, we shall examine where these swings come from and their effects on the trade deficit and economic activity.

17-2 Openness in Financial Markets

Openness in financial markets allows financial investors to hold both domestic assets and foreign assets, to diversify their portfolios, to speculate on movements in foreign interest rates versus domestic interest rates, on movements in exchange rates, and so on.

Diversify and speculate they do. Given that buying or selling foreign assets implies buying or selling foreign currency—sometimes called **foreign exchange**—the volume of transactions in foreign exchange markets gives us a sense of the importance of international financial transactions. In 2013, for example, the recorded *daily* volume of foreign exchange transactions in the world was $5.5 trillion, of which 87%—about $4.8 trillion—involved U.S. dollars on one side of the transaction, and 33% involved the euro.

To get a sense of the magnitude of these numbers, the sum of U.S. exports and imports in 2013 totaled $4 trillion *for the year*, or about $11 billion per day. Suppose the only dollar transactions in foreign-exchange markets had been, on one side, by U.S. exporters selling their foreign currency earnings, and on the other side by U.S. importers buying the foreign currency they needed to buy foreign goods. Then the volume of transactions involving dollars in foreign exchange markets would have been $11 billion per day, or about 0.3% of the actual daily total volume of dollar transactions ($4.8 trillion) involving dollars in foreign exchange markets. This computation tells us that most of the transactions are associated not with trade but with purchases and sales of financial assets. Moreover, the volume of transactions in foreign exchange markets is not only high but also rapidly increasing. The volume of foreign exchange transactions has more than quintupled since 2001. Again, this increase in activity reflects mostly an increase in financial transactions rather than an increase in trade.

◄ Daily volume of foreign exchange transactions with dollars on one side of the transaction: $4.8 trillion. Daily volume of trade of the United States with the rest of the world: $11 billion (0.3% of the volume of foreign exchange transactions).

For a country, openness in financial markets has an important implication. It allows the country to run trade surpluses and trade deficits. Recall that a country running a trade deficit is buying more from the rest of the world than it is selling to the rest of the world. To pay for the difference between what it buys and what it sells, the country must borrow from the rest of the world. It borrows by making it attractive for foreign financial investors to increase their holdings of domestic assets—in effect, to lend to the country.

Let's start by looking more closely at the relation between trade flows and financial flows. When this is done, we shall then look at the determinants of these financial flows.

The Balance of Payments

A country's transactions with the rest of the world, including both trade flows and financial flows, are summarized by a set of accounts called the **balance of payments**. Table 17-3 presents the U.S. balance of payments for 2014. The table has two parts, separated by a line. Transactions are referred to either as **above the line** or **below the line**.

The Current Account

The transactions above the line record payments to and from the rest of the world. They are called **current account** transactions.

■ The first two lines record the exports and imports of goods and services. Exports lead to payments from the rest of the world, imports to payments to the rest of the

Table 17-3 The U.S. Balance of Payments, 2014, in Billions of U.S. Dollars		
Current Account		
Exports	2343	
Imports	2851	
Trade balance (deficit = −)(1)		− 508
Income received	823	
Income paid	585	
Net income (2)		238
Net transfers received (3)		− 119
Current account balance (deficit = −)(1) + (2) + (3)		− 389
Capital Account		
Increase in foreign holdings of U.S. assets (4) (*)	1031	
Increase in U.S. holdings of foreign assets (5)	792	
Capital account balance (7) = (4) − (5)		239
Statistical discrepancy (= capital account balance − current account balance)		150
*including an increase in foreign holdings of U.S. assets of $54 billion from net transactions in financial derivatives		
Source: US Bureau of Economic Analysis, September 17, 2015.		

MyEconLab Real-time data

world. The difference between exports and imports is the *trade balance*. In 2014, imports exceeded exports, leading to a U.S. *trade deficit* of $508 billion—roughly 3% of U.S. GDP.

- Exports and imports are not the only sources of payments to and from the rest of the world. U.S. residents receive income on their holdings of foreign assets, and foreign residents receive income on their holdings of U.S. assets. In 2014, income received from the rest of the world was $823 billion, and income paid to foreigners was $585 billion, for a net **income balance** of $238 billion.

- Finally, countries give and receive foreign aid; the net value of these payments is recorded as **net transfers received**. These net transfers amounted in 2014 to –$119 billion. This negative amount reflects the fact that, in 2014, the United States was—as it has traditionally been—a net donor of foreign aid.

Can a country have:
A trade deficit and no current account deficit?
A current account deficit and no trade deficit?
(The answer to both questions: yes.)

The sum of net payments to and from the rest of the world is called the **current account balance**. If net payments from the rest of the world are positive, the country is running a **current account surplus**; if they are negative, the country is running a **current account deficit**. Adding all payments to and from the rest of the world, net payments from the United States to the rest of the world were equal in 2014 to $-$508 + $238 - $119 = -$389$ billion. Put another way, in 2010, the United States ran a current account deficit of $389 billion—roughly 2.3% of its GDP.

The Capital Account

The fact that the United States had a current account deficit of $389 billion in 2014 implies that it had to borrow $389 billion from the rest of the world—or, equivalently, that net foreign holdings of U.S. assets had to increase by $389 billion. The numbers below the line describe how this was achieved. Transactions below the line are called **capital account** transactions.

In the same way that if you spend more than you earn, you have to finance the difference.

The increase in foreign holdings of U.S. assets was $1,031 billion. Foreign investors, be they foreign private investors, foreign governments, or foreign central banks, bought $1,031 billion worth of U.S. stocks, U.S. bonds, and other U.S. assets (including $54 billion from net transactions in financial derivatives). At the same time, there was an increase in U.S. holdings of foreign assets of $792 billion. U.S. investors, private and public, bought $792 billion worth of foreign stocks, bonds, and other assets. The result was an increase in net U.S foreign indebtedness (the increase in foreign holdings of U.S. assets, minus the increase in U.S. holdings of foreign assets), also called **net capital flows** to the United States, of $1,031 - $792 = 239 billion. Another name for net capital flows is the **capital account balance**. Positive net capital flows are called a **capital account surplus**; negative net capital flows are called a **capital account deficit**. So, put another way, in 2014, the United States ran a capital account surplus of $239 billion.

A country that runs a current account deficit must finance it through positive net capital flows. Equivalently, it must run a capital account surplus.

Shouldn't net capital flows (equivalently, the capital account surplus) be exactly equal to the current account deficit (which we saw previously was equal to $389 billion in 2014)?

In principle, yes. In practice, no.

The numbers for current and capital account transactions are constructed using different sources; although they should give the same answers, they typically do not. In 2014, the difference between the two—called the **statistical discrepancy**—was $150 billion, about 39% of the current account balance. This is yet another reminder that, even for a rich country such as the United States, economic data are far from perfect. (This problem of measurement manifests itself in another way as well. The sum of the current account deficits of all the countries in the world should be equal to zero. One country's deficit should show up as a surplus for the other countries taken as a whole. However, this is not the case in the data. If we just add the published current account deficits of all the countries in the world, it would appear that the world is running a large current account deficit!)

Some economists speculate that the explanation lies in unrecorded trade with Martians. Most others believe that mismeasurement is the explanation.

Now that we have looked at the current account, we can return to an issue we touched on in Chapter 2, the difference between gross domestic product (GDP), the measure of output we have used so far, and **gross national product (GNP)**, another measure of aggregate output.

GDP measures *value added domestically*. GNP measures the *value added by domestic factors of production*. When the economy is closed, the two measures are the same. When the economy is open, however, they can differ. Some of the income from domestic production goes to foreigners; and domestic residents receive some foreign income. Thus, to go from GDP to GNP, one must start from GDP, add income received from the rest of the world, and subtract income paid to the rest of the world. Put another way, GNP is equal to GDP plus net payments from the rest of the world. More formally, denoting these net income payments by NI.

$$GNP = GDP + NI$$

In most countries, the difference between the GNP and GDP is small (relative to GDP). For example, in the United States, you can see from Table 17-3 that net income payments were equal to $238 billion. GNP exceeded GDP by $238 billion, or about 1.4% of GDP. For some countries, however, the difference can be large. This is explored in the Focus box on page 382 "GDP versus GNP: The Example of Kuwait."

The Choice between Domestic and Foreign Assets

Openness in financial markets implies that people (or financial institutions that act on their behalf) face a new financial decision: whether to hold domestic assets or foreign assets.

It would appear that we actually have to think about at least *two* new decisions, the choice of holding *domestic* money versus *foreign* money, and the choice of holding *domestic* interest-paying assets versus *foreign* interest-paying assets. But remember why people hold money: to engage in transactions. For someone who lives in the United States and whose transactions are mostly or fully in dollars, there is little point in holding foreign currency. Foreign currency cannot be used for transactions in the United States, and if the goal is to hold foreign assets, holding foreign currency is clearly less desirable than holding foreign bonds, which pay interest. This leaves us with only one new choice to think about, the choice between domestic interest-paying assets and foreign interest-paying assets.

Two qualifications, from Chapter 4:

Foreigners involved in illegal activities often hold dollars because dollars can be exchanged easily and cannot be traced.

And in times of high inflation, people sometimes switch to a foreign currency, often the dollar, for use even in some domestic transactions.

For now, lets think of these assets for now as domestic one-year bonds and foreign one-year bonds. Consider, for example, the choice between U.S. one-year bonds and U.K. one-year bonds, from the point of view of a U.S. investor.

■ Suppose you decide to hold U.S. bonds.

Let i_t be the one-year U.S. nominal interest rate. Then, as Figure 17-7 on page 382 shows for every dollar you put in U.S. bonds, you will get $(1 + i_t)$ dollars next year. (This is represented by the arrow pointing to the right at the top of the figure.)

■ Suppose you decide instead to hold U.K. bonds.

To buy U.K. bonds, you must first buy pounds. Let E_t be the nominal exchange rate between the dollar and the pound. For every dollar, you get E_t pounds. (This is represented by the arrow pointing downward in the figure.)

Let i_t^* denote the one-year nominal interest rate on U.K. bonds (in pounds). When next year comes, you will have $E_t(1 + i_t^*)$ pounds. (This is represented by the arrow pointing to the right at the bottom of the figure.)

MyEconLab Video

GDP versus GNP: The Example of Kuwait

When oil was discovered in Kuwait, Kuwait's government decided that a portion of oil revenues would be saved and invested abroad rather than spent, so as to provide future Kuwaiti generations with income when oil revenues came to an end. Kuwait ran a large current account surplus, steadily accumulating large foreign assets. As a result, it has large holdings of foreign assets and receives substantial income from the rest of the world. Table 1 gives GDP, GNP, and net investment income for Kuwait, from 1989 to 1994 (you will see the reason for the choice of dates).

Note how much larger GNP was compared to GDP throughout the period. Net income from abroad was 34% of GDP in 1989. But note also how net factor payments decreased after 1989. This is because Kuwait had to pay its allies for part of the cost of the 1990–1991 Gulf War and also had to pay for reconstruction after the war. It did so by running a current account deficit—that is, by decreasing its net holdings of foreign assets. This in turn led to a decrease in the income it earned from foreign assets and, by implication, a decrease in its net factor payments.

Since the Gulf War, Kuwait has rebuilt a sizable net foreign asset position. Net income from abroad was 7% of GDP in 2013.

Table 1	GDP, GNP, and Net Income in Kuwait, 1989–1994		
Year	GDP	GNP	Net Income (NI)
1989	7143	9616	2473
1990	5328	7560	2232
1991	3131	4669	1538
1992	5826	7364	1538
1993	7231	8386	1151
1994	7380	8321	941

Source: International Financial Statistics, IMF. All numbers are in millions of Kuwaiti dinars. 1 dinar = $0.3. (2015).

You will then have to convert your pounds back into dollars. If you expect the nominal exchange rate next year to be E_{t+1}^e, each pound will be worth $(1/E_{t+1}^e)$ dollars. So you can expect to have $E_t(1 + i_t^*)(1/E_{t+1}^e)$ dollars next year for every dollar you invest now. (This is represented by the arrow pointing upward in the figure.)

We shall look at the expression we just derived in more detail soon. But note its basic implication already. In assessing the attractiveness of U.K. versus U.S. bonds, you cannot look just at the U.K. interest rate and the U.S. interest rate; you must also assess what you think will happen to the dollar/pound exchange rate between this year and next.

Let's now make the same assumption we made in Chapter 14 when first discussing the choice between short- and long-term bonds. Let's assume that you and other financial investors care only about *the expected rate of return*, ignoring differences in risk, and therefore want to hold only the asset with the highest expected rate of return. In this case, if both U.K. bonds and U.S. bonds are to be held, they must have the same expected rate of return. Arbitrage implies that the following relation must hold:

$$(1 + i_t) = (E_t)(1 + i_t^*)\left(\frac{1}{E_{t+1}^e}\right)$$

Figure 17-7

Expected Returns from Holding One-Year U.S. Bonds versus One-Year U.K. Bonds

MyEconLab Animation

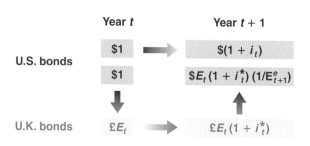

Reorganizing,

$$(1 + i_t) = (1 + i_t^*)\left(\frac{E_t}{E_{t+1}^e}\right) \tag{17.2}$$

Equation (17.2) is called the **uncovered interest parity relation**, or simply the **interest parity condition**.

The assumption that financial investors will hold only the bonds with the highest expected rate of return is obviously too strong, for two reasons:

- It ignores transaction costs. Going in and out of U.K. bonds requires three separate transactions, each with a transaction cost.
- It ignores risk. The exchange rate a year from now is uncertain. For the U.S. investor, holding U.K. bonds is therefore more risky, in terms of dollars, than holding U.S. bonds.

But as a characterization of capital movements among the major world financial markets (New York, Frankfurt, London, and Tokyo), the assumption is not far off. Small changes in interest rates and rumors of impending appreciation or depreciation can lead to movements of billions of dollars within minutes. For the rich countries of the world, the arbitrage assumption in equation (17.2) is a good approximation of reality. Other countries whose capital markets are smaller and less developed, or countries that have various forms of capital controls, have more leeway in choosing their domestic interest rate than is implied by equation (17.2). We shall return to this issue at the end of Chapter 20.

Interest Rates and Exchange Rates

Let's get a better sense of what the interest parity condition implies. First rewrite E_t/E_{t+1}^e as $1/(1 + (E_{t+1}^e - E_t)/E_t)$. Replacing in equation (17.2) gives

$$(1 + i_t) = \frac{(1 + i_t^*)}{[1 + (E_{t+1}^e - E_t)/E_t]} \tag{17.3}$$

This gives us a relation between the domestic nominal interest rate, i_t, the foreign nominal interest rate, i_t^*, and the expected rate of appreciation of the domestic currency, $(E_{t+1}^e - E_t)/E_t$. As long as interest rates or the expected rate of depreciation are not too large—say below 20% a year—a good approximation to this equation is given by:

$$i_t \approx i_t^* - \frac{E_{t+1}^e - E_t}{E_t} \tag{17.4}$$

This is the form of the *interest parity condition* you must remember. Arbitrage by investors implies that *the domestic interest rate must be equal to the foreign interest rate minus the expected appreciation rate of the domestic currency.*

Note that the expected appreciation rate of the domestic currency is also the expected depreciation rate of the foreign currency. So equation (17.4) can be equivalently stated as saying that *the domestic interest rate must be equal to the foreign interest rate minus the expected depreciation rate of the foreign currency.*

Let's apply this equation to U.S. bonds versus U.K. bonds. Suppose the one-year nominal interest rate is 2.0% in the United States and 5.0% in the United Kingdom. Should you hold U.K. bonds or U.S. bonds?

- It depends whether you expect the pound to depreciate relative to the dollar over the coming year by more or less than the difference between the U.S. interest rate and the U.K. interest rate, or 3.0% in this case (5.0% − 2.0%).

The word *uncovered* is to distinguish this relation from another relation called the *covered interest parity condition*. The covered interest parity condition is derived by looking at the following choice: Buy and hold U.S. bonds for one year. Or buy pounds today, buy one-year U.K. bonds with the proceeds, and agree to sell the pounds for dollars a year ahead at a predetermined price, called the *forward exchange rate*. The rate of return on these two alternatives, which can both be realized at *no risk today*, must be the same. The covered interest parity condition is a *riskless arbitrage* condition. It typically holds closely.

Whether holding U.K. bonds or U.S. bonds is more risky actually depends on which investors we are looking at. Holding U.K. bonds is riskier from the point of view of U.S. investors. Holding U.S. bonds is riskier from the point of view of British investors. (Why?)

This follows from Proposition 3 in Appendix 2 at the end of the book.

If the dollar is expected to appreciate by 3% relative to the pound, then the pound is expected to depreciate by 3% relative to the dollar.

Buying Brazilian Bonds

Put yourself back in September 1993 (the very high interest rate in Brazil at the time helps make the point we want to get across here). Brazilian bonds are paying a monthly interest rate of 36.9%! This seems attractive compared to the annual rate of 3% on U.S. bonds—corresponding to a monthly interest rate of about 0.2%. Shouldn't you buy Brazilian bonds?

The discussion in this chapter tells you that to decide you need one more crucial element, the expected rate of depreciation of the cruzeiro (the name of the Brazilian currency at the time; the currency is now called the real) in terms of dollars.

You need this information because, as we saw in equation (17.4), the return in dollars from investing in Brazilian bonds for a month is equal to one plus the Brazilian interest rate, divided by one plus the expected rate of depreciation of the cruzeiro relative to the dollar:

$$\frac{1 + i_t^*}{[1 + (E_{t+1}^e - E_t)/E_t]}$$

What rate of depreciation of the cruzeiro should you expect over the coming month? A reasonable first pass is to expect the rate of depreciation during the coming month to be equal to the rate of depreciation during last month. The dollar was worth 100,000 cruzeiros at the end of July 1993 and worth 134,600 cruzeiros at the end of August 1993, so the rate of appreciation of the dollar relative to the cruzeiro—equivalently, the rate of depreciation of the cruzeiro relative to the dollar—in August was 34.6%. If depreciation is expected to continue at the same rate in September as it did in August, the expected return from investing in Brazilian bonds for one month is

$$\frac{1.369}{1.346} = 1.017$$

The expected rate of return in dollars from holding Brazilian bonds is only $(1.017 - 1) = 1.7\%$ per month, not the 36.9% per month that initially looked so attractive. Note that 1.7% per month is still much higher than the monthly interest rate on U.S. bonds (about 0.2%). But think of the risk and the transaction costs—all the elements we ignored when we wrote the arbitrage condition. When these are taken into account, you may well decide to keep your funds out of Brazil.

- If you expect the pound to depreciate by more than 3.0%, then, despite the fact that the interest rate is higher in the United Kingdom than in the United States, investing in U.K. bonds is less attractive than investing in U.S. bonds. By holding U.K. bonds, you will get higher interest payments next year, but the pound will be worth less in terms of dollars next year, making investing in U.K. bonds less attractive than investing in U.S. bonds.

- If you expect the pound to depreciate by less than 3.0% or even to appreciate, then the reverse holds, and U.K bonds are more attractive than U.S. bonds.

Looking at it another way. If the uncovered interest parity condition holds, and the U.S. one-year interest rate is 3% lower than the U.K. interest rate, it must be that financial investors are expecting, on average, an appreciation of the dollar relative to the pound over the coming year of about 3%, and this is why they are willing to hold U.S. bonds despite their lower interest rate. (Another—and more striking—example is provided in the Focus box "Buying Brazilian Bonds.")

The arbitrage relation between interest rates and exchange rates, either in the form of equation (17.2) or equation (17.4), will play a central role in the following chapters. It suggests that, unless countries are willing to tolerate large movements in their ex-

If $E_{t+1}^e = E_t$, then the interest ▶ parity condition implies $i_t = i_t^*$.

change rate, domestic and foreign interest rates are likely to move largely together. Take the extreme case of two countries that commit to maintaining their bilateral exchange rates at a fixed value. If markets have faith in this commitment, they will expect the exchange rate to remain constant, and the expected depreciation will be equal to zero. In this case, the arbitrage condition implies that interest rates in the two countries will have to move exactly together. Most of the time, as we shall see, governments do not make such absolute commitments to maintain the exchange rate, but they often do try to avoid large movements in the exchange rate. This puts sharp limits on how much they can allow their interest rate to deviate from interest rates elsewhere in the world.

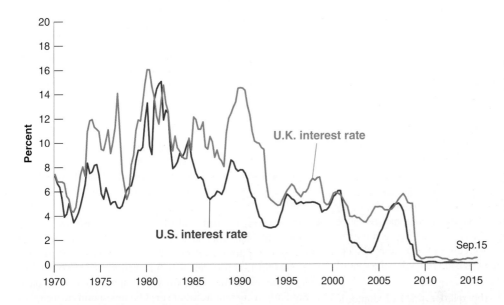

Figure 17-8

Three-Month Nominal Interest Rates in the United States and in the United Kingdom since 1970

U.S. and U.K. nominal interest rates have largely moved together over the last 40 years.

Source: U.S. 3-Month Treasury Bill Rate Series WTB3MS; Federal Reserve Economic Data (FRED); U.K. 3-Month Treasury Bill Rate Series IUQAAJNB, Bank of England.

MyEconLab Real-time data

How much do nominal interest rates actually move together in major countries? Figure 17-8 plots the three-month nominal interest rate in the United States and the three-month nominal interest rate in the United Kingdom (both expressed at annual rates) since 1970. The figure shows that the movements are related but not identical. Interest rates were high in both countries in the early 1980s, and high again— although much more so in the United Kingdom than in the United States—in the late 1980s. They have been low in both countries since the mid-1990s. At the same time, differences between the two have sometimes been quite large. In 1990, for example, the U.K. interest rate was nearly 7% higher than the U.S. interest rate. (At the time of writing, both countries are at the zero lower bound, and one-year rates are close to zero.) In the coming chapters, we shall return to why such differences emerge and what their ◄ implications may be.

Meanwhile, do the following: Look at the back pages of a recent issue of *The Economist* for short-term interest rates in different countries relative to the United States. Assume uncovered interest parity holds. Which currencies are expected to appreciate against the dollar?

17-3 Conclusions and a Look Ahead

We have now set the stage for the study of the open economy:

- Openness in goods markets allows people and firms to choose between domestic goods and foreign goods. This choice depends primarily on the *real exchange rate*— the relative price of domestic goods in terms of foreign goods.
- Openness in financial markets allows investors to choose between domestic assets and foreign assets. This choice depends primarily on their relative rates of return, which depend on domestic interest rates and foreign interest rates, and on the expected rate of appreciation of the domestic currency.

In the next chapter, Chapter 18, we look at the implications of openness in goods markets. In Chapter 19, we further explore openness in financial markets. In Chapter 20, we discuss the pros and cons of different exchange rate regimes.

Summary

- Openness in goods markets allows people and firms to choose between domestic goods and foreign goods. Openness in financial markets allows financial investors to hold domestic financial assets or foreign financial assets.

- The nominal exchange rate is the price of the domestic currency in terms of foreign currency. From the viewpoint of the United States, the nominal exchange rate between the United States and the United Kingdom is the price of a dollar in terms of pounds.

- A nominal appreciation (an appreciation, for short) is an increase in the price of the domestic currency in terms of foreign currency. In other words, it corresponds to an increase in the exchange rate. A nominal depreciation (a depreciation, for short) is a decrease in the price of the domestic currency in terms of foreign currency. It corresponds to a decrease in the exchange rate.

- **MEL** **Video** The real exchange rate is the relative price of domestic goods in terms of foreign goods. It is equal to the nominal exchange rate times the domestic price level divided by the foreign price level.

- A real appreciation is an increase in the relative price of domestic goods in terms of foreign goods (i.e., an increase in the real exchange rate). A real depreciation is a decrease in the relative price of domestic goods in terms of foreign goods (i.e., a decrease in the real exchange rate).

- The multilateral real exchange rate, or real exchange rate for short, is a weighted average of bilateral real exchange rates, with the weight for each foreign country equal to its share in trade.

- The balance of payments records a country's transactions with the rest of the world. The current account balance is equal to the sum of the trade balance, net income, and net transfers the country receives from the rest of the world. The capital account balance is equal to capital flows from the rest of the world minus capital flows to the rest of the world.

- The current account and the capital account are mirror images of each other. Leaving aside statistical problems, the current account plus the capital account must sum to zero. A current account deficit is financed by net capital flows from the rest of the world, thus by a capital account surplus. Similarly, a current account surplus corresponds to a capital account deficit.

- Uncovered interest parity, or interest parity for short, is an arbitrage condition stating that the expected rates of return in terms of domestic currency on domestic bonds and foreign bonds must be equal. Interest parity implies that the domestic interest rate approximately equals the foreign interest rate minus the expected appreciation rate of the domestic currency.

Key Terms

openness in goods markets, 369

tariffs, 369

quotas, 369

openness in financial markets, 369

capital controls, 369

openness in factor markets, 369

North American Free Trade Agreement (NAFTA), 369

tradable goods, 371

real exchange rate, 372

nominal exchange rate, 373

appreciation (nominal), 373

depreciation (nominal), 373

fixed exchange rates, 373

revaluation, 373

devaluation, 373

real appreciation, 375

real depreciation, 375

bilateral exchange rate, 377

multilateral exchange rate, 377

multilateral real U.S. exchange rate, 377

trade-weighted real exchange rate, 377

effective real exchange rate, 377

foreign exchange, 378

balance of payments, 379

above the line, 379

below the line, 379

current account, 379

income balance, 380

net transfers received, 380

current account balance, 380

current account surplus, 380

current account deficit, 380

capital account, 380

net capital flows, 380

capital account balance, 380

capital account surplus, 380

capital account deficit, 380

statistical discrepancy, 380

gross national product (GNP), 381

uncovered interest parity
relation, 383

interest parity condition, 383

Questions and Problems

MyEconLab Visit www.myeconlab.com to complete similar Quick Check problems and get instant feedback.

1. Using the information in this chapter, label each of the following statements true, false, or uncertain. Explain briefly.

a. If there are no statistical discrepancies, countries with current account deficits must receive net capital inflows.

b. Although the export ratio can be larger than one—as it is in Singapore—the same cannot be true of the ratio of imports to GDP.

c. The fact that a rich country like Japan has such a small ratio of imports to GDP is clear evidence of an unfair playing field for U.S. exporters to Japan.

d. Uncovered interest parity implies that interest rates must be the same across countries.

e. The nominal exchange rate in this chapter is defined as the domestic currency price of a unit of foreign currency.

f. The nominal exchange rate and the real exchange rate always move in the same direction.

g. The nominal exchange rate and the real exchange rate usually move in the same direction.

h. If the dollar is expected to appreciate against the yen, uncovered interest parity implies that the U.S. nominal interest rate must be greater than the Japanese nominal interest rate.

i. Given the definition of the exchange rate adopted in this chapter, if the dollar is the domestic currency and the euro the foreign currency, a nominal exchange rate of 0.75 means that 0.75 dollars is worth 0.75 euros.

j. A real appreciation means that domestic goods become less expensive relative to foreign goods.

2. Consider two fictional economies, one called the domestic country and the other the foreign country. Given the transactions listed in (a) through (g), construct the balance of payments for each country. If necessary, include a statistical discrepancy.

a. The domestic country purchased $100 in oil from the foreign country.

b. Foreign tourists spent $25 on domestic ski slopes.

c. Foreign investors were paid $15 in dividends from their holdings of domestic equities.

d. Domestic residents gave $25 to foreign charities.

e. Domestic businesses borrowed $65 from foreign banks.

f. Foreign investors purchased $15 of domestic government bonds.

g. Domestic investors sold $50 of their holdings of foreign government bonds.

3. Each of the governments of Brazil and Turkey has issued bonds in Brazilian real (BRL) and Turkish liras (TRY), respectively. Assume that both are one-year bonds, i.e. paying the face value of the bonds in one year.

Suppose that the exchange rate (E) is 1 Brazilian Real = 0.79 Turkish Lira.

The following table shows the face value and price for both bonds:

	Face Value	Price
Brazil	BRL 10,000	BRL 9,630
Turkey	TRY 10,000	TRY 9,450

a. Calculate the nominal interest rate for each of the bonds.

b. Given that the condition of interest rate parity persists, calculate the exchange rate one year from now.

c. If you expect the real to depreciate in comparison to the lira, which bond should you buy?

d. Assume that you are a Brazilian investor. You exchange the reals for liras and buy the Turkish bond. One year from now it turns out that the exchange rate (E) is 0.75, i.e. 0.75 liras buy one real. What is your realized rate of return in reals compared to the realized rate of return you would have made had you held the Brazilian bond?

e. Explain whether the differences in the rates of return in the previous question are or are not consistent with the uncovered interest rate parity condition.

MyEconLab Visit www.myeconlab.com to complete all Dig Deeper problems and get instant feedback.

4. Consider a world with three equal-sized economies (A, B, and C) and three goods (food, clothes, and cars). Assume that consumers in all three economies want to spend an equal amount on all three goods.

The following table shows the value of production of each good in the three economies.

	A	B	C
Food	10	0	5
Clothes	5	10	0
Cars	0	5	10

a. What is the GDP in each economy? Assume that the total value of GDP is consumed and no country borrows from abroad. How much will consumers in all of the three economies spend on each of the goods?

b. What is the trade balance in each country if none of the 3 countries borrows from abroad? What goods will be traded in the world? What will be the pattern of trade between the 3 nations?

c. Will there be a zero trade balance between any of the three countries? Explain your answer.

d. Due to their large intra-trade volume, the EU-28 (the 28 nations of the EU, which may change following the Brexit results) has a small trade balance deficit. The EU-28 has a trade deficit with some of its trading partners and a trade surplus with others, but the trade deficit is much larger specifically with China. Suppose the EU-28 eliminates its overall trade deficit with the world as a whole. Do you expect the EU-28 to have a zero trade balance with every one of its partners? Does the especially large trade deficit with China indicate that China does not allow EU-28 goods to compete on an equal basis with Chinese goods?

5. *The exchange rate and the labor market*
   Suppose the domestic currency depreciates (i.e., E falls).
   Assume that P and P* remain constant.
   a. How does the nominal depreciation affect the relative price of domestic goods (i.e., the real exchange rate)? Given your answer, what effect would a nominal depreciation likely have on (world) demand for domestic goods? on the domestic unemployment rate?
   b. Given the foreign price level, $P*$, what is the price of foreign goods in terms of domestic currency? How does a nominal depreciation affect the price of foreign goods in terms of domestic currency? How does a nominal depreciation affect the domestic consumer price index? (*Hint*: Remember that domestic consumers buy foreign goods (imports) as well as domestic goods.)
   c. If the nominal wage remains constant, how does a nominal depreciation affect the real wage?
   d. Comment on the following statement. "A depreciating currency puts domestic labor on sale."

EXPLORE FURTHER

6. *Retrieve the nominal exchange rates between the euro (EUR) and the South African rand (ZAR) from the European Central Bank statistics section: "Euro foreign exchange reference rates." It is quoted as ZAR per 1 EUR.*
   a. According to the terminology of the chapter when the exchange rate is quoted as ZAR per EUR which of the two currencies is treated as the domestic currency?
   b. Plot the ZAR per EUR curve since 1995. During which times did the rand appreciate? During which periods did the rand depreciate?
   c. One way of boosting its economy is for the South African government to make its commodities more attractive. Does this require an appreciation or depreciation of the rand?
   d. What has happened to the rand since the global financial crisis of 2008? Has it appreciated or depreciated and is this good or bad for South Africa?

7. *The International Monetary Fund provides a number of publications on its Web site (www.imf.org). Extract from the Statistical Appendix of the World Economic Outlook (WEO) the table titled "Balances on Current Account," which lists current account balances around the world. Use the data for the most recent year to answer parts (a) through (c).*
   a. What is the sum of the world current account balances? Does the sum of the current account balances round the world equal zero as noted in the chapter? What are the sources of this discrepancy and what would it imply?
   b. Compare the regions of the world in terms of borrowing and lending.
   c. Egypt and Tunisia are two nations that have emerged from popular revolutions in 2010–2011. How do their current account balances reflect the economic impact of these uprisings?
   d. The WEO usually provides projections for the following two years. What is the projected outlook in terms of regional borrowing/lending? How do you explain the projected changes for fuel and non-fuel export earnings?

8. *Saving and Investment throughout the world*
   Refer once more to the publications of the International Monetary Fund on its Web site (www.imf.org). Extract from the Statistical Appendix of the World Economic Outlook (WEO) the table titled "Summary of Net Lending and Borrowing" which lists savings and investment (as a percentage of GDP) around the world. Use the data for the most recent year to answer parts (a) and (b).
   a. Does world saving equal investment?
   b. How does the UK saving compare to its investment? How is the UK able to finance its investment? (We explain this in the next chapter, but you might be able to figure it out by now.)
   c. From the World Bank Database compare GDP and GNP (also known as GNI or Gross National Income) for China and Germany for the periods 2006–2010 and 2011–2015. For each of these countries is GDP higher or lower than GNP? What is the reason for the differences?

Further Readings

· ·

■ If you want to learn more about international trade and international economics, a very good textbook is by Paul Krugman, Marc Melitz, and Maurice Obstfeld. Prentice Hall, *International Economics, Theory and Policy*, 10th ed. (2014).

■ If you want to know current exchange rates between nearly any pair of currencies in the world, look at the "currency converter" on http://www.oanda.com/currency/converter/.

The Goods Market in an Open Economy

I n 2009, countries around the world worried about the risk of a recession in the United States. But their worries were not so much for the United States as they were for themselves. To them, a U.S. recession meant lower exports to the United States, a deterioration of their trade position, and weaker growth at home.

Were their worries justified? Figure 17-1 from the previous chapter certainly suggested they were. The U.S. recession clearly led to a world recession. To understand what happened, we must expand the treatment of the goods market in Chapter 3 of the core and account for openness in the analysis of goods markets. This is what we do in this chapter.

Section 18-1 characterizes equilibrium in the goods market for an open economy.

Sections 18-2 and **18-3** show the effects of domestic shocks and foreign shocks on the domestic economy's output and trade balance.

Sections 18-4 and **18-5** look at the effects of a real depreciation on output and the trade balance.

Section 18-6 gives an alternative description of the equilibrium that shows the close connection among saving, investment, and the trade balance.

18-1 The *IS* Relation in the Open Economy

When we were assuming the economy was closed to trade, there was no need to distinguish between the *domestic demand for goods* and the *demand for domestic goods*; they were clearly the same thing. Now, we must distinguish between the two. Some domestic demand falls on foreign goods, and some of the demand for domestic goods comes from foreigners. Let's look at this distinction more closely.

"The domestic demand for goods" and "the demand for domestic goods" sound close but are not the same. Part of ▶ domestic demand falls on foreign goods. Part of foreign demand falls on domestic goods.

The Demand for Domestic Goods

In an open economy, the **demand for domestic goods**, Z, is given by

$$Z = C + I + G - IM/\varepsilon + X \qquad (18.1)$$

The first three terms—consumption, C, investment, I, and government spending, G—constitute the total **domestic demand for goods**, domestic or foreign. If the economy were closed, $C + I + G$ would also be the demand for domestic goods. This is why, until now, we have only looked at $C + I + G$. But now we have to make two adjustments:

In Chapter 3, I ignored the real exchange rate and subtracted *IM*, not *IM*/ε. But I was cheating; I did not want to have to talk about the real exchange rate—and complicate matters— ▶ so early in the book.

- First, we must subtract imports—that part of the domestic demand that falls on foreign goods rather than on domestic goods.

    We must be careful here. Foreign goods are different from domestic goods, so we cannot just subtract the quantity of imports, IM. If we were to do so, we would be subtracting apples (foreign goods) from oranges (domestic goods). We must first express the value of imports in terms of domestic goods. This is what IM/ε in equation (18.1) stands for. Recall from Chapter 17 that ε, the real exchange rate, is defined as the price of domestic goods in terms of foreign goods. Equivalently, $1/\varepsilon$ is the price of foreign goods in terms of domestic goods. So $IM,(1/\varepsilon)$—or, equivalently, IM/ε—is the value of imports in terms of domestic goods.

- Second, we must add exports—that part of the demand for domestic goods that comes from abroad. This is captured by the term X in equation (18.1).

Domestic demand for goods ▶
$C + I + G$
  − Domestic demand for foreign goods (imports), *IM*/ε
  + Foreign demand for domestic goods (exports), *X*
  = Demand for domestic goods
    $C + I + G - IM/\varepsilon + X$

The Determinants of *C*, *I*, and *G*

Having listed the five components of demand, the next task is to specify their determinants. Let's start with the first three: C, I, and G. Now that we are assuming the economy is open, how should we modify our earlier descriptions of consumption, investment, and government spending? The answer: not very much, if at all. How much consumers decide to spend still depends on their income and their wealth. Although the real exchange rate surely affects the *composition* of consumption spending between domestic goods and foreign goods, there is no obvious reason why it should affect the overall *level* of consumption. The same is true of investment; the real exchange rate may affect whether firms buy domestic machines or foreign machines, but it should not affect total investment.

This is good news because it implies that we can use the descriptions of consumption, investment, and government spending that we developed earlier. Therefore, I assume that domestic demand is given by:

$$\text{Domestic demand:} \quad C + I + G = C(Y - T) + I(Y, r) + G$$
$$(+) \qquad (+,-)$$

I again cheat a bit here. Income should include not only domestic income but also net income and transfers from abroad. For ▶ simplicity, I ignore these two additional terms here.

Consumption depends positively on disposable income, $Y - T$ and investment depends positively on production, Y, and negatively on the real policy rate, r. Note that I leave aside some of the refinements I introduced earlier, i.e the presence of a risk premium which we focused on in Chapters 6 and 14, and the role of expectations which we focused on in Chapters 14 to 16. I want to take things one step at a time to understand the effects of opening the economy; I shall reintroduce some of those refinements later.

The Determinants of Imports

Imports are the part of domestic demand that falls on foreign goods. What do they depend on? They clearly depend on domestic income. Higher domestic income leads to a higher domestic demand for all goods, both domestic and foreign. So a higher domestic income leads to higher imports. They also clearly depend on the real exchange rate— the price of domestic goods in terms of foreign goods. The more expensive domestic goods are relative to foreign goods—equivalently, the cheaper foreign goods are relative to domestic goods—the higher is the domestic demand for foreign goods. So a higher real exchange rate leads to higher imports. Thus, we write imports as:

Recall the discussion at the start of this chapter. Countries in the rest of the world worry about a U.S. recession. The reason: A U.S. recession means a decrease in the U.S. demand for foreign goods.

$$IM = IM(Y, \varepsilon) \qquad (18.2)$$
$$(+, +)$$

- An increase in domestic income, Y (equivalently, an increase in domestic output—income and output are still equal in an open economy) leads to an increase in imports. This positive effect of income on imports is captured by the positive sign under Y in equation (18.2).
- An increase in the real exchange rate, ε (a real appreciation), leads to an increase in imports, IM. This positive effect of the real exchange rate on imports is captured by the positive sign under ε in equation (18.2). (As ε goes up, note that IM goes up, but $1/\varepsilon$ goes down, so what happens to IM/ε, the *value* of imports in terms of domestic goods, is ambiguous. We return to this point shortly.)

The Determinants of Exports

Exports are the part of foreign demand that falls on domestic goods. What do they depend on? They depend on foreign income. Higher foreign income means higher foreign demand for all goods, both foreign and domestic. So higher foreign income leads to higher exports. They depend also on the real exchange rate. The higher the price of domestic goods in terms of foreign goods, the lower the foreign demand for domestic goods. In other words, the higher the real exchange rate, the lower are exports.

MyEconLab Video

Let Y^* denote foreign income (equivalently, foreign output). We therefore write exports as

Recall that asterisks refer to foreign variables.

$$X = X(Y^*, \varepsilon) \qquad (18.3)$$
$$(+, -)$$

- An increase in foreign income, Y^*, leads to an increase in exports.
- An increase in the real exchange rate, ε, leads to a decrease in exports.

Putting the Components Together

Figure 18-1 puts together what we have learned so far. It plots the various components of demand against output, keeping constant all other variables (the interest rate, taxes, government spending, foreign output, and the real exchange rate) that affect demand.

In Figure 18-1(a), the line DD plots domestic demand, $C + I + G$ as a function of output, Y. This relation between demand and output is familiar from Chapter 3. Under our standard assumptions, the slope of the relation between demand and output is positive but less than one. An increase in output—equivalently, an increase in

Figure 18-1

The Demand for Domestic Goods and Net Exports

(a), The domestic demand for goods is an increasing function of income (output).

(b) and (c), The demand for domestic goods is obtained by subtracting the value of imports from domestic demand and then adding exports.

(d), The trade balance is a decreasing function of output.

MyEconLab Animation

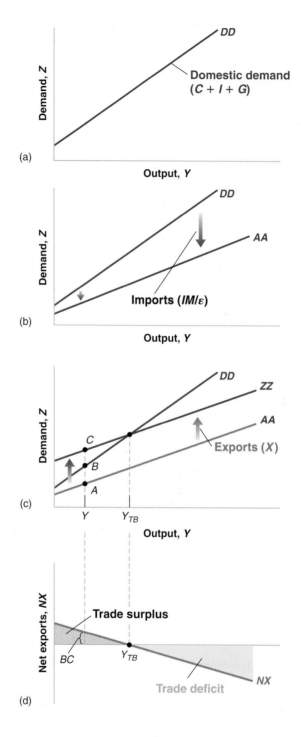

income—increases demand but less than one-for-one. (In the absence of good reasons to the contrary, we draw the relation between demand and output, and the other relations in this chapter, as lines rather than curves. This is purely for convenience, and none of the discussions that follow depend on this assumption.)

To arrive at the demand for domestic goods, we must first *subtract imports.* This is done in Figure 18-1(b) and it gives us the line *AA.* The line *AA* represents the domestic demand for domestic goods. The distance between *DD* and *AA* equals the value of imports, IM/ε. Because the quantity of imports increases with income, the distance between the two lines increases with income. We can establish two facts about line AA, which will be useful later in the chapter:

For a given real exchange rate ε, IM/ε—the value of imports in terms of domestic goods—moves exactly with IM, the quantity of imports.

- AA is flatter than DD. As income increases, some of the additional domestic demand falls on foreign goods rather than on domestic goods. In other words, as income increases, the domestic demand for domestic goods increases less than total domestic demand.

- As long as some of the additional demand falls on domestic goods, AA has a positive slope. An increase in income leads to some increase in the demand for domestic goods.

Finally, we must *add exports*. This is done in Figure 18-1(c) and it gives us the line ZZ, which is above AA. The line ZZ represents the demand for domestic goods. The distance between ZZ and AA equals exports, X. Because exports do not depend on domestic income (they depend on foreign income), the distance between ZZ and AA is constant, which is why the two lines are parallel. Because AA is flatter than DD, ZZ is also flatter than DD.

From the information in Figure 18-1(c) we can characterize the behavior of net exports—the difference between exports and imports $(X - IM/\varepsilon)$—as a function of output. At output level Y, for example, exports are given by the distance AC and imports by the distance AB, so net exports are given by the distance BC.

Recall that *net exports* is synonymous with trade balance. Positive net exports correspond to a trade surplus, whereas negative net exports correspond to a trade deficit.

This relation between net exports and output is represented as the line NX (for Net eXports) in Figure 18-1(d). Net exports are a decreasing function of output. As output increases, imports increase and exports are unaffected, so net exports decrease. Call Y_{TB} (TB for trade balance) the level of output at which the value of imports equals the value of exports, so that net exports are equal to zero. Levels of output above Y_{TB} lead to higher imports and to a trade deficit. Levels of output below Y_{TB} lead to lower imports and to a trade surplus.

18-2 Equilibrium Output and the Trade Balance

The goods market is in equilibrium when domestic output equals the demand—both domestic and foreign—for domestic goods.

$$Y = Z$$

Collecting the relations we derived for the components of the demand for domestic goods, Z, we get

$$Y = C(Y - T) + I(Y, r) + G - IM(Y, \varepsilon)/\varepsilon + X(Y^*, \varepsilon) \qquad (18.4)$$

This equilibrium condition determines output as a function of all the variables we take as given, from taxes to the real exchange rate to foreign output. This is not a simple relation; Figure 18-2 represents it graphically, in a more user-friendly way.

In Figure 18-2(a), demand is measured on the vertical axis, output (equivalently production or income) on the horizontal axis. The line ZZ plots demand as a function of output; this line just replicates the line ZZ in Figure 18-1(c); ZZ is upward sloping, but with slope less than 1.

Equilibrium output is at the point where demand equals output, at the intersection of the line ZZ and the 45-degree line: point A in Figure 18-2(a), with associated output level Y.

Figure 18-2(b) replicates Figure 18-1(d), drawing net exports as a decreasing function of output. There is in general no reason why the equilibrium level of output, Y, should be the same as the level of output at which trade is balanced, Y_{TB}. As we have drawn the figure, equilibrium output is associated with a trade deficit, equal to the

The equilibrium level of output is given by the condition $Y = Z$. The level of output at which there is trade balance is given by the condition $X = IM/\varepsilon$. These are two different conditions.

Figure 18-2

Equilibrium Output and Net Exports

The goods market is in equilibrium when domestic output is equal to the demand for domestic goods. At the equilibrium level of output, the trade balance may show a deficit or a surplus.

MyEconLab Animation

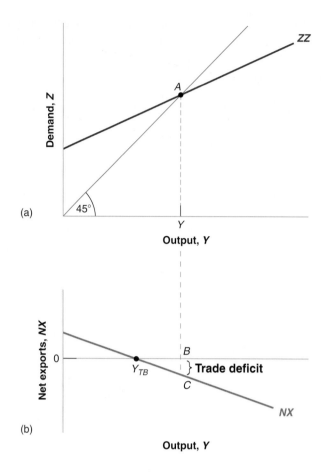

(a)

(b)

distance BC. Note that we could have drawn it differently, so equilibrium output was associated instead with a trade surplus.

We now have the tools needed to answer the questions we asked at the beginning of this chapter.

18-3 Increases in Demand—Domestic or Foreign

How do changes in demand affect output in an open economy? Let's start with an old favorite—an increase in government spending—then turn to a new exercise, the effects of an increase in foreign demand.

Increases in Domestic Demand

As in the core, we start with just the goods market, and introduce financial markets and ▶ labor markets later on.

Suppose the economy is in a recession and the government decides to increase government spending in order to increase domestic demand and, in turn, output. What will be the effects on output and on the trade balance?

The answer is given in Figure 18-3. Before the increase in government spending, demand is given by ZZ in Figure 18-3(a), and the equilibrium is at point A, where output equals Y. Let's assume that trade is initially balanced—even though, as we have seen, there is no reason why this should be true in general. So, in Figure 18-3(b), $Y = Y_{TB}$.

What happens if the government increases spending by ΔG? At any level of output, demand is higher by ΔG, shifting the demand relation up by ΔG from ZZ to ZZ'.

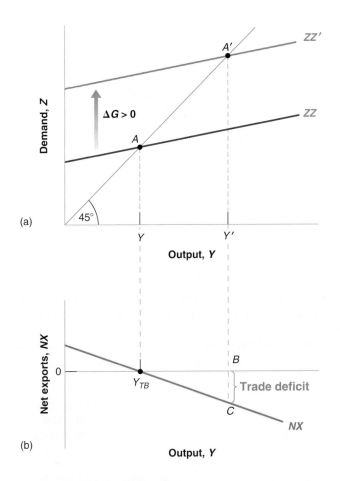

Figure 18-3

*The Effects of an Increase
in Government Spending*

An increase in government
spending leads to an increase
in output and to a trade deficit.

MyEconLab Animation

The equilibrium point moves from A to A', and output increases from Y to Y'. The increase in output is larger than the increase in government spending: There is a multiplier effect.

So far, the story sounds the same as the story for a closed economy in Chapter 3. However, there are two important differences:

- There is now an effect on the trade balance. Because government spending enters neither the exports relation nor the imports relation directly, the relation between net exports and output in Figure 18-3(b) does not shift. So the increase in output from Y to Y' leads to a *trade deficit* equal to BC: Imports go up, and exports do not change.   ◀ *Starting from trade balance, an increase in government spending leads to a trade deficit.*

- Not only does government spending now generate a trade deficit, but the effect of government spending on output is smaller than it would be in a closed economy. Recall from Chapter 3 that the smaller the slope of the demand relation, the smaller the multiplier (for example, if ZZ were horizontal, the multiplier would be 1). And recall from Figure 18-1 that the demand relation, ZZ, is flatter than the demand relation in the closed economy, DD. This means the *multiplier is smaller in the* ◀ *open economy.*   *An increase in government spending increases output. The multiplier is smaller than in a closed economy.*

The trade deficit and the smaller multiplier have the same origin. Because the economy is open, an increase in demand now falls not only on domestic goods but also on foreign goods. So when income increases, the effect on the demand for domestic goods is smaller than it would be in a closed economy, leading to a smaller multiplier. And because some of the increase in demand falls on imports—and exports are unchanged— ◀ the result is a trade deficit.   *The smaller multiplier and the trade deficit have the same origin. Some domestic demand falls on foreign goods.*

These two implications are important. In an open economy, an increase in domestic demand has a smaller effect on output than in a closed economy, and an adverse effect on the trade balance. Indeed, the more open the economy, the smaller the effect on output and the larger the adverse effect on the trade balance. Take the Netherlands, for example. As we saw in Chapter 17, the Netherlands' ratio of exports to GDP is very high. It is also true that the Netherlands' ratio of imports to GDP is very high. When domestic demand increases in the Netherlands, much of the increase in demand is likely to result in an increase in the demand for foreign goods rather than an increase in the demand for domestic goods. The effect of an increase in government spending is therefore likely to be a large increase in the Netherlands' trade deficit and only a small increase in its output, making domestic demand expansion a rather unattractive policy for the Netherlands. Even for the United States, which has a much lower import ratio, an increase in demand will be associated with a worsening of the trade balance.

Increases in Foreign Demand

Consider now an increase in foreign output, that is, an increase in Y^*. This could be due to an increase in foreign government spending, G^*—the policy change we just analyzed, but now taking place abroad. But we do not need to know where the increase in Y^* comes from to analyze its effects on the U.S. economy.

Figure 18-4 shows the effects of an increase in foreign activity on domestic output and the trade balance. The initial demand for domestic goods is given by ZZ in

Figure 18-4

The Effects of an Increase in Foreign Demand

An increase in foreign demand leads to an increase in output and to a trade surplus.

MyEconLab Animation

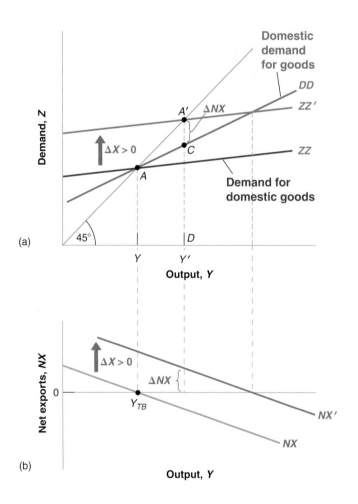

The Open Economy   **Extensions**

Figure 18-4(a). The equilibrium is at point A, with output level Y. Let's again assume trade is balanced, so that in Figure 18-4(b) the net exports associated with Y equal zero $(Y = Y_{TB})$.

It will be useful below to refer to the line that shows the *domestic demand for goods* $C + I + G$ as a function of income. This line is drawn as DD. Recall from Figure 18-1 that DD is steeper than ZZ. The difference between ZZ and DD equal net exports, so that if trade is balanced at point A, then ZZ and DD intersect at point A.

Now consider the effects of an increase in foreign output, ΔY^* (for the moment, ignore the line DD; we only need it later). Higher foreign output means higher foreign demand, including higher foreign demand for U.S. goods. So the direct effect of the increase in foreign output is an increase in U.S. exports by some amount, which we shall denote by ΔX.

- For a given level of output, this increase in exports leads to an increase in the demand for U.S. goods by ΔX, so the line showing the demand for domestic goods as a function of output shifts up by ΔX, from ZZ to ZZ'.
- For a given level of output, net exports go up by ΔX. So the line showing net exports as a function of output in Figure 18-4(b) also shifts up by ΔX, from NX to NX'.

The new equilibrium is at point A' in Figure 18-4(a), with output level Y'. The increase in foreign output leads to an increase in domestic output. The channel is clear. Higher foreign output leads to higher exports of domestic goods, which increases domestic output and the domestic demand for goods through the multiplier.

What happens to the trade balance? We know that exports go up. But could it be that the increase in domestic output leads to such a large increase in imports that the trade balance actually deteriorates? No: The trade balance must improve. To see why, note that, when foreign demand increases, the demand for domestic goods shifts up from ZZ to ZZ'; but the line DD, which gives the *domestic demand for goods* as a function of output, does not shift. At the new equilibrium level of output Y', domestic demand is given by the distance DC, and the demand for domestic goods is given by DA'. Net exports are therefore given by the distance CA'—which, because DD is necessarily below ZZ', is necessarily positive. Thus, while imports increase, the increase does not offset the increase in exports, and the trade balance improves.

DD is the domestic demand for goods. ZZ is the demand for domestic goods. The difference between the two is equal to the trade deficit.

Y^* directly affects exports and so enters the relation between the demand for domestic goods and output. An increase in Y^* shifts ZZ up. Y^* does not affect domestic consumption, domestic investment, or domestic government spending directly, and so it does not enter the relation between the domestic demand for goods and output. An increase in Y^* does not shift DD.

MyEconLab Video

An increase in foreign output increases domestic output and improves the trade balance.

Fiscal Policy Revisited

We have derived two results so far:

- An increase in domestic demand leads to an increase in domestic output but leads also to a deterioration of the trade balance. (We looked at an increase in government spending, but the results would have been the same for a decrease in taxes, an increase in consumer spending, and so on.)
- An increase in foreign demand (which could come from the same types of changes taking place abroad) leads to an increase in domestic output and an improvement in the trade balance.

These results, in turn, have two important implications. Both have been in evidence in the recent crisis.

First, and most obviously, they imply that shocks to demand in one country affect all other countries. The stronger the trade links between countries, the stronger the interactions, and the more countries will move together. This is what we saw in Figure 17-1. Although the crisis started in the United States, it quickly affected the rest of the world. Trade links were not the only reason; financial links also played a central role. But the evidence points to a strong effect of trade, starting with a decrease in exports from other countries to the United States.

Fiscal Stimulus and Structural Reforms amid Negative Interest Rates

To combat the ills of the global financial crisis, 2007–2008, fiscal and monetary agents around the world successfully implemented stimulus packages that helped the international economy to emerge out of the worst global recession in history. As real interest rates were still above the zero bound levels, central banks cut policy rates. To provide further economic stimulus, central banks also employed unconventional monetary policy measures, hence, expanding their balance sheets as a result of quantitative easing or large-scale foreign exchange purchases. Also, most nations simultaneously introduced fiscal stimulus packages by decreasing taxes and/or increasing public spending. However, nations that employed milder stimulus packages were unable to refurbish their economies and fell into severe debt crises.

Despite these stimulus packages, since mid-2014, several economies are suffering from deflation and GDP slowdown. The global economy has been grappling with the combined ills of declining macroeconomic growth rates in Chinese and emerging market economies, the inability of low oil prices to boost growth, and decelerating global aggregate demand rates. With this gloomy outlook, some central banks added another dimension to their toolkit by resorting to negative nominal policy interest rates. In an attempt to prevent the Eurozone from falling into a deflationary spiral, in mid-2015, the European Central Bank (ECB) took the lead in applying a negative interest rate (NIR) to some amounts of the legal reserve balances that central banks hold with the ECB. Soon the central banks of Switzerland, Denmark, Sweden, Japan, and Hungary followed suit. Adopting NIRs was aimed to encourage private investment, increase consumer spending, support price stability, and reduce exchange rate appreciation to enhance exports and growth.

Many economists criticize the NIR strategy on the premise that it is unsustainable and may have been avoided had governments adopted more expansionary fiscal policies and introduced visionary structural reforms. Allianz' chief economic adviser, Mohamed El-Erian, said: "The system isn't built to operate with negative nominal rates." Financial experts also caution that NIRs prevent financial services, like insurance companies and pension funds, from getting the yields they need to thrive. Opponents of the NIR strategy argue that individuals will be discouraged to save and may even hoard cash outside the financial sector. Moreover, NIRs are apt to cause political problems as savers should be rewarded for the risk of placing their money in financial system.

On the flip side, proponents of negative interest rates maintain that so far central banks have only cut deposit rates on cash held by the commercial banks that exceeded the legal reserve requirement. This is to encourage commercial banks to make these excess funds available for lending to consumers and businesses at lower costs in order to stimulate growth and avoid deflation. Moreover, commercial and saving banks have not passed negative rates to their savers and retail customers in the fear of major deposit withdrawals. Advocates of NIRs further argue that even in the case that banks pass on these NIRs to their clients, savers and stock market traders do not have to pull their money out of the financial sector, as they could earn higher returns in more risky assets.

However, with the mounting criticism of negative rate policies, central bankers are pressurizing their fiscal agent counterparts to rapidly reverse NIR policies, specifically requesting their governments to introduce more interventionist expansionary fiscal policies and to endorse structural reforms. When negative interest rates can lead to a deflationary trap, fiscal policies should aim directly at stimulating aggregate demand. These expansionary policies must include a temporary increase in government spending and tax cuts. Yet tax reductions must be aimed directly at stimulating aggregate demand rather than aggregate supply. Examples of such demand side tax cuts are lower sales, personal income taxes, and investment tax credits.

For more discussion at the time, see: Jose Viñals, Simon Gray, and Kelly Eckhold "The Broader View: The Positive Effects of Negative Nominal Interest Rates," in *IMF Direct – The International monetary Fund's Global Economy Forum*, April 10, 2016. (https://blog-imfdirect.imf.org/2016/04/10/the-broader-view-the-positive-effects-of-negative-nominal-interest-rates/).

Second, these interactions complicate the task of policy makers, especially in the case of fiscal policy. Let's explore this argument more closely.

Start with the following observation: Governments do not like to run trade deficits and for good reasons. The main reason: A country that consistently runs a trade deficit accumulates debt vis-à-vis the rest of the world, and therefore has to pay steadily higher interest payments to the rest of the world. Thus, it is no wonder that countries prefer increases in foreign demand (which improve the trade balance) to increases in domestic demand (which worsen the trade balance).

But these preferences can have disastrous implications. Consider a group of countries, all doing a large amount of trade with each other, so that an increase in demand in any one country falls largely on the goods produced in the other countries. Suppose all these countries are in recession and each has roughly balanced trade to start. In this case, each country might be reluctant to take measures to increase domestic demand. Were it to do so, the result might be a small increase in output but also a large trade deficit. Instead, each country might just wait for the other countries to increase their demand. This way, it gets the best of both worlds, higher output and an improvement in its trade balance. But if all the countries wait, nothing will happen and the recession may last a long time.

Is there a way out? There is—at least in theory. If all countries coordinate their macroeconomic policies so as to increase domestic demand simultaneously, each can increase demand and output without increasing its trade deficit (vis-à-vis the others; their combined trade deficit with respect to the rest of the world will still increase). The reason is clear. The coordinated increase in demand leads to increases in both exports and imports in each country. It is still true that domestic demand expansion leads to larger imports; but this increase in imports is offset by the increase in exports, which comes from the foreign demand expansions.

In practice, however, **policy coordination** is not so easy to achieve.

Some countries might have to do more than others and may not want to do so. Suppose that only some countries are in recession. Countries that are not in a recession will be reluctant to increase their own demand; but if they do not, the countries that expand will run a trade deficit vis-à-vis countries that do not. Or suppose some countries are already running a large budget deficit. These countries might not want to cut taxes or further increase spending as this would further increase their deficits. They will ask other countries to take on more of the adjustment. Those other countries may be reluctant to do so.

Countries also have a strong incentive to promise to coordinate and then not deliver on their promise. Once all countries have agreed, say, to an increase in spending, each country has an incentive not to deliver, so as to benefit from the increase in demand elsewhere and thereby improve its trade position. But if each country cheats, or does not do everything it promised, there will be insufficient demand expansion to get out of the recession.

The result is that, despite declarations by governments at international meetings, coordination often fizzles. Only when things are really bad, does coordination appear to take hold. To understand how the world responded to the global financial crisis, 2007–2008, see the Focus box "Fiscal Stimulus and Structural Reforms amid Negative Interest Rates."

18-4 Depreciation, the Trade Balance, and Output

Suppose the U.S. government takes policy measures that lead to a depreciation of the dollar—a decrease in the nominal exchange rate. (We shall see in Chapter 20 how it can do this by using monetary policy. For the moment we will assume the government can simply choose the exchange rate.)

Recall that the real exchange rate is given by

$$\varepsilon = \frac{EP}{P^*}$$

The real exchange rate, ε (the price of domestic goods in terms of foreign goods) is equal to the nominal exchange rate, E (the price of domestic currency in terms of foreign currency) times the domestic price level, P, divided by the foreign price level, P^*. In the short run, we can take the two price levels P and P^* as given. This implies that the nominal depreciation is reflected one-for-one in a real depreciation. More concretely, if the dollar depreciates vis-à-vis the yen by 10% (a 10% nominal depreciation), and if the price levels in Japan and the United States do not change, U.S. goods will be 10% cheaper compared to Japanese goods (a 10% real depreciation).

Given P and P^*, E increases $\Rightarrow \varepsilon = \frac{EP}{P^*}$ increases.

A look ahead: In Chapter 20, we shall look at the effects of a nominal depreciation when we allow the price level to adjust over time. You will see that a nominal depreciation leads to a real depreciation in the short run but not in the medium run.

Let's now ask how this real depreciation will affect the U.S. trade balance and U.S. output.

Depreciation and the Trade Balance: The Marshall-Lerner Condition

Return to the definition of net exports:

$$NX = X - IM/\varepsilon$$

More concretely, if the dollar depreciates vis-à-vis the yen by 10%:

Replace X and IM by their expressions from equations (18.2) and (18.3):

$$NX = X(Y^*, \varepsilon) - IM(Y, \varepsilon)/\varepsilon$$

As the real exchange rate ε enters the right side of the equation in three places, this makes it clear that the real depreciation affects the trade balance through three separate channels:

U.S. goods will be cheaper in Japan, leading to a larger quantity of U.S. exports to Japan.

Japanese goods will be more expensive in the United States, leading to a smaller quantity of imports of Japanese goods to the United States.

Japanese goods will be more expensive, leading to a higher import bill for a given quantity of imports of Japanese goods to the United States.

- *Exports, X, increase.* The real depreciation makes U.S. goods relatively less expensive abroad. This leads to an increase in foreign demand for U.S. goods—an increase in U.S. exports.
- *Imports, IM, decrease.* The real depreciation makes foreign goods relatively more expensive in the United States. This leads to a shift in domestic demand toward domestic goods and to a decrease in the quantity of imports.
- *The relative price of foreign goods in terms of domestic goods, $1/\varepsilon$ increases.* This increases the import bill, IM/ε. The same quantity of imports now costs more to buy (in terms of domestic goods).

For the trade balance to improve following a depreciation, exports must increase enough and imports must decrease enough to compensate for the increase in the price of imports. The condition under which a real depreciation leads to an increase in net exports is known as the **Marshall-Lerner condition**. (It is derived formally in the appendix, called "Derivation of the Marshall Lerner Condition," at the end of this chapter.) It turns out—with a complication we will state when we introduce dynamics later in this chapter—that this condition is satisfied in reality. So, for the rest of this book, we shall assume that a real depreciation—a decrease in ε—leads to an increase in net exports—an increase in NX.

It is named after the two economists, Alfred Marshall and Abba Lerner, who were the first to derive it.

The Effects of a Real Depreciation

We have looked so far at the *direct* effects of a depreciation on the trade balance—that is, the effects *given U.S. and foreign output*. But the effects do not end there. The change in net exports changes domestic output, which affects net exports further.

Because the effects of a real depreciation are much like those of an increase in foreign output, we can use Figure 18-4, the same figure that we used previously to show the effects of an increase in foreign output.

Just like an increase in foreign output, a depreciation leads to an increase in net exports (assuming, as we do, that the Marshall-Lerner condition holds), at any level of output. Both the demand relation (ZZ in Figure 18-4(a)) and the net exports relation (NX in Figure 18-4(b)) shift up. The equilibrium moves from A to A', and output increases from Y to Y'. By the same argument we used previously, the trade balance improves. The increase in imports induced by the increase in output is smaller than the direct improvement in the trade balance induced by the depreciation.

Let's summarize. *The depreciation leads to a shift in demand, both foreign and domestic, toward domestic goods. This shift in demand leads, in turn, to both an increase in domestic output and an improvement in the trade balance.*

MyEconLab Video

Although a depreciation and an increase in foreign output have the same effect on domestic output and the trade balance, there is a subtle but important difference between the two. A depreciation works by making foreign goods relatively more expensive.

But this means that, for a given income, people—who now have to pay more to buy foreign goods because of the depreciation—are worse off. This mechanism is strongly felt in countries that go through a large depreciation. Governments trying to achieve a large depreciation often find themselves with strikes and riots in the streets, as people react to the much higher prices of imported goods. This was the case in Mexico, for example, where the large depreciation of the peso in 1994–1995—from 29 cents per peso in November 1994 to 17 cents per peso in May 1995—led to a large decline in workers' living standards and to social unrest.

There is an alternative to riots—asking for and obtaining an increase in wages. But, if wages increase, the prices of domestic goods will follow and increase as well, leading to a smaller real depreciation. To discuss this mechanism, we need to look at the supply side in more detail than we have done so far. We return to the dynamics of depreciation, wage, and price movements in Chapter 20.

Combining Exchange Rate and Fiscal Policies

Suppose output is at its natural level, but the economy is running a large trade deficit. The government would like to reduce the trade deficit while leaving output unchanged so as to avoid overheating. What should it do?

A depreciation alone will not do. It will reduce the trade deficit, but it will also increase output. Nor will a fiscal contraction do. It will reduce the trade deficit, but it will decrease output. What should the government do? The answer: Use the right combination of depreciation and fiscal contraction. Figure 18-5 shows what this combination should be.

Suppose the initial equilibrium in Figure 18-5 (a) is at A, associated with output Y. At this level of output, there is a trade deficit, given by the distance BC in Figure 18-5 (b).

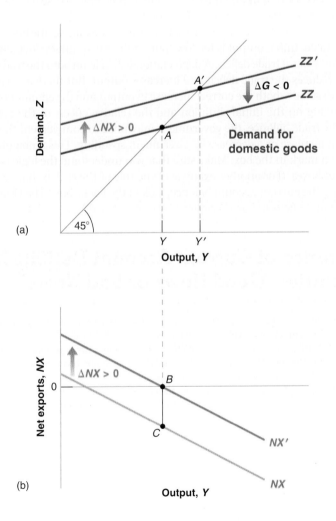

Figure 18-5

Reducing the Trade Deficit without Changing Output

To reduce the trade deficit without changing output, the government must both achieve a depreciation and decrease government spending.

MyEconLab Animation

Table 18-1	Exchange Rate and Fiscal Policy Combinations	
Initial Conditions	**Trade Surplus**	**Trade Deficit**
Low output	ε? $G\uparrow$	$\varepsilon\downarrow$ G?
High output	$\varepsilon\uparrow$ G?	ε? $G\downarrow$

If the government wants to eliminate the trade deficit without changing output, it must do two things:

- It must achieve a depreciation sufficient to eliminate the trade deficit at the initial level of output. So the depreciation must be such as to shift the net exports relation from NX to NX' in Figure 18-5 (b). The problem is that this depreciation, and the associated increase in net exports, also shifts the demand relation in Figure 18-5 (a) from ZZ to ZZ'. In the absence of other measures, the equilibrium would move from A to A', and output would increase from Y to Y'.

- To avoid the increase in output, the government must reduce government spending so as to shift ZZ' back to ZZ. This combination of a depreciation and a fiscal contraction leads to the same level of output and an improved trade balance.

There is a general point behind this example. To the extent that governments care about *both* the level of output and the trade balance, they have to use *both* fiscal policy and exchange rate policies. We just saw one such combination. Table 18-1 gives you others, depending on the initial output and trade situation. Take, for example, the box in the top right corner of the table: Initial output is too low (put another way, unemployment is too high), and the economy has a trade deficit. A depreciation will help on both the trade and the output fronts. It reduces the trade deficit and increases output. But there is no reason for the depreciation to achieve both the correct increase in output and the elimination of the trade deficit. Depending on the initial situation and the relative effects of the depreciation on output and the trade balance, the government may need to complement the depreciation with either an increase or a decrease in government spending. This ambiguity is captured by the question mark in the box. Make sure that you understand the logic behind each of the other three boxes. (For another example of the role of the real exchange rate and output in affecting the current account balance, look at the Focus box "The Disappearance of Current Account Deficits in Euro Periphery Countries: Good News or Bad News?")

A general lesson: If you want to achieve two targets (here, output and trade balance), you better have two instruments (here, fiscal policy and the exchange rate).

FOCUS

The Disappearance of Current Account Deficits in Euro Periphery Countries: Good News or Bad News?

Starting in the early 2000s, a number of Euro periphery countries ran larger and larger current account deficits. Figure 1 shows the evolution of the current account balances of Spain, Portugal, and Greece, from 2000 on. Although the deficits were already substantial in 2000, they continued to increase, reaching 9% of GDP for Spain, 12% for Portugal, and 14% for Greece by 2008.

When the crisis started in 2008, those three countries found it increasingly difficult to borrow abroad, forcing them to reduce borrowing and thus to reduce their current account deficits. And reduce they did. Figure 1 shows that by 2013, the deficits had turned into surpluses in all three countries.

It is an impressive turnaround. Is it unambiguously good news? Not necessarily. The discussion in the text suggests that there are two reasons why a current account may improve. The first is that the country becomes more competitive. The real exchange rate decreases. Exports increase, imports decrease, and the current account balance improves. The second is the country's output decreases. Exports, which depend on what happens in the rest of the world, may remain the same; but imports come down with output, and the current account balance improves.

Unfortunately, the evidence is that the second mechanism has played the dominant role so far.

MEL Video

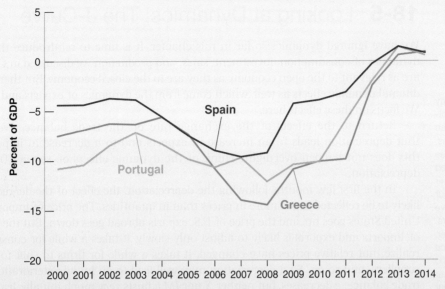

Figure 1 *Euro periphery Current Account Deficits since 2000*

Given that these countries are members of the Euro area, they could not rely on an adjustment of the nominal exchange rate to become more competitive, at least vis-à-vis their Euro partners. They had to rely on a decrease in wages and prices, and this has proven to be slow and difficult (more on this in Chapter 20).

Instead, much of the adjustment has taken place through a decrease in imports, triggered by a decrease in output, an adjustment known as **import compression**. As shown in Figure 2, this has been particularly true of Greece. The figure shows the evolution of imports, exports, and GDP in Greece since 2000. All three series are normalized to equal 1.0 in 2000. Note first how much output has decreased, by roughly 25% since 2008. Note then how imports have moved in tandem with output, also decreasing by 25%. Exports have not

done great either. After sharply decreasing in 2009, reflecting the world crisis and the decrease in demand from the rest of the world, they have not yet recovered to their 2008 level.

In short, the disappearance of the current account deficits in the Euro periphery is, on net, largely bad news. What happens to the current account next depends largely on what happens to output. And this in turn depends on where output is relative to potential output. If much of the decrease in actual output reflects a decrease in potential output, then output will remain low, and the current account surplus will remain. If, as seems more likely, actual output is far below potential output (if there is, in terminology of Chapter 9, a large negative output gap), then unless further real depreciation takes place, the return of output to potential will come with higher imports, and thus a likely return to current account deficits.

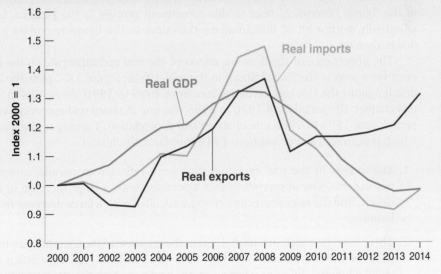

Figure 2 *Imports, Exports, and GDP in Greece since 2000*

Source: IMF, World Economic Outlook.

18-5 Looking at Dynamics: The J-Curve

We have ignored dynamics so far in this chapter. It is time to reintroduce them. The dynamics of consumption, investment, sales, and production we discussed in Chapter 3 are as relevant to the open economy as they are to the closed economy. But there are additional dynamic effects as well, which come from the dynamics of exports and imports. We focus on these effects here.

Return to the effects of the exchange rate on the trade balance. We argued that depreciation leads to an increase in exports and to a decrease in imports. But this does not happen overnight. Think of the dynamic effects of, say, a 10% dollar depreciation.

In the margin:

> And even these prices may adjust slowly. Consider a dollar depreciation. If you are an exporter to the United States, you may want to increase your price less than implied by the exchange rate. In other words, you may decrease your markup to remain competitive with your U.S. competitors. If you are a U.S. exporter, you may decrease your price abroad by less than implied by the exchange rate. In other words, you may increase your markup.

In the first few months following the depreciation, the effect of the depreciation is likely to be reflected much more in prices than in quantities. The price of imports in the United States goes up, and the price of U.S. exports abroad goes down. But the quantity of imports and exports is likely to adjust only slowly. It takes a while for consumers to realize that relative prices have changed, it takes a while for firms to shift to cheaper suppliers, and so on. So a depreciation may well lead to an initial deterioration of the trade balance; ε decreases, but neither X nor IM adjusts very much initially, leading to a decline in net exports $(X - IM/\varepsilon)$.

As time passes, the effects of the change in the relative prices of both exports and imports become stronger. Cheaper U.S. goods cause U.S. consumers and firms to decrease their demand for foreign goods; U.S. imports decrease. Cheaper U.S. goods abroad lead foreign consumers and firms to increase their demand for U.S. goods; U.S. exports increase. If the Marshall-Lerner condition eventually holds—and we have argued that it does—the response of exports and imports eventually becomes stronger than the adverse price effect, and the eventual effect of the depreciation is an improvement of the trade balance.

In the margin:

> The response of the trade balance to the real exchange rate:
> Initially: X, IM unchanged, ε *decreases* $\Rightarrow (X - IM/\varepsilon)$ decreases.
> Eventually: X increases, IM decreases, ε *decreases* $\Rightarrow$ $(X - IM/\varepsilon)$ increases.

Figure 18-6 captures this adjustment by plotting the evolution of the trade balance against time in response to a real depreciation. The pre-depreciation trade deficit is OA. The depreciation initially *increases* the trade deficit to OB: ε decreases, but neither IM nor X changes right away. Over time, however, exports increase and imports decrease, reducing the trade deficit. Eventually (if the Marshall-Lerner condition is satisfied), the trade balance improves beyond its initial level; this is what happens from point C onward in the figure. Economists refer to this adjustment process as the **J-curve**, because—admittedly, with a bit of imagination—the curve in the figure resembles a "J": first down, then up.

The importance of the dynamic effects of the real exchange rate on the trade balance were seen in the United States in the mid-1980s: Figure 18-7 plots the U.S. trade deficit against the U.S. real exchange rate from 1980 to 1990. As we saw in the previous chapter, the period from 1980 to 1985 was one of sharp real appreciation, and the period from 1985 to 1988 one of sharp real depreciation. Turning to the trade deficit, which is expressed as a proportion of GDP, two facts are clear:

1. Movements in the real exchange rate were reflected in parallel movements in net exports. The appreciation was associated with a large increase in the trade deficit, and the later depreciation was associated with a large decrease in the trade balance.

2. There were, however, substantial lags in the response of the trade balance to changes in the real exchange rate. Note how from 1981 to 1983, the trade deficit remained small while the dollar was appreciating. And note how the steady depreciation of

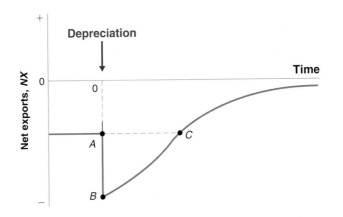

Figure 18-6

The J-Curve

A real depreciation leads initially to a deterioration and then to an improvement of the trade balance.

MyEconLab Animation

the dollar from 1985 onward was not immediately reflected in an improvement in the trade balance before 1987. The dynamics of the J-curve were very much at work during both episodes.

In general, the econometric evidence on the dynamic relation among exports, imports, and the real exchange rate suggests that in all OECD countries, a real depreciation eventually leads to a trade balance improvement. But it also suggests that this process takes some time, typically between six months and a year. These lags have implications not only for the effects of a depreciation on the trade balance but also for the effects of a depreciation on output. If a depreciation initially decreases net exports, it also initially exerts a contractionary effect on output. Thus, if a government relies on a depreciation both to improve the trade balance and to expand domestic output, the effects will go the "wrong" way for a while.

The delays in 1985–1988 were unusually long, prompting some economists at the time to question whether there was still a relation between the real exchange rate and the trade balance. In retrospect, the relation was still there; the delays were just longer than usual.

MyEconLab Video

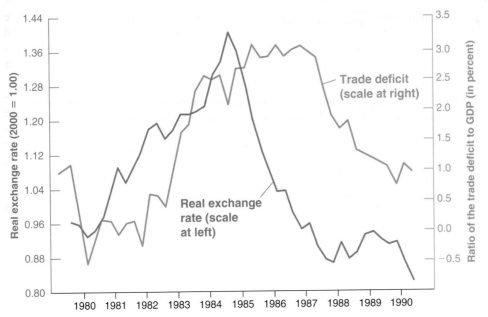

Figure 18-7

The Real Exchange Rate and the Ratio of the Trade Deficit to GDP: United States, 1980–1990

The large real appreciation and subsequent real depreciation from 1980 to 1990 were mirrored, with a lag, by an increase and then a decrease in the trade deficit.

Source: Series GDPDEF, GBRGDPDEFQISMEI and EXUSUK from Federal Reserve Economic Data (FRED).

MyEconLab Real-time data

18-6 Saving, Investment, and the Current Account Balance

You saw in Chapter 3 how we could rewrite the condition for equilibrium in the goods market as the condition that investment was equal to saving—the sum of private saving and public saving. We can now derive the corresponding condition for the open economy, and you will see how useful this alternative way of looking at the equilibrium can be.

Getting there involves some manipulations, but do not worry; the end result is intuitive.

Start from our equilibrium condition

$$Y = C + I + G - IM/\varepsilon + X$$

Move consumption, C, from the right side to the left side of the equation, subtract taxes, T, from both sides, denote net exports $(IM/\varepsilon + X)$ by NX to get

$$Y - T - C = I + (G - T) + NX$$

Recall that, in an open economy, the income of domestic residents is equal to output, Y, plus net income from abroad, NI, plus net transfers received. Denote these transfers by NT, and add NI and NT to both sides of the equation:

$$(Y + NI + NT - T) - C = I + (G - T) + (NX + NI + NT)$$

Note that the term in parentheses on left side is equal to disposable income, so the left side is equal to disposable income minus consumption (i.e., saving, S). Note that the sum of net exports, net income from abroad, and net transfers on the right side is equal to the current account. Denote the current account by CA and rewrite the previous equation as:

$$S = I + (G - T) + CA$$

Reorganize the equation to read:

$$CA = S + (T - G) - I \qquad (18.5)$$

Commentators often do not make a distinction between the trade balance and the current account balance. This is not necessarily a major crime: Because net income and net transfers typically move slowly over time, the trade and the current account balances typically move closely together.

The current account balance is equal to saving—the sum of private saving and public saving—minus investment. A current account surplus implies that the country is saving more than it invests. A current account deficit implies that the country is saving less than it invests.

One way of getting more intuition for this relation is to go back to the discussion of the current account and the capital account in Chapter 17. There we saw that a current account surplus implies net lending from the country to the rest of the world, and a current account deficit implies net borrowing by the country from the rest of the world. So consider a country that invests more than it saves, so that $S + (T - G) - I$ is negative. That country must be borrowing the difference from the rest of the world; it must therefore be running a current account deficit. Symmetrically, a country that lends to the rest of the world is a country that saves more than it invests.

Note some of the things that equation (18.5) says:

■ An increase in investment must be reflected in either an increase in private saving or public saving, or in a deterioration of the current account balance—a smaller current account surplus, or a larger current account deficit, depending on whether the current account is initially in surplus or in deficit.

- A deterioration in the government budget balance—either a smaller budget surplus or a larger budget deficit—must be reflected in an increase in either private saving, or in a decrease in investment, or else in a deterioration of the current account balance.
- A country with a high saving rate (private plus government) must have either a high investment rate or a large current account surplus.

Note also, however, what equation (18.5) does *not* say. It does not say, for example, whether a government budget deficit will lead to a current account deficit, or instead, to an increase in private saving, or to a decrease in investment. To find out what happens in response to a budget deficit, we must explicitly solve for what happens to output and its components using the assumptions that we have made about consumption, investment, exports, and imports. That is, we need to do the complete analysis laid out in this chapter. Using only equation (18.5) can, if you are not careful, be very misleading. To see how misleading, consider, for example, the following argument (which is so common that you may have read something similar in newspapers):

"It is clear the United States cannot reduce its large current account deficit through a depreciation." Look at equation (18.5). It shows that the current account deficit is equal to investment minus saving. Why should a depreciation affect either saving or investment? So, how can a depreciation affect the current account deficit?

The argument might sound convincing, but we know it is wrong. We showed earlier that a depreciation leads to an improvement in a country's trade position and, by implication—given net income and transfers—an improvement in the current account. So what is wrong with the argument? A depreciation actually does affect saving and investment. It does so by affecting the demand for domestic goods, thereby increasing output. Higher output leads to an increase in saving over investment, or equivalently, to a decrease in the current account deficit.

A good way of making sure that you understand the material in this section is to go back and look at the various cases we have considered, from changes in government spending, to changes in foreign output, to combinations of depreciation and fiscal contraction, and so on. Trace what happens in each case to each of the four components of equation (18.5): private saving, public saving (equivalently, the budget surplus), investment, and the current account balance. Make sure, as always, that you can tell the story ◀ in words.

Suppose, for example, that the U.S. government wants to reduce the current account deficit without changing the level of output, so it uses a combination of depreciation and fiscal contraction. What happens to private saving, public saving, and investment?

Let me end the chapter with a challenge. Assess the following three statements and decide which one(s) is (are) right:

- The U.S. current account deficit (which we saw in Chapter 17) shows that the U.S is no longer competitive. It is a sign of weakness. Forget saving or investment. The United States must urgently improve its competitiveness.
- The U.S. current account deficit shows that the United States just does not save enough to finance its investment. It is a sign of weakness. Forget competitiveness. The United States must urgently increase its saving rate.
- The U.S. current account deficit is just a mirror image of the U.S. capital account surplus. What is happening is that the rest of the world wants to put its funds in the United States. The U.S. capital account surplus, and by implication, the U.S. current account deficit, is in fact a sign of strength, and there is no need to take policy measures to reduce it.

Summary

- In an open economy, the demand for domestic goods is equal to the domestic demand for goods (consumption, plus investment, plus government spending) minus the value of imports (in terms of domestic goods), plus exports.

- In an open economy, an increase in domestic demand leads to a smaller increase in output than it would in a closed economy because some of the additional demand falls on imports. For the same reason, an increase in domestic demand also leads to a deterioration of the trade balance.

- An increase in foreign demand leads, as a result of increased exports, to both an increase in domestic output and an improvement of the trade balance.

- Because increases in foreign demand improve the trade balance and increases in domestic demand worsen the trade balance, countries might be tempted to wait for increases in foreign demand to move them out of a recession. When a group of countries is in recession, coordination can, in principle, help their recovery.

- If the Marshall-Lerner condition is satisfied—and the empirical evidence indicates that it is—a real depreciation leads to an improvement in net exports.

- A real depreciation leads first to a deterioration of the trade balance, and then to an improvement. This adjustment process is known as the J-curve.

- The condition for equilibrium in the goods market can be rewritten as the condition that saving (public and private) minus investment must be equal to the current account balance. A current account surplus corresponds to an excess of saving over investment. A current account deficit usually corresponds to an excess of investment over saving.

Key Terms

demand for domestic goods, 390
domestic demand for goods, 390
policy coordination, 399

Marshall-Lerner condition, 400
import compression, 403
J-curve, 404

Questions and Problems

QUICK CHECK

MyEconLab Visit www.myeconlab.com to complete similar Quick Check problems and get instant feedback.

1. Using the information in this chapter, label each of the following statements true, false, or uncertain. Explain briefly.

a. The current U.S. trade deficit is the result of unusually high investment, not the result of a decline in national saving.

b. The national income identity implies that budget deficits cause trade deficits.

c. Opening the economy to trade tends to increase the multiplier because an increase in expenditure leads to more exports.

d. If the trade deficit is equal to zero, then the domestic demand for goods and the demand for domestic goods are equal.

e. A real depreciation leads to an immediate improvement in the trade balance.

f. A small open economy can reduce its trade deficit through fiscal contraction at a smaller cost in output than can a large open economy.

g. The experience of the United States in the 1990s shows that real exchange rate appreciations lead to trade deficits and real exchange rate depreciations lead to trade surpluses.

h. A decline in real income can lead to a decline in imports and thus a trade surplus.

2. Real and nominal exchange rates and inflation

Using the definition of the real exchange rate (and Propositions 7 and 8 in Appendix 2 at the end of the book), you can show that

$$\frac{(\varepsilon_t - \varepsilon_{t-1})}{\varepsilon_{t-1}} = \frac{(E_t - E_{t-1})}{E_{t-1}} + \pi_t - \pi_t^*$$

In words, the percentage real appreciation equals the percentage nominal appreciation plus the difference between domestic and foreign inflation.

a. If domestic inflation is higher than foreign inflation, and the domestic country has a fixed exchange rate, what happens to the real exchange rate over time? Assume that the Marshall-Lerner condition holds. What happens to the trade balance over time? Explain in words.

b. Suppose the real exchange rate is currently at the level required for net exports (or the current account) to equal zero. In this case, if domestic inflation is higher than foreign inflation, what must happen over time to maintain a trade balance of zero?

3. The impact of EU-28 (that is, the 28 member nations of the European Union. The number of member states may change following the Brexit results) slowdown on the Argentinean economy

a. The EU-28 is the second largest trade partner of Argentina in terms of export spending and the third largest trade partner of Argentina in terms of import spending. Go to the Web site of the European Commission (http://ec.europa.eu/) and check the share of EU-28 spending on Argentinean goods relative to the GDP of Argentina in 2014.

b. Assume that the multiplier in Argentina is 1.8 and that a major slowdown in the EU would reduce European imports from Argentina by 3%. What is the impact of the European slump on the GDP of Argentina in comparison to original GDP?

c. Brazil is the largest trade partner of Argentina. Similar to Argentina, the EU-28 slowdown reduces Brazilian exports to the EU. Assume that this reduces the volume of Brazilian imports from Argentina by 6%. How would this further impact the GDP of Argentina in comparison to the original GDP?

d. Some Argentinean economists fear that the EU-28 slowdown will most certainly aggravate the Argentinean macroeconomic problems, eventually causing a total halt in GDP growth. Do you agree with this apprehension?

4. *A further look at Table 18-1 Table 18-1 has four entries. Using Figure 18-5 as a guide, draw the situations illustrated in each of the 4 entries in Table 18-1. Be sure you understand why the direction of change in government spending and the real exchange rate is labeled as ambiguous in each entry.*

DIG DEEPER

MyEconLab Visit www.myeconlab.com to complete all Dig Deeper problems and get instant feedback.

5. *Net exports and foreign demand*

a. Suppose there is an increase in foreign output. Show the effect on the domestic economy (i.e., replicate Figure 18-4). What is the effect on domestic output? On domestic net exports?

b. If the interest rate remains constant, what will happen to domestic investment? If taxes are fixed, what will happen to the domestic budget deficit?

c. Using equation (18.5), what must happen to private saving? Explain.

d. Foreign output does not appear in equation (18.5), yet it evidently affects net exports. Explain how this is possible.

6. *Eliminating a trade deficit*

a. Consider an economy with a trade deficit ($NX < 0$) and with output equal to its natural level. Suppose that, even though output may deviate from its natural level in the short run, it returns to its natural level in the medium run. Assume that the natural level is unaffected by the real exchange rate. What must happen to the real exchange rate over the medium run to eliminate the trade deficit (i.e., to increase NX to 0)?

b. Now write down the national income identity. Assume again that output returns to its natural level in the medium run. If NX increases to 0, what must happen to domestic demand ($C + I + G$) in the medium run? What government policies are available to reduce domestic demand in the medium run? Identify which components of domestic demand each of these policies affect.

7. *Multipliers, openness, and fiscal policy*

Consider an open economy characterized by the following equations:

$$C = c_0 + c_1(Y - T)$$
$$I = d_0 + d_1 Y$$
$$IM = m_1 Y$$
$$X = x_1 Y^*$$

The parameters m_1 and x_1 are the propensities to import and export. Assume that the real exchange rate is fixed at a value of 1 and treat foreign income, Y^*, as fixed. Also assume that taxes are fixed and that government purchases are exogenous (i.e., decided by the government). We explore the effectiveness of changes in G under alternative assumptions about the propensity to import.

a. Write the equilibrium condition in the market for domestic goods and solve for Y.

b. Suppose government purchases increase by one unit. What is the effect on output? (Assume that $0 < m_1 < c_1 + d_1 < 1$. Explain why.)

c. How do net exports change when government purchases increase by one unit?

Now consider two economies, one with $m_1 = 0.5$ and the other with $m_1 = 0.1$. Each economy is characterized by $(c_1 + d_1) = 0.6$.

d. Suppose one of the economies is much larger than the other. Which economy do you expect to have the larger value of m_1? Explain.

e. Calculate your answers to parts (b) and (c) for each economy by substituting the appropriate parameter values.

f. In which economy will fiscal policy have a larger effect on output? In which economy will fiscal policy have a larger effect on net exports?

8. *Policy coordination and the world economy*

Consider an open economy in which the real exchange rate is fixed and equal to one. Consumption, investment, government spending, and taxes are given by

$$C = 10 + 0.8(Y - T), I = 10, G = 10, \text{ and } T = 10$$

Imports and exports are given by

$$IM = 0.3Y \quad \text{and} \quad X = 0.3Y^*$$

where Y^* denotes foreign output.

a. Solve for equilibrium output in the domestic economy, given Y^*. What is the multiplier in this economy? If we were to close the economy—so exports and imports were identically equal to zero—what would the multiplier be? Why would the multiplier be different in a closed economy?

b. Assume that the foreign economy is characterized by the same equations as the domestic economy (with asterisks reversed). Use the two sets of equations to solve for the equilibrium output of each country. [*Hint:* Use the equations for the foreign economy to solve for Y^* as a function of Y and substitute this solution for Y^* in part (a).] What is the multiplier for each country now? Why is it different from the open economy multiplier in part (a)?

c. Assume that the domestic government, G, has a target level of output of 125. Assuming that the foreign government does not change G^*, what is the increase in G necessary to achieve the target output in the domestic economy? Solve for net exports and the budget deficit in each country.

d. Suppose each government has a target level of output of 125 and that each government increases government spending by the same amount. What is the common increase in G and G^* necessary to achieve the target output in both countries? Solve for net exports and the budget deficit in each country.

e. Why is fiscal coordination, such as the common increase in G and G^* in part (d), difficult to achieve in practice?

EXPLORE FURTHER

9. *The trade deficit, current account deficit, and investment*

a. National saving is defined as private saving plus government surplus, that is, $S + T - G$. Using equation (18.5) describe the relation between current account deficit, net investment income, and the difference between saving and investment.

b. Use the World Bank data base (http://data.worldbank.org/) to retrieve annual data for your country for nominal GDP, gross domestic investment (also known as gross capital formation), and net exports since 1996 till to the latest available date. Divide gross domestic investment and net exports by GDP for each year and calculate their values as a percentage of GDP. What period has the largest trade deficit as a percentage of GDP?

c. For each of the periods 2001–2005, 2006–2010, and 2011–2015 calculate the current account balance and the gross domestic investment (gross capital formation) of India as a percentage of GDP. What do the changes in trends over the 15-year period indicate?

d. What problems does a trade deficit pose to an economy? How do the levels of saving and investment determine the severity of implications of a trade deficit?

e. Compare and contrast the levels of GDP and GNP (also known as GNI) of India for each of the periods 2001–2005, 2006–2010, and 2011–2015. Are the values rising or falling over time? What are the implications of these changes?

Further Readings

- A good discussion of the relation among trade deficits, current account deficits, budget deficits, private saving, and investment is given in Barry Bosworth's *Saving and Investment in a Global Economy* (Brookings Institution, 1993).

- For more on the relation between the exchange rate and the trade balance, read "Exchange Rates and Trade Flows: Disconnected?" Chapter 3, World Economic Outlook, International Monetary Fund, October 2015.

APPENDIX: Derivation of the Marshall-Lerner Condition

Start from the definition of net exports

$$NX = X - IM/\varepsilon$$

Assume trade to be initially balanced, so that $NX = 0$ and $X = IM/\varepsilon$ or, equivalently, $\varepsilon X = IM$.

The Marshall-Lerner condition is the condition under which a real depreciation, a decrease in U, leads to an increase in net exports.

To derive this condition, first multiply both sides of the equation above by ε to get

$$\varepsilon NX = \varepsilon X - IM$$

Now consider a change in the real exchange rate of $\Delta\varepsilon$. The effect of the change in the real exchange rate on the left side of the equation is given by $(\Delta\varepsilon) NX + \varepsilon\Delta(NX)$.

Note that, if trade is initially balanced, $NX = 0$, so the first term in this expression is equal to zero, and the effect of the change on the left side is simply given by $\varepsilon\Delta(NX)$.

The effect of the change in the real exchange rate on the right side of the equation is given by $(\Delta\varepsilon) X + \varepsilon\Delta(X) - (\Delta IM)$. Putting the two sides together gives

$$\varepsilon(\Delta NX) = (\Delta\varepsilon) X + \varepsilon(\Delta X) - (\Delta IM)$$

Divide both sides by εX to get:

$$[\varepsilon(\Delta NX)]/\varepsilon X = [(\Delta\varepsilon) X]/\varepsilon X + [\varepsilon(\Delta X)]/\varepsilon X - [\Delta IM]/\varepsilon X$$

Simplify, and use the fact that, if trade is initially balanced, $\varepsilon X = IM$ to replace εX by IM in the last term on the right. This gives

$$(\Delta NX)/X = (\Delta\varepsilon)/\varepsilon + (\Delta X)/X - \Delta IM/IM$$

The change in the trade balance (as a ratio to exports) in response to a real depreciation is equal to the sum of three terms:

- The first term is equal to the proportional change in the real exchange rate. It is negative if there is a real depreciation.
- The second term is equal to the proportional change in exports. It is positive if there is a real depreciation.
- The third term is equal to minus the proportional change in imports. It is positive if there is a real depreciation.

The Marshall-Lerner condition is the condition that the sum of these three terms be positive. If it is satisfied, a real depreciation leads to an improvement in the trade balance.

A numerical example will help here. Suppose that a 1% depreciation leads to a proportional increase in exports of 0.9%, and to a proportional decrease in imports of 0.8%. (Econometric evidence on the relation of exports and imports to the real exchange rate suggest that these are indeed reasonable numbers.) In this case, the right-hand side of the equation is equal to $-1\% + 0.9\% - (-0.8\%) = 0.7\%$. Thus, the trade balance improves, and the Marshall-Lerner condition is satisfied.

Output, the Interest Rate, and the Exchange Rate

In Chapter 18, we treated the exchange rate as one of the policy instruments available to the government. But the exchange rate is not a policy instrument. Rather, it is determined in the foreign exchange market—a market where, as you saw in Chapter 17, there is an enormous amount of trading. This fact raises two obvious questions: What determines the exchange rate? How can policy makers affect it?

These questions motivate this chapter. To answer them, we reintroduce financial markets, which we had left aside in Chapter 18. We examine the implications of equilibrium in both the goods market and financial markets, including the foreign exchange market. This allows us to characterize the joint movements of output, the interest rate, and the exchange rate in an open economy. The model we develop is an extension to the open economy of the *IS-LM* model you first saw in Chapter 5 and is known as the **Mundell-Fleming model**—after the two economists, Robert Mundell and Marcus Fleming, who first put it together in the 1960s. (The model presented here retains the spirit of the original Mundell-Fleming model but differs in its details.)

Section 19-1 looks at equilibrium in the goods market.

Section 19-2 looks at equilibrium in financial markets, including the foreign exchange market.

Section 19-3 puts the two equilibrium conditions together and looks at the determination of output, the interest rate, and the exchange rate.

Section 19-4 looks at the role of policy under flexible exchange rates.

Section 19-5 looks at the role of policy under fixed exchange rates.

19-1 Equilibrium in the Goods Market

Equilibrium in the goods market was the focus of Chapter 18, where we derived the equilibrium condition equation (18.4):

$$Y = C(Y - T) + I(Y, r) + G - IM(Y, \varepsilon)/\varepsilon + X(Y^*, \varepsilon)$$
$$(+) \qquad (+,-) \qquad\qquad (+,+) \qquad (+,-)$$

Goods market equilibrium (*IS*): Output = Demand for domestic goods.

▶ For the goods market to be in equilibrium, output (the left side of the equation) must be equal to the demand for domestic goods (the right side of the equation). The demand for domestic goods is equal to consumption, C, plus investment, I, plus government spending, G minus the value of imports, IM/ε, plus exports, X.

- ■ Consumption, C, depends positively on disposable income $Y - T$.
- ■ Investment, I, depends positively on output, Y, and negatively on the real interest rate, r.
- ■ Government spending, G, is taken as given.
- ■ The quantity of imports, IM, depends positively on both output, Y, and the real exchange rate, ε. The value of imports in terms of domestic goods is equal to the quantity of imports divided by the real exchange rate.
- ■ Exports, X, depend positively on foreign output, Y^*, and negatively on the real exchange rate, ε.

It will be convenient in what follows to regroup the last two terms under "net exports," defined as exports minus the value of imports:

$$NX(Y, Y^*, \varepsilon) = X(Y^*, \varepsilon) - IM(Y, \varepsilon)/\varepsilon$$

We shall assume, throughout the chapter, that the Marshall-Lerner condition holds. Under ▶ this condition, an increase in the real exchange rate—a real appreciation—leads to a decrease in net exports (see Chapter 18).

It follows from our assumptions about imports and exports that net exports, NX, depend on domestic output, Y, foreign output, Y^*, and the real exchange rate ε. An increase in domestic output increases imports, thus decreasing net exports. An increase in foreign output increases exports, thus increasing net exports. An increase in the real exchange rate leads to a decrease in net exports.

Using this definition of net exports, we can rewrite the equilibrium condition as

$$Y = C(Y - T) + I(Y, r) + G + NX(Y, Y^*, \varepsilon) \qquad (19.1)$$
$$(+) \qquad (+,-) \qquad\qquad (-,+,-)$$

For our purposes, the main implication of equation (19.1) is that both the real interest rate and the real exchange rate affect demand, and in turn equilibrium output.

- ■ An increase in the real interest rate leads to a decrease in investment spending, and as a result, to a decrease in the demand for domestic goods. This leads, through the multiplier, to a decrease in output.
- ■ An increase in the real exchange rate leads to a shift in demand toward foreign goods, and as a result, to a decrease in net exports. The decrease in net exports decreases the demand for domestic goods. This leads, through the multiplier, to a decrease in output.

For the remainder of the chapter, we shall simplify equation (19.1) in two ways:

- ■ Given our focus on the short run, we assumed in our previous treatment of the *IS-LM* model that the (domestic) price level was given. We shall make the same assumption here and extend this assumption to the foreign price level, so the real exchange rate, $\varepsilon = EP/P^*$, and the nominal exchange rate, E, move together. A decrease in the nominal exchange rate—a nominal depreciation—leads, one-for-one, to a decrease in the real exchange rate—a real depreciation. Conversely, an increase in the nominal exchange rate—a nominal appreciation—leads, one-for-one, to an increase in the real exchange rate—a real appreciation. If, for notational convenience, we choose P and P^* so that $P/P^* = 1$ (and we can do so because both are index numbers), then $\varepsilon = E$ and we can replace ε by E in equation (19.1).

First simplification: $P = P^* = 1$, so $\varepsilon = E$.

■ Because we take the domestic price level as given, there is no inflation, neither actual nor expected. Therefore, the nominal interest rate and the real interest rate are the same, and we can replace the real interest rate, r, in equation (19.1) by the nominal interest rate, i.

Second simplification: $\pi^e = 0$, so $r = i$.

With these two simplifications, equation (19.1) becomes

$$Y = C(Y - T) + I(Y, i) + G + NX(Y, Y^*, E) \qquad (19.2)$$
$$\quad (+) \qquad (+,-) \qquad\qquad (-,+,-)$$

In words: Goods market equilibrium implies that output depends negatively on both the nominal interest rate and the nominal exchange rate.

By now, you realize that the way to understand various macroeconomic mechanisms is to refine the basic model in one direction, and simplify it in others (here, opening the economy but ignoring risk). Keeping all the refinements would lead to a rich model (and this is what macro econometric models do), but would make for a terrible textbook. Things would become far too complicated.

19-2 Equilibrium in Financial Markets

When we looked at financial markets in the *IS-LM* model, we assumed that people chose only between two financial assets, money and bonds. Now that we look at a financially open economy, we must also take into account the fact that people have a choice between domestic bonds and foreign bonds.

Remember that we have assumed that people are not willing to hold domestic or foreign currency on its own.

Domestic Bonds versus Foreign Bonds

As we look at the choice between domestic bonds and foreign bonds, we shall rely on the assumption we introduced in Chapter 17: Financial investors, domestic or foreign, go for the highest expected rate of return, ignoring risk. This implies that, in equilibrium, both domestic bonds and foreign bonds must have the same expected rate of return; otherwise, investors would be willing to hold only one or the other, but not both, and this could not be an equilibrium. (Like all economic relations, this relation is only an approximation to reality and does not always hold. For more on this, see the Focus box on page 414 "Does the Interest Rate Parity Condition Always Hold for Transitional Economies?")

As we saw in Chapter 17 (equation 17.2), this assumption implies that the following arbitrage relation—the *interest parity condition*—must hold:

$$(1 + i_t) = (1 + i_t^*)\left(\frac{E_t}{E_{t+1}^e}\right) \qquad (19.3)$$

where i_t is the domestic interest rate, i_t^* is the foreign interest rate, E_t is the current exchange rate, and E_{t+1}^e is the future expected exchange rate. The left side of the equation gives the return, in terms of domestic currency, from holding domestic bonds. The right side of the equation gives the expected return, also in terms of domestic currency, from holding foreign bonds. In equilibrium, the two expected returns must be equal.

Multiply both sides by E_{t+1}^e and reorganize to get

$$E_t = \frac{1 + i_t}{1 + i_t^*} E_{t+1}^e \qquad (19.4)$$

The presence of E_t comes from the fact that to buy the foreign bond, you must first exchange domestic currency for foreign currency. The presence of E_{t+1}^e comes from the fact that to bring the funds back next period, you will have to exchange foreign currency for domestic currency.

For now, we shall take the expected future exchange rate as given and denote it as $\bar{E}^e$ (we shall relax this assumption in Chapter 20). Under this assumption, and dropping time indexes, the interest parity condition becomes

$$E = \frac{1 + i}{1 + i^*} \bar{E}^e \qquad (19.5)$$

Does the Interest Rate Parity Condition Always Hold for Transitional Economies?

FOCUS

Interest rate parity is a condition representing an equilibrium state under which investors are assumed to be indifferent to varying interest rates and expected returns available in different countries. There are two assumptions essential for the interest rate parity condition to work. First, capital must be transferable from one currency to another and from one country to the other, without any currency or capital flow restrictions. Second, assets and securities in different countries should be easily comparable on the basis of their riskiness, liquidity, and ease of sale. If these assumptions hold true, then investors in different places would be earning equivalent returns.

However, as discussed in Chapter 14, rational investors do not choose assets simply based on their expected returns as there are many other factors that shape investment decisions. The most important of these factors are risk and liquidity issues and the general policy environment. These are specific to transitional economies that are changing their institutional framework as they move from centrally planned systems to market economies. Transitional nations refer to the former Soviet Union, and its satellite states in Eastern and Central Europe—Poland, Hungary, Bulgaria, and the Czech Republic. These countries suffer from the inherent higher risk of their currencies that stem from active foreign exchange speculation and sudden supply or macroeconomic shocks. There are also political risks that are mainly inflicted by capital controls, or the threat of the imposition of such controls. Moreover, the investment environment in transitional economies is usually unhealthy due to the perceived risks of changes in legislations, taxation, or confiscations. Finally, currency devaluation and transaction costs are other factors that could shape the decisions of rational investors.

The high risks, which are translated in terms of more returns on the assets of transitional economies, have usually attracted many individual investors, investment funds and pension funds to trade in the assets and securities of transitional economies. The most important factors that attract investors' funds to transitional economies are the degree of capital account openness, financial market depth, price stability, and the sustainability of economic development.

Yet, as soon as transitional economies show the first signs of distress, financial uncertainty, and economic slowdown investors choose to forego the high returns and capital flows to the safe harbor of the more liquid and safer trading assets in the relatively advanced and stable economies. Figure 1 shows that after the global financial crisis of 2007, investors have moved their funds from transitional economies to other economies that showed more stability such as China and other Asian emerging market economies.

As government bonds are backed by the fiscal and taxing authorities of nations, it is quite unlikely that governments would default on their bonds. This tempts one to think that government bonds are virtually free from credit risk.

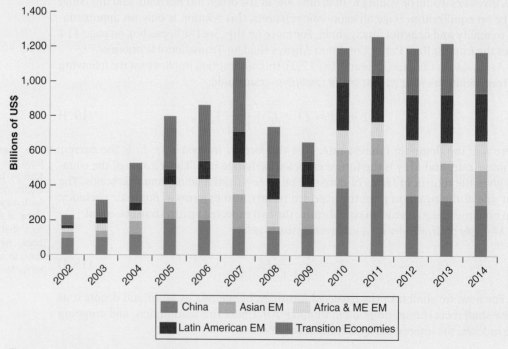

Figure 1 *Net Private Capital Inflows (2002–2014)*

Source: The International Monetary Fund Database.

However, the European sovereign debt crisis of 2009 has uncovered the likelihood of sovereign default. In addition to credit risk all government bonds are exposed to interest-rate risk, inflation risk and foreign exchange rate risk.

When uncertainty increased after the European Debt Crisis of 2014, demand for the German Bunds, U.S. Treasuries and U.K. gilts has increased. Not only are these three economies virtually free of credit risk, but the size and liquidity of these government bond markets has attracted investors. Figure 2 shows that the highest demand for government bonds is in the United States and the United Kingdom, hence explaining how the huge trade deficits that both nations hold are financed by the borrowings from the rest of the world as explained in Chapter 17. By contrast, Germany holds a substantial trade surplus and does not favor borrowing from abroad. This begs the question whether such trade deficits can be sustained in case demand for U.S. and U.K. government bonds falls.

Further reading: After the global financial crisis of 2007/08, many Eastern European nations were harshly impacted by the large capital outflows. Most of these countries had built up unsustainable and shallow financial markets, exposing their economies to huge financial vulnerabilities and economic meltdowns, much worse than those that we studied in Chapter 6. A very comprehensive and succinct read is Anders Åslund's book: The Last Shall Be the First: The East European Financial Crisis, Peterson Institute for International Economics, Washington, D.C., 2010.

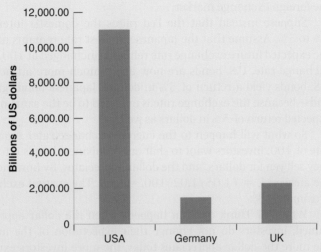

Figure 2 *Outstanding Government Debt Securities as at 2015*

Source: The Bank for International Settlements Statistical Database.

This relation tells us that the current exchange rate depends on the domestic interest rate, on the foreign interest rate, and on the expected future exchange rate.

- An increase in the domestic interest rate leads to an increase in the exchange rate.
- An increase in the foreign interest rate leads to a decrease in the exchange rate.
- An increase in the expected future exchange rate leads to an increase in the current exchange rate.

This relation plays a central role in the real world and will play a central role in this chapter. To understand the relation further, consider the following example:

Consider financial investors—investors, for short—choosing between U.S. bonds and Japanese bonds. Suppose that the one-year interest rate on U.S. bonds is 2%, and the one-year interest rate on Japanese bonds is also 2%. Suppose that the current exchange rate is 100 (one dollar is worth 100 yen), and the expected exchange rate a year from now is also 100. Under these assumptions, both U.S. and Japanese bonds have the same expected return in dollars, and the interest parity condition holds.

Suppose that investors now expect the exchange rate to be 10% higher a year from now, so $\bar{E}^e$ is now equal to 110. At an unchanged current exchange rate, U.S. bonds are now much more attractive than Japanese bonds. U.S. bonds offer an interest rate of 2% in dollars. Japanese bonds still offer an interest rate of 2% in yen, but the yen a year from today are now expected to be worth 10% less in terms of dollars. In terms of dollars, the return on Japanese bonds is therefore 2% (the interest rate) -10% (the expected depreciation of the yen relative to the dollar), or -8%.

So what will happen to the current exchange rate? At the initial exchange rate of 100, investors want to shift out of Japanese bonds into U.S. bonds. To do so, they must first sell Japanese bonds for yen, then sell yen for dollars, and then use the dollars to buy U.S. bonds. As investors sell yen and buy dollars, the dollar appreciates relative to the yen. By how much? Equation (19.5) gives us the answer: $E = (1.02/1.02)110 = 110$. The current exchange rate must increase in the same proportion as the expected future exchange rate. Put another way, the dollar must appreciate today by 10%. When it has appreciated by 10% so $E = \bar{E}^e = 110$, the expected returns on U.S. and Japanese bonds are again equal, and there is equilibrium in the foreign exchange market.

Suppose instead that the Fed raises the domestic interest rate in the U.S. from 2% to 5%. Assume that the Japanese interest rate remains unchanged at 2%, and that the expected future exchange rate remains unchanged at 100. At an unchanged current exchange rate, U.S. bonds are now again much more attractive than Japanese bonds. U.S. bonds yield a return of 5% in dollars. Japanese bonds give a return of 2% in yen, and—because the exchange rate is expected to be the same next year as it is today—an expected return of 5% in dollars as well.

So what will happen to the current exchange rate? Again, at the initial exchange rate of 100, investors want to shift out of Japanese bonds into U.S. bonds. As they do so, they sell yen for dollars, and the dollar appreciates. By how much? Equation (19.5) gives the answer: $E = (1.05/1.02)100 \approx 103$. The current exchange rate increases by approximately 3%.

Why 3%? Think of what happens when the dollar appreciates. If, as we have assumed, investors do not change their expectation of the future exchange rate, then the more the dollar appreciates today, the more investors expect it to depreciate in the future (as it is expected to return to the same value in the future). When the dollar has appreciated by 3% today, investors expect it to depreciate by 3% during the coming year. Equivalently, they expect the yen to appreciate relative to the dollar by 3% over the coming year. The expected rate of return in dollars from holding Japanese bonds is therefore 2% (the interest rate in yen) $+3\%$ (the expected yen appreciation), or 5%.

Make sure you understand the ▶ argument. Why doesn't the dollar appreciate by, say, 20%?

This expected rate of return is the same as the rate of return on holding U.S. bonds, so there is equilibrium in the foreign exchange market.

Note that our argument relies heavily on the assumption that, when the interest rate changes, the expected exchange rate remains unchanged. This implies that an appreciation today leads to an expected depreciation in the future because the exchange rate is expected to return to the same, unchanged, value. We shall relax the assumption that the future expected exchange rate is fixed in Chapter 20. But the basic conclusion will remain: *An increase in the domestic interest rate relative to the foreign interest rate leads to an appreciation.*

MyEconLab Video

Figure 19-1 plots the relation between the domestic interest rate, i, and the exchange rate, E, implied by equation (19.5)—the interest parity relation. The relation is drawn for a given expected future exchange rate, $\bar{E}^e$, and a given foreign interest rate, i^*, and is represented by an upward-sloping line. The higher the domestic interest rate, the higher the exchange rate. Equation (19.5) also implies that when the domestic interest rate is equal to the foreign interest rate ($i = i^*$), the exchange rate is equal to the expected future exchange rate ($E = \bar{E}^e$). This implies that the line corresponding to the interest parity condition goes through point A (where $i = i^*$) in the figure.

What happens to the line if (1) i^* increases? (2) $\bar{E}^e$ increases? ▶

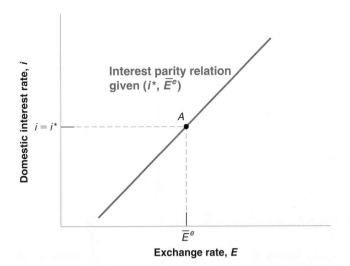

Figure 19-1

The Relation between the Interest Rate and the Exchange Rate Implied by Interest Parity

A higher domestic interest rate leads to a higher exchange rate—an appreciation.

19-3 Putting Goods and Financial Markets Together

We now have the elements we need to understand the movements of output, the interest rate, and the exchange rate.

Goods-market equilibrium implies that output depends, among other factors, on the interest rate and the exchange rate:

$$Y = C(Y - T) + I(Y, i) + G + NX(Y, Y^*, E)$$

Let's think of the interest rate, i, as the policy rate set by the central bank:

$$i = \bar{i}$$

And the interest parity condition implies a positive relation between the domestic interest rate and the exchange rate:

$$E = \frac{1 + i}{1 + i^*} \bar{E}^e$$

Together, these three relations determine output, the interest rate, and the exchange rate. Working with three equations and three variables is not easy. But we can easily reduce them to two by using the interest parity condition to eliminate the exchange rate in the goods-market equilibrium relation. Doing this gives us the following two equations, the open economy versions of our familiar *IS* and *LM* relations:

$$IS: \quad Y = C(Y - T) + I(Y, i) + G + NX\left(Y, Y^*, \frac{1 + i}{1 + i^*} \bar{E}^e\right)$$

$$LM: \quad i = \bar{i}$$

Together, the two equations determine the interest rate and equilibrium output. Using equation (19.5) then gives us the implied exchange rate. Take the *IS* relation first and consider the effects of an increase in the interest rate on output. An increase in the interest rate now has two effects:

Figure 19-2

The IS-LM Model in an Open Economy

An increase in the interest rate reduces output both directly and indirectly (through the exchange rate). The *IS* curve is downward sloping. The *LM* curve is horizontal, as in Chapter 6.

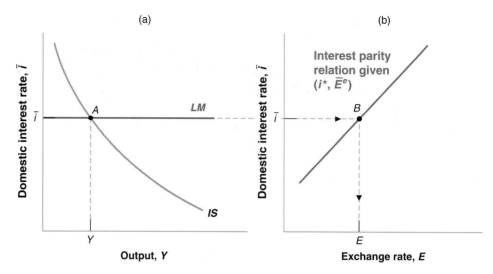

(a)

(b)

The first effect, which was already present in a closed economy, is the direct effect on investment. A higher interest rate leads to a decrease in investment, a decrease in the demand for domestic goods, and a decrease in output.

The second effect, which is only present in the open economy, is the effect through the exchange rate. A higher interest rate leads to an increase in the exchange rate—an appreciation. The appreciation, which makes domestic goods more expensive relative to foreign goods, leads to a decrease in net exports, and therefore to a decrease in the demand for domestic goods and a decrease in output.

Both effects work in the same direction. An increase in the interest rate decreases demand directly and indirectly—through the adverse effect of the appreciation on demand.

The *IS* relation between the interest rate and output is drawn in Figure 19-2(a), for given values of all the other variables in the relation—namely T, G, Y^*, i^*, and $\bar{E}^e$. The *IS* curve is downward sloping. An increase in the interest rate leads to lower output. The curve looks much the same as in the closed economy, but it hides a more complex relation than before. The interest rate affects output not only directly, but also indirectly through the exchange rate.

> An increase in the interest rate leads, both directly and indirectly (through the exchange rate), to a decrease in output.

The *LM* relation is the same as in the closed economy; it is a horizontal line, at the level of the interest rate $\bar{i}$ set by the central bank.

Equilibrium in the goods and financial markets is attained at point A in Figure 19-2(a), with output level Y and interest rate $\bar{i}$. The equilibrium value of the exchange rate cannot be read directly from the graph. But it is easily obtained from Figure 19-2(b), which replicates Figure 19-1 and gives the exchange rate associated with a given interest rate found at point B, given also the foreign interest rate i^* and the expected exchange rate. The exchange rate associated with the equilibrium interest rate $\bar{i}$ is equal to E.

Let's summarize. We have derived the *IS* and the *LM* relations for an open economy:

The *IS* curve is downward sloping. An increase in the interest rate leads both directly and indirectly (through the exchange rate), to a decrease in demand and a decrease in output.

The *LM* curve is horizontal at the interest rate set by the central bank.

Equilibrium output and the equilibrium interest rate are given by the intersection of the *IS* and the *LM* curves. Given the foreign interest rate and the expected future exchange rate, the equilibrium interest rate determines the equilibrium exchange rate.

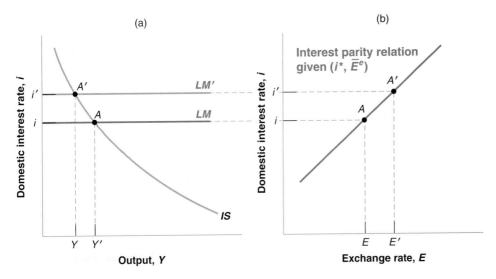

Figure 19-3

The Effects of an Increase in the Interest Rate

An increase in the interest rate leads to a decrease in output and an appreciation.

19-4 The Effects of Policy in an Open Economy

Having derived the *IS-LM* model for the open economy, we can now put it to use and look at the effects of policy.

The Effects of Monetary Policy in an Open Economy

Let's start from the effects of the central bank's decision to increase the domestic interest rate. Look at Figure 19-3(a). At a given level of output, with a higher interest rate, the *LM* curve shifts up, from *LM* to *LM'*. The *IS* curve does not shift (remember that the *IS* curve only shifts if *G* or *T* or *Y** or *i** change). The equilibrium moves from point *A* to point *A'*. In Figure 19-3(b), the increase in the interest rate leads to an appreciation.

◄ A monetary contraction shifts the *LM* curve up. It shifts neither the *IS* curve nor the interest parity curve.

So, in the open economy, monetary policy works through two channels; first, as in the closed economy, it works through the effect of the interest rate on spending; second, it works through the effect of the interest rate on the exchange rate and the effect of the exchange rate on exports and imports. Both effects work in the same direction. In the case of a monetary contraction, the higher interest rate and the appreciation both decrease demand and output.

◄ Can you tell what happens to net exports?

The Effects of Fiscal Policy in an Open Economy

Let's look now at a change in government spending. Suppose that, starting from a balanced budget, the government decides to increase defense spending without raising taxes, and so runs a budget deficit. What happens to the level of output? To the composition of output? To the interest rate? To the exchange rate?

Let us first assume that before the increase in government spending, the level of output, *Y*, was below potential. If the increase in *G* moves output towards potential, but not above potential, the central bank will not be worried that inflation might increase (remember our discussion in Chapter 9, particularly Figure 9-3) and will keep the interest rate unchanged. What happens to the economy is described in Figure 19-4 on page 420. The economy is initially at point *A*. The increase in government spending by,

Figure 19-4

The Effects of an Increase in Government Spending with an Unchanged Interest Rate

An increase in government spending leads to an increase in output. If the central bank keeps the interest rate unchanged, the exchange rate also remains unchanged.

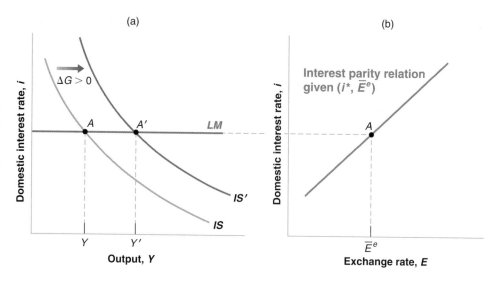

say, $\Delta G > 0$, increases output at a given interest rate, shifting the *IS* curve to the right, from *IS* to *IS'* in Figure 19-4(a). Because the central bank does not change the policy rate, the *LM* curve does not shift. The new equilibrium is at point A', with a higher level of output, Y'. In panel (b), because the interest rate has not changed, neither has the exchange rate. So an increase in government spending, when the central bank keeps the interest rate unchanged, leads to an increase in output with no change in the exchange rate.

> An increase in government spending shifts the *IS* curve ▶ to the right. It shifts neither the *LM* curve nor the interest parity line.

> MyEconLab Video

Can we tell what happens to the various components of demand?

- Clearly, consumption and government spending both increase: Consumption goes up because of the increase in income; government spending goes up by assumption.
- Investment also rises because it depends on both output and the interest rate: $I = I(Y, i)$. Here output rises and the interest rate does not change, thus investment rises.
- What about net exports? Recall that net exports depend on domestic output, foreign output, and the exchange rate: $NX = NX(Y, Y^*, E)$. Foreign output is unchanged, as we are assuming that the rest of the world does not respond to the increase in domestic government spending. The exchange rate is also unchanged, because the interest rate does not change. We are left with the effect of higher domestic output; as the increase in output increases imports at an unchanged exchange rate, net exports decrease. As a result, the budget deficit leads to a deterioration of the trade balance. If trade was balanced to start, then the budget deficit leads to a trade deficit. Note that, although an increase in the budget deficit increases the trade deficit, the effect is far from mechanical. It works through the effect of the budget deficit on output, and in turn, on the trade deficit.

Now assume instead that the increase in *G* happens in an economy where output is close to potential output, Y_n. The government could decide to increase government spending even if the economy is already at potential output for example because it needs to pay for an exceptional event, such as a big flood, and wants to postpone tax increases (more on this in Chapter 22). In this case the central bank will worry that the increase in *G*, by moving the economy above potential output, might push inflation up. It is likely

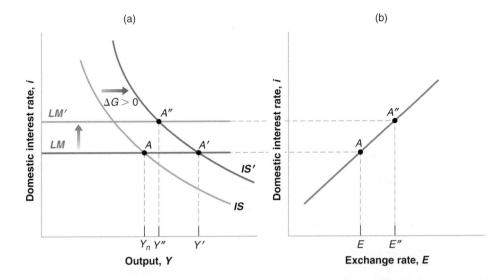

Figure 19-5

The Effects of an Increase in Government Spending when the Central Bank Responds by Raising the Interest Rate

An increase in government spending leads to an increase in output. If the central bank responds by raising the interest rate, the exchange rate will appreciate.

to respond by raising the interest rate. What happens then is described in Figure 19-5. At an unchanged interest rate, output would increase from Y_n to Y' and the exchange rate would not change. But if the central bank accompanies the increase in government spending with an increase in the interest rate, output will increase by less, from Y_n to Y'', and the exchange rate will appreciate, from E to E''.

Again, can we tell what happens to the various components of demand?

- As before, consumption and government spending both increase; consumption goes up because of the increase in income, and government spending goes up by assumption.

- What happens to investment is now ambiguous. Investment depends on both output and the interest rate: $I = I(Y, i)$. Here output rises but so does the interest rate.

- Net exports decrease, for two reasons: Output goes up, increasing imports. The exchange rate appreciates, increasing imports, and decreasing exports. The budget deficit leads to a trade deficit. (Whether however the trade deficit is larger than if the policy rate remained constant is ambiguous. The appreciation makes it worse; but the higher interest rate leads to a smaller increase in output, and thus a smaller increase in imports.)

This version of the *IS-LM* model for the open economy was first put together in the 1960s by the two economists we mentioned at the outset of the chapter, Robert ◄ Mundell, at Columbia University, and Marcus Fleming, at the International Monetary Fund—although their model reflected the economies of the 1960s, when central banks used to set the supply of money, M, rather than the interest rate as they do today (remember our discussion in Chapter 6). How well does the Mundell-Fleming model fit the facts? Typically quite well, and this is why the model is still in use today. Like all simple models, it often needs to be extended. One should incorporate for example the role of risk in affecting portfolio decisions, or the implications of the zero lower bound, two important aspects of the crisis. But the simple exercises we worked through in Figures 19-3, 19-4, and 19-5 are a good starting point to organize thoughts. (See for example the Focus box on page 422 "Fiscal and Monetary Policies Coordination in France (2008–2015)." The Mundell-Fleming model and its predictions pass with flying colors.)

Robert Mundell was awarded the Nobel Prize in Economics in 1999.

Fiscal and Monetary Policies Coordination in France (2008–2015)

France has been adopting one of the most equitable social security systems globally. Since the institution of the Fifth Republic and the advent of the socialist system in the fifties, France's hefty government expenditure on social security and infrastructure have been primarily financed through social contributions and taxation. Today taxes in France are globally acclaimed to be among the highest in the world. Suffice it to say that taxes in France account for 45% of GDP in comparison to an average of 37% in the European Union.

As the Global Financial Crisis struck the global economy, a mix of expansionary fiscal and monetary policies was used to boost economic growth. In the backdrop of the global economic meltdown and lower fiscal revenues, budget deficits deteriorated in most nations of the world. Especially for countries with high levels of real and financial integration, such as the European Union (EU), coordination of economic policy constitutes a major problem. The Stability and Growth Pact (SGP), which is a budget rules agreement between the 28 EU member states, obliges all EU members to stay within the limits on government deficit of 3% of GDP and on public debt of 60% of GDP.

As shown in Table 1, France was unable to meet the European Union's fiscal policy requirements. To arrest this, the European Union has asked member countries with high levels of public debt and budget deficits, such as France, to take measures to limit the government expenditure and increase fiscal earnings. Some countries have implemented significant fiscal consolidation and structural reforms, but others have lagged behind.

There are many reasons why France has found it difficult to comply with the fiscal targets of the EU. The generous social security system that France adopts is undoubtedly behind its consistent budget deficits lying below the 3% limit. Second, subsequent to the 2015 Paris terrorist attacks, France decided to raise its security and military expenditure to combat terrorism. François Hollande, the French president, demanded a deviation from the EU budget-cutting targets and took direct aim at EU budget rules, saying: "The security pact takes precedence over the stability pact. France is at war."

It is true that EU budget rules allow for temporary deviations from fiscal targets in cases of unexpected national emergencies, but the EU called on France to take additional measures to ensure that the 2016 budget will comply with the SGP rules.

Even within the EU, the on-going debate is whether member nations should follow a fiscal austerity program or increase government expenditure in order to boost GDP growth.

When Hollande levied the 75% super-tax in 2012 on individuals earning over €1 million, it was obvious that his socialist government was in favor of an expansionary fiscal policy. Notwithstanding the fact that the controversial super-tax was

Table 1 Emergence of Large French Budget Deficits, 1999–2016 (Percentage of GDP)

	1999	2007	2014	2020* (1984)
Spending	51.0	52.2	57.3	59.0 (23.7)
Tax Revenues	43.9	42.4	45.2	46 (19.2)
Public debt	60	64.2	95.3	95.9 (24.5)
Budget deficit	−2.3	−3.2	−4	−3.2

*Projected

Source: OECD STAT. Revenue Statistics OECD Member Countries. https://stats.oecd.org/Index.aspx?DataSetCode=REV.

Table 2 Major French Macroeconomic Variables, 1999–2015

	1999	2007	2015	2020*
GDP growth (%)	3.4	2.3	0.2	1.4
Unemployment rate (%)	11	7.9	9.3	10.3
Inflation (CPI) (%)	0.2	1.5	0.5	1.2
Interest rate (real) (%)	3.99	4.95	1.59	2.48
	2.5	4.9	6.0	5.1
Nominal effective exchange rate	96.25	106.26	92.35	103.5
Current account balance (% of GDP)	1.18	−0.95	−0.89	−0.34

*Projected

Source: The World Bank Database and the European Central Bank STATS.
Inflation: rate of change of the CPI. The nominal interest rate is the average rate on government bonds for the Euro area. The real interest rate is equal to the nominal rate minus the forecast of inflation by the European Central Bank. The nominal effective exchange rate of the euro is based on weighted averages of bilateral euro exchange rates against 19 trading partners of the euro area. If this index rate goes down, the euro has depreciated.

immediately dropped, as it would have resulted in the escape of top talents, the French argue against the clamor for cuts in fiscal spending.

France is heading towards massive government spending increases coupled with small or no tax rises. In such bleak fiscal conditions, monetary expansion and very low interest rates are vital to ensure that the money supply does not shrink and that recession does not hit the French economy.

The combined effects of low interest rates on the euro and the consistent fiscal expansion were very much in line with what the Mundell-Fleming model determines. Table 2 gives the evolution of the main macroeconomic variables in France from 1999 to 2015.

France has been operating in a deflationary environment from 1999 to 2015. Fiscal and monetary expansion and the lower interest rates that were dictated by the European Central Bank were the methods adopted by the French to combat recession. As the euro depreciated in 2015, the current account balance slightly improved. But in spite of inflationary fiscal and monetary policies, the French economy still suffers from the ills of a slowdown in aggregate demand. This has resulted in a problem of twin budget and trade deficits.

19-5 Fixed Exchange Rates

We have assumed so far that the central bank chose the interest rate and let the exchange rate adjust freely in whatever manner was implied by equilibrium in the foreign exchange market. In many countries, this assumption does not reflect reality. Central banks act under implicit or explicit exchange rate targets and use monetary policy to achieve those targets. The targets are sometimes implicit, sometimes explicit; they are sometimes specific values, sometimes bands or ranges. These exchange rate arrangements (or *regimes*, as they are called) come under many names. Let's first see what the names mean.

Pegs, Crawling Pegs, Bands, the EMS, and the Euro

At one end of the spectrum are countries with flexible exchange rates such as the United States, the United Kingdom, Japan, and Canada. These countries have no explicit exchange rate targets. Although their central banks do not ignore movements in the exchange rate, they have shown themselves quite willing to let their exchange rates fluctuate considerably.

At the other end are countries that operate under *fixed exchange rates*. Those countries maintain a fixed exchange rate in terms of some foreign currency. Some **peg** their currency to the dollar. For example, from 1991 to 2001, Argentina pegged its currency, the peso, at the highly symbolic exchange rate of one dollar for one peso (more on this in Chapter 20). Other countries used to peg their currency to the French franc (most of these are former French colonies in Africa); as the French franc has been replaced by the euro, they are now pegged to the euro. Still other countries peg their currency to a basket of foreign currencies, with the weights reflecting the composition of their trade.

The label *fixed* is a bit misleading. It is not the case that the exchange rate in countries with fixed exchange rates never actually changes. But changes are rare. An extreme case is that of the African countries pegged to the French franc. When their exchange rates were readjusted in January 1994, this was the first adjustment in 45 years! Because these changes are rare, economists use specific words to distinguish them from the daily changes that occur under flexible exchange rates. A decrease in the exchange rate under a regime of fixed exchange rates is called a *devaluation* rather than a depreciation, and an increase in the exchange rate under a regime of fixed exchange rates is called a *revaluation* rather than an appreciation.

Between these extremes are countries with various degrees of commitment to an exchange rate target. For example, some countries operate under a **crawling peg**. The name describes it well. These countries typically have inflation rates that exceed the U.S. inflation rate. If they were to peg their nominal exchange rate against the dollar, the more rapid increase in their domestic price level above the U.S. price level would lead to a steady real appreciation and rapidly make their goods uncompetitive. To avoid this effect,

◄ These terms were first introduced in Chapter 17.

Recall the definition of the real exchange rate $\epsilon = EP/P^*$.
If domestic inflation is higher than foreign inflation:
  P increases faster than P^*.
  If E is fixed, EP/P^* steadily increases.
◄ Equivalently: There is a steady real appreciation. Domestic goods become steadily more expensive relative to foreign goods.

these countries choose a predetermined rate of depreciation against the dollar. They choose to "crawl" (move slowly) vis-à-vis the dollar.

Yet another arrangement is for a group of countries to maintain their bilateral exchange rates (the exchange rate between each pair of countries) within some bands. Perhaps the most prominent example was the **European Monetary System (EMS)**, which determined the movements of exchange rates within the European Union from 1978 to 1998. Under the EMS rules, member countries agreed to maintain their exchange rate relative to the other currencies in the system within narrow limits or **bands** around a **central parity**—a given value for the exchange rate. Changes in the central parity and devaluations or revaluations of specific currencies could occur, but only by common agreement among member countries. After a major crisis in 1992, which led a number of countries to drop out of the EMS altogether, exchange rate adjustments became more and more infrequent, leading a number of countries to move one step further and adopt a common currency, the **euro**. The conversion from domestic currencies to the euro began on January 1, 1999, and was completed in early 2002. We shall return to the implications of the move to the euro in Chapter 20.

We shall look at the 1992 crisis ▶ in Chapter 20.

You can think of countries ▶ adopting a common currency as adopting an extreme form of fixed exchange rates. Their "exchange rate" is fixed at one-to-one between any pair of countries.

We shall discuss the pros and cons of different exchange regimes in the next chapter. But first, we must understand how pegging (also called *fixing*) the exchange rate affects monetary policy and fiscal policy. This is what we do in the rest of this section.

Monetary Policy when the Exchange Rate Is Fixed

Suppose a country decides to peg its exchange rate at some chosen value, call it $\bar{E}$. How does it actually achieve this? The government cannot just announce the value of the exchange rate and remain idle. Rather, it must take measures so that its chosen exchange rate will prevail in the foreign exchange market. Let's look at the implications and mechanics of pegging.

Pegging or no pegging, the exchange rate and the nominal interest rate must satisfy the interest parity condition

$$(1 + i_t) = (1 + i_t^*)\left(\frac{E_t}{E_{t+1}^e}\right)$$

These results depend on the interest rate parity condition, which in turn depends on the assumption of perfect capital mobility—that financial investors go for the highest expected rate of return. The case of fixed exchange rates with imperfect capital mobility, which is more relevant for middle-income countries, such as in Latin America or Asia, is treated in the appendix to this ▶ chapter.

Now suppose the country pegs the exchange rate at $\bar{E}$, so the current exchange rate $E_t = \bar{E}$. If financial and foreign exchange markets believe that the exchange rate will remain pegged at this value, then their expectation of the future exchange rate, E_{t+1}^e, is also equal to $\bar{E}$, and the interest parity relation becomes

$$(1 + i_t) = (1 + i_t^*) \Rightarrow i_t = i_t^*$$

In words: If financial investors expect the exchange rate to remain unchanged, they will require the same nominal interest rate in both countries. *Under a fixed exchange rate and perfect capital mobility, the domestic interest rate must be equal to the foreign interest rate.*

Let's summarize. *Under fixed exchange rates, the central bank gives up monetary policy as a policy instrument.* With a fixed exchange rate, the domestic interest rate must be equal to the foreign interest rate.

Fiscal Policy when the Exchange Rate Is Fixed

If monetary policy can no longer be used under fixed exchange rates, what about fiscal policy?

The effects of an increase in government spending when the central bank pegs the exchange rate are identical to those we saw in Figure 19-4 for the case of flexible exchange rates. This is because if the increase in spending is not accompanied by a change

German Reunification, Interest Rates, and the EMS

Under a fixed exchange rate regime such as the European Monetary System (EMS)—the system which prevailed before the introduction of the euro—no individual country can change its interest rate if the other countries do not change theirs as well. So, how do interest rates actually change? Two arrangements are possible. One is for all the member countries to coordinate changes in their interest rates. Another is for one of the countries to take the lead and for the other countries to follow—this is in effect what happened in the EMS, with Germany as the leader.

During the 1980s, most European central banks shared similar goals and were happy to let the Bundesbank (the German central bank) take the lead. But in 1990, German unification led to a sharp divergence in goals between the Bundesbank and the central banks of the other EMS countries. Large budget deficits, triggered by transfers to people and firms in Eastern Germany, together with an investment boom, led to a large increase in demand in Germany. The Bundesbank's fear that this shift would generate too strong an increase in activity led it to adopt a restrictive monetary policy. The result was strong growth in Germany together with a large increase in interest rates.

This may have been the right policy mix for Germany. But for the other European countries, this policy mix was much less appealing. They were not experiencing the same increase in demand, but to stay in the EMS, they had to match German interest rates. The net result was a sharp decrease in demand and output in the other countries. These results are presented in Table 1, which gives nominal interest rates, real interest rates, inflation rates, and GDP growth from 1990 to 1992 for Germany and for two of its EMS partners, France and Belgium.

Note first how the high German nominal interest rates were matched by both France and Belgium. In fact, nominal interest rates were actually higher in France than in Germany in all three years! This is because France needed higher interest rates than Germany to maintain the Deutsche Mark (DM)/franc parity. The reason is that financial markets were not sure that France would actually keep the parity of the franc relative to the DM. Worried about a possible devaluation of the franc, financial investors asked for a higher interest rate on French bonds than on German bonds.

Although France and Belgium had to match—or, as we have just seen, more than match—German nominal rates, both countries had less inflation than Germany. The result was very high real interest rates, much higher than the rate in Germany: In both France and Belgium, average real interest rates from 1990 to 1992 were close to 7%. And in both countries, the period 1990–1992 was characterized by slow growth and rising unemployment. Unemployment in France in 1992 was 10.4%, up from 8.9% in 1990. The corresponding numbers for Belgium were 12.1% and 8.7%.

A similar story was unfolding in the other EMS countries. By 1992, average unemployment in the European Union, which had been 8.7% in 1990, had increased to 10.3%. The effects of high real interest rates on spending were not the only source of this slowdown, but they were the main one.

By 1992, an increasing number of countries were wondering whether to keep defending their EMS parity or to give it up and lower their interest rates. Worried about the risk of devaluations, financial markets started to ask for higher interest rates in those countries where they thought devaluations were more likely. The result was two major exchange rate crises, one in the fall of 1992, and the other in the summer of 1993. By the end of these two crises, two countries, Italy and the United Kingdom, had left the EMS. We shall look at these crises, their origins, and their implications, in Chapter 20.

Table 1 German Reunification, Interest Rates, and Output Growth: Germany, France, and Belgium, 1990–1992

	Nominal Interest Rates (%)			Inflation (%)		
	1990	1991	1992	1990	1991	1992
Germany	8.5	9.2	9.5	2.7	3.7	4.7
France	10.3	9.6	10.3	2.9	3.0	2.4
Belgium	9.6	9.4	9.4	2.9	2.7	2.4
	Real Interest Rates (%)			GDP Growth (%)		
	1990	1991	1992	1990	1991	1992
Germany	5.8	5.5	4.8	5.7	4.5	2.1
France	7.4	6.6	7.9	2.5	0.7	1.4
Belgium	6.7	6.7	7.0	3.3	2.1	0.8

The nominal interest rate is the short-term nominal interest rate. The real interest rate is the realized real interest rate over the year—that is, the nominal interest rate minus actual inflation over the year. All rates are annual.

Source: OECD Economic Outlook.

Under flexible exchange rates the central bank could respond to an increase in government spending by raising the interest rate, as in Figure 19-5. This option is no longer available under fixed exchange rates because the interest rate must be equal to the foreign rate.

MyEconLab Video

in the interest rate, the exchange rate doesn't move. Thus, when government spending increases whether or not the country pegs its exchange rate makes no difference. The difference between fixed and flexible exchange is the ability of the central bank to respond. We saw in Figure 19-5 that if the increase in government spending pushed the economy above potential output, thus raising the possibility that inflation might increase, the central bank could respond by raising the interest rate. This option is no longer available ► under fixed exchange rates because the interest rate must be equal to the foreign rate.

As this chapter comes to an end, a question should have started to form in your mind: Why would a country choose to fix its exchange rate? You have seen a number of reasons why this appears to be a bad idea:

- By fixing the exchange rate, a country gives up a powerful tool for correcting trade imbalances or changing the level of economic activity.

- By committing to a particular exchange rate, a country also gives up control of its policy rate. Not only that, but the country must match movements in the foreign interest rate, at the risk of unwanted effects on its own activity. This is what happened in the early 1990s in Europe. Because of the increase in demand as a result of the reunification of West and East Germany, Germany felt it had to increase its interest rate. To maintain their parity with the Deutsche Mark, other countries in the European Monetary System (EMS) were forced to also increase their interest rates, something that they would rather have avoided. (This is the topic of the Focus box "German Reunification, Interest Rates, and the EMS.")

- Although the country retains control of fiscal policy, one policy instrument may not be enough. As you saw in Chapter 18, for example, a fiscal expansion can help the economy get out of a recession, but only at the cost of a larger trade deficit. And a country that wants, for example, to decrease its budget deficit cannot, under fixed exchange rates, use monetary policy to offset the contractionary effect of its fiscal policy on output.

So why do some countries fix their exchange rate? Why have 19 European countries—with more to come—adopted a common currency? To answer these questions, we must do some more work. We must look at what happens not only in the short run—which is what we did in this chapter—but also in the medium run, when the price level can adjust. We must look at the nature of exchange rate crises. Once we have done this, we shall then be able to assess the pros and cons of different exchange rate regimes. These are the topics we take up in Chapter 20.

Summary

- In an open economy, the demand for domestic goods, and in turn output, depends both on the interest rate and on the exchange rate. An increase in the interest rate decreases the demand for domestic goods. An increase in the exchange rate—an appreciation—also decreases the demand for domestic goods.

- The exchange rate is determined by the interest parity condition, which states that domestic and foreign bonds must have the same expected rate of return in terms of domestic currency.

- Given the expected future exchange rate and the foreign interest rate, increases in the domestic interest rate lead to an

increase in the exchange rate—an appreciation. Decreases in the domestic interest rate lead to a decrease in the exchange rate—a depreciation.

- Under flexible exchange rates, an expansionary fiscal policy leads to an increase in output. If the fiscal expansion is partially offset by tighter monetary policy, it leads to an increase in the interest rate, and an appreciation.

- Under flexible exchange rates, a contractionary monetary policy leads to a decrease in output, an increase in the interest rate, and an appreciation.

- There are many types of exchange rate arrangements. They range from fully flexible exchange rates to crawling pegs, to fixed exchange rates (or pegs), to the adoption of a common currency. Under fixed exchange rates, a country maintains a fixed exchange rate in terms of a foreign currency or a basket of currencies.

■ Under fixed exchange rates and the interest parity condition, a country must maintain an interest rate equal to the foreign interest rate. The central bank loses the use of monetary policy as a policy instrument. Fiscal policy becomes more powerful than under flexible exchange rates, however, because fiscal policy triggers monetary accommodation, and so does not lead to offsetting changes in the domestic interest rate and exchange rate.

Key Terms

Mundell-Fleming model, 411
peg, 423
crawling peg, 423
European Monetary System (EMS), 424

bands, 424
central parity, 424
euro, 424

Questions and Problems

QUICK CHECK

MyEconLab Visit www.myeconlab.com to complete similar Quick Check problems and get instant feedback.

1. Using the information in this chapter, label each of the following statements true, false, or uncertain. Explain briefly.
   a. The interest rate parity condition means that interest rates are equal across countries.
   b. Other things being equal, the interest parity condition implies that the domestic currency will appreciate in response to an increase in the expected exchange rate.
   c. If financial investors expect the dollar to depreciate against the yen over the coming year, one-year interest rates will be higher in the United States than in Japan.
   d. If the expected exchange rate appreciates, the current exchange rate immediately appreciates.
   e. The central bank influences the value of the exchange rate by changing the domestic interest rate relative to the foreign interest rate.
   f. An increase in domestic interest rates, all other factors equal, increases exports.
   g. A fiscal expansion, all other factors equal, tends to increase net exports.
   h. Fiscal policy has a greater effect on output in an economy with fixed exchange rates than in an economy with flexible exchange rates.
   i. Under a fixed exchange rate, the central bank must keep the domestic interest rate equal to the foreign interest rates.

2. Consider an open economy with flexible exchange rates. Suppose output is at the natural level, but there is a trade deficit. The goal of policy is to reduce the trade deficit and leave the level of output at its natural level.
What is the appropriate fiscal and monetary policy mix?

3. In this chapter, we showed that a reduction in the interest rate in an economy operating under flexible exchange rates leads to an increase in output and a depreciation of the domestic currency.

   a. How does the reduction in interest rates in an economy with flexible exchange rates affect consumption and investment?
   b. How does the reduction in interest rates in an economy with flexible exchange rates affect net exports?

4. Flexible exchange rates and foreign macroeconomic events
   Consider an open economy with flexible exchange rates. Let UIP stand for the uncovered interest parity condition.
   a. In an IS-LM–UIP diagram, show the effect of an increase in foreign output, Y^*, on domestic output (Y) and the exchange rate (E), when the domestic central bank leaves the policy interest rate unchanged. Explain in words.
   b. In an IS-LM–UIP diagram, show the effect of an increase in the foreign interest rate, i^*, on domestic output (Y) and the exchange rate (E), when the domestic central bank leaves the policy interest rate unchanged. Explain in words.

5. Flexible exchange rates and the responses to changes in foreign macroeconomic policy
   Suppose there is an expansionary fiscal policy in the foreign country that increases Y^* and i^* at the same time.
   a. In an IS-LM–UIP diagram, show the effect of the increase in foreign output, Y^*, and the increase in the foreign interest rate, i^*, on domestic output (Y) and the exchange rate (E), when the domestic central bank leaves the policy interest rate unchanged. Explain in words.
   b. In an IS-LM–UIP diagram, show the effect of the increase in foreign output, Y^*, and the increase in the foreign interest rate, i^*, on domestic output (Y) and the exchange rate (E), when the domestic central bank matches the increase in the foreign interest rate with an equal increase in the domestic interest rate. Explain in words.
   c. In an IS-LM–UIP diagram, show the required domestic monetary policy following the increase in foreign output, Y^*, and the increase in the foreign interest rate, i^*, if the goal of domestic monetary policy is to leave domestic output (Y) unchanged. Explain in words. When might such a policy be necessary?

6. *Fixed exchange rates and foreign macroeconomic policy*

Consider a fixed exchange rate system, in which a group of countries (called follower countries) peg their currencies to the currency of one country (called the leader country). Because the currency of the leader country is not fixed against the currencies of countries outside the fixed exchange rate system, the leader country can conduct monetary policy as it wishes. For this problem, consider the domestic country to be a follower country and the foreign country to be the leader country.

a. How does an increase in interest rates in the leader country affect the interest rate and output in the follower country?

b. How does the increase in leader country interest rates change the composition of output in the follower country? Assume the follower country does not change fiscal policy.

c. Can the follower country use fiscal policy to offset the effects of the leader country's reduction in interest rates and leave domestic output unchanged? When might such a fiscal policy be desirable?

d. Fiscal policy involves changing government spending or changing taxes. Design a fiscal policy mix that leaves consumption and domestic output unchanged when the leader country increases interest rates. What component of output is changed?

7. *The exchange rate as a policy tool*

The effectiveness of monetary policy in an open economy is enhanced when the central bank has the flexibility to change the exchange rate and the willingness to change interest rates. Suppose that there is a decrease in consumer confidence in Tunisia given the lengthy political turmoil after the 2010 uprising. This leads households to increase their savings, for a given level of disposable income. Assume that UIP stands for the uncovered interest rate parity condition and its associated curve.

a. Using the AS-AD and *IS-LM-UIP* diagram, show the short run effects of the decline in consumer confidence on output and the exchange rate if the Central Bank of Tunisia does not change interest rates. Explain what happens to output, the interest rate, and the price level in the short run.

b. Now that foreign investors become scared about this country, they require a premium to invest in Tunisia. What happens if the Central Bank of Tunisia is willing to raise interest rates to restore foreign investors' confidence?

c. Compare the response of an economy to a temporary fall in foreign demand for its exports under fixed and flexible exchange rates.

d. What are the advantages and disadvantages of central banks adopting a flexible exchange rate?

EXPLORE FURTHER

8. *Demand for U.K. assets, the pound, and the trade deficit*

This question explores how an increase in global demand for U.K. assets is likely to slow down the depreciation of the British pound. Here we modify the IS-LM-UIP framework (where UIP stands for uncovered interest rate parity) to analyze the effects of an increase in the demand for U.K. assets. Write the uncovered interest rate parity condition as:

$$(1 + i_t) = (1 + i_t)(E_t/E_{t+1}^e) - x$$

Where x represents factors affecting the relative demand for domestic assets. An increase in x means that investors are willing to hold domestic assets at a lower interest rate (given the foreign interest rate and the current and expected exchange rates).

a. Solve the *UIP* condition for the current exchange rate, E_t.

b. Substitute the result from part a in the *IS* curve and construct the *UIP* diagram. As in the text you may assume that P and P^* are constant and equal to one.

c. The British pound has a higher interest rate in comparison to the euro. According to the *UIP* condition, explain whether the expected rate of the pound (E_{t+1}^e) is supposed to appreciate or depreciate in the future. What are the effects on output and net exports? How is this reflected in the *IS-LM-UIP* diagram?

d. Suppose that there are expectations that the expansionary monetary policy by the Bank of England will result in a permanent future increase in the money supply. If the prices of goods and services are fully flexible, do you expect the spot exchange rate to respond immediately?

e. What is the effect of an increase in the demand for domestic assets x? Do you expect that this increase will prevent the depreciation of the pound?

9. *Bond yields and long run currency movements*

a. Go the Web site of *The Economist* (www.economist.com) and find data on 10-year interest rates. Look in the section "Markets & Data" and then the subsection "Economic and Financial Indicators." Look at the 10-year interest rates for the United States, Japan, China, Britain, Canada, Mexico, and the Euro area. For each country (treating the Euro area as a country), calculate the spreads as that country's interest rate minus the U.S. interest rate.

b. From the uncovered interest parity condition, the spreads from part (a) are the annualized expected appreciation rates of the dollar against other currencies. To calculate the 10-year expected appreciation, you must compound. (So, if x is the spread, the 10-year expected appreciation is $[(1 + x)^{10} - 1]$. Be careful about decimal points.) Is the dollar expected to depreciate or appreciate by much against the currency of any of its six major trading partners?

c. Given your answer to part (b), for which country(ies) is a significant appreciation or depreciation of the dollar expected over the next decade? Does your answer seem plausible?

APPENDIX: Fixed Exchange Rates, Interest Rates, and Capital Mobility

The assumption of perfect capital mobility is a good approximation of what happens in countries with highly developed financial markets and few capital controls, such as the United States, the United Kingdom, Japan, and the Euro area. But this assumption is more questionable in countries that have less developed financial markets or have capital controls in place. In these countries, domestic financial investors may have neither the savvy nor the legal right to buy foreign bonds when domestic interest rates are low. The central bank may thus be able to decrease the interest rate while maintaining a given exchange rate.

To look at these issues, we need to have another look at the balance sheet of the central bank. In Chapter 4, we assumed the only asset held by the central bank was domestic bonds. In an open economy, the central bank actually holds two types of assets: (1) domestic bonds and (2) **foreign exchange reserves**, which we shall think of as foreign currency—although they also take the form of foreign bonds or foreign interest-paying assets. Think of the balance sheet of the central bank as represented in Figure 1.

On the asset side are bonds and foreign exchange reserves, and on the liability side is the monetary base. There are now two ways in which the central bank can change the monetary base: either by purchases or sales of bonds in the bond market or by purchases or sales of foreign currency in the foreign exchange market. (If you did not read Section 4-3 in Chapter 4, replace *monetary base* with *money supply* and you will still get the basic argument.)

Perfect Capital Mobility and Fixed Exchange Rates

Consider first the effects of an open market operation under the joint assumptions of perfect capital mobility and fixed exchange rates (the assumptions we made in the last section of this chapter).

- Assume the domestic interest rate and the foreign interest rate are initially equal, so $i = i^*$. Now suppose the central bank embarks on an expansionary open market operation, buying bonds in the bond market in amount ΔB, and creating money—increasing the monetary base—in exchange. This purchase of bonds leads to a decrease in the domestic interest rate, i. This is, however, only the beginning of the story.
- Now that the domestic interest rate is lower than the foreign interest rate, financial investors prefer to hold foreign bonds. To buy foreign bonds, they must first buy foreign currency.

They then go to the foreign exchange market and sell domestic currency for foreign currency.

- If the central bank did nothing, the price of domestic currency would fall, and the result would be a depreciation. Under its commitment to a fixed exchange rate however, the central bank cannot allow the currency to depreciate. So it must intervene in the foreign exchange market and sell foreign currency for domestic currency. As it sells foreign currency and buys domestic money, the monetary base decreases.
- How much foreign currency must the central bank sell? It must keep selling until the monetary base is back to its pre-open market operation level, so the domestic interest rate is again equal to the foreign interest rate. Only then are financial investors willing to hold domestic bonds.

How long do all these steps take? Under perfect capital mobility, all this may happen within minutes or so of the original open market operation. After these steps, the balance sheet of the central bank looks as represented in Figure 2. Bond holdings are up by ΔB, reserves of foreign currency are down by ΔB, and the monetary base is unchanged, having gone up by ΔB in the open market operation and down by ΔB as a result of the sale of foreign currency in the foreign exchange market.

Let's summarize. Under fixed exchange rates and perfect capital mobility, the only effect of the open market operation is to change the *composition* of the central bank's balance sheet but not the monetary base, nor the interest rate.

Imperfect Capital Mobility and Fixed Exchange Rates

Let's now move away from the assumption of perfect capital mobility. Suppose it takes some time for financial investors to shift between domestic bonds and foreign bonds.

Now an expansionary open market operation can initially bring the domestic interest rate below the foreign interest rate. But over time, investors shift to foreign bonds, leading to an increase in the demand for foreign currency in the foreign exchange market. To avoid a depreciation of the domestic currency, the central bank must again stand ready to sell foreign currency and buy domestic currency. Eventually, the central bank buys enough domestic currency to offset the effects of the initial open market operation. The monetary base is back to its pre-open market operation level, and so is the interest rate. The central bank holds more domestic bonds and smaller reserves of foreign currency.

Assets	Liabilities
Bonds Foreign exchange reserves	Monetary base

Figure 1

Balance Sheet of the Central Bank

Assets	Liabilities
Bonds: ΔB Reserves: $-\Delta B$	Monetary base: $\Delta B - \Delta B$ $= 0$

Figure 2

Balance Sheet of the Central Bank after an Open Market Operation, and the Induced Intervention in the Foreign Exchange Market

The difference between this case and the case of perfect capital mobility is that, by accepting a loss in foreign exchange reserves, the central bank is now able to decrease interest rates *for some time*. If it takes just a few days for financial investors to adjust, the trade-off can be very unattractive—as many countries that have suffered large losses in reserves without much effect on the interest rate have discovered at their expense. But if the central bank can affect the domestic interest rate for a few weeks or months, it may, in some circumstances, be willing to do so.

Now let's deviate further from perfect capital mobility. Suppose, in response to a decrease in the domestic interest rate, financial investors are either unwilling or unable to move much of their portfolio into foreign bonds. For example, there are administrative and legal controls on financial transactions, making it illegal or very expensive for domestic residents to invest outside the country. This is the relevant case for a number of emerging economies, from Latin America to China.

After an expansionary open market operation, the domestic interest rate decreases, making domestic bonds less attractive. Some domestic investors move into foreign bonds, selling domestic currency for foreign currency. To maintain the exchange rate, the central bank must buy domestic currency and supply foreign currency. However, the foreign exchange intervention by the central bank may now be small compared to the initial open market operation. And if capital controls truly prevent investors from moving into foreign bonds at all, there may be no need for such a foreign exchange intervention.

Even leaving this extreme case aside, the net effects of the initial open market operation and the following foreign exchange interventions are likely to be *an increase in the monetary base; a decrease in the domestic interest rate; an increase in the central bank's bond holdings; and some—but limited—loss in reserves of foreign currency.* With imperfect capital mobility, a country has some freedom to move the domestic interest rate while maintaining its exchange rate. This freedom depends primarily on three factors:

- The degree of development of its financial markets, and the willingness of domestic and foreign investors to shift between domestic assets and foreign assets.
- The degree of capital controls it is able to impose on both domestic and foreign investors.
- The amount of foreign exchange reserves it holds. The higher the reserves it has, the more it can afford the loss in reserves it is likely to sustain if it decreases the interest rate at a given exchange rate.

With the large movements in capital flows we documented in the chapter, all of these issues are hot topics. Many countries are considering a more active use of capital controls than in the past. Many countries are also accumulating large reserves as a precaution against large capital outflows.

Key Term

foreign-exchange reserves, 429

Exchange Rate Regimes

I n July 1944, representatives of 44 countries met in Bretton Woods, New Hampshire, to design a new international monetary and exchange rate system. The system they adopted was based on fixed exchange rates, with all member countries other than the United States fixing the price of their currency in terms of dollars. In 1973, a series of exchange rate crises brought an abrupt end

MyEconLab Video

©1971 by Ed Fisher/The New Yorker collection/The cartoon Bank

"Then it's agreed. Until the dollar firms up, we let the clamshell float."

to the system—and an end to what is now called "the Bretton Woods period." Since then, the world has been characterized by many exchange rate arrangements. Many countries operate under flexible exchange rates; some operate under fixed exchange rates; some go back and forth between regimes. Which exchange rate regime to choose is one of the most debated issues in macroeconomics and, as the cartoon suggests, a decision facing every country in the world. This chapter discusses this issue.

Section 20-1 looks at the medium run. It shows that, in contrast to the results we derived for the short run in Chapter 19, an economy ends up with the same real exchange rate and output level in the medium run, whether it operates under fixed exchange rates or flexible exchange rates. This obviously does not make the exchange rate regime irrelevant—the short run matters very much—but it is an important qualification to our previous analysis.

Section 20-2 takes another look at fixed exchange rates and focuses on exchange rate crises. During a typical exchange rate crisis, a country operating under a fixed exchange rate is forced, often under dramatic conditions, to abandon its parity and to devalue. Such crises were behind the breakdown of the Bretton Woods system. They rocked the European Monetary System in the early 1990s, and were a major element of the Asian Crisis of the late 1990s. It is important to understand why they happen, and what they imply.

Section 20-3 takes another look at flexible exchange rates. It shows that the behavior of exchange rates and the relation of the exchange rate to monetary policy are more complex than we assumed in Chapter 19. Large fluctuations in the exchange rate, and the difficulties in using monetary policy to affect the exchange rate, make a flexible exchange rate regime less attractive than it appeared to be in Chapter 19.

Section 20-4 puts all these conclusions together and reviews the case for flexible or fixed rates. It discusses two important developments: the use of a common currency in much of Europe, and the move toward strong forms of fixed exchange rate regimes, from currency boards to dollarization.

20-1 The Medium Run

When we focused on the short run in Chapter 19, we drew a sharp contrast between the behavior of an economy with flexible exchange rates and an economy with fixed exchange rates.

- Under flexible exchange rates, a country that needed to achieve a real depreciation (for example, to reduce its trade deficit, or to get out of a recession, or both) could do so by relying on an expansionary monetary policy to achieve both a lower interest rate and a decrease in the exchange rate—a depreciation.
- Under fixed exchange rates, a country lost both of these instruments. By definition, its nominal exchange rate was fixed and thus could not be adjusted. Moreover, the fixed exchange rate and the interest parity condition implied that the country could not adjust its interest rate either; the domestic interest rate had to remain equal to the foreign interest rate.

This appeared to make a flexible exchange rate regime definitely more attractive than a fixed exchange rate regime. Why should a country give up two macroeconomic instruments—the exchange rate and the interest rate? As we now shift focus from the short run to the medium run, you shall see that this previous conclusion needs to be qualified. Although our conclusions about the short run were valid, we shall see that, in the medium run, the difference between the two regimes fades away. More specifically, in the medium run, the economy reaches the same real exchange rate and the same level of output whether it operates under fixed or under flexible exchange rates.

The intuition for this result is actually easy to give. Recall the definition of the real exchange rate:

$$\varepsilon = \frac{EP}{P^*}$$

The real exchange rate, ε, is equal to the nominal exchange rate, E (the price of domestic currency in terms of foreign currency) times the domestic price level, P, divided by the foreign price level, P^*. There are, therefore, two ways in which the real exchange rate can adjust:

- Through a change in the nominal exchange rate E: By definition, this can only be done under flexible exchange rates. And if we assume the domestic price level, P, and the foreign price level, P^*, do not change in the short run, it is the only way to adjust the real exchange rate in the short run.
- Through a change in the domestic price level, P, relative to the foreign price level, P^*. In the medium run, as prices adjust, this option is open even to a country operating under a fixed (nominal) exchange rate. And this is indeed what happens under fixed exchange rates. The adjustment takes place through the price level rather than through the nominal exchange rate.

There are three ways in which a U.S. car can become cheaper relative to a Japanese car. First, through a decrease in the dollar price of the U.S car. Second, through an increase in the yen price of the Japanese car. Third, through a decrease in the nominal exchange rate—a decrease in the value of the dollar in terms of the yen.

The *IS* Relation under Fixed Exchange Rates

In an open economy with fixed exchange rates, we can write the *IS* relation as

$$Y = Y\left(\frac{\bar{E}P}{P^*}, G, T, i^* - \pi^e, Y^*\right) \qquad (20.1)$$
$$(-, \ +,-, \quad -, \quad +)$$

The derivation of equation (20.1) is better left to Appendix 1 at the end of this chapter, titled "Deriving the IS Relation under Fixed Exchange Rates." The intuition behind the equation is straightforward, however. Demand, and in turn, output, depend on:

- Negatively on the real exchange rate, $\bar{E}P/P^*$. $\bar{E}$ denotes the fixed nominal exchange rate; P and P^* denote the domestic and foreign price levels, respectively. A higher real exchange rate implies a lower demand for domestic goods, and in turn lower output.
- Positively on government spending, G, and negatively on taxes, T.
- Negatively on the domestic real interest rate, which itself equal to the domestic nominal interest rate minus expected inflation. Under the interest parity condition and fixed exchange rates, the domestic nominal interest rate is equal to the foreign nominal interest rate i^*, so the domestic real interest rate is given by $i^* - \pi^e$.
- Positively on foreign output, Y^*, through the effect on exports.

Equilibrium in the Short and the Medium Run

Consider an economy where the real exchange rate is too high. As a result, the trade balance is in deficit, and output is below potential.

As we saw in Chapter 19, under a flexible exchange rate regime, the central bank could solve the problem. It could, by decreasing the interest rate, lead to a nominal depreciation. Given the domestic and the foreign price levels, which we assumed were fixed in the short run, the nominal depreciation implied a real depreciation, an improvement in the trade balance and an increase in output.

Under a fixed exchange rate regime however, the central bank cannot move the domestic interest rate. Thus, in the short run, the trade deficit remains, and the country remains in recession.

In the medium run however, prices can adjust. We saw in the core that the behavior of prices is well described by the Phillips curve relation (Chapter 9, equation (9.3)):

$$\pi - \pi^e = (\alpha/L)(Y - Y_n)$$

Making the alternative assumption that expected inflation is equal to last year's inflation leads to more complicated dynamics but to the same medium-run equilibrium.

When output is above potential, the inflation rate (i.e., the rate of change of prices) is higher than expected. When output is below potential, as is the case we are considering here, the inflation rate is lower than expected. In Chapter 9, we saw that the way people formed expectations of inflation has changed over time. When inflation was low and not very persistent, expected inflation was roughly constant, and we could take π^e to be equal to a constant $\bar{\pi}$. When inflation became higher and more persistent, people started expecting inflation this year to be the same as last year, and expected inflation was better captured by $\pi^e = \pi_{-1}$. For simplicity, I shall assume here that expected inflation is constant so that the Phillips curve relation is given by:

$$\pi - \bar{\pi} = (\alpha/L)(Y - Y_n) \tag{20.2}$$

We are now ready to think about the dynamics in the medium run. We need to make some assumption about the initial domestic and foreign inflation rates. Denote the foreign inflation rate by π^*. Suppose that if output was equal to potential output, domestic and foreign inflation would be equal to each other, and both equal to $\bar{\pi}$, so $\pi = \pi^* = \bar{\pi}$. That is, if both economies were operating at potential, inflation rates would be the same, relative price levels would remain constant, and so would the real exchange rate. As we are assuming that we start from a situation where output is below potential, equation (20.2) implies that domestic inflation is lower than it would be if output was at potential, and thus lower than foreign inflation. Put another way, the domestic price level increases more slowly than the foreign price level. This implies that, given the nominal exchange

 $\pi < \pi^* \Rightarrow \bar{E}P/P^* \downarrow$

rate which is fixed, the real exchange rate decreases. As a result, net exports increase over time, and so does output. In the medium run, output is back to potential, domestic inflation is back to $\bar{\pi}$, and thus equal to foreign inflation. With domestic and foreign inflation being equal, the real exchange rate is constant.

To summarize:

- In the short run, a fixed nominal exchange rate implies a fixed real exchange rate.
- In the medium run, the real exchange rate can adjust even if the nominal exchange rate is fixed. This adjustment is achieved through movements in the relative price levels over time.

The Case for and against a Devaluation

The result that, even under fixed exchange rates, the economy can return to potential output in the medium run is important. But it does not eliminate the fact that the process of adjustment can be long and painful. Output may remain too low and unemployment may remain too high for a long time.

Are there faster and better ways to return output to potential? The answer, within the model we have just developed, is a clear yes. Suppose that the government decides, while keeping the fixed exchange rate regime, to allow for a *one-time* devaluation. Given the price level, the devaluation (a decrease in the nominal exchange rate) leads, in the short run, to a real depreciation (a decrease in the real exchange rate), and therefore to an increase in output. In principle, the right size devaluation can thus achieve in the short run what was achieved above only in the medium run, and thus avoid much of the pain. So, whenever a country under fixed exchange rates faces either a large trade

The Return of Britain to the Gold Standard: Keynes versus Churchill

In 1925, Britain decided to return to the gold standard. The **gold standard** was a system in which each country fixed the price of its currency in terms of gold and stood ready to exchange gold for currency at the stated parity. This system implied fixed exchange rates between countries. (If for example, one unit of currency in country A was worth two units of gold, and one unit of currency in country B was worth one unit, the exchange rate between the two was 2 (or ½, depending on which you take as a domestic country).

The gold standard had been in place from 1870 until World War I. Because of the need to finance the war, and to do so in part by money creation, Britain suspended the gold standard in 1914. In 1925, Winston Churchill, then Britain's Chancellor of the Exchequer (the British equivalent of Secretary of the Treasury in the United States), decided to return to the gold standard, and to return to it at the pre-war parity—that is, at the pre-war value of the pound in terms of gold. But because prices had increased faster in Britain than in many of its trading partners, returning to the pre-war parity implied a large real appreciation: At the same nominal exchange rate as before the war, British goods were now relatively more expensive relative to foreign goods. (Go back to the definition of the real exchange rate, $\varepsilon = EP/P^*$: The price level in Britain, P, had increased more than the foreign price level, P^*. At a given nominal exchange rate, E, this implied that ε was higher, that Britain suffered from a real appreciation.)

Keynes severely criticized the decision to return to the pre-war parity. In *The Economic Consequences of Mr. Churchill*, a book he published in 1925, Keynes argued as follows: If Britain were going to return to the gold standard, it should have done so at a lower price of currency in terms of gold; that is, at a lower nominal exchange rate than the pre-war nominal exchange rate. In a newspaper article, he articulated his views as follows:

"There remains, however, the objection to which I have never ceased to attach importance, against the return to gold in actual present conditions, in view of the possible consequences on the state of trade and employment. I believe that our price level is too high, if it is converted to gold at the par of exchange, in relation to gold prices elsewhere; and if we consider the prices of those articles only which are not the subject of international trade, and of services, i.e. wages, we shall find that these are materially too high—not less than 5 per cent, and probably 10 per cent. Thus, unless the situation is saved by a rise of prices elsewhere, the Chancellor is committing us to a policy of forcing down money wages by perhaps 2 shillings in the Pound.

I do not believe that this can be achieved without the gravest danger to industrial profits and industrial peace. I would much rather leave the gold value of our currency where it was some months ago than embark on a struggle with every trade union in the country to reduce money wages. It seems wiser and simpler and saner to leave the currency to find its own level for some time longer rather than force a situation where employers are faced with the alternative of closing down or of lowering wages, cost what the struggle may.

For this reason, I remain of the opinion that the Chancellor of the Exchequer has done an ill-judged thing—ill judged because we are running the risk for no adequate reward if all goes well."

Keynes's prediction turned out to be right. While other countries were growing, Britain remained in recession for the rest of the decade. Most economic historians attribute a good part of the blame to the initial overvaluation.

Source: "The Nation and Athenaeum," May 2, 1925.

---

deficit or a severe recession, there is heavy political pressure either to give up the fixed exchange rate regime altogether, or, at least, to have a one-time devaluation. Perhaps the most forceful presentation of this view was made 90 years ago by Keynes, who argued against Winston Churchill's decision to return the British pound in 1925 to its pre–World War I parity with gold. His arguments are presented in the Focus box "The Return of Britain to the Gold Standard: Keynes versus Churchill." Most economic historians believe that history proved Keynes right, and that overvaluation of the pound was one of the main reasons for Britain's poor economic performance after World War I.

Those who oppose a shift to flexible exchange rates or who oppose a devaluation argue that there are good reasons to choose fixed exchange rates, and that too much willingness to devalue defeats the purpose of adopting a fixed exchange rate regime in the first place. They argue that too much willingness on the part of governments to consider devaluations actually leads to an increased likelihood of exchange rate crises. To understand their arguments, we now turn to these crises: what triggers them and what their implications might be.

20-2 Exchange Rate Crises under Fixed Exchange Rates

Suppose a country has chosen to operate under a fixed exchange rate. Suppose also that financial investors start believing there may soon be an exchange rate adjustment—either a devaluation or a shift to a flexible exchange rate regime accompanied by a depreciation. We just saw why this might be the case:

- The real exchange rate may be too high. Or put another way, the domestic currency may be overvalued, leading to too large a current account deficit. In this case, a real depreciation is called for. Although this could be achieved in the medium run without a devaluation, financial investors conclude that the government will take the quickest way out—and devalue.

    Such an overvaluation often happens in countries that peg their nominal exchange rate to the currency of a country with lower inflation. Higher relative inflation implies a steadily increasing price of domestic goods relative to foreign goods, a steady real appreciation, and so a steady worsening of the trade position. As time passes, the need for an adjustment of the real exchange rate increases, and financial investors become more and more nervous. They start thinking that a devaluation might be coming.

The expression to let a currency "float" is to allow a move from a fixed to a flexible exchange rate regime. A floating exchange rate regime is the same as a flexible exchange rate regime. ▶

- Internal conditions may call for a decrease in the domestic interest rate. As we have seen, a decrease in the domestic interest rate cannot be achieved under fixed exchange rates. But it can be achieved if the country is willing to shift to a flexible exchange rate regime. If a country lets the exchange rate **float** and then decreases its domestic interest rate, we know from Chapter 19 that this will trigger a decrease in the nominal exchange rate—a nominal depreciation.

Because it is more convenient, we use the approximation, equation (17.4), rather than the ▶ original interest parity condition, equation (17.2).

As soon as financial markets believe a devaluation may be coming, then maintaining the exchange rate requires an increase—often a large one—in the domestic interest rate.

To see this, return to the interest parity condition we derived in Chapter 17:

$$i_t = i_t^* - \frac{(E_{t+1}^e - E_t)}{E_t} \qquad (20.3)$$

In Chapter 17, we interpreted this equation as a relation among the *one-year* domestic and foreign nominal interest rates, the current exchange rate, and the expected exchange rate a year hence. But the choice of one year as the period was arbitrary. The relation holds over a day, a week, a month. If financial markets expect the exchange rate to be 2% lower a month from now, they will hold domestic bonds only if the one-month domestic interest rate exceeds the one-month foreign interest rate by 2% (or, if we express interest rates at an annual rate, if the annual domestic interest rate exceeds the annual foreign interest rate by $2\% \times 12 = 24\%$).

Under fixed exchange rates, the current exchange rate, E_t, is set at some level, say $E_t = \bar{E}$. If markets expect the parity will be maintained over the period, then $E_{t+1}^e = \bar{E}$, and the interest parity condition simply states that the domestic and the foreign interest rates must be equal.

Suppose, however, participants in financial markets start anticipating a devaluation—a decision by the central bank to give up the parity and decrease the exchange rate in the future. Suppose they believe that, over the coming month, there is a 75% chance the parity will be maintained and a 25% chance there will be a 20% devaluation. The term $(E_{t+1}^e - E_t)/E_t$ in the interest parity equation (20.3), which we assumed equal to zero earlier, now equals $0.75 \times 0\% + 0.25 \times (-20\%) = -5\%$ (a 75% chance of no change plus a 25% chance of a devaluation of 20%).

This implies that, if the central bank wants to maintain the existing parity, it must now set a monthly interest rate 5% higher than before—60% higher at an annual rate (12 months $\times$ 5% per month); 60% is the interest differential needed to convince investors to hold domestic bonds rather than foreign bonds! Any smaller interest differential, and investors will not want to hold domestic bonds.

What, then, are the choices confronting the government and the central bank?

■ First, the government and the central bank can try to convince markets they have no intention of devaluing. This is always the first line of defense: Communiqués are issued, and prime ministers go on TV to reiterate their absolute commitment to the existing parity. But words are cheap, and they rarely convince financial investors.

■ Second, the central bank can increase the interest rate, but by less than would be needed to satisfy equation (20.3)—in our example, by less than 60%. Although domestic interest rates are high, they are not high enough to fully compensate for the perceived risk of devaluation. This action typically leads to a large capital outflow because financial investors still prefer to get out of domestic bonds and into foreign bonds, since the latter offer higher returns in terms of domestic currency. Thus, investors sell domestic bonds, getting the proceeds in domestic currency. They then go to the foreign exchange market to sell domestic currency for foreign currency, in order to buy foreign bonds. If the central bank did not intervene in the foreign exchange market, the large sales of domestic currency for foreign currency would lead to a depreciation. If the central bank wants to maintain the fixed exchange rate, it must therefore stand ready to buy domestic currency and sell foreign currency at the current exchange rate. In doing so, it often loses most of its reserves of foreign currency. (The mechanics of central bank intervention were described in the appendix to Chapter 19.)

■ Eventually—after a few hours or a few weeks—the choice for the central bank becomes either to increase the interest rate enough to satisfy equation (20.3) or to validate the market's expectations and devalue. Setting a very high short-term domestic interest rate can have a devastating effect on demand and on output—no firm wants to invest; no consumer wants to borrow when interest rates are very high. This course of action makes sense only if (1) the perceived probability of a devaluation is small, so the interest rate does not have to be too high; and (2) the government believes markets will soon become convinced that no devaluation is coming, allowing domestic interest rates to decrease. Otherwise, the only option is to devalue. (All these steps were at the center of the exchange rate crisis which affected much of Western Europe in 1992. See the Focus box on page 438 "The 1992 EMS Crisis.")

To summarize: Expectations that a devaluation may be coming can trigger an exchange rate crisis. Faced with such expectations, the government has two options:

■ Give in and devalue, or
■ Fight and maintain the parity, at the cost of very high interest rates and a potential recession. Fighting may not work anyway; the recession may force the government to change policy later on or force the government out of office.

An interesting twist here is that a devaluation can occur even if the belief that a devaluation was coming was initially groundless. In other words, even if the government initially has no intention of devaluing, it might be forced to do so if financial markets believe that it will devalue. The cost of maintaining the parity would be a long period of high interest rates and a recession; the government might prefer to devalue instead.

They may actually require more than that, given that there is clearly a lot of risk involved. Our computation ignores the risk premium.

In most countries, the government is formally in charge of choosing the parity, the central bank is formally in charge of maintaining it. In practice, choosing and maintaining the parity are joint responsibilities of the government and the central bank.

In the summer of 1998, Boris Yeltsin announced that the Russian government had no intention of devaluing the ruble. Two weeks later, the ruble collapsed.

This should remind you of our discussion of bank runs in Chapter 6. The rumor that a bank is in trouble may trigger a run on the bank and force it to close, whether or not there was truth to the rumor.

The 1992 EMS Crisis

An example of the problems we discussed in this section is the exchange rate crisis that shook the European Monetary System (EMS) in the early 1990s.

At the start of the 1990s, the EMS appeared to work well. The EMS had started in 1979. It was an exchange rate system based on fixed parities with bands. Each member country (among them, France, Germany, Italy, and beginning in 1990, the United Kingdom) had to maintain its exchange rate vis-à-vis all other member countries within narrow bands. The first few years had been rocky, with many realignments—adjustment of parities—among member countries. From 1987 to 1992, however, there were only two realignments, and there was increasing talk about narrowing the bands further and even moving to the next stage—to the adoption of a common currency.

In 1992, however, financial markets became increasingly convinced that more realignments were soon to come. The reason was one we have already seen in Chapter 19, namely the macroeconomic implications of Germany's reunification. Because of the pressure on demand coming from reunification, the Bundesbank (the German central bank) was maintaining high interest rates to avoid too large an increase in output and an increase in inflation in Germany. While Germany's EMS partners needed lower interest rates to reduce a growing unemployment problem, they had to match the German interest rates to maintain their EMS parities. To financial markets, the position of Germany's EMS partners looked increasingly untenable. Lower interest rates outside Germany, and thus devaluations of many currencies relative to the Deutsche Mark (DM), appeared increasingly likely.

Throughout 1992, the perceived probability of a devaluation forced a number of EMS countries to maintain higher nominal interest rates than even those in Germany. Still, the first major crisis did not come until September 1992.

In early September 1992, the belief that a number of countries were soon going to devalue led to speculative attacks on a number of currencies, with financial investors selling in anticipation of an oncoming devaluation. All the lines of defense described earlier were used by the central banks and the governments of the countries under attack. First, solemn communiqués were issued but with no discernible effect. Then, interest rates were increased. For example, Sweden's overnight interest rate (the rate for lending and borrowing overnight) increased to 500% (expressed at an annual rate)! But even such extremely high interest rates were not enough to prevent capital outflows and large losses of foreign exchange reserves by the central banks under pressure.

At that point, different countries took different courses of action. Spain devalued its exchange rate. Italy and the United Kingdom suspended their participation in the EMS. France decided to tough it out through higher interest rates until the storm was over. Figure 1 shows the evolution of the exchange rates relative to the DM for a number of European countries from January 1992 to December 1993. You can clearly see the effects of the September 1992 crisis, highlighted in the figure, and the ensuing depreciations/devaluations.

By the end of September, investors, by and large, believed that no further devaluations were imminent. Some countries were no longer in the EMS. Others had devalued but remained in the EMS, and those that had maintained their parity had shown their determination to stay in the EMS, even if this meant very high interest rates. But the underlying problem—the high German interest rates—was still present, and it was only a matter of time before the next crisis started.

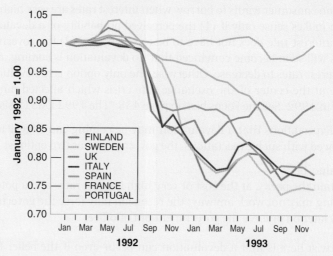

Figure 1 *Exchange Rates of Selected European Countries Relative to the Deutsche Mark, January 1992 to December 1993*

Source: IMF database.

In November 1992, further speculation forced a devaluation of the Spanish peseta, the Portuguese escudo, and the Swedish krona. The peseta and the escudo were further devalued in May 1993. In July 1993, after yet another large speculative attack, EMS countries decided to adopt large fluctuation bands (plus or minus 15%) around central parities, in effect moving to a system that allowed for large exchange rate fluctuations.

This system with wider bands was kept until the adoption of a common currency, the Euro, in January 1999.

To summarize: The 1992 EMS crisis came from the perception by financial markets that the high interest rates forced by Germany upon its partners under the rules of the EMS were becoming very costly.

The belief that some countries might want to devalue or get out of the EMS led investors to ask for even higher interest rates, making it even more costly for those countries to maintain their parity.

In the end, some countries could not bear the cost; some devalued, some dropped out. Others remained in the system, but at a substantial cost in terms of output. (For example, average growth in France from 1990 to 1996 was 1.2%, compared to 2.3% for Germany over the same period.)

20-3 Exchange Rate Movements under Flexible Exchange Rates

In the model we developed in Chapter 19, there was a simple relation between the interest rate and the exchange rate: The lower the interest rate, the lower the exchange rate. This implied that a country that wanted to maintain a stable exchange rate just had to maintain its interest rate close to the foreign interest rate. A country that wanted to achieve a given depreciation just had to decrease its interest rate by the right amount.

In reality, the relation between the interest rate and the exchange rate is not so simple. Exchange rates often move even in the absence of movements in interest rates. Furthermore, the size of the effect of a given change in the interest rate on the exchange rate is hard to predict. This makes it much harder for monetary policy to achieve its desired outcome.

To see why things are more complicated, we must return once again to the interest parity condition we derived in Chapter 17, equation (17.2):

$$(1 + i_t) = (1 + i_t^*)\left(\frac{E_t}{E_{t+1}^e}\right)$$

As we did in Chapter 19 (equation (19.5)), multiply both sides by E_{t+1}^e, and reorganize to get

$$E_t = \frac{1 + i_t}{1 + i_t^*} E_{t+1}^e \qquad (20.4)$$

Think of the time period (from t to $t + 1$) as one year. The exchange rate this year depends on the one-year domestic interest rate, the one-year foreign interest rate, and the exchange rate expected for next year.

We assumed in Chapter 19 that the expected exchange rate next year, E_{t+1}^e, was constant. But this was a simplification. The exchange rate expected one year hence is not constant. Using equation (20.4), but now for next year, it is clear that the exchange rate next year will depend on next year's one-year domestic interest rate, the one-year foreign interest rate, the exchange rate expected for the year after, and so on. So, any change in expectations of *current and future* domestic and foreign interest rates, as well as changes in the expected exchange rate in the far future, will affect the exchange rate today.

Let's explore this more closely. Write equation (20.4) for year $t + 1$ rather than for year t:

$$E_{t+1} = \frac{1 + i_{t+1}}{1 + i_{t+1}^*} E_{t+2}^e$$

The exchange rate in year $t + 1$ depends on the domestic interest rate and the foreign interest rate for year $t + 1$, as well as on the expected future exchange rate in year $t + 2$. So, the expectation of the exchange rate in year $t + 1$ held as of year t, is given by:

$$E_{t+1}^e = \frac{1 + i_{t+1}^e}{1 + i_{t+1}^{*e}} E_{t+2}^e$$

Replacing E_{t+1}^e in equation (20.4) with the expression above gives:

$$E_t = \frac{(1 + i_t)(1 + i_{t+1}^e)}{(1 + i_t^*)(1 + i_{t+1}^{*e})} E_{t+2}^e$$

The current exchange rate depends on this year's domestic and foreign interest rates, on next year's expected domestic and foreign interest rates, and on the expected exchange rate two years from now. Continuing to solve forward in time in the same way (by replacing E_{t+2}^e, E_{t+3}^e, and so on until, say, year $t + n$), we get:

$$E_t = \frac{(1 + i_t)(1 + i_{t+1}^e) \cdots (1 + i_{t+n}^e)}{(1 + i_t^*)(1 + i_{t+1}^{*e}) \cdots (1 + i_{t+n}^{*e})} E_{t+n+1}^e \qquad (20.5)$$

Suppose we take n to be large, say 10 years (equation (20.5) holds for any value of n). This relation tells us that the current exchange rate depends on two sets of factors:

- Current and expected domestic and foreign interest rates for each year over the next 10 years.
- The expected exchange rate 10 years from now.

MyEconLab Video

The basic lesson from Appendix 2: For all the statements, you can put "real" in front of exchange ▶ rates and interest rates, and the statements will also hold.

For some purposes, it is useful to go further and derive a relation among current and expected future domestic and foreign *real* interest rates, the current *real* exchange rate, and the expected future *real* exchange rate. This is done in Appendix 2 at the end of this chapter. (The derivation is not much fun, but it is a useful way of brushing up on the relation between real interest rates and nominal interest rates, and real exchange rates and nominal exchange rates.) Equation (20.5) is sufficient to make three important points, each outlined in more detail below:

- The level of today's exchange rate will move one-for-one with the future expected exchange rate.
- Today's exchange rate will move when future expected interest rates move in either country.
- Because today's exchange rate moves with any change in expectations, the exchange rate will be volatile, that is, move frequently and perhaps by large amounts.

Exchange Rates and the Current Account

Any factor that moves the expected future exchange rate, E_{t+n}^e, also moves the current exchange rate, E_t. Indeed, if the domestic interest rate and the foreign interest rate are expected to be the same in both countries from t to $t + n$, the fraction on the right in equation (20.5) is equal to 1, so the relation reduces to $E_t = E_{t+n}^e$. In words: The effect of any change in the expected future exchange rate on the current exchange rate is one-for-one.

If we think of n as large (say 10 years or more), we can think of E_{t+n}^e as the exchange rate required to achieve current account balance in the medium or long run. Countries cannot borrow—run a current account deficit—forever, and will not want to lend—run a current account surplus—forever either. Thus, any news that affects forecasts of the current account balance in the future is likely to have an effect on the expected future exchange rate, and in turn on the exchange rate today. For example, the announcement of a larger-than-expected current account deficit may lead investors to conclude that a depreciation will eventually be needed to repay the increased debt. Thus, E_{t+n}^{e} will decrease, leading in turn to a decrease in E_t today.

Exchange Rates and Current and Future Interest Rates

Any factor that moves current or expected future domestic or foreign interest rates between years t and $t + n$ moves the current exchange rate, too. For example, given foreign interest rates, an increase in current or expected future domestic interest rates leads to an increase in E_t—an appreciation.

This implies that any variable that causes investors to change their expectations of future interest rates will lead to a change in the exchange rate today. For example, the "dance of the dollar" in the 1980s that we discussed in Chapter 17—the sharp appreciation of the dollar in the first half of the decade, followed by an equally sharp depreciation later—can be largely explained by the movement in current and expected future U.S. interest rates relative to interest rates in the rest of the world during that period. During the first half of the 1980s, tight monetary policy and expansionary fiscal policy combined to increase both U.S. short-term interest rates and long-term interest rates; with the increase in long-term rates reflecting anticipations of high short-term interest rates in the future. This increase in both current and expected future interest rates was, in turn, the main cause of the dollar appreciation. Both fiscal and monetary policy were reversed in the second half of the decade, leading to lower U.S. interest rates and a depreciation of the dollar.

Exchange Rate Volatility

The third implication follows from the first two. In reality, and in contrast to our analysis in Chapter 19, the relation between the interest rate, i_t, and the exchange rate, E_t, is anything but mechanical. When the central bank cuts the policy rate, financial markets have to assess whether this action signals a major shift in monetary policy and the cut in the interest rate is just the first of many such cuts, or whether this cut is just a temporary movement in interest rates. Announcements by the central bank may not be useful. The central bank itself may not even know what it will do in the future. Typically, it will be reacting to early signals, which may be reversed later. Investors also have to assess how foreign central banks will react: whether they will stay put or follow suit and cut their own interest rates. All this makes it much harder to predict what the effect of the change in the interest rate will be on the exchange rate.

Let's be more concrete. Go back to equation (20.5). Assume that $E_{t+n}^{e} = 1$. Assume that current and expected future domestic interest rates, and current and expected future foreign interest rates, are all equal to 5%. The current exchange rate is then given by:

$$E_t = \frac{(1.05)^n}{(1.05)^n} 1 = 1$$

Now consider a reduction in the current domestic interest rate, i_t, from 5% to 3%. Will this lead to a decrease in E_t—to a depreciation—and if so by how much? The answer: It all depends.

Suppose the interest rate is expected to be lower for just one year, so the $n - 1$ expected future interest rates remain unchanged. The current exchange rate then decreases to:

$$E_t = \frac{(1.03)(1.05)^{n-1}}{(1.05)^n} = \frac{1.03}{1.05} = 0.98$$

News about the current account is likely to affect the exchange rate. What would you expect, for example, the effect of the announcement of a major oil discovery to be?

News about current and future domestic and foreign interest rates is likely to affect the exchange rate.

For more on the relation between long-term interest rates and current and expected future short-term interest rates, go back to Chapter 14.

We leave aside here other factors that also move the exchange rate, such as changing perceptions of risk, which we discussed in a Focus box titled "Sudden Stops, Safe Havens, and the Limits to the Interest Parity Condition" in Chapter 19.

If this reminds you of our discussion in Chapter 14 of how monetary policy affects stock prices, you are right. This is more than a coincidence. Like stock prices, the exchange rate depends very much on expectations of variables far into the future. How expectations change in response to a change in a current variable (here, the interest rate) determines the outcome.

The lower interest rate leads to a decrease in the exchange rate—a depreciation—of only 2%.

Suppose instead that, when the current interest rate declines from 5% to 3%, investors expect the decline to last for five years (so $i_{t+4} = \cdots = i_{t+1} = i_t = 3\%$). The exchange rate then decreases to:

$$E_t = \frac{(1.03)^5(1.05)^{n-5}}{(1.05)^n} = \frac{(1.03)^5}{(1.05)^5} = 0.90$$

The lower interest rate now leads to a decrease in the exchange rate—a depreciation—of 10%, a much larger effect.

You can surely think of still more outcomes. Suppose investors had anticipated that the central bank was going to decrease interest rates, and the actual decrease turns out to be smaller than they anticipated. In this case, the investors will revise their expectations of future nominal interest rates *upward*, leading to an appreciation rather than a depreciation of the currency.

When, at the end of the Bretton Woods period, countries moved from fixed exchange rates to flexible exchange rates, most economists had expected that exchange rates would be stable. The large fluctuations in exchange rates that followed—and have continued to this day—came as a surprise. For some time, these fluctuations were thought to be the result of irrational speculation in foreign exchange markets. It was not until the mid-1970s that economists realized that these large movements could be explained, as we have explained here, by the rational reaction of financial markets to news about future interest rates and the future exchange rate. This has an important implication:

A country that decides to operate under flexible exchange rates must accept the fact that it will be exposed to substantial exchange rate fluctuations over time.

20-4 Choosing between Exchange Rate Regimes

Let us now return to the question that motivates this chapter. Should countries choose flexible exchange rates or fixed exchange rates? Are there circumstances under which flexible rates dominate, and others under which fixed rates dominate?

Much of what we have seen in this and the previous chapter would seem to favor flexible exchange rates:

- Section 20-1 argued that the exchange rate regime may not matter in the medium run. But it is still the case that it matters in the short run. In the short run, countries that operate under fixed exchange rates and perfect capital mobility give up two macroeconomic instruments: the interest rate and the exchange rate. This not only reduces their ability to respond to shocks but can also lead to exchange rate crises.
- Section 20-2 argued that, in a country with fixed exchange rates, the anticipation of a devaluation leads investors to ask for high interest rates. This in turn makes the economic situation worse and puts more pressure on the country to devalue. This is another argument against fixed exchange rates.
- Section 20-3 introduced one argument against flexible exchange rates, namely that, under flexible exchange rates, the exchange rate is likely to fluctuate a lot and be difficult to control through monetary policy.

On balance, it therefore appears that, from a macroeconomic viewpoint, flexible exchange rates dominate fixed exchange rates. This indeed is the consensus that has emerged among economists and policy makers. The consensus goes like this:

In general, flexible exchange rates are preferable. There are, however, two exceptions. First, when a group of countries is already tightly integrated, a common currency may be the right solution. Second, when the central bank cannot be trusted to follow a responsible monetary policy under flexible exchange rates, a strong form of fixed exchange rates, such as a currency board or dollarization, may be the right solution.

Let us discuss in turn each of these two exceptions.

Common Currency Areas

Countries that operate under a fixed exchange rate regime are constrained to have the same interest rate. But how costly is that constraint? If the countries face roughly the same macroeconomic problems and the same shocks, they would have chosen similar policies in the first place. Forcing them to have the same monetary policy may not be much of a constraint.

This argument was first explored by Robert Mundell, who looked at the conditions under which a set of countries might want to operate under fixed exchange rates, or even adopt a common currency. For countries to constitute an **optimal currency area**, Mundell argued, they need to satisfy one of two conditions:

> This is the same Mundell who put together the "Mundell–Fleming" model you saw in Chapter 19.

- The countries have to experience similar shocks. We just saw the rationale for this. If they experience similar shocks, then they would have chosen roughly the same monetary policy anyway.
- Or if the countries experience different shocks, they must have high factor mobility. For example, if workers are willing to move from countries that are doing poorly to countries that are doing well, factor mobility rather than macroeconomic policy can allow countries to adjust to shocks. When the unemployment rate is high in a country, workers leave that country to take jobs elsewhere, and the unemployment rate in that country decreases back to normal. If the unemployment rate is low, workers come to the country, and the unemployment rate in the country increases back to normal. The exchange rate is not needed.

Following Mundell's analysis, most economists believe, for example, that the common currency area composed of the 50 states of the United States is close to an optimal currency area. True, the first condition is not satisfied; individual states suffer from different shocks. California is more affected by shifts in demand from Asia than the rest of the United States. Texas is more affected by what happens to the price of oil, and so on. But the second condition is largely satisfied. There is considerable labor mobility across states in the United States. When a state does poorly, workers leave that state. When it does well, workers come to that state. State unemployment rates quickly return to normal, not because of state-level macroeconomic policy, but because of labor mobility.

> Each U.S. state could have its own currency that freely floated against other state currencies. But this is not the way things are. The United States is a common currency area, with one currency, the U.S. dollar.

Clearly, there are also many advantages of using a common currency. For firms and consumers within the United States, the benefits of having a common currency are obvious; imagine how complicated life would be if you had to change currency every time you crossed a state line. The benefits go beyond these lower transaction costs. When prices are quoted in the same currency, it becomes much easier for buyers to compare prices, and competition between firms increases, benefiting consumers. Given these benefits and the limited macroeconomic costs, it makes good sense for the United States to have a single currency.

In adopting the euro, Europe made the same choice as the United States. When the process of conversion from national currencies to the euro ended in early 2002, the euro became the common currency for 11 European countries. (See the Focus box on page 445 "The Euro: A Short History.") The count of countries using the euro at time of writing is now 19. Is the economic argument for this new common currency area as compelling as it is for the United States?

Figure 20-1

The Evolution of the Real Exchange Rate in Spain since 2000

A steady real appreciation from 2000 to 2008 has been followed by a long real depreciation since then.

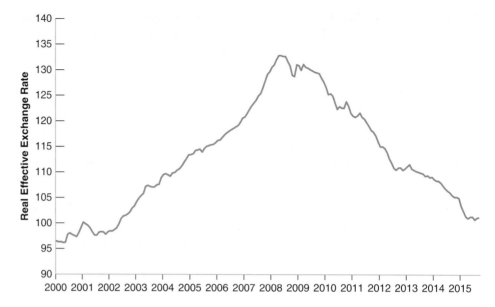

There is little question that a common currency yields for Europe many of the same benefits that it has for the United States. A report by the European Commission estimates that the elimination of foreign exchange transactions within the Euro area leads to a reduction in costs of 0.5% of the combined GDP of these countries. There are also clear signs that the use of a common currency is already increasing competition. When shopping for cars, for example, European consumers now search for the lowest euro price anywhere in the area using the euro. This has already led to a decline in the price of cars in a number of countries.

There is, however, less agreement on whether Europe constitutes an optimal common currency area. This is because neither of the two Mundell conditions appears to be satisfied. European countries experienced very different shocks in the past. Recall our discussion of Germany's reunification and how differently it affected Germany and the other European countries in the 1990s. Furthermore, labor mobility is very low in Europe and likely to remain low. Workers move much less *within* European countries than they do within the United States. Because of language and cultural differences among European countries, mobility *between* countries is even lower.

The worry that this might lead to long slumps in member countries, if they were to be hit by a country-specific adverse shock, was present even before the crisis. But the crisis showed that the worry was indeed justified. A number of countries, Portugal, Greece, and Ireland, which had seen strong demand growth and large increases in current account deficits (see Focus box on current account deficits in Chapter 18), suddenly suffered a sharp decrease in spending, a sharp decrease in output, and increasing difficulty to finance their current account deficits. A large depreciation would have helped them increase demand and improve their current account, but in a common currency, this could only be done through a decrease in prices relative to their Euro partners. The result was a long and painful adjustment process, which, at the time of writing, is far from over. Figure 20-1 shows the evolution of the real exchange rate for Spain. It shows the steady real appreciation associated with a boom until 2008, and the real depreciation since then. Although the real exchange rate has now returned to its value of the early 2000s, the adjustment is far from complete. As we saw in Chapter 1, the unemployment rate in Spain is still a high 21%.

The Euro: A Short History

- As the European Union (EU) celebrated its 30th anniversary in 1988, a number of governments decided the time had come to plan a move to a common currency. They asked Jacques Delors, the President of the EU, to prepare a report, which he presented in June 1989.

  The Delors report suggested moving to a European Monetary Union (EMU) in three stages: Stage I was the abolition of capital controls. Stage II was the choice of fixed parities, to be maintained except for "exceptional circumstances." Stage III was the adoption of a single currency.

- Stage I was implemented in July 1990.

- Stage II began in 1994, after the exchange rate crises of 1992–1993 had subsided. A minor but symbolic decision involved choosing the name of the new common currency. The French liked *Ecu* (European currency unit), which is also the name of an old French currency. But its partners preferred *euro*, and the name was adopted in 1995.

- In parallel, EU countries held referendums on whether they should adopt the **Maastricht treaty**. The treaty, negotiated in 1991, set three main conditions for joining the EMU: low inflation, a budget deficit below 3%, and a public debt below 60%. The Maastricht treaty was not popular, and in many countries, the outcome of the popular vote was close. In France, the treaty passed with only 51% of the votes. In Denmark, the treaty was rejected. The United Kingdom negotiated an "opt out" clause that allowed Britain not to join the new currency union.

- In the mid-1990s, it looked as if few European countries would satisfy the Maastricht conditions. But a number of countries took drastic measures to reduce their budget deficit. When the time came to decide, in May 1998, which countries would be members of the Euro area, 11 countries made the cut: Austria, Belgium, Finland, France, Germany, Italy, Ireland, Luxembourg, The Netherlands, Portugal, and Spain. The United Kingdom, Denmark, and Sweden decided to stay out, at least for the time being. Greece did not qualify initially and didn't join until 2001. (In 2004, it was revealed that Greece had "cooked the books" and understated the size of its budget deficit in order to qualify.) Since then, five more small countries, Cyprus, Malta, Slovakia, Slovenia, and Estonia, have joined.

- Stage III began in January 1999. Parities between the 11 currencies and the euro were "irrevocably" fixed. The new **European Central Bank (ECB)** based in Frankfurt became responsible for monetary policy for the Euro area.

From 1999 to 2002, the euro existed as a unit of account, but euro coins and bank notes did not exist. In effect, the Euro area was still functioning as an area with fixed exchange rates. The next and final step was the introduction of euro coins and bank notes in January 2002. For the first few months of 2002, national currencies and the euro then circulated side by side. Later in the year, national currencies were taken out of circulation.

Today, the euro is the only currency used in the Euro area, as the group of member countries is called. The numbers of countries adopting the euro has now reached 19: Latvia and Lithuania are the latest members.

For more on the euro, go to http://www.euro.ecb.int/. The Wikipedia page on the euro is also very good.

MyEconLab Video

The challenge for the euro, looking forward, is whether such long slumps can be avoided in the future. Reforms are being explored to eliminate some of the factors which made the slump worse in those countries. A number of reforms are being put in place, from a banking union to a fiscal union, which should allow countries to better resist adverse shocks. Whether these measures will be sufficient to be avoid crises in the future remains to be seen.

Hard Pegs, Currency Boards, and Dollarization

The second case for fixed exchange rates is different from the first. It is based on the argument that there may be times when a country may want to limit its ability to use ◀ More on this in Chapter 21. monetary policy.

Look at a country that has had very high inflation in the recent past—perhaps because it was unable to finance its budget deficit by any other means than through money creation, resulting in high money growth and high inflation. Suppose the country decides to reduce money growth and inflation. One way of convincing financial markets that it is serious about doing this is to fix its exchange rate. The need to use monetary policy to maintain the parity then ties the hands of the monetary authority.

Lessons from Argentina's Currency Board

When Carlos Menem became President of Argentina in 1989, he inherited an economic mess. Inflation was running at more than 30% per month. Output growth was negative.

Menem and his economy minister, Domingo Cavallo, quickly came to the conclusion that under these circumstances, the only way to bring money growth—and by implication, inflation—under control was to peg the peso (Argentina's currency) to the dollar, and to do this through a hard peg. So in 1991, Cavallo announced that Argentina would adopt a currency board. The central bank would stand ready to exchange pesos for dollars on demand. Furthermore, it would do so at the highly symbolic rate of one dollar for one peso.

Both the creation of a currency board and the choice of a symbolic exchange rate had the same objective: to convince investors that the government was serious about the peg and to make it more difficult for future governments to give up the parity and devalue; and so by making the fixed exchange rate more credible in this way, decrease the risk of a foreign exchange crisis.

For a while, the currency board appeared to work extremely well. Inflation, which had exceeded 2,300% in 1990, was down to 4% by 1994! This was clearly the result of the tight constraints the currency board put on money growth. Even more impressive, this large drop in inflation was accompanied by strong output growth. Output growth averaged 5% per year from 1991 to 1999.

Beginning in 1999, however, growth turned negative, and Argentina went into a long and deep recession. Was the recession the result of the currency board? Yes and no:

■ Throughout the second half of the 1990s, the dollar steadily appreciated relative to the other major world currencies. Because the peso was pegged to the dollar, the peso also appreciated. By the late 1990s, it was clear that the peso was overvalued, leading to a decrease in demand for goods from Argentina, a decline in output, and an increase in the trade deficit.

■ Was the currency board fully responsible for the recession? No; there were other causes. But the currency board made it much harder to fight it. Lower interest rates and a depreciation of the peso would have helped the economy recover, but under the currency board, this was not an option.

In 2001, the economic crisis turned into a financial and an exchange rate crisis, along the lines we described in Section 20-2:

■ Because of the recession, Argentina's fiscal deficit had increased, leading to an increase in government debt. Worried that the government might default on its debt, financial investors started asking for very high interest rates on government bonds, making the fiscal deficit even larger, and by doing so, further increasing the risk of default.

■ Worried that Argentina would abandon the currency board and devalue to fight the recession, investors started asking for very high interest rates in pesos, making it more costly for the government to sustain the parity with the dollar, and so making it more likely that the currency board would indeed be abandoned.

In December 2001, the government defaulted on part of its debt. In early 2002, it gave up the currency board and let the peso float. The peso sharply depreciated, reaching 3.75 pesos for 1 dollar by June 2002! People and firms that, given their earlier confidence in the peg, had borrowed in dollars found themselves with a large increase in the value of their dollar debts in terms of pesos. Many firms went bankrupt. The banking system collapsed. Despite the sharp real depreciation, which should have helped exports, GDP in Argentina fell by 11% in 2002, and unemployment increased to nearly 20%. In 2003, output growth turned positive and has been consistently high since—exceeding 8% a year—and unemployment has decreased. But it took until 2005 for GDP to reach its 1998 level again.

Does this mean that the currency board was a bad idea? Economists still disagree:

■ Some economists argue that it was a good idea but that it did not go far enough. They argue that Argentina should have simply dollarized (i.e., adopted the dollar outright as its currency and eliminated the peso altogether). Eliminating the domestic currency would have eliminated the risk of a devaluation. The lesson, they argue, is that even a currency board does not provide a sufficiently hard peg for the exchange rate. Only dollarization will do.

■ Other (indeed, most) economists argue that the currency board might have been a good idea at the start, but that it should not have been kept in place for so long. Once inflation was under control, Argentina should have moved from a currency board to a floating exchange rate regime. The problem is that Argentina kept the fixed parity with the dollar for too long, to the point where the peso was overvalued and an exchange rate crisis was inevitable.

The debate about "fix versus flex," about soft pegs, hard pegs, currency boards, and common currencies is unlikely to be settled any time soon.

For a fascinating, fun, and strongly opinionated book about Argentina's crisis, read Paul Blustein's *And the Money Kept Rolling In (and Out): Wall Street, the IMF, and the Bankrupting of Argentina*, Perseus Books Group, 2005.

To the extent that financial markets expect the parity to be maintained, they will stop worrying about money growth being used to finance the budget deficit.

Note the qualifier: "To the extent that financial markets expect the parity to be maintained." Fixing the exchange rate is not a magic solution. The country also needs to convince financial investors that, not only is the exchange rate fixed today, but it will also remain fixed in the future. There are two ways in which it can do so:

- Making the fixed exchange rate be part of a more general macroeconomic package. Fixing the exchange rate while continuing to run a large budget deficit will only convince financial markets that money growth will start again and that a devaluation is soon to come.

- Making it symbolically or technically harder to change the parity, an approach known as a **hard peg**.

An extreme form of a hard peg is simply to replace the domestic currency with a foreign currency. Because the foreign currency chosen is typically the dollar, this is known as **dollarization**. Few countries are willing, however, to give up their currency and adopt the currency of another country. A less extreme way is the use of a **currency board**. Under a currency board, a central bank stands ready to exchange foreign currency for domestic currency at the official exchange rate set by the government. Furthermore, and this is the difference with a standard fixed exchange rate regime, the central bank cannot engage in open market operations (that is, buy or sell government bonds).

Perhaps the best known example of a currency board is that adopted by Argentina in 1991 but abandoned in a crisis at the end of 2001. The story is told in the Focus box "Lessons from Argentina's Currency Board." Economists differ on what conclusions one should draw from what happened in Argentina. Some conclude that currency boards are not *hard* enough. They do not prevent exchange rate crises. So if a country decides to adopt a fixed exchange rate, it should go all the way and dollarize. Others conclude that adopting a fixed exchange rate is a bad idea. If currency boards are used at all, they should be used only for a short period of time, until the central bank has reestablished its credibility and the country returns to a floating exchange rate regime.

When Israel was suffering from high inflation in the 1980s, an Israeli finance minister proposed such a measure as part of a stabilization program. His proposal was perceived as an attack on the sovereignty of Israel, and he was quickly fired.

Summary

- Even under a fixed exchange rate regime, countries can adjust their *real* exchange rate in the medium run. They can do so by relying on adjustments in the price level. Nevertheless, the adjustment can be long and painful. Exchange rate adjustments can allow the economy to adjust faster and thus reduce the pain that comes from a long adjustment.

- Exchange rate crises typically start when participants in financial markets believe a currency may soon be devalued. Defending the parity then requires high interest rates, with potentially large adverse macroeconomic effects. These adverse effects may force the country to devalue, even if there were no initial plans for such a devaluation.

- The exchange rate today depends on both (1) the difference between current and expected future domestic interest rates, and current and expected future foreign interest rates; and (2) the expected future exchange rate.

Any factor that increases current or expected future domestic interest rates leads to an increase in the exchange rate today.
Any factor that increases current or expected future foreign interest rates leads to a decrease in the exchange rate today.
Any factor that increases the expected future exchange rate leads to an increase in the exchange rate today.

- There is wide agreement among economists that flexible exchange regimes generally dominate fixed exchange rate regimes, except in two cases:

1. When a group of countries is highly integrated and forms an optimal currency area. (You can think of a common currency for a group of countries as an extreme form of fixed exchange rates among this group of countries.) For countries to form an optimal currency area, they must either face largely similar shocks, or there must be high labor mobility across these countries.

2. When a central bank cannot be trusted to follow a responsible monetary policy under flexible exchange rates. In this case, a strong form of fixed exchange rates, such as dollarization or a currency board, provides a way of tying the hands of the central bank.

Key Terms

gold standard, 435
float, 436
optimal currency area, 443
Maastricht treaty, 445

European Central Bank (ECB), 445
hard peg, 447
dollarization, 447
currency board, 447

Question and Problems MyEconLab Real-time data exercises are marked 🌐.

QUICK CHECK

MyEconLab Visit www.myeconlab.com to complete similar Quick Check problems and get instant feedback.

1. Using the information in this chapter, label each of the following statements true, false, or uncertain. Explain briefly.

a. If the nominal exchange rate is fixed, the real exchange rate is fixed.

b. When domestic inflation equals foreign inflation, the real exchange rate is fixed.

c. A devaluation is an increase in the nominal exchange rate.

d. Britain's return to the gold standard caused years of high unemployment.

e. A sudden fear that a country is going to devalue leads to an increase in the domestic interest rate.

f. A change in the expected future exchange rate changes the current exchange rate.

g. The effect of a reduction in domestic interest rates on the exchange rate depends on the length of time domestic interest rates are expected to be below foreign interest rates.

h. Because economies tend to return to their natural level of output in the medium run, it makes no difference whether a country chooses a fixed or flexible exchange rate.

i. High labor mobility within Europe makes the Euro area a good candidate for a common currency.

j. A currency board is the best way to operate a fixed exchange rate.

2. Consider a country operating under fixed exchange rates. The IS curve is given by relation (20.1)

$$Y = Y\left(\frac{\bar{E}P}{P^*}, G, T, i^* - \pi^e, Y^*\right)$$
$$(-, +, -, -, +)$$

a. Explain the term $(i^* - \pi^e)$. Why does the foreign nominal interest rate appear in the relation?

b. Explain why when $\dfrac{\bar{E}P}{P^*}$ increases, the IS curve shifts left.

c. In the following table, how is the real exchange rate evolving from period 1 to period 5? What is domestic inflation? What is foreign inflation? Draw an IS-LM diagram with the IS curve in period 1 and the IS curve in period 5.

Period	P	P*	E	π	π*	Real exchange rate ε
1	100.0	100.0	0.5			
2	103.0	102.0	0.5			
3	106.1	104.0	0.5			
4	109.3	106.1	0.5			
5	112.6	108.2	0.5			

d. In the following table, how is the real exchange rate evolving from period 1 to period 5? What is domestic inflation? What is foreign inflation? Draw an IS-LM diagram with the IS curve in period 1 and the IS curve in period 5.

Period	P	P*	E	π	π*	Real exchange rate ε
1	100.0	100.0	0.5			
2	102.0	103.0	0.5			
3	104.0	106.1	0.5			
4	106.1	109.3	0.5			
5	108.2	112.6	0.5			

e. In the table that follows, how is the real exchange rate evolving from period 1 to period 4? What is domestic inflation? What is foreign inflation? What happened between Period 4 and Period 5? Draw an IS-LM diagram with the IS curve in period 1 and the IS curve in period 5.

Period	P	P*	E	π	π*	Real exchange rate ε
1	100.0	100.0	0.5			
2	103.0	102.0	0.5			
3	106.1	104.0	0.5			
4	109.3	106.1	0.5			
5	112.6	108.2	0.46			

3. Policy choices when the real exchange rate is "too high" and the nominal exchange rate is fixed

An overvalued real exchange rate is a rate such that domestic goods are too expensive relative to foreign goods, net exports are too small, and by implication the demand for domestic goods is too low.

This leads to difficult policy choices for the government and central bank. The equations that describe the economy are:

The IS curve:

$$Y = Y\left(\frac{\bar{E}P}{P^*}, G, T, i^* - \pi^e, Y^*\right)$$
$$(-, \ +, -, \quad -, \quad +)$$

The Phillips curves for the domestic and the foreign economy:

Domestic Phillips curve $\pi - \bar{\pi} = (\alpha/L)(Y - Y_n)$

Foreign Phillips curve $\pi^* - \bar{\pi}^* = (\alpha^*/L^*)(Y^* - Y_n^*)$

In the text and in this question, we are going to make two critical assumptions. These are explored in parts (a) and (b). Then we move to the analysis of the policy options when a country is experiencing an overvalued exchange rate.

a. We are going to assume that the foreign economy is always in medium-run equilibrium. What are the implications of that assumption for foreign output and foreign inflation?

b. We are going to assume that the domestic and foreign economies share the same anchored value for the level of expected inflation denoted $\bar{\pi}$ and $\bar{\pi}^*$. What is the implication of that assumption once both the domestic and foreign economies are both in medium-run equilibrium?

c. Draw the IS-LM-UIP diagram for the case where the domestic country has an overvalued nominal exchange rate. What is the key feature of that diagram? Under fixed exchange rates without a devaluation, how does the economy return to its medium-run equilibrium?

d. Draw the IS-LM-UIP diagram for the case where the domestic country has an overvalued nominal exchange rate. Show how the economy can return to its to medium-run equilibrium when a devaluation is a policy choice.

e. Recall that the assumption has been made that interest rate parity holds so $i = i^*$ at all times. Compare the returns on the domestic bond and the returns on the foreign bond in the period of the devaluation. Will bond holders continue to believe there is a completely fixed nominal exchange rate? If bond holders believe another devaluation is possible, what are the consequences for domestic interest rates?

4. Modeling an exchange rate crisis

An exchange rate crisis occurs when the peg (the fixed exchange rate) loses its credibility. Bond holders no longer believe that next period's exchange rate will be this period's exchange rate. The uncovered interest rate parity equation used is the approximation

$$i_t \approx i_t^* - \frac{(E_{t+1}^e - E_t)}{E_t}$$

Period	i_t	i_t^*	E_t	E_{t+1}^e
1		3	0.5	0.5
2		3	0.5	0.45
3		3	0.5	0.45
4		3	0.5	0.5
5	15%	3	0.5	0.4
6		3	0.4	0.4

a. Solve the uncovered interest rate parity condition for the value of the domestic interest rate in period 1.

b. In period 2, the crisis begins. Solve the uncovered interest rate parity condition for the value of the domestic interest rate in period 2.

c. The crisis continues in period 3. However, in period 4, the central bank and government resolve the crisis. How does this occur?

d. Unfortunately, in period 5, the crisis returns bigger and deeper than ever. Has the central bank raised interest rates enough to maintain uncovered interest rate parity? What are the consequences for the level of foreign exchange reserves?

e. How is the crisis resolved in period 6? Does this have implications for the future credibility of the central bank and the government?

5. Modeling the movements in the exchange rate

Equation (20.5) provides insight into the movements of nominal exchange rates between a domestic and a foreign country. Remember that the time periods in equation can refer to any time unit. The equation is:

$$E_t = \frac{(1 + i_t)(1 + i_{t+1}^e)\cdots(1 + i_{t+n}^e)}{(1 + i_t^*)(1 + i_{t+1}^{*e})\cdots(1 + i_{t+n}^{*e})}E_{t+n+1}^e$$

a. Suppose we are thinking of one-day time periods. There are overnight (1-day) interest rates. How do we interpret a large movement in the exchange rate over the course of the day if we do not observe any change in the 1-day interest rate?

b. We learned in Chapter 15 that a one-month (30- or 31-day interest rate) is the average of today's 1-day rate and the expected 1-day rates over the next 30 days. This will be true in both countries. The following headline is observed on February 1: "ECB predicted to cut interest rates February 14, dollar rises." Does the headline make sense?

c. We learned in Chapter 15 that a two-year bond yield is the average of today's one-year interest rate and the expected one-year rate one year from now. This will be true in both countries. The following headline is observed on February 1: "Fed announces that interest rates will remain low for the foreseeable future, dollar falls." Does the headline make sense?

d. The current account is this period's lending to (if positive) or borrowing from (if negative) the rest of the world. Assume the current account is more negative than expected and this is surprising news. Explain why the exchange rate would depreciate on this surprising news.

DIG DEEPER

MyEconLab Visit www.myeconlab.com to complete all Dig Deeper problems and get instant feedback.

6. Realignments of exchange rate

Look at Figure 1 in the box 'The 1992 EMS Crisis." European nominal exchange rates had been fixed between the major currencies from roughly 1979 to 1992.

a. Explain how to read the vertical axis of Figure 1. What country experienced the largest depreciation? What country clearly experienced the smallest depreciation?

b. If two-year nominal interest rates in France and Italy had been similar in January 1992, which country would have generated the highest return on a two-year bond?

c. If the changes in the nominal exchange rates returned countries to medium-run equilibrium, which countries had the largest overvaluations in 1992?

7. Real and nominal exchange rates for Russia and China

Russia and China are two of the largest trading partners and exporters to the European Union. The database of the European Central Bank provides direct quotations of foreign currencies against the euro, which they refer to as the "Euro foreign exchange reference rates". Download the exchange rates for each of the Russian ruble (RUB) per euro and the Chinese yuans per euro for the last 10 years.

a. The exchange rate is defined as the number of Russian rubles per one euro and the number of Chinese yuans per one euro. Redefine the exchange rates as the number of euro cents per rubles and the number of euro cents per yuan. Who does this direct quote of exchange rates benefit?

b. Download and prepare charts depicting exchange rates of the euro against each of the ruble and yuan. Compare and contrast the behavior of each of the ruble and the yuan against the euro. Do you see a period when either of the ruble or lira is pegged? Do you observe a general trend of appreciation or depreciation of the euro against the two currencies? Which country/countries benefit from the changes in the exchange rate?

c. Why do countries resort to devaluing their domestic currencies? When does a depreciated currency lead to inflation? How do inflation measures help to differentiate between nominal exchange rates and real exchange rates? Check the inflation rate of Russia and the EU for last year. Do you expect the real exchange rate between the ruble and the euro to be higher or lower than the nominal exchange rate? Explain your answer.

EXPLORE FURTHER

8. Exchange rates and expectations

In the chapter we emphasized that expectations have an important effect on the exchange rate. In this problem we use data to understand practically the important role of expectations. The results in Appendix 2 at the end of the chapter show that the uncovered interest rate parity condition equation (20.4) can be written as

$$\frac{(E_t - E_{t-1})}{E_{t-1}} = (i_t - i_t^*) - (i_{t-1} - i_{t-1}^*) + \frac{(E_t^e - E_{t-1}^e)}{E_{t-1}^e}$$

The equation implies that the percentage change in the exchange rate (or the appreciation of the domestic currency) is approximately equal to the change in the interest rate differential between domestic and foreign currency rates plus the percentage change in expected exchange rate changes (or the appreciation of the domestic currency). We refer to the interest rate differential as the spread.

a. Go to the Web site of the Central Bank of Sri Lanka (http://www.cbsl.gov.lk/index.asp) and obtain data on the latest issue of the one-year Treasury bill rates in Sri Lanka for the last 10 years. Now go to the Web site of the United Kingdom Debt Management Office (http://www.dmo.gov.uk) and obtain data on the one-year Treasury bill rates in the UK for the same period. Download the data into a spreadsheet. Subtract the Sri Lanka interest rate from the UK interest rate to calculate the spread. Then, for each period calculate the change in the spread from the preceding month. Make sure to convert the interest rate into the proper decimal form.

b. Obtain the exchange rate between the British pound and the Sri Lankan rupee for the same period as part (a). After downloading and entering the data into a spreadsheet, calculate the percentage appreciation/depreciation of the pound for each year. Using the standard deviation function in the software, calculate the standard deviation of the yearly change in the value of the appreciation/depreciation of the pound. The standard deviation is a statistical measure of the variability of a data series.

c. For each year, subtract the spread (part a) from the percentage appreciation/depreciation of the pound (part b). Refer to this difference as the change in expectations. Calculate the standard deviation of the change in expectations. How does the standard deviation of the change in expectations compare to the standard deviation of the yearly change in the value of the appreciation/depreciation of the pound?

As simple as this exercise may be, the essence of this analysis survives in more sophisticated work. Movement in the short-runm interest rates do not account for much of the short-run changes in the exchange rates. Much of the difference is attributed to changes in expectations.

Further Readings

- For an early skeptical view of the euro, read Martin Feldstein, "The European Central Bank and the Euro: The First Year," 2000, http://www.nber.org/papers/w7517, and "The Euro and the Stability Pact," 2005, http://www.nber.org/papers/w11249.

- For a good book on the euro crisis, read Jean Pisani-Ferry, The Euro Crisis and its Aftermath, Oxford University Press, 2014.

APPENDIX 1: Deriving the *IS* Relation under Fixed Exchange Rates

Start from the condition for goods-market equilibrium we derived in Chapter 19, equation (19.1):

$$Y = C(Y - T) + I(Y, r) + G - NX(Y, Y^*, \varepsilon)$$

This condition states that, for the goods market to be in equilibrium, output must be equal to the demand for domestic goods—that is, the sum of consumption, investment, government spending, and net exports. Next, recall the following relations:

- The real interest rate, r, is equal to the nominal interest rate, i, minus expected inflation, π^e (see Chapter 14):

$$r \equiv i - \pi^e$$

- The real exchange rate, ϵ is defined as (see Chapter 17):

$$\varepsilon = \frac{EP}{P^*}$$

- Under fixed exchange rates, the nominal exchange rate, E, is, by definition, fixed. Denote by $\bar{E}$ the value at which the nominal exchange rate is fixed, so:

$$E = \bar{E}$$

- Under fixed exchange rates and perfect capital mobility, the domestic interest rate, i, must be equal to the foreign interest rate, i^* (see Chapter 17):

$$i = i^*$$

Using these four relations, rewrite equation (20.1) as:

$$Y = C(Y - T) + I(Y, i^* - \pi^e) + G + NX\left(Y, Y^*, \frac{\bar{E}P}{P^*}\right)$$

This can be rewritten, using a more compact notation, as:

$$Y = Y\left(\frac{\bar{E}P}{P^*}, G, T, i^* - \pi^e, Y^*\right)$$
$$(-, +,-, \quad -, \quad +)$$

which is equation (20.1) in the text.

APPENDIX 2: The Real Exchange Rate and Domestic and Foreign Real Interest Rates

We derived in Section 20-3 a relation among the current nominal exchange rate, current and expected future domestic and foreign nominal interest rates, and the expected future nominal exchange rate (equation (20.5)). This appendix derives a similar relation, but in terms of real interest rates and the real exchange rate. It then briefly discusses how this alternative relation can be used to think about movements in the real exchange rate.

Deriving the Real Interest Parity Condition

Start from the nominal interest parity condition, equation (19.2):

$$(1 + i_t) = (1 + i_t^*)\frac{E_t}{E_{t+1}^e}$$

Recall the definition of the real interest rate from Chapter 6, equation (6.3):

$$(1 + r_t) = \frac{(1 + i_t)}{(1 + \pi_{t+1}^e)}$$

where $\pi_{t+1}^e \equiv (P_{t+1}^e - P_t)/P_t$ is the expected rate of inflation. Similarly, the foreign real interest rate is given by:

$$(1 + r_t^*) = \frac{(1 + i_t^*)}{(1 + \pi_{t+1}^{*e})}$$

where $\pi_{t+1}^{*e} \equiv (P_{t+1}^{*e} - P_t^*)/P_t^*$ is the expected foreign rate of inflation.

Use these two relations to eliminate nominal interest rates in the interest parity condition, so:

$$(1 + r_t) = (1 + r_t^*)\left[\frac{E_t}{E_{t+1}^e}\frac{(1 + \pi_{t+1}^{*e})}{(1 + \pi_{t+1}^e)}\right] \tag{20.A1}$$

Note from the definition of inflation that $(1 + \pi_{t+1}^e) = P_{t+1}^e/P_t$ and, similarly, $(1 + \pi_{t+1}^{*e}) = P_{t+1}^{*e}/P_t^*$.

Using these two relations in the term in brackets gives:

$$\frac{E_t}{E_{t+1}^e}\frac{(1 + \pi_{t+1}^{*e})}{(1 + \pi_{t+1}^e)} = \frac{E_t}{E_{t+1}^e}\frac{P_{t+1}^{*e}P_t}{P_t^* P_{t+1}^e}$$

Reorganizing terms:

$$\frac{E_t P_{t+1}^{*e} P_t}{E_{t+1}^e P_t^* P_{t+1}^e} = \frac{E_t P_t/P_t^*}{E_{t+1}^e P_{t+1}^e/P_{t+1}^{*e}}$$

Using the definition of the real exchange rate:

$$\frac{E_t P_t/P_t^*}{E_{t+1}^e P_{t+1}^e/P_{t+1}^{*e}} = \frac{\varepsilon_t}{\varepsilon_{t+1}^e}$$

Replacing in equation (20.A1) gives:

$$(1 + r_t) = (1 + r_t^*)\frac{\varepsilon_t}{\varepsilon_{t+1}^e}$$

or, equivalently,

$$\varepsilon_t = \frac{1 + r_t}{1 + r_t^*} \varepsilon_{t+1}^e \qquad (20.A2)$$

The real exchange rate today depends on the domestic and foreign real interest rates this year and the expected future real exchange rate next year. This equation corresponds to equation (20.4) in the text, but now in terms of the real rather than nominal exchange and interest rates.

Solving the Real Interest Parity Condition Forward

The next step is to solve equation (20.A2) forward, in the same way as we did it for equation (20.4). The equation above implies that the real exchange rate in year $t + 1$ is given by:

$$\varepsilon_{t+1} = \frac{1 + r_{t+1}^e}{1 + r_{t+1}^{*e}} \varepsilon_{t+2}^e$$

Taking expectations, as of year t:

$$\varepsilon_{t+1} = \frac{1 + r_{t+1}^e}{1 + r_{t+1}^{*e}} \varepsilon_{t+2}^e$$

Replacing in the previous relation:

$$\varepsilon_t = \frac{(1 + r_t)(1 + r_{t+1}^e)}{(1 + r_t^*)(1 + r_{t+1}^{*e})} \varepsilon_{t+2}^e$$

Solving for ε_{t+2}^e and so on gives:

$$\varepsilon_t = \frac{(1 + r_t)}{(1 + r_t^*)} \frac{(1 + r_{t+1}^e) \cdots (1 + r_{t+n}^e)}{(1 + r_{t+1}^{*e})(1 + r_{t+n}^{*e})} \varepsilon_{t+n+1}^e$$

This relation gives the current real exchange rate as a function of current and expected future domestic real interest rates, of current and expected future foreign real interest rates, and of the expected real exchange rate in year $t + n$.

The advantage of this relation over the relation we derived in the text between the nominal exchange rate and nominal interest rates, equation (20.5), is that it is typically easier to predict the future real exchange rate than to predict the future nominal exchange rate. If, for example, the economy suffers from a large trade deficit, we can be fairly confident that there will have to be a real depreciation—that ε_{t+n}^e will have to be lower. Whether there will be a nominal depreciation—what happens to E_{t+n}^e—is harder to tell. It depends on what happens to inflation, both at home and abroad over the next n years.

Back to Policy

Nearly every chapter of this text has looked at the role of policy. The next three chapters put it all together.

Chapter 21

Chapter 21 asks two questions: Given the uncertainty about the effects of macroeconomic policies, wouldn't it be better not to use policy at all? And even if policy can in principle be useful, can we trust policy makers to carry out the right policy? The bottom lines: Uncertainty limits the role of policy. Policy makers do not always do the right thing. But with the right institutions, policy does help and should be used.

Chapter 22

Chapter 22 looks at fiscal policy. It reviews what we have learned, chapter by chapter, and then looks more closely at the implications of the government budget constraint for the relation between debt, spending, and taxes. It then focuses on the implications and the dangers of high levels of public debt, a central issue in advanced countries today.

Chapter 23

Chapter 23 looks at monetary policy. It reviews what we have learned, chapter by chapter, and then focuses on current challenges. First, it describes the framework, known as *inflation targeting*, that most central banks had adopted before the crisis. It then turns to a number of issues raised by the crisis, from the optimal rate of inflation, to the role of financial regulation and the use of new instruments, known as *macroprudential tools*.

Should Policy Makers Be Restrained?

A t many points in this text, we saw how the right mix of fiscal and monetary policies could potentially help a country out of a recession, improve its trade position without increasing activity and igniting inflation, slow down an overheating economy, and stimulate investment and capital accumulation.

This conclusion, however, appears to be at odds with frequent demands that policy makers be tightly restrained.

In the United States, there are regular calls for the introduction of a balanced-budget amendment to the Constitution to limit the growth of debt. Such a call was the first item in the "Contract with America," the program drawn by Republicans for the mid-term U.S. elections in 1994 and reproduced in Figure 21-1 on page 456. It has regularly resurfaced, most recently in July 2011, when it was proposed by a group of Republicans with close ties to the Tea Party. In Europe, the countries that adopted the euro signed a "**Stability and Growth Pact (SGP)**," which required them to keep their budget deficit under 3% of GDP or else face large fines. As we shall see, that pact eventually failed, but the Europeans have now put in place new ways of making it stronger.

MyEconLab Video

Monetary policy is also under fire. For example, the charter of the central bank of New Zealand, written in 1989, defines monetary policy's role as the maintenance of price stability to the exclusion of any other macroeconomic goal. In the summer of 2011, Governor Rick Perry of Texas, running for the Republican presidential nomination, declared, "If this guy [Fed Chair Ben Bernanke] prints more money between now and the election, I dunno what y'all would do to him in Iowa but we would treat him pretty ugly down in Texas. Printing more money to play politics at this particular time in American history is almost treacherous—or treasonous in my opinion." Rick Perry, and a number of other Republicans, want the Fed Chair to be bound by rules, to have much less discretion.

This chapter looks at the case for such restraints on macroeconomic policy.

Sections 21-1 and **21-2** look at one line of argument, namely that policy makers may have good intentions, but they end up doing more harm than good.

Section 21-3 looks at another—more cynical—line, that policy makers do what is best for themselves, which is not necessarily what is best for the country.

House Republican
Contract with America

A Program for Accountability

We've listened to your concerns and we hear you loud and clear. If you give us the majority, on the first day of Congress, a Republican House will:

Force Congress to live under the same laws as every other American
Cut one out of three Congressional committee staffers
Cut the Congressional budget

Then, in the first 100 days there will be votes on the following 10 bills:

1. Balanced budget amendment and the line item veto: It's time to force the government to live within its means and restore accountability to the budget in Washington.

2. Stop violent criminals: Let's get tough with an effective, able, and timely death penalty for violent offenders. Let's also reduce crime by building more prisons, making sentences longer and putting more police on the streets.

3. Welfare reform: The government should encourage people to work, not have children out of wedlock.

4. Protect our kids: We must strengthen families by giving parents greater control over education, enforcing child support payments, and getting tough on child pornography.

5. Tax cuts for families: Let's make it easier to achieve the American Dream: save money, buy a home, and send their kids to college.

6. Strong national defense: We need to ensure a strong national defense by restoring the essentials of our national security funding.

7. Raise the senior citizens' earning limit: We can put an end to government age discrimination that discourages seniors from working if they want.

8. Roll back government regulations: Let's slash regulations that strangle small business and let's make it easier for people to invest in order to create jobs and increase wages.

9. Common-sense legal reform: We can finally stop excessive legal claims, frivolous lawsuits, and overzealous lawyers.

10. Congressional term limits: Let's replace career politicians with citizen legislators. After all, politics shouldn't be a lifetime job.
(Please see reverse side to know if the candidate from your district has signed the Contract as of October 5, 1994.)

IF WE BREAK THIS CONTRACT, THROW US OUT, WE MEAN IT.

Figure 21-1

The Contract with America

21-1 Uncertainty and Policy

A blunt way of stating the first argument in favor of policy restraints is that those who know little should do little. The argument has two parts: Macroeconomists, and by implication the policy makers who rely on their advice, know little; and they should therefore do little. Let's look at each part separately.

How Much Do Macroeconomists Actually Know?

Macroeconomists are like doctors treating cancer. They know a lot, but there is a lot they don't know.

Take an economy with high unemployment, where the central bank is considering lowering interest rates to increase economic activity. Assume that it has room to decrease the interest rate; in other words, leave aside the even more difficult issue of what to do if the economy is in the liquidity trap. Think of the sequence of links between a reduction in the interest rate that the central bank controls and an increase in output—all the questions the central bank faces when deciding whether, and by how much, to reduce the interest rate:

■ Is the current high rate of unemployment above the natural rate of unemployment, or has the natural rate of unemployment itself increased (Chapter 7)?

■ If the unemployment rate is close to the natural rate of unemployment, is there a significant risk that an interest rate reduction will lead to a decrease in

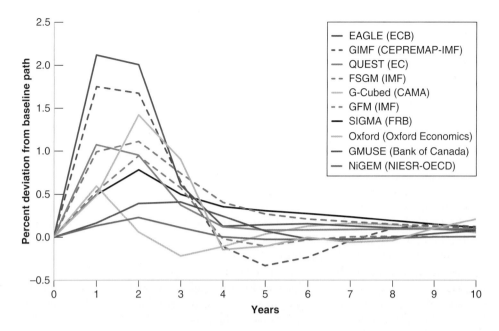

Figure 21-2

The Response of Output to a Monetary Expansion. Predictions from 10 Models

Although all 10 models predict that output will increase for some time in response to a monetary expansion, the range of answers regarding the size and the length of the output response is large.

unemployment below the natural rate of unemployment and cause an increase in inflation (Chapter 9)?

■ What will be the effect of the decrease in the policy rate on the long-term interest rate (Chapter 14)? By how much will stock prices increase (Chapter 14)? By how much will the currency depreciate (Chapters 19 and 20)?

■ How long will it take for lower long-term interest rates and higher stock prices to affect investment and consumption spending (Chapter 15)? How long will it take for the J-curve effects to work themselves out and for the trade balance to improve (Chapter 18)? What is the danger that the effects come too late, when the economy has already recovered?

When assessing these questions, central banks—or macroeconomic policy makers in general—do not operate in a vacuum. They rely, in particular, on macroeconometric models. The equations in these models show how these individual links have looked in the past. But different models yield different answers. This is because they have different structures, different lists of equations, and different lists of variables.

Figure 21-2 gives an example of this diversity. The example comes from an ongoing study coordinated by the IMF, asking the builders of 10 main macroeconometric models to answer a similar question: *Trace out the effects of a decrease in the U.S. policy rate by 100 basis points (1%), for two years.*

Three of these models have been developed and are used by central banks; four have been developed and are used by international organizations, such as the IMF or the OECD, and three have been developed and are used by academic institutions or commercial firms. They have a roughly similar structure, which you can think of as a more detailed version of the *IS-LM-PC* framework we have developed in this text. Yet, as you can see, they give rather different answers to the question. Although the average response is for an increase in U.S. output of 0.8% after one year, the answers vary from 0.1% to 2.1%. And after two years, the average response is for an increase of 1.0%, with a range from 0.2% to 2%. In short, if we measure uncertainty by the range of answers from this set of models, there is indeed substantial uncertainty about the effects of policy.

Should Uncertainty Lead Policy Makers to Do Less?

Should uncertainty about the effects of policy lead policy makers to do less? In general, the answer is: yes. Consider the following example, which builds on the simulations we have just looked at.

In the real world, of course, the Fed does not know any of these things with certainty. It can only make educated guesses. It does not know the exact value of the natural rate of unemployment, or the exact coefficient in Okun's law. ▶ Introducing these sources of uncertainty would reinforce our basic conclusion.

Suppose the U.S. economy is in recession. The unemployment rate is 7% and the Fed is considering using monetary policy to expand output. To concentrate on uncertainty about the effects of policy, let's assume the Fed knows, with certainty, everything else. Based on its forecasts, it *knows* that, absent changes in monetary policy, unemployment will still be 7% next year. It *knows* that the natural rate of unemployment is 5%, and therefore it knows that the unemployment rate is 2% above the natural rate. And it *knows*, from Okun's law, that 1% more output growth for a year leads to a 0.4% reduction in the unemployment rate.

Under these assumptions, the Fed knows that if it could use monetary policy to achieve 5% more output growth over the coming year, the unemployment rate a year from now would be lower by 0.4 times 5% = 2%, so would be down to the natural rate of unemployment, 5%. By how much should the Fed decrease the policy rate?

Taking the average of the responses from the different models in Figure 21-2, a decrease in the policy rate of 1% leads to an increase in output of 0.8% in the first year. Suppose the Fed takes this average relation as holding with *certainty*. What it should then do is straightforward. To return the unemployment rate to the natural rate in one year requires 5% more output growth. And 5% output growth requires the Fed to decrease the policy rate by 5%/0.8% = 6.25%. The Fed should therefore decrease the policy rate by 6.25%. If the economy's response is equal to the *average* response from the 10 models, this decrease in the policy rate will return the economy to the natural rate of unemployment at the end of the year.

Suppose the Fed actually decreases the policy rate by 6.25%. But let's now take into account uncertainty, as measured by the *range* of responses of the different models in Figure 21-2. Recall that the range of responses of output to a 1% decrease in the policy rate varies from 0.1% to 2.1%. This range implies that the decrease in the policy rate leads, across models, to an output response anywhere between 0.625% (0.1 × 6.25%) and 13.1% (2.1 × 6.25%). These output numbers imply, in turn, a decrease in unemployment anywhere between 0.25% (0.4 × 0.625%) and 5.24% (0.4 × 13.1%). Put another way, the unemployment rate a year hence could be anywhere between 1.76% (7% − 5.24%) and 6.75% (7% − 0.25%)!

The conclusion is clear; given the range of uncertainty about the effects of monetary policy on output, decreasing the policy rate by 6.25% would be irresponsible. If the effects of the interest rate on output are as strong as suggested by one of the 10 models, unemployment by the end of the year could be 3.24% (5% − 1.76%) below the natural rate of unemployment, leading to enormous inflationary pressures. Given this uncertainty, the Fed should decrease the policy rate by much less than 6.25%. For example, decreasing the rate by 3% leads to a range for unemployment of 6.9% to 4.5% a year hence, clearly a safer range of outcomes.

This example relies on the notion of *multiplicative uncertainty*, that is, because the effects of policy are uncertain, more active policies lead to more uncertainty. See William Brainard, ▶ "Uncertainty and the Effectiveness of Policy," *American Economic Review* 1967, Vol. 57, No. 2: pp. 411–425.

Uncertainty and Restraints on Policy Makers

Let's summarize: There is substantial uncertainty about the effects of macroeconomic policies. This uncertainty should lead policy makers to be cautious and to limit the use of active policies. Policies should be broadly aimed at avoiding large prolonged recessions, slowing down booms, and avoiding inflationary pressure. The higher unemployment or the higher inflation, the more active the policies should be. One example comes from the recession of 2008–2009 when an unprecedented shift in monetary and fiscal policies probably avoided a repeat of what happened in the 1930s during the Great Depression. But in normal times, macroeconomic policies should stop well short of **fine tuning**, of trying to achieve constant unemployment or constant output growth.

These conclusions would have been controversial 20 years ago. Back then, there was a heated debate between two groups of economists. One group, headed by Milton Friedman from Chicago, argued that because of long and variable lags in the effects of policy on activity, activist policy is likely to do more harm than good. The other group, headed by Franco Modigliani from MIT, had just built the first generation of large macroeconometric models believed that economists' knowledge was becoming good enough to allow for and increasingly fine tuning of the economy. Today, most economists recognize there is substantial uncertainty about the effects of policy. They also accept the implication that, except in special circumstances, such as 2008–2009, this uncertainty should lead to less active policies.

◄ Friedman and Modigliani are the same two economists who independently developed the modern theory of consumption we saw in Chapter 15.

MyEconLab Video

Note, however, that what we have developed so far is an argument for *self-restraint by* policy makers, not for *restraints on* policy makers. If policy makers are benevolent—they care about national well-being—and if they understand the implications of uncertainty—and there is no particular reason to think they don't—they will, on their own, follow less active policies. There is no reason to impose further restraints, such as the requirement that money growth be constant or that the budget be balanced. Let's now turn to arguments for restraints *on* policy makers.

21-2 Expectations and Policy

One of the reasons why the effects of macroeconomic policy are uncertain is the interaction of policy and expectations. How a policy works, and sometimes whether it works at all, depends not only on how it affects current variables but also on how it affects expectations about the future (this was the main theme of Chapter 16). The importance of expectations for policy goes, however, beyond uncertainty about the effects of policy. This brings us to a discussion of *games*.

Until 30 years ago, macroeconomic policy was seen in the same way as the control of a complicated machine. Methods of **optimal control**, developed initially to control and guide rockets, were increasingly being used to design macroeconomic policy. Economists no longer think this way. It has become clear that the economy is fundamentally different from a machine, even from a very complicated one. Unlike a machine, the economy is composed of people and firms who try to anticipate what policy makers will do, and who react not only to current policy but also to expectations of future policy. Hence, macroeconomic policy must be thought of as a **game** between the policy makers and "the economy"—more concretely, the people and the firms in the economy. So, when thinking about policy, what we need is not **optimal control theory** but rather **game theory**.

◄ Even machines are becoming smarter. HAL, the robot in the 1968 movie *2001: A Space Odyssey*, starts anticipating what humans in the space ship will do. The result is not a happy one. (See the movie.)

Warning: When economists say *game*, they do not mean "entertainment"; they mean **strategic interactions** between **players**. In the context of macroeconomic policy, the players are the policy maker on one side and people and firms on the other. The strategic interactions are clear. What people and firms do depend on what they expect policy makers to do. In turn, what policy makers do depend on what is happening in the economy.

Game theory has given economists many insights, often explaining how some apparently strange behavior makes sense when one understands the nature of the game being played. One of these insights is particularly important for our discussion of restraints here. Sometimes you can do better in a game by giving up some of your options. To see why, let's start with an example from outside economics: governments' policies toward hostage takers.

Game theory has become an important tool in all branches of economics. Both the 1994 and the 2005 Nobel Prizes in Economics were awarded to game theorists: in 1994 to John Nash from Princeton, John Harsanyi from Berkeley, and Reinhard Selten from Germany (John Nash's life is ◄ portrayed in the movie *A Beautiful Mind*); in 2005 to Robert Aumann, from Israel, and Tom Schelling, from Harvard.

Hostage Takings and Negotiations

Most governments have a stated policy that they will not negotiate with hostage takers. The reason for this stated policy is clear: to deter hostage taking by making it unattractive to take hostages.

Suppose, despite the stated policy, someone is taken hostage. Now that the hostage taking has taken place anyway, why not negotiate? Whatever compensation the hostage takers demand is likely to be less costly than the alternative (i.e., the likelihood that the hostage will be killed). So the best policy would appear to be: Announce that you will not negotiate, but if someone is taken hostage, negotiate.

On reflection, it is clear this would in fact be a very bad policy. Hostage takers' decisions do not depend on the stated policy but on what they expect will actually happen if they take a hostage. If they know that negotiations will actually take place, they will rightly consider the stated policy as irrelevant. And hostage takings will happen.

So what is the best policy? Despite the fact that once hostage takings have happened and that negotiations typically lead to a better outcome, the best policy is for governments to commit *not* to negotiate. By giving up the option to negotiate, they are more likely to prevent hostage takings to begin with.

Let's now turn to a macroeconomic example based on the relation between inflation and unemployment. As you will see, exactly the same logic is involved.

Inflation and Unemployment Revisited

Recall the relation between inflation and unemployment we derived in Chapter 8 [equation (8.9), with the time indexes omitted for simplicity]:

$$\pi = \pi^e - \alpha(u - u_n) \tag{21.1}$$

Inflation π depends on expected inflation π^e, and on the difference between the actual unemployment rate, u, and the natural unemployment rate, u_n. The coefficient α captures the effect of unemployment on inflation, given expected inflation. When unemployment is above the natural rate, inflation is lower than expected; when unemployment is below the natural rate, inflation is higher than expected.

Suppose the Fed announces it will follow a monetary policy consistent with zero inflation. On the assumption that people believe the announcement, expected inflation (π^e) as embodied in wage contracts is equal to zero, and the Fed faces the following relation between unemployment and inflation:

$$\pi = -\alpha(u - u_n) \tag{21.2}$$

If the Fed follows through with its announced policy, it will choose an unemployment rate equal to the natural rate; from equation (21.2), inflation will be equal to zero, just as the Fed announced and people expected.

Achieving zero inflation and an unemployment rate equal to the natural rate is not a bad outcome. But it would seem the Fed can actually do even better:

■ Recall from Chapter 8 that in the United States, α is roughly equal to 0.5. So equation (21.2) implies that, by accepting just 1% inflation, the Fed can achieve an unemployment rate of 2% below the natural rate of unemployment. Suppose the Fed—and everyone else in the economy—finds the trade-off attractive and decides to decrease unemployment by 2% in exchange for an inflation rate of 1%. This incentive to deviate from the announced policy once the other player has made his move—in this case, once wage setters have set the wage—is known in game theory as the **time inconsistency** of optimal policy. In our example, the Fed can improve the outcome this period by deviating from its announced policy of zero

This example was developed by Finn Kydland, from Carnegie Mellon and now at the University of California–Santa Barbara, and Edward Prescott, then from Minnesota and now at Arizona State University, in "Rules Rather than Discretion: The Inconsistency of Optimal Plans," *Journal of Political Economy*, 1977, 85(3): pp. 473–492. Kydland and Prescott were awarded the Nobel Prize in Economics in 2004.

A refresher: Given labor market conditions and given their expectations of what prices will be, firms and workers set nominal wages. Given the nominal wages firms have to pay, firms then set prices. So prices depend on expected prices and labor market conditions. Equivalently, price inflation depends on expected price inflation and labor market conditions. This is what is captured in equation (21.1).

For simplicity, we assume the Fed can choose the unemployment rate—and, by implication, the inflation rate—exactly. In doing so, we ignore the uncertainty about the effects of policy. This was the topic of Section 21-1, but it is not central here.

If $\alpha = 0.5$, equation (21.2) implies $\pi = -0.5(u - u_n)$. If $\pi = 1\%$, then $(u - u_n) = -2\%$.

inflation: By accepting some inflation, it can achieve a substantial reduction in unemployment.

- Unfortunately, this is not the end of the story. Seeing that the Fed has allowed for more inflation than it announced it would, wage setters are likely to smarten up and begin to expect positive inflation of 1%. If the Fed still wants to achieve an unemployment rate 2% below the natural rate, it will now have to accept 2% inflation because expectations have changed. Accepting an inflation of 1% is no longer enough to sustain lower unemployment. However, if the Fed persists and achieves 2% inflation, wage setters are likely to increase their expectations of future inflation further, and so on.

- The eventual outcome is likely to be persistent high inflation. Because wage setters understand the Fed's motives, expected inflation catches up with actual inflation. The end result is an economy with the *same unemployment rate* that would have prevailed if the Fed had followed its announced policy, but with *much higher inflation.* In short, attempts by the Fed to make things better lead in the end to things being worse.

Remember that the natural rate of unemployment is neither natural nor best in any sense (see Chapter 7). It may be reasonable for the Fed and everyone else in the economy to prefer an unemployment rate lower than the natural rate of unemployment.

How relevant is this example? Very relevant. Go back to Chapter 8: We can read the history of the Phillips curve and the increase in inflation in the 1970s as coming precisely from the Fed's attempts to keep unemployment below the natural rate of unemployment, leading to higher and higher expected inflation, and higher and higher actual inflation. In that light, the shift of the original Phillips curve can be seen as the adjustment of wage setters' expectations to the central bank's behavior.

So what is the best policy for the Fed to follow in this case? It is to make a credible commitment that it will not try to decrease unemployment below the natural rate. By giving up the option of deviating from its announced policy, the Fed can achieve unemployment equal to the natural rate of unemployment and zero inflation. The analogy with the hostage taking example is clear. By credibly committing not to do something that would appear desirable at the time, policy makers can achieve a better outcome; no hostage takings in our previous example, no inflation here.

Establishing Credibility

How can a central bank credibly commit not to deviate from its announced policy?

One way to establish its credibility is for the central bank to give up—or to be stripped by law of—its policy-making power. For example, the mandate of the central bank can be defined by law in terms of a simple rule, such as keeping money growth at 0% forever. (An alternative, which we discussed in Chapter 20, is to adopt a hard peg, such as a currency board or even dollarization. In this case the central bank must keep interest rates equal to foreign rates no matter what.)

Such a law surely takes care of the problem of time inconsistency. But the tight restraint it creates comes close to throwing the baby out with the bath water. We want to prevent the central bank from pursuing too high a rate of money growth in an attempt to lower unemployment below the natural unemployment rate. But—subject to the restrictions discussed in Section 21-1—we still want the central bank to be able to decrease the policy rate by expanding the money supply when unemployment is far above the natural rate, and increase the policy rate by contracting the money supply when unemployment is far below the natural rate. Such actions become impossible under a constant-money-growth rule. There are indeed better ways to deal with time inconsistency. In the case of monetary policy, our discussion suggests various ways of dealing with the problem.

A first step is to make the central bank independent. By an **independent central bank**, we mean a central bank where interest rate and money supply decisions are made independent of the influence of the currently elected politicians. Politicians, who face

Figure 21-3

Inflation and Central Bank Independence

Across OECD countries, the higher the degree of central bank independence, the lower the rate of inflation.

Source: Vittorio Grilli, Donato Masciandaro, and Guido Tabellini, "Political and Monetary Institutions and Public Financial Policies in the Industrial Countries." *Economic Policy*, 1991, 6(13): pp. 341–392.

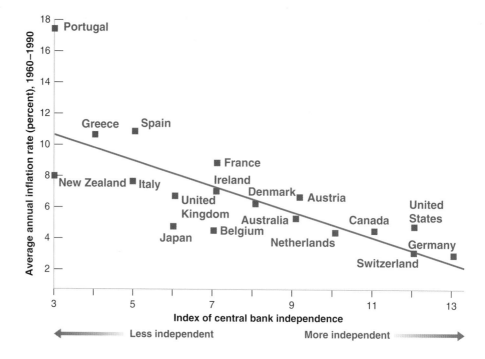

The figure is taken from a 1991 study and thus uses data only up to 1990. More recent evidence yields similar conclusions.

A warning: Figure 21-3 shows correlation, not necessarily causality. It may be that countries that dislike inflation tend both to give more independence to their central bankers and have lower inflation. (This is another example of the difference between correlation and causality—discussed in Appendix 3 at the end of the book.)

frequent reelections, may want lower unemployment now, even if it leads to inflation later. Making the central bank independent, and making it difficult for politicians to fire the central banker, makes it easier for the central bank to resist the political pressure to decrease unemployment below the natural rate of unemployment.

This may not be enough, however. Even if it is not subject to political pressure, the central bank will still be tempted to decrease unemployment below the natural rate. Doing so leads to a better outcome in the short run. So a second step is to give incentives to the central bankers to take the long view—that is, to take into account the long-run costs from higher inflation. One way of doing so is to give them long terms in office, so they have a long horizon and have the incentives to build credibility.

A third step may be to appoint a "conservative" central banker, someone who dislikes inflation very much and is therefore less willing to accept more inflation in exchange for less unemployment when unemployment is at the natural rate. When the economy is at the natural rate, such a central banker will be less tempted to embark on a monetary expansion. Thus, the problem of time inconsistency will be reduced.

These are the steps many countries have taken over the last two decades. Central banks have been given more independence from governments. Central bankers have been given long terms in office. And governments typically have appointed central bankers who are more "conservative" than the governments themselves—central bankers who appear to care more about inflation and less about unemployment than the government does. (See the Focus box "Was Alan Blinder Wrong in Speaking the Truth?")

Figure 21-3 suggests that giving central banks more independence has been successful, at least in terms of achieving lower inflation. The vertical axis gives the average inflation rate in 18 OECD countries over the period 1960–1990. The horizontal axis gives the value of an index of "central bank independence," constructed by looking at a number of legal provisions in the central bank's charter—for example, whether and how the government can remove the head of the bank. There is a striking inverse relation between the two variables, as summarized by the regression line. More central bank independence appears to be systematically associated with lower inflation.

Was Alan Blinder Wrong in Speaking the Truth?

In the summer of 1994, President Bill Clinton appointed Alan Blinder, an economist from Princeton, vice-chairman (in effect, second in command) of the Federal Reserve Board. A few weeks later Blinder, speaking at an economic conference, indicated his belief that the Fed has both the responsibility and the ability, when unemployment is high, to use monetary policy to help the economy recover. This statement was badly received. Bond prices fell, and most newspapers ran editorials critical of Blinder.

Why was the reaction of markets and newspapers so negative? It was surely not that Blinder was wrong. There is no doubt that monetary policy can and should help the economy out of a recession. Indeed, the Federal Reserve Bank Act of 1977 requires the Fed to pursue full employment as well as low inflation.

The reaction was negative because, in terms of the argument we developed in the text, Blinder revealed by his words that he was not a conservative central banker, that he cared about unemployment as well as inflation. With the unemployment rate at the time equal to 6.1%, close to what was thought to be the natural rate of unemployment at the time, markets interpreted Blinder's statements as suggesting that he might want to decrease unemployment below the natural rate. Interest rates increased because of higher expected inflation, and bond prices decreased.

The moral of the story: Whatever views central bankers may hold, they should try to look and sound conservative. This is why, for example, many heads of central banks are reluctant to admit, at least in public, the existence of any trade-off between unemployment and inflation, even in the short run.

Time Consistency and Restraints on Policy Makers

Let's summarize what we have learned in this section:

We have examined arguments for putting restraints on policy makers based on the issue of time inconsistency.

When issues of time inconsistency are relevant, tight restraints on policy makers—like a fixed-money-growth rule in the case of monetary policy, or a balanced-budget rule in the case of fiscal policy—can provide a rough solution. But the solution has large costs because it prevents the use of macroeconomic policy altogether. Better solutions typically involve designing better institutions (like an independent central bank, or a better budget process) that can reduce the problem of time inconsistency, while at the same time allowing the use of policy for the stabilization of output. This is not, however, easy to do.

21-3 Politics and Policy

We have assumed so far that policy makers were benevolent, that is, that they tried to do what was best for the economy. However, much public discussion challenges that assumption. Politicians or policy makers, the argument goes, do what is best for themselves, and this is not always what is best for the country.

You have heard the arguments. Politicians avoid the hard decisions and they pander to the electorate, partisan politics leads to gridlock, and nothing ever gets done. Discussing the flaws of democracy goes far beyond the scope of this book. What we can do here is to briefly review how these arguments apply to macroeconomic policy, then look at the empirical evidence and see what light it sheds on the issue of policy restraints.

Games between Policy Makers and Voters

Many macroeconomic policy decisions involve trading off short-run losses against long-run gains or, conversely, short-run gains against long-run losses.

Take, for example, tax cuts. By definition, tax cuts lead to lower taxes today. They are also likely to lead to an increase in demand, and therefore to an increase in output

Figure 21-4

The Evolution of the U.S. Debt to GDP Ratio since 1900

The three major buildups of debt since 1900 have been associated with World War I, the Great Depression, and World War II. The buildup since 1980 has not been caused by either wars or adverse economic shocks.

Source: Historical Statistics of the United States; U.S. Census Bureau.

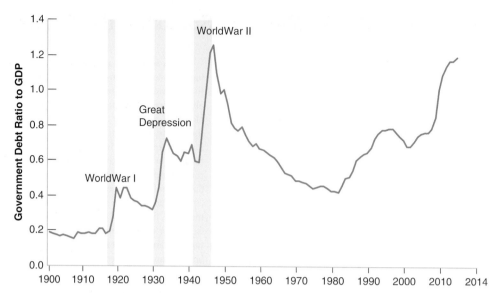

for some time. But unless they are matched by equal decreases in government spending, they lead to a larger budget deficit and to the need for an increase in taxes in the future. If voters are shortsighted, the temptation for politicians to cut taxes may prove irresistible. Politics may lead to systematic deficits, at least until the level of government debt has become so high that politicians are scared into action.

Now move on from taxes to macroeconomic policy in general. Again suppose that voters are shortsighted. If the politicians' main goal is to please voters and get reelected, what better policy than to expand aggregate demand before an election, leading to higher growth and lower unemployment? True, growth in excess of the normal growth rate cannot be sustained, and eventually the economy must return to the natural level of output. Higher growth now must be followed by lower growth later. But with the right timing and shortsighted voters, higher growth can win the elections. Thus, we might expect a clear **political business cycle** (i.e., economic fluctuations induced by political elections) associated with higher growth on average before elections than after elections.

You probably have heard these arguments before, in one form or another. And their logic appears convincing. The question is: How well do they fit the facts?

First, consider deficits and debt. The preceding argument would lead you to expect that budget deficits and high government debt have always been and will always be there. Figure 21-4 takes the long view. It gives the evolution of the ratio of government debt to GDP in the United States beginning in 1900, and shows that the reality is more complex.

Look first at the evolution of the ratio of debt to GDP from 1900 to 1980. Note that each of the three buildups in debt (represented by the shaded areas in the figure) was associated with special circumstances: World War I for the first buildup, the Great Depression for the second, and World War II for the third. These were times of unusually high military spending or unusual declines in output. Adverse circumstances—not pandering to voters—were clearly behind the large deficits and the resulting increase in debt during each of these three episodes. Note also how, in each of these three cases, the buildup was followed by a steady decrease in debt. In particular, note how the ratio of debt to GDP, which was as high as 130% in 1946, was steadily reduced to a postwar low of 33% in 1979.

The more recent evidence, however, fits the argument of shortsighted voters and pandering politicians better. Clearly, the large increase since 2007 is due to the crisis. But leaving it aside, note how the debt-to-GDP ratio increased from 33% in 1980 to

We saw in Chapter 8 that, even if monetary policy is used to increase output in the short run, in the medium run, output returns to its natural level and unemployment to its natural rate.

The precise relation between the evolution of deficits, debt, and the ratio of debt to GDP is explored in detail in Chapter 22. For the moment, all you need to know is that deficits lead to increases in debt.

We discussed the response of fiscal policy to the crisis in Chapter 6.

Table 21-1	Growth during Democratic and Republican Presidential Administrations:1948–2012				
	Year of the Administration				
	First (%)	Second (%)	Third (%)	Fourth (%)	Average (%)
Democratic	2.5	5.4	3.9	3.6	3.9
Republican	3.4	0.7	3.3	3.8	2.8
Average	2.9	3.1	3.6	3.7	3.4

Source: Calculated using Series GDPCA, from 1948 to 2012: Federal Reserve Economic Data (FRED) http://research.stlouisfed.org/fred2/.

63% in 2007. This increase in debt can be largely traced back to two rounds of tax cuts, the first under the Reagan administration in the early 1980s and the second under the Bush administration in the early 2000s. Were these tax cuts, and the resulting deficits and increase in debt, best explained by pandering of politicians to shortsighted voters? We shall argue below that the answer is probably no, and that the main explanation lies in a game between political parties rather than in a game between policy makers and voters.

MyEconLab Video

Before we do so, let us return to the political business cycle argument, that is, that policy makers try to get high output growth before the elections so they will be reelected. If the political business cycle were important, we would expect to see faster growth before elections rather than after. Table 21-1 gives average output growth rates for each of the four years of each U.S. administration from 1948 to 2012, distinguishing between Republican and Democratic presidential administrations. Look at the last line of the table. Growth has indeed been highest on average in the last year of an administration. The average difference across years is relatively small, however; 3.7% in the last year of an administration versus 2.9% in the first year. (We shall return to another interesting feature in the table, namely the difference between Republican and Democratic administrations.) There is little evidence of manipulation—or at least of successful manipulation—of the economy to win elections.

Games between Policy Makers

Another line of argument shifts the focus from games between politicians and voters to games between policy makers.

Suppose, for example, that the party in power wants to reduce spending but faces opposition to spending cuts in Congress. One way of putting pressure both on Congress as well as on the future parties in power is to cut taxes and create deficits. As debt increases over time, the increasing pressure to reduce deficits may well, in turn, force Congress and the future parties in power to reduce spending—something they would not have been willing to do otherwise.

This strategy goes by the ugly name of "Starve the Beast."

Or suppose that, either for the reason we just saw or for any other reason, the country is facing large budget deficits. Both parties in Congress want to reduce the deficit, but they disagree about the way to do it. One party wants to reduce deficits primarily through an increase in taxes; the other wants to reduce deficits primarily through a decrease in spending. Both parties may hold out on the hope that the other side will give in first. Only when debt has increased sufficiently, and it becomes urgent to reduce deficits, will one party give up.

Game theorists refer to these situations as **wars of attrition**. The hope that the other side will give in leads to long and often costly delays. Such wars of attrition happen often in the context of fiscal policy, and deficit reduction occurs long after it should.

Euro Area Fiscal Rules: A Short History

The Maastricht treaty, negotiated by the countries of the European Union in 1991, set a number of convergence criteria that countries had to meet in order to qualify for membership in the Euro area (for more on the history of the euro, see the Focus box "The Euro: A Short History" in Chapter 20). Among them were two restrictions on fiscal policy. First, the ratio of the budget deficit to GDP had to be lower than 3%. Second, the ratio of its debt to GDP had to be less than 60%, or at least "approaching this value at a satisfactory pace."

In 1997, would-be members of the Euro area agreed to make some of these restrictions permanent. The Stability and Growth Pact (SGP), signed in 1997, required members of the Euro area to adhere to the following fiscal rules:

■ That countries commit to balance their budget in the medium run. That they present programs to the European authorities, specifying their objectives for the current and following three years to show how they are making progress toward their medium-run goal.

■ That countries avoid excessive deficits, except under exceptional circumstances. Following the Maastricht treaty criteria, excessive deficits were defined as deficits in excess of 3% of GDP. Exceptional circumstances were defined as declines of GDP larger than 2%.

■ That sanctions be imposed on countries that ran excessive deficits. These sanctions could range from 0.2 to 0.5% of GDP—so, for a country like France, up to roughly 10 billion dollars!

Figure 1 plots the evolution of budget deficits since 1995 for the Euro area as a whole. Note how from 1995 to 2000, budget balances went from a deficit of 7.5% of Euro area GDP to budget balance. The performance of some of the member countries was particularly impressive. Greece reduced its deficit from 13.4% of GDP to a reported 1.4% of GDP. (It was discovered in 2004 that the Greek government had cheated in reporting its deficit numbers and that the actual improvement, although impressive, was less than reported; the deficit for 2000 is now estimated to have been 4.1%.) Italy's deficit went from 10.1% of GDP in 1993 to only 0.9% of GDP in 2000.

Was the improvement entirely due to the Maastricht criteria and the SGP rules? Just as in the case of deficit reduction in the United States over the same period, the answer is no. The decrease in nominal interest rates, which decreased the interest payments on the debt, and the strong expansion of the late 1990s both played important roles. But, again as in the United States, the fiscal rules also played a significant role. The carrot—the right to become a member of the Euro area—was attractive enough to lead a number of countries to take tough measures to reduce their deficits.

Things turned around, however, after 2000. From 2000 on, deficits started increasing. The first country to break the limit was Portugal in 2001, with a deficit of 4.4%. The next two countries were France and Germany, both with deficits in excess of 3% of GDP in 2002. Italy soon followed. In each case, the government of the country decided it was more important to avoid a fiscal contraction that could lead to even slower output growth than to satisfy the rules of the SGP.

Faced with clear "excessive deficits" (and without the excuse of exceptional circumstances because output growth in each these countries was low but positive), European authorities found themselves in a quandary. Starting the excessive deficit procedure against Portugal, a small country, might have been politically feasible, although it is doubtful that Portugal would have ever been willing to pay the fine. Starting the same procedure against the two largest members of the Euro area, France and Germany, proved politically impossible. After an internal fight between the two main European authorities—the European Commission and the European Council—the European Commission wanted to proceed with the excessive deficit procedure, whereas the European Council, which represents the states, did not—the procedure was suspended.

The crisis made it clear that the initial rules were too inflexible. Romano Prodi, the President of the European Commission, admitted to that much. In an interview in October 2002, he stated, "I know very well that the Stability Pact is stupid, like all decisions that are rigid." And the attitudes of both France and Germany showed that the threat to impose large fines on countries with excessive deficits was simply not credible.

For two years, the European Commission explored ways to improve the rules so as to make them more flexible and, by implication, more credible. In 2005, a new, revised SGP was adopted. It kept the 3% deficit and 60% debt numbers as thresholds but allowed for more flexibility in deviating from the rules. Growth no longer had to be less than −2% for the rules to be suspended. Exceptions were also made if the deficit came from structural reforms or from public investment. Fines were gone, and the plan was to rely on early public warnings as well as on peer pressure from other Euro area countries.

For a while, the ratio of the deficit to GDP declined, again largely due to strong growth and higher revenues. The ratio reached a low of 0.5% in 2007. But the crisis, and the associated sharp decrease in revenues, led again to a sharp increase in budget deficits. In 2010, the ratio stood at close to 6%, twice the SGP threshold; 23 out of 27 EU countries stood in violation of the 3% deficit limit, and it was clear that the rules had to be reconsidered. Eventually, in 2012, a new intergovernmental treaty was signed among the member countries of the European Union, the Treaty on Stability, Coordination and Governance in the Economic and Monetary Union, also known as the Fiscal Compact. It has four main provisions:

■ Member countries should introduce a balanced budget rule into national legislation, either through a constitutional amendment or a framework law.

■ Government budgets should be balanced or in surplus. The treaty defines a balanced budget as a budget deficit not exceeding 3.0% of GDP, and a cyclically adjusted

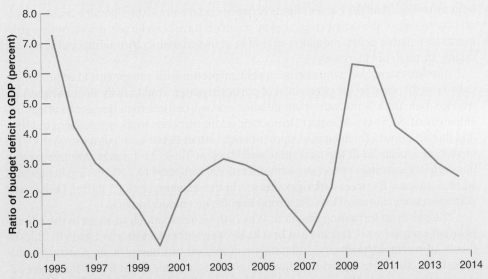

Figure 1

Euro Area Budget Deficit as a Percentage of GDP since 1995

Source: European Central Bank.

deficit not exceeding a country-specific objective, which at most can be set to 0.5% of GDP for states with a debt-to-GDP ratio exceeding 60%, or at most 1.0% of GDP for states with debt levels within the 60% limit.

- Countries whose government debt-to-GDP ratio exceeds 60% must reduce it at an average rate of at least one twentieth (5%) per year of the exceeded percentage points. (So, for example, if the actual ratio of debt to GDP is 100%, they must decrease by at least 0.05 (100 − 60) = 2% of GDP.)

- If a country's budget shows a significant deviation from the second rule, an automatic correction mechanism is triggered with a procedure called *The Excessive Deficit Procedure*. The exact implementation of this mechanism is defined individually by each country, but it has to comply with the basic principles outlined by the European Commission. This convoluted procedure is graphically well explained here: http://ec.europa.eu/economy_finance/graphs/2014-11-10_excessive_deficit_procedure_explained_en.htm.

In 2015 a new criterion had been added to the four, which specifies that in deciding whether a country should be subject to the Excessive Deficit Procedure, its progress in implementing structural reforms (e.g., in the area of pensions, labor, goods, and services markets) will also be considered.

By 2014 the average budget deficit of Euro area countries had fallen to 2.4% but 11 out of 19 Euro member countries were still under the Excessive Deficit Procedure because they were in violation of one or another of the Fiscal Compact Rules. There is wide agreement that the set of rules has become too complex and too confusing, and that the rules have to be simplified. Work is ongoing, but designing a simpler set of rules is proving difficult.

Wars of attrition arise in other macroeconomic contexts; for example, during episodes of hyperinflation. As we shall see in Chapter 22, hyperinflations come from the use of money creation to finance large budget deficits. Although the need to reduce those deficits is usually recognized early on, support for stabilization programs—which include the elimination of those deficits—typically comes only after inflation has reached ◄ such high levels that economic activity is severely affected.

These games go a long way in explaining the rise in the ratio of debt to GDP in the United States since the early 1980s. There is little doubt that one of the goals of the Reagan administration, when it decreased taxes from 1981 to 1983, was to slow down the growth of government spending. There is also little question that, by the mid-1980s, ◄ there was general agreement among policy makers that the deficits should be reduced. But, because of disagreements between Democrats and Republicans about whether this should happen primarily through tax increases or spending cuts, it was not until the late 1990s that deficit reduction was achieved. The motivation behind the Bush administration tax cuts of the early 2000s appears to be similar to those of the Reagan

Another example outside of economics: Think of the 2004–2005 National Hockey League lockout, where the complete season was canceled because owners and players could not reach an agreement. The National Basketball Association faced a similar lockout through the summer of 2011.

See the discussion in the Focus box "Monetary Contraction and Fiscal Expansion: The United States in the Early 1980s" in Chapter 19.

administration. And the current fights between Congress and the Obama administration on how to reduce the deficits triggered by the crisis have been largely driven by disagreements on whether deficit reduction should be achieved mainly through spending cuts or mainly through tax increases.

More on the current U.S. fiscal situation in Chapter 22. ▶

Another example of games between political parties is the movements in economic activity brought about by the alternation of parties in power. Traditionally, Republicans have worried more than Democrats about inflation and worried less than Democrats about unemployment. So we would expect Democratic administrations to show stronger growth—and thus less unemployment and more inflation—than Republican administrations. This prediction appears to fit the facts quite well. Look at Table 21-1 again. Average growth has been 3.9% during Democratic administrations, compared to 2.8% during Republican administrations. The most striking contrast is in the second year: 5.4% during Democratic administrations compared to 0.7% during Republican administrations.

This raises an intriguing question. Why is the effect so much stronger in the administration's second year? It could just be a fluke. Many other factors affect growth. But the theory of unemployment and inflation we developed in Chapter 8 suggests a possible hypothesis. There are lags in the effects of policy, so it takes about a year for a new administration to affect the economy. And sustaining higher growth than normal for too long would lead to increasing inflation, so even a Democratic administration would not want to sustain higher growth throughout its term. Thus, growth rates tend to be much closer to each other during the second halves of Democratic and Republican administrations—more so than during first halves.

Politics and Fiscal Restraints

If politics sometimes lead to long and lasting budget deficits, can rules be put in place to limit these adverse effects?

A constitutional amendment to balance the budget each year, such as the amendment proposed by the Republicans in 1994, would surely eliminate the problem of deficits. But just like a constant-money-growth rule in the case of monetary policy, it also would eliminate the use of fiscal policy as a macroeconomic instrument altogether. This is just too high a price to pay.

A better approach is to put in place rules that put limits either on deficits or on debt. This is, however, more difficult than it sounds. Rules such as limits on the ratio of the deficit to GDP or the ratio of debt to GDP are more flexible than a balanced-budget requirement, but they may still not be flexible enough if the economy is affected by particularly bad shocks. This has been made clear by the problems faced by the Stability and Growth Pact in Europe; these problems are discussed at more length in the Focus box "Euro Area Fiscal Rules: A Short History" on page 466. More flexible or more complex rules, like rules that allow for special circumstances or rules that take into account the state of the economy, are harder to design and especially harder to enforce. For example, allowing the deficit to be higher if the unemployment rate is higher than the natural rate requires having a simple and unambiguous way of computing what the natural rate is, a nearly impossible task.

A complementary approach is to put in place mechanisms to reduce deficits, were such deficits to arise. Consider, for example, a mechanism that triggers automatic spending cuts when the deficit gets too large. Suppose the budget deficit is too large and it is desirable to cut spending across the board by 5%. Members of Congress will find it difficult to explain to their constituency why their favorite spending program was cut by 5%. Now suppose the deficit triggers automatic across-the-board spending cuts of 5% without any congressional action. Knowing that other programs will be cut, members of Congress will accept cuts in their favorite programs more easily. They will also be better able to deflect the blame for the cuts. Members of Congress who succeed in limiting the cuts to their favorite program to, say, 4% (by convincing Congress to make deeper cuts in some other programs so as to maintain the lower overall level of spending) can then return to their constituents and claim they have successfully prevented even larger cuts.

This was indeed the general approach used to reduce deficits in the United States in the 1990s. The Budget Enforcement Act passed in 1990, and extended by new legislation in 1993 and 1997, introduced two main rules:

- It imposed constraints on spending. Spending was divided into two categories: discretionary spending (roughly, spending on goods and services, including defense) and mandatory spending (roughly, transfer payments to individuals). Constraints, called **spending caps**, were set on discretionary spending for the following five years. These caps were set in such a way as to require a small but steady decrease in discretionary spending (in real terms). Explicit provisions were made for emergencies. For example, spending on Operation Desert Storm during the Gulf War in 1991 was not subject to the caps.

- It required that a new transfer program could only be adopted if it could be shown not to increase deficits in the future (either by raising new revenues or by decreasing spending on an existing program). This rule is known as the pay-as-you-go or the **PAYGO rule**.

The focus on spending rather than on the deficit itself had one important implication. If there was a recession, hence a decrease in revenues, the deficit could increase without triggering a decrease in spending. This happened in 1991 and 1992 when, because of the recession, the deficit increased—despite the fact that spending satisfied the constraints imposed by the caps. This focus on spending had two desirable effects: It allowed for a larger fiscal deficit during a recession—a good thing from the point of view of macroeconomic policy; and it decreased the pressure to break the rules during a recession—a good thing from a political point of view.

By 1998, deficits were gone, and for the first time in 20 years, the federal budget was in surplus. Not all of the deficit reduction was due to the Budget Enforcement Act rules. A decrease in defense spending due to the end of the Cold War, and a large increase in tax revenues due to the strong expansion of the second half of the 1990s were important factors. But there is wide agreement that the rules played an important role in making sure that decreases in defense spending and increases in tax revenues were used for deficit reduction rather than for increases in other spending programs.

Once budget surpluses appeared, however, Congress became increasingly willing to break its own rules. Spending caps were systematically broken, and the PAYGO rule was allowed to expire in 2002. The lesson from this, as well as from the failure of the SGP described in the Focus box "Euro Area Fiscal Rules: A Short History," is that, although rules can help, they cannot fully substitute for a lack of resolve from policy makers.

Summary

- The effects of macroeconomic policies are always uncertain. This uncertainty should lead policy makers to be more cautious and to use less active policies. Policies must be broadly aimed at avoiding prolonged recessions, slowing down booms, and avoiding inflationary pressure. The higher the level of unemployment or inflation, the stronger the policies should be. But they should stop short of fine tuning, of trying to maintain constant unemployment or constant output growth.

- Using macroeconomic policy to control the economy is fundamentally different from controlling a machine. Unlike a machine, the economy is composed of people and firms who try to anticipate what policy makers will do and who react not only to current policy but also to expectations of future policy. In this sense, macroeconomic policy can be thought of as a game between policy makers and people in the economy.

- When playing a game, it is sometimes better for a player to give up some of his options. For example, when a hostage taking occurs, it is better to negotiate with the hostage takers. But a government that credibly commits to not negotiating with hostage takers—a government that gives up the option of negotiation—is actually more likely to deter hostage takings.

- The same argument applies to various aspects of macroeconomic policy. By credibly committing not to use monetary policy to decrease unemployment below the natural rate of unemployment, a central bank can alleviate fears that money growth will be high, and in the process decrease both expected and actual inflation. When issues of time inconsistency are relevant, tight restraints on policy makers—such as a fixed-money-growth rule in the case of monetary policy—can provide a rough solution. But the solution can have large costs if it prevents the use of macroeconomic policy altogether. Better methods typically involve designing better institutions (such as an independent central bank) that can reduce the problem of time inconsistency without eliminating monetary policy as a macroeconomic policy tool.

- Another argument for putting restraints on policy makers is that policy makers may play games either with the public or among themselves, and these games may lead to undesirable outcomes. Politicians may try to fool a shortsighted electorate by choosing policies with short-run benefits but large long-term costs—for example, large budget deficits—to be reelected. Political parties may delay painful decisions, hoping that the other party will make the adjustment and take the blame. In cases like this, tight restraints on policy, such as a constitutional amendment to balance the budget, again provide a rough solution. Better ways typically involve better institutions and better ways of designing the process through which policy and decisions are made. However, the design and consistent implementation of such fiscal frameworks has proven difficult in practice, as demonstrated both in the United States and the European Union.

Key Terms

Stability and Growth Pact (SGP), 455
fine tuning, 459
optimal control, 459
game, 459
optimal control theory, 459
game theory, 459
strategic interactions, 459

players, 459
time inconsistency, 460
independent central bank, 461
political business cycle, 464
wars of attrition, 465
spending caps, 469
PAYGO rule, 469

Questions and Problems

QUICK CHECK

MyEconLab Visit www.myeconlab.com to complete similar Quick Check problems and get instant feedback.

1. Using the information in this chapter, label each of the following statements true, false, or uncertain. Explain briefly.
   a. There is so much uncertainty about the effects of monetary policy that we would be better off not using it.
   b. Depending on the model used, a one percentage point reduction in the policy interest rate is estimated to increase output growth in the year of the interest rate cut by as little as 0.1 percentage point.
   c. Depending on the model used, a one percentage point reduction in the policy interest rate is estimated to increase output growth in the year of the interest rate cut by as much as 2.1 percentage points.
   d. Elect a Democrat as president if you want low unemployment.
   e. There is clear evidence of political business cycles in the United States: low unemployment during election campaigns and higher unemployment the rest of the time.
   f. Fiscal spending rules in the United States have been ineffective in reducing budget deficits.

   g. Balanced budget rules in Europe have been effective in constraining budget deficits.
   h. Governments would be wise to announce a no-negotiation policy with hostage takers.
   i. If hostages are taken, it is clearly better for governments to negotiate with hostage takers, even if the government has announced a no-negotiation policy.
   j. There is some evidence that countries with more independent central banks have generally lower inflation.
   k. In a "starve-the-beast" fiscal policy, spending cuts come before tax cuts.

2. Implementing a political business cycle
   You are the economic adviser to a newly elected president. In four years he or she will face another election. Voters want a low unemployment rate and a low inflation rate. However, you believe that voting decisions are influenced heavily by the values of unemployment and inflation in the last year before the election, and that the economy's performance in the first three years of a president's administration has little effect on voting behavior.

Assume that inflation last year was 10%, and that the unemployment rate was equal to the natural rate. The Phillips curve is given by

$$\pi_t = \pi_{t-1} - \alpha(u_t - u_n)$$

Assume that you can use fiscal and monetary policy to achieve any unemployment rate you want for each of the next four years. Your task is to help the president achieve low unemployment and low inflation in the last year of his or her administration.

a. Suppose you want to achieve a low unemployment rate (i.e., an unemployment rate below the natural rate) in the year before the next election (four years from today). What will happen to inflation in the fourth year?

b. Given the effect on inflation you identified in part (a), what would you advise the president to do in the early years of the administration to achieve low inflation in the fourth year?

c. Now suppose the Phillips curve is given by

$$\pi_t = \pi_t^e - \alpha(u_t - u_n)$$

In addition, assume that people form inflation expectations, π_t^e, based on consideration of the future (as opposed to looking only at inflation last year) and are aware that the president has an incentive to carry out the policies you identified in parts (a) and (b). Are the policies you described in those parts likely to be successful? Why or why not?

3. Alcohol consumption produces very negative effects and a high cost for society. The government decides to totally ban alcohol consumption.

What are the advantages of such a policy? What are the disadvantages?

4. New Zealand rewrote the charter of its central bank in the early 1990s to make low inflation its only goal.

Why would New Zealand want to do this?

DIG DEEPER

MyEconLab Visit www.myeconlab.com to complete all Dig Deeper problems and get instant feedback.

5. Consider two groups of countries within the European Union: for the first one, inflation is the absolute target; for the other growth and decrease of unemployment is the main concern. π_{li} (li for low inflation) is the inflation rate limit of the first group and π_{fu} (fu for full employment) is the accepted rate of inflation for the second group. It is clear that

$$\pi_{fu} > \pi_{li}$$

The discussions are balanced between these two groups and no decisive arguments emerge so we can assume that they both have an equal chance to make the decision.

The Philips curve is given by

$$\pi_\tau = \pi_t^e - \alpha(v_t - v_n)$$

The decision is going to be taken in the context of an Euro Union group, the EcoFin, which will announce the economic policy for the coming years. Assume that expectations about inflation in the coming year (represented by π_t^e) are formed before the EcoFin (meaning that wages are already set).

a. Solve for expected inflation, in terms of π_{li} and π_{fu}

b. If the group for full employment prevail, the rate of inflation (π_{fu}) will be accepted. Given the solution for expected inflation in (a), how will the unemployment rate compare to the natural rate of unemployment?

c. What is the answer if the contrary is true?

d. What is the best policy then?

6. Social Stability versus economic modernization as a prisoner's dilemma game

This exercise tries to illustrate a debate in a centralized economy, which is in the process of being modernized, with a single political party. Social stability is the main concern of the government but it is faced by two obstacles: one being support a strengthening of the control of the party (P, party control supporter), the other adopt a more market approach (M, market supporter) with free enterprises and price liberalization.

The following table represents payoffs for each side. Think as payoff a measure of influence in the political governing bodies: if party control supporter accept a weakening of the party and market supporter obtain more market mechanisms, P received a negative payoff of −20 and M a positive payoff of 30.

		Party control (P)			
		more		less	
Market mechanism (M)	more	$P + 10$	$M + 10$	$P - 20$	$M + 30$
	less	$P + 30$	$M - 20$	$P - 10$	$M - 10$

a. If P accept less party control what is the best response of M? Given this response, what is the payoff for the P?

b. If P doesn't accept to alleviate the party control, what is the best answer for M?

c. What will each group do? Is there a way to improve the outcome?

EXPLORE FURTHER

7. Games, pre-commitment, and time inconsistency in the news

Current events offer abundant examples of disputes in which the parties are involved in a game, try to commit themselves to lines of action in advance, and face issues of time inconsistency. Examples arise in the domestic political process, international affairs, and labor-management relations.

a. Choose a current dispute (or one resolved recently) to investigate. Do an internet search to learn the issues involved in the dispute, the actions taken by the parties to date, and the current state of play.

b. In what ways have the parties tried to pre-commit to certain actions in the future? Do they face issues of time inconsistency? Have the parties failed to carry out any of their threatened actions?

c. Does the dispute resemble a prisoner's dilemma game (a game with a payoff structure like the one described in Problem 6)? In other words, does it seem likely (or did it actually happen) that the individual incentives of the parties will lead them to an unfavorable outcome—one that could be improved for both parties through cooperation? Is there a deal to be made? What attempts have the parties made to negotiate?

d. How do you think the dispute will be resolved (or how has it been resolved)?

8. *A specific model: The European Central Bank*
   Created by the Maastricht Treaty on European Union of 1992, the European Central Bank has been set up 1st of June 1998.

a. In your opinion does the following excerpt from the Statute make the ECB goals clear enough?

Article 2 Objectives:

In accordance with Article 105(1) of this Treaty, the primary objective of the ESCB shall be to maintain price stability. Without prejudice to the objective of price stability, it shall support the general economic policies in the Community with a view to contributing to the achievement of the objectives of the Community as laid down in Article 2 of this Treaty (that is, "human dignity, freedom, democracy..."). The ESCB shall act in accordance with the principle of an open market economy with free competition, favoring an efficient allocation of resources, and in compliance with the principles set out in Article 4 of this Treaty.

b. Based on the following excerpts, where would you place the ECB in Graph 21.3? Explain your opinion.

Article 7 Independence:

When exercising the powers and carrying out the tasks and duties conferred upon them by this Treaty and this Statute, neither the ECB, nor a national central bank, nor any member of their decision-making bodies shall seek or take instructions from Community institutions or bodies, from any government of a Member State, or from any other body.

Article 11.2:

The executive board, the President, the Vice-President, and the other members of the Executive Board shall be appointed from among persons of recognized standing and professional experience in monetary or banking matters by common accord of the governments of the Member States at the level of the Heads of State or Government, on a recommendation from the (European) Council after it has consulted the European Parliament and the governing council. Their term of office shall be eight years and shall not be renewable.

Further Readings

- For more model comparisons, you can look at Gunter Coenen et al., Effects of Fiscal Stimulus in Structural Models, in the *American Economic Journal Macroeconomics*, 2012, Vol.4, No. 1, pp: 22–68.
- If you want to learn more about political economy issues, a useful reference is *Political Economy in Macroeconomics* by Alan Drazen, Princeton University Press, 2002.
- For an argument that inflation decreased as a result of the increased independence of central banks in the 1990s, read "Central Bank Independence and Inflation" in the 2009 Annual Report of the Federal Reserve Bank of St. Louis. https://www.stlouisfed.org/annual-report/2009/central-bank-independence-and-inflation.

- A leading proponent of the view that governments misbehave and should be tightly restrained is James Buchanan, from George Mason University. Buchanan received the Nobel Prize in 1986 for his work on public choice. Read, for example, his book with Richard Wagner, *Democracy in Deficit: The Political Legacy of Lord Keynes*, Liberty Fund, 1977.
- For an interpretation of the increase in inflation in the 1970s as the result of time inconsistency, see "Did Time Consistency Contribute to the Great Inflation?" by Henry Chappell and Rob McGregor, *Economics & Politics*, 2004, Vol 16, No. 3, pp: 233–251.

Fiscal Policy: A Summing Up

t the time of writing, fiscal policy is at the center of policy discussions. In most advanced economies, the crisis has led to large budget deficits and a large increase in debt-to-GDP ratios. In Greece, the government has indicated that it will be unable to fully repay its debt and is negotiating with its creditors. The problem goes beyond Greece. In a number of countries, investors are worried about whether debt can indeed be repaid and are asking for higher interest rates to compensate for the risk of default. This calls for governments to reduce deficits, stabilize the debt, and reassure investors. At the same time however, the recovery is weak and a fiscal contraction is likely to slow it down further, at least in the short run. Thus, governments face a difficult choice. Reduce deficits rapidly and reassure markets that they will pay their debt at the risk of lower growth or even a recession, or reduce deficits more slowly to avoid further slowing the recovery at the risk of not convincing investors that debt will be stabilized.

The purpose of this chapter is to review what we have learned about fiscal policy so far, to explore in more depth the dynamics of deficits and debt, and to shed light on the problems associated with high public debt.

Section 22-1 takes stock of what we have learned about fiscal policy in this book so far.

Section 22-2 looks more closely at the government budget constraint and examines its implications for the relation between budget deficits, the interest rate, the growth rate, and government debt.

Section 22-3 takes up three issues for which the government budget constraint plays a central role, from the proposition that deficits do not really matter, to how to run fiscal policy in the cycle, to whether to finance wars through taxes or through debt.

Section 22-4 discusses the dangers associated with high government debt, from higher taxes, to higher interest rates, to default, and to high inflation.

22-1 What We Have Learned

Let's review what we have learned so far about fiscal policy:

- In Chapter 3, we looked at how government spending and taxes affected demand and, in turn, output in the short run.

  We saw how, in the short run, a fiscal expansion—increases in government spending, or decreases in taxes—increases output.

- In Chapter 5, we looked at the short-run effects of fiscal policy on output and on the interest rate.

  We saw how a fiscal contraction leads to lower disposable income, which causes people to decrease their consumption. This decrease in demand leads, in turn, through a multiplier, to a decrease in output and income. At a given policy rate, the fiscal contraction leads therefore to a decrease in output. A decrease in the policy rate by the central bank can, however, partially offset the adverse effects of the fiscal contraction.

- In Chapter 6, we saw how fiscal policy was used during the recent crisis to limit the fall in output.

  We saw that when the economy is in a liquidity trap a reduction in the interest rate cannot be used to increase output, and thus fiscal policy has an important role to play. Large increases in spending and cuts in taxes, however, were not enough to avoid the recession.

MyEconLab Video
- In Chapter 9, we looked at the effects of fiscal policy in the short run and in the medium run.

  We saw that, in the medium run (that is, taking the capital stock as given), a fiscal consolidation has no effect on output but is reflected in a different composition of spending. In the short run however, output decreases. In other words, if output was at potential to start with, the fiscal consolidation, as desirable as it may be on other grounds, initially leads to a recession.

- In Chapter 11, we looked at how saving, both private and public, affects the level of capital accumulation and the level of output in the long run.

  We saw how, once capital accumulation is taken into account, a larger budget deficit, and by implication, a lower national saving rate, decreases capital accumulation, leading to a lower level of output in the long run.

- In Chapter 16, we returned to the short-run effects of fiscal policy, taking into account not only fiscal policy's direct effects through taxes and government spending, but also its effects on expectations.

  We saw how the effects of fiscal policy depend on expectations of future fiscal and monetary policy. In particular, we saw how a deficit reduction may, in some circumstances, lead to an increase in output even in the short run, thanks to people's expectations of higher future disposable income.

- In Chapter 18, we looked at the effects of fiscal policy when the economy is open in the goods market.

  We saw how fiscal policy affects both output and the trade balance, and we examined the relation between the budget deficit and the trade deficit.

- In Chapter 19, we looked at the role of fiscal policy in an economy open in both goods markets and financial markets.

  We saw how, when capital is mobile, the effects of fiscal policy depend on the exchange rate regime. Fiscal policy has a stronger effect on output under fixed exchange rates than under flexible exchange rates.

- In Chapter 21, we looked at the problems facing policy makers in general, from uncertainty about the effects of policy to issues of time consistency and credibility. These issues arise in the analysis of fiscal policy as well as monetary policy. We looked at the pros and cons of putting restraints on the conduct of fiscal policy, from spending caps to a constitutional amendment to balance the budget.

In deriving these conclusions, we did not pay close attention to the government budget constraint—that is, the relation among debt, deficits, spending, and taxes. This relation is important, however, in understanding both how we got to where we are today and the choices faced by policy makers. It is the focus of the next section.

22-2 The Government Budget Constraint: Deficits, Debt, Spending, and Taxes

Suppose that, starting from a balanced budget, the government decreases taxes, creating a budget deficit. What will happen to the debt over time? Will the government need to increase taxes later? If so, by how much?

The Arithmetic of Deficits and Debt

To answer these questions, we must begin with a definition of the budget deficit. We can write the budget deficit in year t as:

$$\text{deficit}_t = rB_{t-1} + G_t - T_t \tag{22.1}$$

All variables are in real terms:

- B_{t-1} is government debt at the end of year $t - 1$, or, equivalently, at the beginning of year t; r is the real interest rate, which we shall assume to be constant here. Thus, rB_{t-1} equals the real interest payments on the government debt in year t.
- G_t is government spending on goods and services during year t.
- T_t is taxes minus transfers during year t.

In words: The budget deficit equals spending, including interest payments on the debt, minus taxes net of transfers.

Note two characteristics of equation (22.1):

- We measure interest payments as real interest payments—that is, the product of the *real* interest rate times existing debt—rather than as actual interest payments—that is, the product of the nominal interest rate and the existing debt. When inflation is high, official measures can be seriously misleading. The correct measure of the deficit is sometimes called the **inflation-adjusted deficit**. In this context, the Focus box "Irresistible Growth of Public Spending Worldwide" shows how the concept of fiscal gap aims to measure the difference between the present value of a government's projected financial expenditure and that of all projected future tax and other receipts.
- For consistency with our definition of G as spending on goods and services, G does not include transfer payments. Transfers are instead subtracted from T, so that T stands for *taxes minus transfers*. Official measures of government spending add transfers to spending on goods and services and define revenues as taxes, not taxes net of transfers.

These are only accounting conventions. Whether transfers are added to spending or subtracted from taxes makes a difference to the measurement of G and T, but clearly does not affect $G - T$, and therefore does not affect the measure of the deficit.

The **government budget constraint** then simply states that the *change in government debt during year t* is equal to the deficit during year t:

$$B_t - B_{t-1} = \text{deficit}_t$$

◄ Do not confuse the words *deficit* and *debt*. (Many journalists and politicians do.) Debt is a stock—what the government owes as a result of past deficits. The deficit is a flow—how much the government borrows during a given year.

◄ Transfer payments are government transfers to individuals, such as unemployment benefits or Medicare.

Let G represent spending on goods and services; Tr, transfers; and Tax, total taxes. For simplicity, assume interest payments rB equal zero. Then

$$\text{Deficit} = G + Tr - Tax$$

This can be rewritten in two (equivalent) ways:

$$\text{Deficit} = G - (Tax - Tr)$$

The deficit equals spending on goods and services minus net taxes—that is, taxes minus transfers. This is the way we write it in the text. Or it can be written as:

$$\text{Deficit} = (G + Tr) - Tax$$

Which is the way it is decomposed in official measures (see for example Table A1-4 in Appendix 1 at the end of the book).

Irresistible Growth of Public Spending Worldwide

The role of the State in economies increases everywhere sharply, even in the economies considered the most "liberal" and less "interventionist." The table below shows two major phenomena: a general increase in the share of public spending to GDP in all economies and a trend toward equalization of this share around 45% of GDP—with some special cases such as the France, where the rate is significantly higher.

What are the causes of this expansion? In the classical era, the State was assumed to have a very limited function under the laissez faire policy. The functions of the State were then restricted to justice, police, and army.

Adolf Wagner, a German fiscal theorist of the nineteenth century, propounded this theory according to which there is a persistent tendency towards an increase in the expenses and functions of the State, owing to the "the pressure for social progress" which call for a growing intervention to achieve a better life for the citizens, what has been denominated as the "Welfare State."

Role of war, urbanization, rural development, population, transport and infrastructure lead to a socialization of expenditures. Apart from performing old functions more efficiently and on a larger scale, a modern State constantly undertakes new functions and added responsibilities day by day. It now embraces many new responsibilities such as free education, social housing, social insurance, unemployment relief, and provisions for underprivileged classes.

Two factors account for the projected increases in outlays relative to GDP for the government's finance: the aging of the population and the rapid growth of health care spending per capita. OECD projections show that public spending on health and long-term care is on course to reach almost 9% of GDP in 2030 and as much as 14% of GDP by 2060.

In a study "Fiscal Consolidation: How Much Is needed to Reduce Debt to a Prudent Level" (*OECD Economics Department Policy Notes*, No. 11, April 2012), the OECD stressed on increasing the importance of health and long-term care spending and pension spending.

The question posed is whether this growth, which seems destined to continue, will face a "natural" limit or if it will cause a major disruption in public finances? In response, some economists (Laurence Kotlikoff and Alan Auerbach) propose the concept of "fiscal gap" that aim to measure the difference between the present value of all of government's projected financial expenditure and the present value of all projected future tax and other receipts, the equivalent of a government's total indebtedness. Thus, the fiscal gap is equivalent to the percentage of increase in taxation or reduction of public expenditures necessary to balance the budget in the long run. However, as we have shown in this chapter to really estimate this fiscal gap, it is necessary to forecast at the same time the growth of the economy and the inflation, and the measure of the "fiscal gap" becomes a controversial topic.

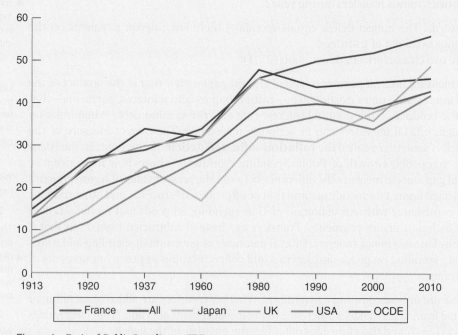

Figure 1   *Ratio of Public Spending to GDP*

Source: Public Spending in the 20th century, V Tanzi, L. Scheknecht.

If the government runs a deficit, government debt increases as the government borrows to fund the part of spending in excess of revenues. If the government runs a surplus, government debt decreases as the government uses the budget surplus to repay part of its outstanding debt.

Using the definition of the deficit (equation (22.1)), we can rewrite the government budget constraint as

$$B_t - B_{t-1} = rB_{t-1} + G_t - T_t \qquad (22.2)$$

The government budget constraint links the change in government debt to the initial level of debt (which affects interest payments) and to current government spending and taxes. It is often convenient to decompose the deficit into the sum of two terms:

■ Interest payments on the debt, rB_{t-1}.
■ The difference between spending and taxes, $G_t - T_t$. This term is called the **primary deficit** (equivalently, $T_t - G_t$ is called the **primary surplus**).

Using this decomposition, we can rewrite equation (22.2) as

$$\underbrace{B_t - B_{t-1}}_{\text{change in the debt}} = \underbrace{rB_{t-1}}_{\text{Interest Payments}} + \underbrace{(G_t - T_t)}_{\text{Primary Deficit}}$$

Or, moving B_{t-1} to the right side of the equation and reorganizing,

$$B_t = (1 + r)B_{t-1} + \underbrace{(G_t - T_t)}_{\text{Primary Deficit}} \qquad (22.3)$$

This relation states that the debt at the end of year t equals $(1 + r)$ times the debt at the end of year $t - 1$ plus the primary deficit during year t, $(G_t - T_t)$. Let's look at some of its implications.

Current versus Future Taxes

Consider first a one-year decrease in taxes for the path of debt and future taxes. Start from a situation where, until year 1, the government has balanced its budget, so that initial debt is equal to zero. During year 1, the government decreases taxes by 1 (think one billion dollars, for example) for one year. Thus, debt at the end of year 1, B_1, is equal to 1. The question we take up: What happens thereafter?

Full Repayment in Year 2
Suppose the government decides to fully repay the debt during year 2. From equation (22.3), the budget constraint for year 2 is given by

$$B_2 = (1 + r)B_1 + (G_2 - T_2)$$

If the debt is fully repaid during year 2, then the debt at the end of year 2 is equal to zero, $B_2 = 0$. Replacing B_1 by 1 and B_2 by 0 and transposing terms gives

$$T_2 - G_2 = (1 + r)1 = (1 + r)$$

To repay the debt fully during year 2, the government must run a primary surplus equal to $(1 + r)$. It can do so in one of two ways: a decrease in spending or an increase in taxes. We shall assume here and in the rest of this section that the adjustment comes through taxes, so that the path of spending is unaffected. It follows that the decrease in taxes by 1 during year 1 must be offset by an increase in taxes by $(1 + r)$ during year 2. ◀

The path of taxes and debt corresponding to this case is given in Figure 22-1 (a): If the debt is fully repaid during year 2, the decrease in taxes of 1 in year 1 requires an increase in taxes equal to $(1 + r)$ in year 2.

Full repayment in year 2:
T_1 decreases by 1 $\Rightarrow$
T_2 increases by $(1 + r)$

Figure 22-1

Tax Cuts, Debt Repayment, and Debt Stabilization

(a), If the debt is fully repaid during year 2, the decrease in taxes of 1 in year 1 requires an increase in taxes equal to $(1 + r)$ in year 2. (b), If the debt is fully repaid during year 5, the decrease in taxes of 1 in year 1 requires an increase in taxes equal to $(1 + r)^4$ during year 5. (c), If the debt is stabilized from year 2 on, then taxes must be permanently higher by r from year 2 on.

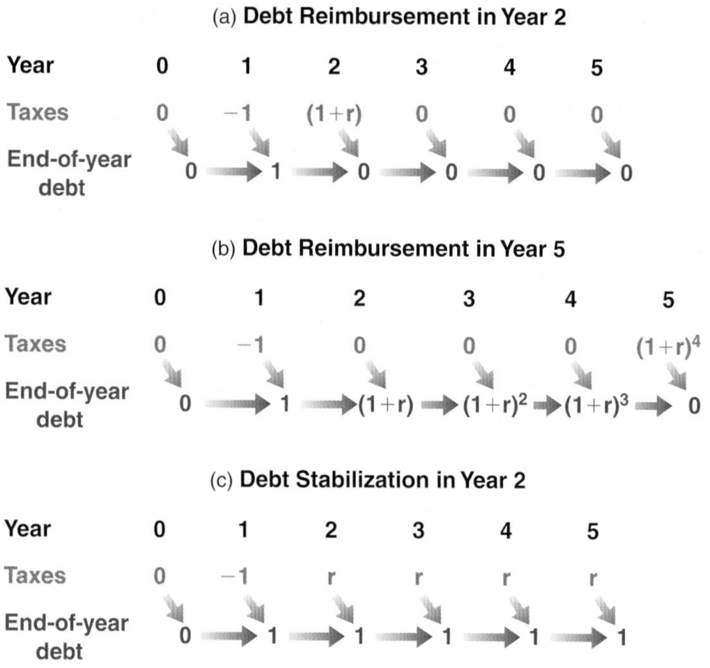

(a) Debt Reimbursement in Year 2

Year	0	1	2	3	4	5
Taxes	0	−1	$(1+r)$	0	0	0
End-of-year debt	0 →	1 →	0 →	0 →	0 →	0

(b) Debt Reimbursement in Year 5

Year	0	1	2	3	4	5
Taxes	0	−1	0	0	0	$(1+r)^4$
End-of-year debt	0 →	1 →	$(1+r)$ →	$(1+r)^2$ →	$(1+r)^3$ →	0

(c) Debt Stabilization in Year 2

Year	0	1	2	3	4	5
Taxes	0	−1	r	r	r	r
End-of-year debt	0 →	1 →	1 →	1 →	1 →	1

Full Repayment in Year t

Now suppose the government decides to wait until year t to repay the debt. From year 2 to year $t - 1$ the primary deficit is equal to zero; taxes are equal to spending, not including interest payments on the debt.

During year 2, the primary deficit is zero. So, from equation (22.3), debt at the end of year 2 is:

$$B_2 = (1 + r)B_1 + 0 = (1 + r)1 = (1 + r)$$

where the second equality uses the fact that $B_1 = 1$.

With the primary deficit still equal to zero during year 3, debt at the end of year 3 is

$$B_3 = (1 + r)B_2 + 0 = (1 + r)(1 + r)1 = (1 + r)^2$$

Solving for debt at the end of year 4 and so on, it is clear that as long as the government keeps a primary deficit equal to zero, debt grows at a rate equal to the interest rate, and thus debt at the end of year $t - 1$ is given by

$$B_{t-1} = (1 + r)^{t-2} \tag{22.4}$$

Despite the fact that taxes are cut only in year 1, debt keeps increasing over time, at a rate equal to the interest rate. The reason is simple; although the primary deficit is equal to zero, debt is now positive, and so are interest payments on it. Each year, the government must issue more debt to pay the interest on existing debt.

In year t, the year in which the government decides to repay the debt, the budget constraint is

$$B_t = (1 + r)B_{t-1} + (G_t - T_t)$$

If debt is fully repaid during year t, then B_t (debt at the end of year t) is zero. Replacing B_t by zero and B_{t-1} by its expression from equation (22.4) gives

$$0 = (1 + r)(1 + r)^{t-2} + (G_t - T_t)$$

Reorganizing and bringing $(G_t - T_t)$ to the left side of the equation implies

$$T_t - G_t = (1 + r)^{t-1}$$

◀ Add exponents: $(1 + r)$ $(1 + r)^{t-2} = (1 + r)^{t-1}$. See Appendix 2 at the end of this book.

To repay the debt, the government must run a primary surplus equal to $(1 + r)^{t-1}$ during year t. If the adjustment is done through taxes, the initial decrease in taxes of 1 during year 1 leads to an increase in taxes of $(1 + r)^{t-1}$ during year t. The path of taxes and debt corresponding to the case where debt is repaid in year 5 is given in Figure 22-1B.

◀ Full repayment in year 5: T_1 decreases by $\Rightarrow$ T_5 increases by $(1 + r)^4$

This example yields our first set of conclusions:

- If government spending is unchanged, a decrease in taxes must eventually be offset by an increase in taxes in the future.
- The longer the government waits to increase taxes, or the higher the real interest rate is, the higher the eventual increase in taxes must be.

Debt Stabilization in Year t

We have assumed so far that the government fully repays the debt. Let's now look at what happens to taxes if the government only stabilizes the debt. (Stabilizing the debt means changing taxes or spending so that debt remains constant from then on.)

Suppose the government decides to stabilize the debt from year 2 on. Stabilizing the debt from year 2 on means the debt at the end of year 2 and thereafter remains at the same level as it was at the end of year 1.

From equation (22.3), the budget constraint for year 2 is

$$B_2 = (1 + r)B_1 + (G_2 - T_2)$$

Under our assumption that debt is stabilized in year 2, $B_2 = B_1 = 1$. Setting $B_2 = B_1 = 1$ in the preceding equation yields

$$1 = (1 + r) + (G_2 - T_2)$$

Reorganizing, and bringing $(G_2 - T_2)$ to the left side of the equation,

$$T_2 - G_2 = (1 + r) - 1 = r$$

To avoid a further increase in debt during year 1, the government must run a primary surplus equal to real interest payments on the existing debt. It must do so in each of the following years as well. Each year, the primary surplus must be sufficient to cover interest payments, leaving the debt level unchanged. The path of taxes and debt is shown in Figure 22-1 C. Debt remains equal to 1 from year 1 on. Taxes are permanently higher from year 1 on, by an amount equal to r; equivalently, from year 1 on, the government runs a primary surplus equal to r.

◀ Stabilizing the debt from year 2 on: T_1 decreases by 1 $\Rightarrow$ $T_2, T_3, \ldots$ increase by r

The logic of this argument extends directly to the case where the government waits until year t to stabilize the debt. Whenever the government stabilizes, it must, each year from then on, run a primary surplus sufficient to pay the interest on the debt.

This example yields our second set of conclusions:

- The legacy of past deficits is higher government debt today.
- To stabilize the debt, the government must eliminate the deficit.
- To eliminate the deficit, the government must run a primary surplus equal to the interest payments on the existing debt. This requires higher taxes forever.

The Evolution of the Debt-to-GDP Ratio

We have focused so far on the evolution of the *level* of debt. But in an economy in which output grows over time, it makes more sense to focus instead on the *ratio of debt to output*.

To see how this change in focus modifies our conclusions, we need to go from equation (22.3) to an equation that gives the evolution of the **debt-to-GDP ratio**—the **debt ratio** for short.

Deriving the evolution of the debt ratio takes a few steps. Do not worry; the final equation is easy to understand.

First divide both sides of equation (22.3) by real output, Y_t, to get

$$\frac{B_t}{Y_t} = (1 + r)\frac{B_{t-1}}{Y_t} + \frac{G_t - T_t}{Y_t}$$

Next rewrite B_{t-1}/Y_t as $(B_{t-1}/Y_{t-1})(Y_{t-1}/Y_t)$ (in other words, multiply the numerator and the denominator by Y_{t-1}):

$$\frac{B_t}{Y_t} = (1 + r)\left(\frac{Y_{t-1}}{Y_t}\right)\frac{B_{t-1}}{Y_{t-1}} + \frac{G_t - T_t}{Y_t}$$

Start from $Y_t = (1 + g)Y_{t-1}$. Divide both sides by Y_t to get $1 = (1 + g)Y_{t-1}/Y_t$. Reorganize to get $Y_{t-1}/Y_t = 1/(1 + g)$. ▶

Note that all the terms in the equation are now in terms of ratios to output, Y. To simplify this equation, assume that output growth is constant and denote the growth rate of output by g, so Y_{t-1}/Y_t can be written as $1/(1 + g)$. And use the approximation $(1 + r)/(1 + g) = 1 + r - g$.

This approximation is derived ▶ as proposition 6 in Appendix 2 at the end of this book.

Using these two assumptions, rewrite the preceding equation as

$$\frac{B_t}{Y_t} = (1 + r - g)\frac{B_{t-1}}{Y_{t-1}} + \frac{G_t - T_t}{Y_t}$$

Finally, reorganize to get

$$\frac{B_t}{Y_t} - \frac{B_{t-1}}{Y_{t-1}} = (r - g)\frac{B_{t-1}}{Y_{t-1}} + \frac{G_t - T_t}{Y_t} \qquad (22.5)$$

This took many steps, but the final relation has a simple interpretation.

The change in the debt ratio over time (the left side of the equation) is equal to the sum of two terms:

■ The first term is the difference between the real interest rate and the growth rate times the initial debt ratio.

■ The second term is the ratio of the primary deficit to GDP.

MyEconLab Video

If two variables (here debt and GDP) grow at rates r and g respectively, then their ratio (here the ratio of debt to GDP) will grow at rate $r - g$. See ▶ proposition 8 in Appendix 2 at the end of this book.

Compare equation (22.5), which gives the evolution of the ratio of debt to GDP, to equation (22.2), which gives the evolution of the level of debt itself. The difference is the presence of $r - g$ in equation (22.5) compared to r in equation (22.2). The reason for the difference is simple. Suppose the primary deficit is zero. Debt will then increase at a rate equal to the real interest rate, r. But if GDP is growing as well, the ratio of debt to GDP will grow more slowly; it will grow at a rate equal to the real interest rate minus the growth rate of output, $r - g$.

Equation (22.5) implies that the increase in the ratio of debt to GDP will be larger:

■ the higher the real interest rate,
■ the lower the growth rate of output,
■ the higher the initial debt ratio,
■ the higher the ratio of the primary deficit to GDP.

Building on this relation, the Focus box "How Countries Decreased Their Debt Ratios after World War II" shows how governments that inherited high debt ratios at the end of the war steadily decreased them through a combination of low real interest rates, high growth rates, and primary surpluses. The next section shows how our analysis can also be used to shed light on a number of other fiscal policy issues.

How Countries Decreased Their Debt Ratios after World War II

After World War II, many countries had high debt ratios, often in excess of 100% of GDP. Yet, two or three decades later, the debt ratios were much lower, often below 50%. How did they do it? The answer is given in Table 1.

Table 1 looks at four countries: Australia, Canada, New Zealand, and the United Kingdom. Column 1 gives the period during which debt ratios decreased. The first year is either 1945 or 1946. The last year is the year in which the debt ratio reached its lowest point; the period of adjustment varies from 13 years in Canada to 30 years in the United Kingdom. Column 2 gives debt ratios at the start and at the end of the period. The most striking numbers here are those for the United Kingdom: an initial debt ratio of 270% of GDP in 1946 and an impressive decline, down to 47% in 1974.

To interpret the numbers in the table, go back to equation (22.5). It tells us that there are two, not mutually exclusive, ways in which a country can reduce its debt ratio. The first is through high primary surpluses. Suppose, for example, that $(r - g)$ was equal to 0. Then the decrease in the debt ratio over some period would just be the sum of the ratios of primary surpluses to GDP over the period. The second is through a low $(r - g)$, so either through low real interest rates or through high growth, or both.

With this in mind, columns 3 to 5 give first the average ratio of the primary balance to GDP, then the average growth rate of GDP and the average real interest rate, over the relevant period.

Look first at primary balances in column 3. Note how all four countries indeed ran primary surpluses on average over the period. But note also that these primary surpluses account only for a small part of the decline in the debt ratio. Look, for example, at the United Kingdom. The sum of the ratios of the primary surpluses to GDP over the period is equal to 2.1% multiplied by 30 = 63% of GDP, so accounting for less than a third of the decline in the debt ratio, 223% $(270\% - 47\%)$ of GDP.

Now look at the growth rates and the real interest rates in columns 4 and 5. Note how high growth rates and how low real interest rates were during the period. Take Australia, for example. The average value of $(r - g)$ during the period was $-6.9\% (-2.3\% - 4.6\%)$. This implies that, even if the primary balance had been equal to zero, the debt ratio would have declined each year by 6.9%. In other words, the decline in debt was not mainly the result of primary surpluses, but the result of sustained high growth and sustained negative real interest rates.

This leads to a final question: Why were real interest rates so low? The answer is given in column 6. During the period, average inflation was relatively high. This inflation, combined with consistently low nominal interest rates, is what accounts for the negative real interest rates. Put another way, a large part of the decrease in debt ratios was achieved by paying bond holders a negative real return on their bonds for many years.

Table 1	Changes in Debt Ratios Following World War II					
	1	2	3	4	5	6
Country	Start/End Year	Start/End Debt Ratio	Primary Balance	Growth Rate	Real Interest Rate	Inflation Rate
Australia	1946 – 1963	92 – 29	1.1	4.6	− 2.3	5.7
Canada	1945 – 1957	115 – 59	3.6	4.3	− 1.4	4.0
New Zealand	1946 – 1974	148 – 41	2.3	3.9	− 2.9	4.9
United Kingdom	1946 – 1975	270 – 47	2.1	2.6	− 1.5	5.5

Columns 2 and 3: Percent of GDP. Columns 4 to 6: Percent.

Source: S. M. A. Abbas et al., "Historical Patterns and Dynamics of Public Debt: Evidence from a New Database," *IMF Economic Review*, 2011, 59 (November): pp. 717–742.

22-3 Ricardian Equivalence, Cyclical Adjusted Deficits, and War Finance

Having looked at the mechanics of the government budget constraint, we can now take up three issues in which this constraint plays a central role.

Ricardian Equivalence

How does taking into account the government budget constraint affect the way we should think of the effects of deficits on output?

One extreme view is that once the government budget constraint is taken into account, neither deficits nor debt have an effect on economic activity! This argument is known as the **Ricardian equivalence** proposition. David Ricardo, a 19th-century English economist, was the first to articulate its logic. His argument was further developed and given prominence in the 1970s by Robert Barro, then at Chicago, now at Harvard University. For this reason, the argument is also known as the **Ricardo-Barro proposition**.

Although Ricardo stated the logic of the argument, he also argued there were many reasons why it would not hold in practice. In contrast, Barro argued that not only the argument was logically correct, but it was also a good description of reality.

The best way to understand the logic of the proposition is to use the example of tax changes from Section 22-2:

- Suppose that the government decreases taxes by 1 (again, think one billion dollars) this year. And as it does so, it announces that, to repay the debt, it will increase taxes by $(1 + r)$ next year. What will be the effect of the initial tax cut on consumption?

See Chapter 15 for a definition of human wealth and a discussion of its role in consumption.

- One possible answer is: No effect at all. Why? Because consumers realize that the tax cut is not much of a gift. Lower taxes this year are exactly offset, in present value, by higher taxes next year. Put another way, their human wealth—the present value of after-tax labor income—is unaffected. Current taxes go down by 1, but the present value of next year's taxes goes up by $(1 + r)/(1 + r) = 1$, and the net effect of the two changes is exactly equal to zero.

Go back to the *IS-LM* model. What is the multiplier associated with a decrease in current taxes in this case?

- Another way of coming to the same answer—this time looking at saving rather than looking at consumption—is as follows: To say that consumers do not change their consumption in response to the tax cut is the same as saying that *private saving increases one-for-one with the deficit*. So the Ricardian equivalence proposition says that if a government finances a given path of spending through deficits, private saving will increase one-for-one with the decrease in public saving, leaving total saving unchanged. The total amount left for investment will not be affected. Over time, the mechanics of the government budget constraint imply that government debt will increase. But this increase will not come at the expense of capital accumulation.

Under the Ricardian equivalence proposition, a long sequence of deficits and the associated increase in government debt are no cause for worry. As the government is dissaving, the argument goes, people are saving more in anticipation of the higher taxes to come. The decrease in public saving is offset by an equal increase in private saving. Total saving is therefore unaffected, and so is investment. The economy has the same capital stock today that it would have had if there had been no increase in debt. High debt is no cause for concern.

How seriously should we take the Ricardian equivalence proposition? Most economists would answer: "Seriously, but surely not seriously enough to think that deficits and debt are irrelevant." A major theme of this book has been that expectations matter, that consumption decisions depend not only on current income but also on future income. If it were widely believed that a tax cut this year is going to be followed by an offsetting increase in taxes *next year*, the effect on consumption would indeed probably be small. Many consumers would save most or all of the tax cut in anticipation of higher taxes next year. (Replace *year* by *month* or *week* and the argument becomes even more convincing.)

Of course, tax cuts rarely come with the announcement of corresponding tax increases a year later. Consumers have to guess when and how taxes will eventually be increased. This fact does not by itself invalidate the Ricardian equivalence argument. No matter when taxes will be increased, the government budget constraint still implies that the present value of future tax increases must always be equal to the decrease in taxes today. Take the second example we looked at in Section 22-2—drawn ◀ in Figure 22-1(b) in which the government waits t years to increase taxes, and so increases taxes by $(1 + r)^{t-1}$. The present value in year 0 of this expected tax increase is $(1 + r)^{t-1}/(1 + r)^{t-1} = 1$—exactly equal to the original tax cut. The change in ◀ human wealth from the tax cut is still zero.

But insofar as future tax increases appear more distant and their timing more uncertain, consumers are in fact more likely to ignore them. This may be the case because they expect to die before taxes go up, or more likely, because they just do not think that far into the future. In either case, Ricardian equivalence is likely to fail.

So, it is safe to conclude that budget deficits have an important effect on activity, although perhaps a smaller effect than you thought before going through the Ricardian equivalence argument. In the short run, larger deficits are likely to lead to higher demand and to higher output. In the long run, higher government debt lowers capital accumulation and, as a result, lowers output.

Recall that this assumes that government spending is unchanged. If people expect government spending to be decreased in the future, what will they do?

The increase in taxes in t years is $(1 + r)^{t-1}$. The discount factor for a dollar t years from now is $1/(1 + r)^{t-1}$. So the value of the increase in taxes t years from now as of today is $(1 + r)^{t-1}/(1 + r)^{t-1} = 1$.

Deficits, Output Stabilization, and the Cyclically Adjusted Deficit

The fact that budget deficits do, indeed, have long-run adverse effects on capital accumulation, and in turn, on output, does not imply that fiscal policy should not be used to reduce output fluctuations. Rather, it implies that deficits during recessions should be ◀ offset by surpluses during booms, so as not to lead to a steady increase in debt.

To help assess whether fiscal policy is on track, economists have constructed deficit measures that tell them what the deficit would be, under existing tax and spending rules, if output were at the potential level of output. Such measures come under many names, ranging from the **full-employment deficit**, to the **mid-cycle deficit**, to the **standardized employment deficit**, to the **structural deficit** (the term used by the OECD). We shall use **cyclically adjusted deficit**, the term we find the most intuitive.

Such a measure gives a simple benchmark against which to judge the direction of fiscal policy. If the actual deficit is large but the cyclically adjusted deficit is zero, then current fiscal policy is consistent with no systematic increase in debt over time. The debt will increase as long as output is below the potential level of output; but as output returns to potential, the deficit will disappear and the debt will stabilize.

It does not follow that the goal of fiscal policy should be to maintain a cyclically adjusted deficit equal to zero at all times. In a recession, the government may want to run a deficit large enough that even the cyclically adjusted deficit is positive. In this case, the fact that the cyclically adjusted deficit is positive provides a useful warning. The warning is that the return of output to potential will not be enough to stabilize the debt. The government will have to take specific measures, from tax increases to cuts in spending, to decrease the deficit at some point in the future.

The theory underlying the concept of cyclically adjusted deficit is simple. The practice of it has proven tricky. To see why, we need to look at how measures of the cyclically

MyEconLab Video

Note the analogy with monetary policy: The fact that higher money growth leads in the long run to more inflation does not imply that monetary policy should not be used for output stabilization. We ignore output growth in this section, and so ignore the distinction between stabilizing the debt and stabilizing the debt-to-GDP ratio. (Verify that the argument extends to the case where output is growing.)

adjusted deficit are constructed. Construction requires two steps: First, establish how much lower the deficit would be if output were, say, 1% higher. Second, assess how far output is from potential.

- The first step is straightforward. A reliable rule of thumb is that a 1% decrease in output leads automatically to an increase in the deficit of about 0.5% of GDP. This increase occurs because most taxes are proportional to output, whereas most government spending does not depend on the level of output. That means a decrease in output, which leads to a decrease in revenues and not much change in spending, naturally leads to a larger deficit.

  If output is, say, 5% below potential, the deficit as a ratio to GDP will therefore be about 2.5% larger than it would be if output were at potential. (This effect of activity on the deficit has been called an **automatic stabilizer**. A recession naturally generates a deficit, and therefore a fiscal expansion, which partly counteracts the recession.)

- The second step is more difficult. Recall from Chapter 7 that potential output is the output level that would be produced if the economy were operating at the natural rate of unemployment. Too low an estimate of the natural rate of unemployment will lead to too high an estimate of potential output and therefore to too optimistic a measure of the cyclically adjusted deficit.

This difficulty explains in part what happened in Europe in the 1980s. Based on the assumption of an unchanged natural unemployment rate, the cyclically adjusted deficits of the 1980s did not look that bad. If European unemployment had returned to its level of the 1970s, the associated increase in output would have been sufficient to reestablish budget balance in most countries. But it turned out, much of the increase in unemployment reflected an increase in the natural unemployment rate, and unemployment remained high during the 1980s. As a result, the decade was characterized by high deficits and large increases in debt ratios in most countries.

Wars and Deficits

Wars typically bring about large budget deficits. As we saw in Chapter 21, the two largest increases in U.S. government debt in the 20th century took place during World War I and World War II. We examine the case of World War II further in the Focus box "Deficits, Consumption, and Investment in the United States during World War II."

Look at the two peaks associated with World War I and World War II in Figure 21-4.

Is it right for governments to rely so much on deficits to finance wars? After all, war economies are usually operating at low unemployment, so the output stabilization reasons for running deficits we just examined are irrelevant. The answer, nevertheless, is yes. In fact, there are two good reasons to run deficits during wars:

- The first is distributional. Deficit finance is a way to pass some of the burden of the war to those alive after the war because they will pay higher taxes once the war is over. It seems only fair for future generations to share in the sacrifices the war requires.
- The second is more narrowly economic. Deficit spending helps reduce tax distortions. Let's look at each reason in turn:

Passing on the Burden of the War

Wars lead to large increases in government spending. Consider the implications of financing this increased spending either through increased taxes or through debt. To distinguish this case from our previous discussion of output stabilization, let's also assume that output is and remains at its potential level.

Deficits, Consumption, and Investment in the United States during World War II

In 1939, the share of U.S. government spending on goods and services in GDP was 15%. By 1944, it had increased to 45%! The increase was due to increased spending on national defense, which went from 1% of GDP in 1939 to 36% in 1944.

Faced with such a massive increase in spending, the U.S. government reacted with large tax increases. For the first time in U.S. history, the individual income tax became a major source of revenues; individual income tax revenues, which were 1% of GDP in 1939, increased to 8.5% in 1944. But the tax increases were still far less than the increase in government expenditures. The increase in federal revenues, from 7.2% of GDP in 1939 to 22.7% in 1944, was only a little more than half the increase in expenditures.

The result was a sequence of large budget deficits. By 1944, the federal deficit reached 22% of GDP. The ratio of debt to GDP, already high at 53% in 1939 because of the deficits the government had run during the Great Depression, reached 110%!

Was the increase in government spending achieved at the expense of consumption or private investment? (As we saw in Chapter 18, it could in principle have come from higher imports and a current account deficit. But the United States had nobody to borrow from during the war. Rather, it was lending to some of its allies. Transfers from the U.S. government to foreign countries were equal to 6% of U.S. GDP in 1944.)

■ It was met in large part by a decrease in consumption. The share of consumption in GDP fell by 23 percentage points, from 74% to 51%. Part of the decrease in consumption may have been due to anticipations of higher taxes after the war; part of it was due to the unavailability of many consumer durables. Patriotism also probably motivated people to save more and buy the war bonds issued by the government to finance the war.

■ It was also met by a 6% decrease in the share of (private) investment in GDP—from 10% to 4%. Part of the burden of the war was therefore passed on in the form of lower capital accumulation to those living after the war.

■ Suppose that the government relies on deficit finance. With government spending sharply up, there will be a large increase in the demand for goods. Given our assumption that output stays the same, the interest rate will have to increase enough so as to maintain equilibrium. Investment, which depends on the interest rate, will decrease sharply.

■ Suppose instead that the government finances the spending increase through an increase in taxes—say income taxes. Consumption will decline sharply. Exactly how much depends on consumers' expectations. The longer they expect the war to last, then the longer they will expect higher taxes to last, and the more they will decrease their consumption. In any case, the increase in government spending will be partly offset by a decrease in consumption. Interest rates will increase by less than they would have increased under deficit spending, and investment will therefore decrease by less.

In short, for a given output, the increase in government spending requires either a decrease in consumption or a decrease in investment. Whether the government relies on tax increases or deficits determines whether consumption or investment does more of the adjustment when government spending increases.

How does this affect who bears the burden of the war? The more the government relies on deficits, the smaller the decrease in consumption during the war and the larger the decrease in investment. Lower investment means a lower capital stock after the war, and therefore lower output after the war. By reducing capital accumulation, deficits become a way of passing some of the burden of the war onto future generations.

> Assume that the economy is closed, so that $Y = C + I + G$. Suppose that G goes up, and Y remains the same. Then, $C + I$ must decrease. If taxes are not increased, most of the decrease will come from a decrease in I. If taxes are increased, most of the decrease will come from a decrease in C.

Reducing Tax Distortions

There is another argument for running deficits, not only during wars but also, more generally, in times when government spending is exceptionally high. Think, for example, of reconstruction after an earthquake or the costs involved in the reunification of Germany in the early 1990s.

The argument is as follows: If the government were to increase taxes to finance the temporary increase in spending, tax rates would have to be very high. Very high tax rates can lead to very high economic distortions. Faced with very high income tax rates, people work less or engage in illegal, untaxed activities. Rather than moving the tax rate up and down so as to always balance the budget, it is better (from the point of view of reducing distortions) to maintain a relatively constant tax rate—to *smooth taxes*. **Tax smoothing** implies running large deficits when government spending is exceptionally high, and small surpluses the rest of the time.

22-4 The Dangers of High Debt

We have seen how high debt requires higher taxes in the future. A lesson from history is that high debt can also lead to vicious cycles, making the conduct of fiscal policy extremely difficult. Let's look at this more closely.

High Debt, Default Risk, and Vicious Cycles

Return to equation (22.5):

$$\frac{B_t}{Y_t} - \frac{B_{t-1}}{Y_{t-1}} = (r - g)\frac{B_{t-1}}{Y_{t-1}} + \frac{(G_t - T_t)}{Y_t}$$

Take a country with a high debt ratio, say, 100%. Suppose the real interest rate is 3% and the growth rate is 2%. The first term on the right is $(3\% - 2\%)$ times $100\% = 1\%$ of GDP. Suppose further that the government is running a primary surplus of 1% of output, so just enough to keep the debt ratio constant (the right side of the equation equals $(3\% - 2\%)$ times $100\% + (-1\%) = 0\%$).

Now suppose financial investors start to worry that the government may not be able to fully repay the debt. They ask for a higher interest rate to compensate for what they perceive as a higher risk of default on the debt. But this in turn makes it more difficult for the government to stabilize the debt. Suppose, for example, that the interest rate increases from 3% to, say, 8%. Then, just to stabilize the debt, the government now needs to run a primary surplus of 6% of output (the right side of the equation is then equal to $(8\% - 2\%) \times 100 + (-6) = 0$). Suppose that, in response to the increase in the interest rate, the government indeed takes measures to increase the primary surplus to 6% of output. The spending cuts or tax increases that are needed are likely to prove politically costly, potentially generating more political uncertainty, a higher risk of default, and thus a further increase in the interest rate. Also, the sharp fiscal contraction is likely to lead to a recession, decreasing the growth rate. Both the increase in the real interest rate and the decrease in growth further increase $(r - g)$, requiring an even larger budget surplus to stabilize the debt. At some point, the government may become unable to increase the primary surplus sufficiently, and the debt ratio starts increasing, leading investors to become even more worried and to require an even higher interest rate. Increases in the interest rate and increases in the debt ratio feed on each other. In short, the higher the ratio of debt to GDP, the larger the potential for catastrophic debt dynamics. Even if the fear that the government may not fully repay the debt was initially unfounded, it can easily become self-fulfilling. The higher interest that the government must pay on its debt can lead the government to lose control of its budget and lead to an increase in debt to a level such that the government is unable to repay the debt, thus validating the initial fears.

This is far from an abstract issue. Let's look again at what happened in the Euro area during the crisis. Figure 22-2 shows the evolution of interest rates on Italian and

This should remind you of bank runs and the discussion in Chapter 6. If people believe a bank is not solvent and decide to withdraw their funds, the bank may have to sell its assets at fire sale prices and become insolvent, validating the initial fears. Here, investors ▶ do not ask for their funds, but for a higher interest rate. The result is the same.

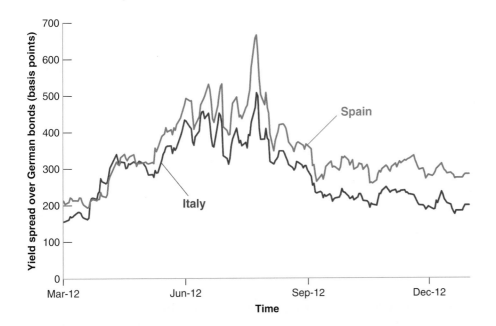

Figure 22-2

The Increase in European Bond Spreads

The spreads on Italian and Spanish two-year government bonds over German two-year bonds increased sharply between March and July 2012. At the end of July, when the European Central Bank stated that it would do whatever was necessary to prevent a breakup of the Euro, the spreads decreased.

Source: Haver Analytics.

Spanish government bonds from March to December 2012. For each country, it plots the difference, also called the **spread**, between the two-year interest rate on the country's government bonds and the two-year interest rate on German government bonds. The reason for comparing interest rates to German interest rates is that German bonds are considered nearly riskless. The spreads are measured, on the vertical axis, in **basis points** (a basis point is a hundredth of a percent).

Both spreads started rising in March 2012. Toward the end of July, the spread on Italian bonds reached 500 basis points (equivalently, 5%), the spread on Spanish bonds 660 basis points (6%). These spreads reflected two worries, first that the Italian and the Spanish governments may default on their debt, and second, that they may devalue. In principle in a monetary union, such as the Euro area, no one should expect a devaluation, unless markets start thinking that the monetary union might break up and that countries might reintroduce national currencies at a devalued exchange rate. This is exactly what happened in the spring and summer of 2012. We can understand why by going back to our discussion of self-fulfilling debt crises earlier in this paragraph. Consider Italy, for instance. In March, the interest on Italian two-year bonds was below 3%; this was the sum of the interest on German two-year bonds, slightly below 1%, plus a 2% risk spread due to investors' concerns about the Italian government's creditworthiness. The country had at the time (and still has) a debt-to-GDP ratio above 130%. With interest below 3% such a high debt burden was sustainable; Italy was generating primary budget surpluses sufficient to keep the debt stable, although at that high level. Italy was fragile (because the debt was so high) but in a "good equilibrium." At this point investors started asking themselves what would happen if, for some reason, interest rates on Italian bonds were to double, reaching 6%. They concluded that if that happened, it was unlikely that Italy would be able raise its primary surplus high enough to keep the debt stable. It was more likely that the country would enter a debt spiral and end up defaulting. At that point Italy might decide to abandon the monetary union and rely on a devaluation to improve its competitiveness and support growth because defaults are usually accompanied by sharp recessions. The fear that this might happen shifted Italy from a "good" to a "bad" equilibrium. As investors recognized that a default and an exit from the euro were a possibility, interest rates jumped to 6% and this increase in interest rates validated the

Go back to Section 20-2 for a discussion of how, under fixed exchange rates, the expectation of a devaluation leads to high interest rates.

By this statement, Mario Draghi meant that the ECB would be ready to buy Spanish or Italian bonds so as to maintain a low yield and go back to the "good equilibrium." In this event, the commitment was enough to decrease rates, and the ECB did not have to intervene if at all.

initial fears. Eventually, it was the European Central Bank (ECB) that shifted Italy back the good equilibrium. On July 26, 2012, the president of the bank, Mario Draghi, clearly said that a break-up of the euro was out of question and that the ECB would do whatever was necessary to avoid it. Investors believed the promise and Italy shifted back to the good equilibrium.

Thus, Italy and Spain succeeded, with the help of the ECB, in avoiding bad debt dynamics and default. What if a government does not succeed in stabilizing the debt and enters a debt spiral? Then, historically, one of two things happens: Either the government explicitly defaults on its debt, or the government relies increasingly on money finance. Let's look at each outcome in turn.

Debt Default

At some point, when a government finds itself unable to repay the outstanding debt, it may decide to default. Default is often partial, however, and creditors take what is known as a **haircut**. A haircut of 30%, for example, means that creditors receive only 70% of what they were owed. Default also comes under many names, many of them euphemisms—probably to make the prospects more appealing (or less unappealing) to creditors. It is called **debt restructuring**, or **debt rescheduling** (when interest payments are deferred rather than cancelled), or, quite ironically, **private sector involvement** (the private sector, that is, the creditors, are asked to *get involved*, i.e. to accept a haircut). It may be unilaterally imposed by the government, or it may be the result of a negotiation with creditors. Creditors, knowing that they will not be fully repaid in any case, may prefer to work out a deal with the government. This is what happened to Greece in 2012 when private creditors accepted a haircut of roughly 50%.

MyEconLab Video

When debt is very high, default would seem to be an appealing solution. Having a lower level of debt after default reduces the size of the required fiscal consolidation and thus makes it more credible. It lowers required taxes, potentially allowing for higher growth. But default comes with high costs. If debt is held, for example, by pension funds, as it is often the case, the retirees may suffer very much from the default. If it is held by banks, then some banks may go bankrupt, with major adverse effects on the economy. If debt is held instead mostly by foreigners, then the country's international reputation may be lost, and it may be difficult for the government to borrow from abroad for a long time. So, in general, and rightly so, governments are very reluctant to default on their debt.

Money Finance

For a refresher on how the central bank creates money, go back to Chapter 4, Section 4-3.

The other outcome is money finance. So far we have assumed that the only way a government could finance itself was by selling bonds. There is however another possibility. The government can finance itself by, in effect, printing money. The way it does this is not actually by printing money itself, but by issuing bonds, and then forcing the central bank to buy its bonds in exchange for money. This process is called **money finance** or **debt monetization**. Because, in this case, the rate of money creation is determined by the government deficit rather than by decisions of the central bank, this is also known as **fiscal dominance** of monetary policy.

The word seignorage is revealing. The right to issue money was a precious source of revenue for the *seigneurs* of the past. They could buy the goods they wanted by issuing their own money and using it to pay for the goods.

How large a deficit can a government finance through such money creation? Let H be the amount of central bank money in the economy. (I shall refer to *central bank money* simply as *money* for short in what follows.) Let ΔH be money creation; that is, the change in the nominal money stock from one month to the next. The revenue, in real terms (that is, in terms of goods), that the government generates by creating an amount of money equal to ΔH is therefore $\Delta H/P$—money creation during the period divided by the price level. This revenue from money creation is called **seignorage**.

$$\text{seignorage} = \frac{\Delta H}{P}$$

Seignorage is equal to money creation divided by the price level. To see what rate of (central bank) nominal money growth is required to generate a given amount of seignorage, rewrite $\Delta H/P$ as

$$\frac{\Delta H}{P} = \frac{\Delta H}{H}\frac{H}{P}$$

In words: We can think of seignorage $(\Delta H/P)$ as the product of the rate of nominal money growth $(\Delta H/H)$ and the real money stock (H/P). Replacing this expression in the previous equation gives

$$\text{seignorage} = \frac{\Delta H}{H}\frac{H}{P}$$

This gives us a relation between seignorage, the rate of nominal money growth, and real money balances. To think about relevant magnitudes, it is convenient to take one more step and divide both sides of the equation by, say, monthly GDP, Y, to get

$$\frac{\text{seignorage}}{Y} = \frac{\Delta H}{H}\left(\frac{H/P}{Y}\right) \qquad (22.6)$$

Suppose the government is running a budget deficit equal to 10% of GDP and decides to finance it through seignorage, so $(\text{deficit}/Y) = (\text{seignorage}/Y) = 10\%$. The average ratio of central bank money to monthly GDP in advanced countries is roughly equal to 1, so choose $(H/P)/Y = 1$. This implies that nominal money growth must satisfy

$$10\% = \frac{\Delta H}{H}\text{ times }1 \Rightarrow \frac{\Delta H}{H} = 10\%$$

Thus, to finance a deficit of 10% of GDP through seignorage, given a ratio of central bank money to monthly GDP of 1, the monthly growth rate of nominal money must be equal to 10%.

This is surely a high rate of money growth, but one might conclude that, in exceptional circumstances, this may be an acceptable price to pay to finance the deficit. Unfortunately, this conclusion could be wrong. As money growth increases, inflation typically follows. And high inflation leads people to want to reduce their demand for money, and in turn the demand for central bank money. In other words, as the rate of money growth increases, the real money balances that people want to hold decreases. If, for example, they were willing to hold money balances equal to one month of income when inflation was low, they may decide to reduce it to one week of income or less when inflation reaches 10%. In terms of equation (22.6), as $(\Delta H/H)$ increases, $(H/P)/Y$ decreases. And so, to achieve the same level of revenues, the government needs to increase ◀ the rate of money growth further. But higher money growth leads to further inflation, a further decrease in $(H/P)/Y$ and the need for further money growth. Soon, high inflation turns into **hyperinflation**, the term that economists use for very high inflation—typically inflation in excess of 30% per month. The Focus box on page 490 "Rules versus Discretion: New Absolute Budgetary Rules in the EU" describes some of the most famous episodes. Hyperinflation only ends when fiscal policy is dramatically improved, and the deficit is eliminated. By then, damage has been done.

This is an example of a general proposition. As you increase the tax rate (here the rate of inflation), the tax base (here real money balances) decreases.

Today, debt is indeed high in many advanced economies, often in excess of 100% of GDP. So what should governments do? The answer is that there is no easy solution. In

Rules versus Discretion: New Absolute Budgetary Rules in the EU

The deterioration in the public finances in Europe led to a strengthening of the fiscal discipline in European Union (EU) through the Stability and Growth Pact (SGP) negotiated after the Greek episode, which was enforced from January 2013. The Pact implements a set of very precise rules in term of objectives, surveillance and assessment. This strengthening is considered as the "price to pay" to ensure the solidity of a union composed of so diverse countries but also the mean to avoid that the rules applied differently in consideration of the economic or political influence of certain countries. As in internal order, the law must be the same for all, and for that they have to be precise and accurate. This updated rules combined a "preventive arm" and a "corrective arm."

The preventive arm set a framework of rules. First, member states are required by the Treaty to keep their general government deficit and debt positions not above the reference values of 3% and 60% of GDP respectively, and to prompt their correction if these two criteria are temporarily not fulfilled. Second they are required to achieve and maintain their medium-term budgetary objective (MTO), which corresponds to a cyclically-adjusted target for the budget balance, to 0.5% of GDP. However, a temporary deviation from these targets could be accepted under exceptional circumstances, which are defined as "major unusual event outside the control" of the government augmented by a "severe economic downturn for the euro area or the European Union as a whole." (Source: Report on public finance in EMU).

On the "corrective arm" side the Treaty set effective enforcement provisions if a country fails to take action to correct its situation and sanctioned it with a penalizing deposit of 0.2% of GDP, which can be transformed in a simple fine if the country persists not to follow the recommendations of the European Commission (EC).

The European Treaty implements an Excessive Deficit Procedure (EDP) to follow-up closely the situation of each country and to formulate the measures to correct the excessive deficit and debt positions (in 2015 nine Member States are examined under EDP).

As these rule become very tight, and taking in account the lessons of the past, the EC fix precise guidance to limit "the margin of interpretation which is left to the Commission, in line with the rules of the Pact." In its communication released on January 2015, the EC shared threefold approach: the understanding of the structural reform, the way to consider the cyclical conditions, and what could constitute exceptional circumstances and the corresponding recommendations.

For the structural reform the EC will take them in account provided "that such reforms (i) are major, (ii) have verifiable direct long-term positive budgetary effects (*It quotes for example pension, healthcare*), including by raising potential sustainable growth (*lower structural unemployment for example*), and (iii) are fully implemented."

In order to assess the appropriate adjustment path for each member state towards its respective MTO, the Pact requires that due consideration be given to the economic situation as well as the sustainability conditions. In principle, member states not having yet reached their MTO are required, as a benchmark, to pursue an annual improvement in the structural budget balance of 0.5% of GDP. The rules also provide that the Commission needs to take into account whether a higher adjustment effort is made in good economic times, whereas effort may be more limited in bad times. Thus, the EC has designed a matrix, as shown in Table 1, which clarifies and specifies the fiscal adjustment requirements under the preventive arm of the Pact.

Table 1 Matrix for Specifying the Annual Fiscal Adjustment towards the Medium-Term Objective (MTO) under the Preventive Arm of the Pact

	Condition	Required Annual Fiscal Adjustment*	
		Debt below 60% and no sustainability risk	Debt above 60% or sustainability risk
Extremely bad times	Real growth < 0 or output gap < −4	No adjustment needed	
Very bad times	−4 ≤ output gap < −3	0	0.25
Bad times	−3 ≤ output gap < −1.5	0 if growth below potential, 0.25 if growth above potential	0.25 if growth below potential, 0.5 if growth above potential
Normal times	−1.5 ≤ output gap < 1.5	0.5	>0.5
Good times	Output gap ≥ 1.5%	>0.5 if growth below potential, ≥0.75 if growth above potential	≥0.75 if growth below potential, ≥1 if growth above potential

*All figures are in percentage points of GDP

Source: European Commission, "Making the Best Use of the Flexibility within the Existing Rules of the Stability and Growth Pact," COM(2015) 12 final provisional, January 2015.

some cases, as for example in Greece, it is clear that debt is unsustainable, and thus debt restructuring in one form or another is needed. In other cases, debt is probably sustainable, but the dangers we just described are there. Should governments generate large primary surpluses to rapidly reduce it? We discussed the dangers of such a policy previously. A large increase in the primary surplus at a time when the policy rate is at the zero lower bound and monetary policy cannot offset the adverse effects of fiscal consolidation, is dangerous and likely to be self-defeating. It is indeed now widely accepted that the strong fiscal consolidation which took place in Europe from 2011 on, known as **fiscal austerity**, was excessive, particularly because it was mainly implemented by raising taxes. There is a large consensus today that debt should be stabilized, but that substantial fiscal consolidation should wait until interest rates are again positive, and monetary policy has enough room to decrease them to offset the adverse effects of consolidation. The path for fiscal policy in Europe is a narrow one, with too much fiscal consolidation potentially triggering another recession, and too little leading to explosive debt dynamics. In any case, the adjustment to lower debt is likely to take a long time. (The Focus box "How Japan Could Stand Such a Huge Debt?" shows how the country faced high debts and adopted a new economic policy to adjust the impact.)

See the discussion of fiscal policy at the zero lower bound, in Chapter 9, Section 9-3.

By the end of its wars against Napoleon in the early 1800s, England had run up a debt ratio in excess of 200% of GDP. It spent most of the 19th century reducing the ratio. By 1900 the ratio stood at only 30% of GDP.

How Japan Could Stand Such a Huge Debt?

Gross public debt of Japan has risen from 70% of GDP in 1992, to 230% of GDP in 2015, the most important by far of the OECD countries. The main reasons of this exceptional increase are of threefold:

- First, the increasing gap between expenditures pushed by rapid population ageing (social security outlays, including cash transfers and in-kind benefits, expand by 10.4 percentage points of GDP between 1992 and 2010) and a decrease in tax revenue (−1.7 percentage points of GDP between 1992 and 2010, primarily due to the fall in taxes on personal and corporate income from 12% of GDP to 8%) – although

the ratio of taxes on GDP is already one of the lowest of OECD: 28.6% of GDP compared to 34.1% on OECD average in 2011.

- Second, the slow economic growth, as its rate has stayed at less than 1% since 1995 – "compensated" on the social ground by the fact that the unemployment rate stay at a low level, around 4%, because of the structure of the population and the behavior of the firms.
- Third, the persistent deflation (consumer price index is negative almost every year since 2000) which doesn't alleviate the debt but let the Bank of Japan monetize part of the debt without causing any drawback.

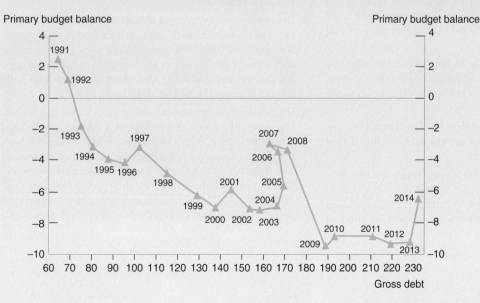

Figure 1

Source: Jones, R. S. and S. Urasawa (2013), "Restoring Japan's Fiscal Sustainability," OECD Economics Department Working Papers, No. 1050, OECD Publishing.

Japan also faces the cost of some catastrophes which represent high public expenditures (more than 5% of GDP according to OECD)

How is it bearable? The factor most frequently quoted is that most of the debt is financed from domestic sources. Direct holdings of government securities by households remained relatively low, but household savings in the form of bank and postal deposits, insurance policies, and pension funds were funneled into government securities through government financial institutions, private banks, and insurance companies. According to OECD, at the end of the third quarter of 2012, about 40% of government bonds were held by Japanese commercial banks, about 10% by the Bank of Japan, about 30% by Japanese insurance and pension funds (including the national pension fund) and about 3% directly by Japanese households.

The main consequence of that is that the rate of interest, corresponding to the risk premium, is very low in Japan: the effective borrowing rate of government bonds is 0.9% in 2014 and thus the interest payments on the debt are much more limited (1.5% GDP) than in other countries which experience lower debt ratio (3% of GDP in US or more than 4% in Italy).

The future may not offer the same facilities; however, all these "favorable" factors may reverse in the near future as the ageing household will save less. Though, if for the past three decades Japan has not had to rely on foreign borrowing to finance its government deficits, it may be obliged to call more for external saving in the near future and its creditworthiness could be challenged on international financial market which are more suspicious about the credibility of the economies.

This risk led Japan to adopt in recent years a new economic policy described as the three arrows: to improve the primary deficit through fiscal measures (yet the consumption tax has been increased), to boost growth and to exit from deflation. The path can only be very narrow. The OECD has studied various scenarios and has found that with a primary balance at zero in 2018, an Increase in growth (1.1%), and a moderate inflation (0.5%), the gross debt could fall under 200% and the net debt around 110%, but not before horizon 2035.

Summary

- The government budget constraint gives the evolution of government debt as a function of spending and taxes. One way of expressing the constraint is that the change in debt (the deficit) is equal to the primary deficit plus interest payments on the debt. The primary deficit is the difference between government spending on goods and services, G, and taxes net of transfers, T.

- If government spending is unchanged, a decrease in taxes must eventually be offset by an increase in taxes in the future. The longer the government waits to increase taxes or the higher the real interest rate, the higher the eventual increase in taxes.

- The legacy of past deficits is higher debt. To stabilize the debt, the government must eliminate the deficit. To eliminate the deficit, it must run a primary surplus equal to the interest payments on the existing debt.

- The evolution of the ratio of debt to GDP depends on four factors: the interest rate, the growth rate, the initial debt ratio, and the primary surplus.

- Under the Ricardian equivalence proposition, a larger deficit is offset by an equal increase in private saving. Deficits have no effect on demand and on output. The accumulation of debt does not affect capital accumulation. In practice however, Ricardian equivalence fails and larger deficits lead to higher demand and higher output in the short run. The accumulation of debt leads to lower capital accumulation, and thus to lower output in the long run.

- To stabilize the economy, the government should run deficits during recessions and surpluses during booms. The cyclically adjusted deficit tells us what the deficit would be, under existing tax and spending rules, if output were at its potential level.

- Deficits are justified in times of high spending, such as wars. Relative to an increase in taxes, deficits lead to higher consumption and lower investment during wars. They therefore shift some of the burden of the war from people living during the war to those living after the war. Deficits also help smooth taxes and reduce tax distortions.

- High debt ratios increase the risk of vicious cycles. A higher perceived risk of default can lead to a higher interest rate and an increase in debt. The increase in debt in turn can lead to a higher perceived risk of default and a higher interest rate. Together, both can combine to lead to a debt explosion. Governments may have no choice than to default or to rely on money finance. Money finance may in turn lead to hyperinflation. In either case, the economic costs are likely to be high.

Key Terms

inflation-adjusted deficit, 475

government budget constraint, 475

primary deficit, 477

primary surplus, 477

debt-to-GDP ratio, 480

debt ratio, 480

Ricardian equivalence, 482

Ricardo-Barro proposition, 482

full-employment deficit, 483

mid-cycle deficit, 483

standardized employment deficit, 483

structural deficit, 483

cyclically adjusted deficit, 483

automatic stabilizer, 484

tax smoothing, 486

spread, 487

basis points, 487

haircut, 488

debt restructuring, 488

debt rescheduling, 488

private sector involvement, 488

money finance, 488

debt monetization, 488

fiscal dominance, 488

seignorage, 488

hyperinflation, 489

fiscal austerity, 491

Questions and Problems

QUICK CHECK

MyEconLab Visit www.myeconlab.com to complete similar Quick Check problems and get instant feedback.

1. Using information in this chapter, label each of the following statements true, false, or uncertain. Explain briefly.

a. The deficit is the difference between real government spending and taxes net of transfers.

b. The primary deficit is the difference between real government spending and taxes net of transfers.

c. The United States has experienced wide fluctuations in the ratio of debt to GDP in the past century.

d. Tax smoothing and deficit finance help spread the burden of war across generations.

e. The government should always take immediate action to eliminate a cyclically adjusted budget deficit.

f. If Ricardian equivalence holds, then an increase in income taxes will affect neither consumption nor saving.

g. The ratio of debt to GDP cannot exceed 100%.

h. A haircut reduces the value of outstanding government debt outstanding.

i. The cyclically adjusted deficit is always smaller than the actual deficit.

j. The inflation-adjusted deficit is always smaller than the actual deficit.

k. When the ratio of debt to GDP is high, the best policy is a fiscal consolidation.

l. A hyperinflation is an inflation rate greater than 30% per month.

m. Hyperinflations may distort prices, but they have no effect on real output.

2. Consider the following statement:

A deficit during a war can be a good thing. First, the deficit is temporary, so after the war is over, the government can go right back to its old level of spending and taxes. Second, given that the evidence supports the Ricardian equivalence proposition, the deficit will stimulate the economy during wartime, helping to keep the unemployment rate low.

Identify the mistakes in this statement. Is anything in this statement correct?

3. High debt in a low-level context

Consider an economy characterized by the following figures (close to the Japanese economy situation in 2013)

Deficit: 7.8%

Net Debt: 123%GNP

Inflation: 0.4%

Interest: 0.25%

a. What is the primary deficit/surplus ratio to GDP?

b. What is the inflation-adjusted deficit/surplus ratio to GDP?

c. Suppose that output is 2% below its natural level. What is the cyclically adjusted, inflation-adjusted deficit/surplus ratio to GDP?

d. Suppose instead that output begins at its natural level and that output growth remains constant at the normal rate of 2%. Ignoring any effect of output on tax revenue; that is, assuming a primary deficit of 7.5% forever, how many years will it take for the debt-to-GDP ratio fall under 60%?

4. A government with a deficit of 3% issues bonds for the deficit amount and asks the central bank to buy the bonds.

Assuming the average ratio of central bank money to monthly GDP (M) is equal to 0.5 and the rate of inflation is 3%,

a. What is the amount of money creation?

b. What is the amount of seignorage?

c. If the central bank money to monthly GDP is equal to 1, deficit is 10% of GDP and inflation is 8%, what are the values derived in parts (a) and (b)?

DIG DEEPER

5. To finance its deficit, a State considers borrowing from a foreign economy. On the national market, the interest rate is 10% and the foreign rate of interest is 5%. The state decided to borrow 1,000 units of the domestic currency for a year (to simplify the calculation, assume that the rate of exchange is 1 unit of national money for 120 foreign units).

As the foreign economy is in a very good situation, the exchange rate of the foreign currency is re-evaluated at 25% during the year.

a. What is the increase in interest charged in the national currency after the re-evaluation?

b. What is the resulting real interest rate of the borrowing?

c. Is it still less costly to borrow in that foreign rate when converting it into domestic currency?

d. If the foreign economy were to devaluate its currency to 25%, what will your answers to parts (a), (b), and (c) be? What will be the expectation about the interest rate of that money?

e. What lessons do you draw for deficit financing?

6. Ricardian equivalence and fiscal policy

First consider an economy in which Ricardian equivalence does not hold.

a. Suppose the government starts with a balanced budget. Then, there is an increase in government spending, but there is no change in taxes. Show in an IS-LM diagram the effect of this policy on output in the short run when the central bank keeps the real interest rate constant. How will the government finance the increase in government spending?

b. Suppose, as in part (a), that the government starts with a balanced budget and then increases government spending. This time, however, assume that taxes increase by the same amount as government spending. Show in an IS-LM diagram the effect of this policy on output in the short run. (It may help to recall the discussion of the multiplier in Chapter 3. Does government spending or tax policy have a bigger multiplier?) How does the output effect compare with the effect in part (a)?

Now suppose Ricardian equivalence holds in this economy. [Parts (c) and (d) do not require use of diagrams.]

c. Consider again an increase in government spending with no change in taxes. How does the output effect compare to the output effects in parts (a) and (b)?

d. Consider again an increase in government spending combined with an increase in taxes of the same amount. How does this output effect compare to the output effects in parts (a) and (b)?

e. Comment on each of the following statements:

i. "Under Ricardian equivalence, government spending has no effect on output."

ii. "Under Ricardian equivalence, changes in taxes have no effect on output."

EXPLORE FURTHER

7. Managing debt ratio

Consider an economy characterized by the following figures:

i. The debt-to-GDP ratio is 50%.

ii. The primary deficit is 3% of GDP.

iii. The normal growth rate is 2%.

iv. The real interest rate is 2%.

a. Using an Excel spreadsheet, compute the debt-to-GDP ratio in 10 years, assuming that: the primary deficit stays at 3% of GDP each year; the economy grows at the normal growth rate in each year; and the real interest rate is constant, at 2%.

b. Suppose the real interest rate increases to 3%, but everything else remains the same as in part (a). Compute the debt-to-GDP ratio in 10 years.

c. Suppose the normal growth rate falls to 1%, and the economy grows at the normal growth rate each year. Everything else remains as in part (a). Calculate the debt-to-GDP ratio in 10 years. Compare your answer to part (b).

d. Return to the assumptions of part (a) and suppose policymakers decide that the debt-to-GDP ratio must be limited to 60%. Verify that reducing the primary deficit to 1% immediately and that maintaining this deficit for 10 years will produce a debt-to-GDP ratio of 60% in 10 years. Thereafter, what value of the primary deficit will be required to maintain the debt-to-GDP ratio of 60%?

e. Continuing with part (d) suppose policy makers wait 5 years before changing fiscal policy. For five years, the primary deficit remains at 3% of GDP. What is the debt-to-GDP ratio in 5 years? Suppose that after five years, policy makers decide to reduce the debt-to-GDP ratio to 60%. In years 6 through 10, what constant value of the primary deficit will produce a debt-to-GDP ratio of 60% at the end of year 10?

f. Suppose that policy makers carry out the policy in parts (d) or (e). If these policies reduce the growth rate of output for a while, how will this affect the size of the reduction in the primary deficit required to achieve a debt-to-GDP ratio of 50% in 10 years?

g. Which policy—the one in part (d) or in part (e)—do you think is more dangerous to the stability of the economy?

8. Comparing fiscal situations in the world

The fiscal situation of economies in the world has been provided in IMF reports and statistics. Refer to the International Financial Statistics and the Fiscal Monitor, available on the IMF Web site, to get the statistical series.

Using these statistics answer the following:

a. Based on the following, compare the United States, Euro Area (EA), and Japan between 2008 and 2015:

i. The nominal deficit

ii. The Cyclically adjusted balance (CAB)

iii. The growth of GDP

b. Compare the ratio to GDP of the gross debt and the net debt of these 3 areas in 2015.

c. Returning to the IMF tables, what can you say about the category of emerging market and middle income economies for their overall fiscal balance, their growth, and their debt GDP ratio if you compare the situation in 2008 with the situation in 2015?

Further Readings

■ The modern statement of the Ricardian equivalence proposition is Robert Barro's "Are Government Bonds Net Wealth?", *Journal of Political Economy*, 1974, Vol. 82, No. 6, pp: 1095–1117.

■ Each year, the Congressional Budget Office publishes *The Economic and Budget Outlook* for the current and future fiscal years. The document provides a clear and unbiased presentation of the current U.S. budget, of current budget issues, and of budget trends available at: http://www.cbo.gov/.

■ For more on the German hyperinflation, read Steven Webb, *Hyperinflation and Stabilization in the Weimar Republic*, Oxford University Press, 1989.

■ A good review of what economists know and don't know about hyperinflation is given in Rudiger Dornbusch, Federico Sturzenegger, and Holger Wolf, "Extreme Inflation: Dynamics and Stabilization," *Brookings Papers on Economic Activity*, 1990 Vol 2, pp: 1–84.

■ For the debate on "fiscal austerity" in Europe, see http://www.voxeu.org/debates/has-austerity-gone-too-far.

Monetary Policy: A Summing Up

The recent crisis has led to a major reassessment of monetary policy. For the two decades before the crisis, most central banks had converged toward a framework for monetary policy, called **inflation targeting**. It was based on two principles: The first was that the primary goal of monetary policy was to keep inflation stable and low. The second was that the best way to achieve this goal was to follow, explicitly or implicitly, an **interest rate rule**, a rule allowing the policy rate to respond to movements in inflation and in activity.

Until the crisis, this framework appeared to work well. Inflation decreased and remained low and stable in most countries. Output fluctuations decreased in amplitude. The period became known as the **Great Moderation**. Many researchers looked for the causes of this moderation, and many concluded that better monetary policy was one of the main factors behind the improvement, consolidating the support for this monetary policy framework.

Then the crisis came. And it has forced macroeconomists and central bankers to reassess along at least two dimensions: The first is the set of issues raised by the liquidity trap. When an economy reaches the zero lower bound, the policy rate can no longer be used to increase activity. This raises two questions: First, can monetary policy be conducted in such a way as to avoid getting to the zero lower bound in the first place? Second, once the economy is at the zero lower bound, are there other tools that the central bank can use to help increase activity?

The second set of issues concerns the mandate of the central bank and the tools of monetary policy. From the early 2000s to the start of the crisis, most advanced economies appeared to do well, with sustained output growth and stable inflation. Yet, as we saw in Chapter 6, behind the scenes, not everything was fine. Important changes were taking place in the financial system, such as the large increase in leverage and the increased reliance on wholesale funding by banks. In many countries, also, there were sharp increases in housing prices. These factors turned out to be at the source of the crisis. This again raises two sets of questions: Looking forward, should the central bank worry not only about inflation and activity, but also about asset prices, stock market booms, housing booms, and risk in the financial sector? And if so, what tools does it have at its disposal?

The purpose of this chapter is to review what we have learned about monetary policy so far, then describe the logic of inflation targeting and the use of an interest rate rule, and finally discuss where we stand on the issues raised by the crisis.

Section 23-1 takes stock of what we have learned so far in this book.

Section 23-2 describes the inflation-targeting framework.

Section 23-3 reviews the costs and benefits of inflation and draws implications for the choice of a target inflation rate.

Section 23-4 describes the unconventional monetary policy measures taken by central banks when they hit the zero lower bound.

Section 23-5 discusses the potential role of central banks in insuring financial stability.

23-1 What We Have Learned

■ In Chapter 4 we looked at money demand and money supply and the determination of the interest rate.

  We saw how the central bank can control the policy rate through changes in the money supply. We saw also that, when the policy rate reaches zero, a case known as the liquidity trap or the zero lower bound, further increases in the money supply have no effect on the policy rate.

■ In Chapter 5 we looked at the short-run effects of monetary policy on output.

  We saw how a decrease in the interest rate leads to an increase in spending and, in turn, to an increase in output. We saw how monetary and fiscal policy can be used to affect both the level of output and its composition.

■ In Chapter 6, we introduced two important distinctions between the nominal and the real interest rate and between the borrowing rate and the policy rate. The real interest rate is equal to the nominal interest rate minus expected inflation. The borrowing rate is equal to the policy rate plus a risk premium.

  We saw that what matters for private spending decisions is the real borrowing rate. We discussed how the state of the financial system affects the relation between the policy rate and the borrowing rate.

■ In Chapter 9 we looked at the effects of monetary policy in the medium run.

  We saw that, in the medium run, monetary policy affects neither output nor the real interest rate. Output returns to potential, and the real interest rate returns to its natural rate, also called the *neutral rate* or the *Wicksellian rate of interest*. Because it does not affect either output or the real interest rate, higher money growth only leads to higher inflation.

  We saw how the zero lower bound may however derail this adjustment. High unemployment may lead to deflation, which, at the zero lower bound, leads to a higher real interest rate, which further decreases demand and further increases unemployment.

■ In Chapter 14 we introduced another important distinction, between short- and long-term interest rates.

  We saw that long-term interest rates depend on expectations of future short-term rates and a term premium. We saw how stock prices depend on expected future short-term rates, future dividends, and an equity premium.

  We saw however how stock prices may be subject to bubbles or fads, making the prices differ from the fundamental values of the stocks.

■ In Chapter 16 we looked at the effects of expectations on spending and output, and the role of monetary policy in this context.

  We saw that monetary policy affects the short-term nominal interest rate, but that spending depends on current and expected future short-term real interest rates.

MyEconLab Video

We saw how the effects of monetary policy on output depend crucially on how expectations respond to monetary policy.

- In Chapter 19 we looked at the effects of monetary policy in an economy open in both goods markets and financial markets.

   We saw how, in an open economy, monetary policy affects spending and output not only through the interest rate, but also through the exchange rate. An increase in money leads both to a decrease in the interest rate and a depreciation, both of which increase spending and output. We saw how, under fixed exchange rates, the central bank gives up monetary policy as a policy instrument.

- In Chapter 20 we discussed the pros and cons of different monetary policy regimes, namely flexible exchange rates versus fixed exchange rates.

   We saw how, under flexible exchange rates, interest rate movements can lead to large changes in exchange rates. We saw how, under fixed exchange rates, speculation can lead to an exchange rate crisis and a sharp devaluation. We discussed the pros and cons of adopting a common currency such as the euro, or even giving up monetary policy altogether through the adoption of a currency board or dollarization.

- In Chapter 21 we looked at the problems facing macroeconomic policy in general, and monetary policy in particular.

   We saw that uncertainty about the effects of policy should lead to more cautious policies. We saw that even well-intentioned policy makers may sometimes not do what is best, and that there is a case to be made for putting restraints on policy makers. We also looked at the benefits of having an independent central bank and appointing a conservative central banker.

In this chapter we extend the analysis to look first at the inflation targeting framework in place before the crisis, and then at the challenges to monetary policy raised by the crisis.

23-2 From Money Targeting to Inflation Targeting

One can think of the goals of monetary policy as twofold: First, to maintain low and stable inflation. Second, to stabilize output around potential—to avoid or at least limit recessions or booms.

Money Targeting

Until the 1980s, the strategy was to choose a target rate of money growth and to allow for deviations from that target rate as a function of activity. The rationale was simple. A low target rate of money growth implied a low average rate of inflation. In recessions, the central bank could increase money growth, leading to a decrease in interest rates and an increase in output. In booms, the central bank could decrease money growth, leading to an increase in interest rates and a slowdown in output.

That strategy did not work well.

First, the relation between money growth and inflation turned out to be far from tight, even *in the medium run*. This is shown in Figure 23-1, which plots 10-year averages of the U.S. inflation rate against 10-year averages of the growth rate of money from 1970 up to the crisis (the way to read the figure: The numbers for inflation and for money growth for 2000 for example are the average inflation rate and the average growth rate of money from 1991 to 2000). The inflation rate is constructed using the consumer price index (CPI) as the price index. The growth rate of nominal money is constructed

Figure 23-1

M1 Growth and Inflation: 10-Year Averages, 1970 to the crisis

There is no tight relation between *M1* growth and inflation,
even in the medium run.

Source: Series CPIAUSL and M1SL
Federal Reserve Economic Data
(FRED) http://research.stlouisfed.
org/fred2/.

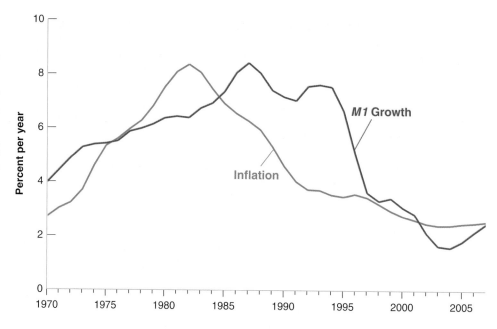

using the sum of currency and checkable deposits, known as **M1**, as the measure for the money stock. The reason for using 10-year averages should be clear. In the short run, changes in nominal money growth affect mostly output rather than inflation. It is only in the medium run that a relation between nominal money growth and inflation should emerge. Taking 10-year averages of both nominal money growth and inflation is a way of detecting such a medium-run relation. The reason for stopping at the crisis is that, as we saw in Chapter 4, when an economy hits the zero lower bound (which the U.S. economy did at the end of 2008), increases in the money supply no longer have an effect on the policy rate, and by implication, the central bank is no longer able to affect output and inflation; so we want to exclude the period during which the U.S. economy was stuck at the zero lower bound.

Figure 23-1 shows that, for the United States, the relation between *M1* growth and inflation was not tight. True, both went up in the 1970s, and both came down later. But note how inflation started declining in the early 1980s, whereas nominal money growth remained high for another decade and came down only in the 1990s. Average inflation from 1981 to 1990 was down to 4%, and average money growth over the same period was still running at 7.5%.

Second, the relation between the money supply and the interest rate *in the short run* also turned out also to be unreliable. A given decrease in money growth in response for example to low activity might lead to different effects on the interest rate, making money growth an unreliable instrument to affect demand and output.

Both problems, namely the poor relation between money growth and inflation in the medium run, and the poor relation of the interest rate to the money supply in the short run, had the same origin, namely *shifts in the demand for money*. An example will help here. Suppose, as the result of the introduction of credit cards, people decide to hold only half the amount of money they held before; in other words, the real demand for money decreases by half. In the short run, at a given price level, this large decrease in the demand for money will lead to a large decrease in the interest rate. In other words, we will see a large decrease in the interest rate with no change in the money supply. In the medium run, at a given interest rate, the price level will adjust, and the real money stock will eventually decrease by half. For a given nominal money stock, the price level will eventually double. So, even if the nominal money stock remains constant, there will still be a period of inflation as the price level doubles. During this period, there will be no tight relation between nominal money growth (which is zero) and inflation (which would be positive).

Throughout the 1970s and the 1980s, these frequent and large shifts in money demand created serious problems for central banks. They found themselves torn between trying to keep a stable target for money growth and staying within announced bands (to maintain credibility), or adjusting to shifts in money demand (to stabilize output in the short run and inflation in the medium run). Starting in the early 1990s, a dramatic rethinking of monetary policy took place based on targeting inflation rather than money growth, and the use of an interest rate rule. Let's look at it more closely.

Inflation Targeting

If one of the main goals of the central bank is to achieve low and stable inflation, why not target inflation directly rather than money growth? And if the way to affect activity in the short run is to rely on the effect of the interest rate on spending, why not focus directly on the interest rate rather than on money growth? This is the reasoning which led to the elaboration of inflation targeting. Central banks committed to achieving a target inflation rate. And they decided to use the interest rate as the instrument to achieve it. Let's look at both parts of the strategy:

Committing to a given inflation target *in the medium run* is hardly controversial. Trying to achieve a given inflation target *in the short run* would appear to be much more controversial. Focusing exclusively on inflation would seem to eliminate any role monetary policy could play in reducing output fluctuations. But in fact, this is not the case.

To see why, return to the Phillips curve relation between inflation, π_t, expected inflation, π_t^e, and the deviation of the unemployment rate, u_t, from the natural rate of unemployment, u_n (equation (8.9)):

$$\pi_t = \pi_t^e - \alpha(u_t - u_n)$$

Let the inflation target be π^*. Assume that, thanks to the central bank's reputation, this target is credible, so that people expect inflation to be equal to the target. The relation becomes:

$$\pi_t = \pi^* - \alpha(u_t - u_n)$$

Note that, if the central bank is able to hit its inflation target exactly, so $\pi_t = \pi^*$, unemployment will be equal to its natural rate. By targeting and achieving a constant rate of inflation in line with inflation expectations, the central bank also keeps unemployment at the natural rate, and by implication keeps output at potential.

Put strongly: Even if policy makers did not care about inflation per se (they do) but cared only about output, inflation targeting would still make sense. Keeping inflation stable is a way of keeping output at potential. This result has been dubbed the **divine coincidence**. With a Phillips curve of the form given in equation (8.9), there is no conflict between keeping inflation constant and keeping output at potential. A focus on keeping stable inflation is thus the right approach to monetary policy, both in the short and the medium run.

This result is a useful benchmark, but it is too strong. Life is not that nice. The main objection is that, as we saw in Chapter 8, the Phillips curve relation is far from an exact relation. There are times when inflation may be above target and output below potential, reintroducing a trade-off between the two goals. The central bank then has to decide whether to focus on decreasing inflation and adopt a tighter monetary policy, or to focus on increasing output and adopt a more expansionary monetary policy. So, although

◄ From Chapter 5, equation (5.3): The real money supply (the left side) must be equal to the real demand for money (the right side):

$$\frac{M}{P} = YL(i)$$

If, as a result of the introduction of credit cards, the real demand for money halves, then

$$\frac{M}{P} = \frac{1}{2} YL(i)$$

In the short run, P does not move, and so the interest rate must adjust. In the medium run, P adjusts. For a given level of output and a given interest rate, M/P must halve. Given M, this implies P must double.

◄ $0 = -\alpha(u_t - u_n) \Rightarrow$
$u_t = u_n$.

some central banks have been given a single mandate, namely stable and low inflation, others, such as the U.S. Fed, have a dual mandate, achieving both stable and low inflation and maintaining output close to potential. Also, all central banks have adopted what is called **flexible inflation targeting**. For the reasons we discussed in Chapter 21, uncertainty about the effects of the interest rate on output and in turn on inflation, central banks do not try to return to target inflation right away. Rather they adjust the interest rate to return to the target inflation rate over time. We now turn to the interest rate rule associated with inflation targeting.

The Interest Rate Rule

Inflation is not under the direct control of the central bank. The policy rate is. Thus, the question is how to set the policy rate so as to achieve the target rate of inflation. The answer is a simple one. When inflation is higher than the target, increase the policy rate to decrease the pressure on prices; when it is below the target rate of inflation, decrease the policy rate. With this in mind, in the 1990s, John Taylor, from Stanford University, suggested the following rule for the policy rate, a rule now known as the **Taylor rule**:

- Let π_t be the rate of inflation and π^* be the target rate of inflation.
- Let i_t be the policy rate, that is, the nominal interest rate controlled by the central bank, and i^* be the target nominal interest rate—the nominal interest rate associated with the neutral rate of interest, r_n, and the target rate of inflation, π^*, so $i^* = r_n + \pi^*$.
- Let u_t be the unemployment rate and u_n be the natural unemployment rate.

Think of the central bank as choosing the nominal interest rate, i. (Recall, from Chapter 4, that, through open market operations, and ignoring the liquidity trap, the central bank can achieve any short-term nominal interest rate that it wants.) Then Taylor argued, the central bank should use the following rule:

$$i_t = i^* + a(\pi_t - \pi^*) - b(u_t - u_n)$$

where a and b are positive coefficients chosen by the central bank.

Let's look at what the rule says:

- If inflation is equal to target inflation ($\pi_t = \pi^*$) and the unemployment rate is equal to the natural rate of unemployment ($u_t = u_n$), then the central bank should set the nominal interest rate, i_t, equal to its target value, i^*. This way, the economy can stay on the same path, with inflation equal to the target inflation rate and unemployment equal to the natural rate of unemployment.
- If inflation is higher than the target ($\pi_t > \pi^*$), the central bank should increase the nominal interest rate, i_t, above i^*. This higher interest rate will lead to an increase unemployment, and this increase in unemployment will lead to a decrease in inflation. The coefficient a should therefore reflect how much the central bank cares about inflation. The higher a, the more the central bank will increase the interest rate in response to inflation, the more the economy will slow down, the more unemployment will increase, and the faster inflation will return to the target inflation rate.

Some economists argue that the increase in U.S. inflation in the 1970s was due to the fact that the Fed increased the nominal interest rate less than one-for-one with inflation. The result, they argue, was that an increase in inflation led to a decrease in the real interest rate, which led to higher demand, lower unemployment, more inflation, a further decrease in the real interest rate, and so on.

    In any case, as Taylor pointed out, a should be larger than one. Why? Because what matters for spending is the real interest rate, not the nominal interest rate. When inflation increases, the central bank, if it wants to decrease spending and output, must increase the *real* interest rate. In other words, it must increase the nominal interest rate more than one-for-one with inflation.

- If unemployment is higher than the natural rate of unemployment ($u_t > u_n$), the central bank should decrease the nominal interest rate. The lower nominal interest rate will lead to an increase output, leading to a decrease in unemployment.

The coefficient b should reflect how much the central bank cares about unemployment. The higher b, the more the central bank will be willing to deviate from target inflation to keep unemployment close to the natural rate of unemployment.

In stating this rule, Taylor did not argue that it should be followed blindly. Many other events, such as an exchange rate crisis or the need to change the composition of spending on goods, and thus the mix between monetary policy and fiscal policy, justify changing the nominal interest rate for other reasons than those included in the rule. But he argued, the rule provided a useful way of thinking about monetary policy. Once the central bank has chosen a target rate of inflation, it should try to achieve it by adjusting the nominal interest rate. The rule it should follow should take into account not only current inflation but also current unemployment.

The logic of the rule was convincing, and, by the mid-2000s, in advanced economies, most central banks had adopted some form of inflation targeting, that is, the choice of an inflation target together with the use of an interest rule.

Then the crisis came and raised many questions, from the choice of the inflation target, to what to do when the interest rate suggested by the interest rule reaches the zero lower bound, to whether and how the central bank should worry about financial stability in addition to inflation and activity. The next section discusses the choice of the inflation target, and the following sections discuss other questions raised by the crisis.

23-3 The Optimal Inflation Rate

Table 23-1 shows how inflation steadily decreased in advanced economies from the early 1980s. In 1981, average inflation in the OECD was 10.5%; in 2014, it was down to 1.7%. In 1981, only two countries (out of the 24 OECD members at the time) had an inflation rate below 5%; in 2014, the number had increased to 33 out of 34.

◀ The country with inflation above 5% was Turkey (8.8%).

Before the crisis, most central banks had aimed for an inflation rate of about 2%. Was this the right goal? The answer depends on the costs and benefits of inflation.

The Costs of Inflation

We saw in Chapter 22 how very high inflation, say a rate of 30% per month or more, can disrupt economic activity. The debate in advanced economies today, however, is not about the costs of inflation rates of 30% or more per month. Rather, it centers on the advantages of, say, 0% versus, say, 4% inflation per year. Within that range, economists identify four main costs of inflation: (1) shoe-leather costs, (2) tax distortions, (3) money illusion, and (4) inflation variability.

Shoe-Leather Costs
Recall that in the medium run, a higher inflation rate leads to a higher nominal interest rate, and so to a higher opportunity cost of holding money. As a result, people decrease

Table 23-1 Inflation Rates in the OECD, 1981–2014					
Year	1981	1990	2000	2010	2014
OECD average*	10.5%	6.2%	2.8%	1.2%	1.7%
Number of countries with inflation below 5%**	2/24	15/24	24/27	27/30	33/34

*Average of GDP deflator inflation rates, using relative GDPs measured at PPP prices as weights.
**The second number denotes the number of member countries at the time.

their money balances by making more trips to the bank—thus the expression **shoe-leather costs**. These trips would be avoided if inflation were lower and people could be doing other things instead, such as working more or enjoying leisure.

During hyperinflations, shoe-leather costs become indeed quite large. But their importance in times of moderate inflation is limited. If an inflation rate of 4% leads people to go to the bank, say, one more time every month, or to do one more transaction between their money market fund and their checking account each month, this hardly qualifies as a major cost of inflation.

Tax Distortions

The second cost of inflation comes from the interaction between the tax system and inflation.

Consider, for example, the taxation of capital gains. Taxes on capital gains are typically based on the change in the price in dollars of the asset between the time it was purchased and the time it is sold. This implies that the higher the rate of inflation, the higher the tax. An example will make this clear:

- Suppose inflation has been running at π% a year for the last 10 years.
- Suppose also that you bought your house for $50,000 10 years ago, and you are selling it today for $50,000 times $(1 + \pi\%)^{10}$; so its real value is unchanged.
- If the capital-gains tax is 30%, the *effective tax rate* on the sale of your house—defined as the ratio of the tax you pay to the price for which you sell your house—is

The numerator of the fraction equals the sale price minus the purchase price. The denominator is the sale price. ▶

$$(30\%) \frac{50{,}000(1 + \pi\%)^{10} - 50{,}000}{50{,}000(1 + \pi\%)^{10}}$$

- Because you are selling your house for the same real price at which you bought it, your real capital gain is zero, so you should not be paying any tax. Indeed, if $\pi = 0$ —if there has been no inflation—then the effective tax rate is 0. But if, for example, $\pi = 4\%$, then the effective tax rate is 9.7%: Despite the fact that your real capital gain is zero, you end up paying a high tax.

The problems created by the interactions between taxation and inflation extend beyond capital-gains taxes. Although we know that the real rate of return on an asset is the real interest rate, not the nominal interest rate, income for the purpose of income taxation includes nominal interest payments, not real interest payments. Or to take yet another example, until the early 1980s in the United States, the income levels corresponding to different income-tax rates were not increased automatically with inflation. As a result, people were pushed into higher tax brackets as their nominal income—but not necessarily their real income—increased over time, an effect known as **bracket creep**.

Some economists argue that the costs of bracket creep were much larger. As tax revenues steadily increased, there was little pressure on the government to control spending. The result, they argue, was an increase in the overall size of the government in the 1960s and 1970s far beyond what would have been desirable.

You might argue this cost is not a cost of inflation per se, but rather the result of a badly designed tax system. In the house example we just discussed, the government could eliminate the problem if it *indexed* the purchase price to the price level—that is, it adjusted the purchase price for inflation since the time of purchase—and computed the tax on the difference between the sale price and the adjusted purchase price. Under this computation, there would be no capital gains and therefore no capital-gains tax to pay. But because tax codes around the world rarely define the tax base in real terms, the inflation rate matters and leads to distortions.

Money Illusion

The third cost comes from **money illusion**—the notion that people appear to make systematic mistakes in assessing nominal versus real changes in incomes and interest rates. A number of computations that would be simple when prices are stable become

Money Illusion

· ·

There is a lot of anecdotal evidence that many people fail to properly adjust for inflation in their financial computations. Recently, economists and psychologists have started looking at money illusion more closely. In a recent study, two psychologists, Eldar Shafir from Princeton and Amos Tversky from Stanford, and one economist, Peter Diamond from MIT, designed a survey aimed at finding how prevalent money illusion is and what causes it. Among the many questions they asked of people in various groups (people at Newark International Airport, people at two New Jersey shopping malls, and a group of Princeton undergraduates) is the following:

Suppose Adam, Ben, and Carl each received an inheritance of $200,000 and each used it immediately to purchase a house. Suppose each sold his house one year after buying it. Economic conditions were, however, different in each case:

- During the time Adam owned the house, there was a 25% deflation—the prices of all goods and services decreased by approximately 25%. A year after Adam bought the house, he sold it for $154,000 (23% less than what he had paid).

- During the time Ben owned the house, there was no inflation or deflation—the prices of all goods and services did not change significantly during the year. A year after Ben bought the house, he sold it for $198,000 (1% less than what he had paid).

- During the time Carl owned the house, there was a 25% inflation—the prices of all goods and services increased

by approximately 25%. A year after Carl bought the house, he sold it for $246,000 (23% more than what he had paid).

Please rank Adam, Ben, and Carl in terms of the success of their house transactions. Assign "1" to the person who made the best deal and "3" to the person who made the worst deal.

In nominal terms, Carl clearly made the best deal, followed by Ben, followed by Adam. But what is relevant is how they did in real terms—adjusting for inflation. In real terms, the ranking is reversed. Adam, with a 2% real gain, made the best deal, followed by Ben (with a 1% loss), followed by Carl (with a 2% loss).

The survey's answers are shown below.

Rank	Adam	Ben	Carl
1st	37%	15%	48%
2nd	10%	74%	16%
3rd	53%	11%	36%

Carl was ranked first by 48% of the respondents, and Adam was ranked third by 53% of the respondents. These answers suggest that money illusion is prevalent. In other words, people (even Princeton undergraduates) have a hard time adjusting for inflation.

Source: Eldar Shafir, Peter Diamond, Amos Tversky, "Money Illusion," *Quarterly Journal of Economics,* 1997, Vol. 112, No. 2, pp: 341–374 by permission of Oxford University Press.

more complicated when there is inflation. When they compare their income this year to their income in previous years, people have to keep track of the history of inflation. When choosing between different assets or deciding how much to consume or save, they have to keep track of the difference between the real interest rate and the nominal interest rate. Casual evidence suggests that many people find these computations difficult and often fail to make the relevant distinctions. Economists and psychologists have gathered more formal evidence, and it suggests that inflation often leads people and firms to make incorrect decisions (see the Focus box "Money Illusion"). If this is the case, then a seemingly simple solution is to have zero inflation.

Inflation Variability

Yet another cost comes from the fact that higher inflation is typically associated with *more variable inflation.* And more variable inflation means financial assets such as bonds, which promise fixed nominal payments in the future, become riskier.

Take a bond that pays $1,000 in 10 years. With constant inflation over the next 10 years, not only the nominal value, but also the real value of the bond in 10 years is known with certainty—we can compute exactly how much a dollar will be worth in 10 years. But with variable inflation, the real value of $1,000 in 10 years becomes uncertain. The more variability there is, the more uncertainty it creates. Saving for retirement becomes more difficult. For those who have invested in bonds, lower inflation than they expected means a better retirement; but higher inflation may mean poverty.

A good and sad movie about surviving on a fixed pension in post-World War II Italy: *Umberto D*, by Vittorio de Sica (1952).

▶ This is one of the reasons retirees, for whom part of their income is fixed in dollar terms, typically worry more about inflation than other groups in the population.

You might argue, as in the case of taxes, that these costs are not due to inflation per se, but rather to the financial markets' inability to provide assets that protect their holders against inflation. Rather than issuing only nominal bonds (bonds that promise a fixed nominal amount in the future), governments or firms could also issue *indexed bonds*—bonds that promise a nominal amount adjusted after inflation so people do not have to worry about the real value of the bond when they retire. Indeed, as we saw in Chapter 14, a number of countries, including the United States, have now introduced such bonds so people can better protect themselves against movements in inflation.

The Benefits of Inflation

This may surprise you, but inflation is not all bad. There are three benefits of inflation: (1) seignorage, (2) (somewhat paradoxically) the use of the interaction between money illusion and inflation in facilitating real wage adjustments, and (3) the option of negative real interest rates for macroeconomic policy.

Seignorage

Money creation—the ultimate source of inflation—is one of the ways in which the government can finance its spending. Put another way, money creation is an alternative to borrowing from the public or raising taxes.

As we saw in Chapter 22, the government typically does not "create" money to pay for its spending. Rather, the government issues and sells bonds and spends the proceeds. But if the bonds are bought by the central bank, which then creates money to pay for them, the result is the same. Other things equal, the revenues from money creation—that is, *seignorage*—allow the government to borrow less from the public or to lower taxes.

Because of quantitative easing (which we shall discuss in the next section) the ratio of the monetary base to GDP is much higher than it was pre-crisis. But it is expected to eventually return to its normal level when the U.S. economy ▶ emerges from the liquidity trap.

How large is seignorage in practice? During hyperinflations, seignorage often becomes an important source of government finance. But its importance in OECD economies today, and for the range of inflation rates we are considering, is much more limited. Take the case of the United States. The ratio of the monetary base—the money issued by the Fed (see Chapter 4)—to GDP is usually around 6%. An increase in the rate of nominal money growth of 4% per year (which eventually leads to a 4% increase in the inflation rate) would lead therefore to an increase in seignorage of ▶ 4% × 6%, or 0.24% of GDP. This is a small amount of revenue to get in exchange for 4% more inflation.

Recall equation (22.6): Let H denote the monetary base—the money issued by the central bank. Then ▶

$$\frac{Seignorage}{Y} = \frac{\Delta H}{PY} = \frac{\Delta H}{H}\frac{H}{PY}$$

where $\Delta H/H$ is the rate of growth of the monetary base, and H/PY is the ratio of the monetary base to nominal GDP.

Therefore, while the seignorage argument is sometimes relevant (for example, in economies that do not have a good tax collection system in place), it hardly seems relevant in the discussion of whether OECD countries today should have, say, 0% versus 4% inflation.

See, for example, the results of a survey of managers by Alan Blinder and Don Choi, in "A Shred of Evidence on Theories of Wage Rigidity," *Quarterly Journal of Economics*, 1990, ▶ Vol. 105, No. 4, pp:1003–1015.

Money Illusion Revisited

Paradoxically, the presence of money illusion provides at least one argument *for* having a positive inflation rate.

To see why, consider two situations: In the first, inflation is 4% and your wage goes up by 1% in nominal terms—in dollars. In the second, inflation is 0% and your wage goes down by 3% in nominal terms. Both lead to the same 3% decrease in your real wage, so you should be indifferent. The evidence, however, shows that many people will accept the real wage cut more readily in the first case than in the second case.

Why is this example relevant to our discussion? As we saw in Chapter 13, the constant process of change that characterizes modern economies means some workers must sometimes take a real pay cut. Thus, the argument goes, the presence of inflation allows for these downward real wage adjustments more easily than if inflation is equal to zero. The evidence on the distribution of wage changes in Portugal under high and low inflation in Chapter 8 suggests that this is indeed a relevant argument.

◀ A conflict of metaphors: Because inflation makes these real wage adjustments easier to achieve, some economists say inflation "greases the wheels" of the economy. Others, emphasizing the adverse effects of inflation on relative prices, say that inflation "puts sand" in the economy.

The Option of Negative Real Interest Rates

Higher inflation decreases the probability of hitting the zero lower bound. This argument, which may be the most important, follows from our discussion of the zero lower bound in Chapter 4. A numerical example will help here.

- Consider two economies, both with a *natural real interest rate equal to 2%*.
- In the first economy, the central bank maintains an average inflation rate of 4%, so the nominal interest rate is on average equal to 2% + 4% = 6%.
- In the second economy, the central bank maintains an average inflation rate of 0%, so the nominal interest rate is on average equal to 2% + 0% = 2%.
- Suppose both economies are hit by a similar adverse shock, which leads, at a given interest rate, to a decrease in spending and a decrease in output in the short run.
- In the first economy, the central bank can decrease the nominal interest rate from 6% to 0% before it hits the liquidity trap, thus achieving a decrease of 6%. Under the assumption that expected inflation does not change immediately and remains equal to 4%, the real interest rate decreases from 2% to −4%. This is likely to have a strong positive effect on spending and help the economy recover.
- In the second economy, the central bank can only decrease the nominal interest rate from 2% to 0%, a decrease of 2%. Under the assumption that expected inflation does not change right away and remains equal to 0%, the real interest rate decreases only by 2%, from 2% to 0%. This small decrease in the real interest rate may not increase spending by very much.

In short, an economy with a higher average inflation rate has more room to use monetary policy to fight a recession. An economy with a low average inflation rate may find itself unable to use monetary policy to return output to the natural level of output. As we saw in Chapter 6, this possibility is far from being just theoretical. At the start of the crisis, central banks quickly hit the zero lower bound, unable to decrease interest rates further. With this experience in mind, the question is whether this should lead central banks to choose higher average inflation in the future. Some economists argue that the current crisis is an exceptional event, that it is unlikely that countries will face a liquidity trap again in the future, and so there is no need to adopt a higher average inflation rate. Others argue that the problems faced by a country in a liquidity trap are so serious that we should avoid taking the risk that it happens again, and that a higher rate of inflation is in fact justified. What is undisputed, though, is that permanently low inflation reduces the central bank's ability to affect the real interest rate.

The Optimal Inflation Rate: The State of the Debate

At this stage, most central banks in advanced economies have an inflation target of about 2%. They are, however, being challenged on two fronts: Some economists want to achieve price stability—that is, 0% inflation. Others want, instead, a higher target rate of inflation, say 4%.

Those who want to aim for 0% make the point that 0% is a different target rate from all others; it corresponds to price stability. This is desirable in itself. Knowing that the price level will be roughly the same in 10 or 20 years as it is today simplifies a number of complicated decisions and eliminates the scope for money illusion. Also, given the time consistency problem facing central banks (discussed in Chapter 21), credibility and simplicity of the target inflation rate are important. Some economists and some central bankers believe price stability—that is, a 0% target—can achieve these goals better than a target inflation rate of 2%. So far, however, no central bank has actually adopted a 0% inflation target.

Those who want to aim for a higher rate argue that it is essential not to fall in the liquidity trap in the future, and that, for these purposes, a higher target rate of inflation, say 4%, would be helpful. They argue that the choice of a 2% target was based on the belief that countries would be unlikely to hit the zero lower bound, and that this belief has proven false. Their argument has gained little support among central bankers, who argue that if central banks increase their target from its current value of 2% to 4%, people may start anticipating that the target will soon become 5%, then 6%, and so on, and inflation expectations will no longer be anchored. Thus, they see it as important to keep current target levels.

This reasoning is sometimes ▶ known as the "slippery slope" argument.

The debate goes on. For the time being, most central banks continue to aim for low but positive inflation—that is, inflation rates of about 2%.

23-4 Unconventional Monetary Policy

When, at the start of the crisis, the interest rate reached the zero lower bound, central banks found themselves unable to decrease it further, and thus lost the use of **conventional monetary policy**. In this book, I have assumed until now that monetary policy became impotent. But this was a simplification. Central banks explored other ways to affect activity, a set of measures known as **unconventional monetary policy**.

The idea was simple. While the policy rate was equal to zero, other interest rates remained positive, reflecting various risk premiums. Although I introduced a risk premium in Chapter 6 in the relation of the borrowing rate to the policy rate, I did not discuss in detail what it depended on, and how it could be affected by monetary policy. In fact, we can think of the premium on an asset as determined by supply and demand for the asset. If the demand for an asset decreases, whether because buyers become more risk averse, or because some investors just decide not to hold the asset, the premium will increase. If, instead, the demand increases, the premium will decrease. This is true whether the increased demand comes from private investors or from the central bank.

This is the logic which led central banks to buy assets other than short-term bonds, with the intention of decreasing the premium on those assets, and thus decreasing the corresponding borrowing rates with the aim of stimulating economic activity. They did this by financing their purchases through money creation, leading to a large increase in the money supply. Although the increase in the money supply had no effect on the policy rate, the purchase of these other assets decreased their premium, leading to lower borrowing rates and higher spending. These purchase programs are known as **quantitative easing**, or **credit easing**, policies.

In the United States, the Fed started its first quantitative easing program in November 2008, even before it had reached the zero lower bound. In what has become known as Quantitative Easing 1 (**QE1** for short), the Fed started buying certain types of mortgage-based securities. We saw the reason for it in Chapter 6: One of the triggers of the crisis was the difficulty of assessing the value of the underlying mortgages on which those securities were based; as a result, many investors had decided to stop holding any kind of mortgage based security, and the premium even on securities which seemed relatively safe had jumped to very high levels. By buying these securities,

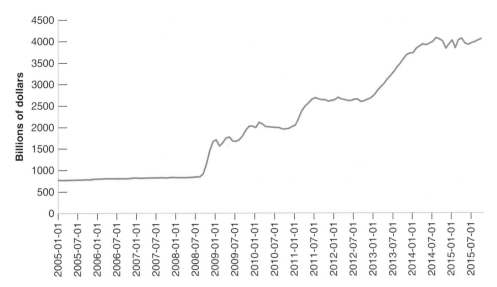

Figure 23-2

The Evolution of the U.S. Monetary Base from 2005 to 2015

As a result of quantitative easing, the monetary base more than quadrupled between 2005 and 2015.

the Fed decreased their premium and limited the effect on the financial system, and on spending. The second quantitative easing program, known as **QE2**, started in November 2010, when the Fed starting buying longer term Treasury bonds, with the intent of decreasing the term premium on these long-term bonds. The third quantitative easing program, **QE3**, started in September 2012, with the further purchase of mortgage-based securities, to decrease the cost of mortgages and further help the housing market to recover.

Much research has gone into assessing the effectiveness of quantitative easing in reducing risk premia. There is wide agreement that QE1 made a large difference. By intervening in a market which had become dysfunctional, the Fed's intervention limited the increase in premiums. The effects of QE2 and QE3, in which the Fed intervened in markets which were no longer dysfunctional, are more controversial. It is widely accepted that they decreased the term premium on long-term government bonds. The question is by how much.

MyEconLab Video

The general assessment of quantitative easing policies, in the United States and elsewhere, is that they had some effect on borrowing rates, and thus monetary policy can still have some effect on activity even at the zero lower bound. But there is also wide agreement that they work in more complicated and less reliable ways than conventional monetary policy. Put another way, the zero lower bound may not make monetary policy impotent, but it surely limits its efficiency.

As a result of these policies, the balance sheet of the Fed is much larger than it was before the crisis. Figure 23-2 shows the evolution of the monetary base (the name for central bank money) since 2005. You can see how until the crisis, it was relatively flat, and how it has increased as a result of quantitative easing, from 850 billion dollars, or about 6.6% of GDP, in September 2008 to 4,000 billion dollars, or about 22% of GDP, at the time of writing. One major issue facing the Fed over the coming years is the rate at which it will want to reduce its balance sheet, and whether it wants to return to the size and composition of balance sheet it had before the crisis. At this stage, banks are willing to hold most of the increase in the money supply in the form of excess reserves at the central bank. Given that the policy rate is equal to zero, banks are indifferent between holding reserves or holding short-term bonds. When the Fed starts increasing the policy rate, and the central bank wants banks to continue to hold these excess reserves, it will have to pay interest on these reserves.

23-5 Monetary Policy and Financial Stability

When the financial crisis started, central banks found themselves confronted not only with a major decline in demand, but also with serious problems within the financial system. As we saw in Chapter 6, the decline in housing prices had been the trigger for the crisis. It was then amplified by failures of the financial system. Opacity of assets led to doubts about the solvency of financial institutions. Doubts about solvency led in turn to runs, in which investors tried to get their funds back, forcing fire sales and generating further doubts about solvency. The first urgent issue facing the central banks was thus what measures to take—beyond the measures already described in the previous sections. The second issue was whether and how, in the future, monetary policy should try to decrease the probability of another such financial crisis. We take both issues in turn:

Liquidity Provision and Lender of Last Resort

Central banks have long known about bank runs. As we saw in Chapter 6, the structure of the balance sheet of banks exposes them to runs. Many of their assets, such as loans, are illiquid. Many of their liabilities, such as demand deposits, are liquid. As their name indicates, demand deposits in particular can be withdrawn *on demand*. Thus, worries, founded or unfounded, by depositors can lead them to want to withdraw their funds, forcing the bank either to close or to sell the assets at fire sale prices. In most countries, two measures have traditionally been taken to limit such runs:

- Deposit insurance, which gives investors the confidence that they will get their funds back even if the bank is insolvent, so that they do not have an incentive to run.
- And, in case the run actually happens, the provision of liquidity by the central bank to the bank against some collateral, namely some of the assets of the bank. This way, the bank can get the liquidity it needs to pay the depositors without having to sell the assets. This function of the central bank is known as **lender of last resort**, and it has been one of the functions of the Fed since its creation in 1913.

What the crisis showed however was that banks were not the only financial institutions that could be subject to runs. Any institution whose assets are less liquid than its liabilities is exposed to similar risks of a run. If investors want their funds back, it may be difficult for the financial institution to get the liquidity it needs. Given the urgency during the crisis, the Fed extended liquidity provision to some financial institutions other than banks. It had little choice than to do so, but, looking forward, the question is what the rules should be, which institutions can expect to receive liquidity from the central bank and which cannot. The question is far from settled. Do central banks really want to provide such liquidity to institutions they do not regulate?

Macroprudential Tools

Starting in the mid-2000s, the Fed became worried about the increase in housing prices. But the Fed and other central banks facing similar housing price increases were reluctant to intervene. This was for a number of reasons: First, they found it difficult to assess whether the price increases reflected increases in fundamentals (e.g., low interest rates) or reflected a bubble (i.e., increases in prices above what were justified by fundamentals). Second, they worried that an increase in the interest rate, although it might indeed stop the increase in housing prices, would also slow down the whole economy and trigger a recession. Third, they thought that, even if the increase in housing prices was indeed a bubble, and the bubble were to burst and lead to a decrease in housing prices later, they could counter the adverse effects on demand through an appropriate decrease in the interest rate.

The crisis has forced them to reconsider. As we saw, housing price declines combined with the build-up of risk in the financial system, led to a major financial and macroeconomic crisis, which they could not avoid, nor counter.

As a result, a broad consensus is emerging along two lines:

- It is risky to wait. Even if in doubt about whether an increase in asset prices reflects fundamentals or a bubble, it may be better to do something than not. Better to stand for a while in the way of a fundamental increase and turn out to be wrong, than to let a bubble build up and burst, with major adverse macroeconomic effects. The same applies to build-ups of financial risk; for example, excessive bank leverage. Better to prevent high leverage, even at the risk of decreasing bank credit, than allow ◀ it to build up, increasing the risk of a financial crisis.

  This has led to the dictum: Better lean [against increases in asset prices] than clean [after asset prices have crashed].

- To deal with bubbles, credit booms, or dangerous behavior in the financial system, the interest rate is not the right policy instrument. It is too blunt a tool, affecting the whole economy rather than resolving the problem at hand. The right instruments are **macroprudential tools**, rules that are aimed directly at borrowers, or lenders, or banks and other financial institutions, as the case may require.

What form might some of the macroprudential tools take? Some tools may be aimed at borrowers:

- Suppose the central bank is worried about what it perceives to be an excessive increase in housing prices. It can tighten conditions under which borrowers can obtain mortgages. A measure used in many countries is a ceiling on the size of the loan borrowers can take relative to the value of the house they buy, a measure known as the maximum **loan-to-value (LTV) ratio**, or maximum LTV for short. Reducing the maximum LTV is likely to decrease demand and thus slow down the price increase. (The Focus box on page 512 "LTV Ratios and Housing Price Increases from 2000 to 2007" examines the relation between maximum LTVs and housing price increases in the period leading up to the crisis.)

- Suppose the central bank is worried that people are borrowing too much in foreign currency. An example will help to make the point. In the early 2010s, more than two-thirds of mortgages in Hungary were denominated in Swiss francs! The reason was simple. Swiss interest rates were very low, making it apparently attractive for Hungarians to borrow at the Swiss rather than the Hungarian interest rate. The risk that borrowers did not take into account, however, was the risk that the Hungarian currency, the forint, would depreciate vis-à-vis the Swiss franc. Such a depreciation took place, increasing, on average, the real value of the mortgages Hungarians had to pay by more than 50%. Many households could no longer make their mortgage payments. This suggests that it would have been wise to put restrictions on the ◀ amount of borrowing in foreign currency by households.

  MyEconLab Video

  This led the Hungarian government to allow for a conversion of mortgages in Swiss francs to mortgages in forints at a better exchange rate. Hungarian households were better off, but the banks that loaned to them were worse off.

Some tools may be aimed at lenders, such as banks or foreign investors:

- Suppose the central bank is worried about an increase in bank leverage. We saw why this should be a concern in Chapter 6. High leverage was one of the main reasons why housing price declines led to the financial crisis. The central bank can impose minimum capital ratios, so as to limit leverage. These may take various forms (for ◀ example, a minimum value for the ratio of capital to all assets, or a minimum value for the ratio of capital to risk weighted assets, with riskier assets having a higher weight). In fact, in a series of agreements known as **Basel II** and **Basel III**, many countries have agreed to impose the same minima on their banks. A more difficult

  Go back to Chapter 6 for a refresher on the relation between leverage and capital ratios.

LTV Ratios and Housing Price Increases from 2000 to 2007

FOCUS

Is it the case that countries that had more stringent restrictions on borrowing had lower housing price increases from 2000 to 2007? An answer is given in Figure 1. The figure, taken from an IMF study, shows the evidence for 21 countries for which the data could be obtained.

The horizontal axis plots the maximum loan-to-value (LTV) ratio on new mortgages across countries. This maximum is not necessarily a legal maximum, but may be a guideline, or a limit over which additional requirements, such as mortgage insurance, may be asked of the borrower. A ratio of 100% means that a borrower may be able to get a loan equal to the value of the house. Actual values vary from 60% in Korea; to 100% in a large number of countries, including the United States; to 125% in The Netherlands. The vertical axis plots the increase in the nominal price of housing from 2000 to 2007 (measuring the real price increase would lead to a similar picture). The figure also plots the regression line, the line that best fits the set of observations.

The figure suggests two conclusions:

The first is that there indeed appears to be a positive relation between the LTV ratio and the housing price increase. Korea and Hong Kong, which imposed low LTV ratios, had smaller housing price increases. Spain and the United Kingdom, with much higher ratios, had much larger price increases.

The second is that the relation is far from tight. This should not come as a surprise, as surely many other factors played a role in the increase in housing prices. But, even controlling for other factors, it is difficult to identify with much confidence the precise effect of the LTV ratio. Looking forward, we shall have to learn a lot more about how an LTV-based regulatory tool might work before it can be used as a reliable macroprudential tool.

Source: Christopher Crowe, Giovanni Dell'Ariccia, Deniz Igan, and Pau Rabanal, "Policies for Macrofinancial Stability: Options to Deal with Real Estate Booms," Staff Discussion Note, International Monetary Fund, February 2011.

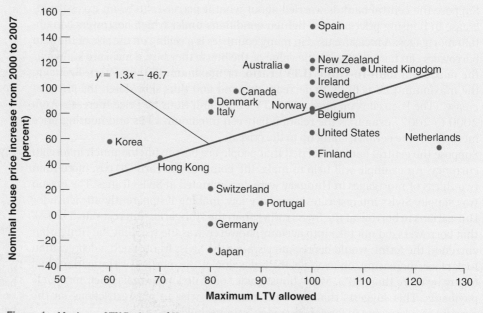

Figure 1 *Maximum LTV Ratios and Housing Price Increases, 2000–2007*

and unresolved issue is whether and how such capital ratios should be adjusted over time as a function of economic and financial conditions (whether, for example, they should be increased if there appears to be excessive credit growth).

■ Suppose the central bank is worried about high capital inflows, as for example, in the Hungarian case we just discussed. The central bank worries that, although investors are willing to lend at low interest rates to the country, they may change their mind, and this might lead to a sudden stop. The central bank may then want to limit the

See the Focus box "Sudden Stops, Safe Havens, and the Limits to the Interest Parity Condition" in Chapter 19.

capital inflows by imposing **capital controls** on inflows. These may take the form of taxes on different types of inflows, with lower taxes on capital flows that are less prone to sudden stops, such as **foreign direct investment** (the purchase of physical assets by foreigners), or a direct limit on the ability of domestic residents to take out foreign loans.

Although there is large agreement that the use of such *macroprudential* tools is desirable, many questions remain:

- In many cases, we do not know how well these tools work (e.g., how much a decrease in the maximum LTV ratio affects the demand for housing, or whether foreign investors can find ways of avoiding capital controls).

- There are likely to be complex interactions between the traditional monetary policy tools and these macroprudential tools. For example, there is some evidence that very low interest rates lead to excessive risk taking, be it by investors or by financial institutions. If this is the case, a central bank that decides, for macroeconomic reasons, to lower the interest rate may have to use various macroprudential tools to offset the potential increase in risk taking. Again, we know little about how best to do it.

- The question arises of whether macroprudential tools should be, together with traditional monetary policy tools, under the control of the central bank or under the control of a separate authority. The argument for having the central bank in charge of both monetary and macroprudential tools is that these tools interact, and thus only one centralized authority can use them in the right way. The argument against it is the worry that such a consolidation of tools may give too much power to an independent central bank.

  At this stage, some countries have taken one route, whereas others have taken another. In the United Kingdom, the central bank has been given power over both monetary and macroprudential tools. In the United States, the responsibility has been given to a council under the formal authority of the U.S. Treasury, but with the Fed playing a major role within the council.

To summarize: The crisis has shown that macroeconomic stability requires the use not only of traditional monetary instruments, but also of macroprudential tools. How best to use them is one of the challenges facing macroeconomic policy makers today.

Summary

- Until the 1980s, the design of monetary policy was focused on nominal money growth. But because of the poor relation between inflation and nominal money growth, this approach was eventually abandoned by most central banks.

- Central banks now focus on an inflation rate target rather than a nominal money growth rate target. And they think about monetary policy in terms of choosing the nominal interest rate rather than choosing the rate of nominal money growth.

- The Taylor rule gives a useful way of thinking about the choice of the nominal interest rate. The rule states that the central bank should move its interest rate in response to two main factors: the deviation of the inflation rate from the target rate of inflation, and the deviation of the unemployment rate from the natural rate of unemployment. A central bank

that follows this rule will stabilize activity and achieve its target inflation rate in the medium run.

- The optimal rate of inflation depends on the costs and benefits of inflation. Higher inflation leads to more distortions, especially when it interacts with the tax system. But higher inflation, which implies higher average nominal interest rates, decreases the probability of hitting the zero lower bound, a bound which has proven costly in the recent crisis.

- When advanced economies hit the zero lower bound, central banks explored unconventional monetary policy tools, such as quantitative easing. These policies worked through the effects of central bank purchases on the risk premiums associated with different assets. These purchases have led to large increases in the balance sheets of central banks. An issue for the future is whether the central banks should reduce those balance sheets, and whether these unconventional measures should be used in normal times.

■ The crisis has shown that stable inflation is not a sufficient condition for macroeconomic stability. This is leading central banks to explore the use of macroprudential tools. These tools can, in principle, help limit bubbles, control credit growth, and decrease risk in the financial system. How best to use them, however, is still poorly understood and is one the challenges facing monetary policy today.

Key Terms

inflation targeting, 497
interest rate rule, 497
Great Moderation, 497
M1, 500
divine coincidence, 501
flexible inflation targeting, 502
Taylor rule, 502
shoe-leather costs, 504
bracket creep, 504
money illusion, 504
conventional monetary policy, 508
unconventional monetary policy, 508

quantitative easing, 508
credit easing, 508
QE1, 508
QE2, 509
QE3, 509
lender of last resort, 510
macroprudential tools, 511
loan-to-value (LTV) ratio, 511
Basel II, 511
Basel III, 511
capital controls, 513
foreign direct investment, 513

Questions and Problems

QUICK CHECK

MyEconLab Visit www.myeconlab.com to complete similar Quick Check problems and get instant feedback.

1. Using the information in this chapter, label each of the following statements true, false, or uncertain. Explain briefly.

a. The most important argument in favor of a positive rate of inflation in OECD countries is seignorage.

b. Fighting inflation should be the Fed's only purpose.

c. Inflation and money growth moved together from 1970 to 2009.

d. Because most people have little trouble distinguishing between nominal and real values, inflation does not distort decision making.

e. Most central banks around the world have an inflation target of 4%.

f. The higher the inflation rate, the higher the effective tax rate on capital gains.

g. The Taylor rule describes how central banks adjust the policy interest rate across recessions and booms.

h. The zero lower bound on the nominal policy rate was expected to be a regular feature of monetary policy when inflation targeting began.

i. Quantitative easing refers to central bank purchases of assets with the intention of directly affecting the yield on these assets.

j. In the crisis, central banks provided liquidity to financial institutions they did not regulate.

k. One consequence of the crisis was higher capital requirements and a more extensive regulatory regime for banks.

2. Breaking the link between money growth and inflation in the medium run

The money demand relationship in Chapter 4 is used implicitly in Figure 23-1. That relation is

$$\frac{M}{P} = Y L(i)$$

The central bank in conjunction with the political authorities chooses an inflation target π^*.

a. Derive the target nominal interest rate in a medium-run equilibrium.

b. Consider medium run equilibria where potential output does not grow. Derive the relation between money growth and inflation. Explain.

c. Now consider medium run equilibria where potential output grows at 3% per year. Now derive the relation between money growth and inflation. Do you expect inflation to be higher or lower than money growth? Explain.

d. Consider Figure 23-1. Look first at the period ending in roughly 1995. How do your results in parts (b) and (c) relate to it?

e. Focus on the case where all money is currency. We can then think of money demand as being the demand for currency (you can refer back to the appendix to Chapter 4 if needed). Over the past 50 years:

i. Automatic tellers have allowed cash to be dispensed outside of regular banking hours.

ii. The use of credit cards for purchases has greatly expanded.

iii. The use of debit cards for purchases has greatly expanded.

iv. Most recently, technology has allowed for small purchases by credit and debit cards by waving the card over a payment terminal near the cash register.

How would each of these innovations affect the demand for currency?

f. The FRED database at the Federal Reserve Bank of St. Louis has a series for currency (MBCURRCIR). Download this series and the series for nominal GDP (GDP). Construct a ratio of currency to nominal GDP. How does this series behave from 1980 to 2015? Are you surprised? Who else besides households and firms holds U.S. currency?

3. Inflation targets

Consider a central bank that has an inflation target, π^*. We studied two versions of the Phillips curve in Chapter 9. The general Phillips curve is

$$\pi_t - \pi_t^e = -\alpha(u_t - u_n)$$

The first version of the Phillips curve in Chapter 9 was

$$\pi_t - \pi_{t-1} = -\alpha(u_t - u_n)$$

The second version of the Phillips curve in Chapter 9 was

$$\pi_t - \bar{\pi} = -\alpha(u_t - u_n)$$

a. How are the two versions of the Phillips curve different?
b. In either version, in principle, the central bank is able to keep the actual rate of inflation in period t equal to the target rate of inflation π^* in every period. How does the central bank carry out this task?
c. Suppose the expected rate of inflation is anchored (does not move) and equal to the target rate of inflation, that is, $\bar{\pi} = \pi^*$. How does this situation make the central bank's task easier?
d. Suppose the expected rate of inflation is last period's rate of inflation rather than the target rate of inflation. How does this make the central banks task more difficult?
e. Use your answer to parts (c) and (d) to answer the question: Why is central bank credibility about the inflation target so useful?
f. In part (b), we asserted that the central bank could always hit its inflation target. Is this likely in practice?
g. One specific problem faced by the central bank is that the natural rate of unemployment is not known with certainty. Suppose the natural rate of unemployment, u_n, changes frequently. How will these changes affect the central bank's ability to hit its inflation target? Explain.

4. Considering the Taylor equation

$i_t = i^* + a\,(\pi_t - \pi^*) + b(U_t - U_n)$
i^* is the target interest rate
i_t is the nominal interest rate fixed by the Central Bank
π_t is the rate of inflation
π^* is the target rate of inflation
U_t is the unemployment rate
U_n is the natural unemployment rate
a and b are fixed according to the preference of the economic policy

a. Calculate the interest rate (i_t) the Central Bank must consider if this rule is applied in the following situation:

Cases	1	2	3	4	5
i^*	2	2	2	2	2
π_t	5	5	2	2	5
π^*	2	2	2	2	2
U_t	8	5	8	8	5
U_n	5	5	5	5	5
a	0.5	0.5	0.5	0.5	1
b	0.5	0.5	0.5	1	0.5

b. Comment on the results observed.

5. Unwinding unconventional monetary policy

It was noted in the text that the Federal Reserve purchased, in addition to Treasury bills, large amounts of mortgage-backed securities and long-term government bonds as part of quantitative easing. Figure 23-2 shows that as of the end of 2015, there were about 4.5 trillion dollars of assets in the monetary base. These assets were roughly distributed as 0.2 trillion in Treasury securities with less than one year to maturity; 2.2 trillion in Treasury securities of more than one year to maturity; and 1.7 trillion in mortgage-backed securities.

a. Why did the Federal Reserve Board buy the mortgage-backed securities?
b. Why did the Federal Reserve Board buy the long-term Treasury bonds?
c. What would you predict as the consequences of the following operation by the Federal Reserve Board: selling 0.5 trillion in mortgage-backed securities and buying 0.5 trillion in Treasury securities with less than one year to maturity?
d. What would you predict as the consequences of the following operation by the Federal Reserve Board: selling 0.5 trillion in Treasury securities with maturity longer than one-year and buying 0.5 trillion in Treasury securities with less than one year to maturity?

6. The maximum loan-to-value ratio

Most home-buyers purchase their home with a combination of a cash down payment and a mortgage. The loan-to-value ratio is a rule that establishes the maximum mortgage loan allowed on a home purchase.

a. If a home costs $300,000 and the maximum loan-to-value ratio is 80% as in Denmark, what is the minimum down payment?
b. If the maximum loan-to-value is reduced, how will this affect the demand for homes?
c. In Chapter 14 you were referred to The Economist House Price Index. Find that index and look at the behavior of house prices in Canada and the United States from 1970 to 2015. On December 10, 2015, the Canadian Minister of Finance announced an increase in the minimum down payment on any portion of a mortgage more than $500,000. (The announcement can be found at http://www.fin.gc.ca/n15/15-088-eng.asp.) Why was this action taken? Do you see an effect on house prices in Canada? What do you conclude?

DIG DEEPER

MyEconLab Visit www.myeconlab.com to complete all Dig Deeper problems and get instant feedback.

7. Saving, inflation and interest

Suppose you want to save to pay the school of your children when they enter university. The fee are €30,000. You save €15,000 and invest them at the interest rate of 8% during 10 years.

The future value of an amount in ten years is given by the formula $FV = Amount \times (1+i)^{10}$

For example the future value of the €10,000 in ten years if the interest rate is 5% is equal to $10\,000 \times (1.05)^{10}$ that is €16,289.

a. Suppose inflation is zero, will the amount saved enough to cover the cost?

b. Suppose now that the inflation is 5% during the ten years and that increase accordingly the university fee. Will your saving be enough then?

c. Approximate how much must you save to equal the amount needed with inflation?

8. Challenging Central Bankers

In a research paper "Central Banks: Powerful, Political and Unaccountable?" Willem H. Buiter, the chief economist of Citigroup, wrote:

Central banks' economic and political importance has grown in advanced economies since the start of the Great Financial Crisis in 2007. An unwillingness or inability of governments to use countercyclical fiscal policy has made monetary policy the only stabilization tool in town. However, much of the enhanced significance of central banks is due to their lender-of-last-resort and market-maker-of-last-resort roles, providing liquidity to financially distressed and illiquid financial institutions and sovereigns. Supervisory and regulatory functions, often deeply political, have been heaped on central banks. Central bankers also increasingly throw their weight around in the public discussion and even the design of fiscal policy and structural reforms, areas which are way beyond their mandates and competence. In this lecture I argue that the preservation of the central bank's legitimacy requires that a clear line be drawn between the central bank's provision of liquidity and the Treasury's solvency support for systemically important financial institutions. Central banks ought not to engage in quasi-fiscal activities.

What information would support this argument? If applied, what will be the consequences of such a policy in comparison to the economic policy practiced? Why do you think central banks are portrayed as such critics? This paper stressed the link between fiscal and monetary policy. Do you think central banks should not interfere with fiscal policies? Do you agree that the monetary policy is the only stabilization tool?

EXPLORE FURTHER

9. From zero lower bound to negative rate

Using data on ECB key interest rate you will find on ECB site (https://www.ecb.europa.eu) state the evolution of the decision of the Bank regarding the deposit facility (that is, the remuneration of the commercial bank deposit on the Central Bank account).

a. Compare this with the decision of Japan's Central Bank introduction of "Quantitative and Qualitative Monetary Easing with a Negative Interest Rate," issued on January 29, 2016, in order to achieve the price stability target of 2% at the earliest possible time.

b. What explanation could you find to explain that the Central Bank impose a negative interest rate on the deposit of the banks?

10. Problem 10 in Chapter 4 asked you to consider the current stance of monetary policy. Here, you are asked to do so again, but with the additional understanding of monetary policy you have gained in this and previous chapters.

a. Go to the Web site of ECB (https://www.ecb.europa.eu) and access the press conference (under media tab), preferably the press conference of March 2016 or a more recent conference.

   i. What are the main concerns of the European Central Bank?

   ii. Is there evidence that the monetary policy decisions are inspired by any economic model, and especially do you think that the Taylor rule could be applied to the decision?

   iii. How negative interest rate policy is justified?

   iv. Does the language raise any issues related to macroprudential regulation of financial institutions?

b. Go to the site of the People's Bank of China and find out what the objective of the monetary policy for the Bank is.

Further Readings

- For an early statement of inflation targeting, read "Inflation Targeting: A New Framework for Monetary Policy?" by Ben Bernanke and Frederic Mishkin, *Journal of Economic Perspectives*, 1997, Vol. 11 (Spring): pp. 97–116. (This article was written by Ben Bernanke before he became Chairman of the Fed.)

- For more institutional details on how the Fed actually functions, see http://www.federalreserve.gov/aboutthefed/default.htm.

- A time frame giving financial developments and the actions of the Fed from 2008 to 2011 is given at http://www.nytimes.com/interactive/2008/09/27/business/economy/20080927_WEEKS_TIMELINE.html.

- A great long read: The description of the problems in the financial sector and of U.S. monetary policy during the crisis by the Chairman of the Fed himself, in "The Courage to Act," by Ben Bernanke, W.W. Norton & Co., Inc., 2015.

Epilogue: The Story of Macroeconomics

MyEconLab Video

W e have spent 23 chapters presenting the framework that most economists use to think about macroeconomic issues, the major conclusions they draw, and the issues on which they disagree. How this framework has been built over time is a fascinating story. It is the story I want to tell in this chapter.

Section 24-1 starts at the beginning of modern macroeconomics—with Keynes and the Great Depression.

Section 24-2 turns to the *neoclassical synthesis*, a synthesis of Keynes's ideas with those of earlier economists—a synthesis that dominated macroeconomics until the early 1970s.

Section 24-3 describes the *rational expectations critique*, the strong attack on the neoclassical synthesis that led to a complete overhaul of macroeconomics starting in the 1970s.

Section 24-4 gives you a sense of the main lines of research in macroeconomics up to the crisis.

Section 24-5 takes a first pass at assessing the effects of the crisis on macroeconomics.

24-1 Keynes and the Great Depression

John Maynard Keynes

The history of modern macroeconomics starts in 1936, with the publication of John Maynard Keynes's *General Theory of Employment, Interest, and Money*. As he was writing the *General Theory*, Keynes confided to a friend: "I believe myself to be writing a book on economic theory which will largely revolutionize—not, I suppose at once but in the course of the next ten years, the way the world thinks about economic problems."

Keynes was right. The book's timing was one of the reasons for its immediate success. The Great Depression was not only an economic catastrophe but also an intellectual failure for the economists working on **business cycle theory**—as macroeconomics was then called. Few economists had a coherent explanation for the Depression, either for its depth or for its length. The economic measures taken by the Roosevelt administration as part of the New Deal had been based on instinct rather than on economic theory. The *General Theory* offered an interpretation of events, an intellectual framework, and a clear argument for government intervention.

The *General Theory* emphasized **effective demand**—what we now call *aggregate demand*. In the short run, Keynes argued, effective demand determines output. Even if output eventually returns to its natural level, the process is slow at best. One of Keynes's most famous quotes is: "In the long run, we are all dead."

In the process of deriving effective demand, Keynes introduced many of the building blocks of modern macroeconomics:

- The relation of consumption to income, and the multiplier, which explains how shocks to demand can be amplified and lead to larger shifts in output.
- **Liquidity preference**, which is the term Keynes gave to the demand for money, explains how monetary policy can affect interest rates and aggregate demand.
- The importance of expectations in affecting consumption and investment; and the idea that *animal spirits* (shifts in expectations) are a major factor behind shifts in demand and output.

The *General Theory* was more than a treatise for economists. It offered clear policy implications, and they were in tune with the times: Waiting for the economy to recover by itself was irresponsible. In the midst of a depression, trying to balance the budget was not only stupid, it was dangerous. Active use of fiscal policy was essential to return the country to high employment.

24-2 The Neoclassical Synthesis

Paul Samuelson

Within a few years, the *General Theory* had transformed macroeconomics. Not everyone was converted, and few agreed with it all. But most discussions became organized around it.

By the early 1950s a large consensus had emerged, based on an integration of many of Keynes's ideas and the ideas of earlier economists. This consensus was called the **neoclassical synthesis**. To quote from Paul Samuelson, in the 1955 edition of his text *Economics*—the first modern economics text:

> "In recent years, 90 percent of American economists have stopped being 'Keynesian economists' or 'Anti-Keynesian economists.' Instead, they have worked toward a synthesis of whatever is valuable in older economics and in modern theories of income determination. The result might be called neo-classical economics and is accepted, in its broad outlines, by all but about five percent of extreme left-wing and right-wing writers."

The neoclassical synthesis was to remain the dominant view for another 20 years. Progress was astonishing, leading many to call the period from the early 1940s to the early 1970s the golden age of macroeconomics.

Progress on All Fronts

The first order of business after the publication of the *General Theory* was to formalize mathematically what Keynes meant. Although Keynes knew mathematics, he had avoided using it in the *General Theory*. One result was endless controversies about what Keynes meant and whether there were logical flaws in some of his arguments.

Franco Modigliani

MyEconLab Video

The *IS-LM* Model

A number of formalizations of Keynes's ideas were offered. The most influential one was the *IS-LM* model, developed by John Hicks and Alvin Hansen in the 1930s and early 1940s. The initial version of the *IS-LM* model—which was actually close to the version presented in Chapter 5 of this book—was criticized for emasculating many of Keynes's insights. Expectations played no role, and the adjustment of prices and wages was altogether absent. Yet the *IS-LM* model provided a basis from which to start building, and as such it was immensely successful. Discussions became organized around the slopes of the *IS* and *LM* curves, what variables were missing from the two relations, what equations for prices and wages should be added to the model, and so on.

Theories of Consumption, Investment, and Money Demand

Keynes had emphasized the importance of consumption and investment behavior, and of the choice between money and other financial assets. Major progress was soon made along all three fronts.

In the 1950s, Franco Modigliani (then at Carnegie Mellon, later at MIT) and Milton Friedman (at the University of Chicago) independently developed the theory of consumption we saw in Chapter 15. Both insisted on the importance of expectations in determining current consumption decisions.

James Tobin, from Yale, developed the theory of investment, based on the relation between the present value of profits and investment. The theory was further developed and tested by Dale Jorgenson, from Harvard. You saw this theory in Chapter 15.

Tobin also developed the theory of the demand for money and, more generally, the theory of the choice between different assets based on liquidity, return, and risk. His work has become the basis not only for an improved treatment of financial markets in macroeconomics, but also for finance theory in general.

James Tobin

Growth Theory

In parallel with the work on fluctuations, there was a renewed focus on growth. In contrast to the stagnation in the pre-World War II era, most countries were experiencing rapid growth in the 1950s and 1960s. Even if they experienced fluctuations, their standard of living was increasing rapidly. The growth model developed by MIT's Robert Solow in 1956, which we saw in Chapters 11 and 12, provided a framework to think about the determinants of growth. It was followed by an explosion of work on the roles saving and technological progress play in determining growth.

Macroeconometric Models

All these contributions were integrated in larger and larger macroeconometric models. The first U.S. macroeconometric model, developed by Lawrence Klein from the University of Pennsylvania in the early 1950s, was an extended *IS* relation, with 16 equations. With

Robert Solow

Lawrence Klein

Milton Friedman

the development of the National Income and Product Accounts (making available better data) and the development of econometrics and of computers, the models quickly grew in size. The most impressive effort was the construction of the MPS model (MPS stands for MIT-Penn-SSRC, for the two universities and the research institution—the Social Science Research Council—involved in its construction), developed during the 1960s by a group led by Modigliani. Its structure was an expanded version of the *IS-LM* model, plus a Phillips curve mechanism. But its components—consumption, investment, and money demand— all reflected the tremendous theoretical and empirical progress made since Keynes.

Keynesians versus Monetarists

With such rapid progress, many macroeconomists—those who defined themselves as **Keynesians**—came to believe that the future was bright. The nature of fluctuations was becoming increasingly well understood; the development of models allowed policy decisions to be made more effectively. The time when the economy could be fine-tuned, and recessions all but eliminated, seemed not far in the future.

This optimism was met with skepticism by a small but influential minority, the **monetarists**. The intellectual leader of the monetarists was Milton Friedman. Although Friedman saw much progress being made—and was himself the father of one of the major contributions to macroeconomics, the theory of consumption—he did not share in the general enthusiasm. He believed that the understanding of the economy remained very limited. He questioned the motives of governments as well as the notion that they actually knew enough to improve macroeconomic outcomes.

In the 1960s, debates between "Keynesians" and "monetarists" dominated the economic headlines. The debates centered around three issues: (1) the effectiveness of monetary policy versus fiscal policy, (2) the Phillips curve, and (3) the role of policy.

Monetary Policy versus Fiscal Policy

Keynes had emphasized *fiscal* rather than *monetary* policy as the key to fighting recessions. And this had remained the prevailing wisdom. The *IS* curve, many argued, was quite steep. Changes in the interest rate had little effect on demand and output. Thus, monetary policy did not work very well. Fiscal policy, which affects demand directly, could affect output faster and more reliably.

Friedman strongly challenged this conclusion. In their 1963 book *A Monetary History of the United States, 1867–1960*, Friedman and Anna Schwartz painstakingly reviewed the evidence on monetary policy and the relation between money and output in the United States over a century. Their conclusion was not only that monetary policy was powerful, but that movements in money did explain most of the fluctuations in output. They interpreted the Great Depression as the result of a major mistake in monetary policy, a decrease in the money supply as a result of bank failures—a decrease that the Fed could have avoided by increasing the monetary base, but had not.

Friedman and Schwartz's challenge was followed by a vigorous debate and by intense research on the respective effects of fiscal policy and monetary policy. In the end, a consensus was reached. Both fiscal policy and monetary policy clearly affected the economy. And if policy makers cared about not only the level but also the composition of output, the best policy was typically a mix of the two.

The Phillips Curve

The second debate focused on the Phillips curve. The Phillips curve was not part of the initial Keynesian model. But because it provided such a convenient (and apparently reliable) way of explaining the movement of wages and prices over time, it had become part of the neoclassical synthesis. In the 1960s, based on the empirical evidence up until then, many Keynesian economists believed that there was a reliable trade-off between unemployment and inflation, even in the long run.

Milton Friedman and Edmund Phelps (from Columbia University) strongly disagreed. They argued that the existence of such a long-run trade-off flew in the face of basic economic theory. They argued that the apparent trade-off would quickly vanish if policy makers actually tried to exploit it—that is, if they tried to achieve low unemployment by accepting higher inflation. As we saw in Chapter 8 when we studied the evolution of the Phillips curve, Friedman and Phelps were definitely right. By the mid-1970s, the consensus was indeed that there was no long-run trade-off between inflation and unemployment.

Edmund Phelps

The Role of Policy

The third debate centered on the role of policy. Skeptical that economists knew enough to stabilize output and that policy makers could be trusted to do the right thing, Friedman argued for the use of simple rules, such as steady money growth (a rule we discussed in Chapter 23). Here is what he said in 1958:

> "A steady rate of growth in the money supply will not mean perfect stability even though it would prevent the kind of wide fluctuations that we have experienced from time to time in the past. It is tempting to try to go farther and to use monetary changes to offset other factors making for expansion and contraction... The available evidence casts grave doubts on the possibility of producing any fine adjustments in economic activity by fine adjustments in monetary policy—at least in the present state of knowledge. There are thus serious limitations to the possibility of a discretionary monetary policy and much danger that such a policy may make matters worse rather than better.
>
> Political pressures to 'do something' in the face of either relatively mild price rises or relatively mild price and employment declines are clearly very strong indeed in the existing state of public attitudes. The main moral to be drawn from the two preceding points is that yielding to these pressures may frequently do more harm than good."

> *Source:* "The Supply of Money and Changes in Prices and Output," Testimony to Congress, 1958.

As we saw in Chapter 21, this debate on the role of macroeconomic policy has not been settled. The nature of the arguments has changed a bit, but they are still with us today.

24-3 The Rational Expectations Critique

Despite the battles between Keynesians and monetarists, macroeconomics at around 1970 looked like a successful and mature field. It appeared to successfully explain events and guide policy choices. Most debates were framed within a common intellectual framework. But within a few years, the field was in crisis. This crisis had two sources:

One was events. By the mid-1970s, most countries were experiencing *stagflation*, a word created at the time to denote the simultaneous existence of high unemployment and high inflation. Macroeconomists had not predicted stagflation. After the fact and after a few years of research, a convincing explanation was provided, based on the effects of adverse supply shocks on both inflation and output. (We discussed the effects of such shocks in Chapter 9.) But it was too late to undo the damage to the discipline's image.

The other was ideas. In the early 1970s, a small group of economists—Robert Lucas from Chicago; Thomas Sargent, then from Minnesota and now at New York University; and Robert Barro, then from Chicago and now at Harvard—led a strong attack against mainstream macroeconomics. They did not mince words. In a 1978 paper, Lucas and Sargent stated:

Robert Lucas

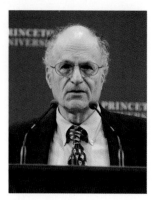

Thomas Sargent

Robert Barro

"That the predictions [of Keynesian economics] were wildly incorrect, and that the doctrine on which they were based was fundamentally flawed, are now simple matters of fact, involving no subtleties in economic theory. The task which faces contemporary students of the business cycle is that of sorting through the wreckage, determining what features of that remarkable intellectual event called the Keynesian Revolution can be salvaged and put to good use, and which others must be discarded."

The Three Implications of Rational Expectations

Lucas and Sargent's main argument was that Keynesian economics had ignored the full implications of the effect of expectations on behavior. The way to proceed, they argued, was to assume that people formed expectations as rationally as they could, based on the information they had. Thinking of people as having *rational expectations* had three major implications, all highly damaging to Keynesian macroeconomics.

The Lucas Critique

The first implication was that existing macroeconomic models could not be used to help design policy. Although these models recognized that expectations affect behavior, they did not incorporate expectations explicitly. All variables were assumed to depend on current and past values of other variables, including policy variables. Thus, what the models captured was the set of relations between economic variables as they had held in the past, under past policies. Were these policies to change, Lucas argued, the way people formed expectations would change as well, making estimated relations—and, by implication, simulations generated using existing macroeconometric models—poor guides to what would happen under these new policies. This critique of macroeconometric models became known as the **Lucas critique**. To take again the history of the Phillips curve as an example, the data up to the early 1970s had suggested a trade-off between unemployment and inflation. As policy makers tried to exploit that trade-off, it disappeared.

Rational Expectations and the Phillips Curve

The second implication was that when rational expectations were introduced in Keynesian models, these models actually delivered very un-Keynesian conclusions. For example, the models implied that deviations of output from its natural level were short lived, much more so than Keynesian economists claimed.

This argument was based on a reexamination of the aggregate supply relation. In Keynesian models, the slow return of output to the natural level of output came from the slow adjustment of prices and wages through the Phillips curve mechanism. An increase in money, for example, led first to higher output and to lower unemployment. Lower unemployment then led to higher nominal wages and to higher prices. The adjustment continued until wages and prices had increased in the same proportion as nominal money, until unemployment and output were both back at their natural levels.

But this adjustment, Lucas pointed out, was highly dependent on wage setters' backward-looking expectations of inflation. In the MPS model, for example, wages responded only to current and past inflation and to current unemployment. But once the assumption was made that wage setters had rational expectations, the adjustment was likely to be much faster. Changes in money, to the extent that they were anticipated, might have no effect on output. For example, anticipating an increase in money of 5% over the coming year, wage setters would increase the nominal wages set in contracts for the coming year by 5%. Firms would in turn increase prices by 5%. The result would be no change in the real money stock, and no change in demand or output.

Within the logic of the Keynesian models, Lucas therefore argued, only *unanticipated changes in money* should affect output. Predictable movements in money should have no effect on activity. More generally, if wage setters had rational expectations, shifts in demand were likely to have effects on output for only as long as nominal wages were set—a year or so. Even on its own terms, the Keynesian model did not deliver a convincing theory of the long-lasting effects of demand on output.

Optimal Control versus Game Theory

The third implication was that if people and firms had rational expectations, it was wrong to think of policy as the control of a complicated but passive system. Rather, the right way was to think of policy as a game between policy makers and the economy. The right tool was not *optimal control*, but *game theory*. And game theory led to a different vision of policy. A striking example was the issue of *time inconsistency* discussed by Finn Kydland (then at Carnegie Mellon, now at University of California–Santa Barbara) and Edward Prescott (then at Carnegie Mellon, now at Arizona State University), an issue that we discussed in Chapter 21. Good intentions on the part of policy makers could actually lead to disaster.

To summarize: When rational expectations were introduced, Keynesian models could not be used to determine policy; Keynesian models could not explain long-lasting deviations of output from the natural level of output; the theory of policy had to be redesigned, using the tools of game theory.

The Integration of Rational Expectations

As you might have guessed from the tone of Lucas and Sargent's quote, the intellectual atmosphere in macroeconomics was tense in the early 1970s. But within a few years, a process of integration (of ideas, not people, because tempers remained high) had begun, and it was to dominate the 1970s and the 1980s.

Fairly quickly, the idea that rational expectations was the right working assumption gained wide acceptance. This was not because macroeconomists believed that people, firms, and participants in financial markets always form expectations rationally. But rational expectations appeared to be a natural benchmark, at least until economists have made more progress in understanding whether, when, and how actual expectations systematically differ from rational expectations.

Work then started on the challenges raised by Lucas and Sargent.

The Implications of Rational Expectations

First, there was a systematic exploration of the role and implications of rational expectations in goods markets, in financial markets, and in labor markets. Much of what was discovered has been presented in this book. For example:

■ Robert Hall, then from MIT and now at Stanford, showed that if consumers are foresighted (in the sense defined in Chapter 15), then changes in consumption should be unpredictable. The best forecast of consumption next year would be consumption this year! Put another way, changes in consumption should be hard to predict. This result came as a surprise to most macroeconomists at the time, but it is in fact based on a simple intuition. If consumers are foresighted, they will change their consumption only when they learn something new about the future. But by definition, such news cannot be predicted. This consumption behavior, known as the **random walk of consumption**, became the benchmark in consumption research thereafter.

Robert Hall

Rudiger Dornbusch

Stanley Fischer

John Taylor

■ Rudiger Dornbusch from MIT showed that the large swings in exchange rates under flexible exchange rates, which had previously been thought of as the result of speculation by irrational investors, were fully consistent with rationality. His argument—which we saw in Chapter 20—was that changes in monetary policy can lead to long-lasting changes in nominal interest rates; changes in current and expected nominal interest rates lead in turn to large changes in the exchange rate. Dornbusch's model, known as the *overshooting* model of exchange rates, became the benchmark in discussions of exchange rate movements.

Wage and Price Setting

Second, there was a systematic exploration of the determination of wages and prices, going far beyond the Phillips curve relation. Two important contributions were made by Stanley Fischer, then at MIT, now governor of the Central Bank of Israel, and John Taylor, then from Columbia University and now at Stanford. Both showed that the adjustment of prices and wages in response to changes in unemployment can be slow *even under rational expectations*.

Fischer and Taylor pointed out an important characteristic of both wage and price setting, the **staggering of wage and price decisions**. In contrast to the simple story we told previously, where all wages and prices increased simultaneously in anticipation of an increase in money, actual wage and price decisions are staggered over time. So there is not one sudden synchronized adjustment of all wages and prices to an increase in money. Rather, the adjustment is likely to be slow, with wages and prices adjusting to the new level of money through a process of leapfrogging over time. Fischer and Taylor thus showed that the second issue raised by the rational-expectations critique could be resolved, that a slow return of output to the natural level of output can be consistent with rational expectations in the labor market.

The Theory of Policy

Third, thinking about policy in terms of game theory led to an explosion of research on the nature of the games being played, not only between policy makers and the economy but also between policy makers—between political parties, or between the central bank and the government, or between governments of different countries. One of the major achievements of this research was the development of a more rigorous way of thinking about fuzzy notions such as "credibility," "reputation," and "commitment." At the same time, there was a distinct shift in focus from "what governments should do" to "what governments actually do," an increasing awareness of the political constraints that economists should take into account when advising policy makers.

In short: By the end of the 1980s, the challenges raised by the rational-expectations critique had led to a complete overhaul of macroeconomics. The basic structure had been extended to take into account the implications of rational expectations, or, more generally, of forward-looking behavior by people and firms. As you have seen, these themes play a central role in this book.

24-4 Developments in Macroeconomics up to the 2009 Crisis

From the late 1980s to the crisis, three groups dominated the research headlines: the new classicals, the new Keynesians, and the new growth theorists. (Note the generous use of the word *new*. Unlike producers of laundry detergents, economists stop short of using "new and improved." But the subliminal message is the same.)

New Classical Economics and Real Business Cycle Theory

Edward Prescott

The rational-expectations critique was more than just a critique of Keynesian economics. It also offered its own interpretation of fluctuations. Lucas argued that instead of relying on imperfections in labor markets, on the slow adjustment of wages and prices, and so on to explain fluctuations, macroeconomists should see how far they could go in explaining fluctuations as the effects of shocks in competitive markets with fully flexible prices and wages.

This research agenda was taken up by the **new classicals**. The intellectual leader was Edward Prescott, and the models he and his followers developed are known as **real business cycle (RBC) models**. Their approach was based on two premises.

The first was methodological. Lucas had argued that, to avoid earlier pitfalls, macroeconomic models should be constructed from explicit microfoundations (i.e., utility maximization by workers, profit maximization by firms, and rational expectations). Before the development of computers, this was hard, if not impossible, to achieve. Models constructed in this way would have been too complex to solve analytically. Indeed, much of the art of macroeconomics was in finding simple shortcuts to capture the essence of a model while keeping the model simple enough to solve (it still remains the art of writing a good textbook). The development of computing power made it possible to solve such models numerically, and an important contribution of RBC theory was the development of more and more powerful numerical methods of solution, which allowed for the development of richer and richer models.

The second was conceptual. Until the 1970s, most fluctuations had been seen as the result of imperfections, of deviations of actual output from a slowly moving potential level of output. Following up on Lucas's suggestion, Prescott argued in a series of influential contributions, that fluctuations could indeed be interpreted as coming from the effects of technological shocks in competitive markets with fully flexible prices and wages. In other words, he argued that movements in actual output could be seen as movements in—rather than as deviations from—the potential level of output. As new discoveries are made, he argued, productivity increases, leading to an increase in output. The increase in productivity leads to an increase in the wage, which makes it more attractive to work, leading workers to work more. Productivity increases therefore lead to increases in both output and employment, just as we observe in the real world. Fluctuations are desirable features of the economy, not something policy makers should try to reduce.

Not surprisingly, this radical view of fluctuations was criticized on many fronts. As we discussed in Chapter 12, technological progress is the result of many innovations, each taking a long time to diffuse throughout the economy. It is hard to see how this process could generate anything like the large short-run fluctuations in output that we observe in practice. It is also hard to think of recessions as times of technological *regress*, times in which productivity and output both decrease. Finally, as we have seen, there is strong evidence that changes in money, which have no effect on output in RBC models, in fact have strong effects on output in the real world. Still, the conceptual RBC approach proved influential and useful. It made an important point, that not all fluctuations in output are deviations of output from its natural level, but movements in the natural level itself.

New Keynesian Economics

The term **new Keynesians** denotes a loosely connected group of researchers who shared a common belief that the synthesis that emerged in response to the rational-expectations critique was basically correct. But they also shared the belief that much remained to be learned about the nature of imperfections in different markets and about the implications of those imperfections for macroeconomic fluctuations.

George Akerlof

Janet Yellen

Ben Bernanke

Paul Romer

There was further work on the nature of **nominal rigidities**. As we saw earlier in this chapter, Fischer and Taylor had shown that with staggering of wage or price decisions, output can deviate from its natural level for a long time. This conclusion raised a number of questions. If staggering of decisions is responsible, at least in part, for fluctuations, why don't wage setters/price setters synchronize decisions? Why aren't prices and wages adjusted more often? Why aren't all prices and all wages changed, say, on the first day of each week? In tackling these issues, George Akerlof (from Berkeley), Janet Yellen (then at Berkeley, now the Chairwoman of the Federal Reserve Board), and N. Gregory Mankiw (from Harvard University) derived a surprising and important result, often referred to as the **menu cost** explanation of output fluctuations.

Each wage setter or price setter is largely indifferent as to when and how often he changes his own wage or price (for a retailer, changing the prices on the shelf every day versus every week does not make much of a difference to the store's overall profits). Therefore, even small costs of changing prices—like the costs involved in printing a new menu, for example—can lead to infrequent and staggered price adjustment. This staggering leads to slow adjustment of the price level and to large aggregate output fluctuations in response to movements in aggregate demand. In short, decisions that do not matter much at the individual level (how often to change prices or wages) lead to large aggregate effects (slow adjustment of the price level, and shifts in aggregate demand that have a large effect on output).

Another line of research focused on the imperfections in the labor market. We discussed in Chapter 7 the notion of *efficiency wages*—the idea that wages, if perceived by workers as being too low, may lead to shirking by workers on the job, to problems of morale within the firm, to difficulties in recruiting or keeping good workers, and so on. One influential researcher in this area was Akerlof, who explored the role of "norms," the rules that develop in any organization—in this case, the firm—to assess what is fair or unfair. This research led him and others to explore issues previously left to research in sociology and psychology, and to examine their macroeconomic implications. In another direction, Peter Diamond (from MIT), Dale Mortensen (from Cornell), and Christopher Pissarides (from the London School of Economics) looked at the labor market as the market characterized by constant reallocation, large flows, and bargaining between workers and firms, a characterization that has proven extremely useful and that we relied upon in Chapter 7.

Yet another line of research, which turned out to be precious when the crisis took place, explored the role of imperfections in credit markets. Most macro models assumed that monetary policy worked through interest rates, and that firms could borrow as much as they wanted at the market interest rate. In practice, many firms can borrow only from banks. And banks often turn down potential borrowers, despite the willingness of these borrowers to pay the interest rate charged by the bank. Why this happens, and how it affects our view of how monetary policy works, was the focus of research by, in particular, Ben Bernanke (then from Princeton, and then Chairman of the Fed, now at the Brookings Institution) and Mark Gertler (from New York University).

New Growth Theory

After being one of the most active topics of research in the 1960s, growth theory had gone into an intellectual slump. Since the late 1980s however, growth theory has made a strong comeback. The set of new contributions went under the name of **new growth theory**.

Two economists, Robert Lucas (the same Lucas who spearheaded the rational-expectations critique) and Paul Romer, then from Berkeley, now at New York University, played an important role in defining the issues. When growth theory faded in the late 1960s, two major issues were left largely unresolved. One issue was the role of increasing returns to scale—whether, say, doubling capital and labor can actually cause output to more than double. The other was the determinants of technological progress. These are the two major issues on which new growth theory concentrated.

The discussions of the effects of research and development (R&D) on technological progress in Chapter 12, and of the interaction between technological progress and unemployment in Chapter 13, both reflect some of the advances made on this front. An important contribution here was the work of Philippe Aghion (then at Harvard University, now at the College de France) and Peter Howitt (then at Brown University), who developed a theme first explored by Joseph Schumpeter in the 1930s, that is, the notion that growth is a process of *creative destruction* in which new products are constantly introduced, making old ones obsolete. Institutions that slow this process of reallocation (for example, by making it harder to create new firms or by making it more expensive for firms to lay off workers) may slow down the rate of technological progress and thus decrease growth.

Philippe Aghion

Research also tried to identify the precise role of specific institutions in determining growth. Andrei Shleifer (from Harvard University) explored the role of different legal systems in affecting the organization of the economy, from financial markets to labor markets, and, through these channels, the effects of legal systems on growth. Daron Acemoglu (from MIT) explored how to go from correlations between institutions and growth—democratic countries are on average richer—to causality from institutions to growth. Does the correlation tell us that democracy leads to higher output per person, or does it tell us that higher output per person leads to democracy, or that some other factor leads to both more democracy and higher output per person? Examining the history of former colonies, Acemoglu argued that their growth performance has been shaped by the type of institutions put in place by their colonizers, thus showing a strong causal role of institutions in economic performance.

Peter Howitt

Toward an Integration

In the 1980s and 1990s, discussions between these three groups, and in particular between new classicals and new Keynesians, were often heated. New Keynesians would accuse new classicals of relying on an implausible explanation of fluctuations and ignoring obvious imperfections; new classicals would in turn point to the ad hocery of some of the new Keynesian models. From the outside—and indeed sometimes from the inside—macroeconomics looked like a battlefield rather than a research field.

Andrei Shleifer

By the 2000s however, a synthesis appeared to be emerging. Methodologically, it built on the RBC approach and its careful description of the optimization problems of people and firms. Conceptually, it recognized the potential importance, emphasized by the RBC and the new growth theory, of changes in the pace of technological progress. But it also allowed for many of the imperfections emphasized by the new Keynesians, from the role of bargaining in the determination of wages, to the role of imperfect information in credit and financial markets, to the role of nominal rigidities in creating a role for aggregate demand to affect output. There was no convergence on a single model or on a single list of important imperfections, but there was broad agreement on the framework and on the way to proceed.

A good example of this convergence was the work of Michael Woodford (from Columbia) and Jordi Gali (from Pompeu Fabra). Woodford, Gali, and a number of coauthors developed a model, known as the *new Keynesian model*, that embodies utility and profit maximization, rational expectations, and nominal rigidities. You can think of it as a high-tech version of the model that was presented in Chapter 16. This model proved extremely useful and influential in the redesign of monetary policy—from the focus on inflation targeting to the reliance on interest rate rules—that we described in Chapter 23. It led to the development of a class of larger models that build on its simple structure

Daron Acemoglu

but allow for a longer menu of imperfections and thus must be solved numerically. These models, which are now standard work horses in most central banks, are known as "*dynamic stochastic general equilibrium*," (DSGE) models.

24-5 First Lessons for Macroeconomics after the Crisis

Just at the time at which a new synthesis appeared to be in sight and macroeconomists felt that they had the tools to understand the economy and design policy, the crisis started, and, at the time of writing this chapter, is still continuing. We saw in Section 24-1 how the Great Depression had led to a dramatic reassessment of macro-economics and started the Keynesian revolution. You may ask, will this crisis have the same effect on macroeconomics, leading yet to another revolution? It is too early to say, but my guess is probably not a revolution, but a major reassessment nonetheless.

There is no question that the crisis reflects a major intellectual failure on the part of macroeconomics. The failure was in not realizing that such a large crisis *could happen*, that the characteristics of the economy were such that a relatively small shock, in this case the decrease in U.S. housing prices, could lead to a major financial and macroeconomic global crisis. The source of the failure, in turn, was insufficient focus on the role of the financial institutions in the economy. (To be fair, a few macroeconomists, who were looking more closely at the financial system, sounded the alarm; best known among them are Nouriel Roubini, from New York University, and the economists at the Bank for International Settlements in Basel, whose job it is to closely follow financial developments.)

By and large, the financial system, and the complex role of banks and other financial institutions in the intermediation of funds between lenders and borrowers, was ignored in most macroeconomic models. There were exceptions. Work by Doug Diamond (from Chicago) and Philip Dybvig (from Washington University in Saint Louis) in the 1980s had clarified the nature of bank runs (which we examined in Chapter 6). Illiquid assets and liquid liabilities created a risk of runs even for solvent banks. The problem could only be avoided by the provision of liquidity by the central bank if and when needed. Work by Bengt Holmström and Jean Tirole (both from MIT) had shown that liquidity issues were endemic to a modern economy. Not only banks, but also firms could well find themselves in a position where they were solvent, but illiquid, unable to raise the additional cash to finish a project or unable to repay investors when they wanted repayment. An important paper by Andrei Shleifer (from Harvard) and Robert Vishny (from Chicago) called "The Limits of Arbitrage" had shown that, after a decline in an asset price below its fundamental value, investors might not be able to take advantage of the arbitrage opportunity; indeed, they may themselves be forced to sell the asset, leading to a further decline in the price and a further deviation from fundamentals. Behavioral economists (for example, Richard Thaler, from Chicago) had pointed to the way in which individuals differ from the rational individual model typically used in economics, and had drawn implications for financial markets.

Thus, most of the elements needed to understand the crisis were available. Much of the work, however, was carried out outside macroeconomics, in the fields of finance or corporate finance. The elements were not integrated in a consistent macroeconomic model, and their interactions were poorly understood. Leverage, complexity, and liquidity, the factors which, as we saw in Chapter 6, combined to create the crisis, were nearly fully absent from the macroeconomic models used by central banks.

After eight years since the start of the crisis, things have changed dramatically. Not surprisingly, researchers have turned their attention to the financial system and the nature of macro financial linkages. Further work is taking place on the various pieces, and these pieces are starting to be integrated into the large macroeconomic models. The

Michael Woodford

MyEconLab Video

Jordi Gali

lessons for policy are also being drawn, be it on the use of *macroprudential* tools or the dangers of high public debt. There is still a long way to go, but, in the end, our macroeconomic models will be richer, with a better understanding of the financial system. Yet, one has to be realistic. If history is any guide, the economy will be hit by yet another type of shock we have not thought of.

The lessons from the crisis probably go beyond adding the financial sector to macroeconomic models and analysis. The Great Depression had, rightly, led most economists to question the macroeconomic properties of a market economy and to suggest a larger role for government intervention. The crisis is raising similar questions. Both the new classical and new Keynesian models had in common the belief that, in the medium run at least, the economy naturally returned to its natural level. The new classicals took the extreme position that output was always at its natural level. The new Keynesians took the view that, in the short run, output would likely deviate from its natural level. But they maintained that, eventually, in the medium run, natural forces would return the economy to the natural level. The Great Depression and the long slump in Japan were well known; they were seen however as aberrations and thought to be caused by substantial policy mistakes that could have been avoided. Many economists today believe that this optimism was excessive. After seven years in the liquidity trap in the United States, it is clear that the usual adjustment mechanism—namely, a decrease in interest rates in response to low output—is not operational. It is also clear that the room for policy, be it monetary policy, or fiscal policy, is also more limited than previously thought.

Bengt Holmström

If there is a consensus, it might be that with respect to small shocks and normal fluctuations, the adjustment process works; but that, in response to large, exceptional shocks, the normal adjustment process may fail, the room for policy may be limited, and it may take a long time for the economy to repair itself. For the moment, the priority is for researchers is to better understand what has happened, and for policy makers to use as best they can, the monetary and fiscal policy tools they have, to steer the world economy back to health.

Jean Tirole

Summary

- The history of modern macroeconomics starts in 1936, with the publication of Keynes's *General Theory of Employment, Interest, and Money*. Keynes's contribution was formalized in the *IS-LM* model by John Hicks and Alvin Hansen in the 1930s and early 1940s.

- The period from the early 1940s to the early 1970s can be called the golden age of macroeconomics. Among the major developments were the development of the theories of consumption, investment, money demand, and portfolio choice; the development of growth theory; and the development of large macroeconometric models.

- The main debate during the 1960s was between Keynesians and monetarists. Keynesians believed developments in macroeconomic theory allowed for better control of the economy. Monetarists, led by Milton Friedman, were more skeptical of the ability of governments to help stabilize the economy.

- In the 1970s, macroeconomics experienced a crisis. There were two reasons: One was the appearance of stagflation, which came as a surprise to most economists. The other was a theoretical attack led by Robert Lucas. Lucas and his followers showed that when rational expectations were introduced, (1) Keynesian models could not be used to determine policy, (2) Keynesian models could not explain long-lasting deviations of output from its natural level, and (3) the theory of policy needed to be redesigned using the tools of game theory.

- Much of the 1970s and 1980s was spent integrating rational MEL expectations into macroeconomics. As is reflected in this text, Video macroeconomists are now much more aware of the role of expectations in determining the effects of shocks and policy and of the complexity of policy than they were two decades ago.

- Recent research in macroeconomic theory, up to the crisis, proceeded along three lines: New classical economists explored the extent to which fluctuations can be explained as movements in the natural level of output, as opposed to movements away from the natural level of output. New Keynesian economists explored more formally the role of market imperfections in fluctuations. New growth theorists explored the determinants of technological progress.

- These lines were increasingly overlapping, and, on the eve of the crisis, a new synthesis appeared to be emerging.

- The crisis reflects a major intellectual failure on the part of macroeconomics: the failure to understand the macroeconomic importance of the financial system. Although many of the elements needed to understand the crisis had been developed before the crisis, they were not central to macroeconomic thinking and were not integrated in large macroeconomic models. Much research is now focused on macro financial linkages.

- The crisis has also raised a larger issue, about the adjustment process through which output returns to its natural level. If there is a consensus, it might be that with respect to small shocks and normal fluctuations, the adjustment process works, and policy can accelerate this return; but that, in response to large, exceptional shocks, the normal adjustment process may fail, the room for policy may be limited, and it may take a long time for the economy to repair itself.

Key Terms

business cycle theory, 518
effective demand, 518
liquidity preference, 518
neoclassical synthesis, 518
Keynesians, 520
monetarists, 520
Lucas critique, 522
random walk of consumption, 523

staggering (of wage and price decisions), 524
new classicals, 525
real business cycles, 525
RBC models, 525
new Keynesians, 525
nominal rigidities, 526
menu costs, 526
new growth theory, 526

Further Readings

- Two classics are J. M. Keynes, *The General Theory of Employment, Interest, and Money*, Palgrave Macmillan, 1936, and Milton Friedman and Anna Schwartz, *A Monetary History of the United States*, Princeton University Press, 1963. Warning: The first makes for hard reading, and the second is a heavy volume.

- For an account of macroeconomics in texts since the 1940s, read Paul Samuelson's, "Credo of a Lucky Textbook Author," *Journal of Economic Perspectives*, 1997, Vol. 11 (Spring): pp: 153–160.

- In the introduction to *Studies in Business Cycle Theory*, MIT Press, 1981, Robert Lucas develops his approach to macroeconomics and gives a guide to his contributions.

- The paper that launched real business cycle theory is Edward Prescott, "Theory Ahead of Business Cycle Measurement," *Federal Reserve Bank of Minneapolis Review*, 1996 (Fall), pp: 9–22. It is not easy reading.

- For more on new Keynesian economics, read David Romer, "The New Keynesian Synthesis," *Journal of Economic Perspectives*, 1993, Vol. 7 (Winter), pp: 5–22.

- For more on new growth theory, read Paul Romer, "The Origins of Endogenous Growth," *Journal of Economic Perspectives*, 1994, Vol. 8 (Winter), pp: 3–22.

- For a detailed look at the history of macroeconomic ideas, with in-depth interviews of most of the major researchers, read Brian Snowdon and Howard Vane, *Modern Macroeconomics: Its Origins, Development and Current State*, Edward Elgar Publishing Ltd., 2005.

- For two points of view on the state of macroeconomics pre crisis, read V. V. Chari and Patrick Kehoe, "Macroeconomics in Practice: How Theory Is Shaping Policy," *Journal of Economic Perspectives*, 2006, Vol. 20, No. 4, pp: 3–28; and N. Greg Mankiw, "The Macroeconomist as Scientist and Engineer," *Journal of Economic Perspectives*, Vol. 20, No. 4, pp: 29–46.

- For a skeptical view of financial markets and the contributions of Thaler and Shleifer among others, read *The Myth of the Rational Market. A History of Risk, Reward, and Delusion on Wall Street* by Justin Fox, Harper Collins Publishers, 2009.

- For an assessment of macroeconomic policy post-crisis, read *In the Wake of the Crisis: Leading Economists Reassess Economic Policy*, edited by Olivier Blanchard et al., MIT Press, 2012. If you want to learn more about macroeconomic issues and theory:

- Most economics journals are heavy on mathematics and are hard to read. But a few make an effort to be more friendly. The *Journal of Economic Perspectives*, in particular, has nontechnical articles on current economic research and issues. The *Brookings Papers on Economic Activity*, published twice a year, analyze current macroeconomic problems. So does *Economic Policy*, published in Europe, which focuses more on European issues.

- Most regional Federal Reserve Banks also publish reviews with easy-to-read articles; these reviews are available free of charge. Among these are the *Economic Review* published by the Cleveland Fed, the *Economic Review* published by the Kansas City Fed, the *New England Economic Review* published by the Boston Fed, and the *Quarterly Review* published by the Minneapolis Fed.

- More advanced treatments of current macroeconomic theory—roughly at the level of a first graduate course in macroeconomics—are given by David Romer, *Advanced Macroeconomics*, 4th ed., McGraw-Hill, 2011, and by Olivier Blanchard and Stanley Fischer, *Lectures on Macroeconomics* (1989).

Appendices

APPENDIX 1 An Introduction to National Income and Product Accounts

This appendix introduces the basic structure and the terms used in the national income and product accounts. The basic measure of aggregate activity is gross domestic product (GDP). The **national income and product accounts (NIPA)**, or simply **national accounts** are organized around two decompositions of GDP.

One decomposes GDP from the *income side*: Who receives what?

The other decomposes GDP from the *production side* (called the *product side* in the national accounts): What is produced, and who buys it?

The Income Side

Table A1-1 looks at the income side of GDP—who receives what.

The top part of the table (lines 1–8) goes from GDP to national income—the sum of the incomes received by the different factors of production:

■ The starting point, in line 1, is **gross domestic product (GDP)**. GDP is defined as *the market value of the goods and services produced by labor and property located in the United States.*

■ The next three lines take us from GDP to **gross national product (GNP)** (line 4). GNP is an alternative measure of aggregate output. It is defined as *the market value of the goods and services produced by labor and property supplied by U.S. residents.*

Until the 1990s, most countries used GNP rather than GDP as the main measure of aggregate activity. The emphasis in the U.S. national accounts shifted from GNP to GDP in 1991. The difference between the two comes from the distinction between "located in the United States" (used for GDP) and "supplied by U.S. residents" (used for GNP). For example, profit from a

Table A1-1 GDP: The Income Side, 2014 (billions of dollars)		
From gross domestic product to national income:		
1 **Gross domestic product (GDP)**	17,348	
2 Plus: receipts of factor income from the rest of the world		854
3 Minus: payments of factor income to the rest of the world		−591
4 Equals: **Gross national product**	17,611	
5 Minus: consumption of fixed capital		2747
6 Equals: **Net national product**	14,865	
7 Minus: Statistical Discrepancy		−212
8 Equals: **National income**	15,077	
The Decomposition of National Income:		
9 Indirect taxes	1,265	
10 Compensation of employees	9,249	
11 Wages and salaries		7,478
12 Supplements to wages and salaries		1,771
13 Corporate profits and business transfers	2,073	
14 Net interest	532	
15 Proprietors' income	1,347	
16 Rental income of persons	610	

Source: Survey of Current Business, July 2015, Tables 1-7-5 and 1-12.

U.S.-owned plant in Japan is not included in U.S. GDP, but is included in U.S. GNP.

So, to go from GDP to GNP, we must first add **receipts of factor income from the rest of the world**, which is income from U.S. capital or U.S. residents abroad (line 2); then subtract **payments of factor income to the rest of the world**, which is income received by foreign capital and foreign residents in the United States (line 3).

In 2014, payments from the rest of the world exceeded receipts to the rest of the world by $263 billion, so GNP was larger than GDP by $263 billion.

■ The next step takes us from GNP to **net national product (NNP)** (line 6). The difference between GNP and NNP is the depreciation of capital, called **consumption of fixed capital** in the national accounts.

■ Finally, lines 7 and 8 take us from NNP to **national income** (line 8). National income is defined as the *income that originates in the production of goods and services supplied by residents of the United States.* In theory, national income and NNP should be equal. In practice, they typically differ, because they are constructed in different ways.

NNP is constructed from the top down, starting from GDP and going through the steps we have just gone through in Table A1-1. National income is constructed instead from the bottom up, by adding the different components of factor income (compensation of employees, corporate profits, and so on). If we could measure everything exactly, the two measures should be equal. In practice, the two measures differ, and the difference between the two is called the *statistical discrepancy.* In 2014, national income computed from the bottom up (the number in line 8) was larger than the NNP computed from the top down (the number in line 6) by $212 billion. The statistical discrepancy is a useful reminder of the statistical problems involved in constructing the national income accounts. Although $212 billion seems like a large error, as a percentage of GDP, the error is about 1 percentage point.

The bottom part of the table (lines 9–15) decomposes national income into different types of income.

■ **Indirect taxes** (line 9). Some of the national income goes directly to the state in the form of sales taxes. (Indirect taxes are just another name for sales taxes.)

The rest of national income goes either to employees, or to firms:

■ **Compensation of employees** (line 10), or labor income, is what goes to employees. It is by far the largest component of national income, accounting for 61% of national income. Labor income is the sum of wages and salaries (line 11) and of supplements to wages and salaries (line 12). These range from employer contributions for social insurance (by far the largest item) to such exotic items as employer contributions to marriage fees to justices of the peace.

■ **Corporate profits and business transfers** (line 13). Profits are revenues minus costs (including interest payments) and minus depreciation. (Business transfers, which account for $127 billion out of $2,073 billion, are items such as liability payments for personal injury, and corporate contributions to nonprofit organizations.)

■ **Net interest** (line 14) is the interest paid by firms minus the interest received by firms, plus interest received from the rest of the world minus interest paid to the rest of the world. In 2014, most of net interest represented net interest paid by firms: The United States received about as much in interest from the rest of the world as it paid to the rest to the world. So the sum of corporate profits plus net interest paid by firms was approximately $2,073 billion + $532 billion = $2,605 billion, or about 17% of national income.

■ **Proprietors' income** (line 15) is the income received by persons who are self-employed. It is defined as *the income of sole proprietorships, partnerships, and tax-exempt cooperatives.*

■ **Rental income of persons** (line 16) is the income from the rental of real property, minus depreciation on this real property. Houses produce housing services; rental income measures the income received for these services.

If the national accounts counted only actual rents, rental income would depend on the proportion of apartments and houses that were rented versus those that were owner occupied. For example, if everybody became the owner of the apartment or the house in which he or she lived, rental income would go to zero, and thus measured GDP would drop. To avoid this problem, national accounts treat houses and apartments as if they were all rented out. So, rental income is constructed as actual rents plus *imputed* rents on those houses and apartments that are owner occupied.

Before we move to the product side, Table A1-2 shows how we can go from national income to personal disposable income, which is the income available to persons after they have received transfers and paid taxes.

■ Not all national income (line 1) is distributed to persons.

Some of the income goes to the state in the form of indirect taxes, so the first step is to subtract indirect taxes. (Line 2 in Table A1-2 is equal to line 9 in Table A1-1.)

Table A1-2	From National Income to Personal Disposable Income, 2014 (billions of dollars)	
1	National income	15,077
2	Minus: indirect taxes	−1,265
3	Minus: corporate profits and business transfers	−2,073
4	Minus: net interest	−532
5	Plus: income from assets	2,118
6	Plus: personal transfers	2,529
7	Minus: contributions for social insurance	−1,159
8	Equals: **Personal income**	14,694
9	Minus: personal tax payments	−1780
10	Equals: **Personal disposable income**	12,914

Source: *Survey of Current Business*, July 2015, Tables 1-7-5, 1-12, and 2-1.

Some of the corporate profits are retained by firms. Some of the interest payments by firms go to banks, or go abroad. So the second step is to subtract all corporate profits and business transfers (line 3—equal to line 13 in Table A1-1) and all net interest payments (line 4—equal to line 14 in Table A1-1), and add back all income from assets (dividends and interest payments) received by persons (line 5).

■ People receive income not only from production, but also from public transfers (line 6). Transfers accounted for $2,529 billion in 2014. From these transfers must be subtracted personal contributions for social insurance, $1,159 billion (line 7).

■ The net result of these adjustments is **personal income**, the income actually received by persons (line 8). **Personal disposable income** (line 10) is equal to personal income minus personal tax and nontax payments (line 9). In 2014, personal disposable income was $12,914 billion, or about 74% of GDP.

The Product Side

Table A1-3 looks at the product side of the national accounts—what is produced, and who buys it.

Start with the three components of domestic demand: consumption, investment, and government spending.

■ Consumption, called **personal consumption expenditures** (line 2), is by far the largest component of demand. It is defined as *the sum of goods and services purchased by persons resident in the United States.*

In the same way that national accounts include imputed rental income on the income side, they include imputed housing services as part of consumption.

Owners of a house are assumed to consume housing services, for a price equal to the imputed rental income of that house.

Consumption is disaggregated into three components: purchases of **durable goods** (line 3), **nondurable goods** (line 4), and **services** (line 5). Durable goods are commodities that can be stored and have an average life of at least three years; automobile purchases are the largest item here. Nondurable goods are commodities that can be stored but have a life of less than three years. Services are commodities that cannot be stored and must be consumed at the place and time of purchase.

■ Investment, called **gross private domestic fixed investment** (line 6), is the sum of two very different components.

Nonresidential investment (line 7) is the purchase of new capital goods by firms. These may be either **structures** (line 8)—mostly new plants—or **equipment and software** (line 9)—such as machines, computers, or office equipment.

Residential investment (line 10) is the purchase of new houses or apartments by persons.

■ **Government purchases** (line 11) equal the purchases of goods by the government plus the compensation of government employees. (The government is thought of as buying the services of the government employees.)

Government purchases equal the sum of purchases by the federal government (line 12) (which themselves can be disaggregated between spending on national defense (line 13) and nondefense spending (line 14) and purchases by state and local governments (line 15).

Table A1-3	GDP: The Product Side, 2014 (billions of dollars)		
1	**Gross domestic product**	17,348	
2	Personal consumption expenditures	11,866	
3	Durable goods		1,280
4	Nondurable goods		2,668
5	Services		7,918
6	Gross private domestic fixed investment	2,860	
7	Nonresidential		2,234
8	Structures			507
9	Equipment and Software			1,727
10	Residential		549
11	Government purchases	3,152	
12	Federal		1,220
13	National Defense			748.2
14	Nondefense			471.6
15	State and local		1,932
16	Net exports	−530	
17	Exports		2,342
18	Imports		−2,872
19	Change in business inventories	77	

Source: *Survey of Current Business*, July 2015, Table 1-1-5.

Note that government purchases do not include transfers from the government or interest payments on government debt. These do not correspond to purchases of either goods or services, and so are not included here. This means that the number for government purchases you see in Table A1-3 is substantially smaller than the number we typically hear for government spending—which includes transfers and interest payments.

■ The sum of consumption, investment, and government purchases gives the demand for goods by U.S. firms, U.S. persons, and the U.S. government. If the United States were a closed economy, this would be the same as the demand for U.S. goods. But because the U.S. economy is open, the two numbers are different. To get to the demand for U.S. goods, we must make two adjustments. First, we must add the foreign purchases of U.S. goods, **exports** (line 17). Second, we must subtract U.S. purchases of foreign goods, **imports** (line 18). In 2014, exports were smaller than imports by $530 billion. Thus, **net exports** (or, equivalently, the **trade balance**), was equal to −$530 billion (line 16).

■ Adding consumption, investment, government purchases, and net exports gives the *total purchases of U.S. goods*. Production may, however, be less than purchases if firms satisfy the difference by decreasing inventories. Or production may be greater than

purchases, in which case firms are accumulating inventories. The last line of Table A1-3 gives **changes in business inventories** (line 19), also sometimes called (rather misleadingly) "inventory investment." It is defined as the *change in the volume of inventories held by business*. The change in business inventories can be positive or negative. In 2014, it was small and positive; U.S. production was higher than total purchases of U.S. goods by $77 billion.

The Federal Government in the National Income Accounts

Table A1-4 presents the basic numbers describing federal government economic activity in fiscal year 2014, using NIPA numbers.

The reason for using the fiscal year rather than the calendar year is that budget projections—as presented in Chapter 23—are typically framed in terms of fiscal year rather than calendar year numbers. The fiscal year runs from October 1 of the previous calendar year to September 30 of the current calendar year, so in this case from October 2013 to September 2014.

The reason for using NIPA rather than the official budget numbers is that they are economically more meaningful; that is, the NIPA numbers are a better

Table A1-4	U.S. Federal Budget Revenues and Expenditures, Fiscal Year 2014 (billions of dollars)		
1	Revenues	3,265	
2	Personal taxes	1,396	
3	Corporate profit taxes	417	
4	Indirect taxes	137	
5	Social insurance contributions	1,145	
6	Other	170	
7	Expenditures, excluding net interest payments	3,465	
8	Consumption expenditures	955	
9	Defense		578
10	Nondefense		377
11	Transfers to persons	1,877	
12	Grants to state/local governments	495	
13	Other	129	
14	Primary surplus (+ sign: surplus)	−191	
15	Net interest payments	440	
16	Real interest payments	155	
17	Inflation component	285	
18	Official surplus: (1) minus (7) minus (15)	−631	
19	Inflation adjusted surplus: (18) plus (17)	−476	

Source: *Survey of Current Business*, July 2015, Table 3-2. Inflation adjustment calculated by debt from Table B-22.

representation of what the government is doing in the economy than the numbers presented in the various budget documents. Budget numbers presented by the government need not follow the national income accounting conventions and sometimes involve creative accounting.

In 2014, federal revenues were $3,265 billion (line 1). Of those, personal taxes (also called *income taxes*) accounted for $1,396 billion, or 43% of revenues; social insurance contributions (also called *payroll taxes*) accounted for $1,145 billion, or 35% of revenues.

Expenditures excluding interest payments but including transfer payments to individuals were $3,456 billion (line 7). Consumption expenditures (mostly wages and salaries of public employees and depreciation of capital) accounted for $955 billion, or 28% of expenditures. Excluding defense, expenditures were only $377 billion. **Transfers to persons** (also called *entitlement programs*, mostly unemployment, retirement, and health benefits) were a much larger $1,877 billion. Table A1-3 shows how the expenditures on goods and services by state and local governments are much larger than those of the federal government.

The federal government was therefore running a primary deficit of $191 billion (line 1 minus line 7, here recorded as a negative **primary surplus** in line 14).

Net interest payments on the debt held by the public totaled $440 billion (line 15). The **official deficit** was therefore equal to $631 billion (line 14 plus line 15). We know, however, that this measure is incorrect. It is appropriate to correct the official deficit measure for the role of inflation in reducing the real value of the public debt. The correct measure, the **inflation-adjusted deficit**, namely the sum of the official deficit plus *real* interest payments, was $476 billion (line 19), or 2.7% of GDP.

Warning

National accounts give an internally consistent description of aggregate activity. But underlying these accounts are many choices of what to include and what not to include, where to put some types of income or spending, and so on. Here are five examples.

■ Work within the home is not counted in GDP. If, for example, two women decide to babysit each other's child rather than take care of their own child and pay each other for the babysitting services, measured

GDP will go up, whereas true GDP clearly does not change. The solution would be to count work within the home in GDP, the same way that we impute rents for owner-occupied housing. But, so far, this has not been done.

■ The purchase of a house is treated as an investment, and housing services are then treated as part of consumption. Contrast this with the treatment of automobiles. Despite the fact that they provide services for a long time—although not as long a time as houses do—purchases of automobiles are not treated as investment. They are treated as consumption and appear in the national accounts only in the year in which they are bought.

■ Firms' purchases of machines are treated as investment. The purchase of education is treated as consumption of education services. But education is clearly in part an investment; people acquire education in part to increase their future income.

■ Many government purchases have to be valued in the national accounts in the absence of a market transaction. How do we value the work of teachers in teaching children to read when that transaction is mandated by the state as part of compulsory education? The rule used is to value it at cost, so using the salaries of teachers.

■ The correct calculation of the government's deficit (and debt) is a challenging task. Here is one aspect of the problem: Suppose the teachers in the example are paid partly with cash and partly with the promise of a future retirement pension. There is an important sense that the pension is just like government debt (i.e., a future liability of taxpayers). However, these liabilities are not counted in the deficit measure in Table A1-4 or in our standard measures of public debt. Another problem lies in the treatment of private sector debt guarantees by federal or state government. Should such contingent liabilities be counted as part of public debt?

The list could go on. However, the point of these examples is not to make you conclude that national accounts are wrong. Most of the accounting decisions you just saw were made for good reasons, often because of data availability or for simplicity. The point is that to use national accounts best, you should understand their logic, but also understand the choices that have been made and thus their limitations.

Key Terms

■ national income and product accounts (NIPA), A-1
■ national accounts, A-1
■ gross domestic product (GDP), A-1
■ gross national product (GNP), A-1
■ receipts of factor income from the rest of the world, A-2
■ payments of factor income to the rest of the world, A-2
■ net national product (NNP), A-2
■ consumption of fixed capital, A-2
■ national income, A-2
■ indirect taxes, A-2
■ compensation of employees, A-2
■ corporate profits, A-2
■ net interest, A-2
■ proprietors' income, A-2
■ rental income of persons, A-2
■ personal income, A-3
■ personal disposable income, A-3
■ personal consumption expenditures, A-3
■ durable goods, A-3
■ nondurable goods, A-3
■ services, A-3
■ gross private domestic fixed investment, A-3
■ nonresidential investment, A-3
■ structures, A-3
■ equipment and software, A-3
■ residential investment, A-3
■ government purchases, A-3
■ exports, A-4
■ imports, A-4
■ net exports, A-4
■ trade balance, A-4
■ changes in business inventories, A-4
■ transfers to persons, A-5
■ primary surplus, A-5
■ official deficit, A-5
■ inflation-adjusted deficit, A-5

Further Readings

For more details, read "A Guide to the National Income and Product Accounts of the United States," September 2006 (www.bea.gov/national/pdf/nipaguid.pdf).

APPENDIX 2 A Math Refresher

This appendix presents the mathematical tools and the mathematical results that are used in this text.

Geometric Series

Definition. A geometric series is a sum of numbers of the form:

$$1 + x + x^2 + \cdots + x^n$$

where x is a number that may be greater or smaller than one, and x^n denotes x to the power n; that is, x times itself n times.

Examples of such series are:

■ The sum of spending in each round of the multiplier (Chapter 3). If c is the marginal propensity to consume, then the sum of increases in spending after $n + 1$ rounds is given by:

$$1 + c + c^2 + \cdots + c^n$$

■ The present discounted value of a sequence of payments of one dollar each year for n years (Chapter 14), when the interest rate is equal to i:

$$1 + \frac{1}{1 + i} + \frac{1}{(1 + i)^2} + \cdots + \frac{1}{(1 + i)^{n-1}}$$

We usually have two questions we want to answer when encountering such a series:

1. What is the sum?
2. Does the sum explode as we let n increase, or does it reach a finite limit (and, if so, what is that limit)?

The following propositions tell you what you need to know to answer these questions.

Proposition 1 tells you how to compute the sum:

Proposition 1:

$$1 + x + x^2 + \cdots + x^n = \frac{1 - x^{n+1}}{1 - x} \quad \text{(A2.1)}$$

Here is the proof: Multiply the sum by $(1 - x)$, and use the fact that $x^a x^b = x^{a+b}$ (that is, you must add exponents when multiplying):

$$(1 + x + x^2 + \cdots + x^n)(1 - x) = 1 + x + x^2 + \cdots + x^n$$
$$-x - x^2 - \cdots - x^n - x^{n+1}$$
$$= 1 \qquad\qquad\qquad - x^{n+1}$$

All the terms on the right except for the first and the last cancel. Dividing both sides by $(1 - x)$ gives equation (A2.1).

This formula can be used for any x and any n. If, for example, x is 0.9 and n is 10, then the sum is equal to 6.86. If x is 1.2 and n is 10, then the sum is 32.15.

Proposition 2 tells you what happens as n gets large:

Proposition 2: If x is less than one, the sum goes to $1/(1 - x)$ as n gets large. If x is equal to or greater than one, the sum explodes as n gets large.

Here is the proof: If x is less than one, then x^n goes to zero as n gets large. Thus, from equation (A2.1), the sum goes to $1/(1 - x)$. If x is greater than one, then x^n becomes larger and larger as x^n increases, $1 - x^n$ becomes a larger and larger negative number, and the ratio $(1 - x^n)/(1 - x)$ becomes a larger and larger positive number. Thus, the sum explodes as n gets large.

Application from Chapter 14: Consider the present value of a payment of $1 forever, starting next year, when the interest rate is i. The present value is given by:

$$\frac{1}{(1 + i)} + \frac{1}{(1 + i)^2} + \cdots \quad \text{(A2.2)}$$

Factoring out $1/(1 + i)$, rewrite this present value as:

$$\frac{1}{(1 + i)} \left[1 + \frac{1}{(1 + i)} + \cdots \right]$$

The term in brackets is a geometric series, with $x = 1/(1 + i)$. As the interest rate i is positive, x is less than 1. Applying Proposition 2, when n gets large, the term in brackets equals

$$\frac{1}{1 - \frac{1}{(1 + i)}} = \frac{(1 + i)}{(1 + i - 1)} = \frac{(1 + i)}{i}$$

Replacing the term in brackets in the previous equation by $(1 + i)/i$ gives:

$$\frac{1}{(1 + i)} \left[\frac{(1 + i)}{i} \right] = \frac{1}{i}$$

The present value of a sequence of payments of one dollar a year forever, starting next year, is equal to $1 divided by the interest rate. If i is equal to 5% per year, the present value equals $1/0.05 = 20.

Useful Approximations

Throughout this text, we use a number of approximations that make computations easier. These approximations are most reliable when the variables x, y, and z are small, say between 0 and 10%. The numerical examples in Propositions 3–8 on pages A-8 and A-9 are based on the values $x = 0.05$ and $y = 0.03$.

Proposition 3:

$$(1 + x)(1 + y) \approx (1 + x + y) \qquad (A2.3)$$

Here is the proof. Expanding $(1 + x)(1 + y)$ gives $(1 + x)(1 + y) = 1 + x + y + xy$. If x and y are small, then the product xy is very small and can be ignored as an approximation (for example, if $x = 0.05$ and $y = 0.03$, and then $xy = 0.0015$). So, $(1 + x)(1 + y)$ is approximately equal to $(1 + x + y)$.

For the values x and y, for example, the approximation gives 1.08 compared to an exact value of 1.0815.

Proposition 4:

$$(1 + x)^2 \approx 1 + 2x \qquad (A2.4)$$

The proof follows directly from Proposition 3, with $y = x$. For the value of $x = 0.05$, the approximation gives 1.10, compared to an exact value of 1.1025.

Application from Chapter 14: From arbitrage, the relation between the two-year interest rate and the current and the expected one-year interest rates is given by:

$$(1 + i_{2t})^2 = (1 + i_{1t})(1 + i_{1t+1}^e)$$

Using Proposition 4 for the left side of the equation gives:

$$(1 + i_{2t})^2 \approx 1 + 2i_{2t}$$

Using Proposition 3 for the right side of the equation gives:

$$(1 + i_{1t})(1 + i_{1t+1}^e) \approx 1 + i_{1t} + i_{1t+1}^e$$

Using this expression to replace $(1 + i_{1t})(1 + i_{1t+1}^e)$ in the original arbitrage relation gives:

$$1 + 2i_{2t} = 1 + i_{1t} + i_{1t+1}^e$$

Or, reorganizing:

$$i_{2t} = \frac{(i_{1t} + i_{1t+1}^e)}{2}$$

The two-year interest rate is approximately equal to the average of the current and the expected one-year interest rates.

Proposition 5:

$$(1 + x)^n \approx 1 + nx \qquad (A2.5)$$

The proof follows by repeated application of Propositions 3 and 4. For example, $(1 + x)^3 = (1 + x)^2(1 + x) \approx (1 + 2x)(1 + x)$ by Proposition 4, $\approx (1 + 2x + x) = 1 + 3x$ by Proposition 3.

The approximation becomes worse as n increases, however. For example, for $x = 0.05$ and $n = 5$, the approximation gives 1.25, compared to an exact value of 1.2763. For $n = 10$, the approximation gives 1.50, compared to an exact value of 1.63.

Proposition 6:

$$\frac{(1 + x)}{(1 + y)} \approx (1 + x - y) \qquad (A2.6)$$

Here is the proof: Consider the product of $(1 + x - y)(1 + y)$. Expanding this product gives $(1 + x - y)(1 + y) = 1 + x + xy - y^2$. If both x and y are small, then xy and y^2 are very small, so $(1 + x - y)(1 + y) \approx (1 + x)$. Dividing both sides of this approximation by $(1 + y)$ gives the preceding proposition.

For the values of $x = 0.05$ and $y = 0.03$, the approximation gives 1.02, while the correct value is 1.019.

Application from Chapter 14: The real interest rate is defined by:

$$(1 + r_t) = \frac{(1 + i_t)}{(1 + \pi_{t+1}^e)}$$

Using Proposition 6 gives

$$(1 + r_t) \approx (1 + i_t - \pi_{t+1}^e)$$

Simplifying:

$$r_t \approx i_t - \pi_{t+1}^e$$

This gives us the approximation we use at many points in this text. The real interest rate is approximately equal to the nominal interest rate minus expected inflation.

These approximations are also convenient when dealing with growth rates. Define the rate of growth of x by $g_x \equiv \Delta x / x$, and similarly for z, g_z, and y, g_y. The numerical examples below are based on the values $g_x = 0.05$ and $g_y = 0.03$.

Proposition 7: If $z = xy$ then:

$$g_z \approx g_x + g_y \qquad (A2.7)$$

Here is the proof: Let Δz be the increase in z when x increases by Δx and y increases by Δy. Then, by definition:

$$z + \Delta z = (x + \Delta x)(y + \Delta y)$$

Divide both sides by z.
The left side becomes:

$$\frac{(z + \Delta z)}{z} = \left(1 + \frac{\Delta z}{z}\right)$$

The right-hand side becomes

$$\frac{(x + \Delta x)(y + \Delta y)}{z} = \frac{(x + \Delta x)}{x}\frac{(y + \Delta y)}{y}$$

$$= \left(1 + \frac{\Delta x}{x}\right)\left(1 + \frac{\Delta y}{y}\right)$$

where the first equality follows from the fact that $z = xy$, the second equality from simplifying each of the two fractions.

Using the expressions for the left and right sides gives:

$$\left(1 + \frac{\Delta z}{z}\right) = \left(1 + \frac{\Delta x}{x}\right)\left(1 + \frac{\Delta y}{y}\right)$$

Or, equivalently,

$$(1 + g_z) = (1 + g_x)(1 + g_y)$$

From Proposition 3, $(1 + g_z) \approx (1 + g_x + g_y)$, or, equivalently,

$$g_z \approx g_x + g_y$$

For $g_x = 0.05$ and $g_y = 0.03$, the approximation gives $g_z = 8\%$, while the correct value is 8.15%.

Application from Chapter 13: Let the production function be of the form $Y = NA$, where Y is production, N is employment, and A is productivity. Denoting the growth rates of Y, N, and A by g_Y, g_N, and g_A; respectively, Proposition 7 implies

$$g_Y \approx g_N + g_A$$

The rate of output growth is approximately equal to the rate of employment growth plus the rate of productivity growth.

Proposition 8: If $z = x/y$, then

$$g_z \approx g_x - g_y \qquad \text{(A2.8)}$$

Here is the proof: Let Δz be the increase in z, when x increases by Δx and y increases by Δy. Then, by definition:

$$z + \Delta z = \frac{x + \Delta x}{y + \Delta y}$$

Divide both sides by z.
The left side becomes:

$$\left(\frac{z + \Delta z}{z}\right) = \left(1 + \frac{\Delta z}{z}\right)$$

The right side becomes:

$$\frac{(x + \Delta x)}{(y + \Delta y)}\frac{1}{z} = \frac{(x + \Delta x)}{(y + \Delta y)}\frac{y}{x} = \frac{(x + \Delta x)/x}{(y + \Delta y)/y} = \frac{1 + (\Delta x/x)}{1 + (\Delta y/y)}$$

where the first equality comes from the fact that $z = x/y$, the second equality comes from rearranging terms, and the third equality comes from simplifying.

Using the expressions for the left and right sides gives:

$$1 + \Delta z/z = \frac{1 + (\Delta x/x)}{1 + (\Delta y/y)}$$

Or, substituting:

$$1 + g_z = \frac{1 + g_x}{1 + g_y}$$

From Proposition 6, $(1 + g_z) \approx (1 + g_x - g_y)$, or, equivalently,

$$g_z \approx g_x - g_y$$

For $g_x = 0.05$ and $g_y = 0.03$, the approximation gives $g_z = 2\%$, while the correct value is 1.9%.

Application from Chapter 9: Let M be nominal money, P be the price level. It follows that the rate of growth of the real money stock M/P is given by:

$$g_{M/P} \approx g_M - \pi$$

where π is the rate of growth of prices or, equivalently, the rate of inflation.

Functions

We use functions informally in this text, as a way of denoting how a variable depends on one or more other variables.

In some cases, we look at how a variable Y moves with a variable X. We write this relation as

$$\begin{array}{c} Y = f(X) \\ + \end{array}$$

A plus sign below X indicates a positive relation; an increase in X leads to an increase in Y. A minus sign below X indicates a negative relation; an increase in X leads to a decrease in Y.

In some cases, we allow the variable Y to depend on more than one variable. For example, we allow Y to depend on X and Z:

$$\begin{array}{c} Y = f(X, Z) \\ (+,-) \end{array}$$

The signs indicate that an increase in X leads to an increase in Y, and that an increase in Z leads to a decrease in Y.

An example of such a function is the investment function (5.1) in Chapter 5:

$$\begin{array}{c} I = I(Y, i) \\ (+,-) \end{array}$$

This equation says that investment, I, increases with production, Y, and decreases with the interest rate, i.

In some cases, it is reasonable to assume that the relation between two or more variables is a **linear relation**. A given increase in X always leads to the same increase in Y. In that case, the function is given by:

$$Y = a + bX$$

This relation can be represented by a line giving Y for any value of X.

The parameter a gives the value of Y when X is equal to zero. It is called the **intercept** because it gives the value of Y when the line representing the relation "intercepts" (crosses) the vertical axis.

The parameter b tells us by how much Y increases when X increases by one unit. It is called the **slope** because it is equal to the slope of the line representing the relation.

A simple linear relation is the relation $Y = X$, which is represented by the 45-degree line and has a slope of 1. Another example of a linear relation is the consumption function (3.2) in Chapter 3:

$$C = c_0 + c_1 Y_D$$

where C is consumption and Y_D is disposable income. c_0 tells us what consumption would be if disposable income were equal to zero. c_1 tells us by how much consumption increases when income increases by 1 unit; c_1 is called the *marginal propensity to consume*.

Logarithmic Scales

A variable that grows at a constant growth rate increases by larger and larger increments over time. Take a variable X that grows over time at a constant growth rate, say at 3% per year.

- Start in year 0 and assume $X = 2$. So a 3% increase in X represents an increase of $0.06(0.03 \times 2)$.
- Go to year 20. X is now equal to $2(1.03)^{20} = 3.61$. A 3% increase now represents an increase of $0.11(0.03 \times 3.61)$.
- Go to year 100. X is equal to $2(1.03)^{100} = 38.4$. A 3% increase represents an increase of $1.15(0.03 \times 38.4)$, so an increase about 20 times larger than in year 0.

If we plot X against time using a standard (linear) vertical scale, the plot looks like Figure A2-1(a). The increases in X become larger and larger over time (0.06 in year 0, 0.11 in year 20, 1.15 in year 100). The curve representing X against time becomes steeper and steeper.

Another way of representing the evolution of X is to use a *logarithmic scale* to measure X on the vertical axis. The property of a logarithmic scale is that the same *proportional* increase in this variable is represented by the same vertical distance on the scale. So the behavior of a variable such as X that increases by the same proportional increase (3%) each year is now represented by a line. Figure A2-1(b) represents the behavior of X, this time using a logarithmic scale on the vertical axis. The fact that the relation is represented by a line indicates that X is growing at a constant

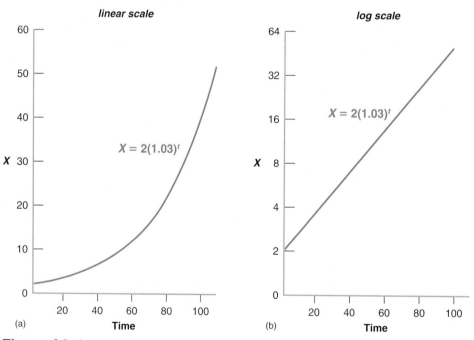

Figure A2-1

(a) The Evolution of X (using a linear scale) (b) The Evolution of X (using a logarithmic scale)

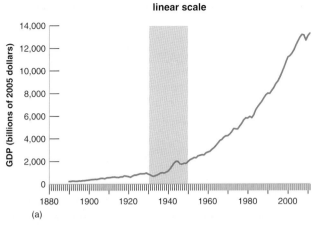

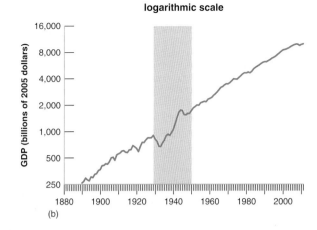

Figure A2-2

(a) U.S. GDP since 1890 (using a linear scale) (b) U.S. GDP since 1890 (using a logarithmic scale)

Source: 1890–1928: Historical Statistics of the United States, Table F1-5, adjusted for level to be consistent with the post 1929 series. 1929–2011: BEA, billions of chained 2005 dollars. http://www.bea.gov/national/index.htm#gdp.

rate over time. The higher the rate of growth, the steeper the line.

In contrast to X, economic variables such as GDP do not grow at a constant growth rate every year. Their growth rate may be higher in some decades, lower in others; a recession may lead to a few years of negative growth. Yet, when looking at their evolution over time, it is often more informative to use a logarithmic scale rather than a linear scale. Let's see why.

Figure A2-2(a) plots real U.S. GDP from 1890 to 2011 using a standard (linear) scale. Because real U.S. GDP is about 51 times bigger in 2011 than in 1890, the same proportional increase in GDP is 51 times bigger in 2011 than in 1890. So the curve representing the evolution of GDP over time becomes steeper and steeper over time. It is difficult to see from the figure whether the U.S. economy is growing faster or slower than it was 50 years or 100 years ago.

Figure A2-2(b) plots U.S. GDP from 1890 to 2011, now using a logarithmic scale. If the growth rate of GDP was the same every year—so the proportional increase in GDP was the same every year—the evolution of GDP would be represented by a line—the same way as the evolution of X was represented by a line in Figure A2-1(b). Because the growth rate of GDP is not constant from year to year—so the proportional increase in GDP is not the same every year—the evolution of GDP is no longer represented by a line. Unlike

in Figure A2-2(a), GDP does not explode over time, and the graph is more informative. Here are two examples.

- If, in Figure A2-2(b), we were to draw a line to fit the curve from 1890 to 1929, and another line to fit the curve from 1950 to 2011 (the two periods are separated by the shaded area in Figure A2-2(b)), the two lines would have roughly the same slope. What this tells us is that the average growth rate was roughly the same during the two periods.

- The decline in output from 1929 to 1933 is visible in Figure A2-2(b). (By contrast, the current crisis looks small relative to the Great Depression.) So is the strong recovery of output that follows. By the 1950s, output appears to be back to its old trend line. This suggests that the Great Depression was not associated with a permanently lower level of output.

Note in both cases how you could not have derived these conclusions by looking at Figure A2-2(a), but you can derive them by looking at Figure A2-2(b). This shows the usefulness of using a logarithmic scale.

Key Terms

- linear relation, A-9
- intercept, A-10
- slope, A-10

APPENDIX 3 An Introduction to Econometrics

How do we know that consumption depends on disposable income?

How do we know the value of the propensity to consume?

To answer these questions and, more generally, to estimate behavioral relations and find out the values of the relevant parameters, economists use *econometrics*—the set of statistical techniques designed for use in economics. Econometrics can get very technical, but we outline in this appendix the basic principles behind it. We shall do so using as an example the consumption function introduced in Chapter 3, and we shall concentrate on estimating c_1, the propensity to consume out of disposable income.

Changes in Consumption and Changes in Disposable Income

The propensity to consume tells us by how much consumption changes for a given change in disposable income. A natural first step is simply to plot changes in consumption versus changes in disposable income and see how the relation between the two looks. You can see this in Figure A3-1.

The vertical axis in Figure A3-1 measures the annual change in consumption minus the average annual change in consumption, for each year from 1970 to 2014. More precisely:

Let C_t denote consumption in year t. Let ΔC_t denote $C_t - C_{t-1}$, the change in consumption from year $t - 1$ to year t. Let $\overline{\Delta C}$ denote the average annual change in consumption since 1970. The variable measured on the vertical axis is constructed as $\Delta C_t - \overline{\Delta C}$. A positive value of the variable represents an increase in consumption larger than average, whereas a negative value represents an increase in consumption smaller than average.

Similarly, the horizontal axis measures the annual change in disposable income, minus the average annual change in disposable income since 1970, $\Delta Y_{Dt} - \overline{\Delta Y_D}$.

A particular square in the figure gives the deviations of the change in consumption and disposable income from their respective means for a particular year between 1970 and 2014. In 2014, for example, the change in consumption was higher than average by \$107 billion, and the change in disposable income was higher than average by \$123 billion. (For our purposes, it is not important to know which year each square refers to, just what the set of points in the diagram looks like. So, except for 2014, the years are not indicated in Figure A3-1.)

Figure A3-1 suggests two main conclusions.

■ One, there is a clear positive relation between changes in consumption and changes in disposable income. Most of the points lie in the upper-right and lower-left quadrants of the figure. When disposable income increases by more than average, consumption also typically increases by more than average; when disposable income increases by less than average, so typically does consumption.

■ Two, the relation between the two variables is good but not perfect. In particular, some points lie in the upper-left quadrant; these points correspond to years when smaller-than-average changes in disposable income were associated with higher-than-average changes in consumption.

Econometrics allows us to state these two conclusions more precisely and to get an estimate of the propensity to consume. Using an econometrics software package, we can find

Figure A3-1

Changes in Consumption versus Changes in Disposable Income, 1970–2011

There is a clear positive relation between changes in consumption and changes in disposable income.

Source: Series PCECCA, DSPIC96 Federal Reserve Economic Data (FRED) http://research.stlouisfed.org/fred2/).

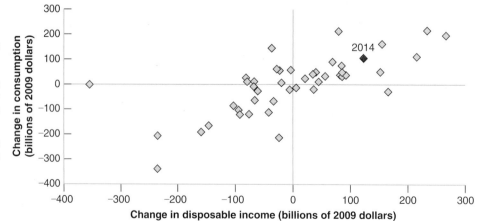

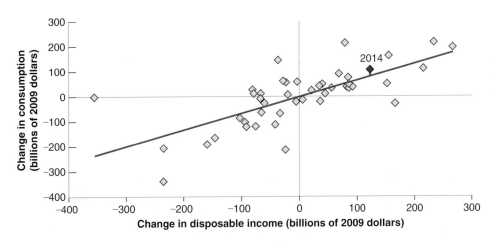

Figure A3-2

Changes in Consumption and Changes in Disposable Income: The Regression Line

The regression line is the line that fits the scatter of points best.

the line that fits the cloud of points in Figure A3-1 best. This line-fitting process is called **ordinary least squares (OLS)**.[1] The estimated equation corresponding to the line is called a **regression**, and the line itself is called the **regression line**.

In our case, the estimated equation is given by

$$(\Delta C_t - \overline{\Delta C}) = 0.66(\Delta Y_{Dt} - \overline{\Delta Y_D}) + \text{residual}$$
$$\bar{R}^2 = 0.51 \qquad \qquad \text{(A3.1)}$$

The regression line corresponding to this estimated equation is drawn in Figure A3-2. Equation (A3.1) reports two important numbers (econometrics packages give more information than those reported above; a typical printout, together with further explanations, is given in the Focus box on page A-14 "A Guide to Understanding Econometric Results").

■ The first important number is the estimated propensity to consume. The equation tells us that an increase in disposable income of $1 billion above normal is typically associated with an increase in consumption of $0.66 billion above normal. In other words, the estimated propensity to consume is 0.66. It is positive but smaller than 1.

■ The second important number is $\bar{R}^2$, which is a measure of how well the regression line fits:

Having estimated the effect of disposable income on consumption, we can decompose the change in consumption for each year into that part that is due to the change in disposable income—the first term on the right in equation (A3.1)— and the rest, which is called the **residual**. For example, the residual for 2014 is indicated in Figure A3-2 by the vertical distance from the point representing 2014 to the regression line.

---

[1] The term *least squares* comes from the fact that the line has the property that it minimizes the sum of the squared distances of the points to the line—thus gives the "least" "squares." The word *ordinary* comes from the fact that this is the simplest method used in econometrics.

If all the points in Figure A3-2 were exactly on the estimated line, all residuals would be zero; all changes in consumption would be explained by changes in disposable income. As you can see, however, this is not the case. $\bar{R}^2$ is a statistic that tells us how well the line fits. $\bar{R}^2$ is always between 0 and 1. A value of 1 would imply that the relation between the two variables is perfect, that all points are exactly on the regression line. A value of zero would imply that the computer can see no relation between the two variables. The value of $\bar{R}^2$ of 0.51 in equation (A3.1) is high, but not very high. It confirms the message from Figure A3-2: Movements in disposable income clearly affect consumption, but there is still quite a bit of movement in consumption that cannot be explained by movements in disposable income.

Correlation versus Causality

What we have established so far is that consumption and disposable income typically move together. More formally, we have seen that there is a positive **correlation**—the technical term for *co-relation*—between annual changes in consumption and annual changes in disposable income. And we have interpreted this relation as showing **causality**—that an increase in disposable income causes an increase in consumption.

We need to think again about this interpretation. A positive relation between consumption and disposable income may reflect the effect of disposable income on consumption. But it may also reflect the effect of consumption on disposable income. Indeed, the model we developed in Chapter 3 tells us that if, for any reason, consumers decide to spend more, then output, and therefore income and, in turn, disposable income will increase. If part of the relation between consumption and disposable income comes from the effect of consumption on disposable income, interpreting

A Guide to Understanding Econometric Results

In your readings, you may run across results of estimation using econometrics. Here is a guide, which uses the slightly simplified, but otherwise untouched computer output for the equation (A3.1):

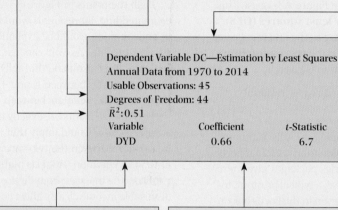

$\bar{R}^2$ is a measure of fit. The closer to 1, the better the fit of the regression line. A value of 0.51 indicates that much but not all of the movement in the dependent variable can be explained by movements in the independent variables.

The period of estimation includes all years from 1970 to 2014. There are therefore 45 **usable observations** used in the regression. **Degrees of freedom** is the number of observations minus the number of parameters to be estimated. There is one estimated parameter here: the coefficient on *DYD*. Thus, there are $45 - 1 = 44$ degrees of freedom. A simple rule is that one needs at least as many observations as parameters to be estimated, and preferably much more; put another way, degrees of freedom must be positive, and the larger the better.

The variable we are trying to explain is called the **dependent variable**. Here the dependent variable is *DC*—the annual change in consumption minus its mean.

Dependent Variable DC—Estimation by Least Squares
Annual Data from 1970 to 2014
Usable Observations: 45
Degrees of Freedom: 44
$\bar{R}^2$:0.51

Variable	Coefficient	*t*-Statistic
DYD	0.66	6.7

The variables that we use to explain the dependent variable are called the **independent variables**. Here there is only one independent variable, *DYD*—the annual change in disposable income minus its mean.

For each independent variable, the computer then gives the estimated coefficient, as well as a *t*-statistic. The *t*-statistic associated with each estimated coefficient tells us how confident we can be that the true coefficient is different from zero. A *t*-statistic above 2 indicates that we can be at least 95% sure that the true coefficient is different from zero. A *t*-statistic of 6.7, as on the coefficient associated with disposable income, is so high that we can be nearly completely sure (more than 99.99% sure) that the true coefficient is different from zero.

equation (A3.1) as telling us about the effect of disposable income on consumption is not right.

An example will help here. Suppose consumption does not depend on disposable income, so that the true value of c_1 is zero. (This is not realistic, but it will make the point most clearly.) So draw the consumption function as a horizontal line (a line with a zero slope) in Figure A3-3. Next, suppose disposable income equals Y_D, so that the initial combination of consumption and disposable income is given by point *A*.

Now suppose that, because of improved confidence, consumers increase their consumption, so the consumption line shifts up. If demand affects output, then income and, in turn, disposable income, increase, so that the new combination of consumption and disposable income will be given by, say, point *B*. If, instead, consumers become more pessimistic, the consumption line shifts down, and so does output, leading to a combination of consumption and disposable income given by point *D*.

If we look at the economy described in the previous two paragraphs, we observe points *A*, *B*, and *D*. If, as we did previously, we draw the best-fitting line through these points, we shall estimate an upward-sloping line, such as

FOCUS

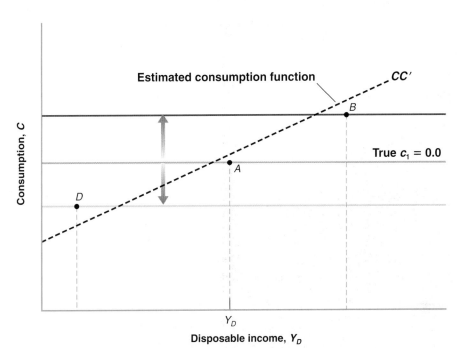

Figure A3-3

A Misleading Regression

The relation between disposable income and consumption comes from the effect of consumption on income rather than from the effect of income on consumption.

CC', and so estimate a positive value for propensity to consume, c_1. Remember, however, that the true value of c_1 is zero. Why do we get the wrong answer—a positive value for c_1 when the true value is zero? Because we interpret the positive relation between disposable income and consumption as showing the effect of disposable income on consumption, where, in fact, the relation reflects the effect of consumption on disposable income; higher consumption leads to higher demand, higher output, and so higher disposable income.

There is an important lesson here: *the difference between correlation and causality*. The fact that two variables move together does not imply that movements in the first variable cause movements in the second variable. Perhaps the causality runs the other way; movements in the second variable cause movements in the first variable. Or perhaps, as is likely to be the case here, the causality runs both ways. Disposable income affects consumption, *and* consumption affects disposable income.

Is there a way out of the correlation-versus-causality problem? If we are interested—and we are—in the effect of disposable income on consumption, can we still learn that from the data? The answer: yes, but only by using more information.

Suppose we *knew* that a specific change in disposable income was not caused by a change in consumption. Then, by looking at the reaction of consumption to *this* change in disposable income, we could learn how consumption responds to disposable income; we could estimate the propensity to consume.

This answer would seem to simply assume away the problem. How can we tell that a change in disposable income is not due to a change in consumption? In fact, sometimes, we can tell. Suppose, for example, that the government embarks on a major increase in defense spending, leading to an increase in demand and, in turn, an increase in output. In that case, if we see both disposable income and consumption increase, we can safely assume that the movement in consumption reflects the effect of disposable income on consumption, and thus estimate the propensity to consume.

This example suggests a general strategy.

- Find exogenous variables—that is, variables that affect disposable income but are not in turn affected by it.
- Look at the change in consumption in response not to all changes in disposable income—as we did in our previous regression—but in response to those changes in disposable income that can be explained by changes in these exogenous variables.

By following this strategy, we can be confident that what we are estimating is the effect of disposable income on consumption, and not the other way around.

The problem of finding such exogenous variables is known as the **identification problem** in econometrics. These exogenous variables, when they can be found, are called **instruments**. Methods of estimation that rely on the use of such instruments are called **instrumental variable methods**.

When equation (A3.1) is estimated using an instrumental variable method—using current and past changes in government defense spending as the instruments—rather than OLS as we did previously, the estimated equation becomes

$$(\Delta C_t - \overline{\Delta C}) = 0.58(\Delta Y_{Dt} - \overline{\Delta Y_D})$$

Note that the coefficient on disposable income, 0.58, is smaller than 0.66 in equation (A3.1). This decrease in the estimated propensity to consume is exactly what we would expect. Our previous estimate in equation (A3.1) reflected not only the effect of disposable income on consumption, but also the effect of consumption back on disposable income. The use of instruments eliminates this second effect, which is why we find a smaller estimated effect of disposable income on consumption.

This short introduction to econometrics is no substitute for a course in econometrics. But it gives you a sense of how economists use data to estimate relations and parameters and to identify causal relations between economic variables.

Key Terms

- ordinary least squares (OLS), A-13
- regression, A-13
- regression line, A-13
- residual $\bar{R}^2$, A-13
- correlation, A-13
- causality, A-13
- usable observations, A-14
- degrees of freedom, A-14
- dependent variable, A-14
- independent variables, A-14
- t-statistic, A-14
- identification problem, A-15
- instruments, A-15
- instrumental variable methods, A-15

Glossary

above the line, below the line In the balance of payments, the items in the current account are above the line drawn to divide them from the items in the financial account, which appear below the line.

accelerationist Phillips curve *See* modified Phillips curve.

adaptive expectations A backward-looking method of forming expectations by adjusting for past mistakes.

aggregate output The total amount of output produced in the economy.

aggregate private spending The sum of all nongovernment spending. Also called *private spending*.

aggregate production function The relation between the quantity of aggregate output produced and the quantities of inputs used in production.

American Recovery and Reinvestment Act (ARRA) The fiscal stimulus program introduced in February 2009 by the U.S. administration.

anchored Inflation expectations are said to be anchored if they do not respond to actual inflation.

animal spirits A term introduced by Keynes to refer to movements in investment that could not be explained by movements in current variables.

appreciation (nominal) An increase in the value of domestic currency in terms of foreign currency. Corresponds to an increase in the exchange rate E, as defined in this text.

appropriability (of research results) The extent to which firms benefit from the results of their research and development efforts.

arbitrage The proposition that the expected rates of return on two financial assets must be equal. Also called *risky arbitrage* to distinguish it from riskless arbitrage, the proposition that the actual rates of return on two financial assets must be the same.

automatic stabilizer The fact that a decrease in output leads, under given tax and spending rules, to an increase in the budget deficit. This increase in the budget deficit in turn increases demand and thus stabilizes output.

autonomous spending The component of the demand for goods that does not depend on the level of output.

backloading A policy is back loaded if it is to be implemented in the future rather than in the present.

balance of payments A set of accounts that summarize a country's transactions with the rest of the world.

balanced budget A budget in which taxes are equal to government spending.

balanced growth The situation in which output, capital, and effective labor all grow at the same rate.

bank reserves Holdings of central bank money by banks. The difference between what banks receive from depositors and what they lend to firms or hold as bonds.

bank run Simultaneous attempts by depositors to withdraw their funds from a bank.

bargaining power The relative strength of each side in a negotiation or a dispute.

base year When constructing real GDP by evaluating quantities in different years using a given set of prices, the year to which this given set of prices corresponds.

Basel II, Basel III International accords, giving recommendations about the regulation of the banking sector.

basis points A basis point is a hundredth of a percent. An increase of the interest rate by 100 basis points is a 1% increase in the interest rate.

behavioral equation An equation that captures some aspect of behavior.

bilateral exchange rate The real exchange rate between two countries.

bond A financial asset that promises a stream of known payments over some period of time.

bond rating The assessment of a bond based on its default risk.

borrowing rate The rate at which consumers or firms can borrow from a financial institution.

bracket creep The increase in the marginal tax rate faced by individuals as their nominal income goes up and tax brackets remain unchanged in nominal terms.

budget deficit The excess of government expenditures over government revenues.

budget surplus *See* public saving.

business cycle theory The study of macroeconomic fluctuations.

business cycles *See* output fluctuations.

capital account The account showing the financial transactions of a country with the rest of the world.

capital account balance The difference between what a country borrows from the rest of the world and what it lends to the rest of the world.

capital account deficit A negative capital account balance.

capital account surplus A positive capital account balance. The country borrows more from the rest of the world than it lends to the rest of the world. A capital account surplus corresponds to a current account deficit.

capital accumulation Increase in the capital stock.

capital controls Restrictions on the foreign assets domestic residents can hold, and on the domestic assets foreigners can hold.

capital ratio Ratio of the capital of a bank to its assets.

cash flow The net flow of cash a firm is receiving.

causality A relation between cause and effect.

central bank money Money issued by the central bank. Also known as the monetary base and high-powered money.

central parity The reference value of the exchange rate around which the exchange rate is allowed to move under a

fixed exchange rate system. The center of the band.

change in business inventories In the national income and product accounts, the change in the volume of inventories held by businesses.

checkable deposits Deposits at banks and other financial institutions against which checks can be written.

churning The concept that new goods make old goods obsolete, that new production techniques make older techniques and worker skills obsolete, and so on.

Cobb-Douglas production function A production function giving output as a weighted geometric average of labor and capital.

collateral The asset pledged in order to get a loan. In case of default, the asset goes to the lender.

collateralized debt obligation (CDO) Security based on an underlying portfolio of assets.

collective bargaining Wage bargaining between unions and firms.

common currency The currency used in the countries which are members of a common currency area.

compensation of employees In the national income and product accounts, the sum of wages and salaries and of supplements to wages and salaries.

confidence band When estimating the dynamic effect of one variable on another, the range of values where we can be confident the true dynamic effect lies.

constant returns to scale The proposition that a proportional increase (or decrease) of all inputs leads to the same proportional increase (or decrease) in output.

consumer price index (CPI) The cost of a given list of goods and services consumed by a typical urban dweller.

consumption (C) Goods and services purchased by consumers.

consumption function A function that relates consumption to its determinants.

consumption of fixed capital Depreciation of capital.

contractionary open market operation An open market operation in which the

central bank sells bonds to decrease the money supply.

conventional monetary policy The use of the policy rate as the main instrument to affect economic activity.

convergence The tendency for countries with lower output per capita to grow faster, leading to convergence of output per capita across countries.

corporate bond A bond issued by a corporation.

corporate profits and business transfers In the national income and product accounts, firms' revenues minus costs (including interest payments) and minus depreciation.

correlation A measure of the way two variables move together. A positive correlation indicates that the two variables tend to move in the same direction. A negative correlation indicates that the two variables tend to move in opposite directions. A correlation of zero indicates that there is no apparent relation between the two variables.

cost of living The average price of a consumption bundle.

coupon bond A bond that promises multiple payments before maturity and one payment at maturity.

coupon payments The payments before maturity on a coupon bond.

coupon rate The ratio of the coupon payment to the face value of a coupon bond.

crawling peg An exchange rate mechanism in which the exchange rate is allowed to move over time according to a prespecified formula.

creative destruction The proposition that growth simultaneously creates and destroys jobs.

credibility The degree to which people and markets believe that a policy announcement will actually be implemented and followed through.

credit easing Monetary policy measures aimed at increasing the supply of credit by banks.

currency Coins and bills.

currency board An exchange rate system in which: (i) the central bank stands ready to buy or sell foreign currency at the official exchange rate; (ii) the central bank cannot engage in open market

operations, that is buy or sell government bonds.

current account In the balance of payments, the summary of a country's payments to and from the rest of the world.

current account balance The sum of net exports, net income, and net transfers from the rest of the world.

current account deficit A negative current account balance.

current account surplus A positive current account balance.

Current Population Survey (CPS) A large monthly survey of U.S. households used, in particular, to compute the unemployment rate.

current yield The ratio of the coupon payment to the price of a coupon bond.

cyclically adjusted deficit A measure of what the government deficit would be under existing tax and spending rules, if output were at its natural level. Also called a *full-employment deficit, mid-cycle deficit, standardized employment deficit*, or *structural deficit*.

debt finance Financing based on loans or the issuance of bonds.

debt monetization The printing of money to finance a deficit.

debt ratio *See* debt-to-GDP ratio.

debt rescheduling The rescheduling of interest payments or payment of principal, typically to decrease current payments.

debt restructuring A decrease in the value of the debt, through a decrease in the value of the principal, or a decrease in interest payments.

debt-to-GDP ratio The ratio of debt to gross domestic product. Also called simply the *debt ratio*.

decreasing returns to capital The property that increases in capital lead to smaller and smaller increases in output as the level of capital increases.

decreasing returns to labor The property that increases in labor leads to smaller and smaller increases in output as the level of labor increases.

deflation Negative inflation.

deflation spiral A mechanism through which deflation increases the real interest rate, which in turn leads to lower activity, and leads to further deflation, a further increase in the real interest rate, etc.

deflation trap The situation of a country subject to a deflation spiral.

degrees of freedom The number of usable observations in a regression minus the number of parameters to be estimated.

demand for domestic goods The demand for domestic goods by people, firms, and governments, both domestic and foreign. Equal to the domestic demand for goods plus net exports.

demand or checkable deposit A bank account that allows depositors to write checks or get cash on demand, up to an amount equal to the account balance.

dependent variable A variable whose value is determined by one or more other variables.

depreciation (nominal) A decrease in the value of domestic currency in terms of a foreign currency. Corresponds to a decrease in the exchange rate E, as defined in this text.

devaluation A decrease in the exchange rate (E) in a fixed exchange rate system.

direct finance Financing through markets, through the issuance of bonds or equities.

discount bond A bond that promises a single payment at maturity.

discount factor The value today of a dollar (or other national currency unit) at some time in the future.

discount rate (i) The interest rate used to discount a sequence of future payments. Equal to the nominal interest rate when discounting future nominal payments and to the real interest rate when discounting future real payments. (ii) The interest rate at which the Fed lends to banks.

discouraged worker A person who has given up looking for employment.

disposable income The income that remains once consumers have received transfers from the government and paid their taxes.

dividends The portion of a corporation's profits that the firm pays out each period to its shareholders.

divine coincidence The proposition that, if inflation remains stable, this is a signal that output is equal to potential output.

dollar GDP *See* nominal GDP.

dollarization The use of dollars in domestic transactions in a country other than the United States.

domestic demand for goods The sum of consumption, investment, and government spending.

durable goods Commodities that can be stored and have an average life of at least three years.

duration of unemployment The period of time during which a worker is unemployed.

dynamics Movements of one or more economic variables over time.

Easterlin paradox The proposition that higher income in a country is not associated with higher levels of happiness.

econometrics Statistical methods applied to economics.

effective demand Synonym for *aggregate demand*.

effective labor The number of workers in an economy times the state of technology.

effective real exchange rate *See* multilateral exchange rate.

efficiency wage theory A theory which argues that a higher wage may lead workers to be more engaged and more productive.

employment The number of people employed.

employment protection The set of regulations determining the conditions under which a firm can lay off a worker.

employment rate The ratio of employment to the labor force.

endogenous variable A variable that depends on other variables in a model and is thus explained within the model.

equilibrium The equality between demand and supply.

equilibrium condition The condition that supply be equal to demand.

equilibrium in the goods market The condition that the supply of goods be equal to the demand for goods.

equipment and software investment The purchase of machines and software by firms.

equity finance Financing based on the issuance of shares.

equity premium Risk premium required by investors to hold stocks rather than short-term bonds.

euro A European currency that replaced national currencies in 11 countries in 2002 and is now used in 15 countries.

Euro area The set of countries sharing the euro as a common currency.

European Central Bank (ECB) The central bank, located in Frankfurt, in charge of determining monetary policy in the euro area.

European Monetary System (EMS) A series of rules that implemented bands for bilateral exchange rates between member countries in Europe that operated from 1979 to roughly 1982.

European Union A political and economic organization of 25 European nations. Formerly called the European Community.

ex-dividend price The price of the stock just after the dividend has been paid.

exogenous variable A variable that is not explained within a model, but rather, is taken as given.

expansion A period of positive GDP growth.

expansionary open market operation An open market operation in which the central bank buys bonds to increase the money supply.

expectations hypothesis The hypothesis that financial investors are risk neutral, which implies that expected returns on all financial assets have to be equal.

expectations-augmented Phillips curve *See* modified Phillips curve.

expected present discount value The value today of current and expected future payments.

expected present discounted value The value today of an expected sequence of future payments. Also called *present discounted value* or *present value*.

exports (X) The purchases of domestic goods and services by foreigners.

extension agreements Agreements to extend the result of negotiations between a set of unions and firms to all firms in a given sector.

external finance Financing of firms through external funds (as opposed to retained earnings).

face value (on a bond) The single payment at maturity promised by a discount bond.

fad A period of time during which, for reasons of fashion or over-optimism, financial investors are willing to pay more for a stock than its fundamental value.

federal deposit insurance Insurance provided by the U.S. government that protects each bank depositor up to $100,000 per account.

federal funds market The market where banks that have excess reserves at the end of the day lend them to banks that have insufficient reserves.

federal funds rate The interest rate determined by equilibrium in the federal funds market. The interest rate affected most directly by changes in monetary policy.

Federal Reserve Bank (Fed) The U.S. central bank.

fertility of research The degree to which spending on research and development translates into new ideas and new products.

final good A good which is used directly for consumption or investment (as opposed to intermediate goods which are used in the process of production.)

financial intermediary A financial institution that receives funds from people, firms, or other financial institutions, and uses these funds to make loans or buy financial assets.

financial investment The purchase of financial assets.

financial wealth The value of all of one's financial assets minus all financial liabilities. Sometimes called *wealth*, for short.

fine-tuning A macroeconomic policy aimed at precisely hitting a given target, such as constant unemployment or constant output growth.

fire sale prices Very low asset prices, reflecting the need for sellers to sell, and the absence of sufficient buyers, because of liquidity constraints.

fiscal austerity A reduction in public spending or an increase in taxes, aimed at reducing the budget deficit.

fiscal consolidation *See* fiscal contraction.

fiscal contraction A policy aimed at reducing the budget deficit through a decrease in government spending or an increase in taxation. Also called *fiscal consolidation*.

fiscal dominance A situation in which monetary policy becomes subordinated to fiscal policy. For example, when the central bank issues money to finance the deficit.

fiscal expansion An increase in government spending or a decrease in taxation, which leads to an increase in the budget deficit.

fiscal multiplier The size of the effect of government spending on output.

fiscal policy A government's choice of taxes and spending.

fixed exchange rate An exchange rate between the currencies of two or more countries that is fixed at some level and adjusted only infrequently.

fixed investment *See* investment (*I*).

fixed investment The purchase of equipment and structures (as opposed to inventory investment).

flexible inflation targeting A way of conducting monetary policy to return inflation to target inflation over time.

float The exchange rate is said to float when it is determined in the foreign exchange market, without central bank intervention.

flow A variable that can be expressed as a quantity per unit of time (such as income).

force of compounding The large effects of sustained growth on the level of a variable.

foreign direct investment The purchase of existing firms or the development of new firms by foreign investors.

foreign exchange Foreign currency; all currencies other than the domestic currency of a given country.

foreign exchange reserves Foreign assets held by the central bank.

four tigers The four Asian economies of Singapore, Taiwan, Hong Kong, and South Korea.

full-employment deficit *See* cyclically adjusted deficit.

fundamental value (of a stock) The present value of expected dividends.

game Strategic interactions between players.

game theory The prediction of outcomes from games.

GDP adjusted for inflation *See* real GDP.

GDP deflator The ratio of nominal GDP to real GDP; a measure of the overall price level. Gives the average price of the final goods produced in the economy.

GDP growth The growth rate of real GDP in year *t*; equal to

GDP in chained (2009) dollars *See* real GDP.

GDP in constant dollars *See* real GDP.

GDP in current dollars *See* nominal GDP.

GDP in terms of goods *See* real GDP.

geometric series A mathematical sequence in which the ratio of one term to the preceding term remains the same. A sequence of the form $1 + c + c^2 + \cdots + c^n$.

GNP *See* Gross National Product.

gold standard A system in which a country fixed the price of its currency in terms of gold and stood ready to exchange gold for currency at the stated parity.

golden-rule level of capital The level of capital at which steady-state consumption is maximized.

government bond A bond issued by a government or a government agency.

government budget constraint The budget constraint faced by the government. The constraint implies that an excess of spending over revenues must be financed by borrowing, and thus leads to an increase in debt.

government purchases In the national income and product accounts, the sum of the purchases of goods by the government plus compensation of government employees.

government spending (G) The goods and services purchased by federal, state, and local governments.

government transfers Payments made by the government to individuals that are not in exchange for goods or services. Example: Social Security payments.

Great Moderation The period of time from the mid-1980s to the mid-2000s when the volatility of output and the volatility of inflation both declined.

gross domestic product (GDP) A measure of aggregate output in the national income accounts. (The market value of the goods and services produced by labor and property located in the United States.)

gross domestic product (GDP) (versus gross national product (GNP)) Gross domestic product measures value added domestically. Gross national product measures value added by domestic factors of production.

gross national product (GNP) A measure of aggregate output in the national income accounts. (The market value of the goods and services produced by labor and property supplied by U.S. residents.)

gross private domestic fixed investment In the national income and product accounts, the sum of nonresidential investment and residential investment.

growth The steady increase in aggregate output over time.

haircut A reduction in the nominal value of debt.

hard peg A fixed exchange rate regime, with a strong commitment of the central bank to maintain the exchange rate fixed.

hedonic pricing An approach to calculating real GDP that treats goods as providing a collection of characteristics, each with an implicit price.

high-powered money *See* central bank money.

hires Workers newly employed by firms.

housing wealth The value of the housing stock.

human capital The set of skills possessed by the workers in an economy.

human wealth The labor-income component of wealth.

hyperinflation Very high inflation.

identification problem In econometrics, the problem of finding whether correlation between variables X and Y indicates a causal relation from X to Y, or from Y to X, or both. This problem is solved by finding exogenous variables, called instruments, that affect X and do not affect Y directly, or affect Y and do not affect X directly.

identity An equation that holds by definition, denoted by the sign.

import compression The decrease in imports coming from a decrease in domestic demand.

imports (Q) The purchases of foreign goods and services by domestic consumers, firms, and the government.

income The flow of revenue from work, rental income, interest, and dividends.

independent variable A variable that is taken as given in a relation or in a model.

index number A number, such as the GDP deflator, that has no natural level and is thus set to equal some value (typically 1 or 100) in a given period.

indexed bond A bond that promises payments adjusted for inflation.

indirect taxes Taxes on goods and services. In the United States, primarily sales taxes.

inflation A sustained rise in the general level of prices.

inflation rate The rate at which the price level increases over time.

inflation targeting The conduct of monetary policy to achieve a given inflation rate over time.

inflation-adjusted deficit The correct economic measure of the budget deficit: The sum of the primary deficit and real interest payments.

insolvency The inability of a debtor, be it a firm, a person, or the government, to repay its debt.

instrumental variable methods In econometrics, methods of estimation that use instruments to estimate causal relations between different variables.

instruments In econometrics, the exogenous variables that allow the identification problem to be solved.

intercept In a linear relation between two variables, the value of the first variable when the second variable is equal to zero.

interest parity condition *See* uncovered interest parity.

interest rate rule A monetary policy rule in which the interest rate is adjusted in response to output and to inflation.

intermediate good A good used in the production of a final good.

internal finance Financing of firms through internal funds (retained earnings).

International Monetary Fund (IMF) The principal international economic organization. Publishes the *World Economic Outlook* annually and the *International Financial Statistics* (IFS) monthly.

inventory investment The difference between production and sales.

investment (I) Purchases of new houses and apartments by people, and purchases of new capital goods (machines and plants) by firms.

IS curve A downward-sloping curve relating output to the interest rate. The curve corresponding to the IS relation, the equilibrium condition for the goods market.

IS relation An equilibrium condition stating that the demand for goods must be equal to the supply of goods, or equivalently that investment must be equal to saving. The equilibrium condition for the goods market.

J-curve A curve depicting the initial deterioration in the trade balance caused by a real depreciation, followed by an improvement in the trade balance.

junior securities Securities being repaid after senior securities in case of insolvency.

junk bond A bond with a high risk of default.

labor hoarding The decision by firms to keep some excess workers in response to a decrease in sales.

labor in efficiency units *See* effective labor.

labor productivity The ratio of output to the number of workers.

labor-market rigidities Restrictions on firms' ability to adjust their level of employment.

layoffs Workers who lose their jobs either temporarily or permanently.

lender of last resort In case a solvent bank cannot finance itself, it can borrow from the central bank, who acts as a lender of last resort.

leverage ratio Ratio of the assets of the bank to its capital (the inverse of the capital ratio).

life (of a bond) The length of time during which the bond pays interest, which ends with the repayment of principal.

life cycle theory of consumption The theory of consumption, developed initially by Franco Modigliani, which emphasizes that the planning horizon of consumers is their lifetime.

linear relation A relation between two variables such that a one-unit increase in one variable always leads to an increase of n units in the other variable.

liquidity An asset is liquid if it can be sold quickly. A financial institution is liquid if it can sell its assets quickly.

liquidity facilities The specific ways in which a central bank can lend to financial institutions.

liquidity preference The term introduced by Keynes to denote the demand for money.

liquidity provision The provision of liquidity to banks by the central bank.

liquidity trap The case where nominal interest rates are equal to zero, and monetary policy cannot, therefore, decrease them further.

***LM* curve** An upward-sloping curve relating the interest rate to output. The curve corresponding to the *LM* relation, the equilibrium condition for financial markets.

loan-to-value (LTV) ratio The ratio of the loan that people can take as a proportion of the value of the house or apartment they buy.

logarithmic scale A scale in which the same proportional increase is represented by the same distance on the scale, so that a variable that grows at a constant rate is represented by a straight line.

long run A period of time extending over decades.

long-term interest rate The interest rate on long-term bonds.

Lucas critique The proposition, put forth by Robert Lucas, that existing relations between economic variables may change when policy changes. An example is the apparent trade-off between inflation and unemployment, which may disappear if policy makers try to exploit it.

M1 The sum of currency, traveler's checks, and checkable deposits—assets that can be used directly in transactions. Also called *narrow money*.

Maastricht treaty A treaty signed in 1991 that defined the steps involved in the transition to a common currency for the European Union.

macroprudential tools The instruments used to regulate the financial system, such as loan-to-value ratios or capital ratio requirements.

Malthusian trap The case of an economy where increases in productivity lead to a decrease in mortality and an increase in population, leaving income per person unchanged.

markup The ratio of the price to the cost of production.

Marshall–Lerner condition The condition under which a real depreciation leads to an increase in net exports.

maturity The length of time over which a financial asset (typically a bond) promises to make payments to the holder.

medium run A period of time between the short run and the long run.

menu cost The cost of changing a price.

mid-cycle deficit *See* cyclically adjusted deficit.

models of endogenous growth Models in which accumulation of physical and human capital can sustain growth even in the absence of technological progress.

modified Phillips curve The curve that plots the change in the inflation rate against the unemployment rate. Also called an *expectations-augmented Phillips curve* or an *accelerationist Phillips curve*.

monetarism, monetarists A group of economists in the 1960s, led by Milton Friedman, who argued that monetary policy had powerful effects on activity.

monetary contraction A change in monetary policy, which leads to an increase in the interest rate. Also called *monetary tightening*.

monetary expansion A change in monetary policy, which leads to a decrease in the interest rate.

monetary-fiscal policy mix The combination of monetary and fiscal policies in effect at a given time.

monetary tightening *See* monetary contraction.

money Those financial assets that can be used directly to buy goods.

money finance The financing of the budget deficit through money creation.

money illusion The proposition that people make systematic mistakes in assessing nominal versus real changes.

money market funds Financial institutions that receive funds from people and use them to buy short-term bonds.

mortgage-based security (MBS) A security based on an underlying portfolio of mortgages.

mortgage lenders The institutions that make housing loans to households.

multilateral exchange rate (multilateral real exchange rate) The real exchange rate between a country and its trading partners, computed as a weighted average of bilateral real exchange rates. Also called the *trade-weighted real exchange rate* or *effective real exchange rate*.

multiplier The ratio of the change in an endogenous variable to the change in an exogenous variable (e.g., the ratio of the change in output to a change in autonomous spending).

Mundell–Fleming model A model of simultaneous equilibrium in both goods and financial markets for an open economy.

narrow banking Restrictions on banks that would require them to hold only short-term government bonds.

national accounts *See* national income and product accounts.

national income In the United States, the income that originates in the production of goods and services supplied by residents of the United States.

national income and product accounts (NIPA) The system of accounts used to describe the evolution of the sum, the composition, and the distribution of aggregate output.

natural rate of interest The rate of interest consistent with a level of demand for goods equal to potential output.

natural rate of unemployment The unemployment rate at which price and wage decisions are consistent.

neoclassical synthesis A consensus in macroeconomics, developed in the early 1950s, based on an integration of Keynes' ideas and the ideas of earlier economists.

net capital flows Capital flows from the rest of the world to the domestic economy, minus capital flows to the rest of the world from the domestic economy.

net exports The difference between exports and imports. Also called the *trade balance*.

net interest In the national income and product accounts, the interest paid by firms minus the interest received by firms, plus interest received from the rest of the world minus interest paid to the rest of the world.

net national product (NNP) Gross national product minus capital depreciation.

net transfers received In the current account, the net value of foreign aid received minus foreign aid given.

neutral rate of interest *See* natural rate of interest.

new classicals A group of economists who interpret fluctuations as the effects of shocks in competitive markets with fully flexible prices and wages.

new growth theory Recent developments in growth theory that explore the determinants of technological progress and the role of increasing returns to scale in growth.

new Keynesians A group of economists who believe in the importance of nominal rigidities in fluctuations, and who are exploring the role of market imperfections in explaining fluctuations.

nominal exchange rate The price of domestic currency in terms of foreign currency. The number of units of foreign currency you can get for one unit of domestic currency.

nominal GDP The sum of the quantities of final goods produced in an economy times their current price. Also known as *dollar GDP* and *GDP in current dollars*.

nominal interest rate The interest rate in terms of the national currency (in terms of dollars in the United States). It tells us how many dollars one has to repay in the future in exchange for borrowing one dollar today.

nominal rigidities The slow adjustment of nominal wages and prices to changes in economic activity.

non-accelerating inflation rate of unemployment (NAIRU) The unemployment rate at which inflation neither decreases nor increases. *See* natural rate of unemployment.

nondurable goods Commodities that can be stored but have an average life of less than three years.

nonhuman wealth The financial and housing component of wealth.

noninstitutional civilian population The number of people potentially available for civilian employment.

nonresidential investment The purchase of new capital goods by firms: structures and producer durable equipment.

North American Free Trade Agreement (NAFTA) An agreement signed by the United States, Canada, and Mexico in which the three countries agreed to establish all of North America as a free-trade zone.

not in the labor force The number of people who are neither employed nor looking for employment.

n-year interest rate *See* yield to maturity.

official deficit The difference between public spending, including nominal interest payments, and public revenues.

Okun coefficient The effect of a change in the rate of growth of output on the change in the unemployment rate.

Okun's law The relation between GDP growth and the change in the unemployment rate.

open market operation The purchase or sale of government bonds by the central bank for the purpose of increasing or decreasing the money supply.

openness in financial markets The opportunity for financial investors to choose between domestic and foreign financial assets.

openness in goods markets The opportunity for consumers and firms to choose between domestic and foreign goods.

optimal control The control of a system (a machine, a rocket, an economy) by means of mathematical methods.

optimal control theory The set of mathematical methods used for optimal control.

optimal currency area The properties of a common currency area needed for it to function smoothly.

ordinary least squares (OLS) A statistical method to find the best-fitting relation between two or more variables.

Organisation for Economic Co-operation and Development (OECD) An international organization that collects and studies economic data for many countries. Most of the world's rich countries belong to the OECD.

Organization of Petroleum Exporting Countries (OPEC) A set of petroleum producing countries, which long acted as a production cartel.

out of the labor force People of working age not working (in the market economy) and not looking for a job.

output fluctuations Movements in output around its trend. Also called *business cycles*.

output gap The difference between actual output and potential output.

output per person A country's gross domestic product divided by its population.

paradox of saving The result that an attempt by people to save more may lead both to a decline in output and to unchanged saving.

parameter A coefficient in a behavioral equation.

participation rate The ratio of the labor force to the noninstitutional civilian population.

patent The legal right granted to a person or firm to exclude anyone else from the production or use of a new product or technique for a certain period of time.

PAYGO rule A budget rule requiring any new spending to be financed by additional revenues.

payments of factor income to the rest of the world In the United States, income received by foreign capital and foreign residents.

peg The exchange rate to which a country commits under a fixed exchange rate system.

permanent income theory of consumption The theory of consumption, developed by Milton Friedman, that emphasizes that people make consumption decisions based not on current income, but on their notion of permanent income.

personal disposable income Personal income minus personal tax and nontax payments. The income available to consumers after they have received transfers and paid taxes.

personal income The income actually received by persons.

Phillips curve The curve that plots the relation between movements in inflation and unemployment. The original Phillips curve captured the relation between the inflation rate and the unemployment rate. The modified Phillips curve captures the relation between (i) the change in the inflation rate and (ii) the unemployment rate.

players The participants in a game. Depending on the context, players may be people, firms, governments, and so on.

policy coordination (of macroeconomic policies between two countries) The joint design of macroeconomic policies to improve the economic situation in the two countries.

policy mix *See* monetary-fiscal policy mix.

policy rate The interest rate set by the central bank.

political business cycle Fluctuations in economic activity caused by the manipulation of the economy for electoral gain.

potential output The level of output associated with the unemployment rate being equal to the natural unemployment rate.

present discounted value *See* expected discounted value.

present value *See* expected present discounted value.

price level The general level of prices in an economy.

price-setting relation The relation between the price chosen by firms, the nominal wage, and the markup.

primary deficit Government spending, excluding interest payments on the debt, minus government revenues. (The negative of the primary surplus.)

primary surplus Government revenues minus government spending, excluding interest payments on the debt.

private saving (S) Saving by the private sector. The value of consumers' disposable income minus their consumption.

private sector involvement A reduction in the value of the debt held by the private sector in case of debt rescheduling or debt restructuring.

production function The relation between the quantity of output and the quantities of inputs used in production.

profitability The expected present discounted value of profits.

propagation mechanism The dynamic effects of a shock on output and its components.

propensity to consume (c_1) The effect of an additional dollar of disposable income on consumption.

propensity to save The effect of an additional dollar of disposable income on saving (equal to one minus the propensity to consume).

property rights The legal rights given to property owners.

proprietors' income In the national income and product accounts, the income of sole proprietorships, partnerships, and tax-exempt cooperatives.

public saving Saving by the government; equal to government revenues minus government spending. Also called the *budget surplus*. (A budget deficit represents public dissaving.)

purchasing power Income in terms of goods.

purchasing power parity (PPP) A method of adjustment used to allow for international comparisons of GDP.

QE1, QE2, QE3 The first, second, and third instances of unconventional monetary policy in the United States during the financial crisis.

quantitative easing Purchases of financial assets by the central bank at the zero lower bound, leading to an increase in the balance sheet of the central bank.

quits Workers who leave their jobs for better alternatives.

quotas Restrictions on the quantities of goods that can be imported.

R^2 A measure of fit, between zero and one, from a regression. An R^2 of zero implies that there is no apparent relation between the variables under consideration. An R^2 of one implies a perfect fit: all the residuals are equal to zero.

random walk The path of a variable whose changes over time are unpredictable.

random walk of consumption The proposition that, if consumers are foresighted, changes in their consumption should be unpredictable.

rate of growth of total factor productivity *See* Solow residual.

rating agencies Firms that assess the credit worthiness of various debt securities and debt issuers.

rational expectations The formation of expectations based on rational forecasts, rather than on simple extrapolations of the past.

rational speculative bubble An increase in stock prices based on the rational expectation of further increases in prices in the future.

real appreciation An increase in the relative price of domestic goods in terms of foreign goods. An increase in the real exchange rate.

real business cycle (RBC) models Economic models that assume that output is always at its natural level. Thus, all output fluctuations are movements of the natural level of output, as opposed to movements away from the natural level of output.

real depreciation A decrease in the relative price of domestic goods in terms of foreign goods. An increase in the real exchange rate.

real exchange rate The relative price of domestic goods in terms of foreign goods.

real GDP A measure of aggregate output. The sum of quantities produced in an economy times their price in a base year. Also known as *GDP in terms of goods, GDP in constant dollars*, or *GDP adjusted for inflation*. The current measure of real GDP in the United States is called GDP in chained (2000) dollars.

real GDP in chained (2000) dollars *See* real GDP.

real GDP per person Ratio of real GDP to population.

real interest rate The interest rate in terms of goods. It tells us how many goods one has to repay in the future in exchange for borrowing the equivalent one good today.

receipts of factor income from the rest of the world In the United States, income received from abroad by U.S. capital or U.S. residents.

recession A period of negative GDP growth. Usually refers to at least two consecutive quarters of negative GDP growth.

regression The output of ordinary least squares. Gives the equation corresponding to the estimated relation between variables, together with information about the degree of fit and the relative importance of the different variables.

regression line The best-fitting line corresponding to the equation obtained by using ordinary least squares.

rental cost of capital *See* user cost of capital.

rental income of persons In the national income and product accounts, the income from the rental of real property, minus depreciation on this property.

research and development (R&D) Spending aimed at discovering and developing new ideas and products.

reservation wage The wage that would make a worker indifferent between working and being unemployed.

reserve ratio The ratio of bank reserves to checkable deposits.

residential investment The purchase of new homes and apartments by people.

residual The difference between the actual value of a variable and the value implied by the regression line. Small residuals indicate a good fit.

revaluation An increase in the exchange rate (*E*) in a fixed exchange rate system.

Ricardian equivalence The proposition that neither government deficits nor government debt have an effect on economic activity. Also called the *Ricardo-Barro proposition*.

Ricardo-Barro proposition *See* Ricardian equivalence.

risk averse A person is risk averse if he or she prefers to receive a given amount for sure to an uncertain amount with the same expected value.

risk premium The difference between the interest rate paid on a given bond and the interest rate paid on a bond with the highest rating.

risk premium on bonds the additional interest rate a bond has to pay, reflecting the risk of default on the bond.

saving The sum of private and public saving, denoted by *S*.

saving rate The proportion of income that is saved.

securitization The issuance of securities, based on an underlying portfolio of assets, such as mortgages, or commercial paper.

seignorage The revenues from the creation of money.

senior securities Securities being repaid before junior securities in case of insolvency.

separations Workers who are leaving or losing their jobs.

services Commodities that cannot be stored and thus must be consumed at the place and time of purchase.

shadow banking system The set of non-bank financial institutions, from SIVs to hedge funds.

share A financial asset issued by a firm that promises to pay a sequence of payments, called *dividends*, in the future. Also called *stock*.

shocks Movements in the factors that affect aggregate demand and/or aggregate supply.

shoe-leather costs The costs of going to the bank to take money out of a checking account.

short run A period of time extending over a few years at most.

short-term interest rate The interest rate on a short-term bond (typically a year or less).

skill-biased technological progress The proposition that new machines and new methods of production require skilled workers to a greater degree than in the past.

slope In a linear relation between two variables, the amount by which the first variable increases when the second increases by one unit.

Solow residual The excess of actual output growth over what can be accounted for by the growth in capital and labor.

spending caps Legislative limits on public spending.

Spread The difference between the interest rate on a risky bond and the interest rate on a safe bond.

Stability and Growth Pact (SGP) A set of rules governing public spending, deficits, and debt in the European Union.

stagflation The combination of stagnation and inflation.

staggering of wage and price decisions The fact that different wages are adjusted at different times, making it impossible to achieve a synchronized decrease in nominal wage inflation.

standard of living Real GDP per person.

standardized employment deficit *See* cyclically adjusted deficit.

state of technology The degree of technological development in a country or industry.

statistical discrepancy A difference between two numbers that should be equal, coming from differences in sources or methods of construction for the two numbers.

steady state In an economy without technological progress, the state of the economy where output and capital per worker are no longer changing. In an economy with technological progress, the state of the economy where output and capital per effective worker are no longer changing.

stock A variable that can be expressed as a quantity at a point in time (such as wealth). Also a synonym for *share*.

stocks An alternative term for *inventories*. Also, an alternative term for *shares*.

strategic interactions An environment in which the actions of one player depend on and affect the actions of another player.

structural change A change in the economic structure of the economy, typically associated with growth.

structural deficit *See* cyclically adjusted deficit.

structural rate of unemployment *See* natural rate of unemployment.

structured investment vehicle (SIV) Financial intermediaries set up by banks. SIVs borrow from investors, typically in the form of short-term debt, and invest in securities.

structures In the national income and product accounts: plants, factories, office buildings, and hotels.

subprime mortgages Mortgages with a higher risk of default by the borrower.

tariffs Taxes on imported goods.

tax smoothing The principle of keeping tax rates roughly constant, so that the government runs large deficits when government spending is exceptionally high and small surpluses the rest of the time.

Taylor rule A rule, suggested by John Taylor, telling a central bank how to adjust the nominal interest rate in response to deviations of inflation from its target, and of the unemployment rate from the natural rate.

technological progress An improvement in the state of technology.

technological unemployment Unemployment brought about by technological progress.

technology frontier The state of technological knowledge.

term structure of interest rates *See* yield curve.

time inconsistency In game theory, the incentive for one player to deviate from his previously announced course of action once the other player has moved.

Tobin's *q* The ratio of the value of the capital stock, computed by adding the stock market value of firms and the debt of firms, to the replacement cost of capital.

total factor productivity (TFP) growth The rate of technological progress.

total wealth The sum of human wealth and nonhuman wealth.

toxic assets Nonperforming assets, from subprime mortgages to nonperforming loans.

tradable goods Goods that compete with foreign goods in domestic or foreign markets.

trade balance The difference between exports and imports. Also called *net exports*.

trade deficit A negative trade balance, that is, imports exceed exports.

trade surplus A positive trade balance, that is, exports exceed imports.

transfers to persons Unemployment, retirement, health, and other benefits paid by the state.

Treasury bill (T-bill) A U.S. government bond with a maturity of up to one year.

Treasury Inflation Protected Securities (TIPS) U.S. government bonds paying the real (rather than the nominal) interest rate.

Troubled Asset Relief Program (TARP) The program introduced in October 2008 by the U.S. administration, aimed at buying toxic assets, and, later, providing capital to banks and other financial institutions in trouble.

***t*-statistic** A statistic associated with an estimated coefficient in a regression that indicates how confident one can be that the true coefficient differs from zero.

unconventional monetary policy Monetary policy measures used to increase economic activity when the policy rate reached the zero lower bound.

uncovered interest parity (UIP) An arbitrage relation stating that domestic and foreign bonds must have the same expected rate of return, expressed in terms of a common currency.

underground economy That part of a nation's economic activity that is not measured in official statistics, either because the activity is illegal or because people and firms are seeking to avoid paying taxes.

Underwater A loan is underwater if its value is higher than the value of the collateral it corresponds to. For example, a mortgage is underwater if its value exceeds the price of the corresponding house.

Unemployment Number of people not working but looking for a job.

unemployment insurance Unemployment benefits paid by the state to the unemployed.

unemployment rate The ratio of the number of unemployed to the labor force.

usable observation An observation for which the values of all the variables under consideration are available for regression purposes.

user cost of capital The cost of using capital over a year, or a given period of time. The sum of the real interest rate and the depreciation rate. Also called the *rental cost of capital*.

value added The value a firm adds in the production process, equal to the value of its production minus the value of the intermediate inputs it uses in production.

wage indexation A rule that automatically increases wages in response to an increase in prices.

wage-setting relation The relation between the wage chosen by wage setters, the price level, and the unemployment rate.

war of attrition When both parties to an argument hold their grounds, hoping that the other party will give in.

wealth *See* financial wealth.

wholesale funding Financing through the issuance of short-term debt than through deposits.

Wicksellian rate of interest *See* neutral, or natural, rate of interest.

Yield The ratio of the coupon payment to the value of the bond.

yield curve The relation between yield and maturity for bonds of different maturities. Also called the *term structure of interest rates*.

yield to maturity The constant interest rate that makes the price of an *n*-year bond today equal to the present value of future payments. Also called the *n-year interest rate*.

zero lower bound The lowest interest rate the central bank can achieve before it becomes more attractive to hold cash than to hold bonds.

Index

A

Above-the-line transactions, 379
Accelerationist Phillips curve, 183
Acemoglu, Daron, 275, 527
Adaptive expectations, 357
Adjustment. *See also* Dynamics of adjustment
   equilibrium output, 78, 80, 83
African countries
   economic growth, 35
   output per capita, 228
Aggregate demand, 518
Aggregate output GDP, 42–46
   determinants of the level of, 56
Aggregate private spending, 353
Aggregate production function, 229–230
Aggregate supply relation, 522
Aghion, Philippe, 298, 527
Akerlof, George, 526
Amendments, balanced budget, 455
American Recovery and Reinvestment Act, 149
Anchored, 203
Animal spirits, 357
Appreciation
   domestic currency, 373
   real, 375
Approximations, A7–A9
Arbitrage
   bond prices and, 313–314
   vs. present value, 314
Argentina
   currency board, 446, 447
   U.S. currency, holders of, 91
Asian countries, output per capita in, 228
Assets
   domestic vs. foreign, 381–383
   financial, 88
Attrition, wars of, 465
Aumann, Robert, 459
Australia, 481
The Australia Bureau of Statistics' Monthly
   Population Surveys (MPS), 160
Austria, unemployment rate in, 188 (figure)
Automatic stabilizer, 484
Autonomous spending, 74, 76 (figure)

B

Backloading, 360
Balance of payments, 379–381
Balance sheet, 94
   central bank, 94
Balanced budget, 74, 455
Balanced growth, 266–267
Bands, 423, 424
Bank runs, 97, 140
Banks
   what they do, 96–99
   world financial crisis, 24–25, 144–149
Bargaining power, 164, 187

Barrel, Ray, 270
Barro, Robert, 521
Basel II, 511
Basel III, 511
Behavioral equation, 70
Belgium, 425
Below-the-line transactions, 379
Bernanke, Ben, 455, 526
Bilateral exchange rates, 377–378
Biogenetic research, 271
Blinder, Alan, 462, 463, 506
Bloom, Nick, 272
Bond prices and yields, 94–95, 310–317
Bond ratings, 312
Bonds, 88, 94–95
   buying Brazilian, 384
   domestic vs. foreign, 413–416
   holding wealth in form of, 88
   interest rate, 88
Borrowing rate, 141
Botswana, 228
Bracket creep, 53, 504
Brazilian bonds, buying, 384
Bretton Woods period, 431–432, 442
Britain. *See also* United Kingdom
   return to gold standard, 435
Bubble, speculative, 325–327
Budget, balanced, 74
Budget deficit, 81. *See also* Deficit(s)
   in Ireland, 361–362
   in United States, 491–492
Budget Enforcement Act of 1990, 469
Budget surplus, 81
Bureau of Labor Statistics (BLS), 52
Business cycle theory, 518
   real, 525
Business cycles, 212
   political, 464
Business transfers, A2

C

Canada, 481
Capital
   consumption of fixed, A2
   decreasing returns to, 230
   golden-rule level of, 253
   output and, 238–243, 264–267
   per worker, 231
   physical vs. human, 254–256
   rental cost of, 342
   steady-state, 243
Capital account, 380–381
Capital account balance, 380
Capital account deficit, 380
Capital account surplus, 380
Capital accumulation, 232, 239, 240–241, 244
   vs. technological progress, 276–278
Capital controls, 369, 513

Capital income, 43
Capital inflows, net private, 414
Capital mobility, 429–430
Capital ratio, 138
Cash flow vs. profitability, 344
Causality, A13–A14
Cavallo, Domingo, 446
Central bank
   equilibrium, achieving, 98–99
   establishing credibility, 461–463
   money, 94–99
Central Europe, 35
Central planning, 35
Chain-type indexes, 62–63
Changes in business inventories, A4
Checkable deposits, 88, 96
China, 33–35
   growth and inflation since 1990, 34 (table)
   growth mechanisms, 275
   technological progress vs. growth, 277–278
Choi, Don, 506
Churchill, Winston, 435
Churning process, 291–293
Civilian population, non-institutional, 158
Clinton-Greenspan policy mix, 124
Cobb, Charles, 259
Cobb-Douglas production function, 259
Collateral, 148
Collateralized debt obligations (CDOs), 146
Collective bargaining, 163
Common currency area, 31, 443, 445
Communism, 34, 35
Compensation of employees, A2
Compounding, 225
Computers, pricing of, 47
Confidence band, 125
Congressional Budget Office (CBO), 491, 492
Consols, 309
Constant returns to scale, 230
Consumer Price Index (CPI), 51–52
Consumer spending, 322–323
Consumers, foresighted, 332–337
Consumption, 51–52, 68, 70–72, 332–338
   changes in, A13–A14
   college student problem, 333–334
   component of GDP, 68
   dependent on current income, 333–334
   determinants of, 390–391
   expectations and, 333–334, 337–338
   of fixed capital, A2
   investment decisions and, 352–355, 519
   parameters characterizing the relation
     between disposable income and, 70
   per person, 222–223
   personal consumption expenditures, A3
   rational expectations, 523
   saving rate and, 247–250
   in United States, during World War II, 485
   volatility, 346–347

Consumption basket, 52
Consumption function, 70, 79–80
Contract with America, 455, 456 (figure)
Contraction, monetary, 118, 421–423
Contractionary open market operations, 94
Conventional monetary policy, 508
Convergence of output per person, 226–227
Corporate bonds, 312
Corporate profits, A2
Correlation, A13–A14
Cost of living, 52
Coupon bonds, 312
Coupon payments, 312
Coupon rate, 312
Covered interest parity, 383
Crawling peg, 423–424
Creative destruction, 291–292, 527
Credibility
    of deficit reduction program, 360
    establishing, 461–463
Credit easing, 508. See also Quantitative
    easing
Currency, 88
    common currency areas, 443, 445
    domestic, appreciation and depreciation
        of, 373
    pegging, 423–424
    U.S., holders of, 91
Currency boards, 445–447
Current account, 379–380
    exchange rates and, 440–441
Current account balance, 380
Current account deficit, 380
Current account surplus, 380
Current Population Survey (CPS), 48, 159
Current profit vs. expected profit, 342–344
Current yield, 312
Cyclically adjusted deficit, 483–484

D

Debt
    arithmetic of, 475, 477
    dangers of high, 486–492
    repayment, 477–479
Debt default, 488
Debt finance, 318
Debt monetarization, 488
Debt ratio, 479–481
Debt rescheduling, 488
Debt restructuring, 488
Debt spirals and zero lower bound, 203–206
Debt stabilization, 479
Decisions
    expectations and, 352–355
    investment, 340
Default risk, 311, 487–489
Deficit(s). See also Budget deficit
    arithmetic of, 475, 477
    capital account, 380
    cyclically-adjusted, 483–484
    European Stability and Growth Pact, 455,
        466–467
    measurement of, 476
    trade, 395, 406, 407
    in United States during World War II, 485
    wars and, 484–485
Deficit reduction, 358–363, 468–469
Deflation, 51, 53

in the Great Depression, 205–206
    Phillips curve relation and, 190–191
    zero lower bound and, 135–136
Deflation spiral, 204
Deflation trap, 204
Delors, Jacques, 445
Demand, 67. See also Aggregate demand
    domestic, increases in, 394–396
    foreign, increases in, 396–397
Demand deposits, 139–140
Demand for bank money, 97
Demand for central bank money, 98–99
Demand for domestic goods, 390
Demand for goods, 70–73
Demand for money, 88–91, 97–99, 519
    deriving, 89–91
    interest rate and, 91–94
    M1 growth and inflation, 500 (figure)
Demand for reserves, 98, 99
Denmark, unemployment rate in, 188 (figure)
Deposits, demand, 139–140
Depreciation
    capital stock, 339
    domestic currency, 373
    real, 375, 400–401
    trade balance, output, and, 399–402
Depression. See Great Depression
Devaluation, 373
    case for and against, 434–435
Development economics, 229
Diamond, Doug, 528
Diamond, Peter, 526
Direct finance, 137
Discipline device, unemployment as, 172
Discount bonds, 312
Discount factor, 306
Discount rate, 306
Discounted values, expected present,
    306–310, 330
Discouraged workers, 48, 160
Disposable income, 70
    changes in, A13–A14
    parameters characterizing the relation
        between consumption and, 70
Dividends, 318
Divine coincidence, 501
Dollar GDP, 44, 45
Dollarization, 445, 447
Domestic assets, 381–383
Domestic bonds vs. foreign bonds, 413–416
Domestic demand, increases in, 390, 394–396
Domestic goods, 372
    demand for, 394–396
    vs. foreign goods, 372
Dornbusch, Rudiger, 524
Douglas, Paul, 259
Durable goods, A3
Dybvig, Philip, 528
Dynamic stochastic general equilibrium, 528
Dynamics of adjustment, 78

E

Early 2000s recession. See 2001 recession
Earnings losses, 293
Easterlin, Richard, 224
Easterlin paradox, 224
Eastern Europe, 213
Econometrics, 77, A12–A16

Economic activity
    hyperinflation, 489
    stock market and, 321
Economic crisis, 24–33
    from housing problem to financial crisis,
        144–149
    lessons from, 528–529
    new classical economics and real business
        cycle theory, 525
    new growth theory, 526–527
    new Keynesian economics, 525–526
    synthesis of theories, 527–528
Economic growth, 270
Economic Report of the President, 38
The Economist, 38
Ecuador, 91
Education
    income inequality, 295
    relative wages by, 293 (figure)
Effective demand, 518
Effective labor, 262–263
Efficiency units, labor in, 263
Efficiency wages, 164–165, 526
    Henry Ford and, 165
El-Erian, Mohamed, 399
El Salvador, 91
Employees, compensation of, A2
Employment, 47
Employment decline, in relation to output, 126
Employment insurance, 167, 187
Employment rate, 160
EMS. See European Monetary System
Endogenous growth, 256
Endogenous variables, 72
Equatorial Guinea, 228
Equilibrium
    federal funds market and federal funds
        rate, 99–100
    in financial markets, 115, 116, 413–416
    in goods market, 73, 412–413
    in short and medium run, 433–434
Equilibrium condition, 73
Equilibrium interest rate, 91–94
Equilibrium output
    algebraic equations, 74
    determination of, 73–80, 82
    in goods market, 73, 412–413
    graphical depictions, 75–77
    time for output to adjust, 78, 83
    trade balance and, 393–394
Equipment and software, A3
Equity finance, 318
Equity premium, 319
EU27. See European Union
Euro, 29–33
    benefits of, 32–33
    conversion to, 425
    history of, 445
    Stability and Growth Pact, 455, 466–467
Euro area, 29
    map of, 30
Euro area fiscal rules, history of, 466–467
Euro periphery countries, disappearance of
    account deficits in, 402–403
Europe
    bond spreads, 487
    collective bargaining, 164
    growth over two millennia, 227
    unemployment, 31–32, 187–188

European Central Bank (ECB), 31, 445, 121
European Central Bank Euro Interbank
    Rates (1999–2005), 121 (figure)
European Commission (EC), 490
European Monetary System (EMS), 424
    exchange rate crisis, 438–439
    German unification and, 425
European Monetary Union (EMU), 445
European Union (EU), 29–33
    budgetary rules in, 490–491
    economic performance, 29–31
    output 1990–2015, 29 (table)
    Stability and Growth Pact, 455, 466–467
    unemployment, 31–32
Ex-dividend price, 319
Excessive Deficit Procedure (EDP), 490
Exchange rate. *See also* Real exchange rate
    bilateral, 377–378
    combined with fiscal policies, 401–402
    fixed, 373, 424, 426, 433, 436–437
    flexible, 439–442
    forward, 383
    GDP per person, 220–221
    history, 431–432
    interest rate and, 383–385
    multilateral, 377–378
    nominal, 372–377
    pegging, 423–424
    volatility of
Exchange rate movements under flexible
    exchange rates, 439–442
Exchange rate regimes, choosing between,
    442–443, 445, 447
Exogenous variables, 72
Expansionary open market operations, 94
Expansions, 46
Expectations, 337–338
    about the future, role of, 359–363
    decisions and, 352–355
    deficit reduction, output, and, 358–363
    monetary policy, output, and, 355–358
    policy and, 459–463
    role of, 203
    static, 340, 350, 357
Expectations-augmented Phillips curve, 183
Expectations hypothesis, 313
Expected present discounted values, 306–
    310, 330
Exports, 69, 370–372, A4
    from China, 33
    determinants of, 391
    exceeding GDP, 372
Extension agreements, 187

F

Face value, 312
Factor market, openness in, 369
Fads (stock prices), 327
Federal deposit insurance, 97, 140
Federal funds market, 99
Federal funds rate, 99–100, 322
Federal Reserve Bank (Fed), 87. *See also*
    Central bank
Federal Reserve Bank of St. Louis, 38
Federal Reserve Board. *See also* Central
    bank
    currency, 91
    currency in circulation, 91

    negative reaction to, 463
    uncertainty, 458
Federal Reserve Economic Database
    (*FRED*), 38
Feldstein, Martin, 248
Final good, 43
Financial intermediaries, 96
    roles of, 137–141, 145–147
Financial investment, 68–69, 89
Financial markets
    balance of payments, 379–381
    capital account, 380–381
    current account, 379–380
    demand for money, 88–91
    domestic bonds vs. foreign bonds,
      413–416
    domestic vs. foreign assets, 381–383
    equilibrium in, 99–100, 413–416
    exchange rates and interest rates, 383–385
    federal funds market and rate, 99–100
    interest rate determination, 91–101
    LM relation and, 114–118
    monetary policy and open market
      operations, 94–96
    openness in, 369, 378–385
    putting together goods markets and,
      417–418
    supply and demand for central bank
      money, 98–100
Financial shocks and policies, 142–143
Financial wealth, 89, 332
Fine tuning, 459
Finland, unemployment rate, 188 (figure)
Fire sale prices, 139
Fiscal austerity, 491
Fiscal consolidation, 116, 206–207
    IS relation and, 352–355
    monetary policy and output, 355–358
Fiscal contraction, 116
Fiscal dominance, 488
Fiscal expansion, 116
    in France, 422–423
Fiscal multipliers, 363
Fiscal policy, 72, 149, 397–399, 473
    combined with exchange rate, 401–402
    dangers of high debt, 486–492
    effects in open economy, 419–421
    under fixed exchange rates, 424, 426
    government budget constraint, 475–480
    interest rate and, 116–118
    vs. monetary policy, 520
    restraints, 468–469
    Ricardian equivalence, 482–483
Fiscal stimulus, 398
Fischer, Stanley, 524
Fixed exchange rates, 373, 423–426
    capital mobility and, 429–430
    fiscal policy under, 424, 426
    IS relation under, 433, 451
Fixed investment, 68
Fleming, Marcus, 411, 421
Flexible inflation targeting, 502
Float, 436
Flow, 89
Force of compounding, 225
Ford, Henry, 165
Foreign assets, 381–383
Foreign bonds vs. domestic bonds, 413–416
Foreign demand, increases in, 396–397

Foreign direct investment, 513, 270
Foreign exchange, 378
Foreign-exchange reserves, 429
Foreign goods, 370–372
Forward exchange rate, 383
France
    capital accumulation and growth after
      World War II, 244
    German unification, interest rates, and
      EMS, 425
    Monetary policy coordination and fiscal
      expansion, 422–423
    output per person since 1950, 223 (table)
    output per worker and technological
      progress, 276 (table)
    recession of 2001, 120–122
    unemployment rate, 188 (figure)
Friedman, Milton, 184, 332, 459, 519–521
Full-employment deficit, 483
Fully funded system, 248
Functions, A9–A10
Fundamental value of stocks, 324

G

Gali, Jordi, 527, 528
Game theory, 459, 523
Garber, Peter, 325
GDP. *See* Gross domestic product
*The General Theory of Employment, Interest,
    and Money* (Keynes), 80, 109, 518
Geometric series, 77, 308, A7
German Chancellor Schröder, 120
Germany
    EMS currency crisis, 438–439
    recession of 2001, 120–122
    spread, 487
    unemployment rate, 188 (figure)
    unification, 425
Gertler, Mark, 526
Getty, J. Paul, 89
Global financial crisis, 414–415
Global Financial Stability Report (GFSR), 39
GNP. *See* Gross national product
Goffe, Bill, 39
Gold standard, Britain's return to, 435
Golden-rule level of capital, 247, 248, 253
Goods
    demand for, 70–73
    demand for domestic, 390
    domestic vs. foreign, 372
    final, 43
    intermediate, 42
    tradable, 371
Goods market
    domestic vs. foreign goods, 372
    equilibrium in, 73–82, 393–394, 412–413
    exports and imports, 370–372
    IS relation and, 110–114, 390–393
    openness in, 369, 370–378
    putting together financial markets and,
      417–418
Government, role in choosing output, 82
Government bonds, 312
    interest-rate risk, 414–415
    yield curve, 318
Government budget constraints, 475–480
Government Expenditure in France and
    Germany (1999–2002), 121 (figure)

Government purchases, A3–A4
Government spending, 69, 72–73
  choosing output level and, 82
  decrease in, 361–362
  determinants of, 390–391
  effects of increase in, 419–420
  in national income accounts, A4–A5
  plus taxes, fiscal policy described by,
    72–73
Government transfers, 69
Graph, equilibrium, 75–77. *See also*
    Equilibrium
Great Depression, 529
  deflation in, 205–206
  fears of, 79–80
  Keynes and, 518
  monetarists' view, 520
  natural employment rate and, 190–191
Great Moderation, 497
Greece
  debt-to-GDP ratio, 473
  unemployment rate, 188 (figure)
Greenspan, Alan, 124
Gross Capital Formation (GCF), 341
Gross domestic product (GDP), A1–A2
  composition of, 68–69
  debt-to-GDP ratio, 479–481
  exports exceeding, 372
  to GNP, A1–A2
  vs. GNP, in Kuwait, 382
  hedonic pricing and, 47
  level vs. growth rate, 46
  national income and product accounts
    (NIPA), A1–A6
  nominal and real, 44–46
  production and income, 42–44
  in United States, 45, 45 (figure), 46 (figure),
    220 (figure), A11 (figure)
Gross domestic product (GDP) deflator, 51
Gross national product (GNP), 42, A1–A2
Gross private domestic fixed investment, A3
Growth, 219, 229–233
  across millenia, 227
  aggregate production function, 229–230
  among rich countries, 223–227, 276–278
  balanced, 266–267
  capital accumulation vs. technological
    progress, 276–278
  endogenous, models of, 256
  happiness and, 224–225
  importance of institutions for, 273–276
  money, 499–501
  OECD countries, 227–229
  output per worker and capital per
    worker, 231
  post-World War II, in France, 244
  productivity, 28–29
  returns to scale and returns to factors,
    230–231
  in rich countries since 1950, 223–228
  sources of, 231–233
Growth rate, technological progress and,
    261–278
Growth theory, 519

H
Haircut, 488
Hall, Robert, 523

Hansen, Alvin, 109, 519
Hard peg, 445, 447
Harsanyi, John, 459
Hedonic pricing, 47
Hicks, John, 109, 519
High-powered money, 98
Hires, 158
*Historical Statistics of the United States,
    Colonial Times to 1970*, 39
Holland. *See also* Netherlands
  tulip bubble, 325
Holmström, Bengt, 528, 529
Hong Kong, 512
Hostage takings and negotiations, 460
Household Finance and Consumption
    Survey (HFCS), 333
Housing prices, 143–145
  maximum loan-to-value (LTV) ratios,
    511, 512
Housing wealth, 332
Howitt, Peter, 527
Human capital, 254
  endogenous growth, 256
  extending the production function, 254–255
  output and, 254–256
Human wealth, 332
Hyperinflation(s), 489

I
Identification problem, A15
Identity, 70
Illiquidity, 139–141
Import compression, 403
Imports, 69, 370–372, A4
  determinants of, 391
Income, 67
  consumption and current, 337–338
  determinants of, 390–391
  disposable, 70
  GDP as sum of, 44
  national income and product accounts,
    A1–A3
  real, 113–114
  wealth, money, and, 89
Income balance, 380
Independent central bank, 461–462
Index number, 51
Indexed bonds, 312
India, 35
Indirect taxes, A2
Inequality. *See also* Wage inequality
  income, technology role in, 295
  and the top 1%, 297–298
Inflation, 53. *See also* Deflation; Hyperinflation(s)
  accounting, 477
  benefits of, 506–507
  bracket creep, 53
  China, 34, 34 (table)
  costs of, 503–506
  economists' view of, 53
  European Union, 29 (table), 30
  expected, 132–136, 178–180
  medium-run output and, 202, 203
  money growth and, 499–501
  Okun's law, 53
  Phillips curve and, 54–55, 188–190
  unemployment and, 27 (table), 180–183,
    195–196, 460–461

  in United States, 27 (table), 178 (figure),
    180–181
Inflation-adjusted deficit, 475
Inflation expectations, 203
Inflation rate, 27, 51–53
  optimal, 503–508
Inflation targeting, 497
  from money targeting to, 499–503
Inflation variability, 505–506
Insolvency, 138
Institutions, technological progress, and
    growth, 273–276
Instrumental variable methods, A15
Instruments, A15
Insurance
  deposit, 97
  unemployment, 187
Interest parity condition, 383, 413–415
Interest rate(s), 202
  on bonds, 88
  constant, 308–309
  demand for money and, 98
  determination of, 91–100
  equilibrium, 98–102
  exchange rates and, 383–385, 429–430,
    441–442, 451–452
  fiscal policy and, 116–118
  German unification and, 425
  investment dependent on, 110–111
  monetary policy and, 118
  money supply and, 96
  negative, 398
  nominal and real, 132–136, 309–310
  parity, 414–415
  real, 451–452, 507
  real money, real income and, 113–114
  wealth in money vs. bonds, 88
  zero, 309
  zero lower bound and, 27–28, 135–136
Interest rate rule, 497, 502–503
Intermediate good, 42
International Monetary Fund (IMF), 38–39
Internet resources, macroeconomic data, 38–39
Inventories, 73, 78
  business, changes in, A4
Inventory, 69
Inventory investment, 69, 111
Investment, 68–69, 72, 89, 338–345, 519
  capital accumulation and, 240–241
  China, 34, 35
  consumption decisions and, 346–347, 352
  current vs. expected profit, 342–344
  deficit reduction and, 123
  dependent on sales, 110–111
  determinants of, 390–391
  equaling saving, 81
  goods market, 110–111
  interest rates and, 111
  nominal, 89–91
  profit and sales, 344–345
  saving, trade balance, and, 406–407
  savings and current account balance,
    406–407
  stock market and, 341–342
  in United States during World War II, 485
  volatility, 346–347
Investment decisions, 340
Ireland
  deficit reduction in, 361–362

unemployment, 187–188
unemployment rate, 188 (figure)
IS curve
 deriving, 113
 expectations and, 354–355
 shifts of, 113–114
 tax increase effect, 116–118
IS-LM model, 109, 116–118, 519
 dynamics, 124–126
 extending the, 141–143
 for open economy, 419, 420 (figure)
IS-LM-PC model, 198–201
IS relation
 expectations and, 352–355
 under fixed exchange rates, 433, 451
 goods market and, 81, 110–114
 LM relations and, 116–118
 in open economy, 390–393
IS-LM model
 fiscal policy and interest rate, 116–118
 monetary policy and activity, 118
Israel, 447
Italy
 bond spreads, 487
 unemployment rate, 188 (figure)

J

J-curve, 404–405
Japan
 collective bargaining, 164
 gross public debt of, 491
 natural rate of unemployment, 189
 output per person since 1950, 223 (table)
 output per worker and technological
  progress, 276 (table)
Job destruction, 293
Jorgenson, Dale, 519
Junior securities, 146
Junk bonds, 312

K

Kenya, property rights in, 273
Keynes, John Maynard, 80, 82, 109, 435,
 518, 520
Keynesians, 520
 new, 525–526
Klein, Lawrence, 519, 520
Krugman, Paul, 244
Kuwait, GDP vs. GNP in, 382
Kuznets, Simon, 42
Kydland, Finn, 460, 523

L

Labor, decreasing returns to, 231
Labor force, 158
 unemployment rate and, 47–51
Labor hoarding, 201
Labor in efficiency units, 263
Labor income, 43
Labor market
 general considerations, 157–161
 institutions, 32
 wage-and price-setting, 175–176
Labor-market rigidities, 32, 186
Labor productivity, 167
Labor-supply relation, 175–176

Lamont, Owen, 344
Layoffs, 159
 costs of, 187
Lehman Brothers, 25, 79–80
Lender of last resort, 510
Lending and leverage, 139–141
Lerner, Abba, 400
Level of transactions, 88
Leverage, 145
 choice of, 138
 lending and, 139–141
Leverage ratio, 138
Life cycle theory of consumption, 332
Linear relation, 71
Liquidity, 139–141
Liquidity facilities, 148
Liquidity preference, 518
Liquidity provision, 140, 510
Liquidity trap, 100–102
LM curve
 deriving, 115–116
 shifts of, 114
 tax increase effect, 116–118
LM relation and financial markets, 114–118
Loan-to-value (LTV) ratio, 511, 512
Loans, 97
Logarithmic scales, 219, A10–A11
Long run, 56
Lucas, Robert, 256, 357, 521, 522, 525–526
Lucas critique, 522
Lustig, Nora, 295
Luxembourg, 188

M

M1, 500
Maastricht Treaty, 445, 466
Macroeconometric models, 519–520
Macroeconomic policy
 expectations and, 459–463
 politics and, 463–469
Macroeconomic policy coordination, 399
Macroeconomic policy makers
 games they play, 463–465, 467–468
 knowledge base, 456–457
 restraints on, 458–459, 463
 uncertainty and, 458–459
Macroeconomics
 developments in, up to the 2009 crisis,
  524–528
 new growth theory, 526–527
Macroprudential tools, 510–513, 529
Maddison, Angus, 39
Malthus, Robert, 227
Malthusian trap, 227
Management, innovation, and imitation, 272
Management practices and technological
 progress, 272
Mankiw, N. Gregory, 526
Mao Tse-tung, 275
Marginal propensity to consume, 71
Market economy, 35
Markup, 168
Marshall, Alfred, 400
Marshall-Lerner condition, 400, 410
Maturity, bond, 310
Mavrody, Sergei, 325
Medium run, 56
 flexible vs. fixed exchange rates, 432–436

Medium-run equilibrium, 201, 212
 dynamics and the, 201–206
Medium-term budgetary objective (MTO), 490
Menem, Carlos, 446
Menu cost, 526
Mexico, depreciation of peso in 1990s, 401
Mid-cycle deficit, 483
Minimum wages, 187
MMM pyramid, 325
Modified Phillips curve, 183
Modigliani, Franco, 332, 459, 519, 520
Monetarists, 520–521
Monetary base, 98
Monetary contraction, 118
Monetary expansion, 118
 response of output to, 457 (figure)
 stock market and, 321–322
Monetary policy coordination and fiscal
 expansion in France, 422–423
Monetary-fiscal policy mix, 119, 122–124
A Monetary History of the United States
 (Friedman and Schwartz), 520
Monetary policy, 355–358
 conventional, 508
 design of, 499–503
 effects in open economy, 419
 expectations, output, and, 355–358
 and financial stability, 510–513
 vs. fiscal policy, 520
 interest rate and, 118
 limits of, 148
 open market operations and, 94–96
 short-run and medium-run effects, 212
 unconventional, 148, 508–509
Monetary tightening, 118
Money demand. *See* Demand for money
Money finance, 488–491
Money growth, 499–501
Money illusion, 504–505
Money market funds, 88–89
Money supply, 91–94, 98–99
Money targeting, 499–501
Mortensen, Dale, 526
Mortgage-based security (MBS), 145–146
Mortgage lenders, 144
Mortgages, subprime, 143–145
MPS model, 520
Multilateral exchange rates, 377–378
Multilateral real U.S. exchange rate, 377
Multiplicative uncertainty, 458
Multiplier(s)
 in algebraic equations, 74
 fiscal, 363
Mundell, Robert, 411, 421, 443
Mundell-Fleming model, 411

N

n-year interest rate, 314
Narrow banking, 140
Nash, John, 459
National accounts. *See* National income and
 product accounts
National Basketball Association (NBA), 467
National Economic Trends, 38
National income and product accounts (national
 income accounts), 42, 520, A1–A6
*National Income and Product Accounts of the
 United States*, 38

Natural rate of interest, 202
Natural rate of unemployment, 171
    across countries, 186
    equilibrium real wages and unemployment,
        170–171
    Japan, 189
    oil prices and, 209–210, 212
    Phillips curve and, 183–185
    price-setting relation, 169–170
    productivity and, 287–291
    variations over time, 186, 188
    wage-setting relation, 168–169
Negative interest rate (NIR), 398
Negotiation, hostage taking and, 460
Neoclassical synthesis, 518–521
Net capital flows, 380
Net exports, 69, A4
Net interest, A2
Net national product (NNP), A2
Net transfers received, 380
Netherlands, 187–188. See also Holland
Neutral rate of interest, 202
New classical economics, 525
New growth theory, 526–527
New Keynesian economics, 525–526
New Zealand, 481
News articles, stock market and, 323
Nikkei Index, 324
NIPA. See National income and product
    accounts
Nominal exchange rates, 372–377
Nominal GDP, 44–46, 51
Nominal income, 89–91
Nominal interest rates, 132–136, 309–310, 330
    expected present discounted value, 330
Nominal rigidities, 526
Non-accelerating, inflation rate of
    unemployment (NAIRU), 185
Non-institutional civilian population, 158
Nondurable goods, A3
Nonhuman wealth, 332
Nonresidential investment, 68, A3
North American Free Trade Agreement
    (NAFTA), 369
North Korea, institutions in, 275
Not in the labor force designation, 48

O

OECD. See Organisation for Economic
    Co-operation and Development
OECD Economic Outlook, 38
OECD Employment Outlook, 38
Oil prices, changes in, 207–212
Okun, Arthur, 54
Okun coefficient, 201
Okun's law, 53
    across time and countries, 200–201
Open economy
    fiscal policy in, 419–421
    IS-LM model in, 420 (figure)
    IS relation in, 390–393
    monetary policy effects in, 419
Open market operations, 94
    monetary policy and, 94–96
Openness
    in factor markets, 369
    in financial markets, 369, 378–385
    in goods markets, 369, 370–378

Optimal control theory, 459, 523
Optimal currency area, 443
Ordinary least squares (OLS), A13
Organisation for Economic Co-operation and
    Development (OECD), 38, 120
    growth, 227–229
    inflation rates in, 503, 503 (table)
    ratio of exports to GDP, 371
Organization of Petroleum Exporting
    Countries (OPEC), 219
Ortiz-Juarez, Eduardo, 295
Out of the labor force, 158
Output, 26–27. See also Aggregate output;
    Equilibrium output; Steady-state output
    capital and, 238–241, 254–256, 264–267
    China, 33, 34, 34 (table)
    deficit reduction and, 358–363
    depreciation, trade balance and, 399–402
    determining, 111–113
    dynamics, 78, 124–126
    financial shocks and, 142–143
    GDP and, 42
    interest rate and, 111–113
    investment and, 239–240
    monetary policy, expectations, and, 355–358
    productivity, unemployment, and, 284–286
    savings rate and, 243–246, 250–253
Output expansion, 361–362
Output fluctuations, 212
Output gap, 199
Output growth, 27
Output per hour worked, 223
Output per person, 220–223
    across countries, 227–229
    across millenia, 227
    convergence of, 226–227
    in OECD countries, 227–229
    in rich countries, 223, 225–227
Output per worker, 223, 231

P

Paradox of saving, 82, 83
Participation rate, 49, 158
Patents, 271
PAYGO rule, 469
Payments
    balance of, 379–381
    constant interest rates and, 308–309
Pegging
    of currency, 423–424
    exchange rate, 423–424
    hard, 445, 447
Permanent income theory of
    consumption, 332
Perry, Rick, 455
Personal consumption expenditures, A3
Personal disposable income, A3
Personal income, A3
Phelps, Edmund, 171, 184, 521
Phillips, A. W., 177
Phillips curve, 54–55, 177, 180–183, 198–199,
    201, 520–521
    the apparent trade-off and its
        disappearance, 180–183
    deflation and, 190–191
    Friedman's critique, 184
    inflation and, 54–55, 188–190
    mutations, 180–183

natural rate of unemployment and, 183–185
    rational expectations and, 522–523
Physical capital, 254–256
    endogenous growth, 256
    extending the production function,
        254–255
    output and, 254–256
Piketty, Thomas, 297, 341
Pissarides, Christopher, 526
Plain, Nigel, 270
Players, 459
Policy
    expectations and, 459–463
    politics and, 463–469
    role of, 521
    theory of, 524
    uncertainty and, 456–459
Policy coordination, 399
Policy mix, 455
    Clinton-Greenspan, 124
    monetary-fiscal, 119, 122–124
Policy rate, 141
Political business cycle, 464
Politics, macroeconomic policy and, 463–469
Portugal, 188, 438, 439
Potential output, 199
PPP. See Purchasing power parity
Prescott, Edward, 460, 523, 525
Present value(s), 307–310
    bonds prices as, 311–312
    deriving, 330
    of expected profits, 339–340, 350
    nominal vs. real interest rates and, 309–310
    stock prices as, 318–321
    utilization of, 306–310
Price determination, production function, 167
Price indexes, 51–52
Price level, 51
    expected, 166
Price-setting relation, 169–170, 287–288
Prices. See also specific prices
    wages, unemployment and, 166
Primary deficit, 477
Primary surplus, 477
Private saving, 81
Private sector involvement, 488
Private spending, 353
Product side, national accounts, A3–A4
Production, 51, 52, 67. See also Output
Production function, 167
    aggregate, 229–230
    Cobb-Douglas, 259
    extending the, 254–255
    price determination, 167
    technological progress and, 262–264
Productivity
    natural rate of unemployment and,
        287–291
    output, unemployment, and, 284–286
Productivity growth, low, 28–29
Profit
    corporate, A2
    current vs. expected, 342–344
    expected present value of profits under
        static expectations, 350
    investment and expectations of, 338–339
    sales and, 344–345
Profit income, 43
Profitability vs. cash flow, 344

Propagation mechanisms, 213
  shocks and, 212–213
Propensity to consume, 71
Propensity to save, 82
Property rights, protection of, 273–276
Proprietor's income, A2
Public saving, 81
Purchasing power parity (PPP), 33, 221–223
  construction of, 222
Pure inflation, 53

Q

Quantitative easing, 508
Quantitative Easing 1 (QE1), 508–509
Quantitative Easing 2 (QE2), 509
Quantitative Easing 3 (QE3), 509
Quits, 159
Quotas, 369

R

Random walk, 321
Random walk of consumption, 523
Rating agencies, 146
Rational expectations, 357, 358
  critique of, 521–524
  integration of, 523–524
  Phillips curve and, 522–523
Rational speculative bubbles, 325, 327
Real appreciation, 375
Real business cycle (RBC) models, 525
Real depreciation, 375
Real exchange rate, 372–377, 451–452
  and domestic and foreign real interest
    rates, 451–452
Real GDP, 44–46, 51
  computing, 44, 47
  construction of, 62–63
Real GDP in chained (2009) dollars, 45
Real GDP per capita, 46
Real income, 113–114
Real interest rates, 132–136, 309–310, 330,
    451–452. See also Interest rate(s)
  expected present discounted value, 330
  negative, 507
  real exchange rate and, 451–452
Real money, 113–114
Real wages, 53
  equilibrium, 170–171
  natural rate of unemployment and, 288–289
Receipts of factor income from the rest of the
    world, A2
Recessions, 46
  2001–02 recession, 120–122
  Euro market members and, 33
Regression, A13
Regression line, 183, A13
Relative price, 45
Rental cost, 342
Rental income of persons, A2
Repayment, debt, 477–479
Research and development (R&D), 268–269
Research process, 268–269
  fertility of, 269–270
Research results, appropriability of, 270–271
Reservation wage, 164
Reserve ratio, 98
Reserves, 97
  demand for, 98

Residential investment, 68, A3
Residual, A13
  Solow, 281
Retail sales, 346
Returns to capital, decreasing, 230
Returns to factors, 230–231
Returns to labor, decreasing, 231
Returns to scale, constant, 230–231
Revaluations, 373
Ricardian equivalence, 482–483
Ricardo, David, 482
Ricardo-Barro proposition, 482
Risk, 136–137
  bonds and, 311, 315–316
  default, 487–489
  stock prices and, 324–327
Risk aversion, 136
Risk premium, 136–137, 312
Romer, Paul, 256, 526
Roubini, Nouriel, 39, 528
Rules vs. discretion, in EU, 490–491
Russia
  MMM pyramid, 325
  U.S. currency, holders of, 91

S

Sales
  investment dependent on, 110–111
  profit and, 344–345
Samuelson, Paul, 177, 518
Sargent, Thomas, 357, 521
Saving, 89
  investment, trade balance, and, 406–407
  investment equaling, 81
  paradox of, 82, 83
  private, 81
  public, 81
Saving rate, 232, 237
  consumption and, 247–250
  dynamic effects of an increase in, 251–253
  dynamics of capital and output, 241–244
  effect on steady-state output, 250–251,
    267–268
  implications of alternative, 241–248
  output in relation to, 243–246, 250–253
  steady-state, 243
  United States, 253
Schelling, Tom, 459
Schumpeter, Joseph, 291, 527
Schwartz, Anna, 520
Securitization, 145–146
Seignorage, 488–489, 506
Selten, Reinhard, 459
Senior securities, 146
Separations, 158
Services, A3
Shadow cost, 342
Shafir, Eldar, 505
Shares, 318
Shiller, Robert, 326
Shleifer, Andrei, 527, 528
Shocks, 212–213
  labor market, 187
Shoe-leather costs, 503–504
Short run, 56
Short-run equilibrium, 201, 212
Siler, Pamela, 270
Skill premium, 295

Skill-biased technological progress, 296
Smooth landing, 316
Solow, Robert M., 177, 229, 281, 519
Solow residual, 281
Solvency, 138
South Korea, institutions in, 275
Soviet Union, 244
Spain
  bond spreads, 487
  EMS crisis, 438
  unemployment rate, 31 (figure), 188 (figure)
Spending
  aggregate private, 353
  autonomous, 74
Spending caps, 469
Spread, 487
Stability and Growth Pact (SGP), 422, 455,
    466–467
Stagflation, 210, 521
Staggering of wage and price decisions, 524
Stalinist growth, 244
Standard of living, 220–223
  increase in, since 1950, 225–226
Standard & Poor's (S&P), 312
Standard & Poor's 500 (S&P 500), 318
Standardized employment deficit, 483
Starve the Beast, 465
Static expectations, 340, 350, 357
Statistical Abstract of the United States, 38
Statistical discrepancy, 380
Statistics, economic, 38
Steady state (of the economy), 243
  Cobb-Douglas production function and, 259
Steady-state capital, 243
Steady-state output, 243
  saving rate and, 250–251, 267–268
Stock indexes, 318
Stock market
  economic activity and the, 321
  increase in consumer spending and the,
    322–323
  investment and the, 341
  monetary expansion and the, 321–322
  well-functioning, 321
Stock prices
  from 2007 to 2010, 25
  bubbles and fads, 324–327
  movements in, 318–323
  as present values, 318–321
Stocks, 89, 318
Stone, Richard, 42
Strategic interactions, 459
Structural change, 291
Structural deficit, 483
Structural rate of unemployment, 171
Structured investment vehicles (SIVs), 145
Structures, A3
Subprime mortgages, 143–145
Supply. *See* Aggregate supply
Surpluses
  budget, 81
  capital account, 380
Survey of Current Business, 38
Sweden, 188, 438

T

Tariffs, 369
Tax distortions, 485–486, 504

Taxes, 72
    current vs. future, 477–480
    effect on *IS* curve, 113, 116–118
    government control of output, 82
    indirect, A2
    in national income accounts, A4–A5
Taylor, John, 524
Taylor rule, 502
Tea Party, 455
Technological change, 270
Temporary employees, 189
Technological progress
    vs. capital accumulation, 276–278
    churning, inequality, and, 291–298
    constructing a measure of, 281
    determinants of, 268–272
    growth and, 232, 261
    institutions and, 273–276
    output, capital, and, 264–267
    production function and, 262–264
    real business cycle models and, 525
    real GDP and changes in market, 47
    savings rate and, 267–268
    skill-biased, 296
Technological unemployment, 287
Technology
    changes in, 270
    in income inequality, 295
    output in relation to, 230
    state of, 230, 262
Technology frontier, 272
Term structure of interest rates, 311
Thaler, Richard, 528
Time consistency and restraints on policy
    makers, 463
Time inconsistency, 460, 523
Tirole, Jean, 528, 529
Tobin, James, 340, 519
Tobin's *q*, 341, 342
Total wealth, 332
Toxic assets, 146
Tradable goods, 371
Trade balance, 69, A4
    depreciation, output, and, 399–402
    equilibrium output and, 393–394
    saving, investment, and, 406–407
    wage inequality, increasing, 296
Trade deficit, 69, 395
Trade surplus, 69
Transfers, business, A2
Transitional economies, 414–415
Treasury bills (T-bills), 95, 312
Treasury bonds, 312
Treasury notes, 312
Troubled Asset Relief Program (TARP), 148
Trust fund, 248
Tulipmania, 325
Tversky, Amos, 505
2001–02 recession, 120–122

U

Unconventional monetary policy, 148,
    508–509
Uncovered interest parity, 383
Underwater, 144

Unemployment, 47
    duration of, 159
    economists' view of, 49–51
    equilibrium real wages and, 170–171
    in Europe, 31–32, 187–188
    happiness and, 50
    inflation and, 195–196, 460–461
    insurance, 167
    job destruction, churning, and earnings
        losses, 293
    movements in, 161–163
    output and, 284–286
    technological, 287
    wages, prices and, 166
Unemployment rate, 27, 47–51, 158,
    166–167. *See also* Natural rate of
    unemployment
    computing, 48
    labor force and, 48–49
    natural, 168–171
    1996-2014, 162 (figure)
    vs. output growth in U.S., 1960-2014, 54
        (figure)
    structural, 171
    U.S., 1960-2014, 49 (figure)
    wages and, 166
United Kingdom
    debt ratios after World War II, 481
    gold standard, 435
    nominal and real interest rates, 385 (figure)
    output per person since 1950, 223 (table)
    output per worker and technological
        progress, 276 (table)
    unemployment, 187, 188
    unemployment rate, 188 (figure)
United States, 26–29
    balanced budget, 455
    budget deficit, 491–492
    consumption during World War II, 485
    country composition of exports and
        imports in 2014, 377 (table)
    deficit reduction in, 468–469
    Department of Commerce, 38
    economic statistics, 38
    employment, unemployment and
        nonparticipation rates (1996-2014), 159
        (figure)
    exports-to-GDP ratios since 1960, 371
        (figure)
    growth, unemployment, and inflation
        1990-2015, 27 (table)
    housing price increases, 326–327
    income adjustment from GDP to GNP,
        A1–A2
    inflation in, 178 (figure), 180–181
    nominal and real interest rates, 134–135,
        385 (figure)
    output per person since 1950, 223 (table)
    output per worker and technological
        progress, 276 (table)
    property rights in, 273
    saving rate, 237
    unemployment, 49
    unemployment rate 1948-2014, 161 (figure)
United States currency, holders of, 91
User cost, 342

V

Value added, GDP as sum of, 43
Van Reenen, John, 272
Variables
    endogenous, 72
    exogenous, 72
Volatility
    of consumption and investment,
        346–347
    exchange rate, 441–442
Voters, policymakers and, 463–465

W

Wage decisions, staggering of, 524
Wage determination, 163–167
    bargaining, 164
    efficiency wages, 164–165
    expected price level, 166
    unemployment and prices, 166
    unemployment insurance, 167
    unemployment rate, 166–167
Wage indexation, 189–190
Wage inequality
    increase in, 292–296
    and the top 1%, 297–298
Wage-setting relation, 168–169, 175–176,
    287–288
Wages, real, 170–171, 288–289
Wang, Chengqi, 270
Wars and deficits, 484–485
Wealth
    in the form of bonds, 88
    income, money, and, 89
    types of, 332
Web sites, for macroeconomic issues, 39
Wei, Yingqi, 270
Wicksellian rate of interest, 202
Woodford, Michael, 527, 528
Workers
    bargaining power, 164
    discouraged, 48, 160
    flows of, 158–161
    output and capital per, 231
World Economic Outlook (WEO), 38–39
*The World Economy: A Millennial
    Perspective*, 39

Y

Yellen, Janet, 526
Yeltsin, Boris, 325, 437
Yield curve, 311
    interpreting, 316–317
    AAA-rated central government bonds,
        317
Yield to maturity, 311

Z

Zero interest rates, 309
Zero lower bound, 100, 317
    debt spirals and, 203–206
    deflation and, 135–136
    interest rates and, 27–28, 135–136

Credits

Material from the International Monetary Fund appears on the following text pages. Courtesy of International Monetary Fund: 23, 31, 35, 43, 52, 56, 72, 73, 77, 81, 97, 98, 101, 114, 117, 119, 122, 136, 139, 142, 146, 165, 170, 172, 181, 185, 203, 212, 221, 228, 248, 253, 273, 278, 283, 297, 323, 324, 331, 332, 343, 347, 357, 358, 360, 363, 370, 381, 386, 391, 397, 400, 405, 416, 420, 426, 431, 440, 440, 444, 445, 455, 459, 465, 474, 480, 483, 488, 498, 509, 511, 517, 519, 528, and 529.

p. 3:	Open Your Eyes: O. Blanchard
p. 4:	Photo of Olivier Blanchard: O. Blanchard
p. 48:	NON SEQUITUR © 2006 Wiley Ink, Inc.. Dist. By UNIVERSAL UCLICK. Reprinted with permission. All rights reserved.
p. 67:	TOLES © 1991 The Washington Post. Reprinted with permission of UNIVERSAL UCLICK. All rights reserved.
p. 221:	Dana Fradon/The New Yorker Collection/The Cartoon Bank
p. 271:	Chappatte in "L'Hebdo", Lausanne - www.globecartoon.com
p. 292:	Chappatte in "Die Weltwoche", Zurich - www.globecartoon.com
p. 323:	Tribune Media Services, Inc. All Rights Reserved. Reprinted with permission.
p. 335:	Roz Chast/The New Yorker Collection/The Cartoon Bank
p. 431:	Ed Fisher/The New Yorker Collection/The Cartoon Bank
p. 518:	J. M. Keynes: Bettmann/Corbis
	P. Samuelson: Rick Friedman/Corbis
p. 519:	F. Modigliani: Plinio Lepri/AP Images
	J. Tobin: AP Images
	R. Solow: Ira Wyman/Sygma/Corbis
p. 520:	L. Klein: B Thumma/AP Images
	M. Friedman: Chuck Nacke/Alamy Stock Photo
p. 521:	E. Phelps: James Leynse/Corbis
	R. Lucas: Ralf-Finn Hestoft/Corbis
p. 522:	T. Sargent: Peter Foley/Corbis
	R. Barro: Imaginechina/Corbis
p. 523:	R. Hall: Robert Hall
p. 524:	R. Dornbusch: Luca Bruno/AP Images
	S. Fischer: Achmad Ibrahim/AP Images
	J. Taylor: Susana Gonzalez/Bloomberg/Getty Images
p. 525:	E. Prescott: Giuseppe Aresu/AP Images
p. 526:	G. Akerlof: Kurt Rogers/San Francisco Chronicle/Corbis
	J. Yellen: Photo courtesy of Janet Yellen, Chair of the Board of Governors of the Federal Reserve System.
	B. Bernanke: Aurora Photos/Alamy Stock Photo
	P. Romer: Larry Busacca/Getty Images
p. 527:	P. Aghion: Dr. Philipe Aghion
	P. Howitt: Dr. Peter Howitt
	A. Shleifer: Dr. Andrei Schleifer
	D. Acemoglu: Daron Acemoglu/Peter Tenzer
p. 528:	M. Woodford: Dr. Michael Woodford
	J.Gali: Arne Dedert/picture-alliance/dpa/AP Images
p. 529:	B. Holmström: Dr. Bengt Holmström
	J. Tirole: Pascal Le Segretain/WireImage/Getty Images

Symbols Used in This Book

Symbol	Term	Introduced in Chapter
$(\ )^d$	Superscript d means demanded	
$(\ )^e$	Superscript e means expected	
A	Aggregate private spending	16
	Also: Labor productivity/states of technology	7, 12
α	Effect on the inflation rate of the unemployment rate, given expected inflation	8
B	Goverment debt	22
C	Consumption	3
CU	Currency	4
c	Proportion of money held as currency	4
c_0	Consumption when disposable income equals zero	3
c_1	Propensity to consume	3
D	Checkable deposits	4
	Also: Real dividend on a stock	14
$\$D$	Nominal dividend on a stock	14
δ	Depreciation rate	11
E	Nominal exchange rate (price of domestic currency in terms of foreign currency)	17
$\bar{E}$	Fixed nominal exchange rate	19
E^e	Expected future exchange rate	17
ε	Real exchange rate	17
G	Government spending	3
g_A	Growth rate of technological progress	12
g_K	Growth rate of capital	12
g_N	Growth rate of population	12
g, g_y	Growth rate of output	8
H	High powered money/monetary base/ central bank money	4
	Also: Human capital	11
I	Fixed investment	3
IM	Imports	3
i	Nominal interest rate	4
i_1	One-year nominal interest rate	14
i_2	Two-year nominal interest rate	14
i^*	Foreign nominal interest rate	17
	Also: Target interest rate for central bank	
K	Capital stock	10

Symbol	Term	Introduced in Chapter
L	Labor force	2
M	Money stock (nominal)	4
M^d	Money demand (nominal)	4
M^s	Money supply (nominal)	4
m	Markup of prices over wages	7
N	Employment	2
N_n	Natural level of employment	9
NI	Net income payments from the rest of the world	
NX	Net exports	18
P	GDP deflator/CPI/price level	2
$P*$	Foreign price level	17
π	Inflation	2
Π	Profit per unit of capital	15
Q	Real stock price	14
$\$Q$	Nominal stock price	14
R	Bank reserves	4
r	Real interest rate	6
S	Private saving	3
s	Private saving rate	11
T	Net taxes (taxes paid by consumers minus transfers)	3
Tr	Government transfers	22
θ	Reserve ratio of banks	4
U	Unemployment	2
u	Unemployment rate	2
u_n	Natural rate of unemployment	7
V	Present value of a sequence of real payments z	14
$\$V$	Present value of a sequence of nominal payments $\$z$	14
W	Nominal wage	7
Y	Real GDP/Output/Production	2
$\$Y$	Nominal GDP	2
Y_D	Disposable income	3
Y_L	Labor income	15
Y_n	Natural level of output	9
$Y*$	Foreign output	18
X	Exports	3
Z	Demand for goods	3
z	Factors that affect the wage, given unemployment	7
	Also: A real payment	14
$\$Z$	Nominal payment	14

Flexible Organization

Macroeconomics, seventh edition is organized around two central parts: A core and a set of two major extensions. The text's **flexible organization** emphasizes an integrated view of macroeconomics, while enabling professors to focus on the theories, models, and applications that they deem central to their particular course.

The flowchart below quickly illustrates how the chapters are organized and fit within the book's overall structure. For a more detailed explanation of the **Organization**, and for an extensive list of **Alternative Course Outlines**, see pages **14–15** in the preface.

INTRODUCTION

A Tour of the World **Chapter 1**
A Tour of the Book **Chapter 2**

THE CORE

The Short Run
The Goods Market **Chapter 3**
Financial Markets I **Chapter 4**
Goods and Financial Markets: The *IS-LM* Model **Chapter 5**
Financial Markets II: The Extended *IS-LM* Model **Chapter 6**

The Medium Run
The Labor Market **Chapter 7**
The Phillips Curve, the Natural Rate of
Unemployment, and Inflation **Chapter 8**
From the Short to the Medium Run: The *IS-LM*
PC Model **Chapter 9**

The Long Run
The Facts of Growth **Chapter 10**
Saving, Capital Accumulation, and Output **Chapter 11**
Technological Progress and Growth **Chapter 12**
Technological Progress: The Short, the Medium, and the
Long Run **Chapter 13**

EXTENSIONS

EXPECTATIONS
Financial Markets and Expectations **Chapter 14**
Expectations, Consumption, and Investment **Chapter 15**
Expectations, Output, and Policy **Chapter 16**

THE OPEN ECONOMY
Openness in Goods and Financial Markets **Chapter 17**
The Goods Market in an Open Economy **Chapter 18**
Output, the Interest Rate, and the Exchange Rate **Chapter 19**
Exchange Rate Regimes **Chapter 20**

BACK TO POLICY

Should Policy Makers Be Restrained? **Chapter 21**
Fiscal Policy: A Summing Up **Chapter 22**
Monetary Policy: A Summing Up **Chapter 23**

EPILOGUE

The Story of Macroeconomics **Chapter 24**